PAROIMIA

Purdue Studies in Romance Literatures

Editorial Board

Íñigo Sánchez Llama, Series Editor
Elena Coda
Paul B. Dixon
Beth Gale

Patricia Hart
Gwen Kirkpatrick
Allen G. Wood

Howard Mancing, Consulting Editor
Floyd Merrell, Consulting Editor
Joyce L. Detzner, Production Editor

Associate Editors

French
Jeanette Beer
Paul Benhamou
Willard Bohn
Thomas Broden
Gerard J. Brault
Mary Ann Caws
Glyn P. Norton
Allan H. Pasco
Gerald Prince
Roseann Runte
Ursula Tidd

Italian
Fiora A. Bassanese
Peter Carravetta
Benjamin Lawton
Franco Masciandaro
Anthony Julian Tamburri

Luso-Brazilian
Fred M. Clark
Marta Peixoto
Ricardo da Silveira Lobo Sternberg

Spanish and Spanish American
Catherine Connor
Ivy A. Corfis
Frederick A. de Armas
Edward Friedman
Charles Ganelin
David T. Gies
Roberto González Echevarría
David K. Herzberger
Emily Hicks
Djelal Kadir
Amy Kaminsky
Lucille Kerr
Howard Mancing
Floyd Merrell
Alberto Moreiras
Randolph D. Pope
Elżbieta Skłodowska
Marcia Stephenson
Mario Valdés

 volume 83

PAROIMIA

Brusantino, Florio, Sarnelli, and Italian Proverbs From the Sixteenth and Seventeenth Centuries

Daniela D'Eugenio

Purdue University Press
West Lafayette, Indiana

Copyright ©2021 by Purdue University. All rights reserved.

♾ The paper used in this book meets the minimum requirements of American National Standard for Information Sciences—Permanence of Paper for Printed Library Materials, ANSI Z39.48-1992.

Printed in the United States of America
Template for interior design by Anita Noble;
template for cover by Heidi Branham.
Cover image:
Le cento novelle da messer Brugiantino dette in ottava rima
Publisher: Francesco Marcolini, Venezia, 1554
Courtesty of the Trustees of the Boston Public Library, Rare Books.

Library of Congress Cataloging-in-Publication Data

Names: D'Eugenio, Daniela, author. | Brusantino, Vicenzo, active 16th century. Cento novelle.
Title: Paroimia : Brusantino, Florio, Sarnelli, and Italian proverbs from the sixteenth and seventeenth centuries / Daniela D'Eugenio.
Other titles: Brusantino, Florio, Sarnelli, and Italian proverbs from the sixteenth and seventeenth centuries | Purdue studies in Romance literatures ; v. 83.
Description: West Lafayette, IN : Purdue University Press, 2021. | Series: Purdue studies in Romance literatures ; volume 83 | Includes bibliographical references and index.
Identifiers: LCCN 2021019920 | ISBN 9781612496719 (hardcover) | ISBN 9781612496726 (paperback) | ISBN 9781612496733 (epub) | ISBN 9781612496740 (pdf)
Subjects: LCSH: Florio, John, 1553?-1625. Firste fruites. | Florio, John, 1553?-1625. Second frutes. | Sarnelli, Pompeo, 1649-1724. Posilecheata. | Proverbs, Italian--History and criticism. | Italian literature--16th century--History and criticism. | Italian literature--17th century--History and criticism.
Classification: LCC PN6470 .D48 2021 | DDC 850.9--dc23
LC record available at https://lccn.loc.gov/2021019920

To Genoveffa

> Voi sapete ch'in ogni lingua non c'è più bella gratia, che l'usar, et nel parlare, et nel scrivere, di bei e spessi proverbi.
>
> You know that in every language there is no more beautiful grace than using beautiful and frequent proverbs, both in speaking and in writing.
>
> Charles Merbury, *Proverbi Vulgari*

Contents

- xi Acknowledgments
- xiii Foreword
- xix Criteria for Transcription
- xxi Notes on Quotations, Translations, and Abbreviations
- 1 **Chapter One**
  Literary History and Theories of Paremias
  - 1 Paremiography: Literature of Paremias and Literature with Paremias
    - 1 The Classical and Middle Ages
    - 6 The Renaissance and Early Modern Period
    - 15 The Nineteenth, Twentieth, and Twenty-First Centuries
  - 16 Paremiology: Defining Paremias
    - 16 The Classical and Middle Ages
    - 19 The Renaissance and Early Modern Period
    - 23 The Twentieth and Twenty-First Centuries
    - 26 Temistocle Franceschi's Paremiology
    - 30 Variations of Paremias in Genre, Culture, and Language
    - 33 Paremiological Categorizations: Proverbs, Proverbial Phrases, and Wellerisms
- 41 **Chapter Two**
  Vincenzo Brusantino's *Le cento novelle*: Paremias and Tridentine Ethics in Reinterpreting the *Decameron*
  - 41 Brusantino's "Translation" of Boccaccio's *Decameron*
    - 43 The Defining Attributes of Brusantino's *Le cento novelle*
    - 47 Rewriting the *Decameron* through Octaves and Paremias
  - 51 *Le cento novelle*: A Stylistic and Social Adaptation of the *Decameron*
  - 57 Introductory Allegories and Paremias: Brusantino's Ethical Perspective
    - 61 Celebrated Love
    - 68 Condemned Love
    - 74 Lascivious Love and Religion

vii

Contents

      86 Jealousy Rebuked
      89 Religious Matters
      96 The Power of the Word
  101 Embedded Paremias: Brusantino's Personal Innovations and His Adaptations of Boccaccio's Paremias to the Octave
  116 Brusantino's Ethical Language in His Paremias

121 Chapter Three

John Florio's *Firste Fruites* and *Second Frutes*: Paremias and Elizabethan Teaching of the Italian Language

  121 Florio's Activity in England
  125 Teaching the Italian Language with Paremias: Florio's Innovative Approach
      131 Florio's Paremias in His *Fruits*
      140 The Sources of Florio's Paremias and Dialogues
      146 Solomon's and Yeshua Ben Sira's Paremias in *Firste Fruites*
  151 Translating Paremias
      153 *Firste Fruites*
      158 *Second Frutes*
  161 Paremias in Context
      161 Paremiac Dialogues in *Firste Fruites*
      172 Paremiac Dialogues in *Second Frutes*
      184 Contextual Comparisons with *Giardino di ricreatione*

195 Chapter Four

Pompeo Sarnelli's *Posilecheata*: Paremias and the Multifaceted Neapolitan Baroque

  195 Sarnelli's Literary Presence
      198 Literature in Neapolitan Dialect and Sarnelli's Fables
  202 The Prefatory Letter: Paremias Praising the Neapolitan Dialect
  210 The Introductory Banquet: Tripartite Paremias to Marvel
  227 The Five Fables: Paremias as Moral, Social, and Linguistic Tools
      229 *Cunto* 1: *La piatà remmonerata*
      234 *Cunto* 2: *La vajassa fedele*

    239 *Cunto 3: La 'ngannatrice 'ngannata*
    243 *Cunto 4: La gallenella*
    248 *Cunto 5: La capo e la coda*

253 Conclusion

269 Index of Paremias in *Le cento novelle*, *Firste Fruites*, *Second Frutes*, and *Posilecheata*

    269 Vincenzo Brusantino: *Le cento novelle*'s Paremias
        269 Introductory Paremias for Each Novella and Final List of Paremias at the End of Each Day
        286 Embedded Paremias in *Le cento novelle* Compared with Boccaccio's Paremias
        293 New Paremias Introduced by Brusantino
    294 John Florio: A Selection of Paremias in *Firste Fruites* and *Second Frutes* Compared with *Giardino di ricreatione*
        374 Numerical Paremias
    381 Pompeo Sarnelli: A Selection of *Posilecheata*'s Paremias
        383 Paremias at the End of the Five *cunti*
        383 Tripartite Paremias
        384 Paremias in Other Languages

385 Notes

465 Works Consulted

535 Index of Names

Acknowledgments

I would like to thank my advisor at the City University of New York, Dr. Hermann Haller, and the members of my dissertation committee, Dr. Monica Calabritto, Dr. Clare Carroll, and Dr. Nicoletta Maraschio, who read this work in its thesis form and consistently offered comments and suggestions on its expanded version. I am grateful to Dr. Paolo Cherchi, who granted me the pleasure of long conversations on proverbs and literature at large, and Dr. Piero Fiorelli for our discussions on Serdonati and Salviati. Many other people contributed to the success of this project in different ways. I thank Dr. Paolo Fasoli, Dr. Timothy Graham, Dr. Giancarlo Lombardi, Dr. Tina Matarrese, Dr. Rosanna Pettinelli, Dr. Matthias Roick, Dr. Paolo Rondinelli, and Dr. Antonio Vinciguerra. My heartfelt gratitude goes to Dr. Lynn Ramey and the Department of French and Italian at Vanderbilt University for their generous support. I am deeply grateful to the Renaissance Society of America and the Newberry Library for granting me a short-term fellowship in Summer 2016. I likewise would like to thank the Renaissance Studies Certificate Program at the Graduate Center for selecting me for the Renaissance and Early Modern Travel and Research Grant in Spring 2017. I am immensely grateful to the library assistants at the Accademia della Crusca, Biblioteca Nazionale Centrale di Firenze, Biblioteca Riccardiana, Boston Public Library, Herzog August Bibliothek, and Newberry Library. In 2018, Accademia della Crusca awarded my dissertation its "Premio Giovanni Nencioni," an award for a dissertation on Italian linguistics discussed abroad. This prize allowed me to spend a month at the institution and to conduct further research for this book. I would like to extend my thanks to the two anonymous reviewers of my article "*Lengua che no' la 'ntienne, e tu la caca.* Irony and Hilarity of Neapolitan Paroemias in Pompeo Sarnelli's *Posilecheata* (1684)." Chapter 4 of this book is loosely based on this article, which appeared in *Humour in Italy Through the Ages*. My gratitude goes to Dr. John Bradley and Dr. Simone McCarter of the Vanderbilt University Writing Studio and to Dr. Deena Levy for their linguistic help with my manuscript. Finally, thank you L., C., and P. for supporting me through all of this.

Foreword

> ... al giuoco de' proverbi, nel quale ciascuno ha da dire un proverbio e dipoi si fa interpretare ciò che con tal proverbio si sia voluto intendere ...
>
> ... in the game of proverbs, in which everyone shares a proverb and then asks the others to interpret what was meant by that proverb ...
>
> Girolamo Bargagli
> *Dialogo de' giuochi che nelle vegghie sanesi si usano di fare*

In his book *Dialogo de' giuochi che nelle vegghie sanesi si usano di fare* (1572), Girolamo Bargagli recounts a delightful conversation during a nightly vigil between members of the Intronati Academy in Siena. While they talk about the origins, typologies, and rules of pastimes, they mention a game that is usually proposed to entertain and please members of a convivial group. This pastime requires that a member of the group recites a decontextualized proverb while the others discern its meaning: "... al giuoco de' proverbi, nel quale ciascuno ha da dire un proverbio e dipoi si fa interpretare ciò che con tal proverbio si sia voluto intendere ..." ("... in the game of proverbs, in which everyone shares a proverb and then asks the others to interpret what was meant by that proverb ..."; 164: par. 156). The participants attempt to guess the message that the proverb supposedly conveys and, in doing so, enjoy themselves.

The necessity of interpreting a proverb to supply its most appropriate meaning demonstrates the ambiguity of its message. Francesco Petrarca comments on the inherent difficulty of understanding proverbial expressions in his poem *Mai non vo' più cantar com'io soleva* entirely based on proverbs: "Intendami chi può, ch'i m'intend'io" (RVF, CV, v. 17; "Let he who's able understand, because I understand myself"). Despite the general belief that tradition permanently determines their interpretation, proverbs are in fact malleable. They adapt to diverse situations and contexts, convey multiple messages and describe reality with a range of references and images. When proverbs are inserted into a context, certain verbal and textual aspects guide the reader or listener towards a specific interpretation of their meaning, which is, indeed, tightly linked to that context. When they are decontextualized, instead, as in Bargagli's and Petrarca's examples, their message is less clearly distinct. This book argues and, subsequently, demonstrates that context plays a crucial role in defining proverbs as well as in determining their interpretation. While examining accounts of proverbs in a variety of literary genres, it provides stylistic and linguistic analyses of their structures and messages as they relate to specific contexts. Not only do these analyses take into consideration the effects and the adaptations of proverbs to a contextual situation, but they also investigate their borrowings from previous sources and the representation of their author's perspectives, which are frequently disguised behind societal wisdom and communal knowledge.

Beginning in the first decades of the twentieth century with the emergence of the scholarly study of proverbs, two typologies of examination have appeared: those that focus on literary sources and those that concentrate on language. Linguistic examination usually explores the language used to express proverbs, describing it both diachronically and synchronically, while literary investigation mostly engages in the critical evaluation of written proverbs and their origins. This means that, with a linguistic analysis, proverbs are evaluated for their stylistic features, morphological aspects, vocabulary, prosodic elements, modes of use, and local and regional variants. Such a typology of investigation primarily deals with spoken proverbs, which linguistics interprets as cultural and anthropological products of a community. According to this approach, the examination of proverbs featured within a literary work is decontextualized, which results in the loss of their textual context and of their multiple layered meanings. Instead, if proverbs are placed within their literary context, the reciprocal relationship with the text and the narrative becomes evident. When this literary investigation is combined with the linguistic one, the stylistic and rhetorical aspects of proverbs can emerge along with the author's mentality, social position, and literary standing. Such a methodology provides insight into the changes and transformations that occur as proverbs adapt to different languages or styles and, simultaneously, reveals idiosyncrasies and specific aspects of each linguistic and rhetorical code. The contemporaneous scholarship of Temistocle Franceschi offers a clear-cut yet broad definition of the contextual analysis of proverbs, and it is within this framework that the paremias are examined in this book. Specifically, Franceschi's invented term *paremia*—a calque from the Greek word παροιμία used to indicate both proverbs and gnomic sentences—describes proverbs as cultural and linguistic elements whose meaning is the result of a metaphorical process that differs from the specific meaning of each constituent word. This definition suggests that considering the context is a fundamental step towards an appropriate evaluation of all of those expressions that are heavily influenced by the contextual situation in which they appear. The word paremia indeed acts as an overarching category including proverbs, proverbial phrases, and wellerisms, which will be the focus of the next chapters' investigation.

To demonstrate the validity of a literary and linguistic methodology, this book takes into account four early modern texts: Vincenzo Brusantino's *Le cento novelle* (1554), John Florio's *Firste Fruites* (1578) and *Second Frutes* (1591), and Pompeo Sarnelli's *Posilecheata* (1684). These works present a wide range of paremias from diverse geographical areas including Ferrara, London, and Naples. They span a period of 130 years, bridging two centuries that thrived with collections of paremias and with the use of paremias in literary texts. Since Brusantino, Florio, and Sarnelli made use of previous works and sources, critics often dismissed the three authors as passive imitators of important Italian texts: Giovanni Boccaccio's *Decameron* for Brusantino, a wide range of literary texts for Florio, and Giambattista Basile's *Lo cunto de li cunti* for Sarnelli. In response, this book highlights how, much to the contrary, *Le cento novelle*, *Firste Fruites*, *Second Frutes*, and *Posilecheata* demonstrate significant uniqueness. Through paremias, the three authors transform language and literature in order to convey textual and authorial elements, as well as societal and cultural perspectives. Brusantino uses paremias to introduce an ethical perspective in Boccaccio's *Decameron*; Florio presents them to teach the Italian culture and language in England; and Sarnelli uses paremias to comment on linguistic practices and depict regional aspects of Baroque Naples more effectively. Brusantino, Florio, and Sarnelli consciously create new works, thereby satisfying both their view of literature and language, and the demands of the public by means of the instructive messages of their expressions.

Foreword

In the middle of the sixteenth century, Brusantino rewrote the *Decameron*, transforming its metric structure from prose to poetry. In transferring Boccaccio's work from the tradition of short stories to that of chivalric poems, he conceives of *Le cento novelle* as fusing together the prosaic form of the original text and the metrical and poetic aspects of the chivalric genre. Being born in Ferrara, he was influenced by the long-standing production of chivalric poems in octaves and innovated it by means of his moral perspectives. The allegories and paremias—which Brusantino invented and placed at the beginning of each novella—resulted from his own personal reading of the *Decameron*. He twisted the message of Boccaccio's stories to express an ethical content intended for a society that was just starting to feel the effects of the Catholic Reformation but was not yet experiencing the full Tridentine ideology.

Florio, an English-born immigrant to Soglio (in Italian-speaking Switzerland), was exposed to the Italian language during his early life and became an acclaimed teacher, translator, and linguist. Wishing to spread Italian culture in sixteenth-century London, he supported and promoted it through dictionaries, bilingual manuals, and translations. His texts are the product of a scholar living outside of Italy who is conscious of the cultural, linguistic, and communicative validity of paremias in teaching Italian to an English audience. In *Firste Fruites* and *Second Frutes*, Florio succeeded in writing two pedagogical manuals appropriate for those Elizabethan people who wished to learn the Italian language through popular culture and authorial literature. Additionally, his English translation of Italian paremias attempted to make the Italian language immediately accessible to his Anglophone students, as well as provide English words and phrases to the many Italian people living in London.

Sarnelli, a native of Apulia, hence an outsider to the Neapolitan area, adopted the Neapolitan dialect in his works because it was geographically and culturally more central than the peripheral dialect of his native area. In order to declare it superior to other available and more prestigious dialects, he used the Neapolitan language in different genres, including the newly experimental fable—much like his predecessor Basile in *Lo cunto de li cunti*. This allowed Sarnelli an immense degree of experimentation and innovation, which was in line with the Baroque spirit at the end of the seventeenth century. Some of his paremias in *Posilecheata* are *ex novo* creations in Neapolitan, whereas others are translations in Neapolitan from originals in other languages. Together, they evoke the expressive accumulation of content, the sumptuous rhetoric, the hilarious and dynamic multiplication of reality, and the "linguistic freedom" distinctive of the Neapolitan culture and dialect.

As Brusantino, Florio, and Sarnelli reinvent the meaning of paremias within the contexts of their respective texts, their work illustrates how paremias take on a specific significance. Their paremias introduce moral content and transmit simplified and easily-recognizable concluding messages more effectively than non-proverbial expressions. When they are enclosed in the development of the discourse, paremias are "narrative propellers" and, as such, cause a shift in the course of events or lead the way to a new topic. When the three authors introduce morphologic, lexical, or syntactical variations, paremias become emotional devices as well. This is because those variations usually emphasize, increase, or transform the effect that the expression has on its audience and in that specific context. The three authors' paremias are far from being immutable in their structure and message. They are selected "on the basis of what the situation requires rather than simply or solely because of either a given proverb's semantic fit or its 'truth' in some abstract sense" (Kirshenblatt-Gimblett 115). Hence, their paremias experience a flexible and fluid transition from one entity to another, which makes their works innovative and personal.

The following chapters demonstrate the vitality and constant rebirth of paremias throughout the centuries in their sociocultural and literary contexts. The first introductory chapter, "Literary History and Theories of Paremias," is a historical account of the fields of paremiography and paremiology,[1] whose analyses are organized into three macro-sections: classical and medieval periods, early modern period, and the contemporary period. This chapter lays the critical and literary foundation for the subsequent examination of paremias by introducing Franceschi's methodology in combination with an emic (or internal) and contextual analysis of proverbs. The other three chapters contain the critical evaluations of Brusantino's, Florio's, and Sarnelli's paremias in the context of their texts, linguistic choices, and communities that they aimed to reach. Chapter 2, "Vincenzo Brusantino's *Le cento novelle*:

Paremias and Tridentine Ethics in Reinterpreting the *Decameron*," introduces Brusantino's paremias through his poetic adaptation of Boccaccio's text. The text's critical exploration also brings to light the proto-Tridentine approach that the author adopts in his own 100 introductory paremias, as well as in those proverbs that he borrows from the *Decameron*. Chapter 3, "John Florio's *Firste Fruites* and *Second Frutes*: Paremias and Elizabethan Teaching of the Italian Language," presents Florio's pedagogical theories in his two language manuals. A comparison with Florio's 1591 collections of paremias, *Giardino di ricreatione*, reveals the validity of the contextual analysis in demonstrating the changes that contextualized paremias undergo in his *Fruits*. The fourth chapter, "Pompeo Sarnelli's *Posilecheata*: Paremias and the Multi-Faceted Neapolitan Baroque," places paremias within the context of the comic and explosive use of the Neapolitan dialect. This reflects the exaltation of Naples, its culture, and its community vis-à-vis the rest of the peninsula, and represents the author's creativity with a language that never gained either literary status or public recognition. Finally, an appendix concludes the book and collates the three authors' paremias allowing for further comparisons and explorations.

The analysis of the paremias of Brusantino, Florio, and Sarnelli, and, more broadly speaking, of paremias from sixteenth- and seventeenth-century Italy, contributes to our knowledge of Renaissance and Baroque paremiography. As this book offers insights on the fluidity among cultures, languages, and literatures and illustrates the relationship between paremias and contexts, it gives voice to the innumerable shapes that paremias assume and the countless messages that they continue to convey. *Abuso no quita uso* ("Abuse does not eliminate use"), says a Spanish expression: the more a paremia is used, the more it is subject to transformation due to its constant reuse in various situations (Flonta, *A Dictionary of English and Romance Languages* x).

Criteria for Transcription

The transcription of the original sources is semi-diplomatic and tends to adhere as faithfully as possible to the texts. However, a few linguistic aspects have been modernized. The vowel *u* and the consonant *v* are distinguished, including titles of works. Apostrophes and accents have been added or removed according to the rules of modern Italian, except for quotations in dialect. Double consonants may present a great deal of variation but have been preserved to allow linguistic analyses. For the same reason, Latinized word forms have been maintained, including etymological and para-etymological uses of the letter *h*. Abbreviations have been resolved, and separation between words has been introduced. Punctuation and capital letters are usually modernized, especially when they differ greatly from contemporary uses.

Notes on Quotations, Translations, and Abbreviations

Throughout the book, the number in parenthesis for citations from Brusantino's *Le cento novelle* refers to the page number in its 1554 edition. All of the original quotations from Boccaccio's *Decameron* are taken from Vittore Branca's work (Boccaccio, *Decameron* [1980]). For citations from Florio's *Firste Fruites* and *Second Frutes*, the numbers reproduce the page numbers of the 1578 and 1591 original editions, respectively. For *Firste Fruites*, the quotations follow the original numeration in sheets (*recto* [r] and *verso* [v]), whereas *Second Frutes* and *Giardino di ricreatione* adopt the original numeration in pages. The numbers beside the paremias listed in *Giardino di ricreatione* indicate the page number of the collection's edition published at the end of *Second Frutes*. For citations from Sarnelli's *Posilecheata*, the numbers refer to the page number and the paragraph number in Enrico Malato's 1986 critical edition of the collection (Sarnelli, *Posilecheata* [1986]). All quotations from Basile's *Lo cunto de li cunti* come from Carolina Stromboli's work (Basile, *Lo cunto de li cunti* [2013]); the first number refers to the page and is followed by the number of the paragraph. For Emmanuele Rocco's *Vocabolario del dialetto napolitano*, any reference from letters A-FEL comes from the 1882–91 edition; for the other letters, the recent edition by Antonio Vinciguerra is used.

When they are unavailable, the translations are my own and literal, unless otherwise specified. I refer to the English translation of Boccaccio's *Decameron* from George McWilliam's edition, published originally in 1972 by Penguin Books. An English translation of Brusantino's *Le cento novelle* does not exist. For Florio's *Firste Fruites* and *Second Frutes*, the English translation is that which Florio provides, and the original spelling is not modified. Ruth Bottigheimer's 2012 book, *Fairy Tales Framed*, offers the translation only of the prefatory letter and the final paragraphs of the introduction to Sarnelli's *Posilecheata* (76–79). The English translation of Basile's *Lo cunto de li cunti* comes from Nancy Canepa's edition of the collection (Basile, *The Tale of Tales*).

Other English translated works used in the book include the 1998 edition of the Bible, William Barker's rendering of Erasmus von Rotterdam's *Adagia* (Erasmus, *The Adages of Erasmus*), Harold Butler's translation of Marcus Fabius Quintilianus's *Institutio*

xxi

Notes on Quotations, Translations, and Abbreviations

oratoria, John Fitch and Jeffrey Henderson's rendering of Lucius Annaeus Seneca's *Tragedies* and Richard Gummere's work on his *Ad Lucilium Epistulae Morales*, James May and Jakob Wisse's edition of Marcus Tullius Cicero's *Orator* (Cicero, *On the Ideal Orator*) and David Bailey's edition of his *Letters to Atticus*, David Raeburn's work on Publius Naso Ovidius's *Metamorphoses*, and C. H. Scott and Anthony Mortimer's translation of Cecco Angiolieri's sonnets. For Italian works, the book refers to Steven Botterill's English translation of Dante Alighieri's *De vulgari eloquentia*, Joseph Consoli's edition of *Novellino*, Allen Mandelbaum's translation of Dante's *Divine Comedy*, Mark Musa's rendering of Petrarca's *Canzoniere*, Ralph Nash's work on Jacopo Sannazaro's *Arcadia*, Charles Stanley Ross's translation of Matteo Maria Boiardo's *Orlando innamorato*, and Joseph Tusiani's edition of Luigi Pulci's *Morgante*.

The following abbreviations are used throughout the book:
CC   *Lo cunto de li cunti* (Basile)
CN   *Le cento novelle* (Brusantino)
DBI   *Dizionario biografico degli italiani*
DEI   *Dizionario etimologico della lingua italiana*
Dec.   *Decameron* (Boccaccio)
FF   *Firste Fruites* (Florio)
GDLI   *Grande dizionario della lingua italiana*
GR   *Giardino di ricreatione* (Florio)
ODEP   *Oxford Dictionary of English Proverbs*
OED   *Oxford English Dictionary*
P   *Posilecheata* (Sarnelli)
RVF   *Canzoniere* or *Rerum vulgarium fragmenta* (Petrarca)
SF   *Second Frutes* (Florio)
TLF   *Trésor de la Langue Français*
Voc. Cr. *Vocabolario degli Accademici della Crusca*

The book may refer to both Florio's *Firste Fruites* and *Second Frutes* as simply *Frutes* and to Basile's *Lo cunti de li cunti* as *Cunto*.

Other abbreviations included in the book are:
par.   paragraph(s)
r   recto (when it follows a page number)

Notes on Quotations, Translations, and Abbreviations

s.l.	sub litera (to indicate the letter under which a word or expression is listed in a dictionary or encyclopedia)
s.v.	sub voce (to indicate an entry in a dictionary or encyclopedia)
v	verso (when it follows a page number)
v.	verse (to indicate the line of a poem)
vv.	verses (to indicate the lines of a poem)

All proverbs in the book are in italics; their translation is not italicized. All of the expressions that Florio highlights with an asterisk in *Second Frutes* are included in the chapters and in the list of paremias in the Index; the asterisk is reproduced beside them. In the chapters and in the Index of Paremias, the expressions are transcribed as they appear in the original texts: in lines for *Le cento novelle*; as continuous text for *Firste Fruites*, *Second Frutes*, *Giardino di ricreatione*, and *Posilecheata*.

Chapter One

Literary History and Theories of Paremias

> Proverbs and proverbial phrases usually take their original from places and persons, but then there is something of action that attends the proverb, which often being conceal'd requires a note or illustration, the circumstances of the fact being too many for the proverb to contain.
>
> Giovanni Torriano, *Piazza universale di proverbi italiani*

Paremiography: Literature of Paremias and Literature with Paremias[1]

The Classical and Middle Ages

As Teodor Flonta argues in the introduction to his 2001 *A Dictionary of English and Romance Languages Equivalent Proverbs*, paremias have existed since societies began forming and giving themselves rules for communal living (ix–xi). However, we only have evidence of their existence from the period of the Sumerian civilization, during which they were recorded in cuneiform inscriptions.[2] In ancient Greece, paremias and maxims were frequently gathered from a variety of authors and genres, including works from Hesiod, Aeschylus, Sophocles, Herodotus, Aristophanes, Euripides, and Menander. Even though structured collections of moral paremias existed in Greek,[3] they did not experience the abundant growth that occurred in the Roman world. The first two Latin accounts of sententious expressions are those by Appius Claudius Caecus (fl. 312–279 B.C.E.), who released a book called *Sententiae*, and by Quintus Ennius (239–169 B.C.E.), who wrote a collection of moral sayings called *Protrepticus*. Latin comedies were filled with paremias and *sententiae*,[4] which contributed to the expressiveness of the texts and the hilarious depiction of life and society. The works of Titus Maccius Plautus (c. 254–184 B.C.E.)

and Publius Terentius (fl. 82–35 B.C.E.) reveal this paremiac use. Authors also inserted paremias in other genres intending to offer moral suggestions or advice for everyday living. For instance, Publius Vergilius Maro enriched his *Georgica* (29 B.C.E.) with many paremias providing recommendations for agricultural techniques and a prosperous peasant life.[5]

While there is no evidence of Lucius Apuleius Madaurensis's supposed work *De proverbiis*, Lucius Annaeus Seneca (4 B.C.E.–65 A.D.) resorted to proverbial expressions quite frequently in his works, especially his *suasoriae* and *controversiae*.[6] Collections of his proverbs and anthologies of his *sententiae* and *loci communi* started circulating from the fifteenth century for pedagogical purposes, primarily teaching students Latin grammar and offering them moral guidance in life.[7] Seneca employed paremias to reinforce a theme, provide epigrammatic comments, and introduce rhetorical paradoxes.[8] In his epistle 33 from *Ad Lucilium Epistulae Morales* ("Letters on Ethics to Lucilius"), he mentions that children memorize proverbs because of their condensed structure: "facilius … singula insidunt circumscripta et carminis modo inclusa" ("single maxims sink in more easily when they are marked off and bounded like a line of verse"; par. 6). Seneca foregrounds this discourse within a consideration on the progressive autonomy of the human mind. He posits that if in childhood proverbs work to express ideas because the mind cannot hold long structures, in adulthood people should produce thoughts of their own and not simply recycle others' words. Even though Seneca consistently references proverbs, Dionysius Cato (third–fourth century A.D.) is considered the most prolific Latin writer of paremias and sayings. He is known for his *Carmen de moribus* and, primarily, for his *Disticha Catonis*.[9] His works were appreciated in the Middle Ages—and in the Renaissance too—for their moralizing intent, severely pedagogical tone, and rhythmic structure, as well as their caustic and solemn content. Therefore, medieval grammar books frequently relied on Cato's paremias to provide students moral examples of individual and societal conduct (Gehl par. 2.02 and 2.14–2.15).[10]

Alongside Cato, collections of famous *sententiae* and expressions used as sources of maxims and proverbs included Valerius Maximus's *Dicta et facta memorabilia* (first century A.D.), Sextus

Julius Frontinus's (35–105 A.D.) *Strategemata*, and even Gaius (or Titus) Arbiter Petronius's *Satyricon* (first century A.D.) with its everyday sententious and witty expressions.[11] Maximus's writings informed later works, such as the thirteenth-century *Fiori e vita di filosofi e d'altri savi e d'imperadori* and collections of exemplary sentences for preachers (D'Agostino, *Fiori e vita di filosofi*). A fundamental source for paremias in the Middle Ages, though, were religious texts (including the Bible), whose maxims and sayings were intended to help students learn moral precepts. In the *Old Testament*, Solomon's *Proverbs* is composed of nine collections of paremias by diverse authors and periods for a total of almost 3,000 one-line maxims (according to 1 Kings 4:32–33). Among these nine collections, only the second and the fifth are attributed to Solomon, the wise King of Israel. His paremias provide useful teachings by focusing on the positive outcome of faithful and upright behavior vis-à-vis the negative results of bad manners that are far from God's precepts. As such, they serve to expose people to existential wisdom for their final reward (*Proverbs* 1:5–6).[12] The other Sapiential books, i.e., *Ecclesiastes*, *Job*, *Wisdom*, and *Sirach* or *Ecclesiasticus*, along with the *Psalms* and sparingly the *Song of Songs*, list a considerable number of proverbs, maxims, and sententious sayings.[13] In the *New Testament*, paremias are scattered, yet fill the *Acts of the Apostles* (20:35), the *Apocalypse*, the *Letters*, as well as the gospels of Matthew (a few selected ones are 6:21–25; 7:17–20; 12:30–74; 13:12; 20:16; 22:14; 24:28; 25:29), Mark (4:25), Luke (6:45; 8:18; 17:37; 19:26), and John (a reference to speaking in proverbs is 16:25).[14]

Similarly, medieval laic collections gathered pearls of wisdom, as well as paremias related to common life and people. Petrarca's great-grandfather, Garzo, a notary in Incisa (Tuscany), collected 240 proverbs, organizing them alphabetically and structuring them in rhymed distiches of five, six, seven, or eight syllables.[15] An almost identical structure informs *Proverbia que dicuntur super natura feminarum*, circulating in the twelfth century and written in a Northern Italian vernacular (Tobler). In this text, paremias on the nature of women are organized into 189 rhymed quatrains of alexandrine verses. *Conti morali dell'anonimo senese* belongs to the thirteenth century and gathers twelve surviving edifying stories with final moral closings that resemble maxims (Segre and Marti). In the second half of the fourteenth century, Paolo di messer Pace

Chapter One

da Certaldo's *Libro di buoni costumi* gathered 388 "molti buoni assempri e buoni costumi e buoni proverbi e buoni ammaestramenti" ("many good examples and good customs and useful proverbs and valuable precepts"), meant to benefit those adhering to their principles.[16]

The most well-known medieval collection of proverbs is, however, *Dialogus Salomonis et Marcolfi* (eleventh century), which started to circulate widely in the thirteenth century when copies in Latin and in the vernacular (*El dyalogo de Salomon e Marcolpho*) were printed in Venice.[17] The work contrasts two typologies of wisdom in a lively and tense exchange of rhetorical lines, initially characterized by a playful atmosphere but later leading to dramatic tones. King Solomon's wisdom is composed of erudite paremias, many of biblical origins, whereas Marcolfo's arises from the worldly experience of rural people.[18] Solomon's paremias are also the subject of a thirteenth-century collection by Girardo Patecchio da Cremona, *Splanamento de li Proverbii de Salamone*, which gathers distiches of alexandrine verses for a total of 607 lines. This collection contains a translation of Solomon's paremias in a Northern dialect, interspersed with expressions from *Ecclesiastes*, *Disticha Catonis*, and *Proverbia que dicuntur super natura feminarum* (Contini, vol. 1: 557–83). The later 1533 *Annotationi di Antonio Brucioli sopra i proverbii di Salomo* translates all of the 31 chapters of "i salutiferi Proverbii di Salomo" ("health-bearing proverbs by Solomon"; *iir*) into Tuscan vernacular. Brucioli asserts that these holy *sententiae* can guide to eternity those willing to apply them constantly. Following the list of proverbs in each chapter, with the exception of the last two chapters, Brucioli provides a short commentary for most of the expressions to explain difficult words and concepts, or reveal the depth and solemnity of their messages.[19] Published by Aurelio Pincio's printing press, the work was intended to educate the masses and make the Bible accessible to everyone in the Ferrara of Renée of France.[20] Brucioli's 1546 *Commento in tutti i Sacrosanti libri del vecchio et nuovo Testamento* provides more extensive explanations of a selection of Solomon's proverbs with a specific focus on their wisdom, usefulness, and divine messages.

Paremias also appeared in genres that were originally linked to oral traditions, especially short stories. The first important paremiac examples are featured in the *Decameron* (1349–53), in which

Boccaccio employed proverbs and sayings in those privileged places that the rhetorical doctrine of *dispositio* reserved for the refined morality of *sententiae* (Chiecchi, "Sentenze e proverbi" 145).[21] In these instances, paremias either start a narration or otherwise comment on a specific event in a comic, ironic, or moralizing way. The expressions gathered in Boccaccio's work frequently refer to the vast circulation of popular sayings and emphasize the role of the populace as the true repository of wisdom and common knowledge. For example, the proverbial phrase introducing Maestro Alberto's novella (Dec. I.10) is said to be common among people as it expresses the idea that women always make the worst choices and select the worst options in everything: "… acciò che per voi non si possa quello proverbio intendere che comunemente si dice per tutto, cioè che *le femmine in ogni cosa sempre pigliano il peggio*" ("Wherefore… in order that people should not associate you with the proverb commonly heard on everyone's lips, namely that women are always worsted in any argument"; Dec. I.10.8). Similarly, Boccaccio opens Friar Alberto's novella (Dec. IV.2) with a supposedly very common proverb: "Usano i volgari un così fatto proverbio: *Chi è reo e buono è tenuto, può fare il male e non è creduto*" ("There is a popular proverb which runs as follows: 'He who is wicked and held to be good, can cheat because no one imagine he would'"; Dec. IV.2.5). Giuseppe Chiecchi argues that the use of the word "volgari" ("vulgar") does not mean that Boccaccio adheres to a popular linguistic program. The author rather shows how proverbs rhetorically refer to a specific characterization of people, events, and attitudes ("Sentenze e proverbi" 136–41). For the most part, characters who are simple or not as well educated as noble characters can more profoundly understand how reality works and achieve its true representation and description through paremias. In this aspect, Boccaccio initiated a trend that would run through all major collections of short stories up until the end of the sixteenth century (Bruscagli, "La novella e il romanzo" 838–39 and 902–7).[22] As Paola Manni states, the *Decameron* was "una vera miniera di modi di dire, locuzioni, proverbi, buona parte dei quali vengono per la prima volta immessi nel circuito della letteratura volgare" ("a true treasure trove of sayings, phrases, proverbs, most of which are for the first time inserted in the circuit of vernacular literature"; 294).

Chapter One

The Renaissance and Early Modern Period

Paremias were used extensively in fourteenth-, fifteenth-, and sixteenth-century *cantari novellistici* and in chivalric poems, which were originally oral much like collections of short stories. Luigi Pulci's *Morgante* (1483), which belongs to the Florentine tradition of chivalric poems, abounds with Tuscan proverbs, popular idiomatic expressions, and maxims, especially comic ones (Ankli). Written during the same period, but in Ferrara, Boiardo's *Orlando innamorato* (1483; 1495) uses paremias extensively in depicting Astolfo and Orlando (Bruscagli, *Studi cavallereschi* 106–7). Conversely, in fellow-citizen Ludovico Ariosto's *Orlando furioso* (1516; 1521; 1532), paremias serve as moral openings and closing remarks both in cantos and in single octaves (Soletti, "«Come raccende il gusto il mutar esca»" 142–43). In Francesco da Ferrara Cieco's *Libro d'arme e d'amore, nomato Mambriano* (1509),[23] Cassio da Narni's *Morte del Danese* (1521), and Brusantino's *L'Angelica innamorata* (1550), the authors insert proverbs, along with allegories and formulaic openings, at the beginning of the cantos to summarize their moral content. This tendency influences Brusantino in his *Le cento novelle,* and can be seen in other genres as well, especially in fables.[24]

By the end of the fifteenth and the beginning of the sixteenth centuries, the proliferation of collections of paremias in Latin and in vernaculars was remarkable. Generally, these collections included maxims (moral utterances without any metaphorical meaning, commonly used by a community),[25] apothegms (a famous person's memorable, anecdotal, and sententious saying, usually witty),[26] and aphorisms (expressions containing rules of life). These collections were aimed to provide delight through the narration of genuine events and anecdotes associated with ancient and classical wisdom or through the presentation of characters remarkable for their witty comments and hilarious quotations. Examples include Poggio Bracciolini's *Liber facetiarum* (1438–52), Arlotto Mainardi's *Motti e facezie del Piovano Arlotto* (1450–70), Ludovico Carbone's *Le facetie* (1466–71), Antonio Cornazzano *De proverbiorum origine* and *Proverbi in facetie* (second half of the fifteenth century), Angelo Poliziano's *Detti piacevoli* (1470s), and Giovanni Pontano's *De sermone*[27] (1499).[28]

In the fifteenth century, three collections of Latin paremias stood out from the others: Lorenzo Lippi's *Liber Proverbiorum*, which was already circulating in the 1470s at Lorenzo de' Medici's court; Niccolò Angeli's *Proverbiorum collectanea*, written between 1486 and 1492; and Polidoro Vergili's *Proverbiorum libellus*, released in 1498.[29] Drawing from ancient sources as well as contemporary works, Lippi's *Liber Proverbiorum* gathered 100 brief *sententiae*, mostly to use in public discourses. Progressively more substantial, Angeli's *Proverbiorum collectanea* contained 263 *sententiae*, of which many (between 100 and 140) were exact copies of Poliziano's *Detti piacevoli* and appeared in the same order. In his *Proverbiorum libellus*, humanist Vergili collected 305 Latin proverbs, first listing them alphabetically and, then, providing literary references, contextual uses, and explanations of difficult *loci* as part of a rhetorical exercise. The great number of manuscripts and the appreciation that contemporaneous scholars and authors expressed for these three collections attest to the great interest in paremiography in the decades before the publication of Erasmus von Rotterdam's work on proverbs (1500).

Despite not being the first collection of Latin expressions, *Adagiorum Collectanea* (also known as *Adagia*), later titled *Adagiorum Chiliades* (by Venetian Aldo Manuzio in 1508), is one of the most influential collections of paremias.[30] In 1536, after 26 reprints, the last edition was released: the collection had been greatly expanded to approximately 4,150 *sententiae* examined comparatively, a quantity unequalled in the classical period or in the Renaissance.[31] In other words, *Adagia* was a compilation of the moral treasure of antiquity (Erasmus, *Collected Works of Erasmus* [*Prolegomena to the Adages*] 38–83; Rico 130), offering a paremiographic exemplar to imitate and a compendium of expressions that could be researched in national and local traditions[32] (Tosi, "Gli «Adagia» di Erasmo" 44).[33] As such, it promoted the revival of letters in Europe, despite being listed in Pius IV's 1564 *Index librorum prohibitorum*, as well as in the later 1596 issue by Pope Clement VIII under the category "Certorum auctorum libri prohibiti" ("Prohibited books of sure authors").[34] In Erasmus's collection, an explanation follows each paremia and usually provides an indication of its literal meaning and figurative usage, when present. At times, the commentary contains a detailed description of the sources or offers information about the ancient world. Some explanations even resemble a treatise, in which the author expresses his personal reflections on political, moral, and social issues. The collection, though, lacks organizational criteria: paremias do not follow an alphabetical order and are collected alongside maxims, phrases, metaphors, mottos, and even single words. Expressions such as *Labyrithus* ("A labyrinth") or *Sileni Alcibiadis* ("The Sileni of Alcibiades"),[35] devoid of any moral or metaphorical intent, appear beside true figurative phrases, including *Simile gaudet simili* ("Like rejoices in like") and *Piscem natare doces* ("You are teaching a fish to swim").

After 1500, Italy experienced an increasingly large interest in anecdotes, paremias, apothegms, and maxims, and consequently collections of paremias thrived. At the beginning of the century, they mostly gathered witty and comic expressions that could combine the useful with the agreeable (Speroni, *Wit and Wisdom* 1–2).[36] Among the others,[37] Aloyse Cynthio de gli Fabritii's collection, *Libro della origine delli volgari proverbi* (1526), dedicated to Pope Clement VII, presents ironic, sarcastic, and comedic scenes to illustrate the message traditionally attached to 45 paremias. As Cynthio declares in his preface and introductory sonnet, *Alli blateratori et sgridatori del libro et dello autore morditori* ("To those who blabber and reprimand the book and castigate the author"), the book might hurt the honor of women and harshly condemns the fallacious behavior not only of members of the clergy but also aristocrats and the populace (31; 34).[38] Cynthio organizes his paremias in 194 chapters in a *terza rima* pattern (ABACBC tercets) and structures their explanation in three *cantiche*, which he always concludes with "Così è nato il proverbio" ("The proverb originated this way"). For all of the proverbs, he invents a social and historical context, including hilarious characters and events. In doing so, he reconstructs the expressions' origins, heavily relying on a dialogic pattern that makes the style fast paced and lively. By drawing from classical fables and Boccaccio's *Decameron*, and by experimenting with Florentine vernacular and dialect forms, Cynthio uses paremias as bridges to expose the social situation of his time and, simultaneously, create an enjoyable reading experience.[39]

Shaped by epistolography, paremias characterize Antonio Bonagiunti Vignali's 1557 famous letter composed of 365 proverbs ("Lettera di Antonio Vignali Arsiccio Intronato in proverbii").[40] In this epistle, paremias are not pure rhetorical and stylistic exercises, but they are also tools that transmit meaningful ironic messages. The paremias' meaning can be ambiguous, given the lack of an explicit context and the infinite possibilities of paremiac application. However, the textual organization, the historical context, and the author's social and political standpoint clarifies the intended meaning of all of the expressions (Pignatti "Frottola e proverbio" 269–72).[41] First, Vignali arranges the paremias according to their meaning, as an act of mnemonic reference, either because one paremia logically depends on the other or because two expressions share the same structure. Second, since he writes a letter to a "gentilissima Madonna" ("a very gentle lady") who happens to symbolize the city of Siena, the listed paremias reveal Vignali's negative attitude toward its citizens and provide moral lessons on everyday social life.[42]

Between the sixteenth and seventeenth centuries, six paremiographers were prominent for the size of their own collections: Lionardo Salviati, Orlando Pescetti, Agnolo (or Angelo) Monosini, Tomaso Buoni, Francesco Serdonati, and Francesco Lena.[43] Salviati supervised the first systematic and large collection of Italian vernacular paremias (Fiorelli, "La raccolta di proverbi di Francesco Serdonati" 221). As a small codex (Cl. I 394), now kept in the Biblioteca Comunale Ariostea in Ferrara, it gathered 3,131 Tuscan paremias, to which five different people contributed in the period from 1588–89 until after the 1612 publication of the *Vocabolario degli Accademici della Crusca*.[44] Organized alphabetically, only by their first letter, Salviati's paremias seem to be listed as a repository of expressions for a future lexicographic undertaking. They are either presented with a succinct explanation or comment, or they do not present any additional information, as can be seen in one of the most important pages of the manuscript from a philological perspective (67): *Come l'huom salvatico. Si rallegra del mal tempo* ("Like the wild man. He welcomes the bad weather"), *Can che morde non abbaia invano* ("A dog that bites does not bark in vain"), *Come una serpe tra l'anguille* ("Like a snake between eels"), *Chi s'appella ha mala novella* ("He who protests has bad news"), *Chi s'impaccia co' grandi maestri, l'ultimo a tavola e 'l primo a' capestri* ("He who gets in the way of the great masters is the last at the table and the first at the noose"), *Cotal grado ha chi tigna pettina* ("Such is ever the requital of those that comb scurfy heads"), meaning that he who is of service to ungrateful or unworthy people is repaid with ingratitude, *Can che lecchi cenere non gli fidar farina* ("To a dog that licks ashes do not trust flour"), *Chi vuol de' pesci bisogna che s'immolli* ("He who wants the fish must get wet"), *Chi fa la notte dimenare il letto, il giorno lo tien fermo a suo dispetto* ("He who makes the bed wiggle during the night, the day holds it in spite").

Expanding the paremias collected by Salviati, Orlando Pescetti published his collection *Proverbi italiani* in 1598. The collection of almost 6,550 paremias listed expressions without any organizational methods or classifying criteria (254–58).[45] Seldom paremias are described succinctly or reference a comparable expression in Latin. For instance, Pescetti pairs *Non ha sale in zucca* ("He does not have salt in his head") with *Caput vacuum cerebro* ("Head empty of brain") to indicate a foolish person. This characteristic anticipates a feature of his later shorter collection of proverbs for children who needed to learn grammar, titled *Proverbi italiani e latini* (Pignatti, *Etimologia e proverbio* 254–63). In this bilingual work from 1602, each paremia in vernacular is provided with a Latin correspondent that conveys the same or a similar meaning.[46] For instance, the Latin paremia *Ex minimo artificio noscitur artifex* ("From a small artifice the architect is recognized") accompanies the Italian expression *Chi vuol conoscere s'è buon scrittore, gli dia la penna in mano* ("He who wishes to know if he is a good writer, give him a pen"). Both express the message that one could detect someone's profession from small details. However, the Latin paremia refers to a general creator, whereas the Italian equivalent specifically mentions a writer, probably an indirect reference to Pescetti's own literary production. The collection was likely meant to provide students with a structure that could be analyzed syntactically and that could help reinforce their linguistic and syntactical skills, while, at the same time, offering pedagogical and moral content (Messina Fajardo 9). Thanks to Pescetti, paremiography shifts into a utilitarian discipline; that is, the use of proverbs is leveraged for the pedagogical benefit of both individuals and society as a whole (Pignatti, *Etimologia e proverbio* 262). This is also expressed in his 1592 *Orazione dietro al modo dell'istituire la gioventù* as a method to increase the young students' virtue and knowledge. Pescetti exhorts teachers to require students to learn a proverb each day by heart and to continue studying them through the years along with two new Greek words (C4).[47]

At the beginning of the seventeenth century, Monosini released his *Flos Italicae Linguae Libri novem* (1604), a collection of roughly 4,000 paremias and *sententiae*, organized into nine books.[48] The collection gathers Latin, Greek, and vernacular paremias provided with etymological and literary excursuses and examined in their morphological, syntactical, and lexical aspects. For instance, Florio's paremia *Chi ben vive ben muore* ("He who lives well, dies well"; FF [28]*r*) features here in the fifteenth sermon on prodigality, *De prodigalitate*. The expression is said to come from those excerpts of Menander's comedies (*Menandri sententiae*) that Joannes Stobaeus reported in his Ανθολογιον ("Anthologion") or *Florilegium* of excerpts, mainly from ethical pagan authors of antiquity. Monosini reports the following trilingual comparison, with the Greek coming from Menander's fragments and the Italian and Latin translation provided by himself: *Chi ben vive, ben muore. Βίου δικαίου γίγνεται τέλοσ καλόν. Iustae vitae honestus est finis* ("He who lives well, dies well. An honest life becomes a good conclusion. Honesty is the aim of a correct life"; Third Book, 146: no. 243).[49] Proverbs, proverbial phrases, sayings, puns, riddles, and other linguistic expressions represent Monosini's exaltation of the everyday Florentine language, its creativity, and its patrimony of *riboboli* and cultural traditions (Fiorelli, "Tra il proverbio e la regola di diritto" 193; Pignatti, *Etimologia e proverbio* 106). His use of Latin and Greek demonstrates how he aimed to reach a wider public of Italians as well as foreigners for whom Latin was the *lingua franca*. As such, his paremias illustrate the possibility of the Florentine vernacular serving as the language of the Italian peninsula and representing the culture of a nation to-be (83).[50]

In the same year as Monosini's *Flos*, Buoni released his work entitled *Nuovo thesoro de' proverbii italiani*, which collects not only ornaments of the language[51] but also precepts that transmit universal values thought to be broadly helpful to humanity (Pignatti, *Etimologia e proverbio* 306–16).[52] Buoni was the first to differentiate—at least in title if not consistently throughout the entire sections—between the various types of paremias. The subdivisions include *Proverbii tolti dagli animali* ("Proverbs coming from animals"), *Proverbi tolti dalla moltitudine delle cose dell'universo* ("Proverbs coming from the multitude of things in the universe"), *Sentenze proverbiose* ("Proverbial sentences"), *Modi*

Chapter One

di dire proverbiosi per similitudine ("Proverbial sayings by similitude"), and *Detti traslati* ("Figurative sayings").[53] They consist of a considerable number of expressions, first listed within the subsections and, then, all adequately interpreted and commented. One example is *Chi non ha memoria, habbia gambe* ("He who does not have memory, let him have legs"). Buoni interprets the expression as referring to the relationship between masters and servants: when the servants forget their duties because they do not remember their masters' orders, they need to go back to their tasks (metaphorically, through their legs) in order to fulfill them.

Detailed explanations are also present in Serdonati's collection, assembled just before 1610 and now preserved in Rome at the Biblioteca Vaticana and in Florence at the Biblioteca Nazionale, the Biblioteca Laurenziana, and the Accademia della Crusca. Serdonati's work gathers almost 26,000 Tuscan paremias, making it an extraordinary collection in the field of Italian paremiography (Biffi, "La raccolta di proverbi"). For almost every collected paremia, Serdonati provides literary and historical references and a great number of synonymic variants, which frequently attest to minimal morphological variation. This attention to detail, which anticipates the Baroque tendency for accumulation and elaboration, is evident when Serdonati's proverbs are compared with Salviati's. For instance, Serdonati explains Salviati's paremia mentioned above, *Chi s'impaccia co' gran maestri, è l'ultimo a tavola e prima a' capestri* ("He who gets in the way of the great masters is the last at the table and the first at the noose"), extensively. He even resorts to another proverb in order to convey its meaning: "Gli uomini mezzani non deono di leggieri conversare co' grandi e potenti, perché nelle prosperità tengono l'ultimo luogo e son poco stimati, e nell'avversità sono i primi a patire, ché *le mosche*, come dice il proverbio, *si posano addosso a' cavalli magri*" ("The men of middle social status should not engage in light conversations with great and powerful people, because, in prosperous times, they keep the last place and are little esteemed and, in adverse times, they are the first to suffer, since, as the proverb says, Unto the lean horses, always resort the flies").[54]

At the end of the seventeenth century,[55] just a few years after the third edition of the Accademia della Crusca's dictionary was published in 1691, Lena released his *Proverbi italiani e latini* (1694), one of the largest bilingual collections of the century with more than 10,000 paremias.[56] The author specifies that he drew the expressions from classical poets and authors, and organized them in alphabetical order even within each letter. As in similar bilingual collections, the Latin paremias are connected to the equivalent Italian expressions by means of their message, without a word-by-word correspondence. An example may be a proverb that describes the indifference of a major element towards a minor one: Lena pairs an expression that Sarnelli uses in his *Posilecheata* (P 169.81), *La luna non cura l'abbaiar de cani* ("The moon does not care about the barking of dogs"), with the Latin *Culicem non curat elephantus* ("The elephant does not worry about the gnat"; b. 3, 2). In his letter to the reader, Lena appeals to the consciousness of his audience in pointing out any possible omissions in his collection. He justifies himself stating that a proverb is "un detto, che diversamente suona in diversi paesi, anzi varia tra gli autori della stessa nazione" ("a saying that sounds different in different nations and, actually, varies among the authors of the same nation"; A4v). Therefore, Lena admits that it is impossible to gather all of the available expressions, even though he is familiar with collections of paremias and works containing paremias. Specifically, he mentions Monosini's *Flos*, Gilles Ménage's index of Italian sayings,[57] and the 1688 edition of Lippi's *Malmantile racquistato*. This last work presents many paremias in Lippi's dedicatory letter to Leopoldo de' Medici as well as commentaries to proverbs, sayings, and idiomatic expressions for the understanding of the large public.[58] Compared to Pescetti's work, Lena's intent in his collection is less pedagogical. Rather, his paremias are cultural and social repositories, which identify a community of speakers and represent its knowledge and wisdom.

For all the collections published after 1612, the *Vocabolario degli Accademici della Crusca* constitutes a valuable source of paremiac expressions (Biffi, "La raccolta di proverbi"; Guidotti). Although it is true of all five editions of the dictionary, the first one exemplifies an innovative approach to paremiography. The consistent presence of paremias begins with its title: *Vocabolario degli Accademici della Crusca, con tre indici delle voci, locuzioni e proverbi latini, e greci posti per entro l'opera* ("Dictionary of the academicians of the Crusca with three indexes of the Latin and Greek entries, phrases, and proverbs, inserted in the work"). This reflected the Crusca's interest in spoken and popular language as well as other communicative expressions that do not necessarily belong to sophisticated literature. The compilers followed a method of classification that distinguished between proverbs, proverbial phrases, proverbial locutions, precepts, and sayings appearing in the dictionary's entries. As the secretary of the Academy Bastiano de' Rossi reports in his diary, each compiler had to "far menzione ne' Prolegomeni del proverbio minutissimamente, e quindi accennare che sia proverbio, che sentenzia proverbiale, che precetto, detto, o locuzione proverbiale" ("mention the proverb in its smallest details in the preliminary remarks and, then, specify if it is a proverb, a proverbial sentence, a precept, a saying, or a proverbial phrase"; 1602–06; Aresti 295; Guidotti 313; Parodi S. 337). In the preface, the academicians state that they gathered both facetious and serious proverbs alongside sayings and proverbial phrases. All of these expressions may be present either within the body of their main verb listed as a dictionary's entry, or within the body of their main noun, or else in both (Voc. Cr. *a*4r). The major sources for the paremias in the 1612 edition of the *Vocabolario* appear to be Monosini's *Flos* and Salviati's collection. In the *Indice de' proverbi latini e greci* ("Index of the Latin and Greek proverbs"), the academicians emphasize that, whenever they did not specify the author of a paremia, either the expression was very famous or derived from Monosini's *Flos* or "il libro de gli Adagi" ("The Book of the Adages"), clearly Erasmus von Rotterdam's *Adagia* (i2r).[59] Monosini's work is mentioned as the collection to which the reader should refer to find etymological explanations for all of those paremias that are not devoted to a thorough description.[60] Though not cited as a source, Salviati's collection is equally referenced in the *Vocabolario*: fifty-three percent of his paremias, specifically 279 out of 527, are found in the dictionary with minor discrepancies. These include punctuation, vocabulary, syntax, and occasional transformations of an expression's structure to fit the context of the commentary in the dictionary's entries (Biffi, "La raccolta di proverbi" 291–93). The authors of the paremias, however, are never specified, since the members of the Academy considered the proverbial expressions as "maniere di favellare" ("ways of speaking").[61] Alessandro Aresti argues that, in fact, proverbs and proverbial phrases are not distinguished and, thus, the label "proverb" is applied to any expression that conveys a moral message or transmits useful life suggestions (298–99).

The Nineteenth, Twentieth, and Twenty-First Centuries

In the nineteenth century, many collections of Italian paremias were published, consistent with the romantic tendency to discover popular origins and preserve the cultural aspects of local communities.[62] Two distinctive ones emerged primarily due to the great number of expressions that they gathered. The first collection, called *Proverbi*, appeared in 1853 by the Tuscan poet Giuseppe Giusti.[63] This work presented nearly 3,000 paremias in alphabetical order, which Gino Capponi later organized thematically in his 1871 supervised publication known as *Proverbi Toscani*. Giusti rarely explains the listed paremias, except for thirty-eight *Illustrazioni* ("Illustrations"), in which he describes the paremias' meanings, uses, and literary references in detail (*Proverbi* 217–62). Since his paremias belong to everyday language, Giusti includes useful teachings and suggestions intended for a wide audience. A few decades later, in 1883 the writer Gustavo Strafforello published an extensive and encyclopedic work on paremias in two volumes, entitled *La sapienza del mondo*. The work catalogues collections of paremias in Italian, Latin, dialects, and many foreign languages, which Strafforello accessed through his translations and his collaborations in lexicographic projects (xiii–xxv). Its core is an alphabetical list of proverbs in Italian, some of which are originally in Italian and others are translated from other languages. Paremias are gathered in accordance with a lexical criterion and, therefore, appear under an entry, which is generally the central term of the proverb (noun, verb, or adverb). They do not follow an alphabetical principle inside each section, and explanations and examples are included occasionally.[64]

In the twentieth century, paremiographers continued collecting national as well as local paremias and introduced spoken accounts alongside written expressions. Simultaneously, paremiologists persisted in speculating about their constituent characteristics, attempting to delimit the field and clarify the dichotomy between proverbial expressions and other forms of communication. The difficulty in finding a clear-cut definition for paremias and their different typologies lies in their shared features that differ in degree of intensity and often-untraceable origins. The following paragraphs briefly overview the theoretical and taxonomical speculations regarding paremias, from the classical period to the most recent considerations on paremiology.[65]

Chapter One

Paremiology: Defining Paremias
The Classical and Middle Ages

The introductory paragraph of the first and still most comprehensive study on proverbs in the English-speaking world, Archer Taylor's 1931 *The Proverb*, raises an important question on the definition of proverbs. Taylor challenges the foundational characteristics that traditionally distinguish proverbs from other paremias:

> The definition of a proverb is too difficult to repay the undertaking; and should we fortunately combine in a single definition all the essential elements and give each the proper emphasis, we should not even then have a touchstone. An incommunicable quality tells us this sentence is proverbial and that one is not. Hence no definition will enable us to identify positively a sentence as proverbial. (3)

Similarly, Italian paremiographer Alberto Mario Cirese highlights the indefiniteness of the field:

> La prima difficoltà in cui ci si imbatte studiando i proverbi è proprio quello di stabilire (sia pure in linea preliminare ma con un minimo di precisione) di che cosa ci si stia occupando o di che cosa ci si debba occupare. (*I proverbi* 1)
>
> The first difficulty that one encounters when studying proverbs is precisely that of establishing (albeit in a preliminary way but with a minimum of precision) what one is dealing with, or should be dealing with.

Providing an exhaustive and clear-cut definition of proverbs is not an easy task given the precariousness of their nature and the varied taxonomies of different languages and cultures (Del Ninno 387). Proverbs entail a variety of aspects, many of which are specifically cultural and folkloristic. Therefore, this status as proverb is difficult to recognize outside the community and context in which the expression is created. Additionally, the denomination "proverb" often includes expressions that share a few similarities with actual proverbs but present dissimilar structure and meaning. Frequently, scholars use the available terminology differently, so that, as Cirese argues, it is challenging to establish the subject and define its typological boundaries.

As mentioned before, the "Scuola Geoparemiologica Italiana," which Franceschi established in the 1980s to promote the study and analysis of Italian proverbs geographically, recently adopted the term *paremia* to solve these issues. The term substitutes for the common Italian word *proverbio* and encompasses all those expressions that share distinctive features.[66] The Greek word παροιμία ("paroimia") combines the suffix παρα- ("similar to," "akin") and the noun οἴμη, which indicates a song or an oral account appointed to instruct.[67] Hence, paremias are characterized by spoken elements and deliver pedagogical content. To these aspects, Franceschi would add a linguistic characterization that explains the structure of all paremiac expressions.

In the Greek world, παροιμίαι ("paroimiai") were not distinguished from maxims, apothegms, and aphorisms. Generally, since paremias were defined by popular and oral transmission of knowledge, they were not considered suitable for elevated works of rhetoric (Kindstrand 71). Aristotle was the first to provide examples of παροιμίαι and to analyze them as a paremiologist in a lost work called Παροιμίαι.[68] In his *Rhetoric*, he differentiates between examples and enthymemes and evaluates their role in rhetorical discourses and syllogistic reasoning (1393a–b). Enthymemes, i.e., rhetorical arguments (as opposed to demonstrative ones), include, on one hand, references to past events and, on the other, pure inventions, which incorporate similes and fables. In particular, fables are said to be fruitful in deliberative or decisional discourses because they can be invented infinitely. Enthymemes, similes, and fables impart a solemn and sententious character to the orator's performance and, at the same time, help persuade the orator's public and effectively direct the human mind to a specific reaction. Enthymemes also include maxims, which, since they appeal to universal concepts and are well-known statements, become optimal tools for moral and ethical topics. Even though many species of maxims exist, each suitable for a specific context, speaking in maxims is appropriate only for those older in years, experienced on the subject, and willing to transmit some useful and ethical advice (1394a–1395b). When he describes paremias, Aristotle writes that they connect two distant worlds that are seemingly unrelated. As much as poetry, the metaphorical process allows for a portion of the paremia's meaning to be associated with an external entity and to deliver a successful message (1413a). Moreover, as metaphors, paremias resemble ambiguous expressions or *aenigmata*, which embellish the literary discourse, infusing it with effectiveness and sharpness while, at the same time, making it enjoyable to the readers (Di Capua 50–57).

In Latin, two words were used to indicate the Greek παροιμία: *proverbium* and *adagium*. The etymology of *proverbium* highlights the presence of words: *verbum pro verbo* means a word taking the place of or substituting for another word. Thus, a proverb essentially transmits another, metaphorical, meaning, which differs from the meaning of each of its lexical components. Since they are *verba* ("spoken words"), the word *proverbia* also refers to spoken utterances and, indirectly, to works rooted in orality. Unlike *proverbium*, which became common after Marcus Tullius Cicero, the term *adagium* was quite widespread in the Middle Ages and early modern period. The etymology, which traces back to *ad agendum aptum* ("good at doing"), emphasizes the moral, ethical, and practical aspects of these expressions. Therefore, it was perfectly suitable for the religious and moral atmosphere of medieval and Renaissance times (Kelso 412).[69]

The most renowned Latin authors speculated over paremias and proverbs in their works, providing well-fitting classifications, mostly related to oratorical and rhetorical practices. In his *De oratore,* Cicero includes paremias in a group of words or phrases that, as witty remarks and jokes, are able to ridicule and defeat an adversary orator (*On the Ideal Orator,* II.60.244). Paremias belong to "ridiculum in dicto" ("mockery found in words"), which a biting expression causes, and are opposed to "ridiculum in re" ("mockery found in events"), which includes anecdotes on human behavior. Only those expressions (paremias included) that are "peracutum et breve" ("extremely ingenious and short") and characterized by "dicacitas" ("nipping sharpness") can be successful means for rhetorical purposes (II.54.218).

If Seneca does not offer any critical reflections on the definition of proverbs, this does not occur with Marcus Fabius Quintilianus, who follows and adapts Aristotle's description of paremias to the rhetorical context of his *Institutio oratoria*.[70] In Book 5, he defines παροιμία as "genus illud, quod est velut fabella brevior et per allegoriam accipitur" ("that class of proverb which may be regarded as an abridged fable and is understood allegorically"; V.11.21). Moreover, he considers paremias as *figurae* or tropes,[71] because of their process of allegorical and metaphorical interpretation, and links them to fairy tales thanks to the concise morality that they express.[72] In Book 6, while emphasizing their laughable aspect, he adds that "proverbia oportune aptata, ut homini nequam lapso et ut adlevaretur roganti «tollat te qui non novit»" ("a neat application of proverbs may also be effective, as when one man replied to another, a worthless fellow, who had fallen down and asked to be helped to his feet, 'Let someone pick you up who does not know you'"; VI.3.98). When talking about *urbanitas*, which is a certain witty flavor necessary in appealing conversations, Quintilianus proves that paremias adapt to a variety of situations easily. Moreover, paremias elegantly contribute to a humorous tone, hence attracting the listeners and persuading them to accept the orator's opinion (Di Capua 81).[73]

In the thirteenth century, anthologies of maxims and sayings by Greek and Latin philosophers, Roman emperors, and wise people from all ages (mostly, called *Fiori*) transported classical *sententiae* into the context of the city-states at the time. Authors did not provide the gnomic sentences that they were translating in vernacular with a specific definition regarding their structure, content, or purpose. Instead, they preferred to present them as didactic tools for rulers and people involved in the local government. The same occurred with proverbs from the Old and New Testament, which appeared as vernacular quotations on the moral and ethical behaviors that a good citizen should possess. Since medieval collectors were interested less in the taxonomy of paremias and more in pedagogical adaptations of classical and biblical sources, these collections of quotations took the form of primarily moral treatises (D'Agostino, "Letteratura di proverbi" 107–13).

The Renaissance and Early Modern Period

It is in the humanistic and early modern period when many paremiographers, while collecting proverbial expressions, also offered paremiological speculations. Lippi, as the first to gather a systematic collection of paremias, provides a cultural and social definition of paremias. In his dedicatory letter to Lorenzo il Magnifico, he repeatedly emphasizes the benefits of proverbs in human life:

> Proverbia probata verba dicuntur, quae multum prudentiae, plurimum sapientiae in se continent. Multa enim quae ad praeceptiones et institutiones vitae pertinere videntur,

Chapter One

> complectuntur. ... Proverbia prae istis (dicta, dicteria, facetiae, ledoriae, responsa, ioci, sales) longe excellentiora duxi et plurimum humanae vitae profutura iudicavi. (*Liber proverbiorum* 417–18)

> Proverbs are said esteemed words, because they include much good sense and the greatest wisdom in themselves. Indeed, they include many that appear to pertain to precepts and principles of life. ... I have inferred that proverbs are by far much more excellent in comparison with these (sayings, clever remarks, witty comments, vehement quips, answers, jokes, wisecracks) and I have judged that they will be very much profitable to human life.

In referring to the meaning of οἴμη (which is the root of the Greek word παροιμία) as a didactic oral account, Lippi highlights the usefulness of proverbs to instruct (Rondinelli, "Il *Liber proverbiorum*" 16).

Given his role in creating the structure of collections of proverbs, Erasmus was also a pioneer in offering a poignant definition of paremias that will become the basis for sixteenth- and seventeenth-century paremiographers. In the section of his *Adagia* titled "Quid sit paroemia" ("What a paremia is"), Erasmus states that a paremia is a "celebre dictum, scita quapiam novitate insigne" ("a saying in popular use, remarkable for some shrewd and novel turn"; *Desiderii Erasmi Roterdami Opera Omnia, Adagia* 2–13). This definition underscores the witty novelty that a saying or a *dictum* (once again, a reference to something said or pronounced) requires to be called a paremia. Erasmus's explanation is sufficiently broad to cover different typologies of expression, such as proverbs, proverbial phrases, idioms, maxims, and mottos, and to permit inclusion of all of them in his work. Commenting on their usefulness, Erasmus lists four elements that paremias cover: love of knowledge ("ad philosophiam"), also including perspectives on cultural and social issues; arts of rhetoric and persuasion ("ad persuadendum"); decorum and grace of the narration ("ad decus et gratiam orationis"); and understanding of good authors ("ad intelligendos optimos quosque auctores"), both ancient and contemporaneous. When describing how novelty distinguishes paremias from other expressions, Erasmus links this *novitas* to evasive allusions ("allusio"), an uncommon phrasing ("eloquendi novitas"), and humor, wit, or irony ("ridiculum"). However, much like Aristotle and Quintilianus, an interpretative process, which accounts for metaphors, allegories, or hyperboles, is the most fruitful way to create new paremiac meanings (*The Adages of Erasmus*, chapters III and IV). It is, indeed, through a process of interpretation that paremias may express all of the potential figurative meanings that their literal message does not convey.[74]

Many Italian paremiographers draw from Erasmus's definition, yet complement it with sociocultural elements. Among them, Vergili points out that distinctive features of paremias are their passage from individual to authorial utterances, their subsequent commonality among people in different contexts, and their aspect of proposing a guide or rule for morality:

> Nam quum huiuscemodi proverbia primum a viris tum sapientissimis dicta, tum a rerum natura orta, mox a scriptoribus passim usurpata in ore fere omnium versari, nec omnino intelligi animadverterem, sub hisque pariter aureas (ut ita dicam) sententias ac praecepta. (*Proverbiorum libellus* aiiv)[75]

> Indeed, since I notice that proverbs of this kind, which, first, are both spoken by the wise men and derive from the very nature of things, then are used by the authors everywhere, transfer almost to the mouth of everybody, nor are understood completely, and within them they are equally golden (as I may so say) maxims and precepts.

In *Proverbi italiani e latini*, Pescetti describes a proverb as a "detto commune, contenente per lo più qualche moralità, o ricordo giovevole al viver humano" ("a common saying, mostly containing some morals, or memories that benefit the human living"; a2). This definition combines ethics, tradition, and usefulness as essential aspects of proverbs, thus adding a social component that will become common in later paremiographic works. Following Erasmus almost *verbatim*, Bargagli in his *Dialogo* defines proverbs as "un celebrato detto per una certa novità notabile; perciò che bisogna che il proverbio sia usitato e in bocca del popolo, ma che sia detto e composto in un certo modo non commune né ordinario" ("a saying remarkable for some noteworthy novelty; hence it is necessary that the proverb is used and in the mouth of the people, but that it is said and composed in a certain way, which is not common or ordinary"; 141–42, section P "Giuochi gravi"). The Sienese author also attempts a distinction between different typologies of paremias, stating that short sayings (or mottos), fables, parables, jargon, and in particular *sententiae* resemble proverbs (163: par. 150; see Pignatti, "Frottola e proverbio" 260–69). Finally, in his *Flos Italicae Linguae*, Monosini offers a theoretical definition of paremias that identifies commonality and figurative meaning as classifying characteristics.[76] According to the Tuscan scholar, proverbs should be distinguished from paremias, the latter of which encompasses the former. His definition of *proverbium* recalls that of Erasmus:

> Proverbium est dictum alicuius totius nationis consensus celebre non vulgari quadam venustate insigne. ... Populare quiddam est proverbium et commune. ... Natura venusta est proverbium. (Third Book 95–96)

> A proverb is a saying remarkable for some agreement of an entire nation and distinguished by a certain unusual beauty. ... A certain proverb is popular and common. ... A proverb is attractive by nature.

Instead, he describes *paroemiae* by referring to tropes, as Quintilianus does:

> Paroemia est proverbium, quodam figurae involucro aliud significans, atque ipsa verba sonent. Per quam definitionem hoc nimirum expressum cupimus, ea tantum proverbia paroemiae nominae esse appellanda, quae vel allegoria, vel metaphora, vel hyperbole et huiusmodi tropis insignita sint. (Third Book 96)

> Paroemia is a proverb that, through the cover of a trope, means something different from its own meaning. With this definition, we desire to make it undoubtedly clear that only those expressions which are distinguished by an allegory, a metaphor, a hyperbole, or any kind of trope, should be called paroemia.

These two definitions reveal Monosini's intention to organize his expressions in a way that could fulfill his desire to collect all the available ones in the field of paremiography (Pignatti, *Etimologia e proverbio* 208).

The entry "proverbio" in the 1612 edition of the *Vocabolario degli Accademici della Crusca* introduces the metaphorical interpretation as a demonstrative function leading to a better understanding of the expression's moral content. Similar to

Monosini and distancing themselves from the classical tradition, the Crusca academicians do not recognize the trope as an essential aspect of paremias. They define proverb as "breve, e arguto detto, ricevuto comunemente, che, per lo più, sotto parlar figurato, comprende avvertimenti attenenti al vivere umano" ("a short and sharp saying, commonly accepted, which, mostly by means of figurative language, includes suggestions on human life"; s.v. *proverbio*).[77] This entry's body highlights how, upon their interpretation, it is possible to tease out the figurative connotations of paremias and, consequently, reveal their useful message on everyday living and to all human beings (Pignatti, *Etimologia e proverbio* 218–26).

Beyond the peninsula, Florio inserts the entry *proverbio* in his 1598 bilingual dictionary *A Worlde of Wordes*. His definition of the word, however, describes more its different typologies than speculating about its essence: "[A] proverb, an adage, a short wittie saying, a common saying, an old said saw." The focus on the way proverbs are used is present in the body of the entry *proverbioso* as well, in which Florio highlights the comic, ironic, and derogatory purposes that paremias achieve alongside moralizing tones: "[F]ull of proverbs, quips or sententious sayings, tants, frumps or skoffes."

The Twentieth and Twenty-First Centuries

In the twentieth and twenty-first centuries, paremiologists try to limit the field of paremiac studies by identifying those aspects that unequivocally characterize paremias. The most mentioned characteristic is the preservation of ancient popular memory through a temporal, pedagogical, and "valuable ethical precept" (Kelso 415). Furthermore, metric and linguistic elements are identified as those that usually hold together the condensed structure of paremiac expressions and make them immediately distinct from other forms of communication. To these two aspects paremiologists add the logical and psychological choices that direct the creation of paremias and their subsequent recognition by individuals and communities.[78]

In his article "The Wisdom of Many and the Wit of One," Archer Taylor, recalling Vergili, asserts that "[a] proverb is wise; it belongs to many people; it is ingenious in form and idea; and it was first invented by an individual and applied by him to a particular situation" (3–4).[79] In his above-mentioned work *The Proverb*, he declares that a satisfying description could be that a proverb is "a saying current among the folk," a sort of *vox populi* (3).[80] Nonetheless, he specifies that such a statement does not account for many other elements that play a significant role in shaping proverbs. One of them is the expression's epigrammatic structure; the other is the human experience and the practical common sense that proverbs, and all paremias, communicate (172).[81] Rooted in centuries of speculations on the pedagogical character of proverbs, Taylor's definition confirms that these expressions are life lessons associated with a specific situation (87–88).

From the line of investigation that gives emphasis to cultural perspectives, Salvatore Trovato's introduction to his volume *Proverbi locuzioni modi di dire nel dominio linguistico italiano* (1999) provides significant insights. Trovato argues that proverbial expressions are a "precipitato culturale" ("cultural precipitate"), since they are deeply embedded in the culture that creates them. He promotes the idea that the paremia's meaning presents a "speculative relation" with its context (viii). Ultimately, this means that the expression's message results from an adaptation of its structure and meaning to the contextual situation; this adaptation is based on the expression's semantic coherence with the surrounding text (Renzi et al., vol. 1: 163–64).[82]

In the same years as Trovato's cultural and contextual speculations on paremias, Mirko Grimaldi proposes to examine spoken proverbs through an emic approach ("Atlante Paremiologico Italiano"). In order to frame his theoretical background, he refers to two American linguists who suggest analyzing languages in a social context, William Labov and Kenneth Pike. Labov coins the term "sociology of language," which "deals with large-scale social factors, and their mutual interaction with language and dialect" (183). In other words, investigating the social aspects of languages reveals those extra-linguistic forms that interact with and within that language and that participate equally in defining its elements, paremias included.[83] Borrowing from Pike's ideas in *Language in Relation to a Unified Theory of the Structure of Human Behavior* (1967), Labov introduces the concept of an emic analysis of language. Pike indeed distinguishes between etic and emic analyses in scientific research on anthropological and behavioral issues by way of reproducing the linguistic opposition that exists between phonetics and phonemics. Just as phonetics examines theoretical representations of phones, the etic approach searches for universal concepts, ultimately valid for each culture. On the contrary, as much as phonemics looks at the contextual relationship between opposing phonemes, the emic approach purports to capture the distinctive features of each individual group, which are not predicted but, rather, discovered. This approach implies an internal view that privileges specific circumstances over general deductions. By extending Pike's and Labov's considerations to linguistics, Grimaldi asserts that the emic approach aims to study languages as tools to explore communities and understand their vision of reality. Such a methodology describes cultures with the same internal logic and cognitive system that characterize them ("Atlante Paremiologico Italiano" 26–27).[84] The emic approach, which Grimaldi applies to spoken paremias, is also useful when studying written paremias. The context represents the social reality in which the paremias are embedded and the internal view that is necessary in order to grasp the "community" of paremias in the text.[85] Such an analysis permits evaluating various contextual aspects: how the presence of paremias is pertinent to the text; how the text affects the paremias; and how the paremias influence the content and purpose of the text, as well as the reader's reaction to it.[86]

On the other side of the spectrum, some paremiologists privilege the linguistic aspects of the paremias above cultural elements, especially because linguistics defines paremias more precisely and scientifically. Cirese claims that recurrent aspects of paremias include brevity, broad use, pedagogical purpose, wit, figurative meaning, and an experience-based message oriented to everyday life (*I proverbi* 3). He draws this definition from James Kelso's entry on proverbs in the *Encyclopedia of Religion and Ethics* (1908–26). Here, Kelso states that, despite the inner difficulties in offering a formal description of proverbs, four elements can be teased out: brevity or conciseness, sense,[87] piquancy or salt, and popularity (412). Cirese seizes this terminology to structure his own definition, according to which brevity, sense, and piquancy concern the internal properties of a proverb because they exemplify its linguistic representation. Among these internal qualities, brevity symbolizes the expression's coherence and conciseness ("content"), whereas sense and piquancy refer to the expression's "form" (*I proverbi* 12). Popularity, on the other hand, concerns what Cirese calls external properties. Such properties include elements to which the proverb is subjected independent of its internal qualities, including its acceptance and use in the community. The combination of both internal and external properties under certain rules guarantees the development of a proverbial expression. The minimal requested association has at least an internal property and an external one (14). However, in many cases, proverbs display three primary properties: an internal one related to form, an internal one related to content, and an external one. Consequently, the most common combination of these properties includes brevity, sense, and popularity (16). Hierarchically, the external property (popularity) is secondary to the internal ones (brevity, sense, and piquancy), whereas, inside the internal properties, the formal internal quality (brevity) has priority over the content-related ones (sense and piquancy). Cirese, evidently, looks at proverbs primarily as linguistic expressions, first in structure and organization and, then, in content and message.

Similarly, Giorgio Qualizza bestows a privilege upon textual structure over cultural and social messages in his study of proverbs (178). He lists three constituent factors that characterize proverbs: brevity, generalization of a rule of behavior, and comprehensibility.[88] First, brevity, meaning lack of redundancy, enables proverbs to express normative messages in a condensed way. Secondly, when they generalize a way of behaving, they mostly intend to prevent a person from doing something wrong rather than inciting correct or positive actions. A typical structure "if …, then …" expresses, in the main sentence, the consequences of a bad behavior described in the subordinate sentence (179). Finally, comprehensibility allows for the proverb's intelligibility to the sociolinguistic group in which it is used. Qualizza successfully connects language and culture, but still emphasizes that the expression's effectiveness in a community depends mostly on textual and linguistic elements.

Temistocle Franceschi's Paremiology

Synthesizing centuries of discussions in the field, Franceschi's theoretical approach offers a comprehensive terminology and describes paremias as cultural and linguistic units within a society.[89] His 1999 essay "L'Atlante paremiologico italiano e la geoparemiologia" provides the most comprehensive and innovative definition of paremias and of their contextual interpretation.[90] He argues that paremias are not exclusively cultural products of popular wisdom, namely a "fatto sociale" ("social event"; see also Bessi 13). Paremias are also communicative and, most importantly, linguistic events to study in their phonetic, morphologic, and syntactic structure. They aim to teach and send out a moral message, yet they are also expressions of the language ("L'atlante paremiologico italiano" 4–5). The combination of anthropological research with linguistic investigation discloses the paremias' shift from the extra-linguistic or "poetic" area, namely the folkloristic context, to the linguistic area, which defines their structure and message (Franceschi et al., 371). Franceschi describes this transition as follows:

> La sua evoluzione potrebbe raffigurarsi su un piano inclinato che scenda dal primo al secondo dei nostri settori demologici. Su di esso, dall'area «poetica» in cui di solito nasce, il proverbio scorre gradualmente verso quella linguistica, ch'è il suo punto d'arrivo. Che è la strada percorsa ormai da tempo (di solito, sino in fondo) da casi più semplici: vocaboli, e locuzioni, figurati. (Franceschi et al., 372)

> The evolution of paremias could be pictured as an inclined surface that descends from the first to the second of our folkloric areas. On this surface, from the poetic area, in which they are usually born, the paremias gradually descend towards the linguistic area, which is their arrival point. This is the path that, for a long time, the simplest structures underwent (usually up to the end): figurative words and phrases.

Franceschi's definition of paremias combines conciseness, analogical processes, efficacy and usefulness, and figurative interpretation:

> [Attribuiamo alle paremie] il valore di breve e conciso insieme allologico (ossìa inteso a comunicare altro da sé) di struttura proverbiale, che in un determinato idioma è convenzionalmente usato in riferimento allusivo ad altro insieme semantico (con cui viene analogicamente correlato), per esprimere in modo indiretto, sintetico ed efficace un parere, un commento, un consiglio. ("L'atlante paremiologico italiano" 10)[91]

> [We confer paremias] the value of brief and concise allological units (which are called to communicate more than merely the words) with a proverbial structure that, in a language, is conventionally used as an allusive reference to another semantic

Chapter One

> unit (to which it is connected via analogy). This unit expresses an opinion, a comment, or a recommendation in an indirect, synthetic, and effective way.

To further prove his point, Franceschi describes this passage as a transition from the lexical to the rhetorical code. The language is composed of two different codes: the "vocabolario" ("the lexical code or lexicon") and the "dizionario" ("the rhetorical code or dictionary"). On one hand, the lexical code incorporates the terms of the language that are monoverbal (made of one word) and unmotivated (or non-metaphorical). They are simple linguistic and graphic representations of a sign, which also include phonemes and graphemes organized to constitute a word. On the other hand, the rhetorical code gathers those expressions that are motivated (by an interpretative process based on figures of speech) and syntagmatic sequences (because of their syntactic relationships) that represent rhetorical signs. Inside the rhetorical code, the "codice paremiaco" ("the paremiac code") includes those expressions whose meaning is figurative ("L'atlante paremiologico italiano" 7).

A three-step process "transfers" paremias from the original "poetic" area to the "linguistic" one. The literal meaning of a paremia, which is the first step of this process, is additional as far as it is the sum of each of the expression's components. It does not yet require a figurative interpretation, for it is indeed tightly bound to the situation that creates the paremia (Jolles 150). The second step addresses the abstraction of the paremia's meaning from the initial circumstance to a figurative and non-compositional level. Non-compositional level refers to the expression's metaphorical or allegorical meaning rather than the literal meaning of each of its individual lexical components. Tradition, unanimous acceptance, and continuous repetition by the community solidify the paremia's significance in a conventional and immediately-recognizable meaning. However, paremias contain infinite metaphorical meanings and semantic references when they are not associated with a context: "Il proverbio è per sua natura ambiguo, giacché si presta ad applicazioni i cui confini non sono predeterminabili" ("The proverb is ambiguous by nature, since it lends itself to applications whose boundaries cannot be determined in advance"; Franceschi, *Atlante paremiologico italiano* xxxviii).[92] Hence, the third and last step brings the paremia to a defined situation again.[93] Its meaning still maintains a relationship with the conventionalized meaning, but is only and exclusively appropriate to that specific situation. The situational context filters the polysemy of meanings that a paremia can express, while simultaneously actualizing its "valore paremiologico" ("paremiologic value").[94] This latter corresponds to the "gamma dei possibili riferimenti semantici d'un detto proverbiale convenzionalmente sottesa alla lettura del testo" ("the range of possible semantic references of a proverbial expression that are conventionally linked to the text's reading"; Franceschi, "L'atlante paremiologico italiano" 8).[95] Franceschi's definition recognizes in paremias the capacity to offer concrete immediacy that could be applied to a vast array of cultural and literary situations (Franceschi et al., 375–76). The process of adaptation to the context requires an inductive passage from the particular (original situation) to the universal (metaphorical sphere) and to the particular again (the contextual situation), in a dynamic and fluid interaction. Moreover, it speaks of the primordial mechanism of figurative language for aesthetic purposes (Casadei, *Metafore ed espressioni idiomatiche* 1), which, as unconscious as it is, explains the conspicuous use of paremias and metaphorical structures in communication (Franceschi et al., 371).[96]

An application of Franceschi's three-step process is the contextual evaluation of a proverb that Florio uses in his *Firste Fruites*. The expression, *Chi tardi arriva mal alloggia*, takes on a specific meaning when it appears in the distinct context of the manual's chapter 5:

> Io voglio parlar a quella donna.
> Madonna, io vi amo cordialmente, io voria che io fosse vostro marito, io vi ameria e serviria fedelmente.
> Io sono molto obligato a voi per il vostro ben volere.
> Io vi ringratio per la vostra cortesia.
> Ma non sapete come dice il proverbio?
> Non certo: come dice?
> *Chi tardi arriva mal alloggia.*
> Come, dunche io arivo tardi.
> Sì certo a dirvi la verità.
> Dunche voi siete promessa.
> Signor sì, longo tempo fa. (FF 4*v*–5*r*)

> I will speake to that woman.
> Madame, I love you hartily, I would I were your husband, I woulde love you and serve you faithfully.
> I am very much bounde to you for your good wil.
> I thanke you for your courtesie.
> But knowe you not what the proverbe saith?
> No truely: how saith it?
> Who commeth late, lodgeth ill.
> Why then I arrive late.
> Yea certaine, to tel you truly.
> Why then you are promised.
> Yea, Sir, long ago.

In this conversation, the proverb refers to a man who wishes to marry a woman but eventually discovers that she had been promised to another man. The conventionalized meaning is still present and influences the direction in which the interpretation should go. The proverb does not, generically, refer to a person who arrives late and receives the worst offer but, specifically, to a man who lingers too long before proposing to a woman, who is by that time, unfortunately, already officially engaged. The contextual meaning shapes the conventionalized meaning in ways that it could have never been expressed otherwise and makes it more appropriate for the specific scene.

Variations of Paremias in Genre, Culture, and Language

When Franceschi's paremiological perspective is matched with Grimaldi's emic approach, both anthropological and linguistic aspects can be introduced as key factors causing variations of paremias. Since Franceschi and Grimaldi primarily study spoken utterances of paremias, they include community, familial ties, and personal considerations among the anthropological factors. For the linguistic elements, they mention phonologic, morpho-syntactic, and semantic modifications, which usually result in twisting the paremia's message for contextual or ideological purposes (Franceschi, "L'atlante paremiologico italiano" 16–17).[97] This implies defining variation as a productive tool for continuous innovation, as well as maintenance of local identities.[98]

Within paremiac variation, the afore-mentioned linguist Qualizza records a list of changes that paremias undergo in the meanings they convey. Two of them entail a "modificazione parziale del testo letterale e nessuna modificazione del significato" ("partial modification of the literal text and no change in the paremia's meaning") and a "modificazione totale del testo letterale e nessuna modificazione del significato" ("total modification of the literal text and no change in the paremia's meaning"; 188). The first case is the most frequent and generates the greatest number of variants. One example might be the slight difference between a paremia used in Florio's *Second Frutes* (*A carne di lupo convien dar dente di cane*; "To wolfe's flesh a man must applie a dogg's tooth"; SF 20) and the same paremia listed in *Giardino di ricreatione* (*A carne di lupo, dente di cane*; "To wolfe's flesh, dogg's tooth"; GR 1). This modification does not affect the message that the paremia transmits. It rather illustrates the flexibility of its constituent terms, which can be inserted within a textual context without changing the expression's structure. Qualizza's second case illustrates what occurs in Florio's *Fruits* and in Sarnelli's *Posilecheata*, when the two authors translate their paremias from one language to another. More than simply modifying the original text, the paremia shifts from one sociolinguistic level to another. This explains why their textual modification is total. For instance, Florio translates his Italian paremia *Si puol cacciar chiodo con chiodo* in English as *One nayle is driven out with an other* (FF 34r). Similarly, Sarnelli, renders the Tuscan expression *Tre cose non sono stimate, forza di bastagio, consiglio di poverhuomo et bellezza di puttana* in Neapolitan as *Tre cose non songo stemmate: forze da vastaso, consiglio de poverommo e bellezza de pottana* ("Three things are not valued: the strength of a porter, the advice of a poor man, and the beauty of a whore"; P 13.9). Both examples illustrate how the meaning of the expressions is unchanged, even though two different linguistic systems are involved.

Another instance identified by Qualizza explains the polysemy that paremias display when the expression undergoes "nessuna modificazione del testo letterale e parziale modificazione del significato" ("no modification of the literal text and partial modification of its meaning"; 188). As discussed previously, paremias are open to different interpretations as well as diverse contextual actualizations of their meaning, without any modification of the paremiac structure or of its constituent terms (190–91). For instance, Brusantino adopts the paremia *Bocca basciata non perde ventura*, which he finds in the *Decameron* (Dec. II.7.122), and slightly changes it for the new context of his *Le cento novelle*: *Bocca basciata non perde fortuna* (CN 97). Despite the minor lexical change of "fortuna" with its synonym "ventura" ("luck"), both paremias communicate the same literal meaning: "A kissed mouth does not lose luck." In the two contexts the story is the same, yet its general point and its reception are different, given the different social and cultural contexts of the two works. The paremias as well send out a slightly dissimilar message in accordance with their contexts, as well as the works in which they appear.

The paremias of Brusantino, Florio and Sarnelli experience all of these variations, while shifting through various linguistic, literary, and cultural codes. This ultimately results in multiple transformations in the paremias' expression, meanings, and values. As Angela Albanese argues, proverbs are "fuori-testo nel testo" ("outside-text inside the text"), since they create a complete and meaningful text inside the larger text that contains them ("I centomila miliardi di proverbi" 7). Yet, paremias are in conversation with the hosting (textual and social) context in a "dialogic relationship" (Bakhtin, *Speech Genres* 115).[99] Taking into account all of these aspects with an internal perspective that is sensitive to contextual situations allows for a comprehensive examination of paremias.

Although Brusantino does not provide a literal translation of Boccaccio's text, he calls his *Le cento novelle* a translation of the *Decameron*. In fact, he refers to translation as "traductio" rather than "translatio,"[100] i.e., a transformation or passage across different codes or systems. In this case, the passage occurs from one genre (short story) to another (chivalric poem) through their reciprocal combination. Gianfranco Folena calls such a translation "poetic" because the signifiers are transferred into a different language and assume a different form (*Volgarizzare e tradurre* 23). Brusantino's process transforms the *Decameron* into a new rhetorical structure adapted to a new contextual situation that is suitable for a different public than the original text. When inserted into the poetic structure of the *Le cento novelle* (octaves of hendecasyllables), paremias change their syntactic and rhythmic organization, yet without losing their distinctive features or their message. Their "translation" is not a faithful or word-by-word process, but rather a transferral, which means that it is the result of a balance between linguistic, cultural, and contextual elements.

In Florio's *Firste Fruites* and *Second Frutes*, paremiac modifications result from a cross-cultural and cross-linguistic adaptation.

Florio translates paremias from Italian to English to make them comprehensible for a community of speakers based on different values. At the same time, he offers paremias to Italian expatriates, who were losing contact with their national culture. Florio's translations can be literal, when they transfer the structure and language of the original Italian paremias into the target one. Alternatively, they may be cultural, when the English equivalents convey the content and the meaning of the Italian paremias but not their structure.

In *Posilecheata*, Sarnelli translates paremias available in other languages (mostly, Greek, Latin, Spanish, and Tuscan) into the Neapolitan dialect and adapts them to the new literary, social, and anthropological context. On one hand, Sarnelli's paremias represent the identity of the Neapolitan people; on the other, accumulation of proverbial expressions suggests Sarnelli's fascination with the Baroque representation of multiple realities, linguistic games, and playful aspects of the dialect (Getto 276, 300). For this purpose, Sarnelli creates many paremias *ex novo* or transforms traditional paremias to craft synonymic structures almost excessively.

Paremiological Categorizations: Proverbs, Proverbial Phrases, and Wellerisms

Before analyzing Brusantino's, Florio's, and Sarnelli's paremias, it is necessary to clarify which typologies the macro-category of paremias incorporates. The most universally-recognized group of paremias includes proverbs. Whether they are delivered orally or in a written form, proverbs respond to traditions and folklore by expressing moral maxims, offering advice, describing aspects of human life, or conveying witty assessments. From a structural perspective, they present a topic-and-comment organization of their content. The "topic," which is usually in a preeminent position, is the explicit and known part of a proverb, whereas the "comment," which usually follows, concludes the thought and requires an interpretational process to clarify the implicitness of the entire expression (Franceschi, "L'atlante paremiologico italiano" 13; A. Taylor, *The Proverb* 135–64). For instance, in the proverb *Chi frequenta la cucina sente da fumo* ("Those who spend time in the kitchen smell of smoke"; SF 94), the main topic, already known, is "chi frequenta la cucina"; the comment, "sente da fumo," adds

33

more information to the topic and leads to the interpretational process: "If we engage with something/someone, we show traces of this relationship." Prosodic and metrical elements generally define proverbs (Franceschi et al., 450): usually the two parallel hemistiches are linked by a final rhyme, assonance, or consonance that facilitate their memorization. Two examples come from Brusantino's *Le cento novelle*: *E a le giovene donne i buon bocconi e di noi vecchie sono i stranguglioni* ("And to the young women good morsels and to us old ones hiccups"; CN 289), which declares the differences between youngsters and the elderly in terms of what they can obtain from life, and *Chi va al letto la sera senza cena intorno tutta notte si dimena* ("Who fasting goes to bed, uneasy lies his head around all night"; CN 145), which addresses the consequences of an improper lifestyle. The metrical and syntactical structure of both expressions remind us that they are undoubtedly proverbs.

In many instances, however, the label "proverbs" includes other typologies that are not clearly separated from actual proverbs. Even though these expressions share their non-compositional meaning (i.e., they are figurative), they present a different structure and have different purposes. As demonstrated in Erasmus's *Adagia* and in all of the early modern collections of paremias, during the Renaissance there was no distinction between different categories. Humanistic paremias included proverbs, proverbial phrases, sayings, metaphors, idiomatic expressions, and witty and facetious remarks (Lippi, *Liber proverbiorum* 142–43; Rondinelli, "Il concetto di proverbio" 167–78). It is only in the nineteenth century that paremiographers become aware of these structural and interpretational differences. Giusti, for instance, states that proverbs convey general precepts or instructions, whereas other sayings require elucidation since they are more rooted in local traditions (*Proverbi*). Sayings like *Conoscere i polli* ("To know one's chickens," meaning to be aware of one's manners and qualities), *Mettere il becco in molle* ("To soak the beak," meaning to chat a lot), and *Scorgere il pelo nell'ovo* ("To see the hair in the egg," meaning to be excessively picky) are informed by a figurative meaning, but devoid of moral aspirations, which is instead what characterizes proverbs.

Critics use different titles for such expressions, including sayings, locutions, idiomatic expressions, proverbial expressions, or proverbial phrases.[101] A. Taylor refers to them as "fixed, conventional phrases,"[102] whose "purpose is to describe the situation, not to convey an ethical or moral lesson" (*The Proverb* 129–30).[103] He highlights that these expressions might be more common than proverbs, probably due to their greater flexibility to adapt to different situations (184–200). The strong syntactic and morphological ties they establish with the context define their structure and, at the same time, cause an endless number of variations (Mieder and Dundes 5).[104] A proverbial phrase like *Dar di becco in ogni cosa* ("To stick one's nose into everything") allows for a great degree of transformation when inserted into a given syntactic form. In that context, for instance, it might agree with the number of the subject or the tense of the verbs.[105] Andreas Langlotz, who chooses the title "idiomatic expressions," comments on their "idiomatic creativity" or "lexicogrammatical malleability" (8).[106] According to him, idiomatic expressions can present modifications in syntax, morphology, and occasionally vocabulary, which supports Franceschi's and Grimaldi's idea of paremiac variation. The idiomatic expressions may generate synonymic variants or they may purportedly become ambiguous and hence convey additional meanings to the literal one (177–78). The variant that results is an occasional and temporary alternative expression, created for the sake of a specific socio-pragmatic or textual context.

The American structuralist linguist Charles Hockett defines idioms (a synonym for proverbial phrases) as "a grammatical form—single morpheme or composite form—the meaning of which cannot be derived from its structure" (222; also in Casadei, *Metafore ed espressioni idiomatiche* 23–24 and Vietri, *Lessico e sintassi* 22–24). Those expressions that present both a literal meaning and a conventionalized meaning can be interpreted literally or idiomatically based upon their context (Hockett 223). For instance, Florio's proverbial phrase *A tal carne tal coltello* (SF 46) and Sarnelli's expression *Scotolare sto sacco e bedere se nc'era porvere o farina* (P 182.15) can be interpreted literally as "To such knife, this meat" (or "A nail can be extracted with another nail") and "To beat the bag and see if there was dust or flour," respectively. However, in Florio's and Sarnelli's texts, the two expressions are taken metaphorically. Florio's proverbial phrase refers to someone's appropriate answer to a provocation. Sarnelli's means that it is

35

necessary to "shake" things to evaluate their real nature; in fact, he employs the expression when a few fairies decide to test a young woman in *cunto* 5.[107]

The most comprehensive analysis of Italian idiomatic expressions, i.e., proverbial phrases, is Federica Casadei's 1996 volume, *Metafore ed espressioni idiomatiche*.[108] She defines idioms as "espressioni polilessicali che abbinano un significato fisso a un significato convenzionale tipicamente non letterale" ("multi-lexical expressions that combine a fixed meaning with a conventionalized meaning, which is typically not literal"; 13–14). Therefore, idioms are sequences of terms, distinguished by a non-compositional meaning that can be related to their single components only figuratively. Casadei argues for a dichotomy between "sentence meaning," that which is the compositional or literal meaning of the expression, and "utterance meaning," that which is expressed in a specific context (19, 57). In order to perceive its non-literal meaning, the receiver of an idiomatic expression needs to account for non-linguistic aspects. In spoken utterances, pragmatics contribute to an appropriate interpretation of idiomatic expressions (23); in written utterances, instead, extra-linguistic elements are crucial and include the narration, the style, the genre, and the objectives of the work.[109]

In addition to proverbial phrases, a consistent group of expressions in the category of paremias are wellerisms.[110] The name "wellerism" comes from Sam Weller, the main character in Charles Dickens's 1836 *Pickwick Papers*. Weller frequently tells anecdotes, jokes, and witty remarks related to historical figures, well-known characters, or even invented people. An almost fixed formula characterizes his quotations, always introduced by "as so and so said," and makes them similar to a *micro-récit* ("micro-narration"; Cirese, "Il wellerismo" 157–59; see also Aquilecchia). Usually, in Italian the expression presents a proper or common name and a famous saying or sentence with paremiac meaning, and is preceded or followed by "come disse," "come diceva," or "disse" ("as he/she said," "as he/she used to say," "he/she said"). Moritz Haupt was the first to use the term "wellerism" in 1876 in reference to Theocritus's fifteenth idyll. Here, one of the characters, Prassìnoa, uses the expression, "All inside, as the bridegroom said when he locked the bedroom door," which presents a similar structure to what will later be called "wellerism" (57: v. 77). Before adopting the

English terminology (Corso; Speroni, "Five Italian Wellerisms," *The Italian Wellerism*, "Wellerismi tolti dai proverbi inediti di F. Serdonati"), Italian wellerisms were confused with proverbs based on fables or else conveying moral and practical suggestions.[111] As a result, they were frequently referred to as parables or anecdotal examples and were considered sources of exemplary behaviors through which two realities are compared: the one that is stated in the wellerism and the one to which the wellerism is applied (Corso 4). In discussing this typology of paremia, Raffaele Corso claims that wellerisms can be either proverbs or proverbial phrases, whereas Franca Brambilla Ageno considers them an exclusive subgroup of proverbial phrases ("Premessa a un repertorio di frasi proverbiali" 244). Brambilla Ageno's point of view appears to be more convincing: wellerisms lack a pedagogical dimension, which instead characterizes proverbs, and do not feature metrical or rhythmic elements much like proverbial phrases.[112] However, wellerisms share with both proverbs and proverbial phrases that their conventionalized meaning needs to be contextualized in order to express specific semantic aspects (Speroni, "Five Italian Wellerisms" 54). Even though the polysemy of their meanings and their ambiguity is less than what is possible with other paremias, wellerisms can nonetheless display a variety of meanings. What differs from proverbs and proverbial phrases is their purpose: wellerisms usually present a satirical, ironic, comic, or humorous twist, which proverbs and proverbial phrases may have but not necessarily convey.[113]

In his chapter on wellerisms, A. Taylor defines these expressions as a "very curious proverbial type ... well represented in English and American oral tradition" (*The Proverb* 200). He argues that this typology was already present in the classical world and flourished in German and Scandinavian countries, yet with limited lifespan and success.[114] Exceptions are those wellerisms that allude to well-known subjects and, thus, do not require any additional commentary (216). Only witty wellerisms or wellerisms with an appeal that went beyond the local community were later accepted largely (Franceschi et al., 370: footnote 68). The others—Taylor claims—were completely forgotten, once the premises for their birth faded away or remained constrained inside their "narrow confines" of use (*The Proverb* 216). Consequently, tracing the origins of a wellerism is difficult because its history is frequently obscure.

Chapter One

Carlo Lapucci suggests that the humorous tone in wellerisms derives from incongruity: specifically, a serious assertion (the famous saying or sentence with paremiac meaning) is placed in a scene (introduced by the formula "come disse/come diceva") in which one would anticipate a different saying. The result of this discrepancy is then a pun that provides comic relief.[115] This happens, for instance, in Florio's *Second Frutes*, in which one of the characters of chapter 6 uses the wellerism, *Per tutto c'è da fare, diceva colui che ferrava le oche* ("Every man hath somthing to do, quoth he that shod his geese"; SF 84), to refer to his frequent commitments. The formality of the context vis-à-vis the popular aspect of the wellerism creates a humorous juxtaposition.

The presence of comedy is a crucial aspect for Charles Speroni, too. In his 1953 book on *The Italian Wellerism*, he defines wellerisms as a "special type of dialogued proverb" (1)[116] and highlights their pleasant rather than moralizing nature (3–6).[117] This explains why wellerisms reached their greatest success in the sixteenth century. In the 1500s and in the first decades of the 1600s, there was, indeed, an efflorescence of comic and carnivalesque genres, and collections of paremias began to feature a considerable number of these expressions.[118] In collections published after the seventeenth century, however, the number of wellerisms drastically decreased. Their frequent references to characters or events known only by people of a specific community made it challenging to understand them in other cultures (2; see also footnote 8).[119] Only in the nineteenth century are wellerisms mentioned in Giusti's 1853 edition of *Proverbi* even though they constitute a very small portion of the entire work.

Speroni distinguishes four groups of expressions that might resemble wellerisms but are in fact "false wellerisms"—a categorization that is particularly useful in analyzing Florio's paremias. The first group of false wellerisms includes paremias that are attributed to an unidentified person and introduced by such formulas as "come disse colui" ("as that person said"), "come disse quello" ("as that one said"), "come diceva quell'uomo" ("as that man used to say"). If they were proper wellerisms, this would mean that wellerisms could be created out of any paremia. The second group contains those wellerisms that feature the present indicative of the verb "dire" ("to say") instead of the imperfect or past. The introductory formula "come dice" ("as he/she says"), according to Speroni, indicates that the wellerism belongs to a community and is conceived as a general statement rather than one attributed to a specific person or character. The third group includes sayings that belong to an ancient moralist, such as Cato's *sententiae*, whereas the fourth contains sentences or passages from an authorial text (*The Italian Wellerism* 5).

As happens with all paremias, users commonly accept the wellerisms' conventionalized meaning. Yet, only the contextual situation allows for this conventionalized meaning to be actualized. Such a characteristic confirms the infinite transformations and adaptations that paremias face to different degrees according to their structure, origin, and content. The following chapters demonstrate and discuss these transformations and adaptations, along with the use, function, and significance of paremias, through the examples provided by the works of Brusantino, Florio, and Sarnelli.

Chapter Two

Vincenzo Brusantino's *Le cento novelle*
Paremias and Tridentine Ethics in Reinterpreting the *Decameron*

> Difatto troverai qui, oltre un tesoro di lingua viva e schiettissima, una raccolta d'utili insegnamenti a portata di tutti, un manuale di prudenza per ogni caso spettante alla vita pubblica e privata.
>
> In fact, you will find here, besides a treasure of lively and frank language, a collection of useful lessons for everyone, a manual of prudence for every case concerning public and private life.
>
> Giuseppe Giusti, *Lettera proemiale ad Andrea Francioni*

Brusantino's "Translation" of Boccaccio's *Decameron*

The Ferrara native Vincenzo Brusantino (also known as Vincenzo Brusantini and Vincenzo Brugiantini[1]) is a forgotten sixteenth-century author. In his time, he was dismissed as an unrefined writer and an imitator of previous masterpieces of Italian literature.[2] As a close friend of Pietro Aretino, he spent some time in Venice, where he established a connection with the printing house of Francesco Marcolini, future editor of Brusantino's two main literary works.[3] Unable to find a court in which to thrive, Brusantino wandered through various places until he returned to his home city, probably in the early 1540s. It was in this period of relatively stable life that he began writing his most well-known work, a chivalric poem entitled *L'Angelica innamorata*.[4] He published it in December 1550 and dedicated it to his protector, Ercole II d'Este, Duke of Ferrara, Modena and Reggio from 1534 to 1559.[5] The author defines the 37 cantos of this poem as a continuation of Ariosto's *Orlando furioso* and its unresolved conclusion. In 1554, Brusantino released another project of reworking and adapting available literary material, *Le cento novelle da messer Brugiantino dette in ottava rima. Et tutte hanno la allegoria, con il proverbio a proposito della novella*, which is the first integral transformation

Chapter Two

of Boccaccio's *Decameron* into a chivalric poem. He dedicated the work to the Duke of Parma and Piacenza, Ottavio Farnese (1524–86), and never reprinted it due to scarce public appeal.[6]

References to Brusantino's *Le cento novelle* are very rare. Contemporaries considered it a worthless literary exercise and a minor work, merely a sterile and impersonal copy of Boccaccio's collection of short stories without any innovative additions.[7] It is only in modern times that scholars began to show more interest in *Le cento novelle* and in its editorial and interpretative aspects. Rosanna Pettinelli engaged in a critical study of Brusantino's work in her 2004 book *Forme e percorsi dei romanzi di cavalleria: da Boiardo a Brusantino*. A chapter in this text, entitled "Vicende editoriali attorno alle *Cento novelle da messer Vincenzo Brugiantino dette in ottava rima*" (165–80), outlines the publication history of the *Decameron*'s editions. Pettinelli illustrates how Brusantino simplifies the corollary elements of the original text (i.e., the proem and the introduction) while, at the same time, changing the meaning of some stories. In another chapter of the book, "Fra Boccaccio e Ariosto. Modi di ricezione dell'oralità nelle *Cento novelle* di Vincenzo Brusantino" (181–98), Pettinelli argues that Brusantino enriches Boccaccio's text with oral elements. First, the octave is a popular poetic form associated with the oral tradition of troubadours and chivalric poems. Moreover, introductory allegories and paremias translate the orality of the work and imbue the content of the stories with ethical tones. Marcolini, who had been fulfilling the public's demands for books written in vernacular since 1534, was particularly eager to print marginal poetic works. He specifically sought for texts that experimented with new forms and genres and, simultaneously, conveyed moral messages. Brusantino's *Le cento novelle* fit this description nicely as it delivered a sense of novelty and ethics in such a canonized text as Boccaccio's *Decameron*.[8] In 2010, Maiko Favaro published an article with the captivating title, "Il *Decameron* in veste di poema: *Le cento novelle* di Vincenzo Brusantino," in which he calls attention to Brusantino's predilection for chivalric poems. This preference probably derives from Brusantino's connection to the court in Ferrara or from his friendship with Aretino, who, at the time, had already published his four chivalric narratives, *Orlandino* (1530), *Marfisa* (1532), *Lagrime di Angelica* (1535), and *Astolfeide*

(1540).[9] Relatedly, in his 2014 article "Nuova veste, nuova via o nuova vita? L'illusione di Vincenzo Brusantino riscrittore in ottave del *Decameron*" Paolo Procaccioli discusses how much each one of the interested parties, i.e., Brusantino and Marcolini, contributes to the structure of *Le cento novelle* by comparing Brusantino's work with similar ones in the period and listed in Marcolini's catalogue. He also interprets Brusantino's adaptation as the result of a combination between a story singer, a writer, and an editor, which does not manage, however, to reach success. Sandra Carapezza's more recent article, "Il *Decamerone furioso* di Vincenzo Brugiantino," illustrates the connections between Boccaccio's work and *Orlando furioso* that can be found in *Le cento novelle*. In particular, her study demonstrates that some of Brusantino's interpolations clearly recall lexical elements of Ariosto's chivalric poem.

The Defining Attributes of Brusantino's *Le cento novelle*

Brusantino's work bears a title that focuses on the structure and content of the collection (the 100 stories) rather than on its chronometric structure (the *Decameron*). Along with *Cento*, *Cento novelle* was the most common alternative title to *Decameron* in the sixteenth-century editions of Boccaccio's collection[10] (Bragantini, "Su alcune edizioni" 345).[11] Already in the dedicatory letter to *Le cento novelle*, Brusantino states that he "translated the *Decameron* in octaves:" "[H]o tradotto il Decamerone in ottava rima" (CN 3). Then, before the proem, he again refers to his work's adaptation from Boccaccio's collection: *Le cento novelle di Messer Giovanni Boccaccio ridotte in ottava rima da Messer Vincenzo Brugiantino* ("The one hundred novellas by Giovanni Boccaccio adapted in octaves by Vincenzo Brugiantino"; CN 5). The use of the verbs "tradurre" ("to translate") and "ridurre" ("to adapt"), both coming from the Latin "ducere" ("to conduct or to lead"), raises the question of how Brusantino considers his reinterpretation of Boccaccio's text. While the prefix "trans-" conveys the idea of a movement across different entities, the prefix "re-" indicates an opposing direction, meaning that something shifts to a condition or situation different and away from the original one. By means of "translating" the *Decameron*, Brusantino creates a hybrid and compound text in which he blends a plurality of genres, traditions, and styles in order to achieve his narrative goals (Bagni in Sportelli 6; Carapezza).[12]

Chapter Two

When Brusantino rewrites Boccaccio's text, he adopts the Italian language or, more precisely, the Florentine vernacular (Stussi, "Lingua"). Despite scant, yet recognizable regional elements from the sixteenth-century Paduan area, Brusantino produces an endolinguistic translation that occurs within ("endo-") the same linguistic code (Nasi, "L'onesto narrare" 87). The process happens diachronically as *Le cento novelle* "translates" a text that was written two centuries before and transforms it from prose to poetry to fulfill the desires of a different community of readers. Brusantino changes Boccaccio's *Decameron* into a more popularized text that could attract a wider audience. His personal additions, i.e., allegories and paremias at the beginning of each canto, represent this aspect. At the same time, they constitute the most important feature of his stylistic, rhetorical, cultural, and ideological adaptation of the original text for his Tridentine society.

Recurring elements open and close the ten days of *Le cento novelle*.[13] A few introductory octaves are separated from the first novella of the day and some concluding ones immediately follow the reaction of the *brigata* to the last recounted story. All of these octaves appear to be more succinct versions than the introductions and conclusions to each novella in the *Decameron*. Brusantino's novellas are also shorter because he omits certain details of Boccaccio's stories. At the end of each day, however, the *brigata* recites the same songs, all of which Brusantino converts into sonnets. With regard to the text's organization, paratextual elements—specifically images (when present),[14] captions, allegories, and paremias—determine a structure within the cantos and the days in a more visible way than in the *Decameron*. As such, they achieve three goals: attract the readers' eye and attention, guide them visually and thematically through the text of each novella, and assign relevance to elements that are crucial to the interpretation of *Le cento novelle*. In other words, they make the intention of Brusantino's transformation explicit and contribute to shaping the work's message and reception. Much like the *Decameron*, *Le cento novelle*'s captions not only summarize the content of the stories but also complement them with their brief and concise narrative liveliness (D'Andrea).[15] The allegories in prose and the paremias in distiches of rhymed hendecasyllables—announced by the words *allegoria* and *proverbio* in capital letters—expand those moralizing introductions that Boccaccio inserts in the narration of some of his stories or introduce a different perspective.[16] For instance, the renowned novella of Griselda and her husband Gualtieri, the Marquis of Saluzzo (Dec. X.10), opens with the succession of the three parts in *Le cento novelle* (CN 542):

Caption

Il Marchese di Saluzzo, da prieghi de' suoi huomini constretto di pigliar moglie, per prenderla a suo modo piglia una figliuola di uno villano, della quale ha dui figliuoli, li quali li fa aveduto de occiderli; poi mostrandoli lei esser rincresciuta e haver altra moglie presa a casa facendosi ritornar la propria figliuola come sua moglie fusse, lei havendo in camiscia cacciata, et da ogni cosa trovandola paciente, più cara che mai in casa tornatasi, i suoi figliuoli grandi le mostra, et come Marchesana l'honora, et fa honorare.

The Marquis of Saluzzo, overborne by the entreaties of his vassals, consents to take a wife and, being minded pleasing himself in the choice of her, takes a husbandman's daughter. He has two children by her, both of whom he makes her believe that he has put to death. Afterward, feigning to be tired of her, and to have taken another wife at home, he turns her out of doors in her shift, and brings his daughter into the house in guise of his bride; but, finding her patient under it all, he brings her home again more beloved than ever, and shows her her children, now grown up, and honors her, and causes her to be honored, as Marchioness.

Allegory

Per il Marchese di Saluzzo si tolle il pazzo che volendo talvolta far esperienza de le cose fuora di ordine con gran maraviglia fa stupire ogniuno de il saggio esprimentato, soportando con lunga pacienza, al fine con bona sorte ritorna in bono stato.

Through the Marquis of Saluzzo, the mad person is depicted who, wishing sometimes to experience extraordinary things, makes everyone marvel at what he has experimented and, after enduring patience, in the end returns in good condition with good luck.

Proverb

De cose fuor di mondo e di credenza
Non deve l'huom mai farne esperienza.

The man never has to experience things out of this world and of his beliefs.

In all of the stories, the allegory and the paremia are distinguished typographically. The allegories are written in a small font, whereas

Chapter Two

the paremias are enclosed inside a rectangle (except for a few cases) and in a larger font. In so doing, Brusantino assigns paremias a greater role than that of Boccaccio's captions and makes them the central element of his text. This is even more evident if one considers that the reader is called to reconstruct the expression's message from the connection that the proverb has with the novella it introduces.

A list of all of the epithets for women and the introductory paremias of the ten novellas in each day appears after the tenth

> **PROVERBI DELLA**
> *Sesta Giornata.*
>
> Nouella prima.
> Di Horetta, & il Caualliero
>
> Nouella sesta.
> De Michele Scalza, e certi gioueni
>
> Resti il vile, & insipido di gire
> Onde ne appar virtù, gratia, e disire.
>
> Ingegno spesso, alta virtude gioua
> Prouar cosa impossibile con proua.
>
> Nouella seconda.
> De Cisti fornaio & Geri Spina.
>
> Nouella settima.
> De Madõna Felippa del statuto Pratese
>
> Accorta cortesia sempre sta in ponto
> De sua gran nobiltade a render conto.
>
> Spesso troua beltà con sentimento
> Del fallo suo la scusa in vn momento.
>
> Nouella terza.
> De Monna Nona de Pulci, et del vesco.
>
> Nouella ottaua.
> De Fresco che cõforta la nepote che si spec
> (chi
>
> L'animo accorto è sempre più abondante
> Di effetti, e di risposte in vno instante.
>
> A l'inganno non gioua mai ragione
> Che sempre seguir vuol sua operione.
>
> Nouella quarta.
> De Chichibio Cuoco di Curado
>
> Nouella nona.
> De Guido (caualcāti che dice villania ad al-
> (cuni cauallieri.
>
> Muta spesso l'accorto in gran piacere
> L'ire, e li sdegni, ne le voglie altiere.
>
> Spesso oprime virtude l'ignoranza
> Talmente che la fa de morti stanza.
>
> Nouella quinta.
> De Forese Rabatta, & Giotto depintore
>
> Nouella decima.
> Di Frate Cipola che mostra i Carboni per la
> (penna
>
> S'altrui schernir si vuol del mal espresso
> Bisogna pria esaminar se stesso.
>
> A l'hippocrito gioua esser sagace
> Se vuol far creder col suo modo audace.

Figure 1: *Le cento novelle,* final list of paremias for day 6, Boston Public Library, G.16.66. Courtesy of the Trustees of the Boston Public Library, Rare Books. Source: archive.org/details/lecentonovelleda00brus

novella of each section.[17] Here, a sentence introduces the paremias and summarizes the plot of each story in a more succinct way than the caption that introduces the actual stories in Boccaccio's text (Fig. 1). Brusantino uses the final list of paremias to index the stories and provide unity and coherence to the entire text. In *Le cento novelle*, the stories do not exclusively need a reference to their actual content in order to be identified, as is necessary in the *Decameron*. The message provided by the associated paremia suffices to express the novella's overall meaning. Moreover, listing paremias at the end of each day mirrors the generalized ethical tone in *Le cento novelle*. These lists offer a summary of the moralizing content of the whole day and, at the same time, help the reader to remain conscious of the moral underpinnings of Brusantino's text throughout the entire reading process. Because of this structure, each day of *Le cento novelle* appears as a separate and autonomous unit, whose confines are defined by the introductory caption and the final list of paremias and epithets. This organization is likely to derive from Francesco Alunno's *Le ricchezze della lingua volgare* (1543), a dictionary with detailed entries of the vernacular words used by Boccaccio in his prosaic texts. Listed in two different final indexes provided with explanations and examples, Alunno collects *Proverbi et motti usati dal Boccaccio* ("Proverbs and mottos used by Boccaccio"; 222v–23r) and *Proverbi triti et noti* ("Trite and known proverbs"; 223r–23v), demonstrating how the author's proverbs could be considered as separate units within the narration. For a public that sought extra-textual elements, stylistic patterns, and expressions of moral conduct, *Le cento novelle*'s textual and typographical aspects supplied a guide to the exploration of the work and to its greater accessibility and comprehensibility.[18]

Rewriting the *Decameron* through Octaves and Paremias

Brusantino is not the first author to introduce octaves in the text of the *Decameron,* as well as paremias and allegories at the beginning of stories or cantos. He is, however, the first to collect and combine different traditions in an original and innovative way. That *Le cento novelle* was doomed to failure was not a direct consequence of this experiment, which presented all of the necessary elements to succeed. It was probably due to Brusantino's lack of coherence in the moral process of reinterpretation, his non-compliance with Pietro Bembo's linguistic norm from *Prose della volgar lingua* (1525), and his scarcely refined humanistic aesthetic. The latter is reflected in Brusantino's frequently convoluted style, far from reproducing Ariosto's elegant and flawless "ottava d'oro" ("gold octave"). Moreover, the absence of glosses and annotations, a feature that was common at the time in new publications of the *Decameron*, might have affected the reception of *Le cento novelle*, which undoubtedly did not experience the same European diffusion as Boccaccio's *Decameron* in terms of manuscript copies, translations, and reinterpretations.[19]

The first vernacular renditions of Boccaccio's text are poetic. The presence of many examples of poetic rewritings in vernacular is evidence that the organization and style of the *Decameron* could be easily adapted to poetry.[20] Not only single episodes but also entire novellas were transformed into recited poems in verse.[21] One of the first instances is *cantari novellistici*—melodic poems in octaves based on novellas—which were performed mostly in the sixteenth century, though their tradition spans the late fourteenth through the seventeenth century. *Cantari novellistici* were simplified and popular versions of Boccaccio's stories, usually anonymous, which rendered the *Decameron*'s novellas more accessible for the immediate consumption of a non-aristocratic public.[22] The octave—the meter that Boccaccio had used in his two epic poems, *Filostrato* (1337) and *Teseida* (1340–41)—also contributed to make a rather difficult text available to this public (Balduino in Picone and Bendinelli Predelli 25–47; Gorni; Roggia 106–9). The rhymed structure based on the *ottava rima* was considered the best option for a number of reasons. First, it was easy to listen to and memorize. Second, it could convey the refined prose and concepts of Boccaccio's texts in a more understandable, immediate, and effective form (Benucci et al., xxxi). Stylistically, the novellas and the *cantari* were connected by means of a conversion, a substitution of one text with another text, in which the original format transformed into the new genre, while still preserving its essence (De Robertis 21).[23]

In general, a combination of pedagogical objectives and entertainment determined the success of *cantari novellistici*. The *Decameron*'s novellas were selected either because they already had a known tradition of adaptations, or because their stories were likely to please the readers with comic elements, examples of feminine cleverness, and a strong sense of morality (Parma, "Fortuna spicciolata del *Decameron*" [2003] 220). The last of these aspects explains why many *cantari* are adapted from Days I, II, III, IV, V, VII, and X in the *Decameron*, which are indeed devoted to tricks played by men and women, individual shrewdness, fortune, love, and munificent deeds. Among the most famous *cantari*, which total eighteen, are *Masetto da Lamporecchio* (novella III.1) and *Lusignacca* (novella V.4).[24] Both of these adaptations rely on hilarious and rather straightforward stories of human desire and sexual satisfaction, despite religious or social ties. *Guiscardo e Gismonda* (novella IV.1), *Nastagio degli Onesti* (novella V.8), and *Griselda* (novella X.10) are exemplary among *cantari* based on tragic and serious stories. Novella II.10 also enjoyed great success generating two different *cantari novellistici*: *La storia di messer Ricciardo da Chinzica* and the *Novella di Paganino e di messer Ricciardo*, which were both produced between 1500 and 1515.

As oral artifacts, *cantari novellistici* abound with moral insertions and paremias.[25] Similar to Brusantino's *Le cento novelle*, they combine a poetic structure with the search for ethical and moral perspectives. A few *cantari* are even tightly interconnected with a paremia and vice versa. For instance, *La historia nova che insegna alle donne come se ametere el diavolo in nelo inferno* is based upon the *Decameron*'s novella III.10 featuring Alibech and Rustico. Boccaccio's story is in turn inspired by or at least draws inspiration from a *cantare* called *Canzone dell'indovinello*, whose central section corresponds with Boccaccio's text.[26] Another *cantare*, *Cantare del cercare Maria per Ravenna*, specifically originates from a proverbial phrase, which corresponds to its title, and elucidates the meaning of the expression as the story unfolds.[27] This *cantare* recounts the events of a young boy falling in love with a young girl who is forced to marry an old man. Upon feigning to be a servant, the young boy enters the woman's house, fulfills his desires, and finally kills the old husband and lives a happy life with his beloved. The story conveys a clear message: if one engages in an impossible enterprise, he suffers the consequences of his actions. In other words, older men should avoid marrying younger women because harm can follow (Romagnoli, *La istoria di Maria per Ravenna*). This is, indeed, the most common meaning associated with the proverbial phrase *Cercare Maria per Ravenna* ("To look for Maria throughout Ravenna"), since it relates to the old husband's final punishment, i.e., death.[28]

Chapter Two

In the sixteenth century, alongside "riduzioni in rima" ("renderings in rhyme"), scholars started reinterpreting Boccaccio's entire text in prose (Pettinelli, *Forme e percorsi* 166–74). Between 1531 and 1545, the *Decameron* saw the greatest number of editions and underwent major additions as editors wished to experiment with a variety of forms (Richardson, *Print Culture* 92–93). One of their main concerns was to make Boccaccio's text available to non-Tuscans, hence to a wider audience who might have been accustomed to a different dialect or vernacular. At the time, editors were "expected not just to take responsibility for the text but also to compile such things as glossaries and annotations" (Richardson, "Editing the *Decameron*" 22; see also Corsaro). For this purpose, they included a wide range of linguistic glosses, brief explanations of difficult passages, and commentaries for paremias. Interpretation of proverbs and proverbial phrases aimed to reduce the ambiguity deriving from the expressions' different connotations and sought to clarify the moral messages of the text. These "edits" occur in a few examples of Boccaccio's collection printed at Giovanni Giolito's Venetian printing press (Pastorello 178–84), as well as Ludovico Dolce's 1541 edition by Curzio Traiano Navò.[29] Other instances are the 1538 edition curated by Brucioli under the protection of Renée of France,[30] the 1542 edition by Brucioli,[31] and the 1546 edition by Francesco Sansovino[32] (later reprinted in 1548 and 1550). Paremias and allegories are also present in two other Venetian publications: the 1549 edition, which Sansovino curates in collaboration with Venetian editor Giovanni Griffio,[33] and Girolamo Ruscelli and Vincenzo Valgrisi's 1552 edition.[34] Finally, proverbs are especially prominent in the 1552 edition by Giolito and Dolce, which, in this context, stands out among the others because it probably constituted the basis for the layout and typology of the paratextual elements in *Le cento novelle*.[35] According to Pettinelli, Brusantino's textual and linguistic choices, especially for expressionistic purposes, seem to align with this publication (*Forme e percorsi* 168–72, 188–94).

Introductory paremias and allegories are included in some of the most important sixteenth-century editions of *Orlando furioso* as well. Not surprisingly, these works were produced in the same presses that were engaging in new editions of the *Decameron*.[36] In considering *Le cento novelle*, the 1542 *Orlando furioso* text curated by Giolito and Dolce constitutes an important source given the many similarities between the two works.[37] Both editions introduce allegories to emphasize the moral and didactic tone of the text and make more acceptable certain aspects in the original texts that society would have considered unethical.[38] Dolce's exposition of proverbs and *sententiae* also recalls Brusantino's final list of paremias at the end of each day, as they both represent a collection of honest teachings and topics for conversations (Javitch 35).

From an editorial and pedagogical perspective, the fact that paremias and allegories introduce many sixteenth-century editions of both the *Decameron* and *Orlando furioso* suggests that scholars and editors were attempting to speak to a specific audience. On one hand, a group of readers at the time engaged primarily in reading chivalric poems evoking classical sources; for them, allegories and paremias were unnecessary.[39] On the other hand, a different group of readers was not as interested in Greek and Latin *topoi* and instead, sought a mixture of stories about everyday lives and stories with classical references. For this audience, the authors and editors recognized that paremias were crucial pedagogical tools to transmit moral messages and stimulate ethical reflections on human life. Paremias also constituted cross-cultural and cross-societal tools that could bridge the distance between the more educated audience and what Francesco Bruni calls "pubblico mezzano" ("middle public"; *Boccacio* 37).[40] Brusantino went beyond Boccaccio's intended audience, i.e., the merchants,[41] and extended the mercantile wisdom to all social classes, in a sort of paremiographic democracy appropriate for the "middle public" to which he intended to speak.[42] In Brusantino's estimation, this should have opened up the *Decameron* to a more popular audience and to a wider reception, which unfortunately did not occur.

Le cento novelle: A Stylistic and Social Adaptation of the *Decameron*

Brusantino's *Le cento novelle* is a direct product of the Este court in Ferrara. The city's fascination with chivalric topics, both in the "matièrie de Bretagne" and the "matièrie de France," resulted in a considerable presence of French books in the libraries of the Este family. This attraction, then, paved the way for the flourishing sixteenth-century production of chivalric poems and epic romances ("romanzi cavallereschi" and "poemi epici"; Villoresi

26–27). By that time, the public had been exposed to many examples of works that continued Boiardo's and Ariosto's stories, as well as complete rewritings of the two poems, including, among others, Francesco Berni's 1541 *Rifacimento* (Flamini 141–68; Foffano 116–205). Ferrara must have affected Brusantino in his selection of the chivalric poem as the genre that he superimposes on Boccaccio's *Decameron* and through which he defines the organization and structure of his own work (Favaro 97).[43] This influence also derived from the city's religious status during the reign of Ercole II d'Este. After John Calvin visited Ferrara in 1536, Ercole's wife, Renée of France, started to develop a fascination for the Calvinist ideology and created a network of relationships with her compatriots who had been expatriated for religious reasons. As a duchy that had received investment by the Pope, Ferrara was profoundly connected to the State of the Church. This explains why the diffusion of Protestantism in Ferrara and the duchess's hospitality to all those persecuted by the Church of Rome constituted a menace to the legitimacy of the duchy. It is possible that Brusantino's ethical orientation in the *Decameron* was meant to highlight Ferrara's observance of the Church's creed and the city's intention to become the symbol of a renewed Christianity. In fact, *Le cento novelle* occurred at a time when the city was hosting many heretical personalities and Renée had been arrested as a heretic (Caponetto; Roveri; *Schifanoia* 175–254).

It is arguable that Tullia D'Aragona's criticism of Boccaccio's text also played a role in Brusantino's choice of genre for his *Le cento novelle*. In the same period when Brusantino was engaged in his *Le cento novelle*, D'Aragona was reinterpreting a moralizing and prosaic story in verse (Villoresi 77–79). Her *Il Meschino, altramente detto il Guerrino*, posthumously published in 1560, freely elaborated upon Andrea da Barberino's text *Guerino decto Meschino* (written around 1410 but printed in 1473). In her introductory letter to the readers, D'Aragona attacks the *Decameron* for two reasons: the genre of the work and the content of the stories. D'Aragona does not appreciate Boccaccio's selection of prose as a genre since it made it impossible for the collection to receive the greatest praise in the literary world. As a response to this, in her own work she introduces the verse because it is more pleasing to the ears, leaves a greater sign in the soul, and is read much more desirously than prose (D'Aragona xxv). Since writings in verse are more memorable, they are the perfect tools to attract the readers and, at the same time, convey ethical and useful teachings (Tomasi 220). Furthermore, D'Aragona criticizes the lascivious, dishonest, and immoral topics that Boccaccio introduces in his stories. In opposition, her reinterpretation of da Barberino's work aims to release a text entrenched in moral considerations. According to her, the religious elements of her (and da Barberino's) story, the valor and virtue of the main character, and the chastity of the recounted events would have made the work a perfect moral reading for the public.

When appropriating the *Decameron*, Brusantino makes a similar choice in genre and moral content to D'Aragona's. As for the metric structure, the Ferrarese author changes the prosaic text of the *Decameron* into octaves of rhymed hendecasyllables. The meter gives coherence to the text and links the stories to the introductory paremias, which follow the same prosodic and metrical scheme. The octaves are organized in ABABABCC and the paremias as distiches with a rhyme different from that of the text. Boccaccio's narrative structure does not force Brusantino to disrupt the unity that the metrical limits of the octave establish. In *Le cento novelle*, octaves always contain an autonomous section, and the narration never goes beyond them. Every thought concludes within the last verse of the octave and the progression of the octaves guarantees the development of the story. Because of the independent structure of the stanzas, paremias that appear at the end of an octave as narrative and moral closures are confined to the structure of a distich or a single verse (Roggia 101).[44]

As for content, Brusantino does not need to restructure the *Decameron*'s novellas since they already possess the two fundamental elements for successful novellas: pleasantness and variety. According to Francesco Bonciani's *Lezione sopra il comporre delle novelle* (1574), pleasantness and variety are essential for instructing the audience and satisfying its appetite in accordance with the Horatian concept—contained in *Ars poetica* (also known as *Epistula ad Pisones*)—"prodesse" ("to be useful") and "delectare" ("to delight"; *Ars poetica* 333; Favaro 100; Ordine 99–135). The *Decameron*'s stories are the perfect example of an enjoyable text with a great selection of useful and applicable plots, themes, characters, and objectives. Boccaccio already emphasizes the usefulness of his own novellas when in the proem he specifies that the *Decameron* is "in soccorso e rifugio di quelle che amano" ("succor and diversion for the ladies, but only for those who are in love"; Dec. Proemio.13). His stories could mitigate and sweeten the amorous sufferings of women, and, at the same time, fill their minds with useful teachings. This practical and beneficial value of the *Decameron*'s stories acquires even more significance in Brusantino's adaptation since he refashions their message and morphs them into something ethically oriented for his readers.

Brusantino's interpretation of the *Decameron*, however, completely differs from what will happen just a few decades after the publication of *Le cento novelle*. Beginning in the 1570s, the pervasive religious and moral atmosphere promoted by the Counter-Reformation led to the release of many moralized and "purged" versions of the *Decameron*. The most famous ones, recognized in a canonical triad, are Vincenzo Borghini and the *Deputati*'s 1573 edition (see Boccaccio, *Decameron* [1573]), Salviati's 1582 *Decameron* "rassettato" ("revised"), and Luigi Groto's (also known as Cieco d'Adria) posthumous edition in 1588 and 1590 (but actually written before Salviati's edition in 1574–84; see Boccaccio, *Decameron* [1588]). In these three editions, the curators eliminated all of the indecent references to sexual matters or, when impossible to change, transferred the setting of the stories to faraway lands. They also rewrote any anti-religious event or character description with an eye towards more religious alternatives. Borghini's edition had political relevance in the Tuscan Grand Duchy of Cosimo I. It was, indeed, the first edition of the *Decameron*, although being a "rassettatura," to be published in Florence after the last 1557 integral one by Paulo Gherardo's Venetian press (Bongi, vol. 1: xxxvi). As such, it represented a counterpart to the plethora of Venetian editions of Boccaccio's work (Mordenti 255–56), as well as an evident maneuver to enable Florence to regain its cultural and literary centrality. The *Deputati* also promoted the philological restoration of the original text by correcting those mistakes that the publishing tradition had introduced. Despite all this, their edition did not enjoy great success and was never republished after its first printing. It even faced censorship in the 1596 *Index librorum prohibitorum* of Pope Clement VIII, since the *Decameron*'s text was still presenting too many references to lascivious and dishonest aspects (Fragnito, *La Bibbia al rogo* 272; *Church, Censorship and Culture* 219–21).

Le cento novelle

Conversely, Salviati's edition, which Francesco I de' Medici, Grand Duke of Tuscany, commissioned in 1580, became the real edition of the Counter-Reformation (Brown, "Aims and Methods," "I veri promotori"). Salviati showed great attention to reconstruct Boccaccio's words, expressions, and sayings even in his own additions and despite the expurgation he was applying (Chiecchi and Troisio 27). His edition represented the new religious spirit in the second decade of the sixteenth century and, therefore, was printed repeatedly in subsequent years, ultimately marking Florence as the place for reviewing and transforming Boccaccio's text. Oppositely, Groto's edition, realized in the north of the Italian peninsula, was the least successful. The author removed any references to the Church, ecclesiastical world, and members of the clergy, along with immoral acts and topics, and replaced them with completely different plots and events, mostly informed by fairy-tale settings. This made his work the furthest from the original and probably, because of it, the least read. Another example can be added to these three works. After Groto's attempt, in 1594 Francesco Dionigi da Fano printed his polemically-titled work *Decamerone spirituale* at the Venetian printing press of Giovanni Varisco (Cherchi, "Il *Decamerone spirituale*"). The author intended to present a text full of scriptural and patristic references on moral themes, in which no narrative digressions or delightful moments were allowed. As Dionigi da Fano declares in the frontispiece, his 100 "ragionamenti" ("reasonings")—and not novellas any longer—should have profited those who wished to live in the proper and redeeming Christian way, which also included the Sapiential wisdom of Solomon's proverbs. Even though *Decamerone spirituale* reflected the spirit and tone of the harsh moralistic 1590 *Index* by Pope Sixtus V, it did not circulate much, which is evidenced by the scarcity of information on both the work and its author.

According to Carlo Dionisotti, at the time when Brusantino was working on his *Le cento novelle*, a rewriting of the *Decameron* such as those that Borghini, Salviati, Groto, and Dionigi da Fano carried out would have been impossible and illogical (189). Between 1545 and 1555, literary enterprises did not yet attempt to adhere to the religious and political implications of the Counter-Reformation. Texts were still exempt from Pope Paul IV's 1559 harsh castigation of the *Decameron* (Paulin or Roman Index) and the more moderate Pope Pius IV's 1564 Index (Tridentine Index),

Chapter Two

which accepted a possible future publication of the *Decameron* after an official expurgation ("donec corrigatur et expurgetur," "until it is corrected and purged"). Brusantino, and contemporary authors, did not yet employ the new moral character of society as a weapon against established texts as do writers in subsequent years. Later textual examples will illustrate how Brusantino's mentality is, indeed, not far from Boccaccio's separation between the world of men and the world of religion (Baratto 53). The author of *Le cento novelle* recognizes the power and force of love and sympathizes with the immoral behavior of some members of the Church. This explains why Brusantino does not restructure the entire content of the stories but rather keeps many of the anti-religious and irreverent allusions, and just as many erotic scenes. However, a strong sense of ethics inspires him and makes him evaluate certain behaviors and events through his critical lens. He elevates Boccaccio's literary message to a level that celebrates human ethical manners and pronounces a judicial opinion on those that society would have considered unethical and incorrect. From his perspective, ethical behaviors would guarantee a peaceful relationship between members of society, especially those committed to marriage and religion.[45]

In this context, *Le cento novelle*'s introductory allegories and paremias may expose the unethical aspects of a story or a character's behavior which does not receive any judgement in the *Decameron*. They may also approve of the punishment that a character faces due to his or her lack of religious or matrimonial ethics. More than moralizing Boccaccio's text, as the available criticism on *Le cento novelle* argues (Perocco, "La moralità rimata" [1987, 1997]; Favaro), Brusantino intends to reveal the different levels of interpretation and the different messages that Boccaccio's text conveys for the benefit of the ethically-inclined members of his own society (Matarrese, *Parole e forme* 40–41; Pettinelli, *Forme e percorsi* 168). His paremias represent the structure, the purpose, and the intention of *Le cento novelle*, which is heavily based upon its original but also differs from it in linguistic expression (poetry), overall interpretation, and reception.

Introductory Allegories and Paremias: Brusantino's Ethical Perspective

By inserting allegories and paremias into the *Decameron*, Brusantino does not aim to create "un ponte verso l'utilizzo esterno del testo" ("a bridge toward the external use of the text"), as was the case of Brucioli's and Sansovino's editions of the *Decameron*. In *Le cento novelle*, Brusantino is rather concerned with the correct interpretation of Boccaccio's text according to his own views. Therefore, his allegories and paremias guarantee "l'accertamento della sua lettura" ("verification of its [of the text] reading"; Bragantini, "Su alcune edizioni" 345). This suggests that the author guides the readers' experience of the collection through these two paratextual elements. Nothing ironic or laughable is present in Brusantino's use of paremias, as it was instead for *cantari*, for chivalric poems such as *Morgante* and *Orlando innamorato*, or for parodic rewritings of chivalric texts in vernacular and local dialects.[46] Nothing is seen of the desecrating laughter and cynic destruction of the knights' ideal world that characterizes his friend Aretino's 1540 *Orlandino* (Luzio). Brusantino's allegories and paremias are rather the voice of the author interpreting the *Decameron* within an ethical perspective and with a precise pedagogical intent.

The 100 allegories generally explain the symbols and highlight the meanings of the stories. The preposition "per" ("through, by means of") introduces almost all of the allegories and is followed by the name of the character that allegorically reflects a type or an entity. The verb is most frequently impersonal or passive: for instance, "si mette" ("one refers to"), "si tassa" or "si taccia" ("one accuses"), "si intende" ("one understands"), "è interpretato" ("one interprets"), "si (di)nota" ("one notices"), "si tol[l]e" and "vien[e] tolta/o" ("one infers"), with a predominance of "si tole." This explains how, through the characters, the reader can experience a deeper allegorical meaning, which always finds a perfect connection in the subsequent paremia.[47]

The 100 paremias represent *captatio benevolentiae* ("winning of goodwill") and attract the readers' attention with a similar pedagogical purpose. As they provide a summary of the stories, they extract and fix, in a memorable structure, the *exemplum* ("exemplary message") that is behind each story.[48] Furthermore, they offer instructions on how to read the text by showing which aspects should be considered central in the stories' interpretation, and which are secondary. Brusantino selects a specific message from Boccaccio's stories and then creates paremias that express an appropriate meaning for that context, frequently including his own position on ethics. Given that paremias have a diegetic or presentational function, Brusantino's introductory proverbs refer to what are key moments or characters for the author. At the same time, the content of the ten stories of each day explains the paremias, since the novellas demonstrate the proverbs' truthfulness and applicability to those specific contexts.[49] As Pettinelli argues, the mutual relationship between the content of the story and the introductory paremias makes these proverbs "una morale da legarsi, nella memoria, alle singole novelle" ("a moral to connect to the single novellas by memory"; *Forme e percorsi* 183–84).

Paremias also work as bridges between the *Decameron* and *Le cento novelle*. As previously discussed, the dialogue between Boccaccio's text and Brusantino's reinterpretation is constant. For instance, when an introductory paremia is already present in the *Decameron* at the beginning of a novella, Brusantino may eliminate it and confirm the message that the expression conveys with a different synonymic paremia. Alternatively, he may emphasize another aspect of the story through his own introductory proverb. This is the case of novella II.9, in which Brusantino does not include the proverbial phrase that introduces Boccaccio's story on the adventures of Bernabò of Genoa, his wife, and Ambrogiuolo: *Lo 'ngannatore rimane a piè dello 'ngannato* ("A dupe will outwit his deceiver"; Dec. II.9.3; Boccaccio, *Decameron* [1980] 284: footnote 4). Boccaccio's proverbial phrase probably derives from Chapter XII, v. 20 of Solomon's *Proverbs* and is later used by Franco Sacchetti to conclude the eighteenth novella of his *Le Trecento Novelle* on the tricks that Basso della Penna plays to some people from Genova and, in a similar format, by Pulci in his *Morgante* ("ingannato è chi inganna," "Those who want to cheat are cheated first"; I.4.37.6). The expression communicates that the deceiver is in turn deceived and receives an adequate punishment for the bad actions he committed; indeed, he is bowed down at the feet of the deceived (GDLI, s.v. *ingannatore*, n. 4). Although Brusantino does not adopt Boccaccio's paremia, its meaning is not lost in *Le cento novelle* because the introductory proverb for the novella rephrases it. Brusantino emphasizes how Bernabò's wife positions herself above everyone, even above her husband's double deceit:

> *Resta l'ingannator del mal accinto*
> *Da l'ingannato spesso oppresso e vinto.* (CN 108)
>
> The deceiver, who is shrouded in evil, often remains oppressed and defeated by the deceived.

(*II.9*: "*Bernabò of Genoa is tricked by Ambrogiuolo, loses his money and orders his innocent wife to be killed. She escapes, however, and, disguising herself as a man, enters the service of the Sultan. Having traced the swindler, she lures her husband to Alexandria, where Ambrogiuolo is punished and she abandons her disguise, after which she and Bernabò return to Genoa, laden with riches.*")[50]

According to Strafforello's 1883 *La sapienza del mondo*, the Latin equivalent for Brusantino's proverb is *Fraude sua capti cadunt Pelasgi* ("Pelasgians fall as they are taken by their own deceit"; s.v. *ingannare-ingannato*; see also Singer et al., s.v. *trügen*, 3.2.92–97). By substituting Boccaccio's paremia and placing it in a more evident position, Brusantino's proverb makes its meaning central to the entire structure of the story.[51]

When Brusantino selects and invents his introductory paremias, he has a specific objective in mind. Favaro claims that Brusantino wishes to emphasize the moral elements already present in Boccaccio's stories and, at the same time, castigate vices in a harsher way than Boccaccio (103). Consequently, Brusantino's text offers a greater distinction between virtues and vices, and eliminates those gray areas that Boccaccio introduces to reflect on human behavior (Favaro 104; Perocco, "La moralità rimata" [1987] 300). Favaro also comments that Brusantino's autobiographical and personal experiences dictate many of these moral changes, specifically his relationship with Ercole II and his life as a high-ranking courtier forced to wander in search of a court. While this tendency acknowledges some of Brusantino's textual changes, it can also be argued that Brusantino's alterations of the original text, and subsequently of the paremias that he creates, concern the social and cultural understanding of ethical behaviors and norms of conduct in the second half of the sixteenth century. This suggests that Brusantino's community is not necessarily embedded in the religious ethos of the Counter-Reformation but is, nevertheless, sensitive to those aspects that are recognized as fundamental for well-being in society.

Through the introductory paremias, Brusantino addresses the ethical and unethical aspects of human behavior.[52] Much like commonplace books that constituted repositories of wisdom and ready examples to use, Brusantino's proverbs serve as an "index" of good and evil. Aside from fortune, which can have both positive and negative outcomes, the author identifies the unethical sphere as involving hypocrisy and avarice (already recognized by Favaro 105), greed, ambition, deceit and consequent shame, scorn, simplicity and credulity, ignorance, and cowardice. Also included are behaviors related to wantonness, immoderate desire, jealousy, and envy. The ethical aspects are, instead, fewer in number and consist of virtue, talent, industry, generosity and magnanimity, courtesy, nobility, honesty, faith, valor, and perspicacity. It often occurs that Brusantino adapts the content of the text to the message of the introductory paremias. Except for a few cases of carelessness, he usually reinforces, in the text of the novellas, the praise or blame of the main concept that the paremia emphasizes. According to Daniel Javitch, the combination of the pedagogical purpose of the introductory allegories and paremias and the ethical coherence of the narration, as it is in *Le cento novelle*, makes Boccaccio's *Decameron* "more ethically assimilable" (33).

If Boccaccio looks more at the physical exigencies of people and at their inclinations, a societal perspective inspires Brusantino. Boccaccio does not clearly condemn unethical members of the clergy, unless the story appears in a day devoted to tragic novellas. He also intersperses his novellas with an ironic and humorous tone to ridicule certain characters, primarily priests, nuns, and monks. This occurs in *Le cento novelle* too, in which Brusantino occasionally inserts minor comic and ironic elements. He also surprisingly preserves certain salacious, irreverent, and improper references to sex, the human body, and religion. As such, these elements contribute to making *Le cento novelle* regain a sense of the levity and ironic verve that characterize Boccaccio's text. At the same time, comic and sexual moments popularize the text and satisfy the requests of the "pubblico mezzano" by guaranteeing immediate pleasure and amusement.

If Borghini and the *Deputati* could find a "convergenza tra la ricchezza polimorfa della narrativa e l'univocità del controllo morale" ("convergence between the polymorphic narrative wealth and the univocal moral control"; Chiecchi and Troisio 35), Brusantino introduces scarce, yet evident, moments of polymorphic ideology within a sturdy univocal-ethical frame that legitimizes it. The readers may enjoy these stories, laugh over them, as the members of the *brigata* do, and quietly wink at certain human qualities. However, they should always keep in mind the general point of the stories, as expressed by the introductory allegories and paremias. Brusantino does not approve of or justify committing adultery, breaking the vow of chastity, lacking devotion, ridiculing someone, and taking advantage of a potentially profitable circumstance. Indeed, these behaviors and actions may endanger the prosperity of the community and disintegrate civic order. Through the experiences of Boccaccio's characters, the readers of *Le cento novelle* can achieve catharsis: they can perceive the usefulness of the stories and the ethical message of the paremias, and thus learn from them and apply them in their social life.

Celebrated Love

On the topic of love, Brusantino seems to accept the genuine feeling of innocent love, which emerges among young people, both women and men. He likewise consents to the erotic needs that all individuals experience (Baratto 102). This explains why he maintains, unmodified, the novella at the beginning of the fourth day of the *Decameron* (also known as "novella delle papere," "novella of the goslings"), which describes the irresistible natural force of love, even between those who have never been exposed to it.

Love appears to be a noble feeling for Brusantino when it is devoted to a good cause, meaning that it is related to ethical etiquette in courtly society. An example of this can be found in novella V.9. Here, the anguish that Federigo degli Alberighi experiences because of Monna Giovanna's obstinacy not to love him, brings him to undertake extreme actions, including sacrificing his best companion, the falcon. Considering the honorable task of serving one's lover in any possible way, Brusantino deems Federigo's gesture as courteous and esteemed. The introductory paremia demonstrates the author's perspective:

Proverbio

> *Non deve a l'alta et honorata impresa*
> *Un magnanimo cor mancar di spesa.* (CN 283)

Chapter Two

> A magnanimous heart must not fail to pay for a high and honorable enterprise.

(*V.9: "In courting a lady who does not return his love, Federigo degli Alberighi spends the whole of his substance, being left with nothing but a falcon, which, since his larder is bare, he offers to his lady to eat when she calls to see him at his house. On discovering the truth of the matter, she has a change of heart, accepts him as her husband, and makes a rich man of him."*)

Since Federigo and Monna Giovanna's story is an example of love oriented toward the soul's satisfaction and is far from any immediate physical gratification, it is ethically admissible. Most of all, it is useful on a bigger societal scale because it does not disrupt the *status quo* that tradition imposes, and also promotes ethical engagement.

Courtly love may be vindictive when it is not reciprocated. Since not to return the love of people who have expressed their feeling is considered to be unethical, Brusantino allows for its revenge in certain contexts. The introductory paremia of novella V.8 illustrates how the author finds it acceptable to frighten a cruel and insensitive heart, that of Paolo Traversari's daughter, which cannot be opened by love:

Proverbio

> *S'amor non pol a un cor ingrato et empio*
> *Giovaralli timore e crudel scempio.* (CN 279)
>
> If love cannot do anything with an ungrateful and cruel heart, fear and harsh torment will be of help.

(*V.8: "In his love for a young lady of the Traversari family, Nastagio degli Onesti squanders his wealth without being loved in return. He is entreated by his friends to leave the city, and goes away to Classe, where he sees a girl being hunted down and killed by a horseman, and devoured by a brace of hounds. He then invites his kinsfolk and the lady he loves to a banquet, where this same girl is torn to pieces before the eyes of the beloved, who, fearing a similar fate, accepts Nastagio as her husband."*)

Boccaccio's fantastic representation of the afterlife for unloving people during a banquet rightly responds to those who deny the advances of loving feelings. Despite the harsh methods that Nastagio degli Onesti uses to generate fear in the other, Brusantino permits them because courtly love cannot remain unsatisfied. Both Federigo and Nastagio are courteous men: the latter is an example of total abnegation in love and the former is a model of correct punishment for the negation of love (Baricci). Brusantino declares their behavior as ethically correct and even liable to imitation by those who are in love.

In expressing and acting upon love, novella VI.7 provides a surprising instance of accepted adultery. Brusantino introduces Madonna Filippa's story with the two usual paratextual elements:

Allegoria

> Per Madonna Filippa chiamata in giuditio si dinota la bona innamorata che, quantunque habbia offeso, pur fidata in sue buone ragioni et amici del fallo riuscisse con buona prova.
>
> Through Madonna Filippa, called to trial, the good female lover is shown, who, despite having offended someone, since she is well-trusted in her good reasons and friends, would manage to come out of her fault with appropriate evidence.

Proverbio

> *Spesso trova beltà con sentimento*
> *Del fallo sua la scusa in un momento.* (CN 311)
>
> Often beauty consciously finds an excuse to its fault instantly.

(*VI.7*: "*Madonna Filippa is discovered by her husband with a lover and called before the magistrate, but by a prompt and ingenious answer she secures her acquittal and causes the statute to be amended.*")

Brusantino praises the cleverness of Madonna Filippa, who, despite admitting her wrongdoings in marriage, is nonetheless conscious of her good reasons for engaging in an extra-marital affair. If she satisfied her husband, she should have the chance to put her excess of sexual desire to use with another man and "not give it to the dogs" (Dec. VI.7.17; CN 313). Relying on the power of her words, Madonna Filippa makes everyone in court favor her behavior and "accept" her fault, and so she can escape death.

Boccaccio sheds an extremely good light on Madonna Filippa, disapproving of her husband's simple and narrow-minded behavior and praising her cleverness. Similarly, Brusantino focuses on the woman's good quality, that she is in love, and not on her dishonesty (Baratto 59). Brusantino is neither condemning Madonna Filippa nor praising her. He is in a neutral position and, although not accepting her behavior fully, still recognizes the validity and reality of her human feelings.[53] The author acknowledges Filippa's quick-wittedness (in the proverb "in un momento," "instantly") and consequently, her verbal and rhetorical skills in escaping a dangerous situation. This aligns with the sixth day's topic on characters who avoid attack or embarrassment through clever remarks. In Madonna Filippa's story, which might be seen as immoral or incongruent in the eyes of those who read *Le cento novelle*, Brusantino celebrates the power that beauty, talent, and wit have on turning events to one's own advantage, as stated in the introductory paremia. Whereas Boccaccio appreciates female empowerment and the right to sexual satisfaction, Brusantino accepts the naturalness and spontaneity of love. Since Madonna Filippa's choices do not disrupt the institution of the family (she has devoted herself to her husband and he is content with her), Brusantino believes her requests to be fair, as the adjective "bona" ("good") in the allegory expresses. This demonstrates how Brusantino is not indifferent to women's exigencies, as might seem from the introductory allegories and paremias of other novellas. Instead, he accepts the value and strength of their feelings when love is directed to satisfy natural desires.

A similar acknowledgment of love occurs in novella II.10. In this story, Paganino kidnaps Ricciardo di Chinzica's wife, Bartolomea, who, upon tasting the pleasure of a mighty body, decides not to return to her husband. The introductory allegory and paremia in *Le cento novelle* both praise passionate love and natural desires and, at the same time, repudiate the boastful behavior of an elderly person willing to compete with youth:

Allegoria

> Per Paganino vien tolto lo sfrenato disio; per la moglie di Riciardo viene tolta la lascivia, la quale sempre voria star nel vano suo diletto; per Riciardo si tole la vecchiezza che mostra li espressi falli a volersi porre a prova con la lasciva gioventude.
>
> Through Paganino one infers the unrestrained desire; through Ricciardo's wife one infers the lasciviousness, which would always want to be in pleasure; through Ricciardo one infers the old age, which shows evident mistakes when it wishes to test itself with lascivious youth.

Proverbio

> *Debbe il vecchio fuggir con fiere voglie*
> *Di farsi gioven donna amica e moglie.* (CN 116)
>
> The old man must escape with haughty desires to have a young woman as friend and wife.

(*II.10:* "*Paganino of Monaco steals the wife of Messer Ricciardo di Chinzica, who, on learning where she is, goes and makes friends with Paganino. He asks Paganino to restore her to him, and Paganino agrees on condition that he obtains her consent. She refuses to go back with Messer Ricciardo, and after his death becomes Paganino's wife.*")

More specifically, the introductory paremia recommends against marriages between old men and young women, while indirectly confronting the public with the consequences of such a union.

In the *Decameron*, Boccaccio uses the word "gelosia" ("jealousy") for the first time when Paganino da Monaco takes Bartolomea away. Ricciardo di Chinzica, Bartolomea's husband, is said to be "sì geloso che temeva dell'aere stesso" ("he was jealous of the very air"; Dec. II.10.14). Instead, Brusantino mentions jealousy earlier in the text, when Ricciardo teaches his wife all the festivities that prevent them from consummating their marriage: "apparia sempre pieno di affanno e gelosia" ("he always looked full of worry and jealousy"; CN 117). Thanks to this statement, *Le cento novelle*'s readers must confront the inappropriateness of the marriage between Ricciardo and Bartolomea earlier in the narration than the *Decameron*'s. As a result, the audience sympathizes with Bartolomea and excuses more easily her decision to remain with her kidnapper.

Boccaccio identifies Ricciardo's despair for the loss of his wife through a paremia. Before the kidnapping, Ricciardo replies to anyone asking about his conjugal situation with a proverbial phrase: Il mal furo non vuol festa ("There's never any rest for the bar"; Dec. II.10.42; CN 120; Chiecchi, "Sentenze e proverbi" 139; Rondinelli, "«Ho udito dire mille volte...»" 306). One interpretation argues that the paremia, expressly created by Boccaccio for this novella, contains an ironic allusion to the law and the court, which Ricciardo represented as a judge ("foro:" court). The accented vowel in u ("foro" > "furo") would be the result of a supposedly Pisan pronunciation of the word and, thus, be part of Boccaccio's dialectical characterization intended for satirical

Chapter Two

purposes (Bruni, *Boccaccio* 368–70, "Caratterizzazione"). The paremia's message transcends from Ricciardo's intimate reflection about his marriage to a more bureaucratic level: the court does not want to engage with a party. This means that, when Ricciardo is living with his wife, he prefers the law to his wife; he is indeed compliant with any form of religious and civil festivities, mostly fasts and vigils, which would not allow Bartolomea to satisfy her physical desires. By saying that the court is not inclined to celebrate, Ricciardo compares his failure to be a judicious husband with the failure of all practices in the tribunal. In other words, the most sophisticated rhetorical techniques cannot win the heart of a woman if she is subjected to excessive restriction and to jealousy. The latter is inadmissible in Brusantino's perspective.

Another interpretation of the paremia reads "foro" as a hole (Boccaccio, *Decameron* [1980] 314: footnote 2). Given that the storyteller of the day is Dioneo, the paremia would have a comic allusion to the female sexual organs. However, the most recent analyses of the paremia argue that, in fact, "furo" comes from the Latin "fur," which was used in medieval times to indicate a thief. In this meaning, the proverbial phrase probably recalls Ricciardo's incorrect idea that he could have satisfied his wife completely, despite his age. In so thinking, he robbed her of the true pleasures of marriage. The paremia could also refer to Paganino's kidnapping of Bartolomea. The fact that the thief "does not wish for festivities" recalls Paganino's constant ability to satisfy Bartolomea's desires, regardless of religious or moral views (Bartoli 129–30).[54]

In *Le cento novelle*, a lexical addition makes the original proverbial phrase lose some of its straightforwardness, while at the same time acquiring a specific relevance to the text of Brusantino's story:

Il mal loro non vol vigilia o festa. (CN 120)[55]
The evil hole/court enjoys no vigil or holiday.

In order to obtain a hendecasyllable, Brusantino lengthens the paremia and introduces the word "vigilia" ("vigil") to indicate that Ricciardo's theft includes both the proper festivities and the vigils. This could have two possible meanings: Ricciardo refuses Bartolomea anything that she could possibly ask for or Paganino is so eager to satisfy Bartolomea's needs that he looks at neither festivities nor their vigils. Considering the introductory paremia, i.e., old men should refrain from relationships with young women, both interpretations fit this message: either Ricciardo steals Bartolomea's age, desires, and needs, or Paganino is willing, prepared, and able to please her. Once again, Ricciardo's unhappy situation at the end of the story is sensible and reasonable as is Paganino and Bartolomea's marriage.

To conclude the story, Brusantino adopts Boccaccio's concluding paremia and transforms it into two rhymed hemistiches. A comparison between the two texts illustrates it:

Decameron

> Per la quale cosa, donne mie care, mi pare che ser Bernabò disputando con Ambruogiuolo *cavalcasse la capra inverso il chino*. (Dec. II.10.43)
>
> So it seems to me, dear ladies, that our friend Bernabò, by taking the course he pursued with Ambrogiuolo, was riding on the edge of a precipice.

Le cento novelle

> Ser Bernardo con Ambrogiuol meschino
> *Cavalcò mal la capra inverso il chino.* (CN 120)
>
> Ser Bernabò with miserable Ambrogiuolo rode on the edge of a precipice badly.

Recalling a character's poor judgment from the previous novella, Dioneo compares Ricciardo with Bernabò. In story II.9, while arguing with Ambrogiuolo about the faithfulness of their wives, Bernabò does not make the right choice when deciding to bet that his own would be honest with him (Dec. II.9.11–22; CN 109–10). The proverbial phrase, *Cavalcare la capra verso il chino* ("To ride the goat downhill"), means to be wrong or act unreasonably. This is a similar behavior to someone who tries to mount a goat down the slope of a hill and experiences an uncomfortable ride (GDLI, s.v. *capra*, n. 6). As he blames Ricciardo from II.10 for his choice to marry a younger woman, Dioneo also states that Ricciardo should accept the consequences of his not being able to keep up with his wife's energy and vitality, a mistake that Bernabò makes—more so if the ride is "mal" ("badly"). The adverb that Brusantino adds to the original proverbial phrase emphasizes how much Ricciardo was a fool if he thought that he could have won over young Bartolomea. Displaying jealousy and pretending to be better than his age demonstrates his ignorance and proves to be fatal to him. Brusantino does not condemn Paganino and Bartolomea's love, although it is adulterous, lascivious, and

Chapter Two

therefore unethical, because jealousy justifies their choice. The disruption of Ricciardo and Bartolomea's marriage does not affect society probably because a new, stable, loving couple is born.

Condemned Love

Brusantino condemns love obtained in a deceitful or unnatural way because it unsettles the society's ethical order. He disapproves of love that deceives a person, acts in opposition to familial interests and friendships, or is contrary to the laws of the Church. He rejects such expressions of love because they do not reveal the beauty of passion but are instead informed by the human mind's wickedness. In these instances, Brusantino alters Boccaccio's text when it favors such behaviors by either introducing a different end to the stories or expressing his position in the allegory and paremia at the beginning of the novella.

The two introductory elements for novella V.4 demonstrate that love, when uncontrolled, is unjustifiable:

Allegoria

> Per Ricciardo che è trovato da Litio da Valbuona è interpretato lo desir sfrenato, qual, tratto dal piacere, non riguarda a danno e dispiacere dove più da sorte che da ragione portato riuscisse di periglio.

> Through Ricciardo, whom Litio da Valbuona finds, one interprets the uncontrollable desire, which, deriving from pleasure, does not pay attention to either harm or displeasure in those occasions in which, guided by chance more than by reason, it would become dangerous.

Proverbio

> *A lo sfrenato ardir spesso gli vale*
> *Condur chi non gli pensa in molto male.* (CN 261)

> Because of unrestrained audacity, it often happens that it ends very badly for he who does not think about it.

(*V.4: "Ricciardo Manardi is discovered by Messer Lizio da Valbona with his daughter, whom he marries, and remains on good terms with her father."*)

In this novella, Ricciardo sneaks inside through Caterina's balcony at night in order to sleep with her. When the following morning Caterina's parents find the two embraced, they forgive them and allow them to get married. Despite the happy conclusion, Brusantino castigates the couple's love because it could lead to some real damage.

Brusantino follows Boccaccio's story almost completely. However, he changes a few aspects when describing the feelings between the two lovers in order to highlight their bodily appetites and tumultuous feelings. When Caterina demands that Ricciardo finds a way to satisfy their love, her talk is longer than in the *Decameron*. She aims to show how an irrational force arouses her and prevents her from seeing the unpredictable consequences of their decision. Moreover, Brusantino's words are very descriptive as they increasingly picture Ricciardo and Caterina's lack of restraint. Ricciardo is said to want to "sfogar tanto martire" ("vent such a pain") and to make Caterina grow "di più ardore ... e di doppia fiamma" ("with greater passion ... and a double loving flame"; CN 263). Brusantino even makes the description of the central scene of the novella more judgmental than Boccaccio's by means of a calculated use of words:

Decameron

> ... senza alcun cosa addosso s'addormentarono, avendo la Caterina col destro braccio abracciato sotto il collo Ricciardo e con la sinistra mano presolo per quella cosa che voi tra gli uomini più vi vergognate di nominare. (Dec. V.4.30)

> They eventually fell asleep without a stitch to cover them ... Caterina had tucked her right arm beneath Ricciardo's neck, whilst with her left hand she was holding that part of his person which in mixed company you ladies are too embarrassed to mention.

Le cento novelle

> E stando ignudi a l'uno e a l'altro in braccio
> La Caterina s'havea tolta in mano
> Quella cosa che a voi vergogna e impaccio
> Donne nomarla chiar vi par sì strano. (CN 264)

> And, while they were both lying naked embracing each other,
> with her hand Caterina had grabbed
> that part of his person which you, women, find it so strange
> to name clearly to your shame and discomfort.

Because he adds bother ("impaccio") to the original shame ("vergogna"), Brusantino makes the verbal reference to the masculine sexual organs more burdensome than it is in the *Decameron*. This

Chapter Two

happens because the two lovers' behavior is unethically lascivious and cannot be excused.

On the topic of wantonness, Andreuccio da Perugia's novella (II.5) is another good example of Brusantino's denial of sexual cravings and, simultaneously, appropriation of the *Decameron*'s content. Through the story of the young horse dealer from Perugia in Naples enduring many difficulties and perils, Boccaccio emphasizes Andreuccio's personal growth, his development of survival skills and, most of all, his final ability to take advantage of unpredictable events for his own sake. It is likely that Brusantino judges such aspect of Andreuccio's behavior secondary to the character's lustful appetites. This probably derives from that specific scene in the novella in which Andreuccio thinks that the Sicilian lady is in love with him, and invites him to satisfy her wishes (Favaro 109). Both the introductory allegory and paremia highlight Brusantino's interpretation of the text:

Allegoria

> Per Andreuccio si tassa l'huomo sciocco, che lascia i propri fatti suoi, et si lascia levare alle lascivie de' appetiti, che lo tirano in perdita della robba e della vita, dove rare volte senza buona fortuna non riesce.

> Through Andreuccio one accuses the dumb man, who leaves his own affairs and lets himself reach the lasciviousness of the appetites. These pull him down to the loss of his things and life, in which rarely, without good fortune, he cannot make it.

Proverbio

> *Cade lo sciocco espresso in grave errore*
> *Se sconciamente vuol seguir amore.* (CN 66)

> The openly dumb man falls in serious error if he indecently wants to follow love.

(II.5: "*Andreuccio da Perugia comes to buy horses in Naples, where in the course of a single night he is overtaken by three serious misfortunes, all of which he survives, and he returns home with a ruby.*")

The adverb "sconciamente" ("indecently"), which appears in the paremia, is absent in Boccaccio's original text.[56] In *Le cento novelle*, defining Andreuccio's behavior as indecent guides the reader in interpreting the story. Andreuccio follows love improperly: he is ready to accept the young woman's invitations and to fantasize about its possible evolutions, when instead he should be more cautious and avoid situations that could endanger his own person and property. Andreuccio's sexual desires are even more inappropriate because of his foolishness, which the allegory highlights ("uomo sciocco," "dumb man"). For the events guiding Andreuccio through the streets of Naples and through multiple adventures, Brusantino finds a different explanation than Boccaccio: it is not lack of intelligence, but rather disgraceful lasciviousness.

By way of changing the story's message, Brusantino offers a personal interpretation of the novella's events and main character, as well as the second day. According to him, the theme "misadventures that suddenly end happily" does not mean that the human being can succeed when fortune and cleverness are combined. This is Boccaccio's perspective on Andreuccio, who takes advantage of fortuitous occasions by relying on his newly acquired wisdom. Brusantino does not recognize any positive outcome from Andreuccio's new personality and vision of life. He rather leaves the entire orchestration of events and decisions to the Latin *fortuna* (Branca, *Boccaccio medievale*). As the allegory specifies, Andreuccio experiences misfortune because of his lack of common sense and he is able to emerge from great loss and peril exclusively with the aid of external forces.

The textual changes that Brusantino makes are consistent with the ethical orientation of his story. In the *Decameron*, an old woman accompanying the young and beautiful Sicilian woman recognizes Andreuccio in the crowd and greets him. The Sicilian woman is shrewd enough to gather all the details about the man without arousing the old woman's suspicion. Instead in *Le cento novelle*, the old woman is part of the scheme that the young woman devises and willingly shares all the information she obtains about Andreuccio. Brusantino uses a very harsh vocabulary to describe the Sicilian woman and addresses her as a sly and wicked prostitute (CN 6[7]). While Boccaccio presents the woman's charming manner with Andreuccio, Brusantino highlights her devious mind:

Decameron

> E così detto, da capo il rabbracciò e ancora teneramente lagrimango gli baciò la fronte. (Dec. II.5.24)
>
> And having said all this, sobbing with affection, she embraced him a second time and kissed him once again on the forehead.

Chapter Two

Le cento novelle

> E così detto con nove maniere
> Tornollo ad abbracciar d'amor insana. (CN 69)

> So, saying it with new manners,
> she went back to embrace him, as a person insane with love.

On the other hand, sexual appetites and erotic thoughts enflame Brusantino's Andreuccio:

> E de la caRa donna tutto aRdendo
> In casa aRdito entRò senza taRdare. (CN 68)

> And all burning with passion for the dear woman,
> he entered the house boldly, without delay.

The alliteration of the letter *r* recalls the crackling of fire, something that an enamored heart experiences. Not only is Andreuccio burning in the flames of love, but he is also ready to satisfy the young woman fully. Brusantino disapproves of this behavior and, therefore, condemns it.

In Brusantino's range of unacceptable typologies of love, there is also homosexual love. Novella V.10 is an intricate story of adulterous love between a young man and a woman. The woman's husband, after discovering the fact, invites the two to continue loving each other, so that he could enjoy the young man's body himself. In the *Decameron*, the moral of Boccaccio's story shows how both women and men have identical physical needs and how they can reach a compromise to satisfy them. Brusantino does not agree with this reading and expresses his opinion clearly in the introductory allegory and paremia:

Allegoria

> Per la donna de Pietro da Venciolo si tole la lascivia, per Pietro il desiderio contra natura, il qual talmente nel suo error s'immerge che non cura al onor suo biasmo per seguitare il vitioso suo disio.

> Through Pietro da Venciolo's wife one infers the lasciviousness, and the desire against nature through Pietro, who immerses himself in his mistake so much that he does not care about the blame against his honor in order to pursue his immoral desire.

Proverbio

> Di vergogna non cura l'alma insana
> Ne escie del fango mai come la rana. (CN 287)

> The insane mind does not care about shame nor does it ever emerge from the mud like the frog.

(*V.10: "Pietro di Vinciolo goes out to sup with Ercolano, and his wife lets a young man in to keep her company. Pietro returns, and she conceals the youth beneath a chicken coop. Pietro tells her that a young man has been discovered in Ercolano's house, having been concealed there by Ercolano's wife, whose conduct she severely censures. As ill luck would have it, an ass steps on the fingers of the fellow hiding beneath the coop, causing him to yell with pain. Pietro rushes to the spot and sees him, thus discovering his wife's deception. But in the end, by reason of his own depravity, he arrives at an understanding with her."*)

The harsh vocabulary in the allegory and paremia, including "error" ("mistake"), "biasmo" ("blame"), "vitioso" ("immoral"), and "vergogna" ("shame"), highlights Brusantino's rejection of same-sex love. Pietro's homosexual tendencies are a desire against natural laws, and hence are unethical. His feelings are even worse since he cares little about his honor and is inclined to forsake it to fulfill his lust.

This story's paremia is the only one out of the 100 introductory proverbs that is not Brusantino's personal creation, but a borrowing from Boiardo's *Orlando innamorato*. Brandimarte uses it when discussing the essence of wicked men in Canto XIX from the second book of the chivalric poem:

> Disse nel suo pensier: «L'omo malvagio
> Non se può stor al male onde è nutrito;
> Né di settembre, né il mese di magio,
> Né a l'aria fredda, né per la caldèna,
> Se può dal fango mai *distor la rana*.» (II.XIX.43)[57]
>
> He thought to himself: "A bad man can't
> escape the foulness of his life,
> not in September, nor in May,
> not in cold, nor when it's hot.
> a frog will never leave the mud!"

Brandimarte thinks that evil men are similar to frogs that never come out of the bog. As the frog hides in the thick mud with every climate and in every season, so a bad man loves his own vileness and cannot separate himself from the harm and negativity with which he always engages. Therefore, he is insensitive to any reprimand and always seeks to excuse his behavior with the bad manners of others (GDLI, s.v. *rana*, n. 11: *La rana ama il pantano*).

The second hemistich of Boiardo's paremia, *Ne escie del fango mai come la rana* ("Nor it ever emerges from the mud like the frog")—which also features in a similar fashion at the beginning of Burchiello's sonnet CXLLX (v. 1; qtd. in Crimi 71)—acquires a specific contextual meaning in the story of Pietro di Vinciolo and his wife. When he scolds his adulterous wife by reprimanding the behavior of another unfaithful woman, he comments that frequently women attribute their own bad deeds to someone else's faults (Dec. V.10.54; CN 291). Pietro's words describing what is perceived as the typical feminine behavior seems to be the textual evidence that justifies Brusantino's introductory paremia. Much like a frog, Pietro's wife and all women hide themselves in the mud of other women's betrayals to feel protected. However, given the tone of the allegory and the text of the novella, it is probable that Brusantino's choice of the paremia is rather directed to a different aspect of the story. In the end, Pietro does not punish his wife, but consents to her relationship so that he can have sexual intercourse with the young man himself "a sodisfacimento di tutti e tre" ("to the mutual satisfaction of all three parties"; Dec. V.10.63). Hiding his sexual orientation but wishing to take advantage of his wife's cheating, he is not dissimilar to a frog in a bog.

Brusantino's interpretation of the story is exclusively ethical. On one hand, the woman's behavior is unethical because she does not respect the commitment of marriage and looks for ways to satisfy her sexual appetites elsewhere (Essary). On the other, Pietro's activities are even more unethical because he follows what was considered an unnatural desire without hesitation. His love is unjustifiable because it cannot be acknowledged in the scope of possible expressions of human feelings in society. As a result, Brusantino denies the two character's feelings and wipes out all of Boccaccio's references to both the power of affection and the happy conclusions of unfortunate love stories, which is the topic of Day V.

Lascivious Love and Religion

When lascivious love involves the Church, Brusantino does not interpret love among or within members of the clergy through the lens of religious sin. The error does not pertain to the religious institution, but rather to individuals and society at large. Breaking the vows of chastity is wrong because the appropriate societal behavior prescribes against it.

As an example, Brusantino does not hesitate to express his disapproval of the main characters' behavior in novella I.4, transforming rather substantially the perspective of the original text. In this story, a monk—and later his superior—engages in sexual intercourses with a beautiful, young woman. Boccaccio views these clergymen humanely because he is conscious that love is an insuperable force almost impossible to suppress. Conversely, Brusantino is straightforward in his castigation. He decides to make the monk and the abbot repent for their sins, eliminates Boccaccio's acknowledgment and acceptance of their behavior, and introduces a correct path to religious observance (Favaro 108). From the beginning, Brusantino prepares his readers for the characters' nature and anticipates the subsequent evolution and resolution of the story. In the introductory allegory, the author specifies that the abbot is a bad man, and this characterization is confirmed throughout the narration. Likewise, in the paremia, he blames the abbot's actions and indirectly comments on his lack of judgment, which prevents him from realizing how foolish it is to blame someone else for a bad action that anyone could potentially commit:

Allegoria

> Per lo abate che volse punier il monaco caduto in peccato dinota l'huomo cattivo che vuole riprender l'altro dove che spesso accade che nel medesimo peccato coperto si ritrova peggio esser incorso.

> Through the abbot, who wished to punish the sinful monk, one notices the bad man who wants to reprimand the other in what it often happens that he, covered in the same sin, finds himself to fall into even worse.

Proverbio
> *Nel riprender altri del mal insano*
> *Il giuditio bisogna haver ben sano.* (CN 26)

> In order to scold someone for his insane evil, one must have healthy judgement.

(*I.4:* "*A monk, having committed a sin deserving of a very severe punishment, escapes the consequences by politely reproaching his abbot with the very same fault.*")

Chapter Two

Under the young monk's fraud, Boccaccio's abbot simply follows his sexual desires when he is left alone with the girl in the cell. Conversely, Brusantino's abbot thinks about having intercourse in advance and plans to enter the monk's cell and possess the girl. In this way, Brusantino does not make the reader experience the empathy that Boccaccio's abbot inspires. The abbot in *Le cento novelle* consciously decides to fulfill his bodily needs beforehand and thus, does not deserve any compassion or excuse. Accordingly, the end of the story in *Le cento novelle* differs greatly from that of the *Decameron*. Boccaccio's abbot and monk reach a compromise and agree not to reveal the event, presumably continuing their meetings with the woman (Dec. I.4.22). Brusantino's abbot, instead, regrets his behavior, makes an ethical choice, and returns to his religious duties, according to which love is directed only to God (CN 28).

In novella III.1 regarding the Church, Brusantino condemns the expression of love since it is cunningly directed to specific members of the Church, i.e., nuns. In this story, Masetto da Lamporecchio, who feigns deafness to be employed as the gardener in a monastery, becomes the nuns' object of desire. In *Le cento novelle*, the introductory allegory emphasizes the dishonesty of Masetto's acts and the paremia condemns the nuns' lack of judgement (Fig. 2):

Allegoria

> Per Masetto da Lamporecchio vien tolta la lascivia, quale sotto più forme cerca di ingannar la castitade, che spesso havendo l'agio risveglia l'animo a far cose dishoneste, non pensate mai.
>
> Through Masetto da Lamporecchio one infers the lasciviousness, which, as it seeks to deceive chastity in different ways, having the comfort often awakens the soul to do dishonest acts, never thought of before.

Proverbio

> *Se castità servar si dee a ragione*
> *Fuggir l'agio bisogna e occasione.* (CN 127)
>
> If one must preserve chastity for a good reason, one needs to escape the comforts and the opportunity.

(III.1: "Masetto da Lamporecchio pretends to be dumb, and becomes a gardener at a convent, where all the nuns combine forces to take him off to bed with them.")

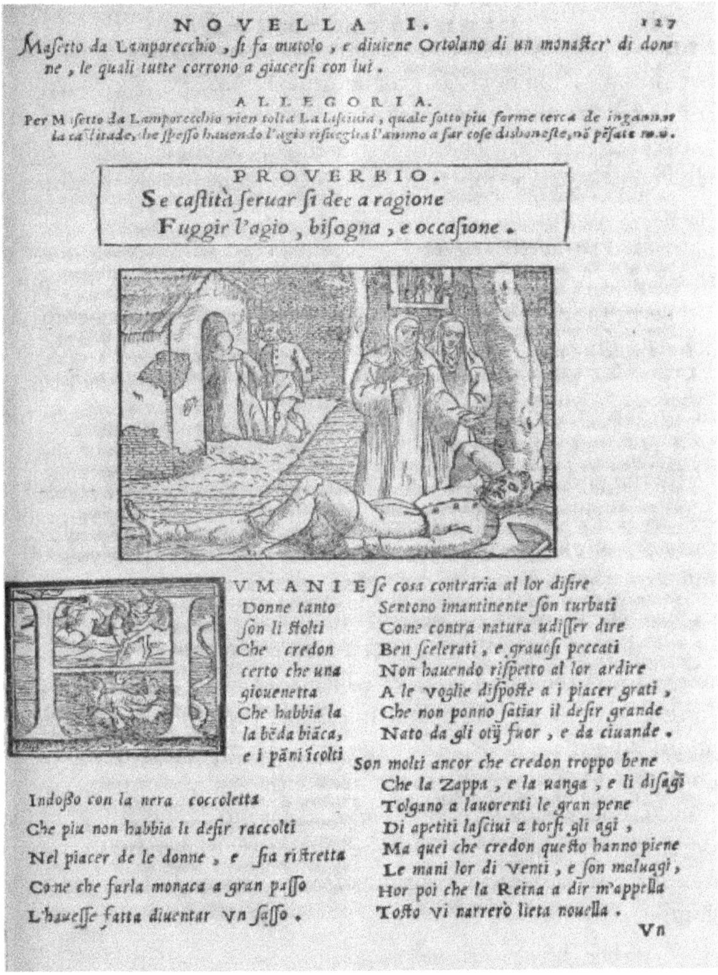

Figure 2: *Le cento novelle*, introductory allegory and paremia for novella III.1, Boston Public Library, G.16.6. Courtesy of the Trustees of the Boston Public Library, Rare Books. Source: archive.org/details/lecentonovelleda00brus

In both paratextual elements, Brusantino rebukes not only Masetto's greed, but also the nuns' departure from their religious paths. As the allegory says, lasciviousness can lead the human soul to corruption and unethical behavior, such as for the nuns not preserving chastity. In order to keep it, as the paremia expresses, the nuns should have avoided the temptations of a young and handsome man available for them.

77

Chapter Two

Daria Perocco claims that the allegory is an example of how Brusantino may insert an inappropriate interpretation at the beginning of his novellas. The allegory's message has no visible connection to the story and seems to express a mere moral stance with no effect on the narration ("La moralità rimata" [1987] 296). However, it is arguable that Brusantino's allegory focuses on an aspect of the novella that might not be the most evident or important, at least according to Boccaccio's text. In *Le cento novelle*, this aspect becomes the central element to analyze and interpret. While in the *Decameron* Boccaccio celebrates Masetto's genius in achieving his goal, regardless of its nature, Brusantino reflects on what is ethical and what is not. By way of judging a behavior that no one in society should exhibit, he aims to teach a lesson to his readers.

By the end of the novella, Brusantino seems to forget the message of the introductory proverb that holds the nuns accountable for staying chaste. He does not condemn the Abbess and the nuns for their choices and actions. His attention goes only and exclusively to Masetto and his unethical decision to fulfill his sexual desires inside a monastery. Because of his behavior, he is not granted the same positive conclusion as in Boccaccio's text. In the *Decameron*, Masetto, living inside the monastery for years and raising many kids, leaves the nuns when he is old, rich, and content with the way he spent his youth in the company of the nuns. Conversely, in *Le cento novelle*, Masetto suffers for all of his deceitful actions. He is rich when he leaves the monastery but, as a sort of Dantesque "contrappasso," at the end of his life he is completely poor:

> Ma che gli avenne al fine io seppi poi
> Che in miseria finì li giorni suoi. (CN 131)
>
> But, later, I knew what happened to him in the end,
> that he spent his last days in misery.

Brusantino's Masetto does not enjoy the wealth that Boccaccio's character gains from the convent. This is Brusantino's lesson about love that is unethically directed to members of a monastery and that disrupts the correct functioning of a community.

Despite the strong ethical atmosphere, this novella is one of the few that foregrounds an exploitation of sexual tensions for comedic purposes and popular appeal. Throughout the story, physical desire ignites both Masetto and the nuns in greater ways than in the *Decameron*. It is interesting to point out that Brusantino develops more explicit sexual content through the same metaphorical vocabulary that Boccaccio employs in other novellas devoted to erotic sequences. This vocabulary is typically associated with sexual scenes in comic, parodic, and dialect literature, as can be seen in Aretino's 1524 *Sonetti lussuriosi* and 1534–36 *Sei giornate* (Porcelli, "Il lessico erotico"; Procaccioli, "Dai *Modi* ai *Sonettti lussuriosi*"). Brusantino's description of Masetto's nudity and of its effects on the Abbess's vulnerable flesh demonstrates this usage:

> E scoperta mostrava quella chiave
> Che era de monache otto contrapeso
> Che la camisia al vento faceva specchio
> De le anguinaglie ignude al petenecchio.
>
> Riguardando madonna quello uccello
> Che a le monache sue cantava in gabbia
> Cade nel apetito dolce e bello
> Che eran l'altre cadute in tanta rabbia. (CN 130)
>
> And he was showing exposed that key
> that was a counterweight for eight nuns,
> because the shirt in the wind mirrored
> the naked groins in the privities.
>
> As the woman was looking again at that bird
> which was singing to her nuns in the cage,
> she falls in the sweet and pleasant appetite
> in which the others had fallen with such avidity.

The semantic area shaped by clearly allusive phallic words, such as "chiave" ("key"), "petenecchio" ("privities"), and "uccello" ("bird"), makes the Abbess's act more reproachable than it is in the *Decameron*. In *Le cento novelle*, succumbing to purely physical needs shows a moral failing, particularly because this makes oneself and others forget about one's duties. Despite its sweetness and pleasantness, this love is unethical, especially because it involves members of the Church.

Novella III.10 is another story devoted to a member of the clergy not respecting his vow of chastity. The actions of the main protagonists are reprehensible because wild desire and wantonness drive them. Rustico, an old hermit tricks a young and naïve woman, Alibech, willing to wander as a hermit herself, into thinking that sexual intercourse represents a holy way to eliminate the devil from the world and express one's love to God—from which the famous expression *Rimettere il diavolo in inferno* ("To put the devil back into Hell") originates. In the introductory allegory and paremia, Brusantino does not account for Alibech's inexperience and, consequently, does not consider her feelings to be as innocent as they are judged to be in the *Decameron*. Additionally, Brusantino emphasizes that Rustico deserves blame, since he falls into temptation and cannot restrain himself from tasting the fruits of love after many years of abstinence:

Allegoria

> Per Alibech dinota la semplice lascivia, per Rustico lo sfrenato disio, il quale tentato per la lascivia ad essersi data in preda et lei più che mai ne lo sfrenato disio compiacendosi, lo invita a li amorosi piaceri.

> Through Alibech one notices the simple lasciviousness and the uncontrollable desire through Rustico, who is tempted by lasciviousness that, open to give itself prey, invites him to loving pleasures, while it pleases itself with unrestrained desire more than ever.

Proverbio

> *Quanto lascivia più in disio si mesce*
> *Tanto la voglia più augumenta e cresce.* (CN 178)

> The more lasciviousness is entangled with desire, the more desire increases and grows.

(III.10: "*Alibech becomes a recluse, and after being taught by the monk, Rustico, to put the Devil back in Hell, she is eventually taken away to become the wife of Neerbal.*")

Despite in the allegory Alibech's lasciviousness is defined as "semplice" ("simple"), meaning not malicious and only driven by natural bodily appetites, she is as guilty as Rustico of "disio" and "voglia" (in the paremia). The use of the verb "tentare" ("to tempt") to describe Rustico's desire, places his act within the religious realm, in which giving into any attraction to the opposite sex is a sin. His trick, however, is not only religious since it affects society and individuals, and thus is an offense against them as well. The women's laughter at Alibech's foolishness, when she returns to her hometown, is the direct consequence of Rustico's unethical and irreverent behavior (Dec. III.10.32–35; CN 182). Indeed, his actions disrupt the central societal tenet of respecting people and showing examples of ethical behavior.

Just as in the previous novella, Brusantino lingers on certain sexual and bodily details when he describes the preliminaries of the love act, something that Boccaccio leaves to the imagination of his readers:

> E mirando la forma di quel peso
> Subitamente fu maravigliata
> E disse, «che cosa è ch'ivi hai sì mossa
> Che spingi inanzi così dura e grossa?»
> ... E come star dovesse insegnò il resto
> A incarcerar quel maledetto e rio
> Che alcia la testa con sì fier disio. (CN 180–81)
>
> And looking at the shape of that weight,
> she was immediately amazed
> and asked: "What is that which you have moved there,
> that you push forward so hard and big?"
> ... And the rest instructed her
> in the art of incarcerating that accused and guilty thing
> that was raising its head with haughty desire.

The noun "peso" ("weight"), the adjectives "dura e grossa" ("hard and big"), and the verbs "mossa" ("moved") and "alcia" ("was raising") define a comic atmosphere in which, however, the sense of error is present as the cluster "maledetto e rio" ("damned and guilty") demonstrates. Although the comedy of these events is lessened in the larger condemnation of the act, it still offers a relief from Brusantino's ethically-charged narration. It represents a way to appeal to a larger audience ("pubblico mezzano") by sweetening the content of the story and, simultaneously, sending a moral message.

In another story, despite following the structure of Boccaccio's novella in detail, Brusantino aggravates the punishment that the main character faces due to his intercourse with a woman. Novella IV.2 features Friar Alberto who feigns to be the Archangel Gabriel in order to descend from the skies and engage in several sexual meetings with beautiful Madonna Lisetta. In the *Decameron*, this novella lightens the somber atmosphere following the tragic story of Guiscardo and Ghismonda (IV.1) and makes the *brigata* merrier. Although Friar Alberto's story deserves a tragic conclusion, Boccaccio's narration transmits a sense of sadness, and almost sympathy, about his destiny. Boccaccio also laughs, yet without critical judgement, over the woman's lack of intelligence and excessive consideration of her own beauty, which brings her to think of herself as a superior and holier human being. On the contrary, in *Le cento novelle* Brusantino judges Friar Alberto harshly for his unethical behavior and his deviant machinations to obtain Madonna Lisetta's sexual favor and condemns the woman's frivolousness. In the allegory, the author mentions the adjective "vile" ("coward") twice to depict Friar Alberto's character, whereas in the paremia, he unrestrainedly accuses Madonna Lisetta of ignorance due to vanity:

Allegoria

> Per Frate Alberto, vien notato lo sfrenato desiderio, posto in un cor vile; per la donna, in la quale s'inamora, s'intende la persuasione di molte sciocche le quali, sotto estremi vanti de la lor fragile bellezza, si lasciano tirar ad opre triste, da genti vili, con biasimo de la lor vergogna.
>
> Through Frate Alberto one notices the unrestrained desire placed in a coward heart; through the woman, with whom he falls in love, one understands the persuasion of many foolish women, who, by means of excessive praise of their fragile beauty, let coward people draw them to sad actions with blame of their shame.

Proverbio

> *Danno e vergogna convien che scocche*
> *Da la persuasion di donne sciocche.* (CN 198)
>
> It's appropriate that harm and shame burst out of the persuasion of foolish women.

(IV.2: *"Fra Alberto, having given a lady to understand that the Angel Gabriel is in love with her, assumes the Angel's form and goes regularly to bed with her, until, in terror of her kinsfolk, he leaps out of the window and takes shelter in the house of a pauper; the latter disguises him as a savage and takes him on the following day to the city square, where he is recognized and seized by his fellow friars, and placed under permanent lock and key."*)

Madonna Lisetta represents all the simpletons who believe everything. In both the *Decameron* and *Le cento novelle*, she lets herself be fooled for the sake of having her beauty recognized and almost rendered supernatural. The result is that the woman, as a vain and characterless "donna zucca al vento" ("flimsy pumpkin lady"; CN 201), is easy to persuade, and thus is driven to commit shameful acts resulting in negative and harmful outcomes. Indeed, after she reveals her meetings with the Angel to her friends, Friar Alberto's trick is discovered, and the friar is brought in a square for public ridicule and then incarcerated until his death.

Brusantino confirms his judgement of the two characters when he adds a proverbial phrase that is absent in the *Decameron*. During her intercourse with Friar Alberto, Madonna Lisetta enjoys making love with a handsome man and, at the same time, experiences the spirituality of the act, thinking that the friar is a real angel—an aspect that Boccaccio's story also presents. Because she satisfies two desires, Brusantino comments:

> *Gli fece far dui chiodi in una calda.* (CN 201)
> She made him do two nails in a hot operation.

Similar to *Fare un viaggio e due servigi* ("To make a trip and fulfill two services"), Brusantino's proverbial phrase, placed at the end of the octave, ironically winks at Madonna Lisetta. She thinks that she is engaging in a heavenly performance on earth when in fact she is simply satisfying her physical desires (GDLI, s.v. *caldo* [2], n. 13).[58]

Brusantino's novella ends as tragically as Boccaccio's.[59] Its conclusion sounds more proverbial than Boccaccio's final words (Boccaccio, *Decameron* [1980] 504: footnote 5):

Decameron

> Così piaccia a Dio che a tutti gli altri possa intervenire. (Dec. IV.2.58)
>
> May it please God that a similar fate should befall each and every one of his fellows.

Le cento novelle

> Che così piaccia a Dio che ciascun vegna
> Ch'in pensar e mal far al cor disegna. (CN 205)
>
> May it please God that a similar fate should befall everyone who puts his mind into bad thoughts and deeds.

Brusantino's final lines look like an *ad hoc* creation for the novella. The consequences of Friar Alberto's behavior should extend to all others who behave in the same way and God should be pleased if harm, sadness, and shame fall upon them. This is the ethical

Chapter Two

message that Brusantino sends to his readers. He essentially communicates that, as a general truth for the entire society, it is better not to engage in similar acts because even God does not wish to absolve those who do.

A similar combination of lasciviousness and religion leads to incontestable condemnation in novella IX.2. This story recounts the adventures of another religious member, the Abbess of a convent, whose illicit affairs are discovered one night after unveiling the long-standing sexual encounters of young nun Isabetta. In the introductory allegory, Brusantino disapproves of Abbess Usimbalda's lust and arrogance in believing that she would be excused for her misconduct. Moreover, in the paremia he points out that the Abbess even excuses her "mistake" for the sake of her own enjoyment:

Allegoria

> Per la Abadessa che riprende la monaca, se intende la superba lascivia, la quale non acorta del suo proprio errore vol gastigare l'altro, e spesse volte accade che nel riprender viene scoperta de maggior eccesso, onde ne resta da doppia vergogna oppressa.
>
> Through the Abbess, who reprimands the nun, one understands the haughty lasciviousness. Since she has not been discovered in her own mistake, she wishes to castigate the other, and often it happens that, in rebuking, she is exposed to be even worse, whence it oppresses her with double shame.

Proverbio

> *Scoperto il reo del suo proprio errore*
> *A la fraude et al mal ne dà favore.* (CN 451)
>
> The guilty person, who has been discovered in his fault, favors the scam and the evil.

(IX.2: *"An abbess rises hurriedly from her bed in the dark when it is reported to her that one of her nuns is abed with a lover. But being with a priest at the time, the Abbess claps his breeches on her head, mistaking them for her veil. On pointing this out to the Abbess, the accused nun is set at liberty, and thenceforth she is able to forgather with her lover at her leisure."*)

According to Brusantino, the nuns are to uphold their moral and ethical conduct not only for all other religious members, but also for society as a whole. The author strongly condemns Abbess Usimbalda for her sin and also for her reproachable deceit and fraud: she has a secret—which is revealed—and she pretends to be perfect and better than all of the other nuns. Her double shame originates from this fact. Brusantino does not mention Isabetta, equally faulty and sinful, probably because her feelings are not malicious.

Although he tends to follow the *Decameron* faithfully, Brusantino changes the tone with which he recounts the events of the novella. On one hand, he emphasizes the young nun Isabetta's beauty and shows an empathetic attitude toward her. On the other hand, he adds more dramatic moments in the various stages of the relationship between her and her lover. In this way, Brusantino highlights the naturalness and spontaneity of Isabetta's love vis-à-vis the Abbess's wickedness. Similar to the previous two examples, Brusantino also includes ironic moments, for instance when he describes the scene of the nuns calling the Abbess and accompanying her to Isabetta's cell:

> [L'Abadessa] dicendo andava ove è la maledetta
> Da Dio con l'altre che erano in furor
> Da far trovare l'Isabetta in fallo
> Con il caro suo amante in mezo al ballo. (CN 452)

> She was going where the woman, damned
> by God, was, with the others who were in frenzy
> to let her find Isabetta fallaciously
> with her dear lover in the middle of the dance.

Brusantino uses a sexual metaphor to describe Isabetta and her lover's intercourse as a dance. The irony of the situation is that the Abbess is ready to accuse the young nun, when, in fact, she is guilty of her own deception. Accordingly, the extent of her indiscretions illustrates a blemish to all of the Church and society.

Boccaccio concludes the narration with the Abbess's final admission of guilt and her authorization of sexual relationships, emphasizing that love is a driving force in human life. Brusantino concludes his story with similar words and even adds a reference to the impossibility of suppressing the stimuli of the flesh in a secure place, such as a convent. The nuns continue to live happily together; the Abbess resumes her sexual encounters without shame, just like Isabetta; and all of the other celibate nuns who did not have a lover start to search for one. Despite the message of the initial allegory and paremia reproaching the nuns' unethical actions, it seems that finally the naturalness of love prevails.

Chapter Two

Jealousy Rebuked

According to Brusantino, jealousy is certainly the most despised shortcoming in human actions. On one hand, the jealous characters of *Le cento novelle* receive the most extreme judgements. On the other, Brusantino allows for a full expression of the feelings that jealousy restrains, as evidenced by those emotions explored in novella II.10 with Ricciardo di Chinzica and his wife Bartolomea. Two other novellas from days III and VII describe the full realization of love despite the jealous behaviors of certain characters. Even though they pertain to two different topics, Brusantino's introductory allegories and paremias for stories III.6 and VII.5 blame jealousy as the evil root that influences the course of events. Therefore, it is worth looking at them comparatively:

III.6
Allegoria

> Per Ricciardo Minutolo, che ama la moglie di Philipello, si mette lo astuto, per la moglie di Philipello si tassa il troppo credere, che per gelosia, talhora corre fuore de li dovuti termini, e crede cose impossibili.

> Through Ricciardo Minutolo, who is in love with Philipello's wife, one refers to the cunning man; through Philipello's wife one accuses the act of believing excessively, which, because of jealousy, sometimes goes out of the required terms and believes in impossible things.

Proverbio

> *Lieve è di astutia ingannar gelosia*
> *Ché il tutto crede quando è in frenesia.* (CN 150)

> Deceiving jealousy requires mild cunning since it believes everything when it is in a frenzy.

(*III.6: "Ricciardo Minutolo loves the wife of Filippello Sighinolfi, and on hearing of her jealous disposition he tricks her into believing that Filippello has arranged to meet his own wife on the following day at a bagnio and persuades her to go there and see for herself. Later she learns she has been with Ricciardo, when all the time she thought she was with her husband."*)

VII.5
Allegoria

> Per il geloso, che in forma di prete confessa la moglie, si dinota la propria gelosia, per la moglie la fraude, la q[ua]l con sua trista

operatione scoperte s'induce a far per modo tale che le vere cose fa conoscer per false.

Through the jealous person, who confesses his wife disguised as a priest, one understands his own jealousy; through the wife one sees the scam, which, by means of unveiled bitter actions, leads to believing as false what is true.

Proverbio

> *La troppo gelosia induce a tale*
> *Che da se stessa se ne causa il male.* (CN 344)

Excessive jealousy leads to such (extreme behaviors) that it causes its own self harm.

(*VII.5: "A jealous husband disguises himself as a priest and confesses his wife, by whom he is given to understand that she loves a priest who comes to her every night. And whilst the husband is secretly keeping watch for him at the front door, the wife admits her lover by way of the roof and passes the time in his arms."*)

In both novellas, the person afflicted by another character's deceptive mind is the jealous person, regardless of gender and social status. In novella III.6, Catella is incredibly jealous of her husband to the point that "ogni uccel che per l'aria volava, che lo togliesse a lei selo credea" ("it seemed to her that every bird that was flying in the air was going to take her husband away from her"; CN 151). Because of it, she is rightly so the recipient of Ricciardo Minutolo's trick. Ricciardo manages to sleep with Catella by deceiving her that she was, in fact, going to the thermal bath with her husband. Likewise, because of his excessive jealousy, the husband in novella VII.5 gives his wife every right to deceive him in order to teach him a lesson. Here, the swindle consists of making the husband wait for her potential lover outside, while she is enjoying herself in her own bed.

The paratextual elements for the stories describe jealousy as a negative feeling that leads to inappropriate and uncontrollable behaviors in society. In the allegories, jealousy makes the mind go "fuori de li dovuti termini" ("out of the required terms"; III.6), believe in "cose impossibili" ("impossible things"; III.6), and consider "le cose vere per false" ("as false what is true"; VII.5). The paremias confirm that, when jealousy is extreme or in a frenzy, it makes someone believe anything and causes a person to be vulnerable and susceptible to deceit or harm. Even though in story III.6 Ricciardo is the allegorical representative of the cunning man, in

Chapter Two

fact it is jealousy that motivates his actions. Thus, Brusantino's introductory paremia focuses more on Catella's jealousy and places Ricciardo's dishonest trick on her secondarily. It seems that the author does not even consider it unethical that deceit brings Catella to cheat on her husband. This occurs in story VII.5 too, as the wife embodies the adulterous and fraudulent person, thus an unethical member of society. The paremia highlights that her husband's jealousy causes more sorrow and distress and, consequently, he deserves to be betrayed in his own house. In the ethical world that Brusantino aims to bring forth, the gravity of the misbehavior that jealousy represents surpasses the gravity of the adulterous relationships, both in social and individual terms.

Although the word "gelosia" ("jealousy") is not mentioned in the introductory allegory and paremia, this feeling dominates story VII.4 and causes young Ghita to deceive her husband. In the allegory, Brusantino recognizes the offensive nature of the wife's act ("ingiurioso"),[60] but places more emphasis on her husband's behavior. The author holds him accountable for both his jealousy and revenge, which require a proper punishment. Along these same lines, the paremia sends out an ethical message about the foolish person whose supposed shrewdness causes harm instead:

Allegoria

> Per Tofano, che chiude la moglie fuor di casa, si tole per lo scempio accorgitore, il quale de l'atto ingiurioso volendo vendicarsi, da astutia et doppia fraude accolto, ritorna in lui tutte le colpe.

> Through Tofano, who shuts his wife outside their house, one infers the foolish deceiver who, wishing to revenge the offending act, pushed by cunning and twofold scam, makes all his faults return upon him.

Proverbio

> *Accorto del suo error lo sciocco viene*
> *Da doppia astutia oppresso in dure pene.* (CN 340)

> The foolish person becoming aware of his mistake is oppressed by a twofold trick causing harsh sufferings.

(*VII.4:* "*Tofano locks his wife out of the house one night, and his wife, having pleaded with him in vain to let her in, pretends to throw herself down a well, into which she hurls an enormous stone. Tofano emerges from the house and rushes to the well, whereupon she steals inside, bolts the door on her husband, and rains abuse upon him at the top of her voice."*)

In Boccaccio's *Decameron*, jealousy does not represent the central point of the story. The last words of the novella, "E viva amore, e muoia soldo, e tutta la brigata" ("Long live love, therefore, and a plague on all skinflints"; Dec. VII.4.31; Boccaccio, *Decameron* [1980] 820: footnote 5), establishes a circular reference to the introductory praise of love in all of its facets:

> O Amore, chenti e quali sono le tue forze, chenti i consigli e chenti gli avvedimenti! Qual filosofo, quale artista mai avrebbe potuto o potrebbe mostrare quegli accorgimenti, quegli avvedimenti, quegli dimostramenti che fai tu subitamente a chi seguita le tue orme? (Dec. VII.4.3)

> O Love, how manifold and mighty are your powers! What philosopher, what artist could ever have conjured up all the arguments, all the subterfuges, all the explanations that you offer spontaneously to those who nail their colours to your mast?

Brusantino maintains this same concept as well as the proverbial phrase *A modo del villan matto, dopo danno fè patto* ("So, like the stupid peasant, he first was mad and then was pleasant"; Dec. VII.4.31) at the end of the novella to emphasize Tofano's change in attitude due to the twofold punishment he receives: "Hor così fece patto pur ritroso dopo il suo male, qual villan matto" ("And so, although recalcitrant, he made a deal after the damage like a mad peasant"; CN 343; see also Boccaccio, *Decameron* [1980] 820: footnote 4). First, his wife's brothers beat him up; next, he is forced to acquiesce to all of his wife's whims and pretend not to notice them. As in the previous examples, novella VII.4 confirms Brusantino's adversarial attitude toward jealous people. In his opinion, nothing justifies jealousy, even though it responds to a supposedly unethical behavior such as adultery. Consequently, even a harsh *beffa* ("trick") is allowed if the recipient of the unethical behavior is jealous (Ferme).

Religious Matters

When he comes to terms with the expression of religious thoughts, Brusantino's adherence to Christian values and rules guides his textual revisions and innovations on the *Decameron*. He may

Chapter Two

modify certain aspects of Boccaccio's stories so that the text acts in accordance with his introductory allegory and paremia or, alternatively, he may follow the original text but twist the message of the novella to comply with his own ethical underpinnings.

In story I.3 in *Le cento novelle*, Brusantino openly declares his opposition to religious discourses and his stance on religion. When Saladin, who is the representative of Islam, asks Melchizedek the Jew to decide which one of the three monotheistic religions is more prestigious than the others, the Jew uses the story of the three rings as a metaphor. The tale narrates a story about a rich man, who does not want to choose only one heir among his three sons, so he gives each a ring signifying full access to his inheritance. Since his sons symbolize the three monotheistic religions, the moral of the story is that Christianity, Judaism, and Islam hold the same hierarchical position and complement each other. In the *Decameron*, in a day devoted by tacit agreement to mottos and verbal stratagems, Boccaccio praises Melchizedek's cleverness and his ability to escape from an unpleasant and entangled circumstance. Conversely, Brusantino openly blames him for his religious views. The introductory allegory and paremia illustrate Brusantino's position and polemic against religions other than Christian:

Allegoria

> Per Melchisedech Giudeo vien tolto il cativo qual voria la miglior fede nascondere tra le due sette, dil che si vede quanto sia la più honorificata et di vigore, et quanto più Dio tegni cura et governo della christiana.

> Through Melchizedek the Jew one infers the evil man since he wanted to hide the best faith among the two sects, from which one sees how this is the most honored and vigorous one and how much God has care and government of the Christian religion.

Proverbio

> *Il dubbio lassa al disputar di fede*
> *Ché sol fedel è quel che 'n Christo crede.* (CN 24)

> Leave the doubt during the dispute of faith because the only faithful is he who believes in Christ.

(I.3: *"Melchizedek the Jew, with a story about three rings, avoids a most dangerous trap laid for him by Saladin."*)

In the two paratextual elements, Saladin is not even mentioned because Brusantino devotes all of his attention to Melchizedek and his attempt to cover the superiority and excellence of the Christian religion. In Brusantino's views, both Judaism and Islam are considered mere sects and do not even qualify as recognized religions. Therefore, they are not liable to become part of a discussion on faith, as stated in the paremia.

The text of the novella confirms Brusantino's lack of consideration for Judaism. The negative characteristics that he associates with Melchizedek suggest the absence of positive qualities in the Jew whatsoever. A comparison between Boccaccio's and Brusantino's texts demonstrates the latter's more critical attitude against him:

Decameron

> E pensossi costui (Melchisedech) avere da poterlo servire, quando volesse, ma sì era avaro che di sua volontà non l'avrebbe mai fatto, e forza non gli voleva fare. (Dec. I.3.7)

> Melchizedek would certainly, he thought, have enough for his purposes, if only he could be persuaded to part with it. But this Melchizedek was such a miserly fellow that he would never hand it over of his own free will, and the Sultan was not prepared to take it away from him by force.

Le cento novelle

> Ma essendo quel hebreo misero e avaro
> Che per cortesia mai faria niente ... (CN 24)

> But since that Jew was so miserable and avaricious
> that he would do nothing out of his kindness ...

Adding the adjective "misero" ("miserable") to the original "avaro" ("avaricious") and using the cluster "per cortesia" ("out of his kindness") instead of "di sua volontà" ("of his own free will") highlight how the Ferrarese author thinks of the Jew as being ontologically devoid of good intentions. Brusantino eliminates any of Boccaccio's references to Melchizedek's verbal skills and prefers focusing on Christianity, the only religion that is worth discussing.

When Boccaccio's stories show clear anti-religious tones against hypocrisy, Brusantino leaves the text unchanged in *Le cento novelle*. One well-fitting example is novella I.6, whose introductory allegory and paremia refer to hypocrisy as the most evil feeling possible. In the story, a friar forces a simple person to penance because of his verbal observation that the wine he was drinking was good enough to be appropriate for Christ. When the person hears about the supposedly philanthropic actions of the Church members, he makes a joke of the friar's stinginess by mentioning the tasteless soup that he gives to the poor and that it will return back to him a hundred times more. Because of the circumstances, Brusantino accepts even a biting remark from a simple person:

Allegoria

> L'uomo a cui viene opposto d'haver errato nella fede, si toglie per la semplicità, il frate che l'accusava si tassa per l'avaritia, la quale per hippocresia non si cura d'alcun biasmo, pur c'habbia il suo intento.

> Through the man who is rebuked for committing mistakes in his faith, one infers of his simplicity; the friar who accused him is blamed for his avarice, which through hypocrisy does not care about any blame as long as he can achieve his intentions.

Proverbio

> *D'ogni religioso opra più ria*
> *Non è presso di lui c'hippocrisia.* (CN 31)

> There is no action more reproachable for a member of the Church than hypocrisy.

(*I.6:* "*With a clever remark, an honest man exposes the wicked hypocrisy of the religious.*")

Throughout the text, Brusantino adds words to express his personal evaluation on the friar's behavior. Thus, the friar's hypocrisy becomes "inferma" ("sick") and "brodaia ... sua immensa" ("his immense broth slop"; CN 33). In order to expose the friar's greed, Brusantino replaces certain veiled, yet more ironic, references to money in the *Decameron* with a clear and direct indication of the object. For instance, Boccaccio writes that the man, in order to be excused from his blasphemy, tries to bribe the friar by giving him "una buona quantità della grascia di san Giovanni Boccadoro" ("a goodly amount of Saint John Golden-Mouth's ointment"; Dec. I.6.9), meaning the florins with the image of the saint. Brusantino, instead, explicitly admits that the man offers the friar "per perdono oro e argento" ("gold and silver in order to be excused"; CN 32), thus augmenting the qualitative value of the bribe. For the same reason, he lingers over the simple man's discourse, emphasizing his jeering tones. Brusantino concludes his speech with a strong mocking and ridiculing vein, which was absent in the *Decameron*:

> E questa è l'importanza che 'n la broda
> Non trovarete mai riva, né proda. (CN 33)
>
> And this is important, that in the broth
> you will never find either the shore or the edge.

In this final distich of the second to last octave, Brusantino uses a poetic term such as "proda" ("shore") to create a rhyme with a common word related to food such as "broda" ("broth"). In doing so, he matches the refined tones of poetic enterprises with the popular level of the novella. The result is a clash between the power of the man's verbal pun and the evidence of the friar's scorn, which makes Brusantino's point of view much more powerful than Boccaccio's.[61]

Among those hypocrite characters who pretend to be excellent observants of the Church's regulations, when they are in fact criminals, the best example is Ser Ciappelletto from novella I.1. In this story, looking for the most wicked man who could exceed the evilness of the inhabitants of Burgundy, Musciatto Franzesi chooses Ser Ciappelletto to help two criminal brothers redeem their money. Once Ser Ciappelletto gets sick, on his deathbed he confesses all his sins by ironically declaring the opposite of what the sin was. His verbal skills are so acute that he is even proclaimed a saint. Brusantino highlights the character's hypocrisy so as to make it the crucial aspect of the novella (Favaro 103–4). Already in the allegory, he mentions that this vice is frequently used against kindness of heart. Such is the case of the confessing Friar who is in the dark about Ciappelletto's ruse and believes all of his words. The introductory paremia further develops the consequences of bad use of the human mind, which only brings evil:

Allegoria

> Per Ser Ciappelletto vien tolta l'hippocrisia, la quale spesse volte inganna la bontade e viene adoperata in così fatti casi che si piglia per Santa, come fu detto santo Ser Ciappelletto.
>
> Through Ser Ciappelletto one infers the hypocrisy, which often deceives kindness and is used on such occasions that it is taken for saintliness, as Ser Ciappelletto was declared a saint.

Chapter Two

Proverbio

> *Credi a gli effetti et non a le parole,*
> *Ché spesso 'l mal e 'l ben ingannar suole.* (CN 13)
>
> Believe the effect, and not the words because they are often accustomed to deceiving good and evil.

(*I.1*: "*Ser Ciappelletto deceives a holy friar with a false confession, then he dies; and although in life he was a most wicked man, in death he is reputed to be a Saint, and is called Saint Ciappelletto.*")

Despite not using the word "hippocrisia" ("hypocrisy"), the paremia mentions how bad deeds and words lead the human mind to be deceived by someone who says one thing yet acts in the opposite way—which is the definition of a hypocrite. When acknowledging this, one should be extremely careful not to believe words, but only facts because the former can be misleading. Therefore, the paremia is a warning to be alert because words can make anything seem possible even if facts cannot substantiate what is said.

By transforming and elaborating various sections of the original text, Brusantino creates a different atmosphere in his version of Ciappelletto's story. In *Le cento novelle*, upon requesting a confessor, Ciappelletto says to the two brothers that he will commit one last sin before dying. Hence, the effect of suspense and surprise that the readers of Boccaccio's story experience during Ciappelletto's paradoxical confession vanishes. Moreover, in Brusantino's text the entire confession, based upon ambiguous terms and references in the *Decameron*, loses its rhetorical power and simply confirms Ciappelletto's wicked soul:[62]

> *E s'al mio ultimo fine un peccato*
> *Farò non spero haver né più né meno,*
> *Ch'ad ogni modo n'ho già tanti oprato,*
> *E fatte tant'ingiurie al ciel sereno.* (CN 16)
>
> And, if in my last days I will commit a sin,
> I hope not to have one more or less,
> since anyway I have already perpetrated many of them
> and done many injustices openly.

In order to show Ciappelletto's ontological brutality, on one hand Brusantino fills his confession with more theological elements. One example is his reference to the sacrifice made by God through his Son: "*Per non offender l'alma, c'hora langue, che Dio ricuperò col proprio sangue*" ("Not to offend the soul, which is languishing now, that God recovered with His own blood"; CN 16). This makes Ciappelletto's discourse even more convincing to the Friar's ears than it was in the original. On the other hand, Brusantino crosses out some of the accusations that Ciappelletto directs at the priest in the *Decameron*, probably to clarify the boundaries between who is lying and who is a faithful devotee. In one of them, Boccaccio's Ciappelletto reproaches the confessor about the way to celebrate the established day of a Christian festivity (Saturdays after the vespers and Sundays). The priest comments that missing them is a minor sin (Dec. I.1.57–60), which is not admissible in Brusantino's logic. Boccaccio's priest also admits that members of the clergy spit on the churches' floor all the time (Dec. I.1.62–64), a reference that is absent in *Le cento novelle*. Brusantino puts aside Boccaccio's view on Ciappelletto's brilliant mind and verbal power, which is the topic of the first day, and rather focuses on his devilish and unethical machinations to absolve himself. For all of these reasons, Brusantino's Ciappelletto is described in more judgmental and unethical terms than in the *Decameron*. This is also visible because, while Boccaccio uses Ciappelletto's first name every time, Brusantino rather describes him with adjectives such as "tristo" ("wretched"), "scelerato" ("wicked"), "falso" ("fake"), and "ghiotto" ("gluttonous").

At the end of the story, Brusantino does not include Panfilo's considerations on the greatness of God, who can forgive anyone, even the most abominable people (Dec. I.1.90). In doing so, the author replaces God's central role in the *Decameron* with the foolishness of those who contribute to Ciappelletto's undeserved fame with his sanctification (CN 10).[63] Brusantino reminds people of the consequences faced by not worshipping God continuously. In other words, one may receive God's grace and love only if one's heart is harmoniously connected to God. The final assertion harshly condemns Ser Ciappelletto to Hell because "his judgement" and mind are devoted to wicked acts. If he were to be saved and sent to Paradise, God would not be distributing his own grace to those who serve him consistently and truly deserve it.[64] Whereas God is prone to accept Ser Ciappelletto among his peers in the *Decameron*, in *Le cento novelle* he is more fair and does not approve his behavior. Once again, this is evidence of the ethical perspective that informs Brusantino's text.

Chapter Two

The Power of the Word

Day VI represents an interesting example of how Brusantino interprets human behaviors and interpersonal relationships within his ethical and societal logic. In those stories that celebrate the clever use of words, Brusantino prefers focusing on aspects other than verbal puns that might emerge from the stories, including primarily the value of virtuous behaviors and the importance of respect for the individual. His message is that sharp rebukes are acceptable only if extreme circumstances require them, otherwise they should be avoided since they tend to hurt people's sensibility and do not show the best human qualities.

A comparison between Boccaccio's captions and Brusantino's introductory paremias for the ten stories of the day already demonstrates how Brusantino adjusts the content of the novellas to be consistent with the objectives of *Le cento novelle* and how he emphasizes certain themes over others that Boccaccio privileges. Boccaccio uses words or phrases that highlight the respectability of the verbal quip ("onestamente," "politely" in VI.9), its swiftness ("sola parola," "single phrase" in VI.2; "presta risposta," "quick retort" in VI.3; "presta parola," "quick word" in VI.4; "presta e piacevol risposta," "prompt and ingenious answer" in VI.7), and its effectiveness ("fa raveder," "shows that he is being unreasonable" in VI.2; "impone silenzio," "puts a stop" in VI.3; "sé campa," "saves himself" in VI.4; "morde," "pokes fun" in VI.5; "vince," "wins" in VI.6; "sé libera," "secures her acquittal" in VI.7; "dice villania," "delivers an insult" in VI.9). When Brusantino adapts these stories to *Le cento novelle*, he shifts the original focus from verbal perspicuity toward religious dishonesty, lack of verbal control, and shame. Of all the stories, only one, namely novella VI.3 on Monna Nonna de' Pulci's rebuke against the bishop of Florence and his inappropriate sexual references, captures the essence of the *Decameron*'s day. Its introductory paremia, *L'animo accorto è sempre più abbondante di effetti e de risposte in uno instante* ("The wise man always abounds more in effects and answers instantly"; CN 303), relates to the quickness and effectiveness of mottos that a "wise" mind generates.

In the first novella of the day, VI.1, Madonna Oretta uses a motto to silence the knight who recounts a story unsuccessfully. Brusantino does not celebrate the woman's graceful rebuke on the knight's inability as a storyteller, but rather highlights the knight's wrongdoing in both the allegory and the paremia:

Allegoria

> Per il cavalier che dice a Horetta dirli una novella si tolle la insipidezza quale ha tal volta ardire di volersi pore a la virtude a paro, onde accortasi de la sua mala gratia resta beffata.

> Through the knight who recounts a story to Oretta one infers the insignificance, which sometimes dares to pose itself at the same level of virtue, whence, realizing its bad grace, is ridiculed.

Proverbio

> *Resti il vile e l'insipido di gire*
> *Onde ne appar virtù, gratia e disire.* (CN 299)

> Let the coward and insignificant person stop to go where virtue, grace, and desire are.

(*VI.1*: "A knight offers to take Madonna Oretta riding through the realm of narrative, but makes such a poor job of it that she begs him to put her down.")

In the *Decameron*, Boccaccio extends his judgment from the knight's verbal skills to his valor in war: "[a] messer lo cavaliere ... forse non stava meglio la spada allato che 'l novellar nella lingua" ("... this worthy knight, whose swordplay was doubtless on par with his storytelling"; Dec. VI.1.9). This reference might explain why Brusantino chooses the adjective "vile" ("coward") for his paremia, in which it appears fairly excessive for a character who does not reveal much of his cowardice while speaking. The Ferrarese author uses this adjective in other stories in *Le cento novelle*, yet with characters who are far worse, including Friar Alberto in IV.2. In Madonna Oretta's story, Brusantino advises any person who falls into the category of "coward and insignificant" to avoid contact with those who are virtuous, i.e., Madonna Oretta. If they engage with such people, they may pay the consequences of their choice. This is what the knight faces in both the *Decameron* and *Le cento novelle*. In Boccaccio's text, however, the knight receives the refined blow that Madonna Oretta gives him, understands it, and even accepts it playfully (Dec. VI.1.12). Hence, he abandons the story he is recounting to start another one. In *Le cento novelle*, the knight does not tell another story but simply starts a new topic of conversation (CN 300). Brusantino suggests that, since his ability as a storyteller is not refined at all, it is better for him to change the typology of his verbal utterances and not simply choose another subject.

Chapter Two

Brusantino frames Madonna Oretta's story in a context that values one's virtuous behaviors in all events of life, even in verbal exchanges. Hence, he interprets the knight's behavior through the lens of ethical etiquette, which is a far less important component in Boccaccio's novella. The author from Certaldo does not aim to compare the knight's virtue with that of Madonna Oretta's. He rather focuses on the characters' rhetorical skills and the swiftness of their minds in finding a solution to an uncomfortable situation. Conversely, Brusantino builds his entire story on the connections between virtue and the ability to use verbal rebukes, which emphasizes the knight's failure and humiliation. This explains why the knight is described as "beffato" ("ridiculed") in the allegory and why he is not a model representative of society.

Brusantino gives his novella VI.5 a similar greater ethical perspective than in the *Decameron*. The novella describes Forese da Rabatta's pun against Giotto's ugliness and the painter's consequent ingenious response. Not only does Boccaccio consider Giotto's great capacity to defend himself from Forese's gratuitous attack but also celebrates Giotto's ability to respond eloquently in turn. Through his words, the author illustrates that appearance is not an equivalent of mental clarity (Dec. VI.5.8), which is one of the messages of the day. Conversely, in *Le cento novelle* the introductory allegory and paremia do not mention Giotto or his sharp mind. They focus, instead, on the societal disrespect that Forese shows through his behavior and his act of deriding Giotto:

Allegoria

> Per Forese da Rabatta, s'intende lo schernitosi, quale non vedendo il proprio difetto schernisce l'altrui, onde nel medesimo effetto schernito dal schernitor resta maggiormente oppresso.
>
> Through Forese da Rabatta one understands the mocked person who, not being able to see his own defect, mocks the other, whence he finds himself greatly oppressed as the mocked person mocks him in a similar fashion.

Proverbio

> *S'altrui schernir si vuol del mal espresso*
> *Bisogna prima esaminar se stesso.* (CN 307)
>
> If one wishes to mock someone of an evident evil, it is necessary to examine oneself first.

(*VI.5*: "Messer Forese da Rabatta and Master Giotto, the painter, returning from Mugello, poke fun at one another's disreputable appearance.")

As the paremia states, in an ethical society based on reciprocal recognition everyone should reflect before accusing someone of his or her same faults. Since Forese ridicules Giotto because of his appearance, without realizing that he is in the same situation, he deserves blame and, most of all, is entitled to be mocked in a similarly harsh way. Both Boccaccio and Brusantino express this idea at the very end of the story by means of a proverbial phrase:

Decameron

> Il che messer Forese udendo il suo error riconobbe, e *vedesi di tal moneta pagato quali erano state le derrate vendute*. (Dec. VI.5.16; Boccaccio, *Decameron* [1980] 740: footnote 3)

> On hearing this, Messer Forese recognized his error, and perceived that he was hoist with his own petard.

Le cento novelle

> Forese alhor conobbe gli errori suoi
> E le sue burle rimanerli a canto
> *Di moneta si vide alhor pagato*
> *De le derate che vende infiammato*. (CN 309)

> Then, Forese recognized that his error
> and jokes would remain by his side
> and perceived that he was hoist
> with his own inflamed petard.

Brusantino's lexical choices for the paremia reveal his greater moralizing attitude. The adjective "infiammato" ("inflamed"), which he adds for metric reasons, emphasizes the inappropriate and excessive force with which Forese ridicules Giotto. Respect for the other should rule any human relationship, so that harm, shame, and blame may be avoided. This is the message that Brusantino's story conveys, ultimately eliminating many of the comedic and verbal elements that Boccaccio's original foregrounds (Bevilacqua).

Comments and considerations on virtue characterize another novella of the day, VI.9. The story recounts the adventures of Guido de' Cavalcanti, son of Cavalcante de' Cavalcanti, who, upon being told that his philosophical speculations on the existence of God are worthless, responds to Betto and his companions with a biting response. Specifically, he tells them that they

Chapter Two

are as dead in their minds as those buried in cemeteries. In the *Decameron*, Boccaccio describes Guido as an Epicurean intellectual, whose mental agility corresponds to his physical agility (Dec. VI.9.12; see also Calvino, "Leggerezza" 12–16). As "leggiadrissimo e costumato e parlante uom molto" ("he was without a peer for gallantry and courtesy and excellence of discourse"; Dec. VI.9.8), Guido is both a courteous man and a brilliant mind, as well as the typical representative of "ingegno" ("intelligence") and "industria" ("industriousness"). These two qualities—which, according to Mario Baratto and Branca, are distinctive in many of Boccaccio's characters (Baratto 27; Branca, *Boccaccio medievale* 27)—help Guido overcome Betto's provocation about his speculative nature in the *Decameron*. On the other hand, Brusantino shifts the focus of his two paratextual elements onto Guido's virtue, which he considers as a tool to defeat the ignorance that pervasively fills his mentally-inert compatriots:

Allegoria

> Per Guido Cavalcanti si tolle la virtude, per gli cavaglieri fiorentini gli schernitori, quali al fine abbattute da la ragione restano impediti et simili alla morte.
>
> Through Guido Cavalcanti one infers the virtue; through the Florentine knights one infers the mockers, who, ultimately defeated by reason, remain obstructed and similar to death.

Proverbio

> *Spesso opprime virtude l'ignoranza*
> *Talmente che fa di morti stanza.* (CN 315)
>
> Often, ignorance oppresses virtue so much that it houses dead people.

(*VI.9: "With a barbed saying, Guido Cavalcanti politely delivers an insult to certain Florentine gentlemen who had taken him by surprise."*)

Le cento novelle's Guido is first an allegorical representation of virtue and then of reason. Within Brusantino's ethical society, his mental acuity is less important than his virtuous behavior as a philosopher and as a member of the community.

It is worth noting that Brusantino removes Guido's speculations aimed at demonstrating that God does not exist (Dec. VI.9.9). Clearly, they would go against Brusantino's views on the Christian religion—much like novella I.3 illustrates—and would be too irreverent. In the *Decameron*, Betto's pun mentions the real nature of Guido's thoughts about God and conforms to the stereotypes about those thinkers philosophically oriented to Epicureanism who speculate over the absence of a supernatural entity:

> Guido, tu rifiuti d'esser di nostra brigata; ma ecco, quando tu avrai trovato che Idio non sia, che avrai fatto? (Dec. VI.9.11)
>
> Guido, you spurn our company; but supposing you find that God doesn't exist, what good will it do you?

Conversely, in *Le cento novelle* the words that Betto and his companions use against Guido concern a more lay and social matter:

> Gli disser, «tu rifiuti esser di nostri
> E pascendo il cervel vano ti mostri». (CN 316)
>
> They told him: "You spurn our company
> and, by satisfying your brain, you show to be frivolous."

Instead of referring to the nonexistence of God, Brusantino makes Betto chide Guido for his supposedly vain thoughts, without specifying that they deal with religious topics. Brusantino does not question that Guido follows Epicureanism but chooses not to include his reflections on God and rather to focus on his virtuous and ethical behavior in society.

Embedded Paremias: Brusantino's Personal Innovations and His Adaptations of Boccaccio's Paremias to the Octave[65]

An analysis of the ways in which Brusantino transforms Boccaccio's paremias demonstrates that he is not simply copying the *Decameron* but rather evidences his personal act of interpretation.[66] For instance, the Ferrarese author does not include the well-known first *sententia* of the *Decameron*, which introduces the preface and offers an interpretative key to the entire collection:

> *Umana cosa è aver compassione degli afflitti.* (Dec. Proemio.2; Boccaccio, *Decameron* [1980] 5: footnote 1)[67]
>
> To take pity on people in distress is a human quality.

The proverbial phrase imitates a line from Guido delle Colonne's *Historia destructionis Troiae*[68] and comes from two works by Boccaccio: *Esposizioni sopra la comedia di Dante* ("Degl'infelici si suole aver compassione," "It is common to sympathize with the afflicted"; Boccaccio, *Tutte le opere* II.litterale.111) and

Chapter Two

Consolatoria ("[N]elle avversità condolersi gli uomini sogliono," "In adversities, men usually console each other"; Boccaccio, *Tutte le opere* 42). Brusantino's *Prohemio* differs from Boccaccio's as far as the introductory description of the plague and of the women suffering from lovesickness is absent. *Le cento novelle* lacks Boccaccio's compassion toward afflicted people, especially those who experienced, as he did, love and its subsequent loss. Brusantino does not seem to address a specific audience. Rather, his readership extends beyond the enclosed walls of rooms in which women spend their time reading the *Decameron* and melancholily weep over their lost love. Brusantino's reading of Boccaccio's text creates a shift in the work's purpose from one that sustains, assists, and provides refuge to women (Dec. Proemio.13) to one that supplies ethical messages to a wider public and offers material for courtly conversation. *Le cento novelle* enlarges the pedagogical intent of Boccaccio's work by opening its stories to any reader who wishes to be guided into a didactic discovery of the text. It seems that Brusantino privileges proverbs over proverbial phrases, probably because of their more explicit moral and ethical messages. Within this logic, he eliminates the proverbial phrase mentioned in the final section of Day III, *Meglio un buon porco che una bella tosa*[69] ("A good fat pig was better than a comely wench"; Dec. III.Concl.18; Boccaccio, *Decameron* [1980] 456: footnote 4). Similarly, he does not keep the two proverbial phrases that feature in the *Decameron*'s novella IX.5: *[E]lla mi verrà dietro come va la pazza al figliuolo* ("She'll cling to me like a mother besotted with her son"; Dec. IX.5.36) and *Menare per lo naso* ("To lead someone by the nose"; Dec. IX.5.43).

The style of the *Decameron* affects the way Brusantino places paremias in his text, both his own and those drawn from Boccaccio's collection. A comparison between the two works reveals the pervasive presence of rhetorical and poetic elements in Boccaccio's prose. Despite his declaration of an "istilo umilissimo e rimesso" ("the most homely and unassuming style"; Dec. IV.Intr.3; Boccaccio, *Decameron* [1980] 460: footnote 2), Boccaccio's language shows evident traces of his attention to rhythm and musicality (Manni 131). Boccaccio himself declares it in the introduction to the fourth day, when he admits that the Muses accompanied him throughout all of his literary production and that he should resort to them even when writing his *Decameron*: "[I]o farei più saviamente a starmi con le Muse in Parnaso che con queste ciance

Le cento novelle

mescolarmi tra voi," in which "voi" refers to "women" ("I would be better advised to remain with the Muses in Parnassus, than to fritter away my time in your company"; Dec. IV.Intr.6).

It is probable that the humanist scholars Paolo da Perugia and Dionigi da Borgo San Sepolcro, whom Boccaccio met at Charles I of Anjou's court, introduced the author to "prosa versificata" ("versified prose") or "prosa rimata" ("rhythmic prose"). Boccaccio must have found it a perfect way to combine his attraction to medieval rhetoric with narrative prose (Branca, *Boccaccio medievale* 58–85; Schiaffini 178–84). In fact, the *Decameron*'s *oratio soluta* ("prosaic style") contains many verses, such as pentasyllables, lines of six syllables, and hendecasyllables. Furthermore, it displays phonetic markers and structures that are typical of poetry. These elements mostly appear in emphatic or heroic moments to elevate the tone, or in comic sections of a speech to highlight the hilarious aspects of the situation.[70] Other than sentences that imitate Latin, Boccaccio places adjectives before nouns and past participles before auxiliary verbs, which all contribute to the poetic flow of his narrative (Manni 253–54; Schiaffini 177). Hyperbatons, chiasmi, antiphrases, and inversions give centrality to a word or create harmonic symmetries among clusters of words, ultimately shaping poetry within prose. In order to intensify the musical intonation of his prose (Manni 254), Boccaccio resorts to *cursus velox* ("quick rhythm"), which, at the time, was reserved for treatises and pontifical documents (E. Parodi 480).[71] He frequently combines it with the conclusive tone of a sentence, as it occurs extensively with the final distiches of octaves in *Filocolo* (Schiaffini 172–73). This use provides fluidity and melodic organization to the narration, similar to those of *artes dictaminis* ("arts of writing"). Simultaneously, it emphasizes the message that the *cursus* conveys by stressing certain words or posing the *ictus* ("accent") over specific letters.[72] Upon reading the prosaic text, the combination of these poetic and rhetorical artifices produces the effect of verses arranged in stanzas. The result is that Boccaccio's work is, in fact, a poetry-prose, a rhythmic prose, or a "prosa adorna di versi" ("prose decorated with verses"; Branca, *Boccaccio medievale* 59).[73]

Because of a structure already based on poetic aspects, the connection between novellas in prose and their poetic renderings in octaves acquires more strength (Branca, *Boccaccio medievale* 65). This occurs with *cantari novellistici* and also includes *Le cento novelle*, whose verses and octaves are crafted to contain

Boccaccio's highly developed narrative and linguistic structures. In Brusantino's work, the canonized aspects of a chivalric poem in octaves engage in a constant dialogue with the distinctive features of a prosaic syntax that is clearly poetic. This generates a hybrid style between prose and poetry, a form of "poesia narrativa"[74] that lacks the "coincidenza di strutture sintattiche e di misure metriche" ("coincidence between syntactic structures and metrical system") characterizing, for instance, *Orlando furioso* (Blasucci 88). All these elements distinguish *Le cento novelle* from previous examples of chivalric poems, making it a *unicum* among the rewritings of the *Decameron*.

When Brusantino finds paremias in the *Decameron*, he either transforms them to fit the verses of his *Le cento novelle* (Pettinelli, *Forme e percorsi* 190) or he paraphrases them to explain their contextual meaning. These expressions still contribute to the development of the stories, clarify an aspect, comment upon an event or a character, conclude a thought, or create a circular structure within the story. However, they result from how Brusantino interprets both the immediate context in which the paremia occurs and the entire text of Boccaccio's collection (De Robertis 17). Generally, proverbial phrases are adjusted to a given context in flexible ways: Brusantino inserts them in one or two lines and modifies them according to syntax and morphology. On the contrary, proverbs already have a defined rhetorical and metrical structure. They present tropes of sound (alliterations, homoeoteleutons, paronomasias; Valesio 133–35), syntactical figures (antitheses, chiasmi, polysyndetons, anaphoras, polyptotons, parallelisms, inversions, separations, and binary structures), and semantic figures (hyperboles, similes, and metaphors; Soletti, "Proverbi"). Additionally, apocopes may give a proverb a broken style, similar to the musical *staccato*, while synalephas may produce a sense of musical *legato* (Menichetti 452). Hence, Brusantino occasionally transforms proverbs in order to adapt them to the meter of the hendecasyllable. A few textual examples may clarify Brusantino's paremiac transformations. In novella I.4, Brusantino renders a proverb a perfect hendecasyllable:

> *[P]eccato celato è mezzo perdonato.* (Dec. I.4.16)
> Sin that is hidden is half forgiven.

> *Peccato ascosto mezo perdonato.* (CN 28)
> Sin hidden, half forgiven.

Boccaccio's paremia derives from Solomon's proverb *Quello che cuopre i peccati suoi, non prospererà, et di quello che confessa et lascia, si harà misericordia* ("Those who conceal their sins will not prosper, but those who confess and renounce them find mercy"; Ch. XXVIII: v. 13 from Brucioli's *Annotationi*). Brusantino adds a synalepha between "peccato" ("sin") and "ascosto" ("hidden") in order to fit the expression into the rhythmic structure of the octave.

Occasionally, the original proverb in the *Decameron* may be difficult to "translate" into two hemistiches of hendecasyllables because it is made of a fixed structure with shorter meters than two pentasyllables and two septenaries.[75] In this case, Brusantino usually inserts words in the proverb, especially if he consciously aims to give it a slightly different meaning. Since Brusantino devotes much attention to the *caesura*, in *Le cento novelle* the syntactical pause frequently coincides with the end of the line and, consequently, the second hemistich of the original proverb occurs in the following verse. This structure is common for those proverbs that conclude an octave. Whenever the pause does not correspond with the end of the line, Brusantino uses a pause where there is no syntactical break in the proverb. In these instances, the syntactical organization in two or more lines may be less fluid than the proverb's conventionalized structure. In story III.1, the Ferrarese author adds a few terms (a verb, an adverb, an article, and two prepositional clusters) in order to obtain two rhymed hendecasyllables out of Boccaccio's original paremia:

> *Chi la sera non cena tutta notte si dimena.* (Dec. III.4.27; Boccaccio, *Decameron* [1980] 366: footnote 7)
>
> He that supper doth not take, in his bed all night will shake.
>
> *Chi va al letto la sera senza cena*
> *Intorno tutta la notte si dimena.* (CN 145)
>
> He that supper doth not take, in his bed all night will shake around.

He adopts a similar process in novella VIII.10, in which he expands the six syllables of Boccaccio's proverb and makes it a distich:

> *Chi ha a far con tosco non vuole esser losco.* (Dec. VIII.10.67; Boccaccio, *Decameron* [1980] 1024: footnote 7)
>
> Honesty's the better line, when dealing with a Florentine.
>
> *Dicendo espresso, non deve esser losco*
> *Chi contrattar ne vuol con huomo tosco.* (CN 442)

Chapter Two

> Clearly saying that he who wants to negotiate with a Tuscan, needs to be honest.

In Brusantino's version, the verb "contrattare" ("negotiate") provides a more specific range of relationships than Boccaccio's more generic "aver a (che) fare" ("to deal/engage"). The two people are engaging in financial affairs and, thus, need to bargain aspects of their financial transactions. It is likely that Brusantino's tendency to clarify made him express the condensed message of Boccaccio's proverb more extensively.

Brusantino mentions one of Boccaccio's most famous paremias, first used in the *Decameron* (D'Agostino, "Letteratura di proverbi" 105), almost in the exact same way as in the original. The paremia refers to the adventures that Alatiel undergoes in novella II.7, passing from man to man because of a series of misadventures, until she returns to her hometown as a virgin and marries her pre-arranged husband (Segre, "Comicità strutturale"). Boccaccio structures the proverb as two hendecasyllables, with an antithetical message expressed by the two hemistiches and an assonance. In *Le cento novelle*, Brusantino follows the proverb's metrical structure and places the expression in the final distich of an octave to emphasize it:[76]

> *Bocca basciata non perde ventura, anzi rinnuova come fa la luna.*
> (Dec. II.7.122; Boccaccio, *Decameron* [1980] 257: footnote 4)

> A kissed mouth doesn't lose its freshness: like the moon it turns up new again.

> *Bocca basciata non perde fortuna*
> *Ma si rinova come fa la luna.* (CN 97)

> A kissed mouth doesn't lose its freshness but like the moon it turns up new again.

Through the paremia, Panfilo refers to his introduction to the novella (Dec. II.7.3–7). There, he talks about the temporal nature of the world: things are all short-lived, except for love, which always renews and constantly becomes more enjoyable, despite any misfortunes. Brusantino's paremia does not differ from the original neither syntactically nor prosodically. However, it faces a few lexical changes, including the substitution of the diphthongized transitive verb "rinnuova" ("renews") with the pronominal "si rinova"[77] and the consequent change of the adverb "anzi" ("rather") with the conjunction "ma" ("but"). Brusantino also replaces "ventura" with "fortuna" ("luck") due to coherence with the final rhyme and, probably, to the more appropriate reference to "fortuna" as the power that directs human life (Baratto 54–57).[78] For these reasons, the proverb acquires new substance in terms of lexical content and interpretative message within Brusantino's context.

While Boccaccio uses metrical elements to make his prose more poetic, at times Brusantino seems to proceed in the opposite direction. Since he was not required to restructure the prose of the original text completely while writing *Le cento novelle*, he could have relied greatly on the many poetic elements and hendecasyllables already present in the *Decameron*. However, he seems to force his text, which is technically more poetic than the original, to be adherent to a prosaic style. As he modifies the structure of many of Boccaccio's paremias, he frequently omits or changes the poetic elements that Boccaccio already places in his text.

An example of this aspect occurs in novella V.9 when Monna Giovanna explains her choice to marry Federigo degli Alberighi to her brothers. In the *Decameron*, the final sentence of her speech contains a paremia structured poetically:

> [M]a io voglio avanti *uomo che abbia bisogno di ricchezza che ricchezza che abbia bisogno d'uomo*. (Dec. V.9.42)

> But I would sooner have a gentleman without riches, than riches without a gentleman.

Monna Giovanna's words come from Lucius Mestrius Plutarchus's life of Themistocles (XVIII), Cicero's *De officiis* (II.20), and Valerius Maximus's *Dicta et facta memorabilia* (Boccaccio, *Decameron* [1980] 691: footnote 1; Rondinelli, "«Ho udito dire mille volte …»" 304–5). The expression captures the essence of courtly love and emphasizes the greater value of the heart over wealth. As such, it represents an appropriate and elevated end for such a refined story. In *Le cento novelle*, Brusantino prefers rephrasing, or rather paraphrasing, the paremia to render it more intelligible to a less cultivated audience. He maintains the meaning, yet without the caustic, short, and effective structure of the original:

> Ma chieggio huomo avanti a cui conviene
> Bisogno di ricchezza e di ricetto
> Che huomo ricco, imperò che 'l bene
> Consiste in virtù più de l'intelletto. (CN 287)

> But I ask more for a man who is appropriately
> needing wealth and shelter

Chapter Two

> than a rich man, considering that the good
> consists in virtue rather than in the intellect.

Brusantino discards the chiasm of Boccaccio's proverb, which could have been inserted in two hendecasyllables with minimal adjustments for metrical reasons. He adds lexical components that make the expression's pedagogical message more intelligible: more than a rich man, a man who needs economic support and protection (this last reference was absent in the *Decameron*) is the perfect husband. According to the elegiac tone of the novella, displaying good manners is more virtuous than possessing intellect, which probably refers to a mind devoted to accumulating riches. The ethical meaning of these lines is incontrovertible, yet the original paremiac structure is missing.

Another paremia, which Boccaccio uses frequently in the *Decameron*, demonstrates Brusantino's transformations of the same expression due to different contexts. *Quale asino dà in parete tal riceve* ("As the ass gives in the wall, so he may receive") appears three times in three different novellas: II.9, V.10, and VIII.8. The paremia, which was a popular expression in Boccaccio's time, conveys the meaning that one receives the fruits of one's actions, just like the donkey that kicks the wall and ends up hurting itself (GDLI, s.v. *asino*, n. 5; Rondinelli, "«Ho udito dire mille volte …»" 304; Voc. Cr. 1612, s.v. *asino*, which reports the Latin *Qui malum dat, malum accipit* "Who gives evil, receives evil"). Alternatively, it may indicate that a person who teases another becomes a recipient of his or her offense (as Serdonati explains it in his collection of proverbs).

In the aforementioned novella II.9 about Bernabò and Ambrogiuolo, Branca demonstrates that Boccaccio frames the section leading to the paremia with a sequence of hendecasyllables (Branca, *Boccaccio medievale* 74). This is clearly visible if the prose is arranged in verses:

> L'altro rispose: «E io fo il somigliante:
> Per ciò che se io credo che la mia
> Donna alcuna sua ventura procacci,
> Ella il fa, e se io nol credo, sì 'l fa:
> E per ciò a fare a far sia: *quale*
> *asino dà in parete tal riceve*.» (Dec. II.9.6; Boccaccio, *Decameron* [1980] 285: footnote 2–5)
>
> "I do the same", said the second man,
> "because whether or not I believe my

Le cento novelle

> wife is behaving herself,
> she will be making the most of her opportunities.
> So it's a case of tit for tat.
> Do as you would be done by, that's my motto."

Brusantino does not maintain this poetic structure, but remodels it, including the paremia itself:

> E per ciò a far questo mi assicura
> *Qual asino essere debbo me ne avedo*
> *Che urti el parete ne la scioglia dura,*
> E così il danno mio bene prevedo. (CN 108)[79]
>
> And, then, I am certain of doing this,
> I notice that I have to be like an ass
> who hits the wall in the hard bump
> and so I foresee my damage well.

In order to create perfect hendecasyllables, Brusantino inserts new elements to the original structure. As a result, the paremia disappears, even though the donkey and the wall persist; furthermore, the expression's message is not as sharp and effective as it was in Boccaccio's text. For instance, Brusantino includes the detail of the donkey kicking the wall in its strong part, probably a threshold made of stone, which is absent in the *Decameron*. This detail emphasizes the pain that the donkey experiences because of his action, and indirectly demonstrates that Brusantino considers Boccaccio's proverb not as an expression of equal opportunities for different sexes, but as transmitting a message of retaliation. Differently from the original, Brusantino's proverb also calls attention to the agency of the first personal subject pronoun: if I am aware ("avedo") of the consequences of my actions, I can foresee ("prevedo") the harm coming from them.

The same paremia appears at the end of novella V.10, which hosts the majority of paremias in the entire *Decameron* and thus in *Le cento novelle*. According to Wilhelm Pötters, since the expression appears at the end of the last story in the fifth day, it falls in the middle of Boccaccio's text as well as in the middle of the space delimited by the proverb's other two mentions in novellas II.9 and VIII.8 (87–88). The expression comments on the wife's adulterous affair, which Pietro di Vinciolo discovers thanks to a donkey:

> Per che così io vi vo' dire, donne mie care, che *chi te la fa, fagliele*; e se tu non puoi, tienloti a mente fin ché tu possa, acciò che *quale asino dà in parete tal riceva*. (Dec. V.10.64; Boccaccio, *Decameron* [1980] 704–5: footnote 5)

> So my advice to you, dear ladies, is this, that you should always give back as much as you receive; and if you can't do it at once, bear it in mind till you can, so that what you lose on the swings, you gain on the roundabouts.

The paremia in question is associated with another proverb, *Chi te le fa, fagliele*, which carries an equivalent meaning. Pietro's wife retaliates against her husband because of his lack of love and ultimately betrays him. However, ironically, she unconsciously chooses someone who could satisfy her husband too. Because of it, it is arguable that the two proverbs transmit a message on sexual justice and equality of genders more than on reciprocal revenge. This time, Brusantino maintains both paremias, yet introducing stylistic changes:

> E per ciò voglio dir donne mie care
> *Fallo a chi te le fa*, et se non poi
> Tientelo a mente né te lo scordare
> Acciò che dopo il fallo non ti annoi
> Perché *quale asino al parete urtare*
> *Simil riceva il danno*, e il mal dapoi.
> Hor sia per questo a tutti quelli essempio
> Che seguitano error sì tristo et empio. (CN 293)

> And, thus, my dear ladies, I would like to say,
> always give back as much as you receive, and, if you can't,
> bear it in mind nor do not forget it,
> so that the consequences won't bother you after the mistake
> because as the ass gives to the wall,
> so he may receive the damage and the evil later.
> Now, let this be an example for all of those
> who carry on such a wretched and bad mistake.

The major change concerns the expression *Chi te le fa, fagliele* (literally, "Who does it to you, just do it to him"). In the *Decameron*, the proverbial phrase is an anacoluthon because the two hemistiches have different subjects ("chi," "who," and "tu," "you"; Manni 302). Conversely, in *Le cento novelle* Brusantino introduces the dative ("a chi," "to whom"), necessary to make the expression syntactically correct. The second proverb, *Quale asino dà in parete tal riceva*, endures only minor lexical modifications in Brusantino's text. These changes include the substitution of the verb "dare" ("to give") with "urtare" ("to hit")[80] and the introduction of the direct object "il danno" ("the damage") after the verb "ricevere" ("to receive"). Evidently, Brusantino chooses not to opt for the original paremia's metrical scheme, in which the proverb without the pronoun "quale" ("as") already forms a hendecasyllable. Instead, Brusantino separates the two sections of the paremia and forms a distich.

The third occurrence of the paremia is in novella VIII.8, in which the expression explains what adultery between two married couples entails:

> [P]er la quale potrete comprendere che assai dee bastare a ciascuno se *quale asino dà in parete tal riceve*, senza volere, soprabondando oltre la convenevolezza della vendetta, ingiuriare, dove l'uomo si mette alla ricevuta ingiuria vendicare. (Dec. VIII.8.3; Boccaccio, *Decameron* [1980] 976: footnote 6)
>
> You will thereby be enabled to apprehend, that when a man seeks to avenge an injury, it should be quite sufficient for him to render an eye for an eye and a tooth for a tooth, without wanting to inflict a punishment out of all proportion to the original offence.

Brusantino restructures the expression's syntax:

> Che comprender per quello hora potrete
> Che assai a ciascadun deve bastare
> Se *qual asino dà urta in parete*
> E *tal riceve* poi nel vendicare. (CN 419)
>
> Now, then, you will understand
> that it is sufficient to everybody
> if as the ass gives to the wall,
> so he may receive in revenging.

The *e* at the beginning of the paremia's second line could be read as the subject pronoun *e'* ("he"), although this option appears less probable. Brusantino never uses the Tuscan form for *egli* > *ei* > *e'* in his paremias. The most probable explanation may be to consider it as the conjunction "and." If so, the paremia would have a structure based on "paraipotassi," or syntactical correlation of two sentences. This would make the paremia closer to spoken language and would intensify its message. The introduction of the cluster "dà urta" ("gives a hit") recalls the verb "urtare" ("to hit") that features in the paremia from story V.10. Its use might result from Brusantino's need to complete the metrical scheme as a hendecasyllable and a verse of five syllables over two lines. As in the previous two examples, Brusantino attentively considers the contexts in which the paremia appears and shows his versatility in changing the expression's structure for metrical and stylistic reasons.

Chapter Two

Major syntactical and metrical changes may occur when Brusantino unwraps the message of a paremia, adding explanatory comments within the expression itself. The result is a loss of the syntactical effectiveness that the paremia imparts in the *Decameron* due to its brevity and, conversely, the presence of a more narrative structure. One example is the opening paremia for the aforementioned story IV.2 about Friar Alberto and Madonna Lisetta. Placed in Pampinea's *incipit* of the novella, a proverb introduces the themes of deception and lies. Despite conducting a criminal life in Imola before moving to Venice, Friar Alberto is not the subject of any doubt. The aura surrounding his religious status confirms his supposedly good behavior as a model of the true Christian:[81]

> Usano i volgari un così fatto proverbio: *Chi è reo e buono è tenuto, può fare il male e non è creduto*. (Dec. IV.2.5)[82]
>
> There is a popular proverb which runs as follows: "He who is wicked and held to be good, can cheat because no one imagines he would."

In *Le cento novelle*, this proverb includes an addition that expands the meaning of the original expression:

> E disse uno proverbio, e tra volgari
> Che *chi è tristo e buono vien tenuto*
> Spesso pone ciascuno in pianti amari
> *E poi far male ché non gli è creduto*. (CN 199)
>
> A proverb among the common people said
> that he who is wicked and held to be good,
> often causes bitter tears in everyone,
> and he can cheat because no one imagines he would.

The components of the proverb are still visible in Brusantino's octave, beginning from the introductory formula, which specifies how what follows is indeed a proverb and largely known among the common people.[83] However, the paremia is extended to occupy three lines of the octaves by means of a verse that Brusantino inserts between the two original hemistiches: "spesso pone ciascuno in pianti amari" ("often causes bitter tears in everyone"). This line changes the poetic nature of the original paremia, which is composed of two verses, specifically an octosyllabic verse and a decasyllable. In the *Decameron*, a *caesura* divides both hemistiches into two parts, which are paralleled by the conjunction "e":

> *Chi è reo e buono è tenuto,*
> *Può fare il male e non è creduto.*

In *Le cento novelle*, the bipartite structure of the two initial hemistiches is lost and the insertion of the paremia in the discourse contributes to its narrative flow and prosaic style. Specific word choices, namely the conjunction "ché" ("because"), contribute to the proverb's narrative flow. For all of these reasons, the structural organization of Brusantino's proverb is less poetic than that of Boccaccio's. In specifying that Friar Alberto can be so harmful as to induce tears, however, Brusantino's paremia augments the dramatic atmosphere in the section. Overall, Friar Alberto's behavior is not detrimental to Monna Lisetta, except for the malevolent laughter that her neighbors direct at her. It is possible that the tears anticipate the sad consequences of Friar Alberto's life and the pain he will suffer after being publicly ridiculed and imprisoned.

Interesting stylistic choices result from Brusantino's adoption of a misogynistic proverb that is contained in novella IX.9 (Chiecchi, "Sentenze e proverbi" 135; Kirkham 249–54; Manni 295). Brusantino slightly adjusts the original expression to fit a distich and, in the process, changes its introductory formula:

> [C]ome che gli uomini un cotal proverbio usino: «*Buon cavallo e mal cavallo vuole sprone e buona femina e mala femina vuol bastone.*» (Dec. IX.9.7)[84]
>
> Although men have a proverb which says: "For a good horse and a bad, spurs are required; for a good woman and a bad, the rod is required."

> Che detto sia per lei simil novella
> Che *a bon cavallo e reo bisogna sprone*
> *E trista e bona donna vuol bastone*. (CN 477)
>
> So let it be said such a novelty
> that for a good horse and a bad, spurs are required,
> for a wicked woman and a good, the rod is required.

For Brusantino, the paremia is no longer a proverb but a "novella," a novelty to say in reference to the story of Melisso and Giosefo asking Solomon for advice about their love life and marriage, respectively. The introductory formula signals the passage from what is known and heard, the proverb in the *Decameron*, to what is instead new, the novella in *Le cento novelle*. In both works, the paremia shows the typical structure of a proverb with a final rhyme and rhythmic elements. Brusantino introduces the chiasm between *bon cavallo—bona donna* ("good horse—good woman")

Chapter Two

and *reo—trista* ("bad—wicked") to substitute for Boccaccio's polysyndeton *Buon cavallo e mal cavallo* ("good horse and bad horse")—*buona femmina e mala femmina* ("good woman and bad woman"). Additionally, Brusantino gives a prominent narrative and metrical position to the paremia, placing it at the end of an octave, when in the *Decameron* Emilia uses it in the middle of her introductory speech on the fragility of women (Dec. IX.9.3–9). Since it stands out, *Le cento novelle*'s paremia becomes the *climax* of the octave and the section of greater narrative tension due to the strong message against women that it conveys (Pettinelli, *Forme e percorsi* 185–86).[85] Women should always be subjected to their husbands and those who do not comply with it should be scared with power and force. Brusantino's expression creates a circular structure with the introductory paremia of the same novella more seamlessly than in the *Decameron*: *Ama e amato serai ben con ragione, la donna rea gastiga col bastone* ("Love and you will be loved reasonably, punish the guilty woman with the stick"; CN 476). In the expression at the beginning of the story, the second hemistich, *La donna rea gastiga col bastone*, expresses the idea that in order to be loved one must be harsh with women and that women are deserving of this behavior.

In reorganizing the original text, Brusantino occasionally inserts paremias that are absent in the *Decameron*. This is the case of the proverbial phrase, *Cadere in piedi come un gatto* ("To fall on one's feet like a cat"), which Brusantino adds to the text of novella II.5, specifically in the moment when Andreuccio falls into the sewer:

> [S]i trovò giuso in un tratto
> *Caduto in piedi proprio come un gatto.* (CN 70)
>
> He found himself down immediately,
> fallen on his feet just like a cat.

While describing the same event, Boccaccio focuses on the fact that Andreuccio is unhurt despite the vertical distance that he covers during his fall:

> [D]i tanto l'amò Idio, che niuno male si fece nella caduta, quantunque alquanto cadesse da alto. (Dec. II.5.38)
>
> Although he had fallen from a goodly height, he mercifully suffered no injury.

"Cadere come i gatti" ("To fall like cats") means to fall straight and, figuratively, to overcome any situation without harm (GDLI, s.v. *gatto* [1], n. 16). Likewise, "cadere in piedi" ("To fall on your feet") means to suffer severe events but to succeed in avoiding complete ruin and be ready to get back on one's feet (GDLI, s.v. *cadere*, n. 12). Brusantino's proverbial phrase summarizes Boccaccio's description in a very effective way and is easy to understand. Brusantino reinvents Boccaccio's text by selecting words and clusters that are appropriate to his own context.[86]

Another paremia that Brusantino adds to the original text is in story I.1, in which it substitutes for a non-proverbial sentence in the *Decameron*. The expression comments on Ciappelletto's wickedness and condenses its message into a hendecasyllabic hemistich:

> [E] a lui non andava per la memoria chi tanto malvagio uom fosse, in cui egli potesse alcuna fidanza avere, che opporre alla loro malvagità si potesse. (Dec. I.1.8)

> He was quite unable to think of anyone he could trust, who was at the same time sufficiently villainous to match the villainy of the Burgundians.

> E come pien d'ingegno e tutto scaltro
> *Pensò a un cauto barbier per rader l'altro.* (CN 14)

> And as a highly talented and shrewd person, he thought of a careful barber to shave the other.

The expression *Un barbier rade l'altro* ("A barber shaves the other") means that a sly person always finds someone who is slyer than himself (GDLI, s.v. *barbiere*, n. 4). In *Le cento novelle*, by adding the adjective "cauto"[87] ("cautious") for metrical purposes, Brusantino conveys his perspective on Ser Ciappelletto and on his being worse than the inhabitants in Burgundy. He is not only a barber able to cut the throats of other barbers, metaphorically meaning that he can overcome the Burgundians, who are quintessentially disloyal, contemptible, and inclined to fighting. He is also cautious, which means that he can detect and choose the best methods to achieve his goals. This raises the question of why Brusantino opts for a proverbial phrase, when, as Perocco argues, Boccaccio's sentence has a clear and identifiable rhythm, which Brusantino could have easily transferred to poetry ("La moralità rimata" [1987] 299). Employing a paremia means creating a relationship with the community and, at the same time, offering a concise structure as an alternative to the sophisticated elaboration of Boccaccio's style. Brusantino's line aims to appeal to a

Chapter Two

broader public, who could immediately identify the meaning of the paremia and its reference or correspondence to everyday life.

Brusantino's Ethical Language in His Paremias

An analysis of all of the proverbs in *Le cento novelle* reveals interesting lexical aspects in Brusantino's linguistic and ethical choices, as well as his exegetical strategies. These instances include the 100 proverbs that Brusantino introduces individually at the beginning of each of the novellas, those proverbs and proverbial phrases that he borrows from the *Decameron* and adopts in his *Le cento novelle*, and also those expressions that he chooses or invents for his text.[88]

When he writes the introductory proverbs, Brusantino uses many words that he does not find in the *Decameron*, even though many of them were already available in Boccaccio's time. Just a few of Brusantino's original words had made their first written appearance in the sixteenth century: "burlare" ("to trick, to mock"; Baldassare Castiglione uses "burlatore" in his *Il libro del cortegiano*), "talmente" ("so much"; first instance in Niccolò Machiavelli), "scaltro" ("shrewd"; used by Bernardo Davanzati), "insognare" ("to dream about something, to imagine, or else not to have the intention to do something"). Notably, Brusantino often combines in his proverbs words that Boccaccio uses separately and never employs in the same clusters that *Le cento novelle* presents. A few examples from Brusantino's work are "sciocco avaro" ("silly avaricious person"; introductory paremia for III.5; CN 146) and "cor altiero" ("arrogant heart"; introductory paremia for III.9 and IV.3; CN 172 and 205). For this last instance, Boccaccio instead uses "altiero animo" in Dec. III.5.13 and "animo altiero/a" ("arrogant soul") in Dec. IV.1.30 and Dec. VIII.7.4. The two lexical choices emphasize how, as in other novellas previously analyzed, Brusantino condemns avarice (III.5), unrequited love (III.9), and jealousy (IV.3) much more than Boccaccio.

The adjective "sfrenato" appears in the *Decameron* in the cluster "sfrenati cavalli" ("uncontrolled horses"; Dec. VII.2.34) and not in "sfrenato ardir" ("unrestrained audacity") as in Brusantino's introductory paremia to novella V.4 (CN 261). Brusantino's choices vis-à-vis Boccaccio's confirms that he considers Ricciardo and Caterina's behavior a mere satisfaction of unethical and lascivious bodily desires. Similarly, in Brusantino's introductory paremia for

I.4, "riprendere" means to reprimand someone of a "mal insano" ("insane evil"; CN 26), which corresponds to the unethical decision of breaking the wows of chastity—an aspect that Boccaccio does not link to the novella. Boccaccio, however, resorts to the verb "riprendere" in a variety of instances. Some of them aim to scold defects (Dec. III.2.3 and Dec. X.9.4) and immoral acts (Dec. III.7.38); some others are not morally-oriented and include reprimanding love (Dec. II.8.41), words (Dec. III.3.34 and Dec. IX.8.28), personality traits (Dec. X.8.108), women (Dec. IV.2.18 and Dec. IV.2.45), and lack of cleverness (Dec. VIII.9.3). An analogous example concerns the verb "saziare" ("to satisfy"), which is linked to "avidità" ("greed") in Brusantino's introductory paremia to story I.5 to describe the King of France's excessive behavior (CN 29). Conversely, in the *Decameron* the verb appears in different formats mainly relating to eyes or anger (Dec. IV.4.24, Dec. III.1.3, Dec. V.2.37, and Dec. IX.5.60).

Another loaded word in Brusantino's ethical world, "ipocresia" ("hypocrisy"), is used in the proverb introducing I.6 to demonstrate the hypocrisy of clergy members (CN 33; also, in Dec. I.6.1 and Dec. I.6.20). Moreover, it occurs in the introductory paremia for story VI.10 because, according to Brusantino, Fra Cipolla exemplifies a hypocritical person (CN 317). Brusantino does not apply it to introduce novella IV.2, as Boccaccio does (Dec. IV.2.5). Interestingly, "castità" ("chastity") does not appear in Brusantino's introductory paremias of those same novellas that mention the word in the *Decameron* (Dec. II.7.24, Dec. III.7.40, Dec. VII.3.11, and Dec. X.5.14). The two authors, though, share the use of the term in Dec. VIII.1.3, which recounts the story of Gulfardo and Gasparruolo's wife. Brusantino also uses the noun at the beginning of novella III.1 and, in doing so, introduces a different ethical perspective on the story of Masetto and the nuns. To highlight positive ethical behaviors, Brusantino clusters "magnanimo cor" ("magnanimous heart") in the introductory paremia to story V.9 to depict praiseworthy Federigo degli Alberighi (CN 283). Boccaccio uses the adjective "magnanimo" in Dec. VIII.7.85 ("io come magnanimo," "as a magnanimous person") and Dec. VIII.7.86 ("io pur magnanimo fossi," "calling me worthy gentleman") both referring to the Florentine scholar in the novella. "Magnanino" also characterizes King Charles's generosity in Dec. X.6.29 ("re magnanino," "great king").

Chapter Two

An interesting line of inquiry on the language of Brusantino's paremias is the comparison between the proverbs at the beginning of each novella and those in the final list for each day.[89] Since the pairs of proverbs differ, through their evaluation Brusantino's lexical and ideological choices emerge along with interesting linguistic variations. It is probable that Brusantino had someone compile the final list in those pages left blank at the end of each day. This person, while reading and copying, rectified some apparent mistakes and changed morphological or syntactical elements of the introductory paremias. Had this person been Brusantino, he would have also adjusted the introductory paremias. Since this does not occur, it can be reasonably argued that the print shop made some of these changes. It is likely that Brusantino's editor, Marcolini, decided to add the final list of paremias and take care of it personally. This would not be surprising, given that Marcolini introduced similar features to other publications that he curated, including the brief descriptions of each canto's topic in his 1553 edition of Brusantino's *L'Angelica innamorata*. Pettinelli, however, claims that it is difficult to identify the person who copied the final list. The differences in linguistic choices could mean uncertainty in embracing a specific linguistic rule or, conversely, its complete refusal (*Forme e percorsi* 187).

Regardless of the identity of the compiler, differences between the introductory paremias and those in the final list frequently include lexical changes. For instance, in story II.10, the introductory paremia suggests that an old man should avoid having a young woman as friend and wife: "farsi gioven donna amica e moglie" ("to have a young woman as friend and wife"; CN 116). In the final iteration, however, the man is advised to not choose a young woman as wife: "torsi donna giovene per moglie" ("to have a young woman as a wife"; CN 124). Evidently, the compiler of the paremia in the final list found it more appropriate to refer to the actual facts recounted in the story, i.e., Ricciardo's marrying his young and beautiful wife. In story I.2, the final paremia introduces a different cluster than the introductory one. Specifically, the final proverb reads "peccato d'opra rea" ("sin originating from a guilty endeavor"), probably because, in the introductory paremia, the copyist interpreted as a sin the "opra rea da religion" ("guilty endeavor committed by religion") that indicates the wickedness of the clergy one could experience during a visit to Rome:

Introductory Paremia

> *Se opra rea da religion si vede*
> *Per questo non si dee mancar di fede.* (CN 21)
>
> If one experiences a guilty endeavor committed by religion, he must not lack faith because of it.

Paremia in the Final List

> *Se gran peccato d'opra rea si vede*
> *Per questo non si de' mancar di fede.* (CN 46)
>
> If one experiences a great sin originating from a guilty endeavor, he must not lack faith because of it.

It is worth noting that, as opposed to the compiler of the final list, Brusantino does not look at the corruption of the Church in Rome as a sin but, similarly to Boccaccio, just as a way to reinforce one's religious faith.

Two different verbal choices in the paremias for story VIII.1 shows Brusantino's ethical views as well:

Introductory Paremia

> *A chi per pregio dona castitade*
> *Ben merta che se gli usi falsitade.* (CN 378)
>
> He who gives his chastity by self-esteem deserves that you use falsehood with him.

Paremia in the Final List

> *A chi per pregio vende castitade*
> *Ben merta che se li usi falsitade.* (CN 444)
>
> He who sells his chastity by self-esteem deserves that you use falsehood with him.

Changing the verb "dona" ("gives") to "vende" ("sells") highlights Gasparruolo's wife's unethical behavior since she trades her marital fidelity for money. Evidently, the compiler attributes more harm to this act than does Brusantino, who already gives more prominence to the woman's corrupted behavior compared to Boccaccio's novella. The author of the *Decameron*, indeed, privileges the perspective of the trick played on the same woman to make her pay for her adulterous thoughts.

Undoubtedly, throughout, Brusantino shows his orientation towards emphasizing good and respectful behaviors in society, both by means of his introductory allegories and paremias and his individual additions to the text. Inspired by the multiple sixteenth-century editions of the *Decameron* and *Orlando furioso*, he aims to release a text that could speak to his contemporaneous public, without being excessively informed by the Counter-Reformation ideology. In doing so, he represents a pioneer in the ethical interpretation of Boccaccio's text and anticipates its later, more moralizing, rewritings.

Chapter Three

John Florio's *Firste Fruites* and *Second Frutes*
Paremias and Elizabethan Teaching of the Italian Language

> Qui Luciano ha un proverbio al quale non corrisponde nessuno de' nostri ch'io sappia, e il proverbio è di quelli che renduti secondo che suonano, o restano insulsissimi o anche senza senso: ora parafrasato e dichiarato nessun proverbio è più proverbio, e pel'ordinario diventa freddura. Sicch'io l'ho saltato di netto: e pure in questa traduzione ho proposto di essere fedelissimo.
>
> Here, Lucian uses a proverb that does not have an equivalent among our proverbs of which I am aware. The proverb is among those that, if they are translated as they sound, either are insignificant or even meaningless. Now, when paraphrased or explained, no proverb is a proverb any longer, and in the common belief it becomes a word pun. Hence, I skipped it without hesitating: and yet I intended to be extremely faithful in this translation.
>
> Giacomo Leopardi, *Come vada scritta la storia*

Florio's Activity in England

John Florio or Giovanni Florio[1] (1553–1625) is the perfect example of a man of letters mediating among multiple cultures and identities. He lived between two languages (Italian and English), two religions (Catholicism and Protestantism), and two homeplaces (London and Soglio in Italian-speaking Switzerland). On one hand, Italian culture, language, and customs influenced him profoundly through his father, Michelangelo Florio. Yet, the younger Florio never experienced Italy personally. British identity, on the other hand, allowed him a constant relationship with the most refined Elizabethan society and, thanks to his intellectual profession, integrated him into the English community. His coat of arms identifies him as a man "Italus ore, Anglus pectore" ("Italian in language, English in the heart"), in which the two

Chapter Three

words "ore" and "pectore" reflect the ambidextrous opposition between that which is pronounced and heard, Italian, and that which is linked to the heart or center of emotions, English.[2] This dichotomy, deriving from Florio's experience as both an immigrant to Soglio and the son of an Italian emigrant in London, makes him the typical Renaissance "go-between" intellectual (Burke, "The Renaissance Translator as Go-Between" 23; Montini, "John/Giovanni" 47–48).[3] Additionally, his bilingualism, as well as his use of Italian as a privileged second-generation learner gives his works an original appeal and distinguishes him in the linguistic and pedagogical scholarship of sixteenth- and seventeenth-century England.[4]

John Florio's father, Michelangelo, a Tuscan native and anti-Trinitarian priest,[5] was forced to leave Florence (or probably Siena or Lucca) in 1550 after embracing the spirit of the Counter-Reformation.[6] In London, which became his new home, he joined an established group of Italian refugees and worked as both a preacher and Italian teacher. These activities offered him the opportunity to disseminate Italian literary culture as well as Counter-Reformation ideals in the city and the surrounding areas, ultimately giving shape to the initial core of the Italian Protestant Church in London. However, after Mary I of Tudor became Queen of England in 1553 and started to reintegrate a strict and observant Catholicism, Michelangelo abandoned England with his one-year-old child. John's father found a place as a pastor in the reformed Swiss town of Soglio, where he remained until his own death in 1565. During his life, Michelangelo distinguished himself by his English translation of Georgius Agricola's *De re metallica* (1556, published in 1563) and, primarily, by the publication of a grammar book on the Tuscan language in 1553, *Regole de la lingua thoscana* (Bocchi 51–64). The work is a balance between Pietro Bembo's influence and Michelangelo's own inclination to promote "living languages" and, in particular, the contemporaneous Tuscan vernacular (Pellegrini, "Michelangelo Florio" 100–3; Wyatt, *The Italian Encounter* 212–13).[7] His son probably gained from him an interest in studying, teaching, and translating languages.[8]

Nineteen-year-old John returned to England in 1572, at a time when Elizabeth I had already reigned for fourteen years, after succeeding Mary I in 1558 (Wyatt, *The Italian Encounter* 101–16,

117–54). He taught French and Italian at Magdalen College in Oxford until 1578, and afterward moved back to London where he became an acclaimed teacher, translator, lexicographer, and linguist (Simonini, "John Florio" 74–75).[9] A friend of Giordano Bruno, John took advantage of close relationships with some of the most influential personalities of the time, including Robert Dudley (Earl of Leicester), Sir Walter Raleigh, Henry Wriothesley (Earl of Southampton), and Queen Anne of Denmark.[10] At the court of the Count of Southampton, he likely met William Shakespeare, who would mock him in the figure of the pedantic schoolmaster in *Love's Labour Lost* (1597).[11] Thanks to Sir Robert Cecil's intermediation, Florio's appointment as a member of the royal court continued even when James I was appointed King of England and Ireland in 1603 (1603–25). However, with the death of King James's wife, Queen Anne of Denmark, in 1619, Florio's active career reached an end and this caused him to spend the last years of his life in complete poverty.

In his multifaceted production, Florio engaged in a variety of textual genres aiming to spread "the Italian Renaissance civilization, universal knowledge, and multilingualism" in London (Florio, *A Worlde of Wordes* [2013] xvi). He produced translations in English, including Jacques Cartier's *A shorte and briefe narration* in 1580,[12] the *Perpetuall and natural prognostications* in 1591 and 1598, and Michel Eyquem de Montaigne's *The essayes* in 1603 (Matthiessen 103–68; Policardi 136–70; and Yates, *John Florio* 213–45). Among the other translations in English that he produced a few years before his death are Boccaccio's *Decameron* in 1620[13]—the first complete translation probably through a French version and not the Italian original—and the first part of Traiano Boccalini's *Ragguagli di Parnaso*, published posthumously in 1626 (see *The new-found politicke*).[14] Florio also engaged in translations from English to Italian, among which the most well-known is his rendering of King James's *Basilikon Doron* (1603; Pellegrini, *John Florio*). Translations were one of the most practiced activities by the same Queen Elizabeth and were heavily associated with language learning since they were considered an excellent method to gain knowledge of a foreign language (Sumillera, "Language Manuals" 67–76).[15] However, the works that assured Florio a considerable place in the realm of language teaching in England

Chapter Three

are his two bilingual manuals for English speakers, *Firste Fruites* (1578) dedicated to Robert Dudley and *Second Frutes* (1591) dedicated to Nicholas Saunders of Charlwood and Ewell.

Renowned is Florio's dictionary *A Worlde of Wordes* (1598), which he later enlarged in *Queen Anna's New World of Words* (1611), dedicated to the same Queen Anne, at the time a student of Giacomo Castelvetro (Butler). *A Worlde of Wordes* represents the first bilingual Italian-English dictionary, published fourteen years before the first edition of the *Vocabolario degli Accademici della Crusca* (1612). Dedicated to the Earl of Southampton, the Earl of Rutland, and the Countess of Bedford, Florio's dictionary gathers more than 40,000 entries, providing its users with a diachronic account of Italian linguistic diversity. Evidently positing his linguistic principles against the monolithic tendencies of the academicians of the Crusca (Wyatt, *The Italian Encounter* 223–54), Florio explains the meaning of each entry at length, inspired by a pedagogical intent (O'Connor, *A History* 19–43; Policardi 109–35). The dictionary's sources include a selection of eclectic books, such as treatises on cooking, riding, animals, and plants, as well as encyclopedic texts that could satisfy Florio's thirst for universality. Among the latter, Alessandro Citolini's *Tipocosmia* and Tommaso Garzoni's *La piazza universale* are those from which Florio drew the most (Florio, *A Worlde of Wordes* [2013] ix; see also Sciarrino in Marrapodi, *Intertestualità shakespeariane* 31–46, specifically 39). As in other works by Florio, the quality and number of texts cited in his dictionary distinguish it from others published previously, an aspect that becomes even greater in the lexicon of his enlarged edition referencing more than 200 sources.[16]

The extent of works consulted also characterizes another encyclopedic work by Florio, his collection of paremias *Giardino di ricreatione*. Probably assembled while the author was working on his language manuals, the collection gathers Italian "proverbii, riboboli, motti, detti, brevi, adagii, e sentenze italiane" ("proverbs, popular idioms, maxims, quotes, short sayings, adages, and Italian *sententiae*"; GR A2r). Dedicated to Sir Edward Dyer, *Giardino* presents 6,150 Italian paremias (or 6,155 according to Gamberini, *Lo studio dell'italiano* 111), which appear at the end of the 1591 edition of *Second Frutes*.[17] Florio organized the collection alphabetically, even though in casual order within individual letters and without explanation, probably because many of the paremias are listed in both *Firste Fruites* and *Second Frutes*. Along with repeating some expressions from *Fruits* identically or with minor changes (specifically 297 according to Gamberini, *Lo studio* 111), Florio also invented many *ex novo*. In England, only two works anticipated Florio's collection and served as sources for his *Giardino*: a small list of Italian paremias translated into English within James Sanford's *The Garden of Pleasure* (1573) and Charles Merbury's *Proverbi Vulgari raccolti di diversi luoghi d'Italia*, which was included in his *A briefe discourse of royall monarchie*[18] (1581).[19] However, thanks to the considerable number of Italian and non-Italian sources, Florio's *Giardino* can be recognized as one of the most complete anthologies of Italian paremias published outside Italy in the sixteenth century, and the work that led to a proliferation of paremiac collections in England and beyond (Pignatti, *Etimologia e proverbio* 350–53).[20]

A distinctive aspect of Florio's production, from his English renderings to his bilingual dictionary, is the frequent use of paremias to enhance the relationship between language and translation. Within this realm, involving adaptations from one culture and language to another, paremias facilitate language teaching and create a fertile space for linguistic and intercultural interpretation. As they promote the rich Italian popular wisdom, they also outline the culture of exchange that existed between Italy and Elizabethan England, especially in language teaching. It is not surprising that even the frontispiece of *Queen Anna's New World of Words* presents a proverb that summarizes Florio's approach to literature, pedagogy, and probably life: *Chi si contenta gode* ("Who lives content, hath all the world at will").

Teaching the Italian Language with Paremias: Florio's Innovative Approach

In the fifteenth century and at the beginning of the sixteenth century, teaching languages and providing contacts with other cultures were considered an enrichment of the intellectual and social life in England. After a century of the undisputed supremacy of French both at a popular level and as an elitist language of literature and conversation, the Tudor dynasty in 1485 started to recognize greater importance to other vernaculars (Simonini, *Italian Scholarship* 17). In this period, the Italian language finally managed to dominate the literary scene and, during the reign of Elizabeth I (1558–1603), progressively became part of aristocratic education, which sought to impart knowledge of books and science.[21] Many noteworthy members of society, including the Queen herself, were able to both converse and write fluently in Italian.[22] Under the guidance of Giovanni Battista Castiglione, known today as "Queen Elizabeth's Master for Italian," Elizabeth opened the court to the profound influence of the Italian culture in all areas, from theater to fashion to language. She exploited the new and generalized deep fascination for what was foreign and not germane to English culture and society and enthusiastically promoted any idea or event that was related to Italy.[23]

Generally, English authors and scholars appreciated the cultural richness of Italy along with the profundity of its literary achievements. At the same time, however, they were concerned about the ethical and moral perspectives of the Italian society (Lievsay, *The Elizabethan Image of Italy* 1–9).[24] Roger Ascham rendered this concern through a spiteful remark about supposed Italian corruption in his *The Scholemaster* (1570). He mentions the paremia, *Un inglese italianato è un diavolo incarnato* ("An Italianate Englishman is a devil incarnate"),[25] to castigate Englishmen for the bad manners they presumably acquired after travelling to Italy: "*Englese italianato è un diabolo incarnato*, that is to say, you remaine men in shape and facion, but becum devils in life and condition" (26).[26] In his letter to the readers of his *Second Frutes*, Florio uses this same paremia more positively to praise his superiority as a speaker of both the Italian and English languages:

> As for me, for it is I, and I am an Englishman in Italiane, I know they [critics] have a knife at command to cut my throat, *Un inglese italianato è un diavolo incarnato*. Now, who the Divell taught thee so much Italian? Speake me as much more, and take all. Meane you the men, or their mindes? Be the men good, and their minds bad? Speake for the men (for you are one) or I will doubt of your minde? Mislike you the language? Why the best speake it best, and hir Maiestie none better, I, but too manie tongues are naught; indeede one is too manie for him that cannot use it well. (SF A2r–A2v)

According to Florio, knowing more languages and mastering them in an appropriate and effective way is more worthy of admiration than a demerit (Florio, *Florio's First Fruites* xxix). In this sense, his paremia conveys the message that being in between two languages and two cultures makes someone a more intelligent and astute person. Both *Firste Fruites* and *Second Frutes* aim to fulfill such objective as they effectively teach the Italian language to help create a well-rounded individual in society.[27]

Teaching was, indeed, the easiest activity for the Elizabethan generation of Italian expatriates. The promotion of education by Elizabeth I, alongside the investment by rich merchants and trade guilds in foreign language pedagogy, created an atmosphere conducive to studying Italian. The majority of refugees from Italy either found a place in private schools or worked as private teachers of noble families' children (Wyatt, *The Italian Encounter* 138; Yates, "Italian Teachers in Elizabethan England" 104). Teaching practices not only guaranteed learners the chance to read Italian works and converse in Italian, but also allowed them to acquire social grace (Engel 518; Pizzoli 58; Rossi, *Ricerche* 96–98).

Similar to other businesses, however, teaching was subject to the demands of the market and was affected by the fierce competition in the field. Since teachers of Italian were often underpaid, they resorted to two ancillary activities to support their livelihood: translations of texts that could not be acquired in the original language (Boutcher, "'A French Dexterity, & an Italian Confidence'"; Policardi 137–70; Wyatt, *The Italian Encounter* 157–202)[28] and publications of different pedagogical instruments (Lawrence 19–29). Many of the masterpieces of Italian literature arrived in England through a pervasive campaign of translation, a process that editors John Wolfe, Thomas Woodcock, and Edward Blount promoted throughout the entirety of the sixteenth and seventeenth centuries (Matthiessen 3; Bellorini, "Le pubblicazioni italiane"; Florio, *A Worlde of Wordes* [2013] xiii; Huffman; Lawrence 187–201; Lievsay, *The Englishman's Italian Books*; and Wyatt, *The Italian Encounter* 185–99). Courtesy books were among the first to be translated. In 1561 Thomas Hoby published the English translation of Castiglione's *Il libro del cortegiano*[29]; in 1576 Richard Peterson reworded into English Giovanni della Casa's *Il galateo*. In 1581 George Pettie engaged with the translation of the first three books of Guazzo's *La civil conversatione*, which was released in its integral edition in 1586 by Bartholomew Young. All of these publications experienced incredible success in

England, ultimately leading the way to conversational and phrase books such as Florio's *Fruits*.[30]

Relatedly, different categories of learners demanded grammar books,[31] language manuals, and dictionaries to facilitate their learning process: those who needed to engage in business relationships and financial enterprises with Italy, primarily merchants; those who wished to visit Italy as part of their education and professional growth; and those who were fascinated by the country and decided to base their education on its literary masterpieces. The combination of educational matters and practical ends greatly affected the way languages were taught and the way bilingual or polyglot textbooks and dictionaries were structured in England. During the Tudor and Stuart periods (mostly from the sixteenth century through the first half of the seventeenth century), a considerable number of pedagogical tools were published (Gamberini, *Lo studio* 45–98; Howatt and Widdowson; Simonini, *Italian Scholarship* 14, 110–14; Sumillera, "Sixteenth-Century").[32] In 1550, William Thomas released the first bilingual grammar book, titled *Principal rules of Italian grammer*.[33] Roger Ascham's above-mentioned *The Scholemaster* (posthumous publication in 1570)[34] was followed by Henry Grantham's *An Italian grammer* in 1575,[35] and in the seventeenth century, by John Sanford's *A grammer* (1605) and Torriano's *New and easie directions for attaining the thuscan tongue* (1639), published just before the progressive disappearance of the Italian language in England.[36]

Aside from these grammar books, manuals based on proverbs offered real instances of the Italian language in context through conversations among different characters. Such manuals derived their structure from medieval debates, Latin colloquia, and conversational books called *manières de langage,* intended to teach Anglophone students to speak and write in French correctly in different contexts (Borello; Meyer; Pizzoli 65–66; Simonini, "The Italian Pedagogy of Claudius Hollyband" 145). The manuals by Huguenot Claude de Sainliens, anglicized Claudius Holyband, were crucial examples for later authors, Florio included. Holyband's *The pretie and wittie historie of Arnalt and Lucenda* (1575) is the first of the series to present pedagogically-driven dialogues. His later *Campo di fior* (1583) offers "a synoptical display of the languages and of pronunciation" through a multilingual compilation of conversations in Latin, Italian, French, and

English (Montini, "Teaching Italian" 521). Lastly, his very popular *The Italian Schoole-maister* (1581) is the equivalent for the Italian language of his two previous works devoted to explaining the grammar of the French language (*The French Littelton* in 1566 and *The French Schoole-maister* in 1573).[37] *The French Littelton* would also become a model for the structure and organization of Florio's *Fruits* because of its rich use of proverbs in context, yet still limited compared to Florio's dialogues.[38] On the verge of the seventeenth century, Benvenuto Italiano's *Il Passagiere/ The Passenger* (1612; heavily influenced by Florio's *Fruits*), Torriano's *The Italian tutor* (1640; see Gamberini, *Lo studio* 150–51), and Pietro Paravicino's *Choice Proverbs and Dialogues in Italian and English* (1660)[39] were the last examples of dialogue manuals in Italian (Gamberini, *Lo studio* 45–98; Pinnavaia; Simonini, "The Genesis of Modern Foreign Language Teaching" and *Italian Scholarship* 42–80).

At the same time when grammar books and language manuals for foreigners were published outside the peninsula, grammar books were also released in the Italian market. Comparatively, the Italian works were more theoretically oriented and disputed which typology of vernacular to use in literature. Because they were intended to promote a regulating approach to the written language, they offered definite rules on Italian syntax and morphology.[40] Their objective was not to teach the vernacular but rather to improve its knowledge, while also engaging in speculation over the "questione della lingua"[41] (Bonomi and Castegnaro 15).[42] Conversely, foreign grammar books, including those produced in England, were far from any theoretical perspective. They were ancillary instruments in the language learning process and primarily explored the practical usage of the language, constantly considering its intended audience and contexts (Marazzini, "The Teaching of Italian"; Palermo and Poggiogalli 37–38; Pizzoli 340).[43] Giovanni Francesco Fortunio's *Regole grammaticali della volgar lingua* (1516) and Bembo's *Prose della volgar lingua* (1525) were known beyond the Italian peninsula, especially because they demonstrated a more open attitude towards communicative functions and actual uses in society than other Italian grammars. Fortunio and Bembo acknowledged the importance of contemporaneous spoken communication, primarily Tuscan, over respect for tradition and the prevalence of literary language[44] (Fornara 56; Gamberini, *Lo studio* 42–43; Vedovelli 48–49).[45] Foreign grammarians accepted their idea of Italian language as an idealization and not as something to promote in their own countries.

A comparison in the use of paremias within pedagogical texts released in Italy and in England is telling of the two different pedagogical methods. In the peninsula, Pescetti's aforementioned *Proverbi italiani e latini* (1602) is the only example of paremias in language teaching, taking the form of a list of expressions in both Italian and Latin. Beginning with the dedicatory letter to Pier Francesco Zino, Pescetti states that proverbs and proverbial phrases are useful for the knowledge of the Italian language and its authors. In his *Orazione*, he emphasizes that they contribute to the "istitutione della vita" ("life institution"; A2r) by instructing young adolescents during their education (Pignatti, *Etimologia e proverbio* 258–63). Since Latin was still the language of educated people and the *lingua franca* in Europe, this compilation not only offered students material for comparison and for better memorization, but also spread paremias across Europe. The objective was two-fold: Italian pupils became skilled in Latin paremias, whereas in other countries the Latin paremias granted an "approximation" to the message of the expressions in vernacular (Fiorelli, "Tra il proverbio e la regola di diritto" 189).

Conversely, outside the peninsula, the attention to the "uso vivo" of the language (Rossi, *Ricerche* 97) led to a greater emphasis on paremias in language manuals for English speakers. Foreign grammars employed paremiac expressions to "expand vocabulary and display popular culture" through "to the laws of dialogue exchanges" (Montini, "Proverbs in John Florio's *Fruits*" 249; see also Gamberini, *Lo studio* 45–129; Mormile and Matteucci 11–34; Pizzoli; Palermo and Poggiogalli; Rossi, *Ricerche* 95–212; Wyatt, *The Italian Encounter* 155–202). Paremias were considered crucial tools for one's eloquence (Manley 249), as well as for one's capability to engage with the target language colloquially and, at the same time, ornately (Speroni, "Giovanni Torriano's *Select Italian Proverbs*" 150). They gave preeminence to spontaneity over awareness of fixed rules and, in general, to culture and communication over grammar (Engel 515). Additionally, proverbs and proverbial phrases transmitted moral and ethical messages "without a trace of the foreign devilry in morals dreaded by [the] elders," namely Ascham's generation (Yates, *John Florio* 36). Florio's predecessors, the same Ascham, but also Gratham, and Holyband, inserted paremias in their works, yet mostly gathered them in bilingual lists.[46] *Firste Fruites* and *Second Frutes*, instead, were the first textbooks featuring paremias in meaningful and real-life conversations. In these manuals, paremias cover many functions: they convey correct grammar, lexicon, and conversational styles and they are tools for cultural exposure (Di Martino, "Florio's *Firste Fruites*" 76–77, "Politeness strategies" 227–28; Policardi 93). They also present definite narratological and social purposes as they summarize or comment upon a concept, become dialogic propellers, represent a moral perspective, allow the expression of oneself with grace and spontaneity, and please the receivers. Thanks to their considerable number, Florio's manuals constitute a collection of culturally-based expressions of the Italian language that go beyond mere linguistic instruction (Engel 509; Tilley 1).

Florio's Paremias in His *Fruits*

Dedicated to lovers of the language, members of courtly circles, attendees of sophisticated meetings, future entrepreneurs, or Grand Tour enthusiasts (Simonini, *Italian Scholarship*; Yates, "Italian Teachers in Elizabethan England"), *Firste Fruites* and *Second Frutes* take place in London in the last decade of the sixteenth century. They contain the Italian and English versions of daily conversations between Elizabethan aristocrats and servants "ideati come esercizi conversazionali senza maestro" ("designed as conversational exercises without a teacher"; Haller, "John Florio e Claudius Holyband" 60). *Firste Fruites* presents forty–four graded conversations, which are much shorter than the twelve conversational exchanges in *Second Frutes* and often resemble concise theatrical pieces (Di Martino, "Politeness strategies" 239).[47] Florio's grammar books contributed to righteous manners in society much like manuals of good behavior that were published in the first half of the sixteenth century, wisdom collections that were inspired by biblical and devotional works since the start of the century, and commonplace books that were at their height between 1580 and 1680 (Considine; Simonini, "Language Lesson Dialogue" 320). Their paremias represented a *vade mecum* of practical suggestions on life conduct and allowed high society an elegant and civil participation in elite events, while also promoting discourses on culture and literature at large and providing expressions of wit.[48]

Chapter Three

From a typographical perspective, *Firste Fruites* is organized synoptically into two columns per page: the left one contains the Italian and the right the English translation. In *Second Frutes*, the two columns, one in Italian and the other in English, appear on two different sheets. In the first manual, the two speakers are a foreigner newly arrived in England and an Englishman willing to offer advice. Their names are not mentioned at the beginning of their lines and, therefore, are not distinguished from other characters' discussions. Differently, in *Second Frutes* the names of the many participants (among them is Nolano, who recalls Giordano Bruno) are spelled out in the caption and their initials are provided before each line in the conversation.[49] This feature helps one to navigate the dialogues of *Second Frutes* more effectively, especially because many speakers usually appear simultaneously and paremias follow each other without a pause. In general, there are fewer paremias in *Firste Fruites* than in *Second Frutes*. The difference in the number of proverbs and proverbial phrases between the two manuals is evident: roughly, 287 in *Firste Fruites* (six are repeated twice) and 517 in *Second Frutes* (twelve are repeated twice). A possible explanation for this could be that Florio was more tentative in his methodological approach to teaching languages in *Firste Fruites* (even though the inclusion of almost 300 paremias is far from being a timid attempt). Later, when working on his *Second Frutes*, his more refined awareness of teaching methods, combined with the larger quantity of paremias that he collected, encouraged him to use proverbs and proverbial phrases profusely and successfully. A last aspect to compare in the two manuals includes their introductory captions. In *Firste Fruites*, the introductory captions that indicate the topics of each dialogue are characterized by their conciseness. They mostly refer to the dynamics of the conversations (interlocutors or registers) or their topics, including references to literary works.[50] Additionally, they frequently mention the linguistic structures used for a specific topic, which could be *sententiae*, paremias, sayings, or mottos, both literary and products of circumstance. Similarly, in *Second Frutes* many introductory captions describe the different registers of the conversation, including the use of proverbs within a facetious dialogue.[51] Other captions address conversations occurring during social and courtly events, as well as daily habits.[52]

In both *Fruits*, proverbs are described as true flowers of rhetoric. As Florio's letter to all Italian gentlemen and merchants states, in

Firste Fruites and *Second Frutes*

Firste Fruites readers find "molti belli proverbi italiani e inglesi, gentili detti, belli motti, belle sentenze, tolti da diversi buoni autori, non solamente profittevole, ma anche dilettevole" ("many beautiful Italian and English proverbs, gentle sayings, beautiful mottos, beautiful sentences, extracted from several good authors, not only profitable, but also delightful"; FF **iii*r*). "Belle sentenze," "gentili detti," and "belli motti" recall the opening caption of the thirteenth-century collection of short stories *Novellino*, which likewise sought to teach life lessons and offer delight to its readers.[53] Another mention of the paremias' origins, as well as authority of the selected sources occurs within *Firste Fruites*'s English dedicatory letter to Robert Dudley. This epistle attests that the book contains "ordinarie answers, together with divers proverbs, sentences, and golden sayinges, used as well as English, and therewithal collected and translated out of sundry the best Italian authors" (FF, *The Epistle Dedicatorie* *iii*v*). Florio also emphasizes this concept in *Second Frutes*'s dedicatory letter to Nicholas Saunders, in which he admits that he "ransackt and rifled all the gardens of fame throughout Italie" (SF A3*r*). By emphasizing the literary derivation of his paremias and sayings, the author intends to protect himself from the accusation of being born outside of Italy, never visiting his father's home country, and therefore not having accessed popular paremias in person. In so doing, he can excuse himself from critics who may point out his limited skills in speaking the Italian language and his lack of proper education in language manual writing (FF, *A tutti i gentilhuomi e mercanti* **ii*v*). Even within the dialogues, when one of the speakers in chapter 6 of the first language manual asks about the provenance of paremias, his interlocutor answers that they come from poets:

> Chi pensate che habbia fatto questi proverbi?
> Io credo qualche poeta. (FF 6*v*)[54]
>
> Who thinke you have made these proverbes?
> I beleeve some poetes.

According to Michael Wyatt, for Florio resorting to paremias means to "lie" in the way poets do, namely by means of figures of speech that create ambiguity. Since the interpretation of these figures and hence, of paremias is not immediate, Florio inserts them into "the larger compass of linguistic activities that constituted his career," i.e., within the pedagogical dialogues of his *Fruits* to guarantee their correct understanding (*The Italian Encounter* 175).

Chapter Three

The way paremias are presented in *Firste Fruites* and *Second Frutes* varies according to the objectives of the two manuals, as well as the characteristics of their respective social contexts. In *Firste Fruites*, the atmosphere is euphuistic and deeply Puritan. A sophisticated phraseology characterizes the manual and its style relies on the beautiful and precious conceits typical of Marinism (Florio, *A Worlde of Wordes* [2013] xv). Dialogues are full of antitheses, alliterations, rhetorical questions, and parallel clauses, resulting in a bombast of language, which is however confined within moralistic intentions (Jeffery 127–28). At the same time, Stilnovistic elements pervade the text, as for example chapter 14, which deals with love between a man and a cruel woman inconsiderate of his affection.[55] Within the dialogues in *Firste Fruites*, the paremias are generally introduced and explained, and their message contextualized. Florio does not present these expressions for aesthetic purposes, though. Similar to Brusantino's introductory paremias, which aim to provide readers with an ethical reading of Boccaccio's stories, Florio uses paremias to determine a "schema di moralità rinascimentale, sotto forma di prontuario di virtù" ("a scheme of Renaissance morality in the form of a handbook on virtue"; Gamberini, *Lo studio* 85). An exemplary instance of this objective is the beginning of chapter 12:

> *Chi sente, vede, et tace, può sempre vivere in pace.*
> Ma *chi fa il contrario sempre viverà in affanni.*
> *Mi par che voi parlate per esperientia.* (FF 10*r*)
>
> Who heares, sees, and holds his peace, may alway live in peace.
> But who doth the contrary, shal alway live in care.
> Me thinkes that you speake by experience.

The reference to the "experience" of living by and through proverbs suggests that applying virtue to one's life guarantees survival in society because "senza virtù non si può far niente che sia buono" ("without virtue nothing can be done that is good"; FF 37*v*).

The stern setting of *Firste Fruites* disappears in *Second Frutes*, whose characters embrace a more frivolous and less moralizing approach to life (Boutcher, "'A French Dexterity, & an Italian Confidence'" 64–68). This probably results from Florio's greater acquaintance with London's society (Yates, *John Florio* 136) and with his public's greater eagerness to read and discuss love poetry than before (Yates, *John Florio* 124). The participants of the dialogues, whose names (Ruspa, Piccinino, Trippa, Roberto, Crusca, Losco, Tinca, Lippa, Scarpa, Polenta, Limbo) seem to recall the sixteenth-century Italian comedy as well as English theater (Perini 182),[56] engage in conversations that are mainly centered upon the theme of love and observe society with light and refined witticism (Gamberini, *Lo studio* 90–92). Florio's greater knowledge of Italian literary sources makes the language of this manual more elaborate and advanced from a pedagogical perspective than the first manual (Montini, "Teaching Italian" 523).[57] Occasionally, paremias are listed for stylistic reasons, without clearly transmitting a message but for the purpose of promoting "graceful conversations" in the style of the "courtesy-book tradition" (Florio, *Second Frutes* Intr.; see also *A Worlde of Wordes* [2013] xii–xv). Since paremias are not part of the narrative and flow of discourse, Donatella Montini calls them "discursive inserts" ("Teaching Italian" 530), while Rinaldo Simonini refers to them as "quotable passages," supplying "quantities of easy erudition and common places" (*Italian Scholarship* 10). Because of this aspect, proverbial expressions are neither introduced nor explained. The following instance from chapter 2 illustrates the absence of explicit presentation and clarification of paremias in an exchange of clever witticism and urban eloquence between Thomaso and Giovanni:

> T. Che andate facendo così solo?
> G. *Io non vorrei esser solo in paradiso.*
> T. *E pur è meglio esser solo che male accompagnato.*
> G. Chi si trova con V.S. è molto bene accompagnato. (SF 14)
>
> T. What are you dooing so alone?
> G. I would be loth to be alone in Paradise.
> T. And yet it is better to be alone than evill acompanied.
> G. He that is with you is very well accompanied.

A similar example demonstrates the subtle paremiac reasonings between Pandolpho and Silvestro on the subject of love:

> P. *Succia amor la borsa, succia amor il cuore.*
> *Pazzo è chi compra con duo sangui amore*, et
> *Per un piacer mille dolori si truova haver chi segue amore.*
> S. *Parole, parole senza sugo, l'amor ci dà la vita.*
> *Et in vita et in morte il tutto amor governa.* (SF 176)
>
> P. Love sacrifices the purse, the heart love sacrificeth.
> A foole he is that love, with double bloodshed buyeth and
> For little pleasure mickle sorow, he shal have that love doth folow.

> S. Al these are but words, by love we live with double breath
> Living in others after death; and love is all in all.

The way paremias are highlighted in *Second Frutes*, that is with an asterisk besides them, seems to confirm their use in conversations. It is possible that while planning his *Giardino di ricreatione*, Florio adopted a method that could allow him to find paremias more easily within his second manual. However, since just a small percentage of paremias included in *Second Frutes* appears in the later collection, it is likely that Florio glossed his paremias to help his readers and invite them to memorize proverbial expressions.[58] By means of gnomic pointing, the dialogues resemble a list of proverbs, yet with a clear difference. Florio's paremias are contextualized and they are organized according to thematic units (and not alphabetically as happens in collections). Such a method makes it difficult for someone looking for a specific paremia in the dialogues, but it is incredibly advantageous for those who wish to engage in conversations and need a ready list of proverbs and proverbial phrases to use in those specific situations (Wyatt, *The Italian Encounter* 167).[59]

The presence of an English translation for all of the paremias as well as the dialogues in *Firste Fruites* and *Second Frutes* may appear to go against full immersion in the target language and culture.[60] As discussed earlier, Florio believed and was particularly engaged in the politics of translating works. In his language manuals, even though the initial language of the translation is Italian, English is the metalanguage that guarantees a correct interpretation of the Italian text for English speakers. Simultaneously, the text in English offers linguistic (lexical and grammatical) support to both English and Italian learners, especially considering the role of *Fruits* as self-study tools.[61] On one hand, translation assured an immediate comprehension of the dialogues; on the other, those who wished to speak the Italian language fluently could practice the topics and structures of the language that Florio had conscientiously selected. From time to time, they could refer to the English translation when the context would be insufficient to decipher the paremias' meanings. Furthermore, the English translation granted access to the Italian language and its wealth of expressions and idioms to those English authors who wished to embellish their works with them, especially those in *Second Frutes*, without knowing the language (Simonini, *Italian Scholarship* 61; Yates, "Italian Teachers in Elizabethan England" 111). Such writers, who were neither learners nor experts of the Italian language, were not requesting a translation that could help them activate a grammatical reflection. Instead, they needed a rendering of the meaning to be sure that the way they were using Italian words, expressions, and idioms in their works was appropriate to the context and the cultural scene. Finally, Italian expatriates and residents in London would have been exposed to input in their native language. The dialogues and their paremias allowed them to refine their competence in English and reestablish or maintain a connection to their homeland, one that was becoming progressively attenuated.

Another aspect seems to contradict the principle of meaningful contextualization of paremias. A few chapters in both *Fruits* stand out for their collation of proverbs and proverbial phrases that are provided without contextualization and thus interrupt the flow of the conversation.[62] This occurs in *Firste Fruites* in chapter 3 (FF 73v–75r), chapter 18 (FF 21v–27r), and particularly in chapter 19 (FF 27r–34v). In this last chapter, the expressions, mostly taken from James Sanford's *The Garden of Pleasure*, are listed alphabetically by their first letter, on the model of Holyband's *The French Littelton* (Pignatti, *Etimologia e proverbio* 346). The beginning of the section provides a good example of the decontextualized organization of Florio's paremias:

> Orsù, io comincio.
> *Ama Dio et non falire, fa pur bene et lassa dire ché non mai potrai falire.*
> Certo bon principio.
> *Al medico et avocato non tener il ver celato.*
> *Aspettare e non venire, star nel letto e non dormire, servire e non gradire son tre cose da morire.*
> *A caval donato non guardar in bocca.* (FF 27r)
>
> Wel I begin.
> Love God and faile not, Do thou wel and let be said, so shalt thou never faile.
> Certis a good beginnyng.
> To tary for a think that cometh not, to lye a bed and sleepe not, to serve wel and not be accepted be three things to dy.
> Looke not at a geven horse in the mouth.

In *Second Frutes*, chapter 6 and parts of chapters 9 and 12 present similar lists of paremiac expressions collected through linguistic or semantic connections (SF 78–110, 138–49, 164–205).

Chapter Three

One instance of such a list comes from chapter 6, in which Stefano pronounces proverbs that refer to Italian cities (Wyatt, *The Italian Encounter* 176–78):

> **In Italia sono troppe feste,*
> *Troppe teste e troppe tempeste.*
> **La Lombardia è il giardino del mondo.*
> **Milan può far, Milan può dire.*
> *Ma non può far di acqua vino.*
> **Tutte le arme di Brescia non armeriano la paura.*
> **Pan padovano, vin vicentino, carne furlana, formaggio piacentino, trippe trevigiane e donne venetiane.*
> **Venetia, chi non ti vede non ti pretia,*
> *Ma chi ti vede ben gli costa.*
> **Bologna la grassa, ma Padova la passa.* (SF 106)
>
> In Italy, too many feasts doe raine,
> Too many stormes, too many a busy braine.
> Lombardy is the garden of the world.
> Millaine may doe, and Millaine may crake,
> But Millaine cannot wine of water make.
> All the armes of Brescia will not arme feare.
> Bread of Padova, wine of Vicentia, flesh of Furly, cheese of Placenza, tripes of Trevise, and women of Venice.
> Who sees not Venice cannot esteeme it,
> But he that sees it payes well for it.
> Fertile is Bologna, but Padova exceeds it.

Chapter 12 is the Petrarchan chapter of the second manual *par excellence* with its listed proverbs concerning matters of love. Silvestro's speech is full of references to Italian poets to praise the eternal value of love:

> **Ama e sarai amato.*
> **Chi non ama essendo amato commette gran peccato.*
> **Et amore è il vero pretio con che si compra*
> **L'aurea catena con che si lega* et
> **La vera calamita con che si trahe amore.* (SF 170)
>
> To love agree, thou lov'd shalt be.
> Who loves not and loved is, he doth (if anie) much amisse.
> For love is the price wherewith we buie,
> Love is the chaine wherewith we tie.
> Love is the adamant whereby we draw kinde love with us to lie.

Conversely, Pandolpho presents a plethora of paremias as he speaks out against love and women:

*L'amor di donna lieve è come vin di fiasco,
La sera è buono et la mattina è guasto.
*Di donna è et sempre fu natura
Odiar chi l'ama e chi non l'ama cura.
*... Sono simili a' cocodrilli
*Che per prender l'huomo piangono e, preso, lo divorano.
*Chi le fugge seguono et chi le segue fuggono.
*O come la bilancia che pende dove più riceve.
*O come il carbone, il quale o tinge o bruscia.
*O come il molino a vento che macina secondo il vento. (SF 174)

The wine of a flaggon and the love of a whore,
At evening is rich, at morning is poore.
It is and even was a woman's fashion,
To love a crosse, to crosse a loving passion.
... They are like cocodrills,
They weepe to winne and wonne they cause to dye.
Follow men flying and men following flye.
Like the ballance, where most it receiveth, there most it inclineth.
Like to a coale, which either burneth or besmeareth.
Like a windmill, which still doth go, as wind doth blow.

The exchange of lines between the two characters illustrates the difference between Petrarchan poetry (Silvestro), which is connected to literary enterprises, and anti-Petrarchan poetry (Pandolpho), which is expressed by means of common and popular wisdom.

Despite the value of anonymous lists of paremias for lexical purposes, dialogues provide more credible reproductions of linguistic usages in line with Florio's pedagogical objectives. In his letter to the English gentlemen in *Firste Fruites* and in the dedicatory epistle in *Second Frutes*, Florio writes that, through paremias, learners are able to achieve the best knowledge of the Italian language and culture. The learners acquire paremias inductively as lexical chunks and discrete units, and do not focus on the grammatical rules behind their structure. The contextual uses make it easier to extrapolate the expressions' meanings from the dialogues and relocate proverbs and proverbial phrases in appropriate contexts. At the same time, these expressions facilitate understanding of how language and culture work and ultimately allow for a more productive learning experience. Although mediated by the written form and thus, not completely spontaneous, Florio exposes his learners to an example of written language that could be defined as "scritto–parlato" ("written–spoken"), borrowing this definition from Giovanni Nencioni's work *Di scritto e di parlato*. Florio's language conveys a sense of naturalness and fluidity and his paremias succeed in demonstrating its liveliness and sociolinguistic aspects.

The Sources of Florio's Paremias and Dialogues

The situational approach that Florio adopts in his *Fruits* emphasizes the linguistic functions that a speaker can express in a variety of circumstances without the intermediation of grammar (Borello 160–61; Montini, "Teaching Italian" 524; Palermo and Poggiogalli 27).[63] Such an approach follows Erasmus's Latin teaching-dialogue model in his *Colloquia*, which is based on greeting *formulae*, brief conversations between different interlocutors, and exchanges of inquiries and replies (Matthiessen 110). Progressively expanded since its first edition in 1518 without the author's permission and despite the condemnation by the Sorbonne in 1526, *Colloquia* experienced great success and was reprinted many times while Erasmus was still alive. The work was indeed perceived as a collection of dialogues on social matters and moral behavior intended to prepare young people for life. Much like Erasmus's *Colloquia*, Florio's dialogues do not contain "le anonime e fredde frasi di un manuale scolastico, bensì espressioni che aderiscono ad una precisa realtà del momento e della quale anzi sono spesso una valida testimonianza" ("the anonymous and cold sentences of a school manual, but rather expressions that adhere to a precise reality in the moment and of which they are often a valid testimony"; Rossi, *Ricerche* 123; see also Vedovelli 93–99). Moreover, they have a "performative aspect" since the speakers become actors and convey linguistic and cultural messages in communicative contexts (Pfister 49; Pizzoli 74–76; Wyatt, *The Italian Encounter* 167). The link between the organization and objectives of Erasmus's work and Florio's manuals is evident, especially because the former provides Florio with a structured model of proverbs, sayings, and *sententiae* embedded within dialogic exchanges.

Another fundamental model for the organization and content of Florio's *Fruits* is Juan Luis Vives's *Linguae latinae exercitatio*, also known as *Los Dialogos*, published in 1538.[64] This text influences Florio in shaping a popular atmosphere, as well as in nourishing the public's requests for moral messages on human life and behavior. It presents twenty-five dialogues in Latin on the most common aspects of sixteenth-century Spanish society.[65] While immersing students in daily-life situations, Vives's grammar book guides learners progressively toward a comprehensive and pragmatic knowledge of Latin language and culture by means of easily-memorized "sententiolas" ("short *sententiae*"). According to Vives, memorization guarantees a more effective language learning process. Consequently, he invites students to learn paremias because they permit them to experience the language thoroughly, expose them to the habits of the target culture, and offer an elaborate way to contribute to conversations (Rossi, *Ricerche* 112).

Lodovico Guicciardini's *L'ore di ricreatione*, published in Antwerp in 1568, could be added to the list of fundamental references for Florio's language manuals (Rossi, *Ricerche* 129–39). Probably a source for Florio's dictionary as well, Guicciardini's work is a collection of 727 classical and contemporaneous short stories, selected according to three specific criteria, as Guicciardini declares in his letter to the readers: their pleasantness and facetiousness, their moral inclinations, and their supposed honest usefulness. By means of apothegms, paremias, mottos, parables, apologues, and *sententiae*, Guicciardini infuses popular and ethical wisdom into the stories, mostly placing moral assertions at their conclusion. Many of Florio's proverbs and proverbial phrases in both *Fruits* come from lists of paremias gathered in two chapters of *L'ore*: "Le sentenzie e' proverbi principali e più piacevoli del prefato Piovano" ("Sententious phrases and primary and pleasant proverbs of the aforementioned Piovano [Arlotto]") and "Ma poiché noi siamo venuti a' proverbii del Piovano, ne metteremo anche qui alquanti che parlando e scrivendo usava talvolta il nostro gran Boccaccio" ("But, since we have come to the point of Piovano's proverbs, we will place some of them here that at times our great Boccaccio used both in speaking and writing"; *L'ore* 77–78[66]). The others derive from the very captions of the stories: for instance, *Chi fa i fatti suoi non s'imbratta le mani* ("He that dooth his own busines, doth not defile his hands"; SF 10, 102; *L'ore* 54); *Le allegreze di questo mondo duran poco* ("The ioyes of this worlde dure but litle"; FF 32r; *L'ore* 254); and *Chi tutto vuol di rabbia muore* ("Who al wil have, through fransie dyeth"; FF 29r), which however presents a different second hemistich from Guicciardini's *Chi tutto il vuole tutto ei perde* ("He who wants all, loses all"; *L'ore* 365).[67]

Chapter Three

While Vives's work provides Florio with a pedagogical structure and immersive approach for his two language manuals, Guicciardini's offers a model for a profitable combination of instruction and delightfulness (Simonini, *Italian Scholarship* 90). Among innumerable examples, an instance from *Firste Fruites* helps to explain how Vives's didactic approach and Guicciardini's broader social intent combines in Florio's work. Two domestic workers talk to each other in chapter 11, devoted to conversing with a servant:

> Ascolta fratello, che fai tu?
> Perché mi domandate?
> Perché io vorei sapere.
> Adunche voi non lo saperete perché *colui che cerca l'altrui facende da tutti li savi è tenuto matto.*
> Certo, tu mi hai colto.
> Perdonatemi, vi dico il vero.
> Così mi pare. (FF 9*v*)

> Hearken brother, what do you?
> Wherefore do you aske me?
> Because I would know.
> Then you shal not know, for because he that seekes to know other men's affayres, of all wise men is counted a foole.
> Now truly you have hit me.
> Pardon me, I tel you the truth.
> So me thinks.

The conversation is both pedagogically useful and socially advantageous. On one hand, it teaches that one risks being rude and making the other person uncomfortable if one inquires too much. On the other, the dialogue does not create any tension between the two speakers, mostly because the paremia "translates" one of the people's opinion anonymously. The proverb embedded in the dialogue offers a way to both communicate successfully and behave delightfully at all levels of social classes (Montini, "Proverbs in John Florio's *Fruits*" 254). This is particularly evident if one considers the audience of Florio's manuals, mostly aristocratic and thus, engaging with servants and maids on a daily basis. As Florio states in the *Epistle to the Reader* in *Second Frutes*, paremias are "the pith, the properties, the proofes, the purities, the elegancies, as the commonest so the commendablest phrases of a language." Hence, "to use them is a grace, to understand them a good" (SF *A1r*).[68] Much like Vives and Guicciardini, Florio offers practical uses of paremias "in actual conversational situations" aiming to contribute to people's societal appeal (Florio, *A Worlde of Wordes* [2013] xiii).

When considering Florio's sources for the paremias and the structure of his two *Fruits*, his acquaintance with Italian literature and with the most well-known authors of pedagogical texts emerges clearly. Dante, Petrarca, Boccaccio, Machiavelli, Ariosto, Tasso, Bruno, as well as Andrea Alciati's *Emblemata* and Cornazzano's *Proverbi in facetie* all contribute to the paremias listed in *Firste Fruites* and *Second Frutes* (Gamberini, *Lo studio* 112–13).[69] Two other crucial sources, Stefano Guazzo's 1574 *La civil conversatione* and 1586 *Dialoghi piacevoli*, provide paremiac examples.[70] In particular, *Dialoghi piacevoli*, under section five "Delle imprese" ("On devices"), reports a conversation about proverbs and their use. According to Guazzo, vulgar and popular proverbs disgrace the tone of high-standard works, but those gathered by Solomon or used by Plato, Plutarchus, and other Greek authors offer moral and allegorical interpretations. They are particularly useful because they are "ben incorporati d'un diletto giovevole e d'un giovamento dilettevole" ("well equipped with pleasant delight and delightful pleasantness"; 50*v*). In like manner, Vignali's "letter in proverbs" is a foundational resource for both *Firste Fruites* and *Second Frutes*, as well as *Giardino di ricreatione*. Out of a total of 24 alike or similar paremias between Vignali and Florio, eight merge in *Firste Fruites*[71]—one is shared by the second manual.[72] All of the others appear only in *Second Frutes* and, if a paremia features in *Giardino*,[73] generally its form is more similar to the one listed by Vignali than its equivalent in *Second Frutes*.[74] It is arguable that the Anglo-Italian author accessed Vignali's letter and consequently, acquainted himself with its many paremias through his knowledge of another work by Arsiccio Intronato. By the end of the sixteenth century, Vignali's dialogue *La cazzaria* (composed around 1525–26) was well known in England, although just a few undated copies were released in the Italian peninsula. Florio demonstrates his knowledge of this text in *A Worlde of Wordes*, in which he includes the entry "cazzaria" and describes it as "a treatise or discourse of pricks."[75]

Many of the paremias that Florio could find in Vignali's letter are also present in Anton Francesco Doni's works, specifically *I marmi* and *La Zucca* (Rees). In *I marmi*, Doni does not introduce

Chapter Three

his proverbs formally; they are rather interspersed in the narration without being set apart. In *La Zucca*, however, the paremiac expressions can be extracted more easily because the author usually introduces them with formulas like "dice bene il proverbio" ("the proverb says it well"), "si dice per proverbio/generalmente" ("it is said with a proverb/generally"), or "si verifica il proverbio" ("the proverb is confirmed"). Moreover, Doni explicitly illustrates or provides a narrative context for 135 expressions in the three sections of his work, *Cicalamenti, Baie,* and *Chiachiere*. Florio shares with Doni's text fourteen of his paremias in *Firste Fruites* (of which two are also listed in the second manual) and nineteen expressions of those listed in *Second Frutes*. Some of these paremias are identical in both *La Zucca*, especially the section *Baie*, and Florio's manuals, despite minor differences.[76] As occurs for Vignali's letter, the paremias listed in *Giardino di ricreatione* resemble the syntax and morphology of the expressions that Doni employs more than those in *Firste Fruites* or *Second Frutes*.[77]

Given the tenor of *Firste Fruites*, some of these paremias display the profound influence of the Spanish euphuistic author Bishop Antonio de Guevara, who in 1529 wrote forty-eight chapters on Marcus Aurelius's life titled *Libro aureo de Marco Aurelio, emperador y eloquentissimo orador* (Policardi 75; Yates, *John Florio* 39–41).[78] Florio does not translate de Guevara's text directly from Spanish, but instead through an Italian rendering of the original work. Among those translations readily available for him at the time, he probably consulted the 1542 work by Mambrino Roseo da Fabriano (de Guevara, *Vita di Marco Aurelio*) or the many editions (1553, 1555, 1556, 1562, and beyond) published in the printing press of Francesco Portonaris da Trino (de Guevara, *Aureo libro di Marco Aurelio*; see also Grendler 300–1, 422–24). Portonaris explains that anyone reading his translation would acquire useful suggestions, concrete rules of life, notable phrases, remarkable sayings, meaningful *sententiae*, and illustrative stories (*A*ir). Indeed, de Guevara's work is filled with recommendations for princes on how to lead a virtuous and upstanding life, as well as on how to govern wisely for the benefit of the people. The primary source of this guidance is Marcus Aurelius, whose letters, writings, and sayings constitute the resource of moral teachings and reflections. In Florio's first manual, all *sententiae*, sayings, and paremias from chapter 36 and the majority from chapters 37 and 38 come from de Guevara's volume. The main topics from this section are God, the church and its ministers, princes and rulers, and human life, as the following examples illustrate:

> Bel detto del detto autore.
> *Iddio non si può ingannare con parole, né corompere con doni, né convincere con prieghi, né spaventar con minaccie, né satisfargli con scuse perché lui sa tutti i pensieri del huomo.*
> Bel detto del detto autore.
> *Le guerre civili le più volte si levano per la superbia de' magiori che per la disobedientia de' minori.* (FF 80v)
>
> A fine saying of the said author.
> God can not be deceyved with woordes, nor corrupted with gyftes, nor overcome with prayers, neither feared with threatenynges, nor satisfied with scuses, for he knoweth al the thoughtes of man.
> A fine saying of the said author.
> The civil warres are often tymes raised through the pride of the greatest than through the disobedience of the least.

The expressions gathered in Florio's chapter 37 from *Firste Fruites*, which is devoted to Plutarchus's political practice for Roman Emperor Caesar Nerva Trajanus, might be inspired by de Guevara's chapter XXXVI in the first book ("Chi fu il grande filosofo Plutarco, quai parole egli disse all'imperator Traiano, et come il buon Prencipe è capo della Repubblica," "Who was the great philosopher Plutarchus, which words he said to Emperor Trajanus, and how the good prince is the head of the Republic"; FF 55r–56v). One of Florio's expressions exhorts people to love genuinely and constantly much like a good emperor should do:

> *Colui che ama di cuore non diviene arogante e nelle prosperità, né si ritira ne la contraria fortuna, non si lamenta nella povertà, non si affligge del poco favore, non si parte nella persecutione, et finalmente l'amor et la vita non hanno fine fin alla sepoltura.* (FF 83v)
>
> He that loveth hartily becometh not arrogant in prosperity, neither withdraweth himselfe in contrary fortunes time, doth not lament in povertie, doth not dispayre through litle favour, doth not depart in tyme of persecution, and lastly love and life end not untyl the grave.

In order to provide the readers with a translation of the Italian quotations from Marcus Aurelius in de Guevara's book, Florio probably read the many English editions of de Guevara's book translated from French by Sir John Bourchier in 1536 (de Guevara,

The golden boke). Among them, Florio might have accessed the 1566 or the 1573 editions, both crafted in the London printing press of John Awdeley, later expanded by Sir Thomas North in his 1557 *The diall of princes* (Franzero 66). Critics argue that Florio's translation of all of these expressions was an intermediary between de Guevara's *Libro aureo* and the emergence of English euphuism, which would reach its efflorescence with John Lyly and his two works, entitled *Euphues: The Anatomy of Wit* (1579) and *Euphues and his England* (1580) (Clarence; Jeffery 117–32; Tilley; Yates, "Italian Teachers in Elizabethan England" 112–13).

Solomon's and Yeshua Ben Sira's Paremias in Firste Fruites

Florio draws some proverbial phrases in *Firste Fruites* from Solomon's *Proverbs* and from *Ecclesiasticus*, also known as the Book of Yeshua (or Jesus) Ben Sira. The two Sapiential books, which fill Florio's eighteenth chapter ("Sentenze umane et divine"; FF 22v–23r), were "the only surviving exemplars of the 'normal' or 'conventional' or even 'lower' wisdom that was the didactic presentation of collection of proverbs" (Sanders 3: footnote 1; see also Corley; Lévi; Sanders 3–26; Skehan and Di Lella 40–45). The organization of the paremias within a conclusive and distinctive section in the manuals recalls the thematic arrangement in the Book of Ben Sira, that is, groups of poetic proverbs conveying practical advice and moral teachings in the form of a discourse, rather than shared as individual sayings (Sanders 15).

More specifically, an opening formula introduces these paremias and establishes their religious origins: "Io comincierò con certe sentenze scritte da Salomone, e da Iesù figliol di Sirach; io comincio" ("I wyl beginne with certaine sentences written by Solomon and by Jesus the sonne of Sirach; I beginne"; FF 22v). The section abounds with numerical paremias and, in particular, with expressions composed of four listed items. Of these items, the first three are associated with a specific aspect, while the fourth represents the opposite. The repeated structure of such expressions and their narrative development make them easily memorable; moreover, the logical concatenation of thoughts and the presence of examples derived from everyday life or aspects of human behavior contribute to their efficacy in proving a point.

From Solomon's *Proverbs*, Florio selects the nineteenth expression on those things that are inexplicable, and changes it slightly

Firste Fruites and *Second Frutes*

in order to generalize the original concept (Roth). This proverb first mentions a number, second a characteristic, and then the list of items that exemplify the characteristic in the quantity originally mentioned:

> Ci sono tre cose che non si possono sapere et la quarta nessuno può intendere, i passi de una aquila volante nel aire, la via de un serpente passando una rocca, la via d'una nave sopra il mare e la via de un giovine ne la sua gioventù. (FF 22v)

> There be three things that can not be knowen, and the fourth no man is able to understand: the steps of an eagle fleeing in the ayre, the waye of a serpent over a rocke, the path of a ship in the sea, and the life of a young man in his youth.

In Brucioli's 1533 *Annotationi*, which was a source for *Queen Anna's New World of Words* (Wyatt, *The Italian Encounter* 415) and may have been one for *Second Frutes* as well, the proverb reads:

> Queste tre cose sono mirabili a me et quattro che io non conobbi. La via de l'aquila nel cielo, la via del serpente sopra 'l sasso, la via de la nave nel cuore del mare, et la via de l'huomo ne la giovane. (Ch. XXX: vv. 18–19)

> These three things are incredible to me and four that I did not know: the path of the eagle in the air, the waye of the serpent on the rock, the path of the ship in the heart of the sea, and the trace of a man in a young girl.

In the other integral translation of the Bible by Giovanni Diodati, which Florio accessed for his dictionary (Wyatt, *The Italian Encounter* 416), the text of the paremia is similar and follows Brucioli's structure (Fiume, *Giovanni Diodati*, "Giovanni Diodati"):

> Queste cose mi sono occulte, anzi io non conosco queste quattro: la traccia dell'aquila nell'aria, la traccia del serpente sopra 'l sasso, la traccia della nave in mezzo del mare, e la traccia dell'huomo nella giovane.

> These things are hidden to me, indeed I do not know these four: the path of the eagle in the air, the path of the serpent on the rock, the path of the ship in the middle of the sea, and the trace of a man in a young girl.

Three other paremias elaborate upon those expressions that Florio read in Solomon's *Proverbs*. The first one of the list is comprised of six members and appears to follow Brucioli's text quite faithfully:

> Sei cose ci sono che Iddio ha in odio et la settima lui ha in abominatione, ciò è: ochi alti, la lingua bugiarda, le mani che spargeno il

> *sangue, i piedi veloci per correre a far male, il cuore che macchina iniquità, il testimonio falso, e colui che mette contentione fra fratelli.* (FF 22v)
>
> There are six things that God hates, and the seventh he abhors, that is: sublime eyes, a lying tongue, hands that scatter blood, feet fast to run and hurt, a heart that drives iniquity, a false witness, and one who puts contentment among brothers.

Brucioli's proverb follows:

> *Sei cose sono quelle che ha in odio il signore et la settima abominatione de l'anima di quello. Gli occhi sublimi, la lingua mendace et le mani che spargono il sangue de lo innocente. Cuore che pensa l'inique cogitationi, piedi che si affrettano di correre al male. Quello che parla le falsità testimone mendace, et quello che mette contentione fra i frategli.* (Ch. VI: vv. 15–18)
>
> Six things are those that the lord hates and the seventh abomination of his soul. The sublime eyes, the mendacious tongue and the hands that scatter the blood of the innocent. A heart that thinks iniquitous thoughts, feet that hurry to run to evil. The mendacious witness who speaks falsehoods and the one who puts contentment among brothers.

The content of Florio's paremia does not change from Brucioli's, and its members, although in a different order, are the same. Florio, though, softens the aberration of the hands that scatter blood because he does not include "de lo innocente" ("of the innocent") in Brucioli. He simplifies the expression's penultimate member since the person that God despises is just a false witness ("testimonio falso") and not a mendacious one who says false things ("che parla le falsità testimone mendace") in Brucioli. Moreover, he makes the person run to do evil ("correre a far male") and not simply run toward the evil ("correre al male") as it is in Brucioli's text.

The other two paremias are loose interpretations of Solomon's expressions:

> *Ci sono tre cose che mai sono satisfatte, et la quarta non dice mai satis, una donna che non è temperata, la terra non è mai sciutta, inferno non è mai satisfatto et il fuoco non ha mai legna assai.* (FF 22v)
>
> There be three things never satisfied, and the fourth never saith [s]o, a woman that is untemperate, the earth that is drie, Hel is never satisfied, and the fire hath never wood yenough.

In Brucioli's editions of *Proverbs*, the text of the expression, coming from the second to last chapter, reads:

> *Il sepolchro e la vulva sterile, la terra non è satiata de l'acque, et il fuoco non dice basta.* (Ch. XXX: v. 16)
>
> The sepulcher and the sterile vulva, the earth is not satiated with the waters, and the fire does not say enough.

Other than eliminating attributes (the reference to the sepulcher) and adding others (Hell that is not satisfied) to the original structure of the expression, Florio provides his paremia with an introduction ("There be three things never satisfied, and the fourth never saith so") that tags it as a numerical paremia. The third expression from Solomon's *Proverbs* already presents a numerical introductory formula in the original text:

> *Per tre cose la terra spesse volte è flagellata, et la quarta è intolerabile, quando che un servitore è fatto signore sopra i beni del suo signore, un pazo cibato con delicateze, un giovine dato a la concupiscentia et una servente fatta herede de la sua signora.* (FF 22v)
>
> For three [t]hinges the earth is oftentimes plagued, and the fourth is intollerable, a servant made lorde over his maister's goods, a foole pampered with delicate meates, a young man addicted to concupiscence, and a damsel made heire unto her mistresse.

Florio may have read the expression in Brucioli's work:

> *Per tre cose si muove la terra et per quattro non può sostenere. Per il servo quando regna et per lo stolto quando sia satollato di pane. Per la odiata quando sia maritata et per la serva quando sia herede de la sua padrona.* (Ch. XXX: vv. 21–23)
>
> For three things the earth is moved, and the fourth it cannot tolerate. For the servant when he rules and for the fool when he is full of bread. For the despised woman when she marries and for the servant when she is heir to her mistress.

Florio modifies one of the three members of the original expression, substituting a despised woman when she marries with a man addicted to concupiscence. He makes the expression say that all of the members are not simply intolerable, but they even plague the earth, which is a much stronger reaction than that expressed by the earth's uncomfortable feeling in Solomon's paremia.

When considering the Book of Ben Sira, Florio mentions openly that just one numerical paremia comes from the Sapiential book. Specifically, the expression appears in its chapter 26 (28), which collects sayings and proverbs on hazards to integrity and friendship, as well as people's proper behavior in society:

> *Due cose, dice Sirach, mi scorrucciano et la terza mi dispiace, quando che homini savii sono disprezati, quando che esperti soldati sono in povertà, quando che un homo declina da la virtù al vitio.* (FF 23r)
>
> Two things saith Sirach, makes me angry, and the third doth displease me, when wise men are despised, when expert souldiours are in povertie, when a man declineth from virtue to vice.

Despite Florio's statement, two other expressions recorded in *Firste Fruites*'s chapter 18 and mentioning that which God likes or dislikes derive from chapter 25 (1–2) in the Book of Ben Sira:

> *Tre cose piacciono a Dio et anche a gli huomini, concordia fra fr[a]telli, amicitia fra vicini, accordo fra il marito e moglie.* (FF 23r)
>
> Three things please both God and man, concord betwene brethren, amitie betweene neighbours, agreement betweene [m]an and wife.
>
> *Tre cose dispiacciono a Dio et a gli huomini, un homo povero superbo, un homo ricco bugiardo et un homo vechio inamorato.* (FF 23r)[79]
>
> Three thinges displease God and man, a poore man proude, a riche man a lyer, and an olde man in love.

The first paremia ("Tre cose piacciono a Dio") comments on topics very common in ancient Israel and for second-century Jews, including close family bonds, kinsmen, blessings of a good marriage, and suitability between husband and wife. Opposite to this, the second paremia ("Tre cose dispiacciono a Dio") discloses Ben Sira's hatred of pride, especially in poor people who should have little to boast of, and of lying, particularly in the rich since, given their status, they should not be inclined to fraudulent activity. The libidinous old man who should be a model of wisdom and virtue is equally despicable to Ben Sira for not respecting his place in society and life.[80] Generally, the structure of these three paremiac borrowings is maintained in Florio's text. However, the narrative voice in two of the listed paremias changes. In the original text, Ben Sira speaks in the first person, hence the aspects that he likes or dislikes are personally enjoyable or regrettable to him. Florio adapts the last two quotations to the structure of the conversation in chapter 18 and attributes them to God. For these same two, he provides a more general appeal, as he relates them not only to a religious entity, God, but also to all of humanity ("a Dio et anche a gli uomini," "to God and also men," and "a Dio et a gli huomini," "to God and to men"). Only the quotation whose origins Florio explicitly states presents a structure with the first person ("makes me [Ben Sira] angry").

Translating Paremias

The introductory quotation of this chapter from Giacomo Leopardi captures an important aspect of the culture of translating paremias.[81] The poet from Recanati raises the question of how paremias can be translated without distorting their original meaning and betraying their effectiveness and communicability for the receiving party. Leopardi admits that it is almost impossible to reproduce the paremia's same linguistic and cultural experience from the original to the target language. On one hand, a literal translation guarantees a word-by-word correspondence that tries to preserve the rhythm but, most of the time, leaves the meaning of the paremia incomprehensible in the second language (Albanese, "I centomila miliardi di proverbi" 9). On the other hand, a paraphrase of the paremia's message reproduces an effect that echoes that of the original (Benjamin 76) by capturing the intentions behind its meaning (Appiah 390). However, such a translation would not do justice to the expression's condensed structure and to its metaphorical interpretation, ultimately resulting in a loss of the paremia's original form and message.[82] Despite a "linguistic clothing" that is not easily interchangeable and a difficulty in rendering the cultural background informing paremias, proverbs and proverbial phrases give shape to an "imaginative world unlimited" that opens up intercultural comparisons (Wyatt, *The Italian Encounter* 166). As Cesare Segre states in his *Le strutture e il tempo*, these imaginative worlds are "possibili infinite parafrasi «oneste» (cioè attentamente fedeli) di uno stesso testo" ("a possible infinite 'honest' [that is, carefully and faithfully rendered] paraphrases of the same text"; 48), which adapt to a specific context and interpretation.

Florio faces these same issues when he translates the Italian paremias of his *Fruits* into their equivalents in English. He aims to create a productive translation that would preserve the text and, at

Chapter Three

the same time, make it readable to English speakers without eliminating cultural and social elements.[83] In *A Worlde of Wordes*, Florio explains the verb "tradurre" as follows: "To bring, to turne, to convert, to convey from one place to another, to bring over. Also to translate out of one tongue into another. Also to bring, convert or transport from one to another, to leade over, to displace and remove from one place to another, to transpose." His definition evidently stems from the etymology of the verb and acknowledges the various interpretations of the word. Specifically, what is considered the most established way to interpret the term (namely, to translate from one language to another) comes after the most general definition of shift or passage from one dimension to another. As Florio openly declares in chapter 18 of his *Firste Fruites*, he does not support literal linguistic translations, especially if paremias are the objects of this operation:

> Ma avvertite prima che un proverbio italiano a dirlo in inglese non può haver quella gratia come ha in italiano, e anche un proverbio inglese a dirlo in italiano non ha quella gratia come ha nel suo natural linguaggio. (FF 27*r*)
>
> But marke first that an Italian proverb, to say it in English, can not have that grace, as it hath in Italian, and also an Englishe proverbe, to say it in Italian, can not have that grace as it hath in their natural language.

In Florio's opinion, paremias are apparently less translatable than other expressions since translation causes their grace to be diminished. That is, their elegance, beauty, and effortless fluency are reduced when their component words shift from one language to another. Such aspects belong to the original culture and language that produced the paremia and are not easily reproduceable in other cultures and languages (Wyatt, *The Italian Encounter* 176).[84] However, Florio continues that translating paremias is still a useful practice:

> Quello non importa, pur che habbi qualche senso con sé, non può se non dare uno certo diletto al ascoltatore. (FF 27*r*)
>
> That skylleth not [i.e., the impossibility of rendering the grace of the original language in the target language], so that it have some sense with it, it can not but yeelde a certaine delight unto the hearer.

As long as the paremia still makes sense, pleasantness can be transmitted and culture interiorized.

It follows that Florio's method of translating paremias is strictly connected to whether he wishes to render their original "grace" in Italian into English or whether he prefers to focus on their contextual meaningfulness. The choice he makes cannot be generalized for *Firste Fruites* or *Second Frutes* in their entirety. Yet, for the majority of translated paremias, Florio adopts a distinctive technique that complies with the diverse objectives of the two language manuals. In *Firste Fruites*, the lower level of the learners' language knowledge and the necessity to present every single aspect of the target language and culture compels him to a more frequent word-by-word translation. The author resorts to two alternatives, even compromising at times the fluidity of the expression in the target language. He opts for a literal translation that does not reproduce the expression's rhythmic and prosodic structure, and thus makes less evident those aspects that are immediately recognizable in a paremia. Alternatively, he adopts a literal translation that preserves the paremia's rhythmic scheme quite faithfully yet rearranges its syntactic structure. In both instances, the result may be a non-paremiac expression for which a metaphorical interpretation is not necessary and which, therefore, fails to reproduce a crucial characteristic of proverbs and proverbial phrases. In contrast, a translation of the paremias' meaning is more frequent in *Second Frutes*. Here, translation does not aim to help learners understand the formal aspects of the language, which they have already acquired by engaging with the dialogues of the first manual. Nor does the translation intend to preserve the expression's original rhythmic and syntactical structure. Instead, it represents an explicative paraphrase that offers learners a way to understand the paremia's message in accordance with its figurative or contextual uses and to reflect on the various topics of conversation. Such a translation privileges semantic features over linguistic ones and reproduces pragmatic, functional, and communicative effects, although the specificity of the original terms is lost.

Firste Fruites

In the first manual, the English proverbs generally do not convey the metaphorical or conventionalized meaning of the original in Italian. The following pair comes from chapter 6 on familiar ways of speaking:

> *Altri fanno conto inanzi l'hoste.* (FF 6*v*)
> Others make their account before the host.

The English expression is a word-by-word translation of the Italian. If one considers Augusto Arthaber's dictionary of proverbs in its 1929 edition, the expression *He that reckons without his host, must reckon again* conveys a metaphorical meaning, while also presenting a topic-comment structure and an organization with two hemistiches as is typical of proverbs (319). Similarly, Jerzy Gluski's expression in his 1971 multilingual and comparative dictionary of proverbs, *To reckon without one's host*, expresses a more effective message in English than Florio's (15–31; ODEP, s.v. *reckons*; Vassano 31–32). The same chapter in *Firste Fruites* offers another example of a literal translation for a common Italian expression:

> *Chi troppo abraccia poco stringe.* (FF 6*v*)
> Who imbraceth much litle closeth.

Arthaber's proverbs, *He that too much embraceth, holds little* and *He that grasps at too much, holds nothing fast* (1371), do not differ much from Florio's English translation. The three of them translate the proverb word for word and do not evoke the expression's figurative meaning, which could be rendered as Gluski and *The Oxford Dictionary of English Proverbs* report: *Grasp all, lose all* (26–11; ODEP, s.v. *grasp*).[85]

In chapter 15, while two interlocutors talk about corruption and the power of money in societal life and relationships, they refer to a proverb that Florio translates literally:

> Ma *dal detto al fatto ci è un grande tratto.* (FF 18*v*)
> But from the said unto the deed there is a gret throw.

The expression could be read in Jacques Yver's 1578 *A courtlie controversie of Cupids cantles*, and also appears in James Sanford's *The Garden of Pleasure* (*From worde to deed is a great space*; 210) and in Torriano's *Select Italian proverbs* (*From the word to the deed, there is a great distance*; 44). Florio inserts the expression in the dialogue to show the correspondence between Italy and England (Gluski 1–1; ODEP, s.v. *word*). Just after one of the speakers pronounces the paremia, the other answers as follows:

> Questo proverbio è vero et usato.
> Ogni dì si usa in Inghilterra. (FF 18*v*)
>
> This proverb is true and used.
> It is used dayly in England.

The interlocutor draws a line that parallels the paremia in Italian with its English equivalent and highlights the commonality of the paremiac expression in both countries. England and Italy share similar paremiac traditions and hence, similar cultures, despite the geographical distance between them.

Florio also opts for a faithful translation for the aforementioned lists of paremias based on numerical members in chapters 18 and 33. Their translations reproduce the original syntax, with minor changes due to the differences between the two languages. From chapter 18:

> *Quatro vie ci sono che nessuno può star fermo sopra, sopra luoghi bagnati, sopra il giaccio, sopra gloria et ambitione, sopra la beltà di una donna.* (FF 24r)
>
> Foure wayes there be, that no man can stand sure on, upon moyst places, upon yse, upon glory and ambition, upon the beautie of a woman.

From chapter 33:

> *Tre bone regole per ogniuno, reggi il tuo volere, tempera la tua lingua, rafrena il tuo ventre.* (FF 75r)
>
> Three good rules for every man, rule thyne owne wyl, temper thy tongue, refrayne thyne owne belly.

In the last paremia from chapter 33, Florio interprets one of the expression's members and unwraps the metonymy that characterizes the Italian original. Hence, his translation is not literal:

> *Tre sorte de huomini possono mentire per auctorità, un medico, un vechio et un che è stato lontano.* (FF 75r)
>
> Three sortes of men may lye by aucthoritie, a phisition, an olde man, and a travayler.

In fact, the traveler belongs to the category of people who have been far away ("un che è stato lontano"). Thus, Florio solves the possible ambiguity of the paremia's last part in the eyes of an Englishman by interpreting it and associating its meaning with a concrete figure.

Occasionally, Florio inserts linguistic material, and he likely does this to make the meaning of the paremia clearer or to offer a synonymic word to his readers. In chapter 11, the translation of a proverbial phrase evidences this practice:

> Ma a *chi non ha danari non ha credito se non di bastonade.* (FF 9v)
> But who hath no money hath no credit but of blowes or stripes.

The word "stripes" is not included in the Italian version but appears in the English translation as a synonym of "blows." Elsewhere in *Firste Fruites*, Florio provides a translation that is half literal and half an interpretation of its conventionalized meaning. From chapter 14 comes a proverb that will also be analyzed later for its contextual significance:

> *Ogniuno tira l'aqua al suo molino*, così fate voi. (FF 14*r*)
> Every man draweth water to hym selfe, and so do you.

Florio preserves the paremia's structure as well as its metaphorical meaning. However, the metaphor in the English version is not concluded since the author does not translate "al suo molino" ("to one's own mill"); he prefers expressing the meaning of drawing water to oneself and hence directs the focus on one's own advantage. In chapter 19, the same paremia in Italian appears with a plural subject:

> *Tutti tirano l'aqua al suo molino.* (FF 33*v*)
> Every one draw water to theyr myl.

This time, the English translation is literal. The structure is also more similar to the current form of the expression, as well as to those historical ones that Gluski reports (28–14: *Every miller draws water to his own mill*; see also ODEP, s.v. *draw*: *To draw water to one's mill*). It is likely that the insertion of the paremia in the decontextualized list of the nineteenth chapter does not require an indication of its figurative meaning. Conversely, the contextualized situation of chapter 14 allows for all of the levels of the paremias' meanings to emerge, including the situational one that should help the language learners understand the paremia's message.

A pair from the same chapter 19 illustrates an act of interpretation forced by the presence of regional linguistic elements:

> *Le bone parole ongino, le cative pongino.* (FF 31*v*)
> Good woords annoynt a man, the yl woordes kyl a man.

In Italian, the form of the two verbs provides information about the origin of the paremia. The absence of anaphonesis clearly indicates that Florio did not select the paremia from a Tuscan source. In fact, the two verbs would have been "ungono" and "pungono" in the Florentine vernacular; the ending in "-ino" suggests instead a Northern provenance. In the English translation, reproducing the original rhyme between the two verbs ("ongino"–"pongino") would have been difficult. Therefore, Florio adds "a man" at the end of the first hemistich to supplement it with an identical rhyme in English. With a method that characterizes *Second Frutes* more, he also intensifies the semantic meaning of the verb "pungere" ("to sting") by translating it into "kill."

In chapter 19, Florio provides the majority of the listed paremias (specifically 273) with the most faithful translation. An example is the following pair that reproduces what today is known as *To kill two flies with one flap* (ODEP, s.v. *kill*):

> È bella cosa pigliar due colombi con una fava. (FF 29v)
> It is a prety thing to catch two doves with one beane.

In *The Booke of Merry Riddles*, an anonymous collection of riddles, comic pronouncements, and useful paremias from which Florio consistently drew examples in English, the listed paremia shows the same structure as that of Florio's and the same introductory formula on the expression's validity: *It is a goodly thing to take two pigeons with one beane* (98). Another paremia translated word by word comes from Boccaccio's *Decameron*, as noted earlier, and is also present in Brusantino's *Le cento novelle* (Dec. III.4.27; CN 145):

> Chi va in letto senza cena tutta la notte si dimena. (FF 29r)
> Who goeth to bed supperlesse shal turne and tosse al night.

A comparison with Arthaber's option, *Who goes to bed supperless, all night tumbles and tosses* (255; also in Gluski 38–17; ODEP, s.v. *goes*), shows how Florio's literal translation eliminates the paremia's original rhyme. However, Florio does not make the expression lose its rhythm since he reproduces the two hemistiches. It is interesting to note that Florio's translation of the same paremia is different in his 1620 English rendering of Boccaccio's text, *The Decameron, containing an hundred pleasant novels*:

> When folke go superles to bed, either they walke in their sleepe, or being awake, talke very idely. (91v)

There, the author does not translate the paremia faithfully, but rather offers a rendering of its message. The consequences of not eating supper are twofold: either it makes sleep difficult or it causes one to stay awake and unable to talk properly.[86]

When considering proverbial phrases, Florio exempts them from a literal translation, given their greater ambiguity not only in content but also in vocabulary. He usually provides a translation of

157

Chapter Three

their contextualized meaning and chooses not to show his beginner students morphological elements and syntactical structures. The following pair comes from chapter 10:

> Voi sete pronto per *darmi la baia*. (FF 8v)
> You are redy to mocke me.

The proverbial phrase is not translated word for word as "to give me a teasing," but is paraphrased in the meaning it conveys, which is to make fun of, fool, or scoff at someone (GDLI, s.v. *bàia* [1]: *voler la bàia* or *recarsi, mettersi qualcosa in bàia*; Voc. Cr., s.v. *baia*). The translation eliminates the different stages of the paremiac interpretation and directly provides its conventional meaning.

Second Frutes

If in *Firste Fruites* Florio translates almost all paremias literally or makes minor additions and/or modifications, in *Second Frutes* he generally renders the meaning of the expressions he uses. The Italian original paremia and its English translation share their contextual meanings since they both appear in the same context; however, they do not share their linguistic elements.

Some of the paremias that Florio employs in his second manual come from the first consistent collection of English proverbs, John Heywood's 1546 *A dialogue*. As Florio declares in his letter to the reader: "The Greekes and Latines thanke Erasmus, and our Englishmen make much of Heywood" (SF A1r). Heywood's preface to his work, indeed, recalls the concepts of fruitfulness, general appeal, profit, and usefulness that Florio emphasizes in his second manual:

> Among other things profiting in our tongue—
> Those which much may profit both old and young,
> Such as on their fruit will feed or take hold—
> Are our common plain pithy proverbs old.
> Some sense of some of which, being bare and rude,
> Yet to fine and fruitful effect they allude.
> And their sentences include so large a reach,
> That almost in all things good lessons they teach. (B2)

A telling example of Florio's translation in *Second Frutes* borrowed from Heywood's work concerns a very common paremia both during Florio's time and today:

Chi va piano va sano. (SF 10)
Soft fier makes sweet malte.

The English paremia evidently follows one of Heywood's lines expressing the idea of moderation and reflection in marrying someone: "Then, such folk see, *soft fire maketh sweet malt,* and that deliberation doth men assist, before they wed, to beware of had I wist" (*A dialogue* Pt. I, Ch. II).[87] The expression's conventionalized meaning corresponds exactly to the conventionalized meaning of the Italian equivalent: something done slowly guarantees a better success and no harm (GDLI, s.v. *piano* [2], n. 34). Language learners would have understood the meaning of the Italian paremia immediately, even though there is no correspondence between the words of the two paremias.

In *Second Frutes*, at times the English translation adds more meanings to the original Italian paremia, as occurs in the following example from chapter 5:

A. Volete voi giuocar a dadi?
S. *Signor no, perché *donna, vino e dado rende l'huomo rovinato.* (SF 72)

A. Will you play at dice?
S. No sir, for women, wine, and dice, will bring a man to lice.

The Italian paremia refers to the adverse consequences that a man faces if he cherishes women, dice, and wine, three things that made Cecco Angiolieri content in his famous sonnet *Tre cose solamente.*[88] The English translation establishes a rhyme ("dice"–"lice") where, in the Italian original, there was only a consonance ("dado"–"rovinato"). Moreover, the word "lice" makes it explicit which "ruin" men experience. Among the possible downfalls of such a dissolute behavior is poverty, which means lack of personal hygiene and therefore, lice. In one instance from chapter 6, Florio ingeniously renders in English the play of words in the Italian version:

*Molti de' nostri che *vanno messeri e tornano seri.* (SF 90)
Men who goe out maisters and returne clearks.

The Italian paremia features a dichotomy between "messeri" ("masters") and "seri," where the latter does not have any meaning. However, because it lacks a part thanks to the apheresis, namely the letters "mes" from "messeri," the word "seri" suggests downgraded "messeri." Since this relationship is untranslatable with two

Chapter Three

equivalent words in English, Florio conveys the most comprehensible meaning possible for his public. An analysis of the context in which the paremia is used clarifies Florio's attempt. Being that Italy did not have a good reputation in civil and behavioral matters, Stefano deems it important to provide guidance to Pietro on how to negotiate these societal aspects during his imminent trip to Italy. Pietro promises not to depart as a respectable person and return as lesser:

> [I]o la prego con le maggior forze che io mi trovo a voler darmi qualche buon ricordo, o civil precetto, come io habbia a governarmi in questa mia preregrinatione, acciò io possa imparar qualche cosa di buono et alla fine tornar a casa con honore, e non come molti de' nostri che *vanno messeri e tornano seri*. (SF 90)

> I beseech you as hartely as may be that it will please you to give me some good remembrance or civill precepts, how I shal behave my selfe in this my travaile, to the end I may learne some good thing and at least returne with some credit, and not doo as many of our country men who goe out maisters and returne clearks.

The degrading influence that Italy is deemed to have over human souls is rendered through professions, specifically the figure of a man who leaves England as a boss and comes back as a subjugated clerk. The ethical and moral message of the paremias in Italian and in English coincide, as they both "translate" someone's loss of status and respect in society. According to Wyatt, this specific example illustrates how Florio's paremias do not distinguish among social classes, something that a courtesy book instead would have emphasized (*The Italian Encounter* 182–84).

Though Florio frequently adopts a translation of the paremias' meaning, he does not follow this approach unconditionally throughout *Second Frutes*. When choosing to translate literally, he does not limit himself to a word-by-word rendering, but rather tends to add something or at least transform the meaning of the paremia slightly. Similar to Brusantino's reinterpretation of the *Decameron*'s text, Florio introduces his own perspective and considers the cultural ambience that will receive his paremias.[89] The following example illustrates how in the English translation he rephrases a reference to a blasphemous behavior, as stated in the Italian paremia, with a description of this same behavior:

> *Io m'accomodo ad ogni cosa e sono come il sacco d'un mugnaio, e non come alcuni che *fanno* tal volta *conscientia di sputar in Chiesa e poi cacheranno su l'altare*. (SF 12)
>
> I aplie my selfe to all, and am like to a miller's sack, and not as some, who sometimes make it a matter of conscience to spitt in the Church and at another time will betray the altar.

The Italian verb "cacare" does not translate "to shite," as Florio does in his *A Worlde of Wordes* (s.v. *cacare*). The entire section is substituted with a translation of the conventionalized meaning of the original: if one defecates on the altar, it means that he betrays and disrespects it (Wyatt, *The Italian Encounter* 178). Even though his *Second Frutes* focuses on less moral topics than those of his *Firste Fruites*, Elizabethan society would have still perceived such an explicit reference to religion as too desecrating.

Paremias in Context

Paremiac Dialogues in *Firste Fruites*

When Florio inserts paremias in his dialogues, he guarantees noticeable linguistic development in their presentation and their explanation due to the graded level of the students engaging with the content of the various chapters. In *Firste Fruites*, an explanation of the paremias' message occurs frequently along with a negotiation of their meaning. The speakers initiate a series of questions and in so doing, constantly guide the students' learning process. This practice slowly decreases in *Second Frutes*, in which formulas of acknowledgment are rarer, if not completely absent (Cerquiglini and Cerquiglini). Generally, the paremias in the second manual do not affect the narrative, but rather are considered as "gems (or conceits) to embellish the language," which more advanced language learners would have appreciated and understood (Simonini, *Italian Scholarship* 60).

In *Firste Fruites*, proverbs and proverbial phrases are usually introduced by formulas that feature the term "proverbio":

> Ma non sapete come dice il proverbio? (FF 5*r*)
> But knowe you not what the proverbe saith?
>
> Quelli verificano il proverbio. Che proverbio volete dire? (FF 6*v*)
> These verifie the proverbe. What proverb wil you say?
>
> Che proverbio è quello? Proverbio che si usa spesso. (FF 14*r*)
> What proverb is that? A proverb that is used often.

Chapter Three

After expressing the paremia, the interlocutors often explicate its meaning in the context of the conversation or respond to it with a brief sentence of acknowledgement. In chapters 18 and 19, for instance, one of the speakers usually pronounces the paremias and the other frequently comments with an assertive statement. A few examples of replies include "certo questo è vero" ("certis that is very true"; FF 22*v*), "questo si vede spesso" ("this is often seene"; FF 23*r*), "un detto verissimo" ("a true saying"; FF 24*r*), "certo bon principio" ("certis a good beginnyng"; FF 27*r*), and "certo tutti boni" ("certis al good"; FF 27*v*). The interlocutor may also answer through an evaluative comment, including "io vorria che queste cose non si usassino" ("I would to God these thinges were not used"; FF 22*v*), "de quelli ce ne sono assai" ("of those there are a great many"; FF 24*r*), "molti fanno queste cose" ("many do these things"; FF 24*v*), and "ma de quelli ce n'è pochi" ("but of those there are few"; FF [26]*r*). Alternatively, he may express an emotion, such as "mi ralegra il core di sentire certe cose" ("it gladdes my hart to heare such things"; FF 23*r*) and "questo mi fa quasi ridere" ("this makes me almost laugh"; FF [26]*r*). These formulas all serve to confirm that the receiver understands the meaning of the paremia, allowing the conversation to continue or turn to another subject.

Both the sentences that introduce a paremia and those that acknowledge the correct interpretation of its meaning serve a variety of functions: they establish the beginning of the paremiac section through an introductory sentence; they demonstrate contact with the source of the paremia or emitter (also called phatic function of the language), which usually leads to the delivery of the expression; they allow for the negotiation and interpretation of the paremia's message (frequently structured in the form of questions and answers); they express appreciation for the paremia (also called emotional function); and finally they permit the acknowledgement and the subsequent comprehension of the expression's meaning. An example of these functions comes from chapter 5 and has already been presented in the first chapter of this book. After a man declares his love to a woman proclaiming a Stilnovistic-like subservience, the woman employs a paremia to declare her unavailability:

> Madonna, io vi amo cordialmente, io voria che io fosse vostro marito, io vi ameria e serviria fedelmente.

> Io sono molto obligato a voi per il vostro ben volere.
> Io vi ringratio per la vostra cortesia.
> Ma non sapete come dice il proverbio? *(introductory sentence; use of the term "proverbio")*
> Non certo: come dice? *(phatic function: contact with the emitter)*
> Chi tardi arriva mal alloggia. *(paremia)*
> Come, dunche io arivo tardi. *(negotiation/interpretation of meaning)*
> Sì certo a dirvi la verità. *(acknowledgment of presumed meaning)*
> Dunche voi siete promessa. *(comprehension of the contextual meaning of the paremia)*
> Signor sì, longo tempo fa. (FF 4v–5r)
>
> Madame, I love you hartily, I would I were your husband, I woulde love you and serve you faithfully.
> I am very much bounde to you for your good wil.
> I thanke you for your courtesie.
> But knowe you not what the proverbe saith?
> No truely: how saith it?
> Who commeth late, lodgeth ill.
> Why then I arrive late.
> Yea certaine, to tel you truly.
> Why then you are promised.
> Yea, Sir, long agoe.

The woman's introductory formula anticipates the paremia by mentioning the term "proverbio" and the very common *verbum dicendi* "dice" ("it says"): "Ma non sapete come dice il proverbio?" ("But knowe you not what the proverbe saith?"). In response, the man establishes contact with the woman by asking her a question in which he leverages a proverb: "Non certo: come dice?" ("No truely: how saith it?"). The paremia *Chi tardi arriva mal alloggia* ("Who commeth late, lodgeth ill") comes next and leads the way to a request for clarification and negotiation of meaning. This consists of a short comment indicating that the receiver of the paremia is on the same page as its source (Grimaldi, "L'ironia nei detti proverbiali" 532): "Come, dunche io arivo tardi" ("Why then I arrive late"). The speaker comprehends the expression's contextual meaning: a man who does not decide to ask for a woman's hand in marriage eventually discovers that she has been promised to another man and finds himself unable to change the reality of having waited too long. As the two speakers understand the message, the conversation proceeds and reveals the identity of the promised spouse.

Chapter Three

Not all introductory formulas present the term "proverbio," though. In chapter 6, a paremia announces an informal scene with two men discussing their menu for the following day:

> Volete farmi un piacere?
> Volentieri se io posso.
> Venite a desinar meco.
> Quando?
> Domani.
> Vi ringratio, io verrò: Che bona cera⁹⁰ haverò io?
> Voi haverete un pezo di carne boina alesso, e un capon arosto.
> Certo questo mi piace.
> Io porterò un fiasco di vino.
> Havetene che sia bono?
> Signor sì, bonissimo.
> Orsù aspettatemi, io venirò, se io non moro questa notte.
> Come fate conto di morir così subitanamente?
> Che so io? Vedo talvolta che *l'huomo compone e Dio dispone. (introductory sentence and paremia)*
> Veramente voi dite il vero. *(acknowledgment of truth)* (FF 6r)

> Wil you do me a pleasure?
> Gladly, if I can.
> Come and dine with me.
> When?
> Tomorow.
> I thanke you, I wil come: what good cheare shal I have?
> You shal have a peese of beefe sodden and a capon rosted.
> Certes this likes me wel.
> I wil bring a bottel of wine.
> Have you any that is good?
> Yea, Sir, very good.
> Wel tary for me, I wil come, if I die not this night.
> What do you make account to die so sodairely?
> What know I? I see sometimes that man doth purpose and God doth dispose.
> Verily you say true.

The formula "vedo talvolta che" ("I see sometimes that") introduces the paremia *L'huomo compone e Dio dispone* ("Man doth compose and God doth dispose") and confirms both the authenticity of its meaning and the commonality of the situation. It is not up to men to decide their own future and destiny, since God frequently has the final answer (GDLI, s.v. *disporre*, n. 12). The assertion, "Veramente voi dite il vero" ("Verily you say true"), acknowledges that the paremia is truthful by repeating the word "vero" as a noun and as an adverb and confirms that the negotiation of meaning was successful.

Tradition, however, does not sustain the form *L'huomo compone e Dio dispone* as it appears in Florio's text. In fact, the paremia usually presents the verb "propone" ("to propose"; *L'uomo propone e Dio dispone*) and not "compone" ("to do"; see Gluski 22–1; ODEP, s.v. *man*). Historically, *Homo proponit sed Deus disponit* derives from two expressions in Solomon's *Proverbs*: *Il cuore de l'huomo penserà la via sua et il signore dirizerà il passo suo* ("A man's heart will think about his way and the Lord will direct his steps"; Ch. XVI: v. 9 from Brucioli's *Annotationi*) and *Nel seno si gitterà la sorte et dal signore è ogni giudicio di quello* ("Fate will be thrown into the womb and its judgment comes from the Lord"; Ch. XVI: v. 33 from Brucioli's *Annotationi*). Still in Latin, but in an English work, the verb "propone" is used in William Langland's *Piers Plowman* (1370–90) when he writes that "*Homo proponit*, quod a poete and Plato he hyght, And *Deus disponit*, quod he lat God done his wille" ("Man proposes, said a poet and his name was Plato, and God disposes, he said, let God fulfil his will"; B, xi: 36–37). The paremia appears in Thomas Haemerkken's (Thomas à Kempis) *The Imitation of Christ* (ca. 1418–27; 1.19.9) and in John Palsgrave's *L'esclaircissement de la langue francoyse* (1530) as *Man proposeth and God disposeth*. Pescetti and Serdonati list the form *L'huom propone e Dio dispone* (Pescetti, *Proverbi italiani raccolti* 2),[91] and so does Florio himself in a second instance in *Firste Fruites* (FF 32v) and in *Giardino di ricreatione* (GR 139): *L'huomo propone e Dio dispone.*

In *Firste Fruites* (6r), the English translation offers the equivalent of the most common form "doth purpose" and not of the expression as it appears in the Italian column ("compone"). It may be that Florio was looking at different literary sources or collections of paremias: the English version was reporting the expression with the verb "purpose," whereas the Italian listed the one with "compone." A second explanation could be that Florio, while writing by memory, may have forgotten the proverb in Italian and did not realize that the English translation was not corresponding to it. Either with the verb "comporre" or the verb "proporre," the ultimate meaning is that God decides and has the last word, which is indeed the message of the expression in the context of the dialogue. Yet, in *L'uomo propone e Dio dispone* ("Man doth purpose

Chapter Three

[sic] and God doth dispose"), God has the last word in permitting what the man has been planning ("propone"). In contrast, in *L'uomo compone e Dio dispone* ("Man doth compose and God doth dispose"), God is depicted as the one who literally dismantles what the man has been constructing over time ("compone").

After this paremia, the two interlocutors continue discussing the growing number of men who are under the influence of fickle fortune. In this instance, they devote greater space to the introductory phase before they pronounce two paremias:

> Io vedo certe persone bizarre che fanno il bravo hoggi, domani sono poveri, altri *fanno conto inanzi l'hoste*, vogliono fare, dire, che e che no, e sono morti. *(introductory sentence and paremia)*
> Di questi ne vedemo l'esperientia giornalmente.
> Quelli verificano il proverbio. *(introductory sentence; use of the term "proverbio")*
> Che proverbio volete dire? *(phatic function: contact with the emitter)*
> Quel proverbio che dice, *Chi troppo abraccia poco stringe*. *(paremia)*
> Certo, questo è bono. *(emotional function: appreciation of paremia)*
> Ma sapete cosa dicea quel altro? *(introductory sentence)*
> Come dice lui, vi prego? *(phatic function: contact with the emitter)*
> Lui dice che *è sempre bono per uno haver due corde per il suo archo*, acciò che se una si rompe lui ne habbia un'altra presta. *(paremia; explanation of meaning)*
> Certo colui la intende. *(comprehension of the contextual meaning of the paremia]*
> È proverbio anticho. (FF 6r–6v)

> I see certain foolish people, that bragge it out to day, and to morowe are poore, others make their account before the host, they wil, do they wil face, and by and by they are dead.
> Of these wee see the experience dayly.
> These verifie the proverbe.
> What proverb wil you say?
> The proverbe that sayth, who imbraceth much litle closeth.
> Certis this is a good one.
> But knowe you how the other said?
> How saith he, I pray you?
> He saith, it is always good for one to have two stringes to his bowe, to the ende that if one breake he may have another ready.
> Certainly he understands it.
> It is an old proverb.

The first paremia of the series, *Far il conto senza l'hoste* ("To make one's account before the host") is listed in both Salviati's and Serdonati's collections and appears in Pulci's *Morgante* during the famous encounter between Margutte and Morgante (I.18.145.5–6).[92] Depending on the context, the proverbial phrase may have different meanings. It suggests that one needs to redo the calculations again if the innkeeper does not agree, which is highly probable if accounts are prepared when he is absent. It can also mean to cheat on the bill by way of making someone else pay more. The 1612 Voc. Cr. (s.v. *oste*) offers a more interpretative explanation: "Determinar da per se di quello a che dee concorrere ancora la volontà d'altri," which means to make decisions on one's own without conferring with the interested parties and waiting for their preferences. In Florio's context, the paremia suggests planning something without great success and without considering possible obstacles. This explains the introductory sentence, which evaluates the eccentricity of certain people who experience misfortune, such as losing everything or dying. The expression exemplifies the message through the situation of a person who tries to adjust the rent or other expenses without consulting the landlord. In so doing, he does not realize that the proprietor will not honor that arrangement and will do the bill of expenses again: *Reckoners without their host much reckon twice*, as Heywood writes (*A dialogue* Pt. I, Ch. VIII). The message of this paremia perfectly matches that of the subsequent expression, *Chi troppo abraccia poco stringe* ("Who imbraceth much litle closeth"). Two sentences introduce the expression by referencing it as a proverb: "Che proverbio volete dire?" ("What proverb wil you say?") and "Quel proverbio che dice" ("The proverbe that sayth"). The expression refers to those who wish to accumulate increasingly and do not consider the consequences of their decisions and acts. Thus, the person who disregards the landlord's policies, ultimately remains without anything (GDLI, s.v. *abbracciare* [1], n. 15). As the conversation progresses, two other questions introduce the last paremia, *È sempre bono per uno haver due corde per il suo archo* ("It is always good for one to have two stringes to his bowe"), and invite the other to quote more paremias: "Ma sapete cosa dicea quel altro? Come dice lui, vi prego?" ("But knowe you how the other said? How saith he, I pray you?"). The interlocutor acknowledges the invitation and pronounces one expression. Immediately following is a

Chapter Three

metaphorical explanation of its meaning by its same source: "acciò che se una si rompe lui ne habbia un'altra presta" ("to the ende that if one breake he may have another ready"). No further clarification is required, since the speaker understands the meaning of the expression: one who pulls the arch too much, risks breaking it (GDLI, s.v. *arco*, n. 23). Hence, having a second cord allows the person to aim again for that which he desires.

Another interesting example of introduction and negotiation of a paremia's meaning during a conversation is found in chapter 14. This is one of the most telling examples of proverbs inserted into the narration for the sake of providing linguistic and cultural material, which is something that informs *Firste Fruites* in its entirety (Fig. 3):

> L'huomo spesse volte si tien certo di qualche cosa e resta ingannato.
> Ma non è così con me.
> Forse voi e [sic] ingannate.
> Imitate il proverbio. *(first introductory sentence; use of the term "proverbio")*
> Che proverbio è quello? *(phatic function: contact with the emitter)*
> Proverbio che si usa spesso. *(second introductory sentence; use of the term "proverbio")*
> Di gratia, recitatelo. *(phatic function: contact with the emitter)*
> *Con il tempo e con la paglia le nespole si matura,* o veramente quest'altro, *Chi va pian va san. (paremias)*
> Non ne sapete altri? *(phatic function: contact with the emitter; introductory sentence)*
> *Ogniuno tira l'aqua al suo molino,* così fate voi. *(paremia)*
> Ma non sapete voi come ogniuno cerca il suo profitto? *(negotiation/interpretation of meaning)*
> Natura ci insegna così. *(acknowledgement of meaning)*
> Ma Dio ci insegna a amar il nostro prossimo, come noi medesimi, e non essere avari.
> Sì, ma pochi sequitano le leggi de Iddio.
> Ce ne sono de li altri che praticano una nuova alchimia.
> Come volete voi dire?
> Dirovi come alcuni fanno. *(introductory sentence)*
> Come ditemi, vi prego? *(phatic function: contact with the emitter)*
> *Imprestar e mai non rendere, assai promettere e poco attendere, ben guadagnar e poco spendere farà presto l'huomo richo. (paremia)*
> Questo è un bello proverbio. *(emotional function: appreciation of paremia)*

Firste Fruites and *Second Frutes*

Ve ne voglio dire due altri belli. *(introductory sentence; implicit use of the term "proverbio")*
Così facendo, mi farete a piacere. *(phatic function: contact with the emitter)*
Chi cerca spesso ingannar altrui opresso resta et ingannato lui. *(paremia)*
Questo è bello e vero. *(emotional function: appreciation of paremia)*
Christo lasciò ne li precetti, voi non far altrui quel che per te non vuoi. *(introductory sentence and paremia)*
Anche questo è bellissimo. *(emotional function: appreciation of paremia)* (FF 13v–14v)

Figure 3: *Firste Fruites*, list of paremias and their translation from chapter 14 (cc. 13v–14r). Courtesy of The Huntington Library, San Marino, California, RB 60820. Source: search.proquest.com/eebo

Man oftentimes holds himselfe sure of something, and then resteth deceyved.
But it is not so with me.
Perhaps you are deceyved.
Imitate the proverbe.
What proverbe is that?
A proverbe that is used often.
I pray you rehearse it.
With time and with straw, meddlers are made ripe, or els this other, who goeth softly, goes wel.

169

> Know you no more?
> Every man draweth water to hym selfe, and so do you.
> But knowe you not howe every man seeketh his owne profite?
> Nature teaches us so.
> But God teacheth us to love our neighbors as ourselves, and not to be so covetous.
> Yea, but few folow the lawes of God.
> There are others that practise a new kynde of alchimistie.
> How is that, that you say?
> I wyl tel you how some do.
> How, I pray you? Tel me.
> To borowe and never geve againe, to promise much and attend litle, to get wel and spend litle, wil quickly make a man rich.
> This is a fyne proverbe.
> I wyl tel you two other fine ones.
> So doing, you shal do me a pleasure.
> Who often seekes others to deceive, doth rest oppressed and deceyved hym selfe.
> That is a fine one, and true.
> Christ left in his preceptes, doo not to others that thou wylt not have done to thy selfe.
> Also this is very fine.

As in the previous example, the introductory sentences of the paremias and their confirmation or appreciation delimit the portions of the dialogue that are devoted to paremias. This structure, which guides the students through the conversation and helps them appreciate the cultural and linguistic aspects of the target language more, begins with multiple contacts with the source of the first paremia: "Imitate il proverbio. Che proverbio è quello?" ("Imitate the proverbe. What proverbe is that?") and "Di gratia, recitatelo" ("I pray you rehearse it"). Then, the proposition of the first paremia follows, along with the proposition of a synonymic paremia introduced by "o veramente" ("or els"): "*Con il tempo e con la paglia le nespole si matura,* o veramente quest'altro *Chi va pian va san*" ("With time and with straw, meddlers are made ripe, or els this other, who goeth softly, goes wel"). Both the paremias express the idea that one achieves what is sought through patience and endurance and that haste is detrimental to the positive development of a situation (GDLI, s.v. *nespola*, n. 8). After a rhetorical question on the source's knowledge of other paremias ("Non ne sapete altri?," "Know you no more?"), the dialogue develops. The interlocutor delivers the paremia, *Ogniuno tira l'aqua al suo molino*

("Every man draweth water to hym selfe") and a negotiation of its meaning follows: "Ma non sapete voi come ogniuno cerca il suo profitto?" ("But knowe you not howe every man seeketh his owne profite?"). Finally, one of the speakers offers acknowledgment and recognition of the paremia's message: "Natura ci insegna così" ("Nature teaches us so"). All of these elements serve to emphasize both the connection between the expressions and their gratuitousness within the conversation. In the second part of the dialogue, an introductory sentence ("Dirovi come alcuni fanno," "I wyl tel you how some do") and a contact with the source ("Come ditemi, vi prego?" "How, I pray you? Tel me") lead to the paremia *Imprestar e mai non rendere, assai promettere e poco attendere, ben guadagnar e poco spendere farà presto l'huomo richo* ("To borowe and never geve againe, to promise much and attend litle, to get wel and spend litle, wil quickly make a man rich"). Once the interlocutor appreciates the expression's beauty ("Questo è un bello proverbio," "This is a fyne proverbe"), the source shares two other paremias: *Chi cerca spesso ingannar altrui opresso resta et ingannato lui* ("Who often seekes others to deceive, doth rest oppressed and deceyved hym selfe") and *Voi non far altrui quel che per te non vuoi* ("Doo not to others that thou wylt not have done to thy selfe"). The other speaker recognizes the elegance of the two expressions, probably because of the ethical message they convey: "bello e vero" ("fine and true") for the first one and "bellissimo" ("very fine") for the second. The reference to Christ's teachings ("Christo lasciò ne li precetti," "Christ left in his preceptes"), as recorded in the apocryphal book of Tobias (4.15), confirms the pedagogical and moralizing nature of these proverbs.

In contrast to proverbs, Florio generally offers proverbial phrases with less contextual evaluation of their meaning. In chapter 10, a woman uses the proverbial phrase, *Dar la baia*, within a sentence that occurs during a love conversation. When a man approaches her, she answers that she is ready to serve him. However, upon receiving gratitude for her courtesy, she comments on the man's act of subjection:

> Certo, signora, vi rendo mille gratie, io so che sete cortese.
> Voi sete pronto per *darmi la baia. (paremia)*
> Non certo, signora, perdonatemi.
> Non mi havete offeso.
> Né ancho cercherò di farlo. (FF 8*v*)

> Certis lady, I render you a thousand thankes, I know you are courteous.
> You are redy to mocke me.
> Not so madam, pardon me.
> You have not offended me.
> Neither wil I seeke to doo it.

The woman's message is evident to the man, who asks neither for additional clarification nor for a confirmation of the proverbial phrase's supposed meaning. However, he replies excusing himself if his assertion has been read as a mockery of the woman's gracious manners. After this exchange, the man dares to ask the woman if she would accept his love, to which she replies that she is not worthy of his feelings. Before the man's puzzlement, the woman states that she was never subject unto love nor does she seek to be such.

Paremiac Dialogues in *Second Frutes*

In opposition to *Firste Fruites*, Florio decreases the number of introductory formulas and frequently presents paremias without any introduction in *Second Frutes*. Here, proverbs and proverbial phrases are not inserted to attract attention and to send a specific linguistic and cultural message, as occurs in the first manual. Rather, Florio integrates these expressions into the conversations and embeds them into the manual's specific social framework (Montini, "Proverbs in John Florio's *Fruits*" 257). Moreover, they do not affect communication or change its dynamics, nor do they contribute to the development of the dialogues. The reader must resort to common knowledge and the surrounding context (often given by other paremias) in order to interpret the meaning of the proposed expressions correctly.

In the first chapter, a sort of *commedia dell'arte* argument arises between Torquato and his servant, Ruspa, who seems not to remember anything and, thus, irritates his master (Wyatt, *The Italian Encounter* 179–80; Fig. 4):

> R. Io non so trovar la chiave.
> T. Dove l'hai posta, trascurato che sei?
> R. Stamane l'ho messa nella scarsella, o io l'ho.
> T. Se' tu così povero di memoria? *(phatic function: contact with the emitter)*
> R. *Io non mi ricordo dal naso alla bocca. (paremia)*
> T. *Tu non farai mai statuti né casa da tre solari. (paremia)*[93]

Firste Fruites and *Second Frutes*

R. Pur che io ne faccia da uno. *(answer to the paremia)*
T. Tre arbori, ti basteranno a far ciò.
R. Molti grandi vengono a star in case così basse.
T. Al corpo di ch'io non vuo' dire, che s'io metto mano ad un bastone, io ti farò ben star in cervello.
R. Io non saprei farci altro.
T. Tu vuoi ch'io dii di piglio a qualche pezzo di legno per pestarti le ossa.
R. Ciò non vorrei già io.
T. *Hora vedo che *chi l'ha da natura fin alla fossa dura*. (paremia)
R. Ecco qui una dozzina di camiscie, due di fazzoletti, altrettanti collari di renza, otto ghimphe o lattuche, co' loro manichetti lavorati di seta, quatro tovaglioli, sei sciugatoi, otto scuffie, tre paia di lenzuola; ecco poi in questa pettiniera i vostri pettini d'avolio e di bosso, le vostre forbicette, con i curaorecchie, et le altre cose. (SF 6–8)

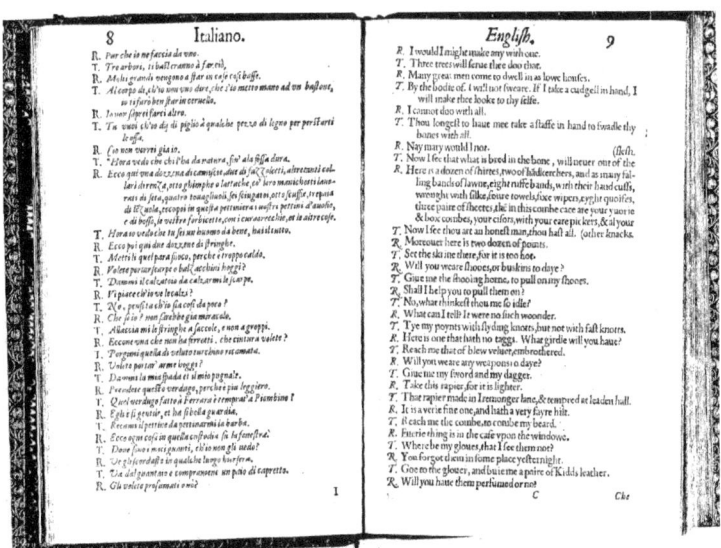

Figure 4: *Second Frutes,* list of paremias and their translation from chapter 1 (pp. 8–9). Courtesy of The Huntington Library, San Marino, California, RB 59806. Source: search.proquest.com/eebo

R. I cannot finde the key.
T. Where hast thou layd it? Thou careles as thou art.
R. I put it in my pocket this morning. Oh I have it.
T. Art thou so short of memory?
R. No man more forgetfull than I.
T. Thou wilt never make statutes, nor houses with three stories.

173

Chapter Three

> R. I would I might make any with one.
> T. Three trees will serve thee doo that.
> R. Many great men come to dwell in as lowe houses.
> T. By the bodie of, I will not sweare, if I take a cudgell in hand, I will make thee looke to thy selfe.
> R. I cannot doo with all.
> T. Thou longest to have mee take a staffe in hand to swaddle thy bones with all.
> R. Nay Mary would I not.
> T. Now I see that what is bred in the bone will never out of the flesh.
> R. Here is a dozen of shirtes, two of handkerchers, and as many falling bands of lawne, eight ruffe bands with their hand cuffs wrought with silke, foure towels, six wipers, eyght quoifes, three paire of sheetes; then in this combe cace are your yvorie and box combes, your cisors, with your eare pickers and al your other knacks.

The first paremia, *Io non mi ricordo dal naso alla bocca* ("No man more forgetfull than I"), relates to someone who is short of memory. The question preceding the expression, "Se' tu così povero di memoria?" ("Art thou so short of memory?"), although it does not serve as an introductory formula and does not feature the word "proverbio," establishes a contact and grants space for an utterance that could confirm its message. At this point, Ruspa asserts that the number of things he remembers is as small as the distance between his mouth and his nose, hence almost nothing. The response to this expression occurs by means of another paremia without any intermediary utterances. *Tu non farai mai statuti né casa da tre solari* ("Thou wilt never make statutes, nor houses with three stories") derives from the proverbial phrase *Havere un cervello da far statuti* ("To have a brain to make statutes"), which means to be shrewd, expert, and forward-looking (GDLI, s.v. *statuto* [1], n. 10). Generally used in an ironic way, Florio's paremia furthers the idea presented in the first expression, i.e., Ruspa is far from being astute. Since "casa da tre solari" refers to a very rich house (because it has three stories), the second part of the paremia suggests that whatever the person plans to do, it would be impossible to accomplish. Ruspa does not need an explanation but responds to the paremia by employing a concept from Torquato's expression to continue its metaphor. He admits that, despite his absent-mindedness, a house with one floor will suffice: "Pur che io ne faccia da uno" ("I would I might make any with

174

one"). The retaliation continues as he asserts that "molti grandi vengono a star in case così basse" ("many great men come to dwell in as lowe houses"), ironically rebutting his master's sentence that a small amount of wood would be enough to build such an insignificant house. When the third paremia is introduced, the comic sketch is almost concluded, with the master threatening to beat Ruspa severely. The proverb *Chi l'ha da natura fin alla fossa dura* ("What is bred in the bone will never out of the flesh") does not affect the conversation this time, but actually serves as a conclusion to the scene. Moreover, it introduces a new section in which Ruspa returns to his work ("Ecco qui una dozzina di camiscie …," "Here is a dozen of shirtes …"). According to Wyatt, the exchange of lines between Torquato and Ruspa describes the relationship of power between them, mediated through the language lesson. Torquato, as the boss, intends to affirm his higher position by appealing to wisdom and using paremias. In response, Ruspa remains unaffected by his master's accusations regarding the insufficient improvement in his behavior and, because of it, can be considered the real ruler of the situation (Wyatt, *The Italian Encounter* 179).

Even when their meaning is obscure, Florio does not explain proverbial phrases explicitly. One example is found in chapter 4, in which six interlocutors spend their time engaging in a pleasant conversation during a meal. They employ a few paremias to comment on a sudden noise coming from the kitchen:

> S. O disgratiato cuoco, egli farebbe venir stizza a un santo.
> H. *Il fuoco aiuta il cuoco. (paremia)
> S. *Anche io so *menar l'oche a bere quando piove. (paremia)*
> T. Qui c'è da mangiar assai e d'avanzo. (SF 52)

> S. O villenous cooke, able to anger a saint.
> H. The fire helps the cooke.
> S. Marie I can leade geese to drinke when it raines to.
> T. Here is too too much meate, and to spare.

All of the assertions are unrelated and, in fact, the reader has the impression that the piece is less of a conversation than a list of phrases. There is no reaction after the first paremia, whose meaning is clear to all of the speakers—especially given the context—nor after the second, whose meaning instead may not be so evident. The 1612 Voc. Cr. (s.v. *papero*) reports the paremia *I paperi voglion menare a ber l'oche* ("The ducks want to lead geese

Chapter Three

to drink") and explains it as "si dice, quando un giovane vuole aggirare un vecchio" ("it is said when a young man wants to fool an old man"). In other words, the ducks' eagerness to convince the geese to drink suggests that inexperienced people pretend to guide those who are more experienced because they are full of themselves (GDLI, s.v. *oca* [1], n. 11). Since in Florio's dialogue the source of the paremia is the "I" in the paremia, a classist undertone seems to be embedded within the expression. Simone, the cook's boss and owner of the house, would be able to teach a cook his art, even though he has never done such a job before. He probably intends to highlight his mental and social superiority and expresses it through a paremia. The conversation resumes just after the paremia when Tancredi appreciates the abundance of available food.

The absence of formulaic introductions and formal explanations of paremias is not a general rule in *Second Frutes*. A few negotiations of meaning occur, especially in the first five chapters, where the speaker may request an explanation or confirm his understanding of the message. Sometimes, a sentence clearly presents a paremia and, in turn, the expression evokes a reaction from the listener. In chapter 2, three such formulas introduce two paremias during a conversation between Thomaso and Giovanni:

> T. È precetto che si possa sapere? *(phatic function: contact with the emitter)*
> G. *Signor sì, e gli mi diceva spesso che *potendo andar per terra, io non dovessi mai andar per acqua.* *(introductory sentence + first paremia)*
> G. *Si suol pur dire che *chi non va per mare non sa ciò che sia il timor di Dio.* *(introductory sentence + second paremia)* (SF 16)
>
> T. Is it a precept that may be knowne?
> G. Yea sir, hee [my father] would often bid me that, if I could goe by land, I should never goe by water.
> G. Yet is it a common saying that he that goes not by sea dooth not knowe what the feare of God is.

Thomaso's formula, "È precetto che si possa sapere?" ("Is it a precept that may be knowne?"), establishes the beginning of the exchange of paremias and serves as a contact with his interlocutor. His words confirm the validity of the first expression from a pedagogical standpoint: the paremia is a precept. Giovanni utters the first expression, *Potendo andar per terra, non andar mai per acqua* ("If one could goe by land, never goe by water"), referencing it to the traditional wisdom of previous generations. His second formula (*Chi non va per mare non sa ciò che sia il timor di Dio*, "He that goes not by sea dooth not knowe what the feare of God is") shares the concept of water and travelling with the first expression: "acqua" ("water") and "andar" ("to go") in the first paremia, and "mare" ("sea") and "va" ("one goes") in the second. For this paremia, the introductory sentence ("si suol pur dire," "it is a common saying") places emphasis on the expression's spoken dimension and common usage among people.

With the exception of chapters 6, 9, and 12, other lists of paremias within a conversation occur in *Second Frutes*. In these instances, Florio occasionally inserts a few sentences to interrupt the sequence and make the conversation livelier. Again, in chapter 2, Thomaso and Giovanni utter a series of expressions related to faithfulness, introducing all of them and acknowledging their meaning. During this dialogue, Thomaso questions the trustworthiness of one of Giovanni's friends, whereas Giovanni believes in the many good words that his friends told him:

> T. *Non sapete che *le belle parole et i cattivi fatti ingannano i savii et i matti?* (phatic function: contact with the emitter = paremia)
> G. *Io lo so, ma *se lui mi batte con la spada, io lo batterò con il fodro.* (acknowledgment and paremia)
> T. *Dunque, volete *rendergli pane per focaccia.* (negotiation/interpretation of meaning = paremia)
> G. *A chi te la fa faglielа, o tientela a mente.* (acknowledgement of meaning = paremia) (SF 18)
>
> T. Wot you not that faire words and fowle deedes are woont to make both fooles and wise men faine?
> G. I knowe it, but, if he beate me with the sword, I will beate him againe with the scabbard.
> T. What will you give him bread for cake then.
> G. If any man wrong thee, wrong him againe, or else be sure to remember it.

Thomaso starts the exchange of paremias with Giovanni by turning a proverbial expression into a question: "Non sapete che *le belle parole et i cattivi fatti ingannano i savii et i matti?*" ("Wot you not that faire words and fowle deedes are woont to make both fooles and wise men faine?"). In doing so, the way he establishes contact with Giovanni coincides with the paremia itself. Giovanni links his expression to the previous with the conjunction "ma" ("but"): "Io lo so, ma *se lui mi batte con la spada, io lo batterò con il fodro*" ("I knowe it, but, if he beate me with the sword, I will beate

Chapter Three

him againe with the scabbard"). He does not express a different point of view on the topic, but rather emphasizes the consequences of his friend's unreliability. In turn, Thomaso acknowledges both the meaning of the expression and the appropriateness of his interlocutor's perspective. He introduces the third paremia using the conjunction "dunque" ("then, so") and highlights how an eye-for-an-eye retribution for someone's offense is justified if promises are not fulfilled: "Dunque, volete *rendergli pane per focaccia*" ("What will you give him bread for cake then"; see Erasmus, *Collected Works of Erasmus, Adages*, vol. 31, I.i.35: 83–85). The section concludes with Giovanni's paremia, *A chi te la fa fagliela, o tientela a mente* ("If any man wrong thee, wrong him againe, or else be sure to remember it"), which repeats and confirms the same message as that of the previous expression. In other words, the majority of all the functions of the discourse in this instance, from asking for the other's attention to the negotiation and confirmation of the expression's meaning, coincides with a paremia.

Similarly, in chapter 1 the acknowledgment of a paremia triggers a concatenation of other expressions related by content or lexicon to the first one. This occurs during a conversation between Torquato and Nolano on getting up in the morning and habits in the bedroom:

> T. Io mi contento di quel poco ch'io ho.
> N. **Chi si contenta gode. (paremia)*
> T. **Cuor contento è manto su le spalle. (acknowledgement of meaning=paremia)*
> N. Perché vi vestite così caldo?
> T. Per viver assai e per seguir il proverbio. *(introductory formula; use of the term "proverbio")*
> N. Come dice cotesto proverbio? *(phatic function: contact with the emitter)*
> T. **Vesti caldo, mangia poco, bevi assai che viverai. (paremia)*
> N. **Chi non sa far i fatti suoi peggio farà quegli d'altrui. (paremia)*
> T. *E *chi fa i fatti suoi non s'imbratta le mani. (paremia)* (SF 10)
>
> T. I am content with that little that I have.
> N. Who lives content, hath all the world at will.
> T. A contented minde is as good as warme cloake.
> N. Why doo you goe so warme?
> T. Because I would live long, and also to folowe the proverb.
> N. What proverb is that, and how saies it?
> T. Cloathe warme, feede sparingly, and drink well, so shalt thou live long.

> N. He that cannot do his own business, will hardly do another man's.
> T. And he that dooth his own busines, doth not defile his hands.

The link between the first two paremias of the quotation is happiness: *Chi si contenta gode* ("Who lives content, hath all the world at will") and *Cuor contento è manto su le spalle* ("A contented minde is as good as warme cloake") share this concept through the verb "contentare" ("be happy") and the adjective "contento" ("happy"), respectively. The first paremia, *Chi si contenta gode*, describes the pleasantness that derives from being content with what one has achieved. In response, the following paremia, *Cuor contento è manto sulle spalle*, relates to the protection from adversity that a positive attitude guarantees (GDLI, s.v. *cuore*, n. 27). The meaning of this second expression leaves Nolano indifferent, even though it is probable that the mention of the cloak invites him to ask about the dress that Torquato is about to wear ("Perché vi vestite così caldo?" "Why doo you goe so warme?"). To answer the question, Torquato uses another expression to reveal his guiding principle of morality in life: "Per viver assai e per seguir il proverbio" ("Because I would live long, and also to folowe the proverb"). After these words, which serve as an introductory sentence, Nolano prompts Torquato to share the proverb: "Come dice cotesto proverbio?" ("What proverb is that, and how saies it?"). To this Torquato replies through a didactic motto offering useful teaching on the best way to dress and eat: *Vesti caldo, mangia poco, bevi assai che viverai* ("Cloathe warme, feede sparingly, and drink well, so shalt thou live long"). The following paremia, *Chi non sa far i fatti suoi peggio farà quegli d'altrui* ("He that cannot do his own business, will hardly do another man's"), shifts to a completely different topic, i.e., people's intrusiveness. The expression, though, is linked to the previous one because it states that those who do not know how to handle their own business are unable to handle others' and may end up losing many opportunities. The final verb, "vivere" ("to live"), creates a context for a discussion of the good and bad in life. In fact, the last proverb of the series, *Chi fa i fatti suoi non s'imbratta le mani* ("He that dooth his owne busines, doth not defile his hands"), connects semantically to the preceding paremia by means of the word "fatti" ("business"). As it expands its meaning, this expression conveys an opposite message: those who are

Chapter Three

able to take care of their own substances, do not get involved in any other form of business, and hence they experience triumph in life.

The explanation of an expression because of its unclear meaning occurs in chapter 5. While Antonio, Samuel, and Crusca discuss games, Antonio asks his servant Crusca how the weather is:

> C. Fa tempo aspro, cattivo, chiuso, oscuro, crudele, e tempestoso.
> A. *Faremo dunque come fanno a Prato. (paremia)*
> S. E come fanno a Prato, quando piove? *(request for clarification)*
> A. Lasciano piovere e stanno in casa. *(clarification of meaning)*
> S. *Chi è coperto quando piove è un matto se si muove, se si muove e si bagna è più che matto se si lagna. (paremia)*
> A. Volete inferire che ci bisogna star in casa. *(request for clarification and negotiation of meaning)*
> S. Signor sì, fin che passi questa burasca. *(acknowledgement of meaning)*
> A. Andiamo dunque nel vostro studio a leggere. (SF 78)
>
> C. It is sharpe, ill, closedarke, cruell, and stormie weather.
> A. We will doe as they doe at Prato then.
> S. And how doe they do at Prato when it raines?
> A. They let it raine and keep home.
> S. Who covered is, when raine dooth fall, a foole he is to stir at al, but if he stir and then bee wet more than a foole he is to fret.
> A. You will infer that a man must keepe home.
> S. Yea sir, until this storme be past.
> A. Then let us goe into your studie to reade.

After Crusca comments on the bad weather, Antonio utters the first paremia *ex abrupto* and without introduction: *Faremo come fanno a Prato* ("We will doe as they doe at Prato"). In the style of *Firste Fruites*, Samuel asks for clarification since supposedly the other people present during the conversation are unable to understand the expression: "E come fanno a Prato, quando piove?" ("And how doe they do at Prato when it raines?"). It may be that, because of the local geographical dimension of the paremia referring to a small town like Prato, the English community in London could have not understood it. Another characteristic of Antonio's utterance makes the expression prone to confusion. *Far come quei da Prato* ("To do it in the way they do in Prato") is usually followed by an explanation, which Antonio includes only in response to Samuel's question: "Lasciano piovere e stanno in casa" ("They

180

let it raine and keep home").[94] When Samuel pronounces another paremia, *Chi è coperto quando piove è un matto se si muove, se si muove e si bagna è più che matto se si lagna* ("Who covered is, when raine dooth fall, a foole he is to stir at al, but if he stir and then bee wet more than a foole he is to fret"), Antonio is unclear about the meaning of the expression. He doubts that he has chosen the correct application of the expression's conventionalized meaning to the context of their conversation, namely that they should stay at home to avoid the rain. By referring to his previous words, "stanno in casa" ("keep home"), he comments: "Volete inferire che ci bisogna star in casa" ("You will infer that a man must keepe home"). Samuel confirms the paremia's correct application and adds a reference to the actual context: Samuel and Antonio should not go outside until the storm passes ("fin che passi questa burasca"), and spend their time reading.

Despite the considerable number of paremias, wellerisms in Florio's *Fruites* are rare.[95] According to A. Taylor, wellerisms offered relatively few opportunities for pedagogical use and their lack of a proper moral message made them "unsuitable for school use" (*The Proverb* 206). Speroni also argues that a wellerism transplanted in a foreign culture is rarely productive: "It is very difficult to appreciate or even to care for the local, and frequently, incongruous and untranslatable, phrases that constitute many wellerisms" (*The Italian Wellerism* 6). This could explain the scarcity of wellerisms in Florio's two language manuals, which were expressly directed to foreign language pedagogy and intended for a public that was unfamiliar with Italian culture. For this reason and given its more advanced instruction, only *Second Frutes* includes three wellerisms. For all of them, Florio extrapolates the proverbial component and places it before the "come disse/come diceva" ("as he/she said," "as he/she used to say") section:

> **Nel mezzo consiste la virtù, disse il diavolo trovandosi fra due Monache.* (SF 48)
>
> Vertue consists in the midst, quoth the divell, when hee found himselfe betweene two nonnes.
>
> **Per tutto c'è da fare, diceva colui che ferrava le oche.* (SF 84)
> Every man hath somthing to do, quoth he that shod his geese.
>
> **Io non so se l'anderà bene, diceva colei che dava un servitiale al suo marito con un buon bastone.* (SF 136)

Chapter Three

> I can not tell how it will falle out, quoth the good wife that gave her husband a glister with a good cudgel.

If their context is acknowledged, their lexical or conceptual connection with previous sentences emerge. In chapter 4, the ironic wellerism on the devil that sits between two nuns shares a word, specifically "mezzo" ("middle"), with the preceding line, which prompts the paremiac utterance. The exchange of lines occurs during a conversation on the topic of convivial food, when Horatio and Simone welcome Melibeo to sit at their table:

> H. Di gratia Signor M., sedete qui nel mezzo tra noi duo.
> M. *Nel mezzo consiste la virtù, disse il diavolo trovandosi fra due Monache
> S. Signori, il buon pro vi possa fare, voi sete tutti i ben venuti. (SF 48)
>
> H. Of courtesie, Master, sit here between us two.
> M. Vertue consists in the midst, quoth the divell, when hee found himselfe betweene two nonnes.
> S. Much good may it doo everie bodie, you are al hartely welcome.

In chapter 8, during a conversation between Giacomo and his servant Lippa, the latter utters a wellerism about a wife getting revenge on her husband. He resorts to it as a skeptical response to his master's willingness to forgive him for his supposed laziness. The link established between Giacomo's sentence and Lippa's wellerism is, therefore, conceptual as the paremia critically comments on an action that seems positive, but in fact hides a very harsh reprimand:

> G. Orsù, vien qua, io ti voglio perdonare, se tu vuoi esser huomo da bene e gettar la poltroneria, l'ocio, e le ciancie da banda.
> L. *Voi mi rompete la testa e poi mi date un empiastro. *Io non so se l'anderà bene, diceva colei che dava un servitiale al suo marito con un buon bastone.*
> G. Rispondi a proposito. Vuoi tacere e ravvederti?
> L. Signor sì, io non vi dirò mai più parola. (SF 136)
>
> G. Goe to, come hether, I will forgive thee if thou wilt become an honest man, and cast idlenes, slouthfulnes, and thy bimble bable aside.
> L. You break my head, and then give me a plaster. I can not tell how it will falle out, quoth the good wife that gave her husband a glister with a good cudgel.

> G. Answere to the purpose, wilt thou holde thy peace and amend?
> L. Yea sir, I will never speake word anie more.

Finally, in chapter 6, once Michele is warmly received, Daniele addresses him by using a wellerism about certain geese. The conceptual connection between the paremia and its surrounding context is being "occupato in qualche negotio importante" ("busied with some waightie matters"). This paremia is an interesting case since Florio changes it for reasons related to contextualization, specifically a dialogue among six speakers on the issue of "familiar and ceremonious compliments." Michele's wellerism has so little impact on the narration that Stefano goes back to talk about Michele's unexpected arrival:

> D. Sete sempre occupato in qualche negotio importante.
> M. **Per tutto c'è da fare, diceva colui che ferrava le oche. (paremia: wellerism)*
> S. Ho a caro che siate giunto così a proposito. (SF 84)
>
> D. You are alwaies busied with some waightie matters.
> M. Every man hath somthing to do, quoth he that shod his geese.
> S. I'm glad you are come so fitlie.

Per tutto c'è da fare, diceva colui che ferrava le oche ("Every man hath somthing to do, quoth he that shod his geese") is derived from its most common form, *Come disse quel che ferrava l'oche. E' ci sarà, che fare* ("As he that shod his geese, there will be something to do"; see Speroni, *The Italian Wellerism* 43). The provenance of the paremia is rather comic, as is the case for almost all wellerisms. A man, apparently not very perspicacious, wants to shoe the feet of his geese. As someone reports, he stretches out on the ground and, looking at the foot of a goose, he acknowledges that the task is more difficult than expected: "E' ci sarà che fare" ("There will be something to do"). Others report that, as soon as the same man lifts the foot of one goose, each of the remaining geese lifts a foot. He then realizes the burden of the undertaking and becomes aware of the difficulty of his initiative. The 1612 Voc. Cr. (s.v. *oca*) lists a third explanation for the wellerism: all the geese together tighten their palms while raising their foot, thus creating a rather laborious situation. In Florio's dialogue, the wellerism has an entirely positive meaning because it emphasizes the advantage of having to deal with occupations that evidently bear wealth and income

Chapter Three

to those who are interested. Michele asserts that he feels lucky to always be busy with *negotia*, or occupations and affairs; it follows that "E' ci sarà che fare" is read literally as a positive illustration of the continual occurrence of problems. This example confirms that, if paremias appear in a meaningful context, their contextualization goes beyond morphological, syntactic, and lexical elements, and they may even express opposite meanings to their common ones.

Contextual Comparisons with *Giardino di ricreatione*

A contextual evaluation of paremias in *Firste Fruites* and *Second Frutes* acquires more significance if their proverbs, proverbial phrases, and wellerisms are compared with each other and with those listed in *Giardino di ricreatione*. In his formal collection of paremias, Florio gathers more than 6,000 proverbial expressions in Italian without contextualizing and translating them in English.[96] Thus, those paremias that present a narrative or dialogic structure in *Firste Fruites* and *Second Frutes* manifest a generalized form and meaning in *Giardino*. Comparing and contrasting modifications of these paremias in terms of morphology, syntax, and vocabulary illustrates the influence of context on their structure and message, as well as their adaptation to the three works' genres and objectives.

Nearly all of the paremias in *Firste Fruites* (specifically, 254 out of 287) appear in *Giardino*. Florio excludes only 33 from the collection although his reasons for doing it remains unclear. The 273 paremias in chapter 19 feature almost entirely in *Giardino* (only 26 paremias do not have an equivalent in the collection) and, specifically, 229 show a perfect correspondence or just minor modifications. The remaining 18 can count on a variant, most of the time a different hemistich,[97] which does not change the expression's meaning.[98] For *Second Frutes*, the number of shared paremias is consistently different: only 274 out of 517 paremias appear in *Giardino*. This aspect supports the speculation that the asterisk beside the paremias is not an indication of which proverbs and proverbial phrases merge into *Giardino*, otherwise most of the remaining 243 paremias would be listed there. The inconsistent use of this paratextual element suggests that the asterisks were aids for readers, who could, without much difficulty, spot a paremia inside the dialogues and use it in their own conversations. They could even be an encouragement to memorize the expressions, something that Florio apparently did not judge crucial in *Firste Fruites*.

As for the title of the collection, these expressions grow in Florio's garden in the form of "fronde, fiori e frutti, vaghe, leggiadri, e soavi" ("fronds, flowers and fruits, loving, graceful, and sweet").[99] Considering the distribution of the two language manuals' paremias in *Giardino*, an interesting characteristic emerges. Each letter of the alphabet features at least one cluster of sequential paremias from the two language manuals. Some letters present even long clusters of expressions, with one under letter L being the most extensive of the entire collection:

> *L'havessi io saputo, sempre è tardi.* (GR 139; FF 34v)
> Have I known it, it's always late.
>
> *La vita passa e la morte viene.* (GR 139; FF 34r)
> Life passes and death comes.
>
> *La maraviglia è figliuola dell'ignoranza.* (GR 139; FF 32v)
> Marvel is the daughter of ignorance.
>
> *La legge nasce dal peccato e lo castiga.* (GR 139; *La legge nasce del peccato et lo gastiga,* FF 32v)
> The law is born of sin and punishes it.
>
> *La vera legge è la natura.* (GR 139; FF 32v)
> The right law is nature.
>
> *La conscientia serve per mille testimoni.* (GR 139; FF 32v)
> Conscience serves for a thousand witnesses.
>
> *L'huomo propone e Dio dispone.* (GR 139; FF 32v)
> The man proposes and God disposes.
>
> *Le allegrezze di questo mondo duran poco.* (GR 139; FF 32r)
> The joys of this world are short-lived.
>
> *La Lombardia è il giardino del mondo.* (GR 139; FF 31v; SF 106)
> Lombardy is the garden of the world.
>
> *Le bugie hanno corte le gambe.* (GR 139; FF 31v)
> Lies have short legs.
>
> *L'ultimo riffugio è la speranza o la morte.* (GR 139; *La speranza è l'ultima cosa de l'huomo,* FF 31v)
> The last refuge is hope or death.

Chapter Three

> *Le buone parole ongono, le cattive pongono.* (GR 139; *Le bone parole ongino, le cattive pongino*, FF 31v; *Delle parole, le buone ongono et le cattive pongono*, SF 176)
> Good words oil, bad sting.
>
> *La robba non è di chi la fa ma di chi la gode.* (GR 139; *La robba non è a chi la fa ma a chi la gode*, FF 31v)
> Things are not for those who gather it, but for those who enjoy it.
>
> *La porta di dietro guasta la casa.* (GR 139; FF 31v)
> The back door mars the house.
>
> *La coda per esser troppo longa alle volte condanna la volpe.* (GR 139; *La coda condanna spesso la volpe a morte per esser tropo lunga*, FF 31v)
> Because it is too long, sometimes the tail condemns the fox.
>
> *L'innocentia porta seco la sua deffensione.* (GR 139; *L'innocentia porta seco la sua d[e]fensione*, FF 31v)
> Innocence bears its defense with itself.
>
> *L'ira placata non rifà l'offese.* (GR 139; *L'ira placata non rifà l'ofese*, FF 31r)
> The anger assuaged does not renue the offense.
>
> *Lui spoglia Pietro per vestir Paolo.* (GR 139; *Lui robba Pietro per pagare san Paulo*, FF 31r)
> He strips Pietro to dress Paolo.

Since these expressions appear in both *Firste Fruites* and *Second Frutes*, it may be suggested that Florio was selecting them in the dialogues and writing them one after the other, without arranging them alphabetically, as is evident from the list in *Giardino*.

Since paremias are situated within a context in both *Fruits*, they show linguistic elements that do not appear in *Giardino*. The most distinctive aspect is the presence of a formula that introduces a subordinate sentence through the conjunction "che" ("that"). Among the most common are "bisogna che" ("it's needed that"), "c'è de gli huomini che" ("there are people who"), "convien/ conviene che" ("it's appropriate that"), "è meglio che" ("it's better that"), "si dice che" ("it's said that"), "non sapete che" ("don't you know that"), "bene dice il savio che" ("the wise person says well that"), "vi converrebbe dire che" ("it would be better for you to say that"), and the authorial "ben dice il Boccaccio che" ("Boccaccio says well that"). One instance is a paremia from *Second Frutes*, which Florio lists in *Giardino* as well:

A carne di lupo convien dar *dente di cane*. (SF 20)
To wolfe's flesh a man must applie a dogg's tooth.

A carne di lupo, dente di cane. (GR 1)
To wolfe's flesh, a dogg's tooth.

In the language manual, the paremia appears in a dialogue between Thomaso and Giovanni in the above-mentioned chapter 2. Here, it acquires a prosaic structure, which differs from the more prosodic with two hemistiches that the paremia shows in *Giardino*. For ease of reference, the section from the conversation in which the paremia appears is displayed here again:

T. **Chi promette e non attende la promessa non val niente.*
G. Sì, ma io mi fido della sua promessa.
T. **Da chi mi fido guardimi Dio ché da chi non mi fido mi guarderò io.*
G. Egli mi dà tante belle parole ch'io non potrei non fidarmi di lui.
T. **Non sapete che le belle parole et i cattivi fatti ingannano i savi e i matti?*
G. **Io lo so, ma se lui mi batte con la spada, io lo batterò con il fodro.*
T. **Dunque, volete rendergli pane per focaccia.*
G. **A chi te la fa, fagliela, o tientela a mente.*
T. Con tale gente bisogna far così.
G. **A carne di lupo convien dar dente di cane.* (SF 18–20)

T. Yea, but a promise not performed is not a rush worth to bee deemed.
G. Yea, but I trust to his promise.
T. From those which I doo trust, good Lord deliver me, from such as I mistrust, ile harmeles care to be.
G. He gives me so many faire words, that I cannot chuse but trust him.
T. Wot you not that faire words and fowle deedes are woont to make fooles and wise man faine?
G. I knowe it, but, if he beate me with the sword, I will beate him againe with the scabbard.
T. What you will give him bread for cake then.
G. If any man wrong thee, wrong him againe, or else be sure to remember it.
T. With such people a man must needes doo so.
G. To wolfe's flesh a man must applie a dogg's tooth.

If all of these paremias contained in this passage are compared with the corresponding equivalent in *Giardino*, it appears that

Chapter Three

they were subject to syntactical transformation when Florio placed them in the dialogical context of his *Firste Fruites* and *Second Frutes*:

   a. **Chi promette e non attende la promessa non val niente.* (SF 18)
      Chi promette e non attende la promessa non val niente. (GR 31)
         A promise not performed is not a rush worth to bee deemed.

   b. **Da chi mi fido guardimi Dio ché da chi non mi fido mi guarderò io.* (SF 18)
      Da chi mi fido guardimi Dio ché da chi non mi fido mi guarderò io. (GR 94)
         From those which I doo trust, good Lord deliver me, from such as I mistrust, ile harmeles care to be.

   c. **Non sapete che le belle parole et i cattivi fatti ingannano i savi e i matti?* (SF 18)
      Belle parole e cattivi fatti ingannano savi et matti. (GR 18)
         Wot you not that faire words and fowle deedes are woont to make fooles and wise man faine?
         Faire words and fowle deedes are woont to make fooles and wise man faine.

   d. **Io lo so, ma se lui mi batte con la spada, io lo batterò con il fodro.* (SF 18)
      Chi percuote con la spada, sarà percosso col fodro. (GR 38)
         I knowe it, but, if he beate me with the sword, I will beate him againe with the scabbard.
         If one beates with the sword, he will be beated with the scabbard.

   e. **Dunque, volete rendergli pane per focaccia.* (SF 18)
      Rendere pane per focaccia. (GR 187)
         What you will give him bread for cake then.
         To give one bread for cake.

   f. **A chi te la fa fagliela, o tientela a mente.* (SF 18)
      A chi te la fa fagliela, o tientela a mente. (GR 4)
         If any man wrong thee, wrong him againe, or else be sure to remember it.

   g. **A carne di lupo convien dar dente di cane.* (SF 20)
      A carne di lupo, dente di cane. (GR 1)
         To wolfe's flesh a man must applie a dogg's tooth.
         To wolfe's flesh, a dogg's tooth.

The examples c, d, e, and g illustrate how the paremias in *Second Frutes* need to conform to the syntax and content of the conversation and present more linguistic substance to run smoothly in the sentence. They can become part of a question (e.g., c), or specify a thought and refer to a specific person and thus, introduce the personal pronouns replacing "chi" ("who") in *Giardino* (e.g., d). They may also introduce a logical inference and a concluding summary (e.g., e), or offer a suggestion (e.g., g).

From *Firste Fruites* comes an example already mentioned in the chapter on the opportunity to be ready to face problems. The expression appears twice in the first manuals and is listed in *Giardino*:

> *È sempre bono per uno haver due corde per il suo archo.* (FF 6v)
> It is alwayes good for one to have two stringes to his bowe.

> *È bon sempre haver due corde per un archo.* (FF 30v)
> It is alwayes good to have two stringes to a bowe.

> *È sempre buono haver due corde per un arco.* (GR 98)
> It is alwayes good to have two stringes to a bowe.

The formula introducing the three expressions with the adverb "sempre" ("always") and the adjective "bono" ("good") highlights their universality and appropriateness. In the instance from chapter 6 (FF 6v), the possessive adjective "suo" in "per il suo archo" ("to his bowe") makes the paremia more personal as it connects with the precedent dative "per uno" ("for one"). In the paremia listed in chapter 19 (FF 30v), Florio does not introduce all of the other prosaic elements that feature in chapter 6. In so doing, he renders the paremia less narrative, as well as more impersonal since it refers to a generic arch ("per un arco") and not to someone's arch ("per il suo archo"). The paremia in *Giardino di ricreatione* seems to combine the two versions resulting in a more general expression. Florio maintains the introductory formula from chapter 6 but keeps the general structure of the paremia from chapter 19. Understandably, *Giardino di ricreatione* is ideologically nearer to the list of proverbs and proverbial phrases in chapter 19 since they both share the decontextualized presence of paremias.

For the same reason, paremias in *Giardino* are frequently more similar, if not equivalent, to those in *Second Frutes*. In one instance, the regional form "sorgi" ("rats") demonstrates equivalence between the expressions in the second manual and the collection:

Chapter Three

> *Gatto guantato non piglia sorzi.* (FF 30r)
> A cat gloved catcheth no mise.
>
> **Gatto guantato non piglia sorgi.* (SF 120)
> A gloved cat dooth never catch good rats.
>
> *Gatto guantato non piglia sorgi.* (GR 107)
> A gloved cat dooth never catch good rats.

Sometimes, however, the opposite occurs and the paremia in *Giardino* clearly derives from an expression in *Firste Fruites*. In one example, a paremia has three members in *Firste Fruites* and *Giardino*, but contains ten members in *Second Frutes* because Florio expands it:

> *Aspettar e non venire, star nel letto e non dormire, servire e non gradire son tre cose da morire.* (FF 27r)
> To tary for a thing that cometh not, to lye a bed and sleepe not, to serve wel and not be accepted, be three things to dy.
>
> **Aspettar e non venire. Star in letto e non dormire. Ben servir e non gradire. Haver cavallo e non vuol ire; e servitor che non vuol ubidire. Esser in prigione e non poter fuggire; et ammalato e non poter guarire. Smarrir la strada quand'un vuol gire. Star alla porta quand'un non vuol aprire; et haver un amico che ti vuol tradire: son dieci doglie da morire.* (SF 12)
> To long for that which coms not. To lye a bed and sleepe not. To serve well and please not. To have a horse that goes not. To keepe a man obeyes not. To lye in iayle and hope not. To bee sich and recover not. To loose one's waye and knowe not. To waite a doore and enter not, and to have a friend we trust not, are ten such spites as hell hath not.
>
> *Aspettare e non venire, star in letto e non dormire, ben servire e non gradire son tre doglie da morire.* (GR 13)
> To tary for a thing that cometh not, to lye a bed and sleepe not, to serve wel and not be accepted, be three pain to dy.

Despite being closer to the paremia in *Firste Fruites*, the paremia in *Giardino* presents a lexical borrowing from *Second Frutes*, namely "doglie" ("pains"), which replaces the more generic "cose" ("things") in the expression from the first language manual. The addition of more elements in the structure of the paremia in *Second Frutes* is an attempt to present the greatest possible number of instances with the same or similar meaning. This satisfies the requests of those in need of a phrase book or conversation manual, an objective that is less perceived in *Firste Fruites* and apparently is not a guiding criterion for the selection of paremias in *Giardino*.

There are many examples of combined paremias in *Second Frutes* as opposed to disjointed ones in *Giardino*. For instance, a paremia from chapter 6 in the language manual corresponds to four distinct paremias in *Giardino*:

> * *Lauda il mare e tienti alla terra; lauda il monte e tienti al piano; lauda la guerra e tienti alla pace; e lauda la moglie ma tienti donzello.* (SF 98)
> Praise the sea, on shore remaine; wonder at hills, keepe on the plaine; commend war, but peace mantaine; honour a wife, but never wed her.
>
> *Lauda la moglie e tienti donzello.* (GR 137)
> Honour a wife, but never wed her.
>
> *Lauda la guerra e tienti alla pace.* (GR 137)
> Commend war, but peace mantaine.
>
> *Lauda il monte e tienti al piano.* (GR 137)
> Wonder at hills, keepe on the plaine.
>
> *Lauda il mare e tienti a terra.* (GR 137)
> Praise the sea, on shore remaine.

Another paremia, from chapter 12, corresponds to two separate paremias in *Giardino* with a slightly different meaning:

> **Freno indorato non migliora il cavallo né guaina d'oro coltello di piombo.* (SF 194)
> A guilded bridle betters not the horse, nor a sheath of gold a leaden knife.
>
> *Freno indorato non migliora il cavallo.* (GR 102; also in SF 122)
> A guilded bridle betters not the horse.
>
> *In guaina d'oro, coltello di piombo.* (GR 123)
> In a sheath of gold, a leaden knife.

In *Second Frutes*, the main clause "non migliora" ("betters not") supports both the first and the second hemistich. The meaning of the second hemistich would be that a good appearance cannot change the real substance of things, much as "a sheath of gold [does not better] a leaden knife." In contrast, *In guaina d'oro, coltello di piombo* in *Giardino* conveys the conventionalized meaning that appearances are not truthful (GDLI, s.v. *guaina*, n. 12).

A final example demonstrates the different contextualizations of a paremia in the two *Fruits* and in the collection, and illustrates how this expression is used as a defense of the author's work in the second language manual. Florio lists it in chapter 19 of *Firste Fruites* and then uses it in the letter to the readers of his *Second Frutes* as well as in *Giardino*:

> *Muro bianco, carta de matti.* (FF 32r)
> A white wal is a foole's paper.
>
> *Muro bianco* is paper good enough for everie *matto*. (SF A2v)
> A white wal is paper good enough for everie foole.
>
> *Muro bianco, carta di matto.* (GR 149)
> A white wal is a foole's paper.

Conventionally, the paremia suggests the idea that it is hard to imagine what a mad mind can do and that no field is immune from the presence of strange people.[100] The form of the paremia is similar in the first language manual and in *Giardino*, in the last of which the preposition "di" ("of") takes the form attested in the Florentine vernacular. The singular adjective "matto" ("fool") however, links the expression in the collection to that in the letter "To the Reader" in *Second Frutes*, in which Florio applies its meaning to literary enterprises. Florio dismembers the paremia and transforms it into a hybrid structure between Italian and English. He plays with its meaning asserting that a mad person could even use a white wall to write and, in so doing, justifies the publication of his own proverb-studded language manuals:

> If they sight and taste be so altred, that neither colour or taste of my frutes will please thee, I greatly force not, for I never minded to be thy fruterer. *Muro bianco* is paper good enough for everie *matto*. Prints were first invented for wise men's use, and not for foole's play. These proverbs and proverbial phrases (hethertoo so peculiar to the Italians that they could never finde the way over the Apenines, or meanes to become familiar to anie other nation) have only been selected and stamped for the wise and not for thee (and therefore hast thou no part in them) who will kindly accept of them ... for the pleasure of which I will shortly send into the world an exquisite Italian and English Dictionary and a compendious Grammer. (SF A2v)

"Crazy people," namely unworthy writers and linguists, pretend to be at the same level of the others and thus do the craziest things ever, such as engaging in a publication. As will be discussed in the following chapter, this topic informs Sarnelli's letter to the readers of his *Posilecheata* as well. Considering that Florio is excusing himself from the accusation of being unworthy of writing a bilingual manual, he ironically admits that the range of possibilities for a "crazy" mind, such as his, is infinite. As a result, he plans to publish an Italian-English dictionary, his *A Worlde of Wordes*, and a grammar, which he never published though. He also shares his Italian proverbs and proverbial phrases with the world, demonstrating the usefulness of his pedagogy and the worthiness of his "muro bianco" ("white wall").

Chapter Four

Pompeo Sarnelli's *Posilecheata*
Paremias and the Multifaceted Neapolitan Baroque

> Quasi tutti e medesimi proverbi o simili, benché con diverse parole, si truovono in ogni nazione; e la ragione è che e proverbii nascono dalla esperienzia o vero osservazione delle cose, le quali in ogni luogo sono le medesime o simili.
>
> The same or similar proverbs, though differently expressed, are found among all nations; and this is because proverbs spring from experience or from the observation of things, which are everywhere the same or similar.
>
> Francesco Guicciardini, *Ricordi*

Sarnelli's Literary Presence

Born in the Apulia region in Polignano (today Polignano a Mare, near Bari),[1] Pompeo Sarnelli (1649–1724) moved to Naples when he was an adolescent. There, he studied theology and law and, after he became a priest in 1669, worked for Cardinal Vincenzo Maria Orsini. In 1689, he refused a position at the bishopric of Termoli; however, in 1692[2] he accepted that same position in Bisceglie after Pope Innocent XII offered it to him. Throughout all his years of activity, Sarnelli wrote several erudite works, including many elegies and odes in Latin, a commentary on Latin poems (*Il filo d'Arianna*), and paraphrases of religious texts (*Salmi penitenziali*). He also published two guides to the city of Naples and surrounding areas in 1685 and, along with Antonio Bulifon, coordinated the second edition of Giovanni Antonio Summonte's *Historia della città e regno di Napoli* (1601–02, 1640–43) and of Ferrante Loffredo's *Antichità di Pozzuoli* (1570), both republished in 1675.[3] One year later, Bulifon printed Sarnelli's *Degli avvenimenti di Fortunato e de' suoi figli*, a personal interpretation of a Spanish story that the author accessed from a French translation

(Gimma 287)[4] and presented at the Accademia degli Scioperati di Rossano of which he was a member.[5]

Sarnelli's reputation as a knowledgeable man of letters and as a clergyman did not protect his main work, *Posilecheata*, a collection of five fables or *cunti* in the Neapolitan dialect, from sinking into oblivion. He printed the collection under the pseudonym Masillo Reppone de Gnanopoli[6] in 1684,[7] fifty years after the posthumous publication of Basile's *Lo cunto de li cunti, overo lo trattienimento de' peccerille* (1634–36).[8] The work is introduced by a prefatory letter addressed to "li vertoluse lejeture" ("the virtuous readers") and concluded by a "scompetura" ("conclusion"). The letter, like the "Proemio" of the *Decameron*, sets the tone of the narration but also, resembles a pseudo-linguistic treatise on sociolinguistic variations in Italy. In the following introduction, *'Ntroduzzione de la Posilecheata e commito d'ammice fatto a Posileco* ("Introduction to *Posilecheata* and banquet amongst friends made in Posillipo"), a carnivalesque dialogue takes place in the context of a formal dinner and serves as a humorous framework for the five fables. Since Sarnelli was considered a mere follower of Basile, the brighter and long-lasting success surrounding *Lo cunto de li cunti* overshadowed his own collection of fables. The inclusion of his work in Thomas Frederick Crane's 1886 article, "Some Forgotten Italian Storytellers," confirms the obscurity that Sarnelli suffered for almost two centuries after the publication of *Posilecheata*. Not even Enrico Malato's 1963 (Sarnelli, *Posilecheata* [1963]) and 1986 Italian translation (Sarnelli, *Posilecheata* [1986]) of the collection helped to promote it in either academic or non-academic venues in the way that Benedetto Croce's Italian edition of Basile's *Lo cunto de li cunti* (*Il Pentamerone* [1925]) did for that text (Rak, *Napoli gentile* 295: footnote 1).

Before modern times, just a few scholars referenced Sarnelli and his production. After Nicola De Donato's 1906 biography of the author, only Benedetto Croce redeemed Sarnelli's work and defined it as an "imitazione intelligente ed elegante" ("intelligent and elegant imitation"; *Saggi sulla letteratura italiana* 74). More recent anthologies of Neapolitan literature and monographs on Baroque fairy tales devoted only short paragraphs to Sarnelli and his collection of fables.[9] In 1984, Rosa Franzese wrote an article on *Posilecheata*'s etiologic stories and fantastic settings in the journal *Napoli Nobilissima*. More than a decade later, Giorgio Fulco dedicated a paragraph to *Posilecheata* in the *Storia della letteratura italiana* published by Salerno and recognized Sarnelli's personal innovation in his imitation of Basile's model (863–64). Hermann Haller reserved a section for Sarnelli in his *The Other Italy* (255–56), and subsequently in its Italian translation *La festa delle lingue* (254–55), thereby according the author a respectable place in the canon of writers in Neapolitan. Along with Raffaele Giglio's and Clara Allasia's articles on the fairy-tale tradition, Bottigheimer included *Posilecheata* in her 2012 book on Italian and French literary and critical works on fairy tales and translated parts of Sarnelli's collection into English (71–79).

As far as Sarnelli's language is concerned, Rocco's 1882–91 *Vocabolario del dialetto napolitano* frequently mentions Sarnelli's *Posilecheata* and reports many of his expressions, including paremias, among the dictionary's entries (Rocco, *Vocabolario* [2018], vol. 1: 41–44; see also Vinciguerra, "Spigolature lessicali napoletane," "Per un'edizione critica"). Similarly, Raffaele Capozzoli in his 1889 *Grammatica del dialetto napoletano* refers to *Posilecheata* to offer examples of Neapolitan morphology, orthography, etymology, and syntax. More recently, Speroni and Vincenzo Valente published articles on aspects of Sarnelli's use of language and paremias. Speroni's 1953 "Proverbi della *Posilecheata*" lists all of the proverbs and proverbial phrases in Sarnelli's work and indicates their possible sources.[10] More generally, Valente's 1977 "La lingua napoletana di Pompeo Sarnelli" analyzes the Neapolitan language in Sarnelli's work and compares and contrasts it with the dialect of earlier authors. Sarnelli's language is frequently mentioned in Adam Ledgeway's 2009 *Grammatica diacronica del napoletano*, which lists *Posilecheata* as a textual source. Likewise, Carolina Stromboli refers to Sarnelli extensively in her 2013 edition of Basile's collection of fables, and Francesco Montuori suggests that Sarnelli's collection is a fundamental work for identifying proverbs of the Campania region (158: footnote 27). According to Montuori, Sarnelli's paremias serve as a testimony to the linguistic creativity of the Neapolitan culture and identity, and simultaneously represent the means to discuss sociocultural issues and practices.

Chapter Four

Literature in Neapolitan Dialect and Sarnelli's Fables

Since the fourteenth century, the Neapolitan dialect attracted many authors, especially those writing in the Florentine vernacular. The very first example of "dialettalità riflessa"[11] ("conscious use of the dialect") is, indeed, the 1339 *Epistola napoletana* by Boccaccio, who signs it with his Neapolitan pseudonym Jannetta di Parisse, literally a small John from Paris (De Blasi, *Storia linguistica* 26–29; Manni 262–65; Paccagnella, *Plurilinguismo letterario*; Sabatini). Tuscan writer Zanobi da Strada provides another example of literary use of the Neapolitan dialect when he recounts to Jacopo Acciaioli (son of Donato Acciaioli the Old) how a woman acquired such a strong Neapolitan accent that her way of speaking was almost unintelligible to his fellow Tuscans (Bianchi et al., 35). In the next century, the interest in the Neapolitan dialect evolved and matured into a specific attention to more popular and spoken linguistic modes of expression. Personal accounts and *mémoires* presented interesting aspects of the local quotidian language in this regard. The most famous example of *mémoire* is Loise De Rosa's *Ricordi*, a collection of five texts written between 1467 and 1475. The work's structure aims to establish a connection with the reader and with those elements of the oral discourse, including paremias, idiomatic expressions, and riddles, that were used to mimic spoken language in written form (50–58).[12]

During the Aragonese domination, beginning with Alfonso I's conquest of the city in 1442, Naples thrived as a cosmopolitan center where different languages came in contact with one another promoting the city's bureaucratic, administrative, cultural, literary, economic, and commercial activities (De Blasi, *Storia linguistica* 45). Along with the other languages that were commonly spoken (namely, Latin, Neapolitan, Florentine, Venetian, French, Provençal, and German), Castilian and Catalan began to be used at court and at the chancellor's office—forming what is called "*koinè* cancelleresca" ("chancery koine"). Only after Naples was annexed by Ferdinand the Catholic in 1503 did the distinctive linguistic panorama of the Neapolitan area become evident. A pronounced diastratic division between varieties spoken by different social groups emerged. Specifically, on one hand, Neapolitan served for oral communication. On the other, Castilian and Catalan represented the prestigious varieties since they exemplified the cohesiveness and unity of Spain, a nation that boasted incredible military strength and domination.[13] From that point forward, speaking Spanish in Naples meant to pay tribute to the dominators and thus, became a common way to communicate in high society. Because of it, dictionaries, grammar books, and conversational texts were published for the sake of disseminating the correct use of the Spanish language amongst the local community (D'Ascoli, *Lingua spagnuola* 8–10).[14]

Because of this administrative situation, the Neapolitan dialect was condemned to a marginal position in literary practices as well. Traditionally, the Florentine vernacular was granted space in Petrarchist literature and in those genres that could count on a secular tradition. For instance, Sannazaro and Tommaso Costo, the latter a member of the Accademia della Crusca, adhered to the Florentine model in their works, *Arcadia* (1504) and *Fuggilozio* (1596) respectively. Similarly, Tasso used standard Florentine in all of his poetic production, from *Gerusalemme liberata* (1581) to *Gerusalemme conquistata* (1593) to his rhymes (1591–93). However, the bland acceptance of Bembo's prescriptions in *Prose della volgar lingua* testifies to how the Neapolitan dialect was resistant to a top-down imposition (Bianchi et al., 83; Haller, *The Other Italy* 244). In the sixteenth and seventeenth centuries, the discussion about the dichotomy between the Neapolitan and Tuscan varieties and the superiority of one over the other became lively (Malato, "La letteratura dialettale campana" 265–66; Vitale, "Di alcune rivendicazioni secentesche"). Partenio Tosco's 1662 *L'Eccellenza della lingua napoletana* is an example of this linguistic debate. Although it was written in Italian for easy access, the work exalted the Neapolitan dialect through lists of words organized in themes. As Manlio Cortelazzo argues, the dialect renounced the competition with Tuscan and chose to explore those literary genres that the elevated literature in standard language had not yet acknowledged (*I dialetti e la dialettologia* 75; see also Rak, *Napoli gentile* 22–25). Authors writing in dialect transferred all of the traditionally-recognized literary forms and topics into their own compositions and gave them a local, and often popular, flavor through language. They intended to explore the infinite expressive potential of the Neapolitan language as a counterpart to the purist Tuscan monopoly (Paccagnella, "Uso letterario dei dialetti"). In order to achieve it, they indulged in a great degree of linguistic experimentation, which allowed them to constantly reinvigorate the dialect in a variety of contexts and uses.

As an antidote to the literary affectation and mawkishness of the Florentine literary tradition (De Blasi, "Notizie sulla variazione diastratica" 95), idiomatic expressions and paremias constituted recurrent elements within texts in the Neapolitan dialect. They expressed the authenticity of the local communities and contributed to the legitimization of the language, demonstrating its ability to compete with other literatures yet preserving its unique qualities (Bianchi et al., 64). For instance, comic poetic exchanges in dialect called *gliommieri* featured paremias, maxims, and idiomatic expressions that were recited for pure amusement. Entertaining songs in dialect called *villanelle*, which recalled oral practices during communal events, heavily employed formulaic and idiomatic language (De Blasi, *Storia linguistica* 57–60; Haller, *The Other Italy* 243–78; Malato, "La letteratura dialettale campana"; Rak, *Napoli gentile* 47–74). Paremias found expression in Neapolitan dialect through theater. This is especially evident in *farze* (or *farcze*) *cavaiole*, a sort of farce that hybridized Neapolitan and Tuscan. Proverbs and proverbial expressions were also used in performances of the *commedia dell'arte* as well as in puppetry to portray the Neapolitan dialect of the mean and vicious character Pulcinella (Rak, *Napoli gentile* 99–134, 240–51).

In the seventeenth century, the presence of bilingual authors became more common. Basile and Giulio Cesare Cortese, himself a member of the Accademia della Crusca, wrote both in Italian and in Neapolitan (Radtke, "La questione della lingua" 82). Along with Felippo de Scafato Sgruttendio, they attempted to create a literary reality that could be deemed as equally respectable as the established literature in Florentine vernacular. By way of reworking traditional genres and by filling them with erudite classical and mythological references, these three authors forged a specific language and style that could give voice to the local and popular culture and satisfy the public's taste for realism. As the crowns of the Neapolitan dialect,[15] they competed with the established triad of the Florentine language, Dante, Petrarca, and Boccaccio, and succeeded in demanding attention from the literary world.

Posilecheata is the direct descendant of these literary experimentations with and in the Neapolitan dialect.[16] For Sarnelli,

Neapolitan becomes a language of inclusion in the culture that accepted and nurtured him after leaving Apulia (Grimaldi, "L'ironia nei detti proverbiali" 533). To his eyes of a non-native speaker, Naples is a linguistic, cultural, and social center to praise and promote (Haller, *The Other Italy* 280).[17] In fact, Naples and the Neapolitan dialect leave a visible trace in all parts of his collection. The recounting of the fables happens in Posillipo, and all of the fables are set in Naples with a limited centrifugal movement toward distant lands. As a collection of fairy tales, the abstract and the fantastic dominate *Posilecheata*. Nonetheless, the stories perceive and describe the true essence of reality, anchored, as they are, in the real world that creates them and constitutes the starting point of their utopian dimension (Canepa, *From Court to Forest* 24). Within this characterization, the dialect gives voice to the lively and colorful community of the Neapolitan people and shapes the Baroque dimension of the collection meant to instruct, amuse, and astonish the audience (Getto 298; Rak, *Napoli gentile* 298; Tarzia 180).[18]

A fundamental feature of the newly-created seventeenth-century genre of the fable (Calvino, *Sulla fiaba* 31–78, 117–34), and in general of Baroque novellas, is indeed the "ricerca dello stupefacente" ("search for the astonishing"; Spera 29; see also Calabrese; Canepa, *From Court to Forest*; Picone and Messerli; and Tarzia). As Giovanni Getto highlights in his 2000 book, *Il barocco letterario in Italia*, trying to channel the Baroque novella inside an historical and literary catalogue is a burdensome enterprise. However, it is possible to underscore some elements that characterize and unify all Baroque short stories, and Baroque literature in general. They offer delight and marvel by reproducing the dynamic spirit of the period. Moreover, their language is characterized by an accumulation of words, ludic enthusiasm for linguistic games, and metaphorical transformation and deformation, which all serve as literary ornaments to the narration (Getto 276, 300). The Baroque overwhelming presence of comic elements, exaggerated rhetoric, and hilarious magnification of reality created polyphonic literary works that could appeal to the different senses of the human being (Albanese, "I centomila miliardi di proverbi" 11). This is particularly true for Basile's language, which is dominated by an absolute linguistic freedom, exploding in a farcical and concrete depiction of popular life. Despite its more subdued nature, Sarnelli's language in *Posilecheata* reveals the same strength and dynamism. His Neapolitan is very controlled and results from his long-standing philological engagement with literary texts and authors.[19] However, this does not prevent Sarnelli from inserting structures typical of spoken and popular language for expressive purposes, especially paremias (Valente, "La lingua napoletana" 260–63).[20]

In the introduction to his edition of Basile's collection, Michele Rak writes that paremias are narrative elements. They resemble micro-stories with a specific and individual dimension, yet they are more flexible than a fixed narration (Basile, *Lo cunto de li cunti* [1986] xlii). While they delimit an autonomous space for themselves, they are in contact with the surrounding context and adapt to the infinite variety of circumstances that take place. Sarnelli's paremias represent perfect illustrations of this adaptability as they transcend specific genres while contemporaneously adapting to the textual, linguistic, stylistic, and cultural exigencies of the different sections of *Posilecheata*.[21]

The Prefatory Letter: Paremias Praising the Neapolitan Dialect

Posilecheata's prefatory epistle represents a manifesto of Sarnelli's polemical and subversive idea of linguistic supremacy and of his attitude toward the Neapolitan language. By offering his own contribution to the Italian "questione della lingua," Sarnelli powerfully and comically compares Neapolitan to other languages with stronger literary traditions and elevates it. The first "victim"[22] of his derision is the dated and antiquated idea of language promoted by the Accademici della Crusca in their two published editions of the *Vocabolario* in 1612 and 1623.[23] The second victims are the Northern dialects, stereotyped as more sophisticated and refined languages than other dialects.

Sarnelli is conscious of the supremacy of the Tuscan vernacular and of the great literary traditions in Lombard and Venetian dialects. In all fairness, literature in Neapolitan embraced more genres and showed more original aspects than dialect literature in Northern Italy. The sole exception was indeed Venice, where production in the local languages was quite robust, especially in theatre (Malato, "La letteratura dialettale campana" 260). Yet, a secular stigma was in place against Neapolitan, which was considered the language only of comedies and less refined literature.[24] Therefore, Sarnelli begins his letter by asserting that those who always engage in grand literature evaluate his *Posilecheata* as a "passiatempo" ("diversion") and do not grant the work the recognition that is typically awarded to other literary works (P 4.3). According to the author, these writers of high-standard literary works are "pennaruli" ("pen-wielders"), a word that he uses as an ironic and derogatory remark for those who hold their pen only after payment. Such men of letters consider literature merely as a lucrative profession yet are always revered because of their established social status.

Two proverbial phrases express Sarnelli's decision to write a work that does not meet the expectations of a public used to those "pen-wielders" and steeped in the Florentine literary tradition. This public is so obtuse and inconsiderate that it does not appreciate the value of his *Posilecheata*:

> Pocca li primme uommene de lo munno porzì songo state cenzorate, essenno 'mpossibbele che *quarche travo rutto no' strida* e che *quarche strenga rotta non se metta 'n dozzana*: anze, trattannose de livre, vide pe infi' a li strunze (parlanno co lleverenzia de le facce voste) che diceno: *Nos coque pomma natamus*. (P 3.2)

> Indeed, the very first men of the world were censored, for it's impossible that there's no beam that doesn't creak or that in a dozen shoelaces there's not a broken one or two. In fact, in the matter of books, you'll see that pieces of shit (speaking with reverence for your faces) will say, "we can swim, too." (Bottigheimer 76)

The paremia, *Il travo rutto stride* ("The broken beam creaks"), conveys the message that anything defective, despite looking as strong as a beam, creaks and shows its flaws. Consequently, when an imperfection occurs, it is impossible to hide it. Critics, who do not excel in their job, are "travi rotte" ("broken beams") and cannot help but express their own, incorrect ideas. In fact, many writers fell victim to these incompetent critics, who blamed them for their supposed imperfections or literary inappropriateness—something false in Sarnelli's opinion. The second paremia, *La strenga rotta se mette 'n dozzana* ("A broken shoelace puts itself in a dozen"), also in Basile's *Muse napolitane* (4.153, 5.381), confirms the first expression's message by referring to blusterous people who cannot avoid intruding in matters that do not concern them. They put themselves in a dozen groups and are, therefore, all together without distinction, much like "stringhe rotte" ("broken shoelaces") that are not separated from the good ones.[25] The critique is even more apparent since some unworthy authors imagine themselves to be "apples," when in fact they are "pieces of shit." *Nos coque pomma natamus*, a phonetic transcription of the Latin expression, *Nos quoque poma natamus* ("We are floating apples"), exemplifies the unrealistic consideration of their worth.[26] Malato traces the phrase to an Aesopian fable that argues against the vanity of praise, and identifies it as a source of a Neapolitan story about a shipwreck that left oranges floating in the water beside some dung. Sarnelli applies the literal meaning of the expression to the context of his prefatory letter, in which he refers to those who are not able to write and dare to criticize other writers. These people deem themselves to be as good as the brightest authors, in the same faulty way that, in the fable, excrement is believed to be apples. By inference, this group of unskilled critics includes those who would attack Sarnelli for the literary enterprise he has undertaken with his *Posilecheata*.

The only way Sarnelli can find a meritorious place in the linguistic canon for Neapolitan and claim the literary dignity of this dialect is to play satirically with the stereotype that the Tuscan tradition created. Sarnelli is aware that the clash between two linguistic codes, especially if one is dialect and another represents the standardized or more prestigious language, is a powerful tool for sarcasm and comedy (Gibellini). After demonstrating that Tuscan cannot be given the label of a more literary language, he emphasizes that his work is a "recreazione leceta ed onesta" ("a legitimate and honest recreation").[27] When he then activates an antagonistic "parodia del diverso" ("parody of the diverse") based on diatopic aspects (Cortelazzo et al., *I dialetti italiani* 1003),[28] he can satirize the canonical literature in Florentine and demolish it. The tools that he uses to achieve his objective are paremias. While they minimize the traditional prestige associated with the language of the city of Florence, Sarnelli's proverbs and proverbial phrases confirm the creative nature of the Neapolitan language, and hence demonstrate the success of his literary operation.

The author sets forth a classical source to strengthen his point and mentions Gnaeus Pompeius Magnus's experience in Naples. Apparently, upon arriving in the city, the Roman statesman fell in love with the local dialect and immediately abandoned Latin.[29] When Cicero scolded him for his decision, Pompeius responded that if Cicero had been acquainted with the Neapolitan language, he himself would have chosen it over Latin because Neapolitan, in fact a combination of Latin and Greek, "sweetens the mouth."[30] Cicero's reprimand of Pompeius is described by means of a proverbial phrase:

> Quanno Cicerone ne le *fece na lavatella de capo senza sapone* ...
> (P 5.7)
>
> As a result, Cicero gave Pompey's head a good washing without soap ... (Bottigheimer 77)

In his dictionary, Rocco (s.v. *sapone*) explains that *Lavare la capo* ("To wash someone his/her head") or *Fare lo contrapilo senza sapone* ("To go against the direction of the hair without soap") suggest doing something easily and without much consideration.[31] However, within the verbal discussion between Cicero and Pompeius, a second meaning for the expression fits the context more, specifically to scold someone (GDLI, s.v. *sapone* [1], n. 5). Sarnelli modifies the expression by replacing the more traditional "lavare" ("to wash") with "fare una lavatella" ("to give a good/kind washing"), in which "lavatella" presents a pun in comparison to the term "lavata" ("a washing").[32] "Lavata" indeed indicates an admonishment that is usually firm and direct, and difficult to soften. "Lavatella" grammatically seems to lessen the meaning of the word or, at least, to make it nicer in order to communicate an affectionate feeling or emotion. However, in Sarnelli's *Posilecheata*, the phrase ironically means that the rebuke is in fact very sharp. Sarnelli states that Cicero is not simply giving Pompeius a washing without soap, but rather a good washing of reproaches (Grimaldi, "L'ironia nei detti proverbiali").

The proverbial phrase, *Fare na lavatella de capo senza sapone* ("To give someone's head a good/kind washing without soap"), achieves many objectives in this section of the prefatory letter. First, it situates Cicero and Pompeius in a colloquial context and in the middle of a linguistic discussion. If Cicero can scold Pompeius for his choice of spoken language, then the paremia also shifts their relationship to a level of friendly banter rather than political association. Second, the "Neapolitanization" of the proverbial phrase makes the entire event local and far from Rome. The contrast between Neapolitan and Latin creates a dichotomy between a highly-recognized language and a dialect. Since Tuscan is not present in the comparison, Neapolitan can compete with Latin and is even the victor of this competition. Third, the presence of the paremia representing Cicero's reproach is fundamental to understanding the meaning of Pompeius's subsequent answer fully. Because of Cicero's disapproval, Pompeius replies in a demonstrative and epideictic way. Without the proverbial phrase, it can be speculated that Pompeius's words would have probably been less passionate and reasoned. Finally, the proverbial phrase makes light of Cicero's inability to convince Pompeius. The great philosopher and rhetorician appears powerless and fails in demonstrating the superiority of Latin over Neapolitan. It is probable that Sarnelli compares Cicero's unsuccessful attempt to convince Pompeius about the superiority of Latin with the defeat of the Tuscan language and the consequent victory of the Neapolitan dialect. The paremia indirectly contributes to the Tuscan-Neapolitan contrast and allows the author of *Posilecheata* to deliver his own successful praise of the Neapolitan language.[33]

The narration continues with Sarnelli's underscoring, much like Pompeius, his loyalty to the Neapolitan language and culture:

> Chi ha fatto lo stromiento co li Toscanise de parlare a lengua loro, s'aggia pacienzia: Io non ce l'aggio fatto, e perzò voglio parlare a lengua de lo pajese mio. E chi no' lo pò sentire, o s'appila l'aurecchie, *o cinco lettere*. (P 7.14)

> If you've made a pact with the Tuscans to speak their language, you'll have to bear with me: I haven't, and I intend to speak in the language of my own country. And if you can't stand hearing it, either plug your ears, or take those five letters and do with them what you wish. (Bottigheimer 78)

Sarnelli's unwillingness to find a compromise demonstrates his intolerance of the Tuscan language. He only offers two possibilities, neither of which is agreeable to speakers of languages other than Neapolitan. The options are either a voluntary choice of deafness or "five letters." In his edition of *Posilecheata*, Malato explains that the meaning of the proverbial phrase *Cinco lettere* is lost and that it might be a periphrasis for the Italian word "merda" ("shit"; P 7.14: footnote 7). In *Vocabolario del dialetto napolitano*, Rocco (s.v. *cinco*) identifies the five letters with "crepa" ("snuff it") and reports Sarnelli's quotation without offering further explanation.[34] Usually, the two words "pazienza" ("patience") and "cinque" ("five") are coupled in the proverbial phrase, *O pazienza o cinque lettere* ("Either patience or five letters"). In Sarnelli's text, the word "pacienzia" refers to those who are able to tolerate the Tuscan language, unlike himself who has lost it and wishes to speak in the language of Naples. In this context, "cinque lettere" means that the alternative to "pazienza" relates to pain, and possible appropriate terms may be "dolor" ("pain") or "morte" ("death"). This is a metaphorical and slightly ironic pain, or death, since it affects only those who do not recognize the value of the Neapolitan language, and thus of Sarnelli's work, as opposed to the artificiality and bookish tradition of the Tuscan language (Valente, "La lingua napoletana"). The paremia *O pazienza o cinque lettere*, being elliptical or monophrastic (since it does not contain a verb and is composed of a main sentence only), is meant to be direct (Bessi 65); however, in this instance, it is more ambiguous than other paremias. Its indeterminant meaning, one that lies somewhere between surrender and irreverence, is also a sentiment that characterizes Sarnelli's entire prefatory letter.

After the Tuscan vernacular, Sarnelli scrutinizes the Northern dialects (Cortelazzo et al., *I dialetti italiani* 226–60; Del Tufo 624–883). He criticizes them in order to heap praise upon the phonetic and morphological regulatory principles of the Neapolitan language. A seventeenth-century dialectology lesson is said to be delivered by a philosopher from Posillipo, who looks like the embodiment of Sarnelli. He speaks to a person from Northern Italy whom he considers a "protoquamquam," ironically meaning that he behaves like a pedant:

> Na vota, cammenanno no cierto felosofo de Posileco pe la Lommardia, perché parlava napoletano chiantuto e majàteco, tutte se ne redevano. Isso, mo, *pe farele toccare la coda co le mmano*, decette a uno che faceva lo protaquamquam: «Vedimmo no poco, de 'ratia, si songo meglio le parole voste o le noste!» (P 6.10)

> Once, when a certain philosopher from Posillipo was walking around in Lombardy, everyone started laughing at him because he was speaking his vigorous and succulent Neapolitan. So, to make sure they'd go off with their tails between their legs, he says to one of them who was acting like a know-it-all: "Now, let's just see, if you please, if your words or ours are better!" (Bottigheimer 77)

Chapter Four

Rocco (s.v. *coda*) explains that the proverbial phrase *Pe farele toccare la coda co le mmano* ("To make someone touch the tail with his/her own hand") means to cause someone to be confused, defeated, and discouraged. In the same dictionary (s.v. *mano* and *toccare*), he describes *Toccare co mano* ("To touch it with your hand") as to make sure of something. Thus, in Sarnelli's context, the expression suggests beating the critics in this linguistic competition and demonstrating to them the unquestionable superiority of the Neapolitan dialect. Neapolitan is said to be "chiantuto e majateco," vigorous, consistent, solid, and flourishing.[35] As Rak argues, "chiantuto" establishes a connection between literature and life, and confirms that literary production in Neapolitan dialect is rooted in geographical, cultural, social, and historical elements (*Napoli gentile* 24). According to Sarnelli, such characteristics are exclusive to Naples and do not pertain to Tuscan or other dialects.[36]

Sarnelli continues his derogatory analysis of the Lombard dialects by means of a harsh linguistic prank. The apocopation of words typical of these vernaculars introduces a comparison between the beauty of Neapolitan and the ungraceful Lombard words. Ultimately, Sarnelli celebrates the Neapolitan phonetic aspects as he considers them more meaningful and productive than those of the Northern dialects:

> «Dì alla 'mpressa le parole meje a lengua toja: Io, Casa, Capo». E lo Lommardo, subeto: «Mi Ca-Cò!» «E si te cacò» decette lo Napoletano «te lo 'mmeretaste!» (P 6.11)

> "Say my words in your language fast: Io, Casa, Capo." And the Lombard right away replied: "Mi Ca-Cò." "If you shat yourself," said the Neapolitan, "you deserved it!" (Bottigheimer 77)

The Neapolitan philosopher skillfully deflects the malevolent laughter originally directed at him by the Lombard person because of his accent and way of speaking. The obscene pun, i.e., demonstrating that the Neapolitan words "io, casa, capo" ("I, house, head") become "mi, ca, co" in Lombard,[37] derides the Northern dialects and their inconvenience and inappropriateness with scatological references. At the same time, the philosopher's words mock the grammar of those who cannot speak the Lombard dialect correctly. He uses the third person singular of the verb "cacare," "cacò" ("to shit"), for the subject pronoun "tu" ("you"), the same form that the Northern speaker employs for the subject pronoun "mi" ("I"). Hence, the philosopher, who is an expert in language and rhetoric, ridicules the ungrammatical way in which people from the north of Italy talk. His wordplay paves the way to the apex of the prefatory letter, which introduces a paremia expressly created for this context.

As Boccaccio's *Decameron* and Basile's *Lo cunto de li cunti* are introduced by a paremia, a proverbial phrase features in the climactic point of *Posilecheata*'s prefatory letter. In the *Decameron*, the expression, *Umana cosa è aver compassione degli afflitti* ("To take pity on people in distress is a human quality"; Dec. Proemio.2), opens a text meant to heal melancholy in the female readers of Boccaccio's text. In Basile's *Cunto*, the proverb, *Chi cerca quello che non deve trova quello che non vuole* ("Those who look for what they should not, find what they would not"; CC I.Intr.1), invites people not to follow and imitate tradition (Guaragnella, "Motti, sentenze e proverbi" 123–25). In *Posilecheata*, the paremia sets the tone of both the letter and the collection with its intensely ironic and hilarious mood that intends to scorn and ridicule. The same philosopher refers to an expression used in an area surrounding Posillipo:

> Pocca se dice a lo pajese che non è mio: *Lengua che no' la 'ntienne, e tu la caca*. Ora vide chi parla a lo sproposeto, nuje o vuje? (P 6.11)

> Because it's said in a town—not mine—that if you don't understand a language, you shit it right out. Now let's see who's talking out of turn, us or you? (Bottigheimer 77)

Malato comments that the paremia was used in Naples in the seventeenth century to indicate the Neapolitan people's indifference to foreign languages (P 6.11–12: footnote 6).[38] In the context of Sarnelli's prefatory letter to *Posilecheata*, the expression affirms that the Northern dialects are unintelligible and that, although a stronger literary tradition supports them, they should be discarded.[39] In the end, the paremia confirms the supremacy of the Neapolitan dialect over any other vernacular by means of a defecatory metaphor.

Sarnelli endorses the rules of his own language in an ironic context, which makes his statement even stronger. He does not focus on the positive aspects of the Neapolitan dialect, but rather, concentrates on negative ones when he describes the language as being corpulent and heavy, hence worthy of common people and suitable for depicting the rural reality instead of the refined world of letters. By way of exalting these supposedly poor characteristics, he ironically denies the other vernaculars any form of linguistic dignity. As paremias convey comedy and sarcasm, create ambiguity, and express in a more tangible way the wisdom of the Neapolitan culture, they help Sarnelli to express a powerful message in crucial sections of his prefatory letter.

The Introductory Banquet: Tripartite Paremias to Marvel

Giving credit to Cicero's words that "comoediam esse imitationem vitae, speculum consuetudinis, imaginem veritatis" ("comedy is an imitation of life, a mirror of customs, and an image of truth"; Donatus 5.1), Sarnelli's '*Ntroduzzione* (P 9–33) is a perfect example of comedy. As Mikhail Bakhtin states, freedom is one of the most appropriate manifestations of the carnival, and laughter becomes the tool for revealing truth and authenticity (*Rabelais and His World* 83–101, 196–303). The banquet described in Sarnelli's introduction represents an explosion of vitality, similar to the overturning of the typical and hierarchical order of life that carnival allows.[40] Facetious use of paremias, word games, and humorous expressions occur against the background of gastronomic erudition and popular atmosphere in which neither decency nor respect are required any longer.[41] The realistic scene and "hyperboles of food" (*Rabelais and His World* 184–85) not only create a comedic effect, but also attest to the inventiveness of the dialect. As argued for the prefatory letter, proverbs and proverbial phrases help demonstrate the linguistic superiority and the greater literary versatility of the Neapolitan language, and enhance pivotal sections in the narration.

In contrast to Boccaccio's frame, Sarnelli's is filled with comic stratagems, which the central character of the scene, doctor Marchionno, employs to benefit himself during the dinner.[42] Moreover, as a response to Basile's fantastic world, *Posilecheata*'s introduction takes place in a concrete context that presents the author under his pseudonym Masillo, his friend Petruccio, doctor Marchionno, and the five storytellers. On July 26, 1684, Masillo accepts his friend Petruccio's invitation to spend time with him in Posillipo. The two friends are unaware, though, that an uninvited host, indeed Marchionno, would join them and stage a gigantic scene in both words and actions. The result is a linguistic and theatrical performance, whose humor results from the absurd and illogical inversion of common sense and from the character's excessiveness of manners.

A sentence that sounds like a didactic saying with prescriptive value opens the introduction and determines the atmosphere of the banquet (Fig. 5):

Figure 5: *Posilecheata,* first page of *'Ntroduzzione de la Posilecheata e comito d'ammice fatto a Posileco.* Courtesy of the Newberry Library, Bonaparte 5634.

Chapter Four

> Na longa vita senza na recreazione, a lo munno, è ghiusto comme a no luongo viaggio senza na taverna pe defrisco, senza n'alloggiamento pe repuoso. (P 9.1)[43]
>
> In the world, a long life without any recreation is as fair as a long journey without a tavern to restore oneself and without a lodging to rest.

The saying admits ironically that those who consider diversion disgraceful are reprehensible men. They always walk with lead on their feet and with a compass in their hands, meaning that they are scrutinizing the world carefully and reducing it to a sort of geometrical and mathematical formula (P 9.1). However, Sarnelli does not agree with the common people's negative judgement against someone who engages in more pleasurable activities. According to him, even the most proper and formal men enjoy a distraction from time to time. A long life without any form of entertainment is as unfair as a long journey without a break. Thus, authors are summoned to produce pleasurable texts that readers can enjoy.

Consistent with his overarching intention, Sarnelli again defends his own work. *Posilecheata* can be classified as an escape into fresh air from the erudite studies to which the author had been devoting himself up until that point. Considering the etymological reasoning that Sarnelli proposes, the idea that his *Posilecheata* can be read as a useful and worthy *divertissement* becomes significant (P 9.2). He explains that the word "Posileco"—the name of the town of Posillipo at Sarnelli's time (nowadays Pusilleco in Neapolitan dialect)—means remedy against melancholy[44] and is an implicit acceptance of entertainment and pleasure.[45] In the title of Sarnelli's collection, the word is given the typical denominative suffix "–ata" that produces feminine words (Renzi et al., vol. 3: 489). This suffix, which is common in improvised constructions that are not highly productive (512–13), makes "Posilecheata" suggest an extemporaneous recreational event dominated by a delightful atmosphere—literally, "to go on a trip in Posillipo in a leisurely way without much programming." As the word also conveys the idea of a relaxed stroll without a clear direction, the description of the banquet in the introduction is subjected to a similar casual atmosphere. Nonetheless, this informality presents a programmatic agenda since it leads to the recounting of the five fables.[46]

From his initial characterization, the reader understands that doctor Marchionno is a meritorious descendant of François Rabelais's Pantagruel in his *La vie de Gargantua et de Pantaguel* (Allasia 262). Bakhtin's "grotesque realism" emerges in his physical appearance as well as in his behavior. Marchionno's voracity is a mainstay for feasts, food, and the pleasure of eating, as well as for an exploitation of each possible aspect of the Neapolitan dialect.[47] With a long speech, he employs all of the tools on which logic and rhetoric can count to illustrate the significance of the number three. As a result, he skillfully dupes his hosts into inviting him to their meal:

> Non sapite vuje, segnorielle mieje, ca a lo 'mmito non deveno essere né manco de le Grazie, né cchiù de le Muse? Azzoè o tre o nove, ma duje è troppo poco. Otra po' che lo numero de lo tre ha cchiù bertute che non hanno tutte le nummere 'n chietta. (P 12.8)

> Don't you know, my lords, that at a banquet there should be neither fewer people than the Graces nor more than the Muses? That is, either three or nine, but two is way too few. Aside from that, the number three possesses more virtues than all the other numbers together.

After this, Marchionno enumerates all the elements of the world with a tripartite structure: the natural principles, the types of animals, the components of the soul, the things that control the world, and so on. He uses a significant quantity of numerical paremias and maxims, specifically tripartite ones, to underscore the properties of the number three. For all of these expressions, an initial proposition, which cites the characteristic(s) of the three things, starts with the word "tre" ("three"); then, the list of the three things themselves follows.[48] Marchionno's hyperbolic use of these paremias in a work that is not technically devoted to them acquires a specific significance. Other than creating a sense of wonderment, their presence results in a powerful comedic effect. Such expressions aim to achieve a goal that could be accomplished efficiently with less waste of energy and linguistic material. It should not be forgotten that the display of wisdom is intended to convince Masillo and Petruccio to invite Marchionno to dinner, a far too easy target for such a demonstration of knowledge and rhetorical skills. Yet, Marchionno exploits the value of the tripartite paremias to the upmost and eventually fulfills his objective, i.e., eating.

Chapter Four

Works and collections that contained tripartite paremias in Italian based on the Latin formula "Tria sunt ..." ("Three are ...") were mostly released in the sixteenth and seventeenth centuries. Chapter 25 of the *Ecclesiastes* and chapter 30 of Solomon's *Proverbs* constituted excellent sources for this typology of paremias.[49] In 1519, the German scholar Ulrich von Hutten's publication *Trias Romana* contained a list of tripartite paremias, specifically 48 Latin *sententiae* followed by 58 German equivalents. These expressions mostly dealt with the immoral customs and the corrupted institutions of Rome (Besso 151–56). Almost a century later, in 1614, G. C. Croce, previously mentioned for his stories on Bertoldo and Bertoldino, published a work titled *Il tre*, featuring 62 paremias from both the oral and the written tradition.[50] Speroni, who republished this text in 1960, mentions that paremias with three elements were particularly suited for moral and didactic purposes and for being easy to remember (G. C. Croce, *Il Tre* [1960] 5).[51]

Although G. C. Croce writes in Tuscan and Sarnelli in Neapolitan—with the exception of the last ten paremias in Croce's work—this paremiac type occurs almost identically in both *Il tre* and *Posilecheata*. Sometimes, the order of the listed things may change (as in examples 1a–1b and 3a–3b), or one item in this list may differ (as the third member in example 2a–2b), or else the items composing the expression may be different but linked by logical connections (as the first two members in example 2a–2b):

    1a. *Tre sono le sue* [dell'anima] *potenze, cioè intelletto, memoria e volontà.* (G. C. Croce, *Il Tre* [1960] n. 3)
    Three are the powers of the human soul, which are intellect, memory, and will.

    1b. *Tre le dute prencepale de l'anema de l'ommo: memmoria, 'ntelletto e bolontà.* (P 12–13.9)
    Three are the primary gifts of the human soul: memory, intellect, and will.

    2a. *Tre parti vuole havere il rufiano, cioè audace, eloquente e paziente nelle bastonate.* (G. C. Croce, *Il Tre* [1960] n. 26)
    Three traits the sycophant should have, which is audacious, eloquent, and patient with beatings.

    2b. *Tre cose abbesognano a lo ruffiano: gran core, assai chiacchiare e poca vregogna.* (P 14.12)
    Three are the things that the sycophant needs: a brazen heart, endless chatter, and little shame.

3a. *Tre cose non sono apprezzate, cioè bellezza di cortigiana, fortezza di facchino e consiglio di fallito.* (G. C. Croce, *Il Tre* [1960] n. 29)
   Three things are not appreciated, which are the beauty of a courtesan, the strength of a porter, and the advice of a poor man.

3b. *Tre cose non songo stemmate: forze da vastaso, consiglio de poverommo e bellezza de pottana.* (P 13.9)
   Three things are not valued: the strength of a porter, the advice of a poor man, and the beauty of a whore.

In the second pair, that the sycophant has a brazen heart (Sarnelli) suggests that he is audacious (Croce) and that he chatters endlessly (Sarnelli) means that he is verbose (Croce). In G. C. Croce's text, the last item of the expression ("paziente nelle bastonate," "patient with beatings") refers to the consequences ("bastonate," "beatings with a stick") that the ruffian often endures because of his behavior. Conversely, Sarnelli's item "poca vregogna" ("little shame") highlights the lack of embarrassment in the ruffian's attitude and, thus, the cause of the beating that Croce mentions. Despite this variation, the paremia's meaning is the same as it warns not to trust such a person as a sycophant.

In 1883, Benedetto Croce published a list of 45 "proverbi trimembri napoletani" ("tripartite Neapolitan proverbs"), which is worth comparing with Marchionno's paremias. Croce transcribed these tripartite expressions from an undated manuscript of Latin, Italian, and Neapolitan proverbs and proverbial phrases gathered by Luca Auriemma ("Proverbi trimembri napoletani"). Vittorio Imbriani later published the list in its entirety in his 1885 edition of Sarnelli's *Posilecheata* (Imbriani, *Posilecheata di Pompeo Sarnelli* 112–17). Unlike G. C. Croce's paremias, some of Auriemma's expressions are not tripartite yet they are based on the juxtaposition of three elements that makes their structure similar to that of a threefold proverb.[52] However, more than half—27 to be exact—present the same organization as those paremias listed in Sarnelli's work. In the following examples, the structural and linguistic commonalities clearly emerge:

4a. *Tre F cacciano l'ommo dalla casa: fummo, fieto, femmena marvasa.* (B. Croce, "Proverbi trimembri napoletani" n. 20)
   Three F's drive the man out of his house: smoke, stench, and an evil woman.

Chapter Four

> 4b. *Tre cose cacciano l'ommo da la casa: fummo, fieto e femmena marvasa.* (P 14.12)[53]
> Three things drive the man out of his house: smoke, stench, and an evil woman.

> 5a. *Tre cose non se ponno annàsconnere: le fusa int'a no sacco, le femmene 'nchiuse a la casa, la paglia into de le scarpe.*
> (B. Croce, "Proverbi trimembri napoletani" n. 24)
> Three things cannot be hidden: purrs inside a bag, women closed in the house, straw in the shoes.

> 5b. *Tre cose non possono stare annascose: le fusa dinto de lo sacco, le femmene 'nchiuse 'n casa e la paglia dintro de le scarpe.* (P 13.10)
> Three things cannot be hidden: purrs inside a bag, women closed in the house, and straw in the shoes.

Except for a few differences in vocabulary, i.e., "into" vs "dinto/dintro" ("inside"; D'Ambra, s.v. *dinto*) and "possono" vs "ponno" ("they can"; Ledgeway 388–89), the examples show similar language. Both Auriemma and Sarnelli use the Italianized feminine article "la" instead of the singular "'a" (which originated in the seventeenth century) or the elided form (common in the sixteenth century; Ledgeway 167–70). They also share the apheresis of the initial "i" in "'nchiuse" ("enclosed"; Ledgeway 102), the word "marvasa" ("evil"; Ledgeway 114), and the assimilation in "annasconnere/annascose" ("to hide/hidden"; Ledgeway 75, 102).[54] Given their similarities, Sarnelli and Auriemma might have referred to a common source of paremias or alternatively, they might have drawn to that common paremiac knowledge or wisdom that characterized the life and literary experience of the Neapolitan society at the time.

One work undoubtedly crosses Sarnelli's path when he enumerates his tripartite paremias: Alunno's *Della fabbrica del mondo* (1546–48). During his tirade, Marchionno declares that, if someone aspires to know all of the other virtues of the number three, he should read *La Fraveca de lo munno* (P 13.11). In fact, Alunno's ninth book, entitled *Quantità* ("Quantity"; section *Tre*: 232r–33r) contains all of the paremias that Marchionno lists, and many more. A comparison of Alunno's and Sarnelli's texts reveals the Neapolitan patina of Sarnelli's paremias vis-à-vis the Tuscan vernacular of Alunno's:

6a. *Tre cose non sono stimate, forza di bastagio, consiglio di poverhuomo et bellezza di puttana.* (Alunno ix: 232v)
Three things are not valued: the strength of a porter, the advice of a poor man, and the beauty of a whore.

6b. *Tre cose non songo stemmate: forze da vastaso, consiglio de poverommo e bellezza de pottana.* (P 13.9; see also example 3b in this chapter)
Three things are not valued: the strength of a porter, the advice of a poor man, and the beauty of a whore.

7a. *Tre cose go[v]ernano il tutto, cioè numero, peso et misura.* (Alunno ix: 232v)
Three things govern the world, which is number, weight, and measure.

7b. *Tre cose squatrano ogne cosa: nummero, piso e mesura.* (P 13.9)
Three things square the world: number, weight, and measure.

8a. *Di tre cose non ti fidare, di medico malato, d'alchimista stracciato e romito grasso.* (Alunno ix: 232v)[55]
You should not trust in three things, the sick doctor, the poor alchemist, and the fat hermit.

8b. *A tre cose non se deve credere, all'archemista povero, a lo miedeco malato e al remito grasso.* (P 13.10)
You should not believe in three things, the poor alchemist, the sick doctor, and the fat hermit.

Since many Neapolitan words used by Sarnelli are not far from their Tuscan equivalents, the similarity between the Neapolitan and Florentine paremias is evident. There are two possible reasons for this characteristic. First, an explanation external to the Neapolitan dialect recognizes that non-indigenous words in Neapolitan were transferred directly from the paremias available in the Florentine vernacular and that this transition left a few remnants of the original language. This demonstration supports the idea that the Neapolitan paremias originated from the Tuscan ones or were translated from them. As such, it contradicts Sarnelli's disparagement of the Tuscan language, as expressed in the prefatory letter, and undermines his efforts to demonstrate the autonomous productivity of the Neapolitan language. The second explanation, internal to the Neapolitan dialect, proposes that Neapolitan words similar to those in the Florentine vernacular should be considered a legacy of previous contact between the two languages. Florentine words would have been progressively assimilated and therefore, not recognized as such any longer in the Neapolitan vocabulary. In other words, terms common to the Neapolitan dialect and Florentine vernacular coexisted for a certain period of time until they were simply integrated into the dialect's lexicon (Montuori 156). This second option argues that, even though Tuscan may represent a catalyzing tool and may have been the original language of Sarnelli's paremias, these expressions became constituent parts of the Neapolitan identity once they were adapted to the phonetic and morphological structures of the dialect.

Despite such linguistic similarities, Alunno's and Sarnelli's organization of their paremias differ, mostly because of the two genres involved. Encyclopedic entries, such as those in *Della fabbrica del mondo*, should include a comprehensive presentation of as much information as possible on a topic. Conversely, a persuasive oration, such as that of Marchionno, can be limited to a reasonable number of expressions to prove a point. In *Della fabbrica*, before mentioning the list of tripartite paremias, Alunno provides a grammatical definition of the number three, as well as the translation into Tuscan of Latin words containing this number.[56] He then argues that in mathematics three is considered a perfect number, which explains the appropriateness of the paremias in an encyclopedic entry on the number three. After demonstrating that everything in nature derives from this number, he lists the actual expressions, providing them with deductive reasonings and examples. In *Posilecheata*, instead, Marchionno does not include any example because he employs the tripartite expressions for the sole purpose of exemplifying a specific structure. An illustration of this is apparent in a paremia that lists the beauties of a woman. To demonstrate the superior value of the number three, Marchionno uses the following expression:

> *Tre bote tre unnece cose fanno bella na femmiena: azzoè tre cose longhe e tre corte; tre larghe, tre strette e tre grosse, tre sottile; tre retonne, tre piccole, tre ghianche, tre rosse, tre negre.* (P 13.11; also in Romagnoli, *Facezie e motti*, story 66)

> Three times eleven things make a woman beautiful: which is three long and three short; three large, three tight, and three big, three thin; three round, three small, three white, three red, three black.

The repetition of the word "tre" is requisite for the expression to be included in Marchionno's speech. The total number of things referenced in this paremia is 33—when considering that there are 11 listed items in multiples of three—and 33 is a perfect number for a collection of expressions based on the number three. In comparison, Alunno's expression presents many more members and does not resemble a paremia:

> *Con tre volte tre 11, che sono 33, si distinguono le parti che dobbono haver la donna a voler essere bella compimento, cioè tre cose lunghe e tre corte si fanno la donna bella; tre larghe, tre strette, tre grosse, tre sottili, tre rotonde, tre picciole, tre bianche, tre rosse, et tre nere, le quali, volendo particolarmente distinguere diremo prima che le tre lunghe sono i capelli, la mano et la gamba; le tre corte sono i denti, l'orecchie et le mammelle; le larghe la fronte, il petto e fianchi; le strette nel traverso, nelle coscie, la terza è poi quella ove natura pose ogni dolcezza; le grosse, con misura però, sono le treccie, le braccia et le coscie; le sottili i capelli, le dita et i labri; le rotonde il collo, le braccia et groppe; le picciole la bocca, il mento et il piede. Le bianche i denti, la gola e la mano. Le rosse le gote, le labra e i capitelli delle mammelle. L'ultimo sono le nere, cioè le ciglia, gli occhi e i peletti della natura, e che siano rari et alquanto crespetti. Et se oltre le trentatre parti sopra dette sono poi accompagnate con la gratia, con la maniera e col leggiadro portamento si può dire con verità quella essere bellissima.* (Alunno ix: 232v)

With three times 11, which are 33, we distinguish the parts that the woman needs to be a beautiful fulfillment, that is three long and three short things make the woman beautiful; three broad, three narrow, three large, three thin, three round, three small, three white, three red, and three black. Wishing to distinguish these parts, first we say that the three long are the hair, the hand, and the leg; the three short are the teeth, the ears, and the breasts; the broad are the forehead, the chest, and hips; the narrow ones in the transverse, in the thighs, and the third is then the one where nature posed every sweetness. The large things, with measure though, are the braids, the arms, and the thighs; the thin are the hair, the fingers, and the lips; the round are the neck, the arms, and the back; the small are the mouth, the chin, and the foot. The white are the teeth, the throat, and the hand. The red are the cheeks, the lips, and the extremities of the breasts. The last are the black ones, that is, the eyelashes, the eyes, and the hairs of nature, and may they be rare and somewhat curly. And if additionally, the thirty-three parts above are accompanied with grace, with manners, and with graceful bearing, you can truly say that woman is beautiful.

Chapter Four

Comparatively, Marchionno's paremia in *Posilecheata* does not specify the various parts of the human body under each category, which instead Alunno includes. Thus, Marchionno's expression explains less than Alunno's entry yet it is more effective and more memorable. Due to the encyclopedic nature of his work, Alunno presents his paremias with many introductory formulas, which serve to make the discourse flow. He also uses transitions, connections, and explicative conjunctions like "cioè" ("that is"). On the contrary, introductory formulas are absent in Marchionno's speech—except for the sentence that introduces the entire list, "Vuj sapite che …" ("You know that …"; P 12.9).

In one case, Sarnelli slightly changes a paremia from Alunno's work to make it conform to those included in the list of tripartite paremias. The expression has already been mentioned in Chapter 3 since Florio lists it in the eighteenth chapter of his *Firste Fruites* (FF 23*r*):

> *Tre cose sommamente dispiacciono a Dio, ricco avaro, povero superbo et vecchio lussurioso.* (Alunno ix: 232*v*)
>
> Three things supremely displease God, a rich avaricious person, a poor proud being, and a lustful old man.
>
> *Tre cose songo 'nsoffribele: ricco avaro, povero soperbio e biecchio 'nnammorato.* (P 13.9)
>
> Three things are unacceptable: a rich avaricious person, a poor proud being, and an enamored old man.

In Alunno's text, God displeases and does not approve of the listed "three things," while in Sarnelli's example the paremia does not contain the reference to God and conveys a common feeling of non-acceptance. Moreover, Sarnelli changes the adjective related to the old man from "lussurioso" ("lustful") to "'nnamorato" ("enamored"). The meaning remains the same: a libidinous old man is undoubtedly in love. However, "lussurioso," coming from the Latin "luxuria" ("excess") and later borrowed by Christianity, is charged with a spiritual meaning and it is, indeed, one of the capital vices. On the contrary, "innamorato" does not present the same religious and moral connotation. This change seems to conform to Sarnelli's general choice to omit paremias related to God and a religious subtext from Alunno's list.[57] It is evident that, when Sarnelli prepared his list of tripartite paremias, he did not simply translate them from Florentine to Neapolitan. He modified their content, making sure to not alter their general message, and adapted them to the new situation. In other words, Sarnelli transferred Alunno's paremias from an encyclopedic entry to the popular, extravagant, carnivalesque, and Neapolitan circumstance of *Posilecheata*'s introduction.

Some of Marchionno's tripartite paremias are also present in a collection entitled *Proverbii attiladi novi et belli quali l'huomo non se ne debbe mai fidare*, which was originally published in Venice in 1586 and then republished in 1865 by Gaetano Romagnoli (*Due opuscoli rarissimi*). A comparison of Sarnelli's Neapolitan expressions with these paremias, originated in Northern Italy and organized in distiches, illustrates how Sarnelli reuses and combines paremias that were available at his time, translates them into dialect, and transforms them into a tripartite structure. For instance, a paremia from *Proverbii attiladi* presents two unrhymed distiches:

> *Archimista povero*
> *e medico amala*
> *Romitto grasso*
> *e matto stiza.* (*Due opuscoli rarissimi* 9)
>
> Poor alchemist
> and sick doctor,
> fat hermit and
> irritable madman.

In his version, Sarnelli does not include the last reference to the maniac:

> *A tre cose non se deve credere, all'archemista povero, a lo miedeco malato e al remito grasso.* (P 13.10; see also example 8b in this chapter)
>
> You should not believe in three things, the poor alchemist, the sick doctor, and the fat hermit.

In *Posilecheata*, the expression presents an explicit connection between its members by way of introducing them with the sentence, "A tre cose non se deve credere" ("You should not believe in three things"). In this way, Marchionno's passionate verbal demonstration can be more effective.

Another text that shares tripartite paremias with Marchionno's speech is Basile's *Lo cunto de li cunti*, specifically *cunto* IV.6 entitled *Le tre corone* ("The Three Crowns"). Here, paremias fill a hyperbolic conversation between a young woman called Marchetta and

Chapter Four

a cruel female ogre. Marchetta prepares a juicy dinner for the ogre so that she, herself, can avoid being eaten. In response, the ogre recites several tripartite expressions, which serve to emphasize her ecstatic disposition before the meal and her exalted praise of Marchetta's food. The ogre is unaware that Marchetta has prepared the succulent dishes and, thus, begins her discourse with the following sentence:

> Io iuro pe le tre parole de Napole ca, si sapesse chi è stato lo cuoco, io le vorria dare le vísole meie. (CC IV.6.29)
>
> I swear on the three words of Naples that if I knew who the cook was, I would give her the pupils of my eyes. (Basile, *The Tale of Tales* 339)

There is more than one hypothesis about what the "three words of Naples" indicate. B. Croce argues that they might be the three epithets "Gentile, Sirena e Sacra" ("gentle, mermaid, and holy") that Friar Manuel Ponze de Soto uses in his 1683 *Memorial de las tres Parténopes* (Basile, *Il Pentamerone* [1925] 190: footnote 2). Evidently, Basile does not extract the three epithets from the friar's eulogy, which was published after *Lo cunto de li cunti*. More probably, he refers to a common tradition before Ponze de Soto's written record. Croce's other conjecture about the origin of these three terms seems more apt. He suggests that the tripartite paremia *Tre cose abbesognano a chi stace a Napole: vruoccole, zuoccole, trapole* ("Three things are needed to those who are in Naples: broccoli, clogs, and traps") might be the source. Hence, the "three words of Naples" would indicate these three rhymed things useful to thrive in the city.[58]

Among the paremias that the ogre pronounces are the following (CC IV.6.28–33): *Pe le tre cannele che s'allumano quanno se fa no strommiento de notte* ("I swear on the three candles that are lit when a contract is signed at night"); *Per li tre parme de funa che danno vota a lo 'mpiso* ("I swear on the three spans of rope wrapped around the hanged man"); *Pe tre cose che la casa strude: zeppole, pane caudo e maccarune* ("I swear on the three things that a house consumes: fritters, warm bread, and macaroni"); *Pe tre cose che cacciano l'ommo da la casa: fieto, fummo e femmena marvasa* ("I swear on the three things that drive a man from his house: stench, smoke, and an evil woman"; see examples 4a and 4b in this chapter); *Pe le tre effe de lo pesce: fritto, friddo e futo* ("I swear on the three F's of fish: fried, frosty, and fresh");[59] *Pe le tre S ch'abbesognano a no 'namorato: sulo, sollicito e secreto* ("I swear on the three S's a lover must be: solitary, solicitous, and secret"; the paremia is also in CC VI.9); *Pe le tre sciorte de perzune che se tene la pottana: smargiasse, belle giuvane e corrive* ("I swear on the three sorts of people a whore takes to: swashbucklers, handsome young men, and dimwits"); *Pe tre cose ch'arroinano la gioventù: iuoco, femmene e taverne* ("I swear on the three things that ruin youth: gambling, women, and taverns"); *Pe tre cose che vole avere lo roffiano: gran core, assai chiacchiere e poca vergogna* ("I swear on the three things that a sycophant should have: a brazen heart, endless chatter, and little shame"; see example 2b); and *Pe le tre cose ch'osserva lo miedeco, lo puzo, la facce e lo càntaro* ("I swear on the three things a doctor checks: the pulse, the face, and the chamber pot"; Basile, *The Tale of Tales* 339–40; see also Speroni, *Proverbs and Proverbial Phrases*). In Basile's text, the tripartite structure is not directly linked to the narrative context *per se*, but is instead a stylistic choice that gives voice to an emotional status. Conversely, in Sarnelli's work Marchionno's paremias are strongly related to the narrative context and underscore the main objective of his monologue. Because of this, the expressions appear very similar to Basile's, but the majority of them starts with the number "tre" (P 14.12). That the structure of the paremias is the same but their order in the two texts is different might indicate that both Basile and Sarnelli were looking at a third source and reused it in accordance with their personal needs. However, there is no evidence to support this idea.

When Marchionno concludes the demonstration of the virtues associated with the number three, the supper can officially begin. For the first course, soup is brought to the table and Marchionno eats it with so much eagerness that Masillo and Petruccio can only enjoy a few sips. In order to tease Marchionno, Petruccio asks if he enjoyed it, to which Marchionno answers by mentioning a Spanish paremia expressing the idea that nothing can be built upon a rounded surface:

> È bona! Ma non è cosa da farence fonnamiento. Non sapite ca dice lo Spagnuolo: *Sobre una cosa redonda no haze buen edificio?* (P 16.18)

> It's good! But it is not a thing to use as foundation. Don't you know what the Spanish people say: "Upon that which is round, you don't make a good building?"

Chapter Four

In Melchor de Santa Cruz de Dueñas and Francisco Asensio y Mejorado's 1777 collection *Floresta española de apotegmas ó sentencias*, this same paremia appears in a similar fashion:

> A un Francés dábanle uvas al principio de comer. Dixo, que no las comia, sino á la postre, porque *sobre cosa redonda no se hace buen edificio*. (Pt. 6 on the table, 255: n. xv)
>
> Grapes were given to a French man to eat at the beginning of the meal, but he said that he would not eat them, if not at the end, because upon that which is round you don't make a good building.

In this quotation, a shrewd French man tries to get a better meal than simple grapes in order to save himself from hunger. Thus, he employs the paremia as a sarcastic way to get his point across. The result of constructing something on a rounded surface would not be a strong building; transitively, to build an entire meal on grapes, which are rounded, would not yield a positive outcome. The meaning of this paremia appears to be that it is unwise to begin something if the foundation is not strong or the prerequisites are not satisfied. Within Sarnelli's context, the message of the expression grants the situation a comic twist. According to Marchionno, a meal cannot rely only and exclusively on soup, because it is an insignificant dish and not sufficiently nutritious. Thus, the indirect message that the paremia conveys is that it is inappropriate to treat a guest badly when, in fact, he should be treated with a proper welcome. In contrast to the quotation from the Spanish collection, in *Posilecheata* there is nothing round, even though the shape of the soup bowl recalls a round surface. However, the contextual meaning is similarly related to food or, more precisely, to obtaining better and more food. The paremia makes Marchionno's request happen: Petruccio asks Cianna to bring a mullet, which the doctor greatly appreciates.[60]

Since later during the dinner Petruccio and Masillo do not give adequate attention to Marchionno's hunger, as in a farce the doctor pretends that a thorn is stuck in his throat for which he needs an enormous quantity of wine to free himself of it. When he receives it, he uses a paremia to comment on the situation:

> Auto ca *chillo de masto Grillo*. (P 18.21; see also footnote 13)[61]
> More than that from doctor Grillo.

Marchionno refers to a story in verse about a doctor called Grillo, originally a farmer, who seemed particularly skilled in solving any sort of medical issues in quite unorthodox ways. After Grillo decides to wander in search of a better life, his wife takes revenge on him. Since the King's daughter has a thorn stuck in her throat, she spreads the voice that her husband is the most knowledgeable doctor available on earth. Called by the King and fearing for his life, Grillo does not perform any medical treatment but instead starts to oil the young woman's backside in such a way that he makes her laugh hard. Upon laughing, the thorn is expelled and the young woman is safe.[62] The comparison with this story makes Marchionno's behavior even more ridiculous than it really is: the doctor declares to be more intelligent than mastro Grillo, who is known to be an impostor. As such, Grillo, and thus Marchionno, is the epitome of the successful mischievous person, who always manages to get what he is looking for, regardless of the methods he uses.

Marchionno reinforces his arrogant and annoying behavior when fried fish is brought to the table. Since he smells a conger eel that is still in the kitchen, he stages a theatrical scene and asks a small fish the whereabouts of his dead father. This supposedly prompts Marchionno to make inquiries about the dish that has not yet been served. In turn, Petruccio teases him with a proverbial phrase, which refers to animals as a metaphor for food or, more precisely, negation of food:

> Ma Petruccio, pe darele cottura e ped annozzarele lo muorzo 'n canna, responnette: «Io no' approvo chillo proverbejo: *Carne giovane e pesce viecchio,* pocca sti pescetielle me piaceno. E così, sio Dottore mio, haje sbagliato o coll'uocchie o co lo naso.» (P 21.29)

> However, Petruccio, in order to bother him and make his morsel go down the wrong pipe, answered: "I do not agree with that proverb: Young meat and old fish, because I like this little fish. So, my dear Doctor, you got it wrong either with your eyes or your nose."

This is the first time in *Posilecheata* that a sentence introduces a paremia with the generalizing term "chillo proverbejo" ("that proverb"). *Carne giovane e pesce vecchio* ("Young meat and old fish") literally remarks on the relative merits of tasty mature fish over soft and young meat. Figuratively, it refers to a relationship between an old man (usually fish is a phallic symbol) and a young woman (indeed, fresh flesh; Lapucci, *Dizionario dei proverbi italiani*, s.l. C: footnote 751).[63] However, there is a specific pragmatic significance to the proverb's use in context. Marchionno naturally prefers a mature fish such as a conger eel to small, fried fish. By saying that he does not approve of the proverbial phrase, Petruccio tries to silence Marchionno. He wishes him to eat the fried food without longing for the huge eel. Thus, the proverbial phrase serves as a tool to drop an unwanted topic, divert attention toward a different matter, and advance the narration.

Despite the effectiveness of Petruccio's expression, Marchionno brings up the topic of food again in the conversation. Upon his request for more wine, Petruccio gives his servant Cianna the key to the canteen so that she can replace the twelve barrels of wine that they already drank:

> Ma pocca *non chiove, ca delluvia*, veccote la chiave de l'autra cantenetta 'n grazia de lo sio dottore. (P 23.35)

> But because it does not rain, but it pours down, here is the key to the other canteen to please the doctor.

The sentence comes from the Neapolitan expression, "I' dico ca chiove, ma no' che delluvia" ("I say it rains, and it does not pour").[64] The paremia literally speaks about weather conditions, but metaphorically refers to something that, despite being useful, is extreme. One recognizes the reality ("rain") but not its exaggeration ("downpour"; Sarnelli, *Posilecheata* [1986] 23: footnote 20), or one believes that there is abundance but not annoying excessiveness. Petruccio twists the original expression making it ironically suitable for the scene. The fact is acknowledged (it definitely rains) but it is not sufficient; thus, its exaggeration (a downpour) is admissible and needs to be considered. Out of metaphor, Petruccio acknowledges that Marchionno receives food in such huge quantities that it seems to pour from the sky directly into his mouth and then, disappearing in his stomach.

As these examples demonstrate, in *Posilecheata*'s introduction the accumulation of paremias and popular expressions illustrates how rich and multiform the Neapolitan language can be.[65] Since reality can be multiplied and even projected on a fantastical world, one paremia is not enough to represent it. A vast number of expressions are needed to give credit to its multiple facets and to the wonders that they allow. As Canepa states, Baroque poetics were based on the pervasive application of *inventio* to rhetoric and on the author's ability to create a marvelous "world of words" (*From Court to Forest* 61). Even though Marchionno is described in grotesque and animalesque terms, all of Sarnelli's admiration is for him as a member of that Neapolitan community that *Posilecheata* recreates. Through the doctor's paremias, the author indirectly illustrates his devotion to the linguistic creativity of the Neapolitan dialect and his appreciation for the popular wisdom that the character discloses.

The Five Fables: Paremias as Moral, Social, and Linguistic Tools

Beginning with the names of the storytellers, Ciulettella, Popa, Tolla, Cecca, and old Cianna (Chlodowski 195),[66] the fairytale-like quality of the five fables is informed by an authentic reality that represents the centennial and genuine Neapolitan wisdom (P 35–207).[67] When Marchionno asks the five women to entertain him and the others with fairy tales in Neapolitan, the only possible alternative is reading Basile's *Cunto* a work that everyone enjoys, including non-Neapolitan readers. However, since none of the characters present possesses the book, Cianna responds that she and her daughters will narrate local tales:

> Chesta è arte nosta! … Anze ste fegliole, s'accossì ve piace, ne decerranno porzine uno ped uno: avarranno perzò pacienzia se non sarranno comme a chille de lo livro, che songo cose stodiate, ma nuje le decimmo a la foretana,[68] accossì comme l'avimmo 'ntiso contare da l'antecestune nuoste. (P 33.58)

> We are certainly skilled in doing that! … And if you like, each of my daughters will tell you one of them. However, you must be patient with us, if they aren't exactly the same as those in the book, which are studied things. We tell them in a country way, the way we heard them told by our forebears.

Cianna's words become intrinsically connected to popular memory, something that does not happen in such a profound way in Basile's *Cunto*. If, as Giorgio Raimondo Cardona argues, the library of orality is memory (36), the spoken word is a direct descendant of the ancestors' wisdom. Hence, sharing tales constitutes a revival of that authenticity whose authority derives from neither literature, nor the learned works of canonized authors (Guaragnella, "Rassegna di proverbi e sentenze" 330). Rather, the voice of the community and, specifically, the voice of the most native community, is the repository of the local traditional knowledge.

In Sarnelli's five *cunti*, the act of recounting fables is linked to the Neapolitan dialect. Marchionno does not refer to tales regarding Neapolitan matters or characters. He specifically requests stories in the language that the five storytellers speak, which also highlights his own interest in the diastratic dimension of the Neapolitan linguistic system (Valente, "La lingua napoletana" 260). The intricacy of the plot, the variety of concepts, and the grace of words then create a perfect balance between enjoyment and didacticism. In this context, paremias represent the language elements best suited to reflect the importance given to orality and morality: they convey comedy, realism, communal cultural and linguistic identity, but also moral teachings and emotional evaluations.

At the beginning of the fables, paremias set the groundwork for the stories' moral, social, and didactic definition. Their position makes them memorable, similar to what is achieved by the introductory paremias in Brusantino's *Le cento novelle* and the expressions enriching the dialogues in Florio's *Fruits*. They permit the reader to "avere una conoscenza preliminare dell'intreccio" ("have a preliminary knowledge of the storyline"; Albanese, *Metamorfosi del Cunto* 73) and offer suggestions about what to focus on in the text and how to interpret it. This, however, does not mean that the story should be confined to only one line of interpretation if others are possible. The paremia rather indicates which one should prevail and highlights the message that the author wishes the readers to analyze most.

When used in the narration, paremias can be moral maxims, ironic assessments, short and frequently witty rhetorical forms, or a means of constructing the varied structures of the fables. They shed light on a particular aspect, offer alternative perspectives or new directions, centralize a concept by adding a specific twist, or move the narration forward. As they actualize their meaning(s) in the stories, they assume specific characteristics within that context and, simultaneously, shape it with their own implications making it more meaningful (Sarnelli, *Posilecheata* [1986] lxiii–lxvii).

When they conclude the stories, paremias caustically summarize the story's meaning and content into a short and effective structure. Alternatively, they offer a moral interpretation or express the text's pedagogical stance in a powerful way.[69] Out of the five final paremias, those at the end of fables 1, 2, and 3 confirm the moral message that was anticipated at the beginning of the story or correspond perfectly to the title of the fable. In these instances, the initial and final paremias create a paremiac circular movement from beginning to end.[70] At times, paremias account for an etiologic description of buildings, statues, and inscriptions in Naples; hence, they give real and human connotations to what is originally fantastic and most of all, make it specific to the city.[71] Independently from their role, all of Sarnelli's final paremias stand out in the first edition of *Posilecheata*: they are in italics and detached from the text of the fables. As such, they become a "suggerimento mnemonico non solo della favola ma, ancor meglio, della sua morale di cui rimangono antichi e tradizionali depositari" ("mnemonic suggestion not only of the fable but, more precisely, of its morality, of which they are ancient and traditional repositories"; Albanese, *Metamorfosi del Cunto* 70).[72]

Cunto 1: *La piatà remmonerata*

Proverbs and proverbial phrases introduce the first tale of *Posilecheata*, *La piatà remmonerata* ("The well-paid devotion"), which Ciulletella recounts:

> Veramente disse buono, e non potea dicere meglio, chillo che decette: *Fa bene e scordaténne*.[73] Pocca quanno manco l'ommo se lo penza trova lo contracammio, se non dall'aute uommene, da lo cielo stisso. E pe lo contrario: *Chi fa male male aspetta*, ché non è possibile *semmenare grano e cogliere ardiche*, o puro *chiantare ardiche e cogliere vruoccole*. (P 35.1)

> In truth he spoke well, and could have not spoken better, he who said: "Do good and then forget about it." Because when a man expects less, he finds repayment, if not from other men, from God himself. And on the contrary, who does bad may expect bad, because it is not possible to sow wheat and harvest nettles, or to sow nettles and harvest broccoli.

Basile's *cunto* 3 features Sarnelli's proverbial phrase, *Fa bene e scordaténne* ("Do good and then forget about it"), and the contrary of Sarnelli's other expression in the quotation (*Chi fa male male aspetta*; "Who does bad may expect bad"): "Ma non dubitare: *chi bene fa bene aspetta; fa' bene e scordatenne*" ("Have no doubts: he who does good, may expect good; do good and then forget about

Chapter Four

it"; CC III.5.37; Basile, *The Tale of Tales* 250). The two expressions, *Chi fa male male aspetta* and *Chi bene fa bene aspetta*, convey the message that people get what they deserve according to their behavior.[74] In Basile's text, the semantic field is positive, meaning that if one does good things, one will also experience them in return: indeed, *Chi bene fa bene aspetta*. Young Nardello frees three entrapped animals, therefore, acts in a good way and receives their help in making a fool of the prince who married the woman he loves. In contrast, the proverb in *Posilecheata*, *Chi fa male male aspetta*, focuses on the negative side: someone who acts in an evil way should expect negative outcomes. Such a meaning applies to Sarnelli's story: an evil husband faces a suitably bad and painful death because of his malicious acts against his wife, both while living with her and later when manipulating facts to implicate her in a homicide that she did not commit.

Sarnelli's other two proverbial phrases, *Semmenare grano e cogliere ardiche* ("To sow wheat and harvest nettles") and *Chiantare ardiche e cogliere vruoccole* ("To sow nettles and harvest broccoli"), suggest that only like can beget like: wheat cannot generate nettle nor can nettle create broccoli. Notably, the paremias at the beginning of *cunto* 4 and *cunto* 5 convey the same message as the expressions introducing the first *cunto*. In *cunto* 4, the text reads:

> Ca l'*ommo comme nasce accossì pasce*. E se maje villano fece azzione de galant'ommo, o fu jannizzero o cuorvo janco: pocca *da le cevettole non nasceno aquele, né da le ciavole palumme*. E perzò se sole dicere: *pratteca co chi è meglio de tene e falle le spese*: perché *chi meglio nasce meglio procede* e *chi dorme co' cane non se nn'auza senza pullece*. (P 141.1)

> Because as a man is born, so he is fed. And if ever a villain behaved as a gentleman, either he was a Janissary or a white crow: because neither from owls can eagles be born nor from magpies doves. So, it's a common saying, associate with those who are better than you and share with them. Because a person who is born better continues to be better, and a person who sleeps with dogs wakes up with fleas.

The paremia opening *cunto* 5 expresses a similar concept:

> Non sempre cammina la regola: *Comm'è la chianta è la scianta*. Perché se vede ca *da le spine nasceno le rose* e *da n'erva fetente nasce lo giglio*. (P 181.12)

> This rule doesn't always work: As the plant is, so is the branch.
> Since one can see that roses bloom from thorny branches and
> the lily blossoms amongst fetid weeds.

The first introductory paremias of *cunto* 4, *Ommo comme nasce accossì pasce* ("Because as a man is born, so he is fed") and *Da le cevettole non nasceno aquele, né da le ciavole palumme* ("Neither from owls can eagles be born nor from magpies doves"), declare that similarity to ancestors is genetic, so men do not change during their lives and always become what is dictated from birth. However, *Chi meglio nasce meglio procede* ("He who is born better continues to be better") and *Chi dorme co' cane non se nn'auza senza pullece* ("He who sleeps with dogs wakes up with fleas") convey a slightly different idea.[75] If not genetic, similarity of intent and behavior can be acquired by continuous relations with someone, regardless of its positive or negative results. Basile, in *cunto* 4, makes the aforementioned dying man express the same concept and give the same advice to his two children: *Chi prattica co lo zuoppo 'n capo dell'anno zoppeca* ("He who associates with a cripple will be limping by the end of the year") and *Chi dorme co cane non se n'auza senza pulece* ("He who sleeps with the dog won't get up without fleas"; CC IV.2.14; Basile, *The Tale of Tales* 306). Sarnelli's *cunto* 5 expresses another exception to the idea that, no matter how you are exposed to different stimuli, you can never change your own nature. If *Da le spine nasceno le rose* ("Roses bloom from thorny branches") and *Da n'erva fetente nasce lo giglio* ("The lily blossoms amongst fetid weeds"), then redemption is possible and upbringing and education can overcome one's essence. The two proverbial phrases indirectly promote the idea that associating with a better person in order to gain something positive from the relationship is better than associating with those who are lesser off. This is the message that the expression, *Pratteca co chi è meglio de tene e falle le spese* ("Associate with those who are better than you and share with them") in *cunto* 4, conveys.

In the first *cunto* of *Posilecheata*, all of the introductory expressions set the ground for the story featuring a generous woman, Pacecca, who always does well, and her mean husband, mastro Cocchiarone, who continuously tries to deceive her. When Pacecca begs her husband to buy her a pair of shoes, since she has donated hers to a poor woman, Sarnelli leaves a tolerant and good-natured comment toward her ingenuity:

> Ma non s'addonava la scura ca lo marito la 'nfenocchiava e decea chelle parole pe *darele la quatra*. (P 37.7)
>
> The unfortunate woman did not realize that her husband was fooling her and was telling her those words to make fun of her.

By promising to buy Pacecca new clothes, mastro Cocchiarone hoodwinks her ("infinocchiare") and "gives her the fourth part" ("darle la quatra"). Both D'Ambra's and Andreoli's dictionaries report the entry "quatra," equivalent of "quadra" ("fourth") in the Neapolitan dialect.[76] They include the proverbial phrase, *Fare na quatra de vierme* ("To make the fourth part of a worm"), which suggests that a person is greatly afraid and experiences an extremely frightening situation.[77] GDLI (s.v. *quadra* [2], n. 9) lists two other meanings for the expression. The first, which does not apply to this context, is to flatter someone. In this meaning, the proverbial phrase appears in Salviati's and Serdonati's collections as a synonym of "to adulate." The second meaning, which Malato adopts in his edition of *Posilecheata*, refers to fooling or deriding someone (P 37.7). This interpretation probably derives from the 1612 Voc. Cr. (s.v. *dare* and *quadra*): "Motteggiare, uccellare e beffare copertamente" ("To jest, to ridicule, and to mock covertly"). In Sarnelli's context, the fact that Pacecca's husband is mocking and deceiving his wife is confirmed by another expression: *Longa se vedde, corta se trovaje* ("Long she saw herself, short she found herself"; P 38.8). Since Pacecca is said to believe that she was wealthy ("longa") when in fact she was a pauper ("corta"), the readers infer that she will be humiliated later in the story. Both paremias function as a prolepsis of the next development of the story and as an indication of how to read and interpret the recounted events.

The fable presents an interesting example of transition between two languages through a paremia that occurs when mastro Cocchiarone abandons a naked Pacecca in the woods. While wandering, she finds a castle, which she is initially scared to access. However, she finally gathers the necessary courage to explore it:

> *[F]ece de la trippa corazzone.* (P 45.32)[78]
> She made heart of her guts.

The paremia, featuring in Basile's *cunto* V.4.53, is the Neapolitan translation of the Spanish expression *Hacer de tripas corazón* ("To make heart of one's guts"; D'Ambra, s.v. *corazzone;* Franciosini, s.v. *tripa*). As such, it shows a phonetic and morphologic adaptation of the word "corazzone," a calque from the Spanish "corazón" ("heart").[79] The literal meaning of the expression is to transform the bowels—the typical place where fear manifests—into the heart, or to let courage come from fear. In a slightly different meaning, Rocco (s.v. *corazzone*) and Malato in his *Vocabolarietto napoletano* (57–58) suggest that the paremia refers to taking advantage of a situation much like the message conveyed by the expression *Fare della necessità virtù* ("To make virtue out of necessity"). In his glossary to Cortese's and Sgruttendio de Scafato's *Opere poetiche*, Malato also includes the meaning "fare buon viso a cattiva sorte" ("to make a good face in front of bad luck"), which refers to the act of trying to minimize the effect of a negative situation by manifesting an opposite feeling (167). The most appropriate interpretation of Sarnelli's paremias would, however, imply that of being fearless enough to pull something out of a sense of dread, as does Pacecca.

As previously discussed, in *Posilecheata* the presence of Spanish paremias does not have any social or political implications; rather, their use derives from aesthetic and stylistic matters.[80] According to Gian Luigi Beccaria, Sarnelli wished to distinguish those expressions from the rest of the text, probably for ironic purposes (*Spagnolo e spagnoli* 259). This does not seem to be the case for *Fece de la trippa corazzone* and for other instances in Sarnelli's collection, though. Another plausible interpretation is that the author meant to render the reading of his text more pleasurable and, thus, enriched its vocabulary with precious and unique non-Neapolitan expressions. He may have also intended to reproduce the linguistic variety of the Neapolitan area by way of including foreign words (*Spagnolo* 264–79). Consequently, mentioning a Spanish paremia would be a conscious choice of plurilingualism. In a work that is already in dialect, inserting expressions from another language, which is also the most prestigious among the foreign ones, would succeed in presenting a multifaceted and composite situation, while also leaving space for new linguistic creations (286–91). Even more so considering that Spanish paremias were circulating widely in Italy in the sixteenth and the seventeenth centuries. Italian authors heavily borrowed from Spanish collections, since they considered the Spanish language better crafted to create proverbs and proverbial phrases.[81] Employing them in the narrative was not exceptional, but rather demonstrated the author's acquaintance with expressions and idioms in a different language.

In Sarnelli's *cunto*, before the final reward Pacecca faces a charge of murder for the death of a young boy, when in fact mastro Cocchiarone killed him to get rid of his wife. When the woman resuscitates the adolescent, he accuses mastro Cocchiarone of being his murderer. Everyone at court would like to castigate him harshly, but Pacecca asks for him to be spared (P 50.71). The final paremia of the *cunto* refers to Pacecca's generous choice, as well as to the content and significance of the entire story:

> *Chi vò male ped aute a sè non jova,*
> *E chi fa bene sempre bene trova.* (P 61.79)
>
> He who wants evil for others does not benefit himself
> and he who does good always finds good.

The meaning of the proverb emerges clearly in the given context: those, like mastro Cocchiarone, who wish bad events upon others, always pay the consequences of their evil acts. Meanwhile, those like Pacecca, who commit themselves to helping others, are rewarded in turn for their worthy actions. In the end, Pacecca marries the Prince of Campochiaro and everyone at court loves her. Conversely, mastro Cocchiarone drowns in a water tank, is transformed into a statue, and is placed before the main sewer in Campochiaro. The proverb summarizes the tale's moral tension and didactic orientation. Simultaneously, it connects with the ethical admonitions of the initial paremiac expressions, speculating over the good and bad resulting from one's actions.

Cunto 2: *La vajassa fedele*

The second *cunto* of Sarnelli's collection, which Popa narrates, presents a specific connection to the characters presented in the frame of the overall collection: indeed, Petruccio bears the same name of the main character of the fairy tale, Petruccia. The fable begins with a rather misogynistic quotation. The author specifies that he borrows it from Sannazaro's *Arcadia*, which in turn originates from Petrarca's *Rerum vulgarium fragmenta*.[82] Sannazaro's lines read that entrusting one's hopes to a woman is impossible and useless, because all of the activities to which love is compared are unreliable:

> Ne l'onda solca e nell'arena semina
> E i vaghi venti cerca in rete accogliere
> Chi sue speranze fonda in cor di femina. (P 63.1)
>
> A furrow in the waves, and seed in the desert sands,
> and the wandering winds in a net he hopes to gather
> who builds his trust upon the heart of a woman.

Sarnelli uses the authority given by literature to argue that he disagrees with the idea that all women are untrustworthy, and promises to illustrate the fallaciousness of Sannazaro's lines by means of the main character of his story. Petruccia is a faithful servant, able to endure privation, and is willing to go beyond her immediate job responsibility in order to serve her mistress fully. This introductory moral quotation, much like those in the first *cunto*, provides the reader with an indication of what to consider while reading the story. However, since the author asserts the opposite through the *cunto*, referring to Sannazaro's lines succeeds in reinforcing the message of the recounted story even further, i.e., the ideal of long-lasting loyalty and submission among women. Moreover, by extracting a verse from a Neapolitan author, Sarnelli confirms the Neapolitan essence of his story vis-à-vis high-level and respected literature. Yet, by contradicting it, he strengthens the identity of his *Posilecheata* in the realm of works written in the Neapolitan dialect.

The storyteller, Popa, recounts the events of *cunto* 2. Seven fairies are called to predict the future of Pomponia, a newly born princess in the reign of Green Land. When the shells of some nuts scattered on the floor hurt one of the fairies, she casts a terrible spell upon Pomponia. The girl will transform into a snake on her first night of marriage and she will remain in that shape for three years, three months, three hours, and three minutes. She will need to find a devoted maid in order to break the spell: a young woman with two uncouth sisters and no male siblings, daughter of an orphan mother without any grandfather and whose face resembles Pomponia's to the smallest details. Only in this way, will she regain her original human body; if not, she will remain a serpent forever.

Comic metaphors co-mingle with paremias concerning food when the King of Red Land selects Pomponia as his future wife. Eager to marry his beautiful daughter to him, Pomponia's father expresses his thoughts on the incredible advantages of such a marriage with a culinary reference:

Chapter Four

> [V]edenno ca sto parentato le 'mportava assaje, e che se l'avesse cercato co lo sprocchetiello no' l'avarria potuto asciare meglio, e che a la figlia *le cadeva lo vruoccolo dinto lo lardo, lo maccarone dinto lo ccaso*. (P 70.20)

> Considering that this relationship mattered a lot to him, and that had he been looking for it carefully, he would have not been able to find a better one, such that it suited his daughter the way broccoli goes with lard and macaroni with cheese.

The two proverbial phrases *Cadere lo vruoccolo dinto lo lardo* ("To suit the way broccoli goes with lard") and *Cadere lo maccarone dinto lo ccaso* ("To suit the way macaroni goes with cheese") comically suggest that someone might experience unexpected good luck or that simply an event occurs conveniently (Rocco, s.v. *caso*).[83] In other words, everything goes into the right place by chance, such as broccoli on lard, or fits perfectly, such as cheese over macaroni pasta (D'Ambra, s.v. *caso*). Pomponia and the King of Red Land are the appropriate match since perfect suitability and profitability bless their marriage.

Elements of the narration related to food are not surprising in a Neapolitan text in which these references constitute the main thread of the various parts of the collection.[84] Food is proverbially mentioned again when Pomponia, who is looking for a faithful servant, tests three sisters from the small village of Villanova. The first sister, Livia, is a rough and poorly educated young girl and does not appreciate the endeavor that she needs to undertake in order to demonstrate her suitability for the task that Pomponia will impose on her. Upon her poor results, Pomponia discharges Livia and sends one of her servants to eavesdrop on the girl's reaction:

> [M]ettenno la lengua 'n mota accommenzaje a ghiastemmare la Prencepessa, comme femmena senza descrezzione, e come ca *lo sazio non crede lo dejuno*, e ca *lo piso de la corona fa calare tal'ommore all'uocchie che non vedeno lo deritto*, e tant'aute felastoccole che non le avarria ditto manco no poeta. (P 74.32)

> Setting her tongue in motion, she started to curse the princess as an insensitive woman, and as a well-fed person who does not believe a starving one, and that the weight of a crown clouds the eyes so that they cannot discern the right way, and many other verses that not even a poet would have been able to declare.

Before being dismissed in favor of her younger sister Petruccia, Livia rebukes Princess Pomponia for not understanding those who are not as wealthy as she is. This is similar to the behavior of a person who can count on a nutritious diet and does not understand the hardship of a famished one, as expressed by the paremia, *Lo sazio non crede lo dejuno* ("A well-fed person does not believe a starving one"; Rocco, s.v. *dejuno*).[85] Livia also argues that those who are healthy or rich do not give credit to complaints from the sick or poor, nor do they believe that they are as sick or as poor as they claim. The proverbial phrase, *Lo piso de la corona fa calare tal'ommore all'uocchie che non vedeno lo deritto* ("The weight of a crown clouds the eyes so that they cannot discern the right way"), underscores this concept even more. It connects the weight of a crown (a coin indeed)[86] to impaired judgement, possibly due to an imbalance of the four Hippocratic humors. Wealth causes anyone to overlook the implicit and correct perspective in a situation: this is Livia's accusation at Pomponia. However, the proverbial phrase may also indicate that an excessive consideration of oneself, as Livia does, leads to inconsiderate and inappropriate behaviors and choices.

Since the third sister of the family, Petruccia, resembles Pomponia greatly, she is elected to become her substitute. Petruccia endures many difficulties, such as pretending to be dead in the eyes of her own mother, living in isolation for three years, replacing Pomponia for the entire length of the spell, and taking care of her in the garden when she is in the shape of a serpent. A paremia, which Basile uses in the eighth eclogue of his *Muse napolitane* (Basile, *Lo cunto de li cunti* [1976], 8.170–71), summarizes the meaning of this sequence of events and the reward that the young woman deserves because of her patience:

> *Male e bene a fine vene.* (P 82.54)[87]
> Bad and good come to an end.

By anticipating the narration, the expression gives advance notice of the final development of the *cunto*, which undoubtedly presents a happy conclusion and a final positive outcome. In fact, the monophrastic paremia concluding the tale demonstrates how loyal servitude pays off. Associated with a fountain in Naples allusively called *Fontana de li serpi* ("The fountain of the snakes"), the expression represents its etiologic explanation, as well as a closure for the events that associate Pomponia and Petruccia:

> *Chi serve fedele aspetta premmio.* (P 93.82)
> He who serves faithfully awaits a reward.

Since the tale reveals that hope can be directed toward faithful people, including women, the proverb proves Sarnelli's introductory assertion true and conversely, contradicts Sannazaro's lines. The message of Sarnelli's proverb recalls that of an expression that Basile uses in the third *cunto* of his second day: *Ogni fatica cerca premio* ("Every job deserves a reward"). In Basile's tale, the paremia does not appear at the end but in the middle of the narration in which it refers to the skills that young Viola employs to free herself from the sexual advances of a prince. Since her aunt is helping the prince in his pursuit, Viola deprives her of her ears and says: "Tienete sso buono veveraggio de la sansaria: *Ogni fatica cerca premio*, a sfrisate de 'nore sgarrate d'aurecchie" ("Here is a generous tip for your matchmaking. Every job deserves a reward: for honor ruined, ears damaged"; CC II.3.20; Basile, *The Tale of Tales* 158). Clearly, Basile is using the paremia ironically: Viola twists the positive meaning of the expression to reproach her aunt, who thus obtains the appropriate reward for acting as an unapproved love intermediary. In contrast, Sarnelli's proverb carries a positive meaning and seeks to highlight the inherent profit of respectful servitude.

Another paremia featuring in the description of Pomponia's spell confirms her successful collusion with Petruccia and the depth of their feelings. Upon Pomponia's regaining her human body, the two women hug each other tightly:

> [P]oje s'abbracciajeno tanto e de tale manera che *parevano l'urmo e la vite.* (P 86.65)
>
> They hugged each other so much and in such a way that they looked like the elm and the vine.

The proverbial phrase comes from an account of the Ovidian myth featuring the Etruscan god Vertumnus and the Roman goddess of fruits, Pomona. In *Metamorphoses* (Book 14, vv. 609–97), the association of the two plants is a symbol of marriage. Both the elm and the vine without each other would not grow appropriately, whereas their combination gives strength to both. Vertumnus, disguised as an old woman, refers to the expression by saying: "Ulmus erat contra speciosa nitentibus uvis" ("That elm tree supported the beautiful clusters of shiny grapes"; v. 661). These words are the pretext to tell Pomona that she should not follow the message of the saying, and thus not marry anyone but him. The image of the two plants growing together also features in Alciati's *Emblemata*, whose emblem CLX bears a motto on the eternity of friendship: *Amicitia etiam post mortem durans* ("Friendship lasting even after death"). The last two lines of the epigram confirms the motto's message that nothing, not even death, can separate good friends: "[E]xemploque monet, tales nos quaerere amicos, quos neque disiungat foedere summa dies" ("[A]nd by its own example it advises us to seek such friends as the last day, death, would not separate from the pact of friendship").[88] The emblem serves as a model of long-standing and strong friendship between two people beyond the passage of time and the end of life, much like the relationship between Petruccia and Pomponia illustrates.

An additional source for this paremia is one of Christ's parables in the Bible, specifically the *Parable of the Fig Tree* (Luke 13:6–9). In this reference the image of mutual support is charged with a negative element. Despite being intertwined, the vine prevents a fig from thriving and bearing fruit. The only solution would be to remove the vine, including its roots, in order to enable the fig to bear fruit again. If one applies the moral of this story to Sarnelli's *cunto*, Petruccia's trust in the girl results in a happy conclusion. This positive ending is possible only because of an extreme act like that of uprooting the vine. Pomponia and the King of Red Land spend a life full of love together, Petruccia marries the King of Red Land's brother, and both couples live together and for a long time in Naples (P 94.83). The moral message of the final proverb and of the tale itself offers an immediate reflection on the meaning of friendship and on the faithfulness of which human beings are capable.

Cunto 3: *La 'ngannatrice 'ngannata*

In the third *cunto*, which is exactly in the middle of the collection, the introductory proverbial phrase sets the tone for the entire fairytale that focuses on instances of friendship or lack thereof. The expression also introduces the relationship between two characters in the story, Menic'Aniello and his friend Marcone as recounted by Tolla:

> *A l'abbesuogne se canosceno l'ammice*, e comme lo buono vino è sempre buono pe nfi' a la feccia, così lo buono amico dura porzí dapo' la morte. (P 96.3)[89]

> When needed, one can really value a friend, and as much as good wine is always perfectly fine up to its dregs, so a good friend lasts even after death.

Since the last reference in the previous tale is to long-lasting and deeply-felt friendship, this proverbial phrase establishes a link between *cunto* 2 and *cunto* 3. The stories exemplify the consequences of two opposite behaviors and feelings of friendship: faithfulness in the second fable and deceit in the third.

The first instance of negative friendship occurs after Menic'Aniello's death, when Marcone confines Menic'Aniello's daughters Lella, Cilla, and Cicia in their own palace and forces them to work. Sarnelli describes the three girls as they talk about their future as spouses yet lack consideration of the consequences of their thoughts. A proverbial phrase, which Florio also uses in *Firste Fruites* (FF 6v), describes their solipsistic reflections:

> [F]acevano lo cunto senza lo tavernaro. (P 98.11)
> They did their calculations without the host.

As illustrated earlier, an appropriate meaning of the proverbial phrase would be to plan something without evaluating its possible difficulties and implications. The three sisters, upon deciding their future on their own, do not evaluate the other person's opinions: specifically, they do not take into account the opinions of their future husbands, who play the role of the innkeepers in the paremia. Sarnelli plays with the correspondence between two homographs: "cunto" as calculation and "cunto" as tale to recount (Andreoli, D'Ambra, and Rocco, s.v. *cunto*). The three sisters are planning their lives and making their own calculations in a rather "unfriendly" way, but they are also the characters of a *cunto* and thus shape Sarnelli's tale while creating their own stories in their minds.

As the fable progresses, the three sisters marry the husbands they chose. However, luck is not on the side of the youngest of them, Cicia, since her husband's stepmother, Pascadozia, hates her and replaces her newly-born twins with two puppies. This second instance of negative friendship causes Cicia to be imprisoned and the two infants, Jannuzzo and Ninella, to be abandoned in the woods. The traumatic event leads to the second part of the narration during which a series of adventures take place for the twins. When a miller's wife finds them, they soon become part of the family. Yet, their desire to search for their own origins makes the two adolescents wander in the world until they decide to reside in Naples. Unbeknownst to them, they end up living in a house just in front of their parents' palace, where Pascadozia dwells. As the two women see each other through the windows, Pascadozia tells Ninella that she would be more beautiful if she possessed three magic elements that could be found only in a distant land. Jannuzzo, as a sort of fairy-tale knight looking for honorable tasks, embarks on long journeys to faraway places in order to find these three objects and satisfy his sister's desires (P 115.55). In contrast to the traditional *quête* of valiant knights in chivalric poems, though, his search is not profitable or honorable, for it just stems from Ninella's capriciousness.

For these reasons, paremias in this section of the fable are linked to emotional states and comment on Jannuzzo's behavior comically or ironically. After two successful journeys to find a singing apple and dancing water, the young adolescent is asked to catch a magic bird able to talk like a human being. Fooled by the beauty of the place, Jannuzzo is transformed into a statue after he dares to touch the animal with his own hands.[90] A proverbial phrase describes Jannuzzo's lack of consideration for his actions and indirectly, depicts him as a naïve boy who does not have much worldly experience. He is said to trust in a rather difficult and challenging undertaking:

> … credennose de *infilare perne a lo junco*. (P 123.83)
> … believing to insert pearls in a reed.

Basile adopts this paremia in his *cunti* II.5 and V.2. In the first fable, the expression appears in the discourse that a snake gives to a peasant named Cola Matteo. The animal asks him to gather all the fruit pits that he can find in the city and to sow them in the park so that "ne vederrai *perne 'nfilate a lo iunco*" ("you'll see pearls strung on rush stems"; CC II.5.15; Basile, *The Tale of Tales* 171). Even though this is thought to be an absurd mission, Cola Matteo is able to accomplish it and experiences the marvels that the snake predicted, i.e., all of the fruit pits turned into precious stones. In fable V.2, the meaning of the expression is the same. When the month of March gives Cianne a stick, it tells him that the object could perform incredible deeds: "Sempre che te vene desederio di quarcosa, e tu dì: «Scorriato, dammene ciento,» e *vederrai perne 'nfilate a lo iunco*" ("Whenever you wish for something just say, 'Flail, give me a hundred of them!' and you'll see the rushes

Chapter Four

strung with pearls"; CC V.2.25; Basile, *The Tale of Tales* 397).⁹¹ In *Posilecheata*, the paremia suggests something different, i.e., that Jannuzzo did not reflect properly on how catching the bird would not be an easy task. Because of his lack of consideration, he now pays the consequences of his poor judgement.

Since the young boy does not come back from his journey, Ninella, disguised as a pilgrim, starts to look for him and arrives at the mountain covered with statues where he is. The entire section contains etiologic stories explaining the origins of statues in Naples and offers a journey through the city of Naples and the Neapolitan region.⁹² Once again, the fantastical world of a fable establishes a link with the real world and makes the tale exclusively Neapolitan. In this context, Naples seems to replace Rome as a *caput mundi*. Its language might not be as polished and refined as the Tuscan vernacular and the Northern dialects, but from a visual perspective the city can count on a recognition that goes beyond other cities. For all of these urban references and the enthusiastic depiction of the area, the fable is said to be the most pleasant, characteristic, and graceful in the collection:

> Fu accossì saporito, coriuso e galante lo cunto de Tolla, che chisto sulo se potea chiammare *lo cunto de li cunte*, avennoce renchiuse tutte le storie de Napole. (my italics; P 138.128)

> Tolla's tale was so tasty, curious, and graceful that this alone could be called the tale of the tales, since it included all the stories of Naples.

This tale generates other tales, as occurs also in Basile's *Lo cunto de li cunti*, and thus serves as a tale *par excellence*. Its importance and centrality derive from its concluding moral message: the story supports that evil people who are not friends rightly face the negative and fatal consequences of their bad actions. It also confirms the message of the initial paremia: those who are friends are reliable, whereas those who deceive others do not deserve anyone's friendship. Pascadozia experiences the latter, as she dies and is transformed into a statue:

> 'Ncoppa a lo ingannator cade lo 'nganno,
> E se tarda, non manca lo malanno. (P 138.127)

> The deceit falls on top of the deceiver, and if it delays, misfortune won't lack.

As the title already anticipates, tricking someone results in being tricked in return. Sarnelli inserts a temporal element within this common expression, which has also been analyzed in Brusantino's *Le cento novelle* (CN 108). If the trick is not played on the trickster soon ("se tarda"), there will, nonetheless, be misfortune and bad luck ("malanno"). The moral message of the proverb and of the entire *cunto* is not to be deceptive and commit tricks because the trickster will always pay for the results of his own actions.

Cunto 4: *La gallenella*

The introductory paremias of *cunto* 4 have already been analyzed while interpreting the first *cunto* of the collection:

> Ca l'*ommo comme nasce accossì pasce*. E se maje villano fece azzione de galant'ommo, o fu jannizzero o cuorvo janco: pocca *da le cevettole non nasceno aquele, né da le ciavole palumme*. E perzò se sole dicere: *prattega co chi è meglio de tene e falle le spese*: perché *chi meglio nasce meglio procede* e *chi dorme co' cane non se nn'auza senza pullece*. (P 141.1)

> Because as a man is born, so he is fed. And if ever a villain behaved as a gentleman, either he was a Janissary or a white crow: because neither from owls can eagles be born nor from magpies doves. So, it's a common saying, Associate with those who are better than you and share with them. Because a person who is born better continues to be better, and a person who sleeps with dogs wakes up with fleas.

Here, it suffices to mention that these expressions outline one of the possible interpretations of the *cunto*. They indeed tell the reader that the moral message of the fable concerns the behavior of a poor person who suddenly becomes rich. Many are the ideal candidates for this behavior, including the two twin protagonists of the story. However, only one, Belluccia, fully demonstrates (and in a negative way) the meaning that these paremias express.

The story narrated by Cecca presents a frame that almost reproduces the same aspects of Sarnelli's collection as a whole. Here too, the act of recounting tales is associated with food and spending time together: Cecca recalls a story that her grandmother used to narrate while she was roasting chestnuts, the memory of which is as vivid as the story itself in Cecca's mind. As she makes a reference to the plague, the incursion of reality into the fairytale ambience is evident. It is probable that the recollection of the pestilence that hit Naples in 1656 was still fresh and might have influenced Sarnelli in its literary description. Compared to the

Chapter Four

famous representation of the 1348 plague in the *Decameron* (Dec. Intr.8–48), Sarnelli's account is less emotional and miserable, yet more popular as the paremias illustrate. For instance, when Death is said to kill both a father and his son at once, Sarnelli uses a proverbial phrase that Basile had already placed in his *cunti* III.6 and IV.9 in a similar form:

> *Fare no viaggio e duje servizie.* (P 143.5)[93]
> To take one journey and perform two services.

Since the expression highlights that Death is not sparing anyone, it acquires a dark connotation: Death's scythe kills two innocent people ("duje servizie") with one blow ("no viaggio"). Simultaneously, the paremia gains a popular focus as it shifts the description of the plague from an historical account to an everyday and common context, thus bringing the entire scene closer to the feelings of the Neapolitan readers of Sarnelli's story.

The death of a Neapolitan couple establishes a link between the plague and the fairytale. Upon dying, Peppone and Zezolla entrust their two children, Sole and Luna,[94] to the care of their wet nurse in the countryside. After raising them to adolescence, the woman decides to bring them back to the city, where she abandons them. As in the third *cunto*, magic animals intervene in the story to support the two young people, now named Cecca and Mineco. Cecca is given a hen, who discovers a secret passage to her parents' palace. Here, a lizard shows her many riches and advises her of her future life. Since Cecca needs to assess her brother's wisdom before disclosing to him the incredible treasure in the palace, she asks him what they should do with the hen. Upon his answer that they should eat it, Cecca scolds Mineco because common sense dictates that the animal should be preserved until it becomes a mother hen. Mineco answers back with a proverbial expression:

> E chi vò aspettare tanto? ... Primma de vedere sto gallinaro sarriamo cennere. Non saje ca se dice: *È meglio la gallina oje che l'uovo craje?* (P 152.31)
>
> And who wants to wait that long? ... Before we go and see these chicks, we would be ashes. Don't you know that it is commonly said, it is better a hen today than an egg tomorrow?

The use of a common proverbial phrase and its actual modification is an interesting case of adaptation that Rocco (s.v. *uovo*) calls "inversione scherzevole" ("playful inversion"). *Meglio n'uovo ogge ca na gallina dimane* ("It is better an egg today than a hen tomorrow"; D'Ambra, s.v. *uovo*) suggests that waiting could not be advantageous if one hopes for future luck or wealth. Since Mineco wishes to eat the hen, and not the egg, he flips over the two parts of the traditional expression and conveys the comic message that it is better to have a hen today than an egg later. Sarnelli's change makes the expression specific to the context of the fable, a sort of paremia translated for the immediacy and contingency of the situation. Despite its humorous message, the proverbial phrase confirms Mineco's immaturity in the given scenario, as opposed to his sister's wisdom. Thus, it shows how he cannot be trusted because he does not have enough good judgement.[95]

When Mineco acquires the necessary wisdom a few years later, Cecca discloses the treasure to him. Remembering the lizard's advice, she convinces him to marry an extremely poor lady called Belluccia. In this section of the story, Sarnelli employs paremias as a repository of ancient wisdom successfully conveying moral messages. When the author comments on Belluccia's sudden jealousy toward Cecca due to her newly acquired wealth, he uses such a proverb:

> Perché li proverbie antiche sempre so' resciute, ca *non se dice lo mutto se non è miezo o tutto*: azzoè ca *non c'è peo de pezzente arresagliuto*, pocca lo grasso le dà subbeto a lo core, e *lo cavallo c'ha uorgio e paglia soperchia tira cauce*. (P 158.48)
>
> Because ancient proverbs always succeeded, since one does not say a motto if it is not half or all of it: which is there is nothing worse than a wealthy villain, since fat immediately strikes one's heart, and the horse that has excessive barley and straw kicks.

Dare il grasso al cuore ("To strike one's heart with fat") means that someone becomes insensible because of sudden prosperity. In the context of the *cunto*, this message transfers to Belluccia's inability to control a surge of pride resulting exclusively from her new social status. The subsequent proverbial phrase, *Lo cavallo c'ha uorgio e paglia soperchia tira cauce* ("The horse that has excessive barley and straw kicks"), further explains this meaning. It depicts the lack of gratitude to those who provide someone with food and shelter, like a horse that is ungrateful to its master and kicks him without appreciating the refinement of the food it receives.[96] Belluccia is a "pezzente arresagliuto" ("enriched villain"), who has accumulated riches all at once and does not behave appropriately in her new status (Rocco, s.v. *arresagliuto*). By seeing wealth ("lo grasso"), she loses her reasoning and common sense. The final paremia of the *cunto*, *Non c'è peo de vellane arresagliute* ("There is nothing worse than a wealthy villain"; P 174.92), is used here with a stronger reference to the social class to which Belluccia belongs (she is a "pezzente," hence a "villain"), and not only to her behavior. The paremia's moral tension creates a circular narrative and moral movement that is resolved at the end of the *cunto* upon Belluccia's cruel death. There, the proverbial phrase demonstrates how prosperity cannot change one's origins, especially if one is poor. Summarizing Belluccia's actions and conveying a message similar to that of *cunto* 3, the paremia serves as a reminder for future generations. The behavior of unreliable people brings evil and harsh consequences, whereas the persistency of fraternal bonds furthers relationships among people and builds reciprocal trust.

Another interesting transformation of a paremia brings Sarnelli to convey irony in the story. Attempting to get Mineco's sister out of the house, Belluccia feeds her serpent's eggs, which make her seem pregnant.[97] Upon succeeding to show how dishonorable Cecca is, Belluccia tries to convince her husband to disown her and reproaches him for his hesitation:

> Meglio che tu te lieve da casa na scrofa ch'essere mostato a dito comm'a ciervo; è meglio che tu lighe no chiappo a lo cannaruozzolo sujo ch'esserete ditto: *L'ommo se lega pe le corna e li vuoje pe le parole*. (P 161.56)

> It is better to deprive your house of a sow rather than be pointed at as a deer; better to have your hands tied than have it said: Men are tied up by horns, oxen by words.

The paremia, *Gli huomini si legano per la lingua* (or *le parole*) *e i buoi per le corna* ("Men are tied up by their tongue [or words], oxen by their horns"), is used by Basile in *cunto* III.2.62 and referred to by Doni in *Chiacchiera XI* of his *Zucca*. The expression signifies that for each person and personality a specific behavior is required (Tosi, "Precedenti classici" 191: par. 3.1). Sarnelli revises the syntax of the expression that results in the form, *L'ommo se lega pe le corna e li vuoje pe le parole* ("Men are tied up by horns, oxen by words"). Rocco's entry *cuorno* helps explain the meaning of this paremiac neologism, especially by comparing it with *Fare corna comm'a boje* ("To grow horns like oxen," meaning to give up). The traditional (or non-inverted) paremia, *Gli huomini si legano per la lingua e i buoi per le corna*, conveys the sense that, in order to dominate people, the only way is to use the language, of which the tongue is the central organ. This offers the idea that someone can employ all of the devices that rhetoric offers. In other words, if animals can be limited only with material things, such as a rope, men can realize their will through words. By inverting the two sections of the paremia, thus the two types of behavior, Sarnelli's Belluccia satirizes the horns, which are culturally associated with sexual betrayal. Appropriately, in this case, Mineco is confronted with fraternal betrayal and social scandal. Words usually restrain men when they are unreasonable; when betrayed, though, men are wild, dangerous, and almost skittish, and therefore, they can only be controlled by a rope in their horns, the same way an ox is fastened to work.[98] Belluccia changes the expression to fit the context of her discourse and, as a result, the paremia sends out a strong message about human social behavior, while at the same time criticizing Mineco's lack of judgment in Belluccia's opinion.

As time progresses and Cecca lives happily married in Foggia, an occasion brings her husband, her daughter, and herself to Naples to do some business with her own brother. While at Mineco's house, when all onlookers are unaware of Cecca's identity, the truth is revealed. Sarnelli uses a meta-narrative technique, which is further emphasized by the fact that the narrator of Sarnelli's story bears the same name of the character in her story, Cecca. The fairytale character Cecca recounts her own story in front of the others. However, this time, the *cunto* is not as spontaneous as the other accounts of storytelling in Sarnelli's collection. Cecca's narration is rather premeditated and discloses her own personal events from the moment in which she was sent away from home. To describe Belluccia's scheming at the time, Cecca uses a proverbial phrase:

> Essa *fice comme fa lo cane ch'abbaja a la luna*. Azzoè che tanta màchene soje ghiezero 'n fummo. (P 169.81)
>
> She did like the dog that barks at the moon, which is that her many machinations went up in smoke.

The explanation, which the conjunction "azzoè" ("that is") introduces, provides the correct interpretation of the paremia in the context of the *cunto*. The conventionalized meaning of the proverbial phrase is to do something without any result, to engage in a useless and ridiculous activity, or to pick on someone who does not have any part in the matter (D'Ambra, s.v. *abbaiare*; GDLI, s.v. *abbaiare* [1], n. 3, and *cane* [1], n. 17).[99] Therefore, the contextual meaning is that Belluccia acted against Cecca but in the end failed in her plans. Ultimately, the expression emphasizes how Cecca is stronger and superior to Belluccia, who is indeed a villain and will always remain one. Just as in traditional fables, the final resolution of Sarnelli's *cunto* vindicates Cecca and results in a positive conclusion for her and her brother Mineco, who can both enjoy their economic treasures and their love lives.

Cunto 5: *La capo e la coda*

Cianna, the oldest woman of the group of five storytellers, recounts the fifth and last tale, the most Baroque of all.[100] As with all of the others, the *cunto* features a proemial message, which contains a paremia, specifically a wellerism:

> Se bè de tutte li vizie se pò dicere chello che decette no cierto foretano de li lupe, che addommannato che nce nne trovasse uno buono, responnette: «*Sempe che so' lupe, malannaggia lo meglio!*», puro l'avarizia è no vizio accossì brutto che fa venire l'avaro 'nzavuorrio a tutte. (P 177.1)
>
> Even though, of all the vices you can say what a certain farmer of wolves said, who, when asked to find a good one, answered: "As long as they are wolves, and may misfortune get the better," yet avarice is such a bad vice that it makes everyone hate the avaricious person.

Lena lists this wellerism twice: *Come disse quel che vendeva i lupi: malanno habbia il meglio, o trist'è quel poco di buon che vi è, Sardi venales alius alio nequior* ("As the one that was selling wolves said: may misfortune get the better, or sad is that little good that there is; Sardinians slaves offered for sale are one more worthless than another"; 140) and *Malanno habbia il meglio: disse quello che vendeva i lupi, Simiarum pulcherrima deformis est* ("May misfortune get the better, the one that was selling wolves said; The most beautiful of the monkeys is shapeless"; 408). The wellerism refers to a bad situation that cannot be ameliorated because, even if there is a small quantity of good, the bad surpasses it. It derives from Benvenuto da Imola and, specifically, relates to a passage in Dante's *Commedia* describing Conte Ugolino's dream while imprisoned in the tower:

> Questi pareva a me maestro e donno,
> Cacciando il lupo e' lupicini al monte
> Per ché i Pisani veder Lucca non ponno. (*Inferno* 33, 28–30)

> This man appeared to me as lord and master;
> he hunted down the wolf and its young whelps
> upon the mountain that prevents the Pisans from seeing Lucca.

Benvenuto da Imola comments on these lines as follows:

> Ideo bene dicit ille qui portabat parvulos lupos ad vendendum. Rogatus ab emptore ut daret sibi unum bonum respondit: *Omnes sunt lupi.*
>
> And so he spoke well who was bringing small wolves. Having been asked by the buyer to give him a good one, he answered: "They are all wolves."

In Sarnelli's context, the paremia means that all of the vices are negative and do not differ from each other. Even if a better one exists, it cannot be praised because it always remains a vice. Among them, avarice is so bad that everyone despises it, and so the wellerism sends out an appropriate message on the impossibility of change for avaricious people. Sarnelli's repulsion for this vice is evident in his disposition against the story's character who embodies it: Roseca-chiuove, literally a person who gnaws nails. Her description recalls a long tradition of *vituperatio ad vetulam* and aims at emphasizing the most repellent attributes of an old woman, whose physical appearance corresponds to the ugliness of her mind and soul (P 178.3).[101]

After the characters' general presentation, the *cunto* portrays Nunziella, Roseca-chiuove's daughter, as the recipient of a contest between three fairies, who wish to test her kindness, generosity, and good-heartedness vis-à-vis her mother's stinginess. The paremias used to describe how Nunziella differs from Roseca-chiuove have already been analyzed in *cunto* one:

> Non sempre cammina la regola: *Comm'è la chianta è la scianta.*[102] Perché se vede ca *da le spine nasceno le rose* e *da n'erva fetente nasce lo giglio.* (P 181.12)
>
> This rule doesn't always work: As the plant is, so is the branch. Since one can see that roses bloom from thorny branches and the lily blossoms amongst fetid weeds.

The introductory formula, "non sempre cammina la regola" ("this rule doesn't always work"), emphasizes that the paremia is a stylistic tool used to illustrate the opposite of what the tale seems to demonstrate. Since it is not always true that children resemble their parents, it is possible that a change occurs and a good branch

Chapter Four

comes out of a bad root. Similarly, Nunziella was born as a rose or a lily from the thorns and weeds of her mother's avarice.

When Nunziella helps a fairy who is disguised as an old woman, her mother throws her out of her house. As Nunziella wanders alone in the woods, she arrives at a river and receives a spell by another fairy. She is given a ring, which allows her to marry a rich merchant, Micco, and lead a pleasant and wealthy life. When one day Micco asks his wife about her previous life, of which he was almost completely in the dark, Nunziella starts worrying about the miserable lies she has been recounting. To express her fear of public shame and poverty, she uses a common proverbial phrase and transforms it into a sarcastic exclamation:

> *Eccote fatto lo becco a l'oca.* (P 189.35)
> Here is that which the beak is done to the goose.

The paremia, *Fare il becco all'oca* ("To make the beak to the goose"), which Basile employs in his *cunto* III.4.13, is a playful way to state that something is over and finished (Voc. Cr. 1612, s.v. *becco*) or that it is well-done and well-concluded (GDLI, s.v. *becco* [1], n. 2; see also Speroni, *Proverbs and Proverbial Phrases* 183). Alternatively, it suggests that something has gone farther than what was originally thought (Rocco, s.v. *becco*), which is the sense that Sarnelli applies to his paremiac instance.[103]

Despite the deceitful circumstances of Nunziella's marriage, as in all other *cunti*, justice is reestablished at the end of this fable, too. Roseca-chiuove is transformed into a toad and continues being stingy, whereas Nunziella enjoys her life together with her husband. The final proverb, which comes from Erasmus's *Adagia*, *Lupus pilum mutat, non mentem* ("A wolf may change his hair, but not his heart"; *Collected Works of Erasmus, Adages*, vol. 34, III.iii.19: 288), harkens back to the introductory paremia of the story. No matter what the appearance is, nature remains the same, especially if avarice comes into play (GDLI, s.v. *lupo*, n. 24; Fig. 6):

> *Lo vizio dello lupo tanto dura,*
> *Che pilo pò mutare e no' natura.* (P 207.79)
>
> The vice of the wolf lasts as long as it can change its hair but not its nature.

Despite changing her essence from a human being to an animal, Roseca-chiuove still lives avariciously, deeply rooted in her vice, with no plans to modify or improve her behavior. As this *cunto* exemplifies, avarice is the worst of all vices because it results in no compassion for the others. The *cunto* represents the proper conclusion of an array of fables thematizing the virtues that one should have (kindness and goodness of heart in *cunto* 1 and faithfulness in ethical behavior in *cunto* 2) and the bad behavior that one should avoid (deceit in *cunto* 3, unsubstantiated boastfulness in *cunto* 4, and avarice in *cunto* 5). Similar to those ethical and unethical behaviors that Brusantino's proverbs describe and the useful and virtuous precepts that Florio's paremias express, Sarnelli's expressions transmit moral lessons to their readers of yesterday and today.

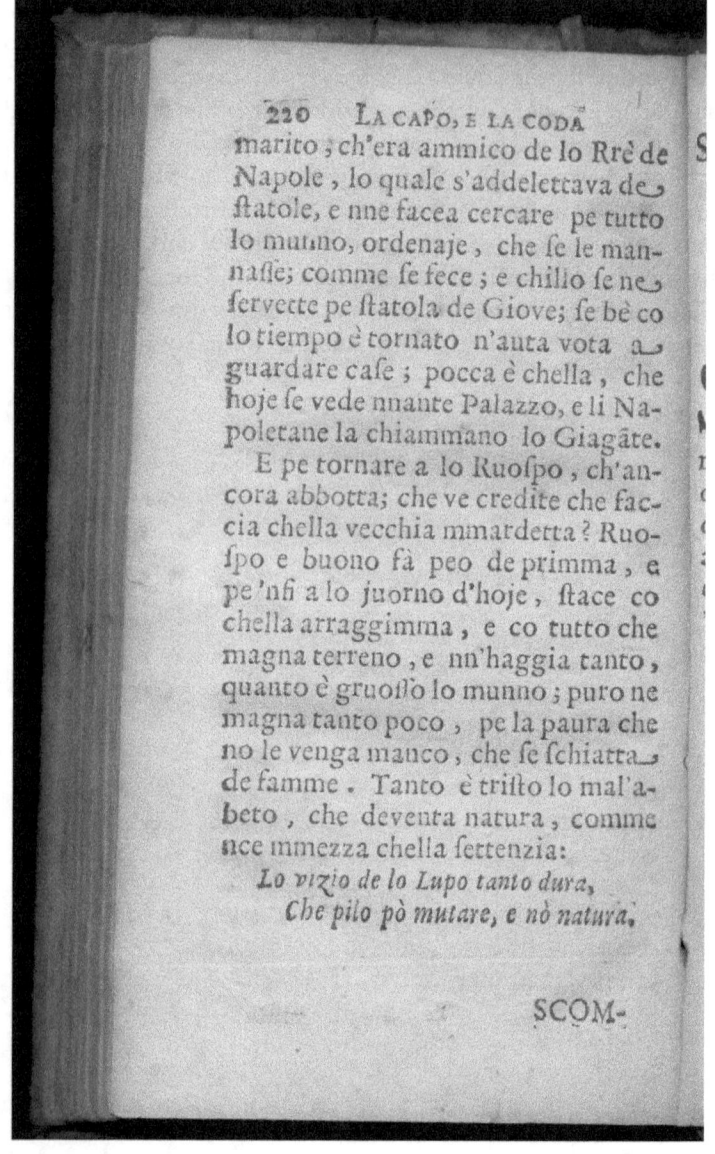

Figure 6: *Posilecheata*, final page with conclusive paremia for the fifth *cunto*, *La capo e la coda*. Courtesy of the Newberry Library, Bonaparte 5634.

Conclusion

> Non ho osservato interamente l'ordine richiesto, a cui d'una in un'altra lingua, gli altri scrittori et concetti trasporta et traduce; anzi talhora levando, talhora aggiungnendo qualche parola, ho mischiato il mio con quello dell'autore, secondo che mi è paruto meglio et di più vaghezza, pur ch'io habbia servata integra la sententia.
>
> I have not entirely observed the required order, in relation to which the other writers transfer and translate concepts from one language to another; rather, sometimes eliminating, sometimes adding a few words, I have mixed mine with that of the author, according to what seemed to me better and more ambiguously attractive, provided that I had preserved the integrity of the sententious phrase.
>
> Lodovico Guicciardini, *Detti et fatti piacevoli et gravi*

A frequently-used Latin paremia, *Polypi mentem obtine*, advised people to "adopt the outlook of the polyp" and thus adjust to the circumstances at hand (Erasmus, *Collected Works of Erasmus, Adages*, vol. 31, I.i.93: 133). Like a polyp, paremias themselves adapt to different contexts: they are polysemic, subject to change, and express a range of contextual meanings. Whether witty or severe, innovative or formulaic, they illuminate reality as a kaleidoscope of intercultural, intertemporal, and intertextual references (Bassnett 89). Contrary to the notion that they are unmodifiable, Brusantino's, Florio's, and Sarnelli's works demonstrate that paremias cross genres and ideologies, and experience different actualizations of their structure and meanings. These transformations reveal the intricacies of the Renaissance and Baroque cultures and result in linguistic variations and creative adaptations to the sociocultural situations.

Conclusion

It may be argued that paremias are rooted in a group identity and speak exclusively to its members. Each culture features its own proverbs and proverbial phrases, which are the result of mostly historical, chronological, and geographical factors. For this reason, Florio provides an explanation for the proverbial phrase *Far come quei da Prato* ("To do it in the way they do in Prato;" SF 78) because its meaning would not have been sufficiently comprehensible to the English community. As Constance Sullivan states, paremias are the "cultural currency at a given historical moment" (83). Yet, many times paremias transcend national, social, and linguistic boundaries and act as a timeless *lingua franca*, written or spoken by different cultures. Many Italian expressions that Florio inserts into the conversations of his *Fruits* are still in current use: an example is the proverb *Chi semina virtù racoglie fama* ("He who soweth virtue reapeth fame"; FF [28]*v*), which is listed in Valter Boggione and Lorenzo Massobrio's *Dizionario dei proverbi* (IX.1.1.19, IX.22.5.13) as well as in Salvatore Battaglia's *Grande dizionario della lingua italiana* (s.v. *virtù*, n. 23). Paremias may belong to multiple cultures and circulate through communities of speakers and writers in a process that ultimately results in diversifications of their meaning. Brusantino's paremias are illustrative: he acquires Boccaccio's original expressions and transfers them to the poetry of his *Le cento novelle*, while simultaneously adding his own introductory proverbs. All of these modifications conform to the needs of a community two centuries later than Boccaccio's audience. For instance, when Brusantino introduces novella V.4 with the proverb, *A lo sfrenato ardir spesso gli vale condur chi non gli pensa in molto male* ("Because of unrestrained audacity, it often happens that it ends very badly for he who does not think about it"; CN 261), he intends to condemn those behaviors that his Counter-Reformation society would have found difficult to approve.

While paremias assume various roles in different contexts, these contexts reciprocally enrich the significance of those expressions, and ultimately, influence the way in which the audience receives them. This explains why, on one hand, decontextualized paremias remain suspended in a potential state. They represent an unreal condition given that, without a context, they can be associated with infinite meanings. On the other hand, contextualized paremias are embedded in real and meaningful situations and acquire a specific contextual meaning appropriate only to that particular context. Written contexts include the immediate sentence or the paragraph in which the paremia appears. Even the larger structure of the work, which comprises its genre and purpose, influences the contextual meaning of paremias. This is the case with the numerical paremias based on the presence of three members that Marchionno uses during his long speech in Sarnelli's *Posilecheata*. Although this typology of proverb does not usually convey comedy, the clash between the situation described in *Posilecheata* and the origins of the expressions, mostly from philosophical concepts and the Old Testament, generates irony. For instance, the numerical paremia, *Tre songo li principie naturale: materia, forma e privazione* ("Three are the natural principles: matter, form, and privation"; P 12.9), which derives from Aristotle's *Metaphysics* (V, 1022 b 22–1023 a 7), is used to address the physiological objective of eating abundantly through soliciting an invitation to dinner. Sarnelli transforms the original philosophical message of the paremia to comment on and create a specific reaction about a hilarious situation.

Within the larger framework of sixteenth- and seventeenth-century paremiography, the paremias of Brusantino, Florio, and Sarnelli combine tradition and personal interpretation. As they appear in different genres, languages, and historical moments, and span 130 years, these paremias reveal the voice of the three authors and shape their texts to suit their audience. Brusantino, Florio, and Sarnelli live in marginal positions, either ideologically or geographically, yet their innovative use of paremias demonstrates their independence from celebrated writers and traditions and their ability to express their individual views within the perspectives of communal knowledge. The contextual analysis of their expressions brings to light Brusantino's work, otherwise unknown, illustrates the modernity of Florio's approach to language pedagogy, and reevaluates Sarnelli as an author of fables distinguished from Basile's *Lo cunto de li cunti*.

In *Le cento novelle*, Brusantino chooses his paremias to express an ethical interpretation of the *Decameron* earlier than the established "rassettature" of Boccaccio's text. The introductory allegories and paremias, most of which he invented, as well as those paremias adapted from the *Decameron* demonstrate that Brusantino is not a simple imitator. These expressions result from his appropriation of the original text in content, structure, and style, mediated through the lens of his poetry "translation." Although his cantos follow the content of Boccaccio's stories, paremias enrich the message of the novellas and express Brusantino's views of the evolving sociocultural contexts. Brusantino consciously blends different traditions, including *cantari novellistici*, previous and contemporary renderings of Boccaccio's *Decameron*, and poetry in octaves of hendecasyllables. While hybridizing all of them (Sportelli 91), he shapes a new literary product, in which past and contemporaneous trends speak concurrently with Brusantino's intent to use paremias and allegories for ethical purposes.

Although he does not share the same humanistic orientation that characterizes Boccaccio, Brusantino is an acute observer of the seventeenth-century Tridentine society. He writes in verse, which was deemed more intelligible and more accessible than prose. He levels the different registers that he finds in the *Decameron*, from Ghismunda's elevated and noble discourse in story IV.1 to the dialect of the "schermaglia erotica" ("erotic skirmish") between Monna Belcolore and the priest of Varlungo in novella VIII.2. He introduces paremias to address those who sought a more concrete experience with literary texts that could influence their lives. Moreover, he develops a deeper sense of morality in the text while still granting himself some comedic moments, mostly through sexual references. This makes him an isolated example among the censors of Boccaccio's work during the Counter-Reformation. However, that *Le cento novelle* represented a mild "rassettatura" of the *Decameron* appealing to a wide audience, did not facilitate its popularity. Brusantino's style did not eliminate the prosaic elements of Boccaccio's narrative and seemed to remain unpoetic. It is also possible that Brusantino's targeted audience did not find his work a true "translation of class" from *Decameron*'s courtly members to "pubblico mezzano" ("middle public"). Considering all of these aspects, *Le cento novelle*'s paremias tell us much about the fortune, tradition, and reception of Boccaccio's text in the sixteenth century. The introductory proverbs provide a range of those values that Brusantino proposed as necessary for an audience in need of more morally-focused messages, primarily wisdom, balance, reflection, and faith. Expressions like *Resta l'ingannator del mal accinto da l'ingannato spesso oppresso e vinto* ("The deceiver, who is shrouded in evil, often remains oppressed and defeated by the deceived"; CN 108) and *Resti il vile e l'insipido di gire onde ne appar virtù, gratia e disire* ("Let the coward and insignificant person stop to go where virtue, grace, and desire are"; CN 299) are telling examples. If one connects these proverbs to the original stories of Boccaccio, Brusantino's ethical interpretation of the *Decameron* clearly emerges.

Similar to *Le cento novelle*, Florio's *Firste Fruites* and *Second Frutes* reinterpret classical, Italian, and English traditions in order to address those in sixteenth-century English society who were interested in learning the Italian language. Unlike previous instructors and scholars, Florio's novelty consisted in his extensive use of paremias, which he considered to be the most effective tool for teaching a foreign language and culture. Paremias fulfilled Florio's goal of spreading knowledge about the Italian language in a society that was thirsty for culturally-rich models to follow and imitate. Employed by Italians living in London and merchants engaging in business deals with locals, these paremias answered to a pragmatic necessity while simultaneously fulfilling the recreational needs of learners and lovers of Italy. Hence, in both *Fruits* they speak to different social classes (Wyatt, *The Italian Encounter* 180). In the first manual, frequently the topics of conversation concern "parlar familiare," i.e., subjects that are familiar and unsophisticated. In the second, servants and maids are included in almost all of the dialogues along with high-class members of society. Although these books address privileged learners, their language and content, including paremias, are available to everyone willing to acquire knowledge about Italy. Compared to Brusantino, Florio's *Fruits* are examples of a "translation beyond class." If there are instances of a lack of social mobility, the message is embedded in the expression and is unrelated to the context of the dialogue. An example comes from chapter 18 of *Firste Fruites*: *Per tre cose la terra spesse volte è flagellata, et la quarta è intolerabile, quando che un servitore è fatto signore sopra i beni del suo signore ... et una servente fatta herede de la sua signora* ("For three thinges the earth is oftentimes plagued, and the fourth is intollerable, a servant made lorde over his maister's goods ... and a damsel made heire unto her mistresse"; FF 22*v*). Here, two members of the numerical paremia express a condemnation of servants who are given power over their masters or mistresses, yet this message does not reflect the tone of the other divine and secular *sententiae* gathered in the chapter.

Considering the structure of the two manuals, the proverbially embedded dialogues in *Firste Fruites* are organized in a clear, pedagogical way as the speakers introduce and explain almost every paremia and make sure that their message is properly received. While shaping communicative contexts that reproduce everyday mundane conversations, the content of the dialogues complies with a stern and morally driven community. Conversely, *Second Frutes* represents a less narrative but more decorative manual, which is primarily perceived as a repository of sayings to embellish literary discourses. In this volume, Florio selects paremias for their form and structure rather than for their message. Consequently, their presence in the text is less influential, especially when compared with *Firste Fruites*. Furthermore, the dissimilar levels of target audiences differentiate the two manual's exposition of the Italian language and culture. In *Firste Fruites*, the cultural aspects that the paremias transmit would be difficult for a learner with only a basic knowledge of the language to grasp. On the contrary, the paremias presented in *Second Frutes* suit the exigencies of advanced students able to read about sophisticated conversations on literary topics. Finally, the translation of paremias evolves from *Firste Fruites* to *Second Frutes*. The choice between a literal translation and a translation based upon the expression's message reflects the shifts that occurred within Elizabethan society. Progressively, paremias convey situations and messages related to culture and language rather than simply describing them. Hence, their translation has less of a memory-facilitating function for educational purposes and instead, performs more of a societal and cultural service.

In Sarnelli's *Posilecheata*, paremias interpret, comment, and offer a Neapolitan perspective on society and language, while displacing the Tuscan-centric tradition and appropriating it to the local dialect and culture. Sarnelli's expressions introduce the moral content of the fables or conclude the stories by providing a summary of their content and stimulating a reflection on their message. The author intersperses paremias in the different parts of his work, both individually and in long lists, to advance or block the narration, introduce ambiguity, promote a new narrative perspective, or emphasize a moral idea. Sarnelli's debt towards

Basile's *Lo cunto de li cunti* is evident, but also highlights his idea of imitation between tradition and innovation, authority of the past and personal choices. The paremias that he creates *ex novo* mostly translate his emotions associated with literary, linguistic, and social instances, or else give voice to the Neapolitan culture propensity toward invective and comedy, especially in the dedicatory letter and the introduction. In the fables, the popular environment, as "translated" by its paremias, does not allow much social movement. Many of the expressions concluding the fables suggest that people should not rise above their social status. An example is the message conveyed by the proverbial phrase at the end of the fourth *cunto*, according to which a poor person who becomes rich is the worst species ever: *Non c'è peo de vellane arresagliute* ("There is nothing worse than a wealthy villain"; P 174.92). Similarly, servants should serve continuously in order to receive a reward for their obedience, as the proverb summarizing the second *cunto* expresses: *Chi serve fedele aspetta premmio* ("He who serves faithfully awaits a reward"; P 93.82). Whether related to the traditional origins of paremias or to Sarnelli's personal approach to life, these paremias describe a society that favors those who are able to commit themselves to faithfulness, continuous effort, and kindness of heart. As might be expected in a work by a religious member, these three concepts coincide with the theological virtues (faith, hope, and charity) of the Catholic Church.

Despite the variety of genres, sources, and objectives, the paremias in Brusantino's, Florio's, and Sarnelli's works share more commonality than they seem to on the surface. From an ideological perspective, Pettinelli's assertion that Brusantino's *Le cento novelle* is a "manuale di comportamenti" ("manual of behavior"; *Forme e percorsi* 168, 182) establishes a connection between Brusantino's text and Florio's *Fruits*. Both works offer a vast number of expressions for almost every occasion. The Ferrarese author speaks for an audience that was beginning to experience the moral convictions promoted by the Tridentine council. A few decades later, Florio writes for the English population who was seeking examples of moral behavior and instances of refined discourse. The two authors achieve this goal by means of paremias that convey ethical messages about personal and social behaviors to learn and put into practice. Hence, their paremias allow people to become better members of society and help them speak in public more

Conclusion

appropriately, while at the same time making them experts in Italian culture.

Considering their dominant semantic fields, the paremias of Brusantino, Florio, and Sarnelli transmit both positive and negative characteristics. On one hand, they convey greed, hypocrisy, dumbness, pride, pretentiousness, and ignorance; on the other, they express patience, generosity, awareness of difficult times, and joy for positive ones. Beauty, women, and love, with the associated semantic fields of courtesy, fidelity, and jealousy, are all found in their paremias. This is particularly evident in Brusantino's proverbs, many of which address the good and bad of love as well as its different typologies. Florio's *Second Frutes* also refers to love through the refined conversations on Petrarchan topics that lead to an exploration of the many facets of this feeling, especially in chapter 12. Furthermore, among Brusantino's introductory proverbs, many are those that refer to Christ, including the expression at the beginning of I.3: *Il dubbio lassa al disputar di fede ché sol fedel è quel che 'n Christo crede* ("Leave the doubt during the dispute of faith because the only faithful is he who believes in Christ"; CN 24). In *Firste Fruites* and *Second Frutes*, the Italian word for Christ features in a few paremias as a way to establish the saying's authority: *Christo lasciò ne li precetti suoi, voi non far altrui quel che per te non vuoi* ("Christ left in his preceptes, Doo not to others that thou wylt not have done to thy selfe"; FF 14v, 28r; SF 102) and *Dice Christo nel Vangelo che l'humiltà apre le porte del cielo, et impara a spese altrui ad esser savio* ("Christ in his Gospell tolde us this, Humilitie brings us to blis, learne always to be wise by other mens harmes"; SF 102).

In Sarnelli's *Posilecheata*, flora and fauna become metaphors for human beings, who need suggestions about how to live or behave. Among the animals described are fish, cats, lions, foxes, crows, hens, dogs, donkeys, oxen, wolves, shrimp, swans, mice, goats, lambs, doves, hawks, and horses. Roses, lilies, figs, broccoli, grass, nettle, and reeds are the most common plants and vegetables present in his paremias. In *Le cento novelle*, only one of the paremias added by Brusantino to Boccaccio's text features an animal, specifically a cat: *Cadere in piedi come un gatto* ("To fall on one's feet like a cat"; CN 70). While there is no mention of flora or fauna in Florio's *Second Frutes*, a group of paremias in chapter 6 describes behaviors related to Italian cities and regions, which do not appear in the works of the other two authors. A few examples are:

Conclusion

*Venetia, chi non ti vede non ti pretia, ma chi ti vede ben gli costa.
*Bologna la grassa, ma Padova la passa.
*Chi ha a far con tosco, non convien esser losco.
*Napolitano, largo di bocca, stretto di mano. (SF 106–08)

Who sees not Venice cannot esteeme it, but he that sees it payes well for it.
Fertile is Bologna, but Padova exceeds it.
Who with a Tuscane hath to mell, had need to heare and see full well.
The Neapolitane is wide mouthed, but narowe handed.

Florio's peripheral position to the Italian peninsula allowed for the presentation of regional variations and local realities, which would have been attractive to his audience. This typology does not appear in the works of Brusantino and Sarnelli, with the exception of those expressions that refer to German or Spanish customs in *Posilecheata*. Sarnelli's two paremias, *Tre cose stanno male a lo munno ... no fiasco 'mmano de no Todisco* ("Three things are bad in the world ... a wicker wine bottle in the hands of a German person"; P 13.10) and *Essere stoccata catalana* ("To be a Catalan thrust"; P 104.28), reflect the international dimension of Naples.

Brusantino, Florio, and Sarnelli make interesting decisions on which typologies of paremias they insert into their works. There are no proverbial phrases in *Le cento novelle* among the introductory expressions, all of which follow the typical structure of proverbs with two hemistiches and a topic and comment organization. Only the four new paremias that Brusantino introduces to Boccaccio's text are proverbial phrases. Conversely, in Florio and Sarnelli, proverbial phrases abound in both conversation and narration. Given the number of paremias, it is surprising that the three works lack wellerisms. Just a few appear in Florio's manuals, while they are completely absent in Brusantino's and Sarnelli's texts. That this typology of paremia provides the narration with a comic and ironic patina may explain their scarce presence in *Le cento novelle*, whose introductory proverbs are primarily ethical in nature. Their absence in Florio's *Fruits* can be explained by the two works' structure of pedagogical language manuals. Wellerisms are, among all paremias, the least translatable because their rendering in another language tends to leave out linguistic and cultural components that are crucial for their intelligibility. Hence, their use would be intimately linked to their local and often regional nature, their cultural specificity, and their reference to a particular

Conclusion

community or group. Because of these characteristics, they would have been appropriate in *Posilecheata*; however, Sarnelli chooses not to select them for his work.

The three authors, though ideologically distinct, share sources and readings for their paremias, which they adapt and revive within their works. Florio's paremias result from a meticulous search through literature, texts containing lists of paremias, collections of proverbs and sayings, and proverb-studded grammar books that were available to him in England. He personally admits that his knowledge of Italian paremiography derives from a continuous acquaintance with texts that could provide him with literary and more popular examples of proverbs and proverbial phrases. Likewise, Brusantino and Sarnelli draw from the literary tradition, as well as from common knowledge and popular expertise. Because of its foundational importance in paremiography, the most common source among the three authors is Solomon's *Proverbs*, which provides both Florio and Sarnelli with many numerical paremias. This collection also offers Brusantino expressions from Boccaccio's text as well as the one-line structure for *Le cento novelle*'s introductory proverbs. For instance, Solomon's *Peccato celato è mezzo perdonato* ("Sin that is hidden is half forgiven"; Ch. XXVIII: v. 13 from Brucioli's *Annotationi*) appears both in novella I.4 of *Decameron* (Dec. I.4.16) and *Le cento novelle* (CN 28), as well as in Florio's *Firste Fruites* (FF 32*v*). Another source common to Brusantino and Florio is Brucioli's 1538 edition of the *Decameron* and his 1533 *Annotationi sopra i proverbii di Salomo*. Even though it cannot be proven that the two authors selected materials from Brucioli's two publications, it is highly possible that his edition of Boccaccio's text was a starting point for Brusantino, specifically his proverbs introducing each canto and the lists of paremias concluding each day. Likewise, Florio may have accessed the several editions of Brucioli's *Annotationi* available in England, which provided him with ready quotations in Italian from the Old Testament.

All three authors share a proverb that conveys a sharp message on the negative consequences of creating a hoax. They adapt the original source from Solomon's *Proverbs* to the specific context of their works yet preserve its general meaning, i.e., that a good person receives the favor of the Lord and a deceitful man faces His condemnation (Ch. XII, v. 20). Brusantino employs it as the

Conclusion

introductory paremia for three of Boccaccio's novellas. Two of these novellas belong to Day 2, dedicated to misadventures that suddenly end happily, and the other comes from Day 8, discussing stories of tricks that women and men play on each other:

> II.1: *Spesso l'ingannator ne resta oppresso e de l'opra sua rende aspro interesso.* (CN 49)
>
> Often the deceiver remains oppressed and from his work he receives a harsh return.
>
> II.9: *Resta l'ingannator del mal accinto da l'ingannato spesso oppresso e vinto.* (CN 108)
>
> The deceiver, who is shrouded in evil, often remains oppressed and defeated by the deceived.
>
> VIII.10: *Merta ben degna laude e grande honore l'ingannato a ingannar l'ingannatore.* (CN 434)[1]
>
> The deceived deserves fair praise and great honor to deceive the deceiver.

Brusantino proposes the expression again at the end of the same story II.9, inheriting it from Boccaccio's text (II.9.75; Monosini 254):

> II.9: *Così al piè resta appresso con furore de l'ingannato il falso ingannatore.* (CN 115)
>
> This way the false deceiver remains furiously at the foot of the deceived.

Florio uses the paremia in chapter 14 of *Firste Fruites*, which concerns amorous conversations. At the end of the dialogue, one of the speakers gives suggestions about how to deal with unrequited love and offers a series of expressions directly connected to the topic, including the one shared with Brusantino's novellas II.1 and II.9:

> *Chi cerca spesso ingannar altrui opresso resta et ingannato lui.* (FF 14*v*, [28]*r*)
>
> Who often seekes others to deceive, doth rest oppressed and deceyved hym selfe.

Finally, Sarnelli employs the paremia to warn those who wish to mislead someone because they will be punished accordingly. At the end of *cunto* 3, Pascadozia receives an adequate proverbial compensation for her misdeeds:

Conclusion

> *'Ncoppa a lo ingannator cade lo 'nganno,*
> *E se tarda, non manca lo malanno.* (P 138.127)[2]
>
> The deceit falls on top of the deceiver, and if it delays, misfortune won't lack.

The three authors' condemnation of deceit manifests cross-geographically and cross-culturally, and evidently refers to their shared ideal for moral and ethical messages.

Alunno's cornerstone publications also appear to be a reference for the three authors. Through Alunno's works, the entire classical tradition in Greek and Latin filtered by Erasmus's works and other consistent collections of paremias converge in the works of Brusantino, Florio, and Sarnelli (Pignatti, *Etimologia e proverbio* 213–28). As one illustration, the lists of proverbs and sayings used by Boccaccio that Alunno supplies in his 1543 *Le ricchezze della lingua volgare* may have been a model for Brusantino's day-concluding lists of paremias. Similarly, Florio and Sarnelli refer to Alunno's 1546–48 *Della fabbrica del mondo* and specifically to the list of three-member expressions gathered in his encyclopedic entry on the number three. Surprisingly, given their biblical tradition, tripartite paremias are instead absent in *Le cento novelle*. Not even the fact that their message is usually connected to suggestions on how to avoid something bad from happening appealed to Brusantino. On the contrary, tripartite expressions fulfill Florio's and Sarnelli's linguistic and pedagogical objectives, in particular to teach how to speak appropriately and in correct Italian (*Firste Fruites* and *Second Frutes*) and to show the rich and productive nature of the Neapolitan culture and language (*Posilecheata*). Sarnelli mentions Alunno as a source of many tripartite paremias in the introduction to his *Posilecheata* and invites his readers to find more of these expressions in *Della fabbrica*. Florio does not quote Alunno directly, but one of his proverbs listed in the section from the Book of Ben Sira also features in Alunno's *Della fabbrica*: *Tre cose dispiacciono a Dio et a gli huomini, un homo povero superbo, un homo ricco bugiardo et un homo vechio inamorato* ("Three things displease God and man, a poore man proude, a riche man a lyer, and an olde man in love"; FF 23r). On the description of the best features that beautiful women possess, both Florio and Sarnelli recall Alunno's words. In chapter 8 of *Second Frutes*, Florio's paremia is loosely inspired by Alunno's:

> *La donna che vuol esser detta bella sopra tutte le bellissime, convien haver trenta cose per le quali vien celebrata Helena. Cioè tre bianche, tre negre, tre rosse, tre corte, tre longhe, tre grosse, tre sottili, tre strette, tre larghe e tre picciole ... Et chi manca alcuna di queste parti non puo vantarsi d'esser bella, ma chi tutte le possiede si può dir bella in ogni perfettione.* (SF 130)
>
> In choyse of faire are thirtie things required. For which (they saie) faire Hellen was admired, three white, three black, three red, three short, three tall, three thick, three thin, three streight, three wide, three small ... Of these who wants so much of fairest wants and who hath all, her beautie perfect vauntes.

Florio does not put an asterisk beside this long and detailed paremia. Probably, he does not consider it to be a proverb like all of the others, but instead regards it as an expression intended to instruct people on how to judge the beauty of women. Moreover, he does not place it along with other paremias with a similar tripartite structure. This occurs in *Posilecheata*, in which Sarnelli provides a shorter version of Alunno's paremia so that it can fit the context of Marchionno's long speech on the number three:

> *Tre bote tre unnece cose fanno bella na femmiena: azzoè tre cose longhe e tre corte; tre larghe, tre strette e tre grosse, tre sottile; tre retonne, tre piccole, tre ghianche, tre rosse, tre negre.* (P 13.11)
>
> Three times eleven things make a woman beautiful: which is three long and three short; three large, three tight, and three big, three thin; three round, three small, three white, three red, three black.

Even though the actual form of the expression resembles a narrative structure rather than a proverb, Sarnelli's paremia is more concise and effective than Florio's expression.

One of the most renowned proverbs in the *Decameron*, *Chi va a letto senza cena, tutta la notte si dimena* ("Who fasting goes to bed, uneasy lies his head around all night"), appears both in *Le cento novelle* (CN 145) and in *Fruits* (FF 29r; SF 150), which demonstrates Florio's borrowing from Boccaccio's text. In these three instances, the proverb is interpreted literally: the characters move around the bed under the grip of hunger because they did not eat anything at night. However, Brusantino's metaphorical hint at the real act of engaging in passionate sexual exchange is absent in Florio's language manual. Here, a character pronounces the proverb while commenting upon a desired dinner that seems not to take place. When a group of friends realizes that they will be going to bed without supper, one of them replies with this proverb in order to soften the tension and find a valid alternative to the unfortunate and unexpected circumstance.[3] The moralizing atmosphere of Elizabethan England when Florio was writing his *Firste Fruites* did not yet allow for explicit sexual references.

Oral sources link Sarnelli and Florio. The parallel between the two authors acquires even more significance if one considers that they wrote in a non-native language. Both were linguistic foreigners and experienced a dual linguistic identity: for Florio, England was the place where he had lived almost all of his life; for Sarnelli, Naples was the city where he had been legally naturalized. Their long lists of paremias provide valuable evidence of the two authors' extensive knowledge of their second language and culture. One instance is represented by the proverbial phrase *D'una fetida herba nasce il giglio* ("The lily is born from fetid grass"; SF 180), which Florio lists in chapter 12 of his *Second Frutes*. As a decontextualized expression, its place in the list derives from the lexicon and message that it shares with the preceding expression, *Da le spine nascon le rose* ("Even of prickles roses doe proceede"; SF 180). Sarnelli's corresponding Neapolitan paremia, *Da n'erva fetente nasce lo giglio* ("The lily blossoms amongst fetid weeds"; P 181.12) is contextualized within *cunto* 5 and refers to the remote possibility that someone can be a better person than his or her parents can.[4]

Brusantino, Sarnelli, and Florio leave us with a strong and substantiated message on paremiography that may still be applicable today. Creativity, change, and evolution distinguish paremias as they are adapted and transformed across periods, users, and genres. Exploring *Le cento novelle*, *Firste Fruites*, *Second Frutes*, and *Posilecheata* opens up new historical, cultural, and linguistic perspectives in the field of paremiography, and emphasizes the importance of a contextual analysis of the expressions found in works of the early modern and Baroque periods and beyond. The innumerable forms that such paremias assume through a continuous process of modification and transformation contribute to the articulated history of the Italian language, as well as to the creation of a linguistic identity during the mid-sixteenth and the late seventeenth centuries. Authors and speakers keep their messages and meanings alive and renew them continually for generations to come. As stated in a proverb, *Chi vivrà vedrà* ("Who will live, will see").

Index of Paremias in *Le cento novelle*, *Firste Fruites*, *Second Frutes*, and *Posilecheata*

Vincenzo Brusantino: *Le cento novelle*'s Paremias

Introductory Paremias for Each Novella	Final List of Paremias at the End of Each Day
I.1	
Credi a gli effetti et non a le parole, Ché spesso 'l mal e 'l ben ingannar suole (CN 13)	Credi a gli effetti e non a le parole, Ché spesso il male e 'l bene ingannar suole (CN 46)
I.2	
Se opra rea da religion si vede Per questo non si dee mancar di fede (CN 21)	Se gran peccato d'opra rea si vede Per questo non si de' mancar di fede (CN 46)
I.3	
Il dubbio lassa al disputar di fede Ché sol fedel è quel che 'n Christo crede (CN 24)	In dubbio lassa il disputar di fede Ché sol fedel è quel che in Christo crede (CN 46)
I.4	
Nel riprender altrui del mal insano Il giuditio bisogna haver ben sano (CN 26)	Nel riprender altrui del male insano Il giuditio bisogna haver ben sano (CN 46)
I.5	
L'avidità che non si satia mai Da continentia viene oppressa assai (CN 29)	L'avidità talhor non satia mai Da continenza vien oppressa assai (CN 46)

I.6	
D'ogni religioso opra più ria Non è presso di lui c'hippo- crisia (CN 31)	De lo religioso opra più ria Non è appresso di lui che hippocresia (CN 46)
I.7	
L'avaritia cagion di tutto il male Spesso più di ragione e virtù vale (CN 33)	L'avaritia cagione di tutto il male Spesso più di ragione e virtù vale (CN 47)
I.8	
Per vergogna tal'hor mostra l'avaro Illustri atti cortesi a ogni altro a paro (CN 37)	Per vergogna talhor mostra l'avaro Illustri atti cortesi a ogni altro a paro (CN 47)
I.9	
Move talhor vergogna un cor cortese E inducel spesso a gloriose imprese (CN 39)	Talhor move vergogna un cor cortese E induce quello a gloriose imprese (CN 47)
I.10	
Chi vuol tal volta vergognar altrui Oppresso resta et ingannato lui (CN 41)	Chi vuol tal volta vergognar altrui Oppresso resta et ingannato lui (CN 47)
II.1	
Spesso l'ingannator ne resta oppresso E de l'opra sua rende aspro interesso (CN 49)	Spesso l'ingannetor ne resta oppresso E de l'opra sua rende aspro interesso (CN 122)

Index of Paremias

II.2	
Spesso governa buona sorte un saggio Per vie non conosciute in qualche oltraggio (CN 53)	Spesso governa buona sorte un saggio Per vie non conosciute in qualche oltraggio (CN 122)
II.3	
Se fortuna travaglia un nobil core Raro è che al fine non gli dia favore (CN 57)	Se fortuna travaglia un nobil core Raro è che al fine non gli dia favore (CN 123)
II.4	
Quando dona fortuna a l'hom ricetto Gli dà favore e aiuto al suo dispetto (CN 63)	Quando dona fortuna a l'hom ricetto Gli dà favore e aiuto al suo dispetto (CN 123)
II.5	
Cade lo sciocco espresso in grave errore Se sconciamente vuol seguir amore (CN 66)	Cade lo sciocco spesso in grave errore Se sconciamente vuol seguir amore (CN 123)
II.6	
De fortuna crudele il fiero oltraggio Patiente sopportar deve l'hom saggio (CN 74)	De fortuna crudele il fiero oltraggio Patiente portar deve l'huomo saggio (CN 123)
II.7	
La bellezza maggior col ciel secondo Vien disiata al fin per tutto 'l mondo (CN 83)	La bellezza maggior col ciel segondo Vien disiata al fin per tutto il mondo (CN 123)

II.8	
Quando vien dal maggior fatta violenza Contra ragion li vol buona patienza (CN 97)	Quando vien da i maggior fatta violenza Contra ragion li vuol buona pacienza (CN 123)
II.9	
Resta l'ingannator del mal accinto Da l'ingannato spesso oppresso e vinto (CN 108)	Resta l'ingannator del mal accinto Da l'ingannato spesso oppresso e vinto (CN 123)
II.10	
Debbe il vecchio fuggir con fiere voglie Di farsi gioven donna amica e moglie (CN 116)	Debbe il vecchio fuggir con fiere voglie De torsi donna giovene per moglie (CN 124)
III.1	
Se castità servar si dee a ragione Fuggir l'agio bisogna e occasione (CN 127)	Se castità servar si dee a ragione Fuggir li agi bisogna e occasione (CN 184)
III.2	
L'avidità talhor fuora del segno Ne capitaria mal senza l'ingegno (CN 132)	L'avidità talhor fuora del segno Ne capitaria mal senza l'ingegno (CN 184)
III.3	
Il troppo creder di una mente insana Fa l'arte sua parer propria ruffiana (CN 135)	Il troppo creder de una mente insana Fa l'arte propria sua parer ruffiana (CN 184)

III.4	
Creder così non si dee facilmente Ché spesso inganna il reo la bona mente (CN 142)	Creder così non si de' facilmente Ché spesso inganna il reo la buona mente (CN 184)
III.5	
Giova l'astutia a un cor nobile e raro Per opprimer amando il sciocco avaro (CN 146)	Giova l'astutia a un cor nobile e raro Per opprimer amando il sciocco avaro (CN 185)
III.6	
Lieve è di astutia ingannar gelosia Ché il tutto crede quando è in frenesia (CN 150)	Lieve è di astutia ingannar gelosia Ché il tutto crede quando è in frenesia (CN 185)
III.7	
L'animo generoso in cor constante Di fede adorna ogni huomo in bel sembiante (CN 157)	L'animo generoso in cor constante Di fede adorna ogni huomo al bel sembiante (CN 185)
III.8	
Facil crede e ogni cosa gli par lieve A lo sciocco se duolo o mal riceve (CN 165)	Facil crede e ogni cosa gli par lieve A lo sciocco se danno o mal riceve (CN 185)
III.9	
Vince l'humanitade il cor altiero Se con sagacità seguita il vero (CN 172)	Vince l'humanitade il cor altiero Se con sagacità seguita il vero (CN 185)

III.10	
Quanto lascivia più in disio si mesce Tanto la voglia più augumenta e cresce (CN 178)	Quanto lascivia più in disio si mesce Tanto la voglia più augumenta e cresce (CN 185)
IV.1	
Non cura crudeltà, sdegno o rea sorte Un generoso cor, né affanno o morte (CN 191)	Non cura crudeltà, sdegno o rea sorte Un generoso cor, né [a]ffanno o morte (CN 240)
IV.2	
Danno e vergogna convien che scocche Da la persuasion di donne sciocche (CN 198)	Danno e vergogna al fin convien che scocche Da la persuasion de donne sciocche (CN 240)
IV.3	
L'ira l'alma impedisce e 'l cor altiero Né lascia de ragion veder il vero (CN 205)	L'ira l'alma impedisce e il cor altiero Né lascia de ragion veder il vero (CN 240)
IV.4	
Quando giustitia amor pone in oblio Manca di fé tal'hor per gran disio (CN 210)	Quando giustitia amor pone in oblio Manca di fé talhor per gran disio (CN 241)
IV.5	
La trista vision mossa talhora Affligge il senso e mai non lo ristora (CN 214)	La trista vision mossa talhora Affligge il senso e mai non lo ristora (CN 241)

IV.6	
Del mal che può avenir ne suol visione Inditio spesso dar con più ragione (CN 217)	Del mal che può avenir ne suol visione Inditio spesso dar con più ragione (CN 241)
IV.7	
Ne tira spesso a una medesma morte Lo sfrenato disio sotto rea sorte (CN 222)	Ne tira spesso a una medesma morte Lo sfrenato disio sotto rea sorte (CN 241)
IV.8	
Per ambition, tal'hor, per alterezza More il perfetto amor di alta vaghezza (CN 225)	Per ambition, talhor, per alterezza More il perfetto amor d'alta vaghezza (CN 241)
IV.9	
De gelosia talhor superbe voglie Tirano al fin amor con fiere doglie (CN 230)	Di gelosia talhor altiere voglie Tiran al fin d'amor superchie doglie (CN 241)
IV.10	
Per burlare talhor si giunge a tanto Che causa morte, over miseria o pianto (CN 233)	Per burlare talhor si giunge a tanto Che causa morte spesso, o duolo o pianto (CN 242)
V.1	
Di rozzo inerto e vil fa spesso amore Generoso e cortese un nobil core (CN 244)	Di rozo inerto e vil fa spesso amore Generoso e cortese un nobil core (CN 294)

Index of Paremias

V.2	
Se con fermezza il cor seguita il vero Ottiene al fine il disiato impero (CN 251)	Se con fermezza il cor seguita il vero Ottiene al fine il disiato impero (CN 294)
V.3	
Se ben non pensa il fin d'ogni suo effetto Non deve il saggio assicurarsi il petto (CN 256)	A non pensar il fin d'ogni suo effetto Non deve il saggio assicurarsi il petto (CN 295)
V.4	
A lo sfrenato ardir spesso gli vale Condur chi non gli pensa in molto male (CN 261)	A lo sfrenato ardir spesso gli vale Condur chi non gli pensa in molto male (CN 295)
V.5	
S'el si porta di fede l'alma accesa S'ottien perserverando ogni alta impresa (CN 266)	S'el si porta di fede l'alma accesa S'ottien perserverando ogni alta impresa (CN 295)
V.6	
Raro è ch'a l'alte imprese pellegrine Non dia favore la fortuna al fine (CN 270)	Rar'è che a le alte imprese pellegrine Non dia favore la fortuna al fine (CN 295)
V.7	
Da lo sfrenato amor guardar si deve Ché danno e biasmo spesso se riceve (CN 274)	Da lo sfrenato amar guardar si deve Ché danno e biasmo spesso si riceve (CN 295)

V.8	
S'amor non pol a un cor ingrato et empio Giovaralli timore e crudel scempio (CN 279)	S'amor non puol a un cor ingrato et empio Giovaralli timore e crudel scempio (CN 295)
V.9	
Non deve a l'alta et honorata impresa Un magnanimo cor mancar di spesa (CN 283)	Non deve a l'alta et honorata impresa Un magnanimo cor mancar di spesa (CN 295)
V.10	
De vergogna non cura l'alma insana Né escie del fango mai come la rana (CN 287)	De vergogna non cura l'alma insana Né escie del fango mai come la rana (CN 296)
VI.1	
Resti il vile e l'insipido di gire Onde ne appar virtù, gratia e disire (CN 299)	Resti il vile et insipido di gire Onde ne appar virtù, gratia e disire (CN 326)
VI.2	
Accorta cortesia sempre sta in ponto Di sua gran nobiltate a render conto (CN 301)	Accorta cortesia sempre sta in ponto De sua gran nobiltate a render conto (CN 326)
VI.3	
L'animo accorto è sempre più abondante Di effetti e de risposte in uno instante (CN 303)	L'animo accorto è sempre più abondante Di effetti e di risposte in uno instante (CN 326)

VI.4	
Muta spesso l'accorto in gran piacere L'ire e gli sdegni ne le voglie altiere (CN 305)	Muta spesso l'accorto in gran piacere L'ire e li sdegni ne le voglie altiere (CN 326)
VI.5	
S'altrui schernir si vuol del mal espresso Bisogna prima esaminar se stesso (CN 307)	S'altrui schernir si vuol del mal espresso Bisogna pria esaminar se stesso (CN 326)
VI.6	
Ingegno spesso e alta virtude giova Provar cosa impossibile con prova (CN 309)	Ingegno spesso alta virtude giova Provar cosa impossibile con prova (CN 326)
VI.7	
Spesso trova beltà con sentimento Del fallo suo la scusa in un momento (CN 311)	Spesso trova beltà con sentimento Del fallo suo la scusa in un momento (CN 326)
VI.8	
A l'inganno non giova mai ragione Ché sempre seguir vuol sua opinione (CN 314)	A l'inganno non giova mai ragione Ché sempre seguir vuol sua openione (CN 326)
VI.9	
Spesso opprime virtude l'ignoranza Talmente che la fa di morti stanza (CN 315)	Spesso oprime virtude l'ignoranza Talmente che la fa de' morti stanza (CN 326)

VI.10	
A l'ipocrito giova esser sagace Se vuol far creder col suo modo audace (CN 317)	A l'hippocrito giova essere sagace Se vuol far creder col suo modo audace (CN 326)
VII.1	
De l'astutia lo sciocco oppresso è quello Che perde al troppo credere il cervello (CN 329)	Da l'astutia lo sciocco oppresso è quello Che perde al troppo credere il cervello (CN 376)
VII.2	
Son de lascivie l'opre così astute Che se ben falla non sono credute (CN 333)	Son de lascivia l'opre così astute Che se ben falla non sono credute (CN 376)
VII.3	
Ingegno et arte spesso ne bisogna Ne li casi amorosi a dir men- zogna (CN 336)	Ingegno et arte spesso ne bisogna Ne li casi amorosi a dir men- zogna (CN 376)
VII.4	
Accorto del suo error lo sciocco viene Da doppia astuzia oppresso in dure pene (CN 340)	Accorto del suo error lo sciocco viene Da doppia astuzia oppresso in dure pene (CN 376)
VII.5	
La troppo gelosia induce a tale Che da se stessa se ne causa il male (CN 344)	La troppo gelosia induce a tale Che da se stessa se ne causa il male (CN 376)

VII.6	
Giova spesso l'astutia in core altiero A fingere e mostrare di falso il vero (CN 350)	Giova spesso l'astutia in core altero A finger e mostrar de falso il vero (CN 376)
VII.7	
Indutta spesso vien simplicitade A patir mal per troppa credultade (CN 353)	Indutta spesso vien simplicitade A patir mal per troppa credultade (CN 376)
VII.8	
Del doppio errore ne resta ingannato L'orgoglio dal cor saggio inamorato (CN 357)	Del doppio errore ne resta ingannato L'orgoglio dal cor saggio inamorato (CN 376)
VII.9	
L'industria più in amor che in altro vale Ché il mal fa creder bene e il bene male (CN 363)	L'industria più in amor che in altro vale Ché il mal fa creder bene e il bene male (CN 376)
VII.10	
Quando d'oprar il mal piglia l'assonto Pensa de l'opra sua non haver conto (CN 371)	Quando di oprar il mal piglia l'assonto Pensa de l'opra sua non haver conto (CN 376)
VIII.1	
A chi per pregio dona castitade Ben merta che se gli usi falsitade (CN 378)	A chi per pregio vende castitade Ben merta che se li usi falsitade (CN 444)

VIII.2	
Più del poter prometter non si deve Ché sfrenato disir fa poi mal greve (CN 380)	Più che 'l poter prometter non si deve Ché sfrenato disir fa poi mal greve (CN 444)
VIII.3	
Semplicitade mai non mutò via Che non mostrasse a i gesti alta pazzia (CN 385)	Semplicitade mai non mutò via Che non mostrasse a i gesti alta pacia (CN 444)
VIII.4	
Ben lice a l'honestà con modo scaltro Fuggir vergogna et por l'uno per l'altro (CN 390)	Ben lice a l'honestà con modo scaltro Fuggir vergogna et por l'uno per l'altro (CN 444)
VIII.5	
Non si muta sciocchezza mai di loco E rende, ovunque appar, solaccio e gioco (CN 394)	Non si muta sciocchezza ma' del loco E rende, ovunque appar, solatio e gioco (CN 444)
VIII.6	
In forma di schernir l'aviditade Roba ingannando la simplicitade (CN 397)	In forma di schernir l'aviditade Robba ingannando la simplicitade (CN 444)
VIII.7	
Se schernito l'amante si sospetta Col generoso cor diè far vendetta (CN 402)	Se schernito l'amante si sospetta Col generoso cor de' far vendetta (CN 444)

VIII.8	
La rea e finta amistade ingannar parme E vendicarse con le sue proprie arme (CN 419)	La rea e finta amistade ingannar parme E vendicarse con le sue proprie arme (CN 444)
VIII.9	
Chi è semplice e saper più si persuade Vergogna e danno, ovunque va, gli accade (CN 422)	Chi è semplice e saper più si persuade Vergogna e danno, ovunque va, li accade (CN 444)
VIII.10	
Merta ben degna laude e grande honore L'ingannato a ingannar l'ingannatore (CN 434)	Merta ben degna laude e grande honore L'ingannato a ingannar l'ingannatore (CN 444)
IX.1	
Le spaventose cose a comandare Con giusta causa si dovrian negare (CN 446)	Le spaventose cose a comandare Con giusta causa si dovrian negare (CN 485)
IX.2	
Scoperto il reo del suo proprio errore A la fraude et al mal ne dà favore (CN 451)	Scoperto il reo del suo proprio errore A la fraude et al mal ne dà vigore (CN 485)
IX.3	
L'astuto inganna col sagace appresso La bontà, la sciocchezza a un modo istesso (CN 454)	L'astuto inganna col sagace appresso La bontà, la sciocchezza a un modo istesso (CN 485)

IX.4	
Non si pol nel giocar haver bon loco Ché mal profitto al fin nasce dal gioco (CN 457)	Non si puol nel giocar haver bon loco Ché mal profitto al fin nasce dal gioco (CN 485)
IX.5	
Da la malitia schiocchezza persuasa Piace a ciascuno eccetto a' suoi da casa (CN 461)	Da la malitia schiocchezza persuasa Piace a ciascuno eccetto a' suoi da casa (CN 485)
IX.6	
Giova l'industria alhor nel mal audace Quando in discordie ree fa nascer pace (CN 467)	Giova l'industria alhor nel male audace Quando in discordie ree fa nascer pace (CN 485)
IX.7	
Spesso l'huomo insognarsi un gran periglio Né puol fuggir pigliando il bon consiglio (CN 471)	Spesso l'huomo insognarsi un gran periglio Né puol fuggir pigliando il bon consiglio (CN 485)
IX.8	
Cade spesso il cattivo in dure pene Se il sagace schernir non si ritiene (CN 473)	Cade spesso il cattivo in dure pene Se il sagace schernir non se ritiene (CN 485)
IX.9	
Ama e amato serai ben con ragione La donna rea gastiga col bastone (CN 476)	Ama e amato serai ben con ragione La donna rea gastiga col bastone (CN 485)

IX.10	
La sciocchezza ingannata in più maniere Spesso con biasmo suo gli dà piacere (CN 480)	La sciocchezza ingannata in più maniere Spesso con biasmo suo li dà piacere (CN 485)
X.1	
Quando del ben servir mal si raduna Non si deve incolpar se non fortuna (CN 487)	Quando del ben servir mal si raduna Non incolpar altrui se non fortuna (CN 551)
X.2	
Tal'hora l'huomo da fier sorte astretto Gli vien fatto appiacer al suo dispetto (CN 490)	Talhora l'huomo da fiera sorte astreto Gli vien fatto servitio al suo dispetto (CN 551)
X.3	
Pien d'invidia talhor ne porta offese A un animo eccellente il men cortese (CN 493)	Pien d'invidia talhor ne porta offese A un animo eccellente il men cortese (CN 551)
X.4	
Non muta effetto in le honorate imprese Un cor inamorato, alto e cortese (CN 499)	Non muta effetto in l'honorate imprese L'inamorato cor saggio e cortese (CN 551)
X.5	
L'impossibil richiesta è cosa lieve A l'amante donar in tempo breve (CN 504)	L'impossibil richiesta ne par lieve A l'amante donar in tempo brieve (CN 551)

X.6	
Dimostra il vecchio per suo grande honore Cortesia grande a lo sforzato amore (CN 508)	Dimostra il vecchio per suo grande honore Cortesia spesso a lo sforzato amore (CN 551)
X.7	
Amor, se in nobil cor il foco accende, Quantunque sia maggior cortesia rende (CN 513)	Amor, se in nobil core il foco accende, Quantunque sia maggior cortesia rende (CN 552)
X.8	
Finta virtude mai non trova loco Senza la cortesia un huom da poco (CN 518)	Finta virtude mai non trova loco Senza la cortesia in huom da poco (CN 552)
X.9	
Non perde cortesia il giusto pregio Servendo a nobil cor famoso e egregio (CN 530)	Non perde cortesia il giusto pregio Servendo a un nobil cor famoso egregio (CN 552)
X.10	
De cose fuor di modo e di credenza Non deve l'huom mai farne esperienza (CN 542)	De cose fuor di modo e di credenza Non deve l'huomo mai farne esperienza (CN 552)

Index of Paremias

Embedded Paremias in *Le cento novelle* Compared with Boccaccio's Paremias

Proemio	
Dec. Proemio.2	Umana cosa è aver compassione degli afflitti
CN	/
I.4	
Dec. I.4.16	Peccato celato è mezzo perdonato
CN 28	Peccato ascosto mezo perdonato È cosa chiara né si saprà mai
I.10	
Dec. I.10.8	Acciò che per voi non si possa quello proverbio intendere che comunemente si dice per tutto, cioè che le femine in ogni cosa sempre pigliano il peggio
CN 42	E acciò per noi non si possa mostrare Il proverbio ch'è noto in quell'etate Che dice che le donne in ogni seggio Communemente pigliano il lor peggio
II.1	
Dec. II.1.2	Chi altrui sé di beffare ingegnò, e massimamente quelle cose che sono da reverire, s'è con le beffe e talvolta col danno sé solo ritrovato
CN 49	Spesse volte, felici donne, aviene Che chi in beffar altrui s'è dilettato In quel che riverir ben si conviene Resta con danno al fin lui sol beffato
Dec. II.1.29	Noi abbiamo costui tratto della padella e gittatolo nel fuoco
CN 52	… come è venuto Della padella in foco in duro stato

Index of Paremias

	II.2
Dec. II.2.7	Mi vivo all'antica e lascio correre due soldi per ventiquattro denari
CN 53	… vivo a la antica et sol mi vale Dodeci un soldo bei dinari piani
	II.7
Dec. II.7.122	Bocca basciata non perde ventura, anzi rinnuova come fa la luna
CN 97	Bocca basciata non perde fortuna Ma si rinova come fa la luna
	II.9
Dec. II.9.3	Suolsi tra' volgari spesse volte dire un cotal proverbio: che lo 'ngannatore rimane a piè dello 'ngannato
CN	/
Dec. II.9.6	Quale asino dà in parete tal riceve
CN 108	E per ciò a far questo mi assicura Qual asino essere debbo me ne avedo Che urti el parete ne la scioglia dura, E così il danno mio bene prevedo
Dec. II.9.75	E così rimase lo 'ngannatore a piè dello 'ngannato
CN 115	Così al piè resta appresso con furore De l'ingannato il falso ingannatore
	II.10
Dec. II.10.42	Il mal furo non vuol festa
CN 120	Il mal [f]oro non vol vigilia o festa
Dec. II.10.43	… mi pare che ser Bernabò disputando con Ambruogiuolo cavalcasse la capra inverso il chino
CN 120	Ser Bernabò con Ambrogiuol meschino Cavalcò mal la capra inverso il chino

	III.1
Dec. III.1.37	Un gallo basta assai bene a diece galline, ma ... diece uomini posson male o con fatica una femina sodisfare
CN 131	... che basta un gallo a dieci gran galline Ma che dieci homin possano il gran peso Di una donna satiar nol trovo in fine
	III.4
Dec. III.4.25	La donna, che motteggevole era molto, forse cavalcando allora la bestia di San Benedetto, o vero di San Giovanni Gualberto ...
CN 145	La donna motteggievole e in diletto (Cavalcandosi alhora senza sella) La buona bestia di San Benedetto Over di San Gualberto ...
Dec. III.4.27	Chi la sera non cena tutta notte si dimena
CN 145	Chi va al letto la sera senza cena Intorno tutta la notte si dimena
	III.5
Dec. III.5.30	È egli meglio fare e pentere che starsi e pentersi
CN 150	Meglio è far e pentirsi il core humano Che star di fare e poi dolersi invano
	III.6
Dec. III.6.43	Egli non può oggimai essere che quello che è stato non sia pure stato
CN 155	... esser non puole Quel ch'è stato non sia ...
	III.10
Dec. III.10.3	... come il diavolo si rimetta in inferno
CN 179	... come il diavol si metta ne l'inferno

Dec. III.10.35	E per ciò voi, giovani donne, alle quali la grazia di Dio bisogna, apparate a rimettere il diavolo in inferno
CN 182	E questo motto per longhe contrade È gito e poi passato qua da mare Per donne apparate con interno Piacer a metter il diavol nello inferno
	III.Conclusione
Dec. III.Concl.18	... fosse meglio un buon porco che una bella tosa
CN	/
	IV.Proemio
Dec. IV.Proemio.33	E quegli che contro alla mia età parlando vanno, mostra mal che conoscano che, perché il porro abbia il capo bianco, che la coda sia verde
CN 189	E quei che dicon contra a la mia etade Non sanno perché il por ha il capo bianco E la coda poi verde ...
	IV.1
Dec. IV.1.23	Amor può troppo più che che né voi né io possiamo
CN 194	... scusavasi per esser infiammato Troppo d'amor, a cui non è cor alto Che durar possa al suo crudele assalto
	IV.2
Dec. IV.2.5	Usano i volgari un così fatto proverbio: Chi è reo e buono è tenuto, può fare il male e non è creduto
CN 199	E disse uno proverbio, e tra volgari Che chi è tristo e buono vien tenuto Spesso pone ciascuno in pianti amari E pol far male ché non gli è creduto
Dec. IV.2.29	Rimase faccendo sì gran galloria che non le toccava il cul la camiscia

CN 202	Né gli toccava la camiscia il cullo
IV.8	
Dec. IV.8.8	Si credeva per la gran ricchezza del figlio fare del pruno un melrancio
CN 227	Dubitò far del melarancio un pruno
IV.10	
Dec. IV.10.15	Egli aveva a buon caviglia legato l'asino
CN 235	Nulla facea che a buona e a gran caviglia Havea l'asin legato …
V.10	
Dec. V.10.14	Pareva pur santa Verdiana che dà beccare alle serpi
CN 289	… parea proprio santa Verdiana Che dà a beccare i serpi a la fontana
Dec. V.10.19	Una femina stancherebbe molti uomini, dove molti uomini non possono una femmina stancare. E per ciò che a questo siam nate, da capo ti dico che tu farai molto bene a rendere al marito tuo pan per focaccia
CN 289	Et una donna sola in tal maniere Stancarebbe più huomini ogni etate Né molti una sol potrian stancare … Onde ti dico che buon pro ti faccia Che se lo fai tu farai molto bene Dar al marito tuo pan per fucaccia
Dec. V.10.21	Alle giovani i buon bocconi e alle vecchie gli stranguglioni
CN 289	E a le giovene donne i buon bocconi E di noi vecchie sono i stranguglioni
Dec. V.10.55	Sì come colui che se' così vago di noi come il can delle mazze
CN 292	Come quel che di donne sei sì vago Come i can de le mazze traditore

Dec. V.10.64	Per che così io vi vo dire, donne mie care, che chi te la fa, fagliele; e se tu non puoi, tienloti a mente fin ché tu possa, acciò che quale asino dà in parete tal riceva
CN 293	E perciò voglio dir donne mie care Fallo a chi te le fa, et se non poi Tientelo a mente né te lo scordare Acciò che dopo il fallo non ti annoi Perché quale asino al parete urtare Simil riceva il danno …
VI.5	
Dec. VI.5.16	Vedesi di tal moneta pagato quali erano state le derrate vendute
CN 309	Di moneta si vide alhor pagato De le derate che vende infiammato
VI.10	
Dec. VI.10.23	Avrebbe condito il calderon d'Altopascio
CN 320	… havrebbe acconciati i calderoni di Altopascio …
VII.4	
Dec. VII.4.31	A modo del villan matto, dopo danno fé patto
CN 343	Hor così fece patto pur ritroso Dopo il suo male, qual villano matto
VII.9	
Dec. VII.9.17	Per lo primo colpo non cade la quercia
CN 365	… a un colpo sol non cade La quercia, onde più darli al fin gli accade
VIII.3	
Dec. VIII.3.35	Avremmo perduto il trotto per l'ambiadura
CN 387	… E havessimo perduto noi il trotto Per cambiadura nostra in questo motto

VIII.6	
Dec. VIII.6.54	... quando tu ci avesti messi in galea senza biscotto
CN 401	... e in galea ne mettessi a tua cagione Senza biscotto con tuo gran piacere
VIII.7	
Dec. VIII.7.3	Spesse volte avviene che l'arte è dall'arte schernita
CN 402	Ben spesso vien schernita L'arte da l'arte ...
Dec. VIII.7.3	Non dico tutti, ma la maggior parte sanno dove il diavolo tien la coda
CN 418	Non sapendo però che sanno bene Li scolari ove il diavolo ne appare E tien la coda ...
VIII.8	
Dec. VIII.8.3	Quale asino dà in parete tal riceve
CN 419	... Se qual asino dà urta in parete E tal riceve poi nel vendicare
Dec. VIII.8.30	M'avete renduto pan per focaccia
CN 421	... mi rendete pan qui per focaccia
VIII.10	
Dec. VIII.10.67	Chi ha a far con tosco non vuole esser losco
CN 442	... non deve esser losco Chi contrattar ne vuol con huomo tosco
IX.3	
Dec. IX.3.5	... andar comperando terra come se egli avesse avuto a far pallottole
CN 454	... comprare Terra come palottole da fare
IX.5	
Dec. IX.5.26	Tutta l'acqua d'Arno non ci laverebbe
CN 463	Perciò che l'acqua d'Arno non seria Bastante di lavar cotanto errore

Dec. IX.5.36	Io le farò giuoco che ella mi verrà dietro come va la pazza al figliuolo
CN	/
Dec. IX.5.43	Parmi che ella ti meni per lo naso
CN	/
IX.7	
Dec. IX.7.8	Chi mal ti vuol mal ti sogna
CN 472	Chi non ti ama mal ti sogna
Dec. IX.7.9	Cotal grado ha chi tigna pettina
CN 472	... tal grado ha chi petinar conviene La tigna per star sempre sul languire
Dec. IX.7.10	Egli avrebbe buon manicar co' ciechi
CN 472	Harebbe buon coi ciechi manicare
IX.9	
Dec. IX.9.7	Come che gli uomini un cotal proverbio usino: Buon cavallo e mal cavallo vuole sprone e buona femina e mala femina vuol bastone
CN 477	Che detto sia per lei simil novella Che a bon cavallo e reo bisogna sprone E trista e bona donna vuol bastone
Dec. IX.9.112	Senno s'insegna a chi tanto non apparò a Bologna
CN 433	Così se insegna il senno a cui bisogna Ché tanto lui non apparò a Bologna

New Paremias Introduced by Brusantino

Pensò a un cauto barbier per rader l'altro (I.1; CN 14)

Caduto in piedi proprio come un gatto (II.5; CN 70)

Gli fece far dui chiodi in una calda (IV.2; CN 202)

Consistè in virtù più de l'inteletto (V.9; CN 287)

John Florio: A Selection of Paremias in *Firste Fruites*[1] and *Second Frutes*[2] Compared with *Giardino di ricreatione*

A bon intenditore meza parola basta (FF Ch. 19: 27v)	A buon intenditore mezza parola basta (GR 1)
A buona derrata pensaci su (SF Ch. 7: 122)	A buona derrata pensavi su (GR 2)
A carne di lupo convien dar dente di cane (SF Ch. 2: 20)	A carne di lupo, dente di cane (GR 1)
A caval donato non guardar in bocca (FF Ch. 19: 27r)	A cavallo donato non guardar in bocca (GR 1)
A cavalli magri sempre vanno le mosche (FF Ch. 19: 27v)	A cavalli magri vanno le mosche (GR 1)
Accenna coppe e poi dà bastoni (SF Ch. 12: 170)	Accennar coppe e dar bastoni (GR 2)
A chi dici il tuo secreto doni la tua libertà (SF Ch. 6: 98)	A chi dici il tuo secreto doni la tua libertà (GR 1)
A chi te la fa fagliela, o tientela a mente (SF Ch. 2: 18)	A chi te la fa fagliela, o tientela a mente (GR 4)
Acqua lontana non spegne fuoco vicino (SF Ch. 7: 122) L'acqua lontana non spegne fuoco vicino (SF Ch. 12: 198)	Acqua lontana non ispegne fuoco vicino (GR 1)
Acquista in giovanezza per viver in vecchiezza (SF Ch. 6: 102)	Acquista in giovanezza per viver in vecchiezza (GR [10][3])

Index of Parenias

Ad altare scarupato non s'accende candela (SF Ch. 6: 98)	Ad altare scaruppato non s'accende candela (GR 2)
Ad amor non mancan brame benché spesso muor di fame (SF Ch. 12: 166)	
Ad arca aperta il giusto pecca (SF Ch. 12: 168)	Ad arca aperta il giusto pecca (GR 3)
A' disgratiati il pan tempesta in forno (SF Ch. 7: 120)	Al disgratiato il pan tempesta in forno (GR 1)
Adorna una simia d'oro che sempre sarà simia (FF Ch. 19: 31v)	Adorna la cimia d'oro e sempre sarà cimia (GR 1)
Ad un vero amore mai nulla manca (SF Ch. 12: 166)	
Affrettiamo il passo perché egli è tra cane e lupo (SF Ch. 10: 150)	
A gatto vecchio sorgio tenerello (SF Ch. 9: 140)	A gatto vecchio sorgio tenerello (GR 2)
A giuocar con voi convien esser astuto volpone (SF Ch. 5: 70)	
Al contrario de' porri, cioè col capo in su (SF Ch. 7: 120)	
Alegreza di cuore fa bella peladura di viso (FF Ch. 19: 27v)	Allegrezza di cuore fa bella pelatura di viso (GR 5)
A lettere di scattole tu pari et in effetti sei un furfante visu, verbo et opere (SF Ch. 8: 135)	

Index of Paremias

Alle noze e alla morte si cognoscono li amici (FF Ch. 19: 27v)	Alle nozze et alla morte si conoscon gl'amici (GR 1)
Allontanati dal dinanzi delle donne, dal di dietro delle mule e da tutti i lati de' monaci (SF Ch. 6: 98)	Guardati dal davanti della donna, dal dietro della mula e da tutti i lati de monaci (GR 110)
Al mal mortal né medico né medicina val (FF Ch. 19: 27v)	A mal mortale né medico né medicina vale (GR 1)
Al manco m'havesse mio padre pisciato al muro (SF Ch. 8: 135)	Tutti non son huomini che pisciano al muro (GR 201) Tutti voglion pisciar al muro (GR 204)
Al medico et avocato non tener il ver celato (FF Ch. 19: 27r)	Al medico et avvocato non tener il ver celato (GR 1)
Ama Dio et non falire, fa pur bene et lassa dire ché non mai potrai falire (FF Ch. 19: 27r)	Ama Dio et non fallire, fa pur bene et lascia dire (GR 7)
Ama e sarai amato (SF Ch. 12: 170) Ama chi ti ama (FF Ch. 19: 27v)	Ama che sarai amato (GR 1)
Ama l'amico tuo con il difetto suo (SF Ch. 6: 104)	Ama l'amico tuo con il diffetto suo (GR 2)
Amami poco et amami longo (FF Ch. 19: 34v)	Amami poco ma continua (GR 7)
Ama per lui et non fallire ché non mai potrai fallire (SF Ch. 6: 92)	
A me non entrerà mai nel capo (SF Ch. 12: 178)	

Index of Paremias

Amor a chi lo serve al fin dà per mercede infamia, gelosia e rotta fede (SF Ch. 12: 166)	Amor dà per mercede gelosia e rotta fede (GR 8)
Amor ci guida et i nostri timidi animi assicura (SF Ch. 12: 168)	
Amor di putana e vin di fiasco, la sera è buono, la matina è guasto (FF Ch. 19: 127v) L'amor di donna lieve è come vin di fiasco, la sera è buono et la mattina è guasto (SF Ch. 12: 174)	Amor di donna è come il vin di fiasco, la sera è buono, la mattina è guasto (GR 13)
Amore è il vero pretio con che si compra l'aurea catena, con che si lega et la vera calamità con cui si trahe amore (SF Ch. 12: 170)	Amore è il vero pretio con che si compra amore (GR 7)
Amor è il nipotino della natura e primogenito di madonna beltà e di diletto suo marito (SF Ch. 12: 166)	
Amore nel principio dolcemente aplaude, poi tesse di nascosto inganno e fraude (SF Ch. 12: 176)	Amore nel principio dolcemente applaude, poi tesse di nascosto inganno e fraude (GR [14][4])

Amore si può dire essere una pillola inzucherata et un dillettoso male ciecho perché ci accieca; sciolto ma gli altri lega; nudo e pur cuopre inganno; un boccone che affoga, un fuoco interno, un capestro di seta, un incanto di Circe, un cane d'Atteonte, una ruota d'Issione, un specchio di Narcisso, un fanciullo, una bagatella, un traditore, un assassino, un tiranno, un micidiale, una sanguisuga, una sirena, una hienna, un basilisco, un cocodrillo, una chimera di natura di lione, di capra, e di dragone; di lione per la sua fierezza, di capra per la sua lussuria, e di dragone per la sua crudeltà; e col suo tentare, piagare, tormentare et uccidere (SF Ch. 12: 164)	
Amor può il tutto et il tutto amor mantiene (SF Ch. 12: 164)	Amore può il tutto et il tutto amor mantiene (GR 4)
Amor vince ogni cosa (FF Ch. 19: 33v)	
Andando per viaggio, ne l'inverno honora il compagno, per non esser il primo ad inciampare ne' cattivi passi; l'istate mettiti inanzi, per non havere la polvere ne gli occhi (SF Ch. 6: 92)	

Index of Paremias

Andarono in trenta per cavar una rapa (SF Ch. 7: 112)	
A novelle di borsa e di San Paolo non bisogna dar più fede che a promesse di fuor'usciti e favole di comedianti (SF Ch. 9: 140)	
A' pazzi si mostra la vergine Maria (SF Ch. 7: 120)	A' pazzi si mostra la vergine Maria (GR 2)
A' porci cadon le miglior pere in bocca (SF Ch. 7: 120)	A' porci cadono le buone pera in bocca (GR 2)
A qual si voglia dolore rimedia la patientia (FF Ch. 19: 27v)	
A scrigno sgangherato non si scrolla sacco (SF Ch. 6: 98)	A scrigno sgangherato non si scrolla sacco (GR 2)
Asino punto bisogna che trotti (FF Ch. 19: 27v)	Asino punto convien che trotti (GR 1)
Aspetta luogo e tempo a far vendett[a] ché non si face mai ben in fretta (FF Ch. 19: 27v) Aspetta tempo e luoco a far vendetta perché non si fece mai bene in fretta (SF Ch. 6: 100)	Aspetta tempo e luoco a far vendetta ché non si fece mai ben in fretta (GR 7)

Aspettar e non venire, star nel letto e non dormire, servire e non gradire son tre cose da morire (FF Ch. 19: 27r) Aspettar e non venire. Star in letto e non dormire. Ben servir e non gradire. Haver cavallo e non vuol ire; e servitor che non vuol ubidire. Esser in prigione e non poter fuggire; et ammalato e non poter guarire. Smarrir la strada quand'un vuol gire. Star alla porta quand'un non vuol aprire; et haver un amico che ti vuol tradire: son dieci doglie da morire (SF Ch. 1: 12)	Aspettare e non venire, star in letto e non dormire, ben servire e non gradire son tre doglie da morire (GR 13)
Aspettar finché sonino le campane (SF Ch. 4: 52)	
Assai aqua corre per il molino che il molinaro non ne sa (FF Ch. 19: 34v)	Assai acqua passa per il molino ch'il molinaio non vede (GR 7)
Assai ben balla a chi fortuna sona (FF Ch. 19: 27v)	Assai ben balla a chi fortuna suona (GR 1)
Assai guadagna chi fortuna perde (FF Ch. 19: 27v)	Assai guadagna chi fortuna passa ma molto più chi le donne lassa (GR 7)
Assai presto si fa quel che si fa bene (FF Ch. 19: 27v)	Presto e bene non si conviene (GR 174)
Assai sa chi non sa se tacer sa (FF Ch. 19: 27v)	Assai sa chi sa se tacer sa (GR 3)

A tal carne tal cortello (SF Ch. 3: 46)	Tal carne, tal cortello (GR 202)
A te tutti i gatti son grigi all'oscuro (SF Ch. 8: 130)	A l'oscuro ogni gatto è grigio (GR 12)
Attaccar dal mal al peggio (SF Ch. 5: 74)	
A tutto è rimedio eccetto che alla morte (FF Ch. 19: 27v)	A tutto è rimedio eccetto alla morte (GR 1)
A uno a uno si fanno li fusi (FF Ch. 19: 27v)	Ad uno ad uno si fanno i fusi (GR 1)
Ave morta non fa mele (FF Ch. 19: 27v)	Senza le api non si ha il miele (GR 190)
Bandiera vechia, honor di capitano (FF Ch. 19: [28][5]r)	Bandiera vecchia, honor di capitano (GR [14])
Barbier giovine e medico vechio (FF Ch. 19: 32r)	Barbier giovane e medico vecchio (GR [14])
Beato il figliuolo di cui il padre va a casa del diavolo (SF Ch. 7: 116)	
Beato voi che godete fino del latte della gallina (SF Ch. 1: 8)	
Bel carro e bei buò e bella moglie a chi la vuò (SF Ch. 12: 184)	Bel carro et be' buò, bella moglie a chi la vuò (GR 18)
Bel cavallo non morire ché l'herba frescha dè venire (SF Ch. 3: 42)	Bel cavallo non morir ché l'herba fresca dee venir (GR 16)
Bella donna è donna et ogni donna molle, et donne d'esser belle mai non son satolle (SF Ch. 12: 194)	

Belle parole e cattivi fatti inganano i savi et i matti (FF Ch. 19: 27v; SF Ch. 2: 18; SF Ch. 6: 102)	Belle parole e cattivi fatti ingannano savi et matti (GR 18)
Bello si fa chi ben amando muore. Più bello si fa chi non amando gode (SF Ch. 12: 166)	Bello sin fa chi ben amando muore (GR [15][6])
Ben faremo, ben diremo, mal va la barca senza remo (FF Ch. 19: [28]r)	Ben diremo, ben faremo, ma mal va la barca senza remo (GR 18)
Ben venga maggio co' suoi fiori (SF Ch. 4: 54)	Ben venga maggio co' suoi fiori (GR 16)
Bisogna che ogni santo abbia la sua candela (SF Ch. 7: 124)	Ogni santo vuol la sua candela (GR 169)
Bisogna ch'il prete viva dell'altare (SF Ch. 7: 124)	Bisogna ch'il prete viva dell'altare (GR 17)
Bisognerebbe haver la patientia di Giobbe a durarla con voi (SF Ch. 8: 136)	
Bocca dolce, mano che molce (SF Ch. 12: 196)	Bocca dolce, bocca di puttana (GR 16)
Bologna la grassa, ma Padova la passa (SF Ch. 6: 106)	Bologna la grassa, Padova la passa (GR 16)
Buon cane rare volte truova buon osso (SF Ch. 7: 120)	Buon cane non truova buon osso (GR [14])
Buonissimo come il pane (SF Ch. 8: 128)	
Buon prò vi faccia come il mele all'orso o l'oglio alle ancione (SF Ch. 4: 56)	

Buon prò vi faccia, ma non come l'herba a' cani (SF Ch. 4: 56)	
Buon viaggio faccia la barca (SF Ch. 4: 54)	
Calabrese, guai a quella casa dove sta un mese, se ci sta un anno ci apporta rovina e danno (SF Ch. 6: 108)	Calabrese, guai a quella casa dove sta un mese, se ci sta un anno c'apporta ruina e danno (GR 45)
Cane che baia non sol nocer (FF Ch. 19: [28]v)	Cane che baia non suol nuocer (GR 30)
Cane vechio non baia in darno (FF Ch. 19: [28]v)	Cane vecchio non baia in darno (GR 21)
Capra al sale, mosca al miele, al sol furfante (SF Ch. 12: 168)	
Carne vecchia fa buon bruodo (SF Ch. 9: 140)	Carne vecchia fa buon brodo (GR 21)
Cascan le rose et restan poi le spine (SF Ch. 6: 104)	Cascan le rose e restan poi le spine, non giudicate nulla inanzi il fine (GR 43)
Castello spesso combattuto alla fine è preso o si rende (SF Ch. 12: 194)	
Caval corrente sepoltura aperta (FF Ch. 19: [28]v)	Cavallo corrente, sepoltura aperta (GR 22)
C'è de gli huomini che vogliono l'uovo e la gallina (FF Ch. 19: 33v)	Voler l'uovo e la gallina (GR 212)

Index of Paremias

Cedi al maggiore, persuadi al minore et consenti a l'uguale e fuggirai il male (SF Ch. 6: 100)	Cedi al maggiore, persuadi al minore e consenti a l'uguale (GR 36)
Cento carra di pensieri non pagano mai un'oncia di debiti (SF Ch. 2: 26)	Cento carra di pensieri non pagan un'oncia di debito (GR 20)
Cera, tela e fustagno, bella botega poco guadagno (FF Ch. 1: [28]*v*)	Cera, tela e fustagno, bella bottega e poco guadagno (GR 30)
Cercar i fatti d'altrui è tempo perso (FF Ch. 19: 29*r*)	
Che colpa n'ha la gatta, se la massaia è matta? (FF Ch. 19: 29*r*) Che colpa n'ha la gatta, se la massara è matta? (SF Ch. 3: 40; Ch. 9: 144)	Che colpa ne ha la gatta, se la massaia è matta? (GR 23)
Chi a l'honor suo manca d'un momento non ripara mai in anni cento (SF Ch. 6: 96)	A l'honor chi manca d'un momento non ripara in anni cento (GR 7)
Chi bellissima nacque povera non nacque (SF Ch. 12: [190][7])	
Chi ben chiude, schifa rìa fortuna (SF Ch. 1: 14)	Buona guardia schifa ria fortuna (GR [15])
Chi bene dona chiaro vende, se villan non è chi prende (SF Ch. 6: 104)	Chi bene dona chiaro vende, se villan non è chi prende (GR 30)
Chi ben e male non può soffrire, a grand'honor non può venire (SF Ch. 6: 100)	Chi ben e mal non può soffrir, a grand'honor non può venir (GR 30)

Chi ben serra ben apre (SF Ch. 1: 14)	Chi ben serra ben apre (GR 27)
Chi ben siede mal pensa (FF Ch. 19: [28]*r*)	Chi ben siede male pensa (GR 27)
Chi [b]en vive ben more (FF Ch. 19: [28]*r*)	Chi ben vive ben muore (GR 23)
Chi beve vino beve sangue e chi acqua cotta flemma (SF Ch. 4: 50)	
Chi cerca spesso ingannar altrui opresso resta et ingannato lui (FF Ch. 14: 14*v*; Ch. 19: [28]*r*)	Chi cerca spesso ingannar altrui oppresso resta et ingannato lui (GR 41)
Chi cerca trova (FF Ch. 19: 34*r*)	Chi cerca truova (GR 20)
Chi compra caro e toglie a credenza, consum'il corpo e perde la semenza (FF Ch. 19: [28]*v*)	Chi compra caro e toglie a credenza, consuma il corpo e perde la semenza (GR 41)
Chi cucina in fretta ha mal stagionate le vivande (SF Ch. 4: 52)	
Chi d'amor vuole diletto convien che porti con sospetto la corazza con l'elmetto e che scherzi raro et giuochi netto, come a mamma fanciullo, avaro all'oro, mosca al tignoso, alla pignatta il cuoco, così l'amante avezzo al foro torna che la facenda dolcemente inforna (SF Ch. 12: 168)	Chi d'amor prende diletto porti sempre con sospetto la corazza con l'elmetto, scherzi raro et giuochi netto (GR 43)

Chi da venti non è e da trenta non sa e da quaranta non ha, né mai sarà né mai saprà né mai haverà (SF Ch. 6: 100)	Chi da venti non è et da trenta non sa et da quaranta non ha, né mai sarà né mai saperà né mai haverà (GR 40)
Chi del suo honore si lascia privare né viva né morta donna si dee più chiamare (SF Ch. 12: 192)	
Chi di gallina nasce convien che razzoli (SF Ch. 12: 178)	
Chi di gatta, o sorgi piglia o graffia (SF Ch. 12: 178)	Chi di gatto nasce, o sorgi piglia o graffia (GR 21)
Chi di paglia fuoco fa, molto fumo e altro non ha (FF Ch. 19: [28]v)	Chi di paglia fuoco fa, molto fumo altro non ha (GR 20)
Chi dorme co' cani si leva co' pulci (SF Ch. 6: 94) Chi va dormir con i cani si leva con i pulici (FF Ch. 19: 29r)	Dove cani ivi pulci (GR 91)
Chi dorme non piglia pesce (FF Ch. 19: 34r; SF Ch. 6: 94)	Chi dorme non piglia pesce (GR 20)
Chi duo lepri cazia, uno perde, l'altro lasia (FF Ch. 19: [28]v)	Chi duo lepri caccia, uno perde e l'altro lascia (GR 24)
Chi è coperto quando piove è un matto se si muove, se si muove e si bagna è più che matto se si lagna (SF Ch. 5: 78)	Chi è coperto quando piove è un matto se si muove. Se si muove et si bagna è un asino se si lagna (GR 41)
Chi è in difetto è in suspetto (FF Ch. 19: [28]v)	Chi è in diffetto è in sospetto (GR 31)

Chi è mostro del corpo è mostro dell'animo (SF Ch. 12: 192)	
Chi è nutrito in corte impara ogni astutia (SF Ch. 4: 56)	
Chi è reo e non è tenuto può far il mal e non è creduto (FF Ch. 19: [28]*r*)	Chi è reo e non è tenuto può far il mal e non è creduto (GR 29)
Chi fa i fatti suoi non s'imbratta le mani (SF Ch. 1: 10; Ch. 6: 102)	Chi fa i fatti suoi non s'imbratta le mani (GR 27)
Chi fa il contrario sempre viverà in affanni (FF Ch. 12: 10*r*)	
Chi fa male odia il lume (FF Ch. 19: [28]*v*)	Chi fa male odia il lume (GR 21)
Chi fa più carezze che non suole t'ha ingannato or ingannar ti vuole (SF Ch. 6: 100)	
Chi fa quel che non debbe gli avvien quel che non crede (FF Ch. 19: 28*r*; SF Ch. 6: 96)	Chi fa quello che non deve gli avien quel che non crede (GR 29)
Chi frequenta la cucina sente da fumo (SF Ch. 6: 94)	Chi cucina pratica sente da fumo (GR 24)
Chi ha a far con tosco non convien esser losco (SF Ch. 6: 108)	Chi ha a far con tosco non convien esser losco (GR 19)
Chi ha buona lancia la pruovi nel muro (FF Ch. 19: [28]*v*)	Chi ha buona lancia la pruovi nel muro (GR 31)

Chi ha cavallo bianco et bella moglie, non si truova mai senza doglie (SF Ch. 12: 190)	Chi ha caval bianco e bella moglie, non è mai senza doglie (GR 30)
Chi ha fiele in bocca non può sputar miele (SF Ch. 12: 170)	Chi ha fiele in bocca non può sputar miele (GR 27)
Chi ha tempo ha vita (FF Ch. 19: [28]*r*)	
Chi ha tempo non aspetti tempo (FF Ch. 19: [28]*v*)	Chi ha tempo non aspetti tempo (GR 27)
Chi tempo ha e tempo aspetta, tempo perde et tempo perso non si racquista mai (SF Ch. 6: 98) Chi tempo ha e tempo aspetta tempo perde (FF Ch. 19: [28]*v*) Chi havendo tempo aspetta tempo, tempo perde, e tempo perso non si riacquista mai (SF Ch. 12: 164)	Chi tempo ha e tempo aspetta, tempo perde, et tempo perso non si racquista mai (GR 41)
Chi in corpo bianco tiene mente negra habbiasi sempre corpo negro finché possegga mente bianca (SF Ch. 12: 196)	
Chi la dura la vince (FF Ch. 19: [28]*r*)	Chi la dura la vince o la perde amaramente (GR 31)
Chi lascia andar la sua moglie ad ogni festa et bere il suo cavallo ad ogni fontana, del suo cavallo haverà una rozza e della sua moglie una puttana (SF Ch. 3: 40)	Chi lascia andar sua moglie ad ogni festa et bere il suo cavallo ad ogni fontana, del suo cavallo haverà una rozza et fra poco della sua moglie una puttana (GR 45)

Index of Paremias

Chi lascia la via vecchia per la nuova spesso ingannato si ritrova (SF Ch. 6: 102) Chi lascia la via vechia per la nuova spesse volte inganato si ritrova (FF Ch. 19: [28]*r*)	Chi lascia la via vecchia per la nuova spesso ingannato si ritrova (GR 41)
Chi lava la testa a un asino perde il sapon et la fatica (FF Ch. 19: 34*r*)	Chi lava la testa a l'asino perd'il sapone e la liscia (GR 27)
Chi le fugge seguono et chi le segue fuggono (SF Ch. 12: 174)	
Chi l'ha da natura fino alla fossa dura (SF Ch. 1: 8)	
Chi mi ama me [sic] ama il mio cane (FF Ch. 19: 29*r*)	Chi ama me ama il mio cane (GR 23)
Chi mi fa meglio che non sole, tradito m'ha o tradir mi vole (FF Ch. 19: [28]*r*)	
Chi monta più alto che non deve cade più basso che non crede (SF Ch. 6: 102)	Chi monta più alto che non deve cade più basso che non crede (GR 36)
Chi muta stato muta conditione (FF Ch. 19: 30*r*)	Chi muta stato muta conditione (GR 21)
Chi non ama essendo amato commette gran peccato (SF Ch. 12: 170)	Chi non ama essendo amato comette gran peccato (GR 33)
Chi non ama il cielo si giacci nell'inferno (SF Ch. 12: 194)	

Chi non cavalca per terra non sa che cosa sia solazzo o piacere (SF Ch. 2: 18)	Chi non cavalca per terra non conosce piacere (GR 31)
Chi non è d'amor soggetto non conosce alcun diletto (SF Ch. 12: 166)	Chi non è d'amor soggetto non conosce alcun diletto (GR 27)
Chi non fa non falla, chi falla s'amenda (FF Ch. 19: [28]v)	Chi non fa non falla e chi non falla non s'amenda (GR 31)
Chi non ha che quatro e spende sette non ha bisogno di borsette (SF Ch. 6: 102)	Chi non n'ha che quatro e ne spende sette non ha bisogno di borsette (GR 42)
Chi non ha cuore habbia gambe (FF Ch. 19: [28]v)	Chi non ha cuore o memoria habbia gambe (GR 20)
Chi non ha danari non ha credito se non di bastonate (FF Ch. 10: 9v)	
Chi non ha figlioli bene gli pasce (FF Ch. 19: [28]v)	Chi non ha figliuoli ben gli pasce (GR 32)
Chi non ha gustato l'amaro non sa che cosa sia il dolce (SF Ch. 8: 130)	
Chi non ha moglie spesso la batte (FF Ch. 19: [28]v)	Chi non ha moglie ben la veste (GR 32)
Chi non ha servito non sa comandare (FF Ch. 19: [28]v)	Chi non ha servito non sa comandare (GR 21)
Chi non può batter il cavallo batta la sella (FF Ch. 19: 29r)	Chi non può batter il cavallo batta la sella (GR 30)

Index of Paremias

Chi non robba non fa robba (FF Ch. 19: 29*r*)	Chi non robba non fa robba (GR 32)
Chi non sa fare i fatti suoi peggio farà quelli d'altrui (SF Ch. 1: 10) Chi non sa far i fatti suoi peggio fa a quegli d'altrui (SF Ch. 6: 104)	Chi non sa fare i fatti suoi peggio farà quelli d'altrui (GR 29)
Chi non s'arischia non s'arichisce (SF Ch. 5: 70)	Chi non s'arischia non guadagna (GR 22)
Chi non si compiace di un cigno qualche corbo gli cavi gl'occhi (SF Ch. 12: 194)	
Chi non va per mare non sa ciò che sia il timor di Dio (SF Ch. 2: 16) Chi non naviga non sa che sia il timor di Dio (FF Ch. 19: 29*r*)	Chi non va per mare non conosce il timor di Dio (GR 24)
Chi non vuol durare fatica in questo mondo non nasca (FF Ch. 19: [28]*r*)	Chi non vuol durar fatica non nasca (GR 30)
Chi non vuole la luce habbisi le tenebre (SF Ch. 12: 194)	
Chi non vuole quando puole, quando vorrà non potrà (SF Ch. 6: 98)	Chi non vuol quando puol, quando vorrà non potrà (GR 27)
Chi non vuol periclitare non si dee metter ad amare (SF Ch. 12: 176)	
Chi nuoce altrui nuoce se stesso (FF Ch. 19: 29*r*)	Chi conosce se stesso altrui non nuoce (GR 22)

Chi paga inanzi tratto trova il lavor mal fatto (SF Ch. 3: 38)	Chi paga inanzi tratto trova il lavor malfatto (GR 24)
Chi pecora si fa il lupo la mangia (SF Ch. 6: 94)	Chi pecora si fa il lupo la mangia (GR 21)
Chi pensa di trovar in una troia purità o in una vacca castità? (SF Ch. 12: 192)	
Chi pratica co' lupi impara a hurlare (SF Ch. 6: 94) Chi è nutrito tra lupi impara a hurlare (SF Ch. 4: 56)	Chi pratica co' lupi impara a hurlare (GR 24)
Chi promette e non attende la promessa non val niente (SF Ch. 2: 18)	Chi promette e non attende la promessa non val niente (GR 31)
Chi, quel sbardellato che non studia altro che la boccolica, le matte lettere e con tanta diligentia va praticando la matematica? (SF Ch. 9: 142)	
Chi segue amor potrà per cimier portar la pentecoste, perché in breve si pente del suo costo (SF Ch. 12: 168)	
Chi semina virtù racoglie fama et vera fama supera la morte (FF Ch. 19: [28]*v*)	Chi semina virtù raccoglie fama et vera fama supera la morte (GR 41)
Chi sente, vede, et tace può sempre vivere in pace (FF Ch. 12: 10*r*)	

Index of Paremias

Chi serv'al comune serv'a nessuno (FF Ch. 19: 29r)	
Chi serve le putane il tempo perde (FF Ch. 19: 29r)	
Chi si allieva il serpe in seno è poi pagato di veleno (SF Ch. 6: 96)	Chi s'allieva il serpe in seno è poi pagato di veleno (GR 22)
Chi si contenta gode (SF Ch. 1: 10; Ch. 2: 28)	Chi si contenta gode (GR 33)
Chi si mette fra la semola è mangiato da' porci (SF Ch. 6: 94)	
Chi s'impaccia con fanciulli con puttane e con fuorusciti, con ingrati, con bugiardi e con sconoscienti si ritrova poi (SF Ch. 9: 140)	
Chi si vuol dar fastidio tutta la sua vita (FF Ch. 19: 30r)	
Chi sta bene non si muova perché movendo se si rompe le gambe, a suo danno (SF Ch. 9: 148)	Chi potendo stare cade tra via, s'ei si rompe il collo a suo danno sia (GR 44)
Chi sta ne l'aqua fino a la gola ben è ostinato se mercé non crida (FF Ch. 19: [28]r) Chi sta nell'acqua fino alla gola ben è ostinato se mercé non grida (SF Ch. 6: 102)	Chi sta nell'acqua fino alla gola ben è ostinato se mercé non crida (GR 41)

313

Chi tardi ariva mal allogia (FF Ch. 5: 5r [Chi tardi arriva ...]; Ch. 19: 29r; SF Ch. 4: 58)	Chi tardi arriva male alloggia (GR 21)
Chi ti vede di giorno non ti cercherà di notte (FF Ch. 19: 29r)	Chi ti vede di giorno non ti cerca di notte (GR 23)
Chi tosto dà due volte dà (SF Ch. 6: 104)	Chi tosto dà due volte dà (GR 20)
Chi troppo abraccia nulla stringe (FF Ch. 19: [28]r) Chi troppo abraccia poco stringe (FF Ch. 6: 6v)	Chi tutto abbraccia nulla stringe (GR 24)
Chi tutto vuol di rabbia muore (FF Ch. 19: 29r)	Chi tutto vuole di rabbia muore (GR 30)
Chi va a Roma e porta buon borsotto, diventa abbate o vescovo di botto (SF Ch. 6: 108)	Chi va a Roma e porta buon borsotto, diventa abate o vescovo di botto (GR 41)
Chi va di notte ha delle botte (SF Ch. 6: 98)	Chi va di notte ha delle botte (GR 31)
Chi va dormir con i cani si leva con i pulici (FF Ch. 19: 29r) Chi dorme co' cani si leva co' pulci (SF Ch. 6: 94)	Dove cani ivi pulci (GR 91)
Chi va et ritorna fa bon viaggio (FF Ch. 19: 29r)	Chi va e torna fa buon viaggio (GR 30)
Chi va in letto senza cena tutta la notte si dimena (FF Ch. 19: 29r; SF Ch. 10: 150)	Chi va in letto senza cena tutta notte si dimena (GR 70)

Chi va pian va san (FF Ch. 14: 14r) Chi va piano va sano (SF Ch. 1: 10)	Chi va piano va sano (GR 20)
Chi vede la bella e non le dona il cuore o non è vivo o non conosce amore (SF Ch. 12: 198)	
Chi vende a credenza spaccia robba assai, l'amico perde, denari non ha mai (SF Ch. 7: 122)	Chi vende a credenza spaccia robba assai, perde gli amici, denari non ha mai (GR 41)
Chi vive a speranza magra fa la danza (SF Ch. 9: 148)	Chi vive in speranza magra fa la danza (GR 22)
Chi vive in corte muore in pagliaro (FF Ch. 19: 29r; SF Ch. 9: 146)	Chi vive in corte muore su 'l pagliaio (GR 24)
Chi vuol dir mal d'altrui prima si pensi di lui (FF Ch. 19: 29r)	Chi vuol dir mal d'altrui prima pensi di lui (GR 31)
Chi vuol sopra sapere per bestia si fa tenere (SF Ch. 6: 98)	Chi vuol sopra sapere per bestia si fa tenere (GR 21)
Christo lasciò ne gli precetti suoi, non far altrui quel che per te non vuoi (SF Ch. 6: 102) Christo lasiò ne li precetti suoi, non far altrui quel che per te non vuoi (FF Ch. 19: [28]r) Christo lasciò ne li precetti suoi, voi non far altrui quel che per te non vuoi (FF Ch. 14: 14v)	Christo lasciò negli precetti suoi, non far altrui quel che per te non vuoi (GR 41)

Ci lasciò quasi la stampa della cuffia (SF Ch. 9: 144)	
Ci vado come la biscia all'incanto (SF Ch. 6: 88)	Andarci come la biscia all'incanto (GR 2)
Col mall'anno e la mala Pasqua che Dio ti dia (SF Ch. 8: 132)	
Colui che cerca l'altrui facende da tutti li savi è tenuto matto (FF Ch. 11: 9v)	Il matto sa meglio i fatti suoi che non sa il savio quegli d'altrui (GR 128)
Colui che vien ultimo serra la porta (FF Ch. 19: 29r)	
Come a bella giovenca torna il toro, al fonte cervo, l'agghiacciato al fuoco, al suo nido l'augello, chierico al coro, al ballo pastorella e barro al giuoco (SF Ch. 12: 168)	
Come corre al buon vin gente todesca (SF Ch. 12: 168)	
Come ha l'uccellaccio la sua canzone, la quale non rende harmonia veruna (SF Ch. 12: 168)	
Come il carbone, il quale o tinge o bruscia (SF Ch. 12: 174)	La puttana è come il carbone, o tinge o bruscia (GR 141)
Come il molino a vento che macina secondo il vento (SF Ch. 12: 174)	

Come il pesce che, cercando fuggir padella, cade nelle bragie (SF Ch. 12: 168)	Lui salta da la padella nelle brascie (GR 140)
Come i piffari da Bologna che non sanno sonare se non sono gonfi e pieni (SF Ch. 4: 52)	
Come la bilancia che prende dove più riceve (SF Ch. 12: 174)	
Come la brutta è mal di stomaco, così la bella è mal di testa, l'una satia e l'alt[r]a cruccia (SF Ch. 12: [190])	Donna brutta è mal di stomaco, donna bella è mal di testa (GR 90)
Come la castagna che di fuori è bella e dentro ha la magagna (SF Ch. 12: 184)	Amor di donna è come la castagna, di fuor è bella e dentro ha la magagna (GR 13)
Come ogni cavallo buon o rio vuol lo sperone, così ogni donna buona o ria vuole il bastone (SF Ch. 12: 182)	
Come quegli da Mantoa che andaron per sonare e furono sonati (SF Ch. 4: 52)	Far come i pifari da Luca che andaron a sonare e furono sonati (GR 106)
Come volete ch'io sappia tener la lingua fra i denti (SF Ch. 8: 132)	

Con arte e con inganno si vive mezo l'anno, con inganno e con arte si vive l'altra parte (FF Ch. 19: [28]r) Ogniuno con arte et con inganno vive mezzo l'anno, e con inganno et con arte vive l'altra parte (SF Ch. 6: 104)	Con arte e con inganno si vive mezzo l'anno (GR 27) Con inganno e con arte si vive l'altra parte (GR 27)
Con il martello d'oro si rompe ogni serratura et si giunge ad ogni altezza (SF Ch. 6: 92)	
Con il tempo e con la paglia le nespole si matura (FF Ch. 14: 14r)	Col tempo e con la paglia si maturano le nespole (GR 27)
Con le sue burle, berte, baie e facetie harebbe fatto smascellare un Heraclito dalle risa (SF Ch. 9: 144)	
Conto fatto, amicitia longa (SF Ch. 7: 122)	Contar spesso è amicitia longa (GR 19)
Contrario oggetto proprio della fede et è infelice et misero chi lor crede (SF Ch. 12: 178)	
Convien star in cervello in questo mondo (SF Ch. 9: 140)	
Convien tener il braccio al petto e la gamba al letto (SF Ch. 3: 44)	Il braccio al petto e la gamba al letto (GR 117)
Corbi con corbi non cavano mai gli ochi (FF Ch. 19: 29r)	Corvi con corvi non si cavano mai gl'occhi (GR 21)

Index of Paremias

Corpo senz'alma e fonte senz'humore, pesce senz'onde e senza gemma anello, si può dir l'huomo che non sente amore (SF Ch. 12: 168)	Corpo senz'alma et fonte senz'humore è quella donna che non sente amore (GR 40)
Corpo vendibile e spirito corruttibile (SF Ch. 12: 196)	
Cortegiano giovine et vecchio mendico (SF Ch. 9: 146)	Otioso giovane, vecchio mendico (GR 173)
Così cieco come chi non vuol vedere (SF Ch. 12: 184)	
Così rade come vien l'anno del Giubileo (SF Ch. 9: 146)	
Credo che fosse madre del gallo che cantò a Pietro (SF Ch. 4: 56)	
Credo che siate fiorentino, poiché sete così ritroso, protervo e fastidioso a contentare (SF Ch. 8: 135)	
Cuor contento è manto su le spalle (SF Ch. 1: 10)	Cuor contento è manto su le spalle (GR 33)
Da' cattivi costumi seguono le buone leggi (SF Ch. 12: 180)	
Da chi mi fido guardimi Dio ché da chi non mi fido mi guarderò io (SF Ch. 2: 18)	Da chi mi fido guardimi Dio ché da chi non mi fido mi guarderò io (GR 94)

319

Index of Paremias

Dal detto al fatto ci è un grande tratto (FF Ch. 15: 18v) Dal ditto al fatto vi è un gran tratto (FF Ch. 19: 29v)	Dal detto al fatto vi è un gran tratto (GR 47)
Da le spine nascon le rose (SF Ch. 12: 180)	
Dalla bellezza nasce la superbia et la superbia dà adito alla lussuria (SF Ch. 12: 192)	
Dalla bellezza vien la tentatione, dalla tentatione il dishonore (SF Ch. 12: 192)	
Dalla campana alla nona non ci passa buona persona (SF Ch. 12: 204)	Da la campana a nona non ci passa buona persona (GR 89)
Dalla nona alla campana sempre passa qualche puttana (SF Ch. 12: 204)	Da nona a campana sempre passa qualche puttana (GR 89)
Dall'avversità nasce la virtù (SF Ch. 12: 180)	
Dalle cose passate si giudicano le presente (FF Ch. 19: 30r)	Dalle cose passate si giudican le presenti (GR 47)
Dal mare salato esce il pesce fresco (SF Ch. 12: 180)	
Da tre cose signor liberaci, da una borsa voda, da un cativo vicino e da una cativa donna (FF Ch. 19: 30r)	
Debbe voler bene al bambino per amor della balia (SF Ch. 4: 56)	

Debbe voler bene al tagliere per amor della carne (SF Ch. 4: 56)	
Delle parole, le buone ongono et le cattive pongono (SF Ch. 12: 176) Le bone parole ongino, le cative pongino (FF Ch. 19: 31v)	Le buone parole ongono, le cattive pongono (GR 139)
De l'ocha mangiane poca (FF Ch. 19: 29v)	De l'oca mangiane poca (GR 88)
Denaro è il principal verbo in questa casa (FF Ch. 19: 30v)	
Dice Aristotine, quando puoi haver del bene tuotene. Dice poi Platon, se non lo tuoi tu sei un coglion (SF Ch. 6: 100)	Dice Aristotine, quando puoi haver del bene tuotene, e dice poi Platon se non lo tuoi tu sei un gran coglion (GR 95)
Dice Christo nel Vangelo che l'humiltà apre le porte del cielo, et impara a spese altrui ad esser savio (SF Ch. 6: 102)	Dice Christo nel Vangelo, l'humiltà apre le porte del cielo (GR 88)
Di denari, senno e fede ce n'è manco che non si crede (SF Ch. 6: 96)	Di denari, senno e fede ce n'è manco che non si crede (GR 88)
Di donna è et sempre fu natura odiar chi l'ama e chi non l'ama cura (SF Ch. 12: 174)	Di donna è et sempre fu natura odiar chi l'ama et chi non l'ama cura (GR 94)
Di donna son nato e da donna son rovinato (SF Ch. 12: 172)	
Di minaccie non temere né di promesse non godere (SF Ch. 6: 94)	Di promesse non godere e di minaccie non temere (GR 88)

Dio guardi me da cinque F, cioè femine, fuoco, fame, frati et fiume (SF Ch. 12: 180)	Dio ci guardi da cinque F: fame, fumo, fiume, frate e femine (GR 90)
Dio vi doni quel guadagno e me guardi da quella perdita (SF Ch. 12: 180)	
Di pochi fidatevi ma da tutti guardatevi (SF Ch. 6: 96)	Di pochi fidati ma da tutti guardati (GR 48)
Di senno è pieno ogni testa (FF Ch. 19: 29v)	Di senno è piena ogni testa (GR 89)
Dita di vischio, se tocca prende, se prende tiene et se tiene si truova tener un bel corno (SF Ch. 12: 196)	
Dolce parole rompono l'ira (FF Ch. 19: 29v)	Dolci parole rompono l'ira (GR 47)
Dolce vivanda bisogna haver salsa brusca (FF Ch. 19: 30r)	Dolce vivanda vuole salsa acerba (GR 47)
Donato è morto, ristoro sta male (FF Ch. 19: 30r)	Donato è morto, ristoro sta male (GR 47)
Donna, forze, occhi, voce, ben corpo, alma, trahe, orba, mastra, strugge, infetta, ancide (SF Ch. 12: 184)	Donna, forze, occhi, voce, ben corpo, alma, trahe, orba, inaspra, strugge, infetta, uccide (GR 94)
Donna fu detta danno (SF Ch. 9: 142)	Donna, danno, dama, dammi (GR 48)
Donna, vino e dado rende l'huomo rovinato (SF Ch. 5: 72)	Bocca, braghe e dado, il tuo fatto è spacciato (GR [14])

Dopo tempesta vien bel tempo (FF Ch. 19: 29v)	Dopo la tempesta viene il bel tempo (GR 47)
Dove ci è nulla il re perde il suo dritto (FF Ch. 19: 29v)	Dove non c'è nulla il re non ha ragione (GR 47)
Dove è amore ivi è Dio e dov'è Dio hai di beni un cornucopia (SF Ch. 12: 166)	
Dove è vita ivi è modo, dove modo ricapito, dove ricapito speranza e dove speranza ivi è consolatione (SF Ch. 9: 148)	
Dove ho l'amore ivi ho il cuore, il qual dimora, non dove vive, ma dove ama (SF Ch. 12: 168)	
Dove non han pasco né ricetto, infin le Furie abandonano i luoghi (FF Ch. 19: 34r)	
Dove non puoi fare con la pelle del lione cerca di fare con quella della volpe (SF Ch. 6: 104)	Dove manca forza di lione habbi l'astutia di volpone (GR 93)
D'una fetida herba nasce il giglio (SF Ch. 12: 180)	Di fetida herba nasce il giglio (GR 89)
Duro con duro non fece mai buon muro (FF Ch. 19: 29v)	Duro con duro non fece mai buon muro (GR 47)
È bella cosa pigliar due colombi con una fava (FF Ch. 19: 29v)	È bella cosa pigliar due colombi con una fava (GR 98)

È bon batter il ferro quando che l'è caldo (FF Ch. 19: 30r)	Batter si deve mentre è caldo il ferro (GR [14])
È egli de' soldati del Tinca (SF Ch. 7: 112)	Soldati del Tinca (GR 194)
Egli debbe dunque haver il mal matino (SF Ch. 8: 128)	
Egli è il diavolo quello haver debiti (SF Ch. 9: 144)	
Egli è il diavolo quel toccar sul vivo (SF Ch. 12: 168)	È il diavolo quello toccar su il vivo (GR 98)
Egli è tanto superbo che havendo bisogno di misericordia grida vendetta (SF Ch. 9: 144)	Haver bisogno di misericordia e cridar vendetta (GR 111)
Egli è una bella cosa il sapersi guardare (SF Ch. 12: 168)	
Egli è un vero diavolo incarnato che infanga i giovani et annega i vecchi (SF Ch. 12: 166)	Amor infanga i gioveni et annega i vecchi (GR 4)
El ben guadagnare fa il bel spendere (FF Ch. 19: 29v)	Il bel guadagnare fa il bel spendere (GR 118)
El dir mal d'altrui è il quinto elemento (FF Ch. 19: 29v)	Il dir mal d'altrui è il quinto elemento (GR 118)
El fine fa il tutto (FF Ch. 19: 29v)	Il fine fa il tutto (GR 114)
El mal va dietro al bene et il bene al male (FF Ch. 19: 29v)	Il mal va dietro al ben, el ben al male (GR 122)

El mal vien per libra e va via per oncie (FF Ch. 19: 29v)	I mali vengono a carra e fuggono a oncia (GR 118)
El pasciuto non crede al digiuno (FF Ch. 19: 29v)	Il pasciuto non crede al digiuno (GR 118)
El pesce grande mangia il piccolo (FF Ch. 19: 29v)	Il pesce grande mangia il piccolo (GR 118)
El pesce guasta l'aqua et la carne la concia (FF Ch. 19: 29v)	Il pescie guasta l'acqua, la carne la concia (GR 118)
El primo capitolo de' matti si è tenersi savio (FF Ch. 19: 29v)	Il primo capitolo de' matti è di tenersi savio (GR 118)
El promette mari e monti (FF Ch. 19: 29v)	Chi promette mari, monti e montagna non ha credito in Bertagna (GR 43)
El promettere è la viglia del dare (FF Ch. 19: 29v)	Il promettere è la vigilia del dare (GR 117)
El vino al sapore, el pane al calore (FF Ch. 19, 29v)	Il vino al sapore, il pane al calore (GR 118)
È meglio assai morire con honore che vivere con vergogna (FF Ch. 19: 29v; Ch. 41: 93v)	Chi troppo nell'honor presume in vergogna muore (GR 23)
È meglio che si dica, qui fuggì Lippa che qui morì Lippa (SF Ch. 8: 136)	
È meglio sdruciolar co' piedi che con la lingua (SF Ch. 6: 96)	È meglio sdrusciolar co' piedi che colla lingua (GR 97)
È morto in letto d'honore (SF Ch. 9: 144)	Chi muore in campo muore in letto d'honore (GR 29)

È più dura la ferita della penna che quella della lancia (SF Ch. 6: 96)	
E pur è meglio esser solo che male accompagnato (SF Ch. 2: 14)	È meglio esser solo che male accompagnato (GR 97)
Era un avarone ch'haverebbe scorticato un pedocchio per haverne la pelle (SF Ch. 7: 116)	
È sempre bono per uno haver due corde per il suo archo (FF Ch. 6: 6*v*) È bon sempre haver due corde per un archo (FF Ch. 19: 30*v*)	È sempre buono haver due corde per un arco (GR 98)
Esperientia è qualche volta pericolosa (FF Ch. 19: 30*r*)	
Essendo a tavola, se c'è poco pane, tienlo in mano; se poca carne prendi l'osso; se poco vino bevi spesso; e non voler mai presentar né sale né testa d'animale a veruno, se prima non ne sei richiesto; e non ragionar mai de' morti a tavola (SF Ch. 6: 94)	
Esser cavallo di Ruggiero (SF Ch. 4: 56)	
Essere un'acqua queta di Toscana (SF Ch. 5: 70)	
È tempo perso a metter aqua nel mare (FF Ch. 19: 34*r*)	Si può aggiunger acqua ma non già crescer il mare (GR 192)

Index of Paremias

E voi potete pisciar in letto e dir ch'havete sudato (SF Ch. 1: 8)	Lui piscia in letto e dice ch'ha sudato (GR 143)
Faccia rara, mente avara (SF Ch. 12: 196)	
Fallando si impara (FF Ch. 19: 30r)	Guastando s'impara (GR 108)
Fame è la miglior salsa (FF Ch. 19: 30r)	Fame è la miglior salsa (GR 101)
Fammi indovino et io ti farò richo (FF Ch. 19: 30r) Fatemi indovino ch'io vi farò ricco (SF Ch. 7: 118)	Fammi indovino, io ti farò ricco (GR 101)
Fanno conto inanzi l'hoste (FF Ch. 6: 6v)	Chi fa conto senza l'hoste due volte lo fa (GR 24)
Far ben non è inganno, buttar via il suo non è guadagno (FF Ch. 19: 30r)	Far bene non è inganno, gittar via il suo non è guadagno (GR 103)
Farebbe spasimare, tramortire e venir meno ogn'huomo quantunque ardito, o almeno lo farebbe fuggire gridando a acorrhuomo (SF Ch. 9: 144)	
Fare come il gambaro (SF Ch. 7: 114)	
Fare di una lancia un fuso (SF Ch. 9: 142)	Far d'una lancia un fuso (GR 105) Fare d'una lancia una spina (GR 103)
Faremo dunque come fanno a Prato (SF Ch. 5: 78)	Se piove facciamo come fanno a Prato (GR 193)

Fare tal conscientia di sputar in Chiesa e poi cacare su l'altare (SF Ch. 1: 12)	Molti fan conscientia di sputar in chiesa e poi cacan su l'altare (GR 149)
Fargli portar il cimier cerviero (SF Ch. 9: 140)	
Fate di necessità virtù (FF Ch. 14: 13v)	Fare di necessità virtù (GR 102)
Fate d'ogni herba fascio (SF Ch. 7: 120)	Fare d'ogni herba fascio (GR 102)
Fatemi indovino ch'io vi farò ricco (SF Ch. 7: 118) Fammi indovino et io ti farò richo (FF Ch. 19: 30r)	Fammi indovino, io ti farò ricco (GR 101)
Febraio curto, pegior de tutti (FF Ch. 19: 30r)	Febraio corto, peggio di tutti (GR 101)
Felice è colui ch'impara a spese altrui (SF Ch. 6: 102)	Felice colui che impara a spese altrui (GR 103)
Foco e stoppa non s'acorda (FF Ch. 19: 30v)	Fuoco e stoppa non s'accordano (GR 102)
Frati osservanti sparagnano il suo e mangiono quel d'altrui (FF Ch. 19: 30r)	Frati osservanti mangiano quel d'altri e sparagnano il loro (GR 103)
Freno indorato non migliora il cavallo (SF Ch. 7: 122) Freno indorato non migliora il cavallo né guaina d'oro coltello di piombo (SF Ch. 12: 194)	Freno indorato non migliora il cavallo (GR 102) In guaina d'oro, coltello di piombo (GR 123)
Fuggi donne, vino e dado, se non il tuo fatto è spacciato (SF Ch. 6: 104)	Bocca, braghe e dado, il tuo fatto è spacciato (GR [14])

Index of Paremias

Fuggi l'acqua quiete, ne la corrente entra sicuramente (SF Ch. 6: 98)	Guardati da l'acqua quiete, nella corrente entra sicuramente (GR 110)
Fuggi le quistioni e non entrar mai in disputa né con hosti né con donne, ma paga et va con Dio (SF Ch. 6: 98)	
Fuggi quel piacer presente che ti dà dolor futuro (FF Ch. 19: 30r; SF Ch. 6: 98)	Fuggi quel piacer presente che ti dà dolor futuro (GR 103)
Gatto guantato non piglia sorgi (SF Ch. 7: 120) Gatto guantato non piglia sorzi (FF Ch. 19: 30r)	Gatto guantato non piglia sorgi (GR 107)
Gente d'Essaù, chi le ha avute una volta non le vuole più (SF Ch. 12: 180)	
Giugno, luglio et agosto, non toccar né donna né mosto (SF Ch. 6: 104)	Giugno, luglio et agosto, non toccar né donna né mosto (GR 110)
Gli amici tuoi pigliali quando vuoi (SF Ch. 6: 104)	Gli amici pigliali quando tu puoi (GR 108)
Grand'amore, gran dolore (FF Ch. 19: 30r)	Grand'amore, gran dolore (GR 107) Dov'è grand'amore, ivi è gran dolore (GR 47)
Grand'e grossa mi faccia Dio che bianca e rossa mi farò io (FF Ch. 19: 30r)	Grande e grassa mi faccia Dio che bella et bianca mi farò io (GR 110)
Gran navi, gran pensieri (FF Ch. 19: 30r)	Gran nave, gran pensiere (GR 108)

Index of Paremias

Gratie non aspettate soglion esser più grate (SF Ch. 6: 104)	Gratie non aspettate sogliono esser più grate (GR 108)
Guancia polita, fronte ardita (SF Ch. 6: 96)	
Guarda bene inanzi che tu salti (FF Ch. 19: 34v)	Guarda inanzi che tu salti (GR 107)
Guardate di non mandarle per la posta delle lumache (SF Ch. 6: 88)	Lui scrive per la posta delle lumache (GR 140)
Guardatevi d'aceto et da vino dolce et da la cholera d'un homo pacifico (FF Ch. 19: 30v)	Guardati d'aceto di vin dolce (GR 107)
Guardatevi dal non ci pensai né vogliate comprar penitentia a troppo alto pretio (SF Ch. 12: 164)	
Guardatevi da questo lupo involto in pelle pecorina, il quale sotto forma di colomba porta coda di scorpione (SF Ch. 12: 170)	Sotto forma di colomba portar coda di scorpione (GR 193)
Guardati da debiti, tempera la voglie e modera la lingua (SF Ch. 9: 144)	
Habbi sempre la mano al cappello et alla borsa (SF Ch. 6: 92)	
Havete buon vicino e per conseguentia buon matino (SF Ch. 4: 56)	
Havete dato su la brocca (SF Ch. 9: 142)	Dare nella brocca (GR 87)
Havete la coscientia del lupo (SF Ch. 7: 120)	

Index of Paremias

Havete tolto una cattiva gatta a pettinare (SF Ch. 12: 172)	Haver mala gatta a pelare (GR 111)
Homo condannato è mezo degolato (FF Ch. 19: 30*v*)	Huomo condannato è mezzo degolato (GR 111)
Homo da confini, overo l'è ladro overo assasino (FF Ch. 19: 30*v*)	Huomo da confino, o ladro o assassino (GR 111)
Homo peloso, o che l'è matto over venturoso (FF Ch. 19: 30*v*)	Huomo peloso, o matto o venturoso (GR 111)
Homo rosso e femina barbata, tre miglia de lontan la saluta (FF Ch. 19: 30*v*)	Huomo rosso e donna barbuta, tre miglia di lontano gli saluta (GR 113)
I denari fanno correre i cavalli (FF Ch. 19: 30*v*)	Denari fanno correr i cavalli (GR 88)
I fatti sono maschi e le parole femine (FF Ch. 19: 32*v*) Le parole sono femine et i fatti sono maschi (SF Ch. 12: 176)	I fatti sono maschi e le parole femine (GR 118)
Il buon marito fa la buona moglie (SF Ch. 12: 192)	
Il corvo per troppo gracchiare del cibo si lascia privare (SF Ch. 6: 100)	Il corvo per troppo gracchiar perde il suo cibo (GR 121)
Il dolce cibo vuol la salsa amara (SF Ch. 12: 168)	Dolce vivanda vuole salsa acerba (GR 47)
Il fine fa tutti equali (FF Ch. 19: 31*r*)	

Il fuoco aiuta il cuoco (SF Ch. 4: 52)	Il fuoco aiuta il cuoco (GR 117)
Il giuoco è un tarlo che rode fin su l'osso (SF Ch. 6: 100)	
Il mal anno che Dio ti dia (SF Ch. 1: 6)	
Il mappamondo né la carta da navicare non la troveria, né Mercurio con tutta quanta la sua malitia (SF Ch. 8: 132)	
Il mio cuoco mi serve bene (SF Ch. 4: 48)	
Il Pensa non harebbe pensato a tanta malitia (SF Ch. 8: 132)	
Il principio è paura, il mezzo peccato et il fine dolore è noia (SF Ch. 12: 170)	
Il ricco quando vuole, il povero quando puole (SF Ch. 6: 84)	
Il savio non si deve vergognar di mutar proposito (FF Ch. 19: 32v)	Il savio non si dee vergognar di mutar proposito (GR 118)
Il secreto è laudabile (FF Ch. 19: 31r)	
Il secreto si deve celare (FF Ch. 19: 31r)	Se vuoi sia secreto non lo dire (GR 193)
Il serpente tra i fiori et l'herba giace (SF Ch. 12: 170)	Il serpente tra fiori e la herba giace (GR 114)

Il spagnolo per star sano fa un buon pasto, un cattivo et un mezzano (SF Ch. 10: 150)	Un buon pasto, un cattivo et un mezzano, mantien l'huomo sano (GR 211)
Il sparagno è il primo guandagno (SF Ch. 6: 102) El sparagno è il primo guadagno (FF Ch. 19: 29v)	Il sparagno è il primo guadagno (GR 118)
Il suo amor si cambia come fa il nuvolo la state (SF Ch. 12: 174)	
Il tempo è padre de la verità e l'esperientia è madre de le cose (FF Ch. 19: 32v)	Il tempo è padre della verità e l'esperientia madre delle cose (GR 127)
Il troppo amore fa spesso occhio ben sano veder torto (SF Ch. 6: 82)	Amor occhio ben sano spesso fa veder torto (GR 3)
Il tutto saporisce e condisce il sale (SF Ch. 4: 52)	Ogni cosa saporisce il sale (GR 172)
Il vitio non è egli maschio et la virtù non è lei femina (SF Ch. 12: 176)	
Il vostro credo non si canta in chiesa (SF Ch. 12: 178)	Il suo credo non si canta in chiesa (GR 124)
I matti fanno le feste e i savi le godeno (FF Ch. 19: 30v)	I matti fanno le feste et i savi le godono (GR 118)
Impara una arte et mettila da parte ché tempo vegnerà che la ti bisognerà (FF Ch. 19: 31r)	Impara l'arte e mettila da parte ché tempo verrà la ti bisognerà (GR 126)

Imprestar e mai non rendere, assai promettere e poco attendere, ben guadagnar e poco spendere, farà presto l'huomo richo (FF Ch. 14: 14r) Imprestar e mai non rendere, assai prometter e poco attendere, ben guadagnar e poco spendere, sono tre cose da inrichirsi (FF Ch. 19: 30v)	
In bocca ha miele et il rasoio alla cintola (SF Ch. 12: 170)	Lui ha miele in bocca et il rasoio alla cintola (GR 140) Oh che mele in bocca e rasoio a cintola (GR 170)
In Cipro è bon mercato di tre cose, sale, zukaro e putane (FF Ch. 19: 30v)	In Cipro sono tre cose a buon mercato, sale, zucchero e puttane (GR 128)
In corpo storto di rado si truova un'anima retta (SF Ch. 12: [190])	
In corte chi non sa non ha (SF Ch. 9: 146)	
In corte chi sa mentire sa regnare (SF Ch. 9: 146)	
In Genova harete aria senza uccelli, marina senza pesce, montagne senza legna, huomini senza rispetto et donne senza vergogna (SF Ch. 6: 108)	

Index of Paremias

In Italia sono troppe feste, troppe teste e troppe tempeste (SF Ch. 6: 106)	In Italia sono troppo teste, troppo feste e troppo tempeste (GR 126)
In ogni luogo guardati da gli huomini rossi, dalle donne barbute e da' segnati da Dio (SF Ch. 6: 98)	
In Roma più vale la cortegiana che la donna romana (SF Ch. 6: 108)	In Roma più vale la cortegiana che la moglie romana (GR 122)
In una mano tiene il pane e con l'altra avventa la pietra (SF Ch. 12: 170)	
In una notte nasce un fungo (FF Ch. 19: 30v)	In una notte nasce un fongo (GR 114)
In virtù et in constantia vive e ciascheduna esser vuol quell'una, quantunque al mondo non sen truovi ch'una (SF Ch. 12: 178)	
Io credo che siate nato con l'amor in bocca, perché sempre date su quella brocca (SF Ch. 12: 168)	
Io credo in Dio e non nelle donne, quantunque ne facessero miracoli o che havessero il pegno in mano (SF Ch. 12: 178)	
Io domando acqua e non tempesta (SF Ch. 9: 138)	S'intende acqua e non tempesta (GR 194)
Io faccio il mestier di Michelazzo, mangio, bevo e vado a solazzo (SF Ch. 7: 114)	Far il mestier di Michelazzo (GR 104)

Io le farò ragione ma non alla todesca (SF Ch. 4: 60)	
Io lo conosco meglio che la madre che l'ha fatto (SF Ch. 7: 116)	
Io non andrei in prigione a ritorre un occhio, s'io ce lo havessi lasciato (SF Ch. 9: 144)	
Io non ci vorrei esser dipinto tanto odio et ho a schifo il luogo (SF Ch. 9: 144)	
Io non ho pelo adosso che ci pensi (SF Ch. 5: 68)	
Io non mi ricordo dal naso alla bocca (SF Ch. 1: 6)	Lui non si ricorda dal naso alla bocca (GR 138)
Io non so se l'anderà bene, diceva colei che dava un servitiale al suo marito con un buon bastone (SF Ch. 8: 136)	Io non so se l'anderà bene, diceva la moglie, che dava un servitiale a suo marito con un bastone (GR 128)
Io non vorrei esser solo in paradiso (SF Ch. 2: 14)	
Io prendo il panno per il verso e lascio correr l'acqua al mare (SF Ch. 9: 142)	
Io sono cavaliero da ogni sella (SF Ch. 3: 46)	Lui è cavagliere da ogni sella (GR 140)
Io stavo fresco s'io giuocavo quel cavallo (SF Ch. 5: 74)	

Io ti farò ben star in cervello (SF Ch. 1: 8)	
I panni rifanno le stanghe (SF Ch. 7: 114)	I panni rifanno le stanghe (GR 114)
I patti rompono le leggi (FF Ch. 19: 32*v*)	I patti rompono le leggi (GR 118) I patti e gl'accordi rompono le leggi (GR 126)
La bella donna è un bel cipresso senza frutto (SF Ch. 12: [190])	
La bella moglie è un dolce veneno (SF Ch. 12: [190])	
La bella robba fa l'huomo ladro (SF Ch. 12: 168) La bella robba fa l'huomo ladro (SF Ch. 12: [190])	La comodità fa l'huomo ladro (GR 130)
La bellezza delle donne è come un fiore che la mattina si mette in seno e la sera si getta in terra (SF Ch. 12: 168)	
La bellezza et l'honestà di rado s'accordano (SF Ch. 12: 192)	Virtù e fortuna di rado s'accordano (GR 213)
La bellissima [donna] è tesoro grandissimo (SF Ch. 12: [190])	
L'abondaza delle cose genera fastidio (FF Ch. 19: 32*r*)	L'abbondantia genera fastidio (GR 138)

Index of Paremias

La coda condanna spesso la volpe a morte per esser troppo lunga (FF Ch. 19: 31v)	La coda per esser troppo longa alle volte condanna la volpe (GR 139)
La conscientia serve per mille testimoni (FF Ch. 19: 32v)	La conscientia serve per mille testimoni (GR 139)
La corte romana non vuole pecora senza lana (SF Ch. 6: 108)	La corte romana non vuole pecora senza lana (GR 145) Corte romana non vuol pecora senza lana (GR 21)
L'acqua lontana non spegne fuoco vicino (SF Ch. 12: 198) Acqua lontana non spegne fuoco vicino (SF Ch. 7: 122)	Acqua lontana non ispegne fuoco vicino (GR 1)
L'acqua marcisce fino i pali (SF Ch. 4: 48)	L'acqua fa marcire i pali (GR 132)
La fame è quella che caccia il lupo del bosco (SF Ch. 7: 124)	La fame fa uscir il lupo del bosco (GR 140)
La legge nasce del peccato et lo gastiga (FF Ch. 19: 32v)	La legge nasce dal peccato e lo castiga (GR 139)
L'alegreze di questo mondo duran poco (FF Ch. 19: 32r)	Le allegrezze di questo mondo duran poco (GR 139)
La lingua corre dove il dente duole (SF Ch. 12: 168)	La lingua corre dove il dente vuole (GR 141)
La lode in corte è cibo delle orecchie et un nome vano (SF Ch. 9: 146)	

La Lombardia è il giardino del mondo (SF Ch. 6: 106) Lombardia è il giardino del mondo (FF Ch. 19: 31v)	La Lombardia è il giardino del mondo (GR 139)
La mala compagnia è quella che mena molti alla forca (FF Ch. 19: 31v)	La mala compagnia mena gl'huomini a le forche (GR 139)
La mala herba cresce presto (FF Ch. 19: 31v)	Herba cattiva tosto cresce (GR 111)
La maraviglia è figliola de l'ignoranza (FF Ch. 19: 32v)	La maraviglia è figliuola dell'ignoranza (GR 139)
L'amaro chi non vuol gustare non gusti il dolce dell'amare (SF Ch. 12: 166)	
L'amor di donna lieve è come vin di fiasco, la sera è buono et la mattina è guasto (SF Ch. 12: 174) Amor di putana e vin di fiasco, la sera è buono, la matina è guast[o] (FF Ch. 19: 27v)	Amor di donna è come il vin di fiasco, la sera è buono la mattina è guasto (GR 13)
L'amor passa il guanto, la scommessa è fatta (SF Ch. 11: 156)	L'amore passa il guanto (GR 138)
La morte de' lupi è sanità de le pecore (FF Ch. 19: 31v)	La morte de' lupi sanità è delle pecore (GR 139)
La morte segue chi la fugge et chi la fugge chiama alle ortiche, che pongono chi le tocca leggiermente ma non offendono chi le preme (SF Ch. 12: 174)	

La necessità non ha legge (FF Ch. 19: 32v; SF Ch. 4: [64][8])	La necessità non ha né re né legge (GR 136)
La notte è madre de' pensieri (FF Ch. 19: 31v)	La notte è madre de' pensieri (GR 138)
La peggior carne che sia al mondo è quella de l'huomo (FF Ch. 19: 31v)	La peggior carne è quella dell'huomo (GR 138)
La porta di dietro guasta la casa (FF Ch. 19: 31v)	La porta di dietro guasta la casa (GR 139)
La povertà non è vitio ma solo in comodità (SF Ch. 6: 104)	Povertà non è vitio (GR 178)
La prima parte del pazzo è di tenersi savio (FF Ch. 19: 32v)	Il primo capitolo de' matti è di tenersi savio (GR 118)
L'aqua fa male, il vino fa cantare (FF Ch. 19: 31r)	L'acqua fa pianger, il vin cantar (GR 135)
L'aqua va al mare (FF Ch. 19: 31r)	Lascia andar l'acqua alla valle (GR 138) Lascia andar l'acqua alla china (GR 144)
La robba non è a chi la fa ma a chi la gode (FF Ch. 19: 31v)	La robba non è di chi la fa ma di chi la gode (GR 139)
Lascia il frutto per le foglie, rogna compra e pesca foglie, un pedante in casa toglie chi ricerca d'haver moglie (SF Ch. 12: 188)	Lascia il frutto per le foglie, rogna compra e pesca doglie, un pedante in casa toglie chi ricerca d'haver moglie (GR 147)
La Spagna, spugna de la nostra etade (SF Ch. 6: 108)	La Spagna, spugna della nostra etade (GR 130)

La speranza è l'ultima cosa de l'huomo (FF Ch. 19: 31v)	L'ultimo riffugio è la speranza o la morte (GR 139)
La terra non avvilisce l'oro (SF Ch. 12: 180)	
Lauda il mare e tienti alla terra; lauda il monte e tienti al piano; lauda la guerra e tienti alla pace; e lauda la moglie ma tienti donzello (SF Ch. 6: 98)	Lauda il mare e tienti a terra (GR 137) Lauda il monte e tienti al piano (GR 137) Lauda la guerra e tienti alla pace (GR 137) Lauda la moglie e tienti donzello (GR 137)
La vera legge è la natura (FF Ch. 19: 32v)	La vera legge è la natura (GR 139)
La vita passa e la morte viene (FF Ch. 19: 34r)	La vita passa e la morte viene (GR 139) Il tempo passa e la morte viene (GR 118)
La vostra voce non entra in paradiso (SF Ch. 12: 178)	
L'avvertito si può dir mezzo munito (SF Ch. 12: 168)	
Le belle parole et i cattivi fatti ingannano i savi et i matti (SF Ch. 2: 18)	Belle parole e cattivi fatti ingannano savi et matti (GR 18)
Le bone parole ongino, le cative pongino (FF Ch. 19: 31v) Delle parole, le buone ongono et le cattive pongono (SF Ch. 12: 176)	Le buone parole ongono, le cattive pongono (GR 139)

Le bugie hanno corte le gambe (FF Ch. 19: 31v)	Le bugie hanno corte le gambe (GR 139)
Le donne sono il purgatorio della borsa, il paradiso del corpo et l'inferno della anima (SF Ch. 12: 174)	
Le donne sono sante in chiesa, angele in strada, diavole in casa, sirene alla finestra, gazze alla porta e capre ne' giardini (SF Ch. 12: 174)	
Le donne sono simili a' cocodrilli che per prender l'huomo piangono e, preso, lo divorano (SF Ch. 12: 174)	
Lei fa come l'insegna dello spetiale, cioè né ben né male (SF Ch. 9: 144)	
Lei fa le fusa storte e manda il suo marito in Cornovaglia senza barca (SF Ch. 9: 142)	Fare le fusa storte (GR 103) Andar senza barca in Cornovaglia (GR 2)
Le lettere sono de li studiosi, le richeze de i soleciti, il mondo de' presuntuosi, il paradiso de' divoti (FF Ch. 19: 31v)	Il mondo è de' prosuntuosi, il paradisio de' devoti, le lettere sono de' studiosi e le richezze de' solleciti (GR 127)
Le parole sono femine et i fatti sono maschi (SF Ch. 12: 176) I fatti sono maschi e le parole femine (FF Ch. 19: 32v)	I fatti sono maschi e le parole femine (GR 118)

Le perle crescono nelle conche, le gemme nelle rupi, l'oro et l'argento nelle mine et il miele è prodotto dalle api (SF Ch. 12: 180)	
Le più limpide acque scatturiscono da le più dure pietre (SF Ch. 12: 180)	
L'hai tolta bella, a tuo danno sia (SF Ch. 12: [190])	L'hai tolta bella? A tuo danno (GR 140)
L'havessi io saputo, vien troppo tardi (FF Ch. 19: 34*v*)	L'havessi io saputo, sempre è tardi (GR 139)
L'huomo propone e Dio dispone (FF Ch. 19: 32*v*) L'huomo compone e Dio dispone (FF Ch. 6: 6*r*)	L'huomo propone e Dio dispone (GR 139)
L'infante brugiato teme il foco (FF Ch. 19: 31*r*)	
L'Inghilterra è il paradiso delle donne, il purgatorio de gli huomini et lo inferno de' cavalli (SF Ch. 12: 204)	
L'ingiuria che non vuoi vendicare non la voler mai publicare (SF Ch. 6: 100)	La ingiuria non publicare che non vuoi vendicare (GR 131)
Lingua bardella e che in fretta favella (FF Ch. 19: 31*v*)	Lingua bardella, per sette saltella (GR 139)

Lingua chieditrice, pensier espilatrice (SF Ch. 12: 196)	
L'innocentia porta seco sua d[e]fensione (FF Ch. 19: 31v)	L'innocentia porta seco la sua deffensione (GR 139)
L'ira placata non rifà l'ofese (FF Ch. 19: 31r)	L'ira placata non rifà l'offese (GR 139)
L'ochio del patron ingrassa il cavallo (FF Ch. 19: 31v)	L'occhio del patrone ingrassa il cavallo (GR 138)
L'odor de gli odori si è il pane; il sapore de sapori si è il sale; l'amor de gli amori sono i figliuoli (FF Ch. 40: [90]⁹v)	
L'orbo mangia molte mosce (FF Ch. 19: 34r)	Chi è cieco mangia molte mosche (GR 29)
L'oro ha la istessa virtù che ha la carità, cioè cuopre una infinità di peccati (SF Ch. 6: 92)	
Lui è come un stizon di fuoco, alluma altrui et si brucia se stesso (FF Ch. 19: 34r)	
Lui è povero come Iob (FF Ch. 19: 31r)	
Lui ha due faccie sotto una beretta (FF Ch. 19: 31r)	Due visi sotto una beretta (GR 90)
Lui mette il carro inanzi al cavallo (FF Ch. 19: 31r)	Metter il carro inanzi i buo' (GR 150)

Lui porta fuoco in una mano et aqua in l'altra (FF Ch. 19: 31r)	Haver acqua nell'una e fuoco nell'altra mano (GR 113)
Lui robba Pietro per pagar san Paulo (FF Ch. 19: 31r)	Lui spoglia Pietro per vestir Paolo (GR 139)
Madonna Ingordigia con sua sirocchia Avaritia, che poco fa si sono maritate a quei che come cavalli mordono et piangono (SF Ch. 3: 38)	
Maggior fretta minor atto e per troppo spronar la fuga è tarda (SF Ch. 1: 8)	Maggior fretta, minor atto (GR 151) Per troppo spronar la fuga è tarda (GR 177)
Mal anno e mala moglie non manca mai (FF Ch. 19: 32r)	Mal anno e mala moglie non manca mai (GR 151)
Maritasi un donna, over compra una nave (FF Ch. 19: 30v)	
Matto per natura e savio per scritura (FF Ch. 19: 32r)	Matto per natura e savio per scrittura (GR 151) Essere savio per scrittura e matto per natura (GR 98) Savio per lettera e matto per natura (GR 192)
Medico pietoso fa la piaga tegnosa (FF Ch. 19: 32r)	Medico pietoso fa la piaga rognosa (GR 151)

Meglio è dar la lana che la pecora (FF Ch. 19: 32r)	È meglio donar la lana che la pecora (GR 97)
Meglio è esser confessore che martire (FF Ch. 19: 32r)	È meglio esser confessore che martire (GR 97)
Meglio è haver mezzo un pane che non ne haver niente (FF Ch. 19: 34v)	Meglio è un pezzo di pane che niente (GR 151)
Meglio è un magro accordo che una grassa sentenza (FF Ch. 19: 32r)	Meglio è magro accordo che grassa sententia (GR 151)
Anche io so menar l'oche a bere quando piove (SF Ch. 4: 52)	Anche io so menar l'oche a bere quando piove (GR 5)
Mettere il borsotto nel borsetto (SF Ch. 9: 142)	
Metti il matto sul bancho, o gioca di piede o di canto (FF Ch. 19: 32r)	
Miglior medicina che pisciar chiaro per poter far le fiche al medico (SF Ch. 4: 60)	Piscia chiaro e fa le fiche al medico (GR 175)
Milan può far, Milan può dire, ma non può far di acqua vino (SF Ch. 6: 106)	Milan può far, Milan può dir, ma non può far d'aqua vin (GR 152)
Minor pena Tantalo pate nell'inferno che non fa chi sta di donna al governo (SF Ch. 12: 174)	Minor pena Tantalo pate nell'inferno che non fa chi sta di donna al governo (GR 155)

Index of Paremias

Misero chi speme in cor di donna pone (SF Ch. 3: 28) Misero è quello che speme in cuor di donna pone (SF Ch. 12: 178)	Misero chi speme in cor di donna pone (GR 151)
Misuratene sempre tre prima che tagliarne uno (SF Ch. 6: 96)	
Mi vorreste render pane per focaccia (SF Ch. 10: 152) Rendergli pan per focaccia (SF Ch. 2: 18)	Rendere pane per focaccia (GR 187)
Molte volte le ciancie riescono a lancie (SF Ch. 6: 96)	Spesso le ciancie riescono a lancie (GR 195)
Muro bianco, carta de matti (FF Ch. 19: 32r)	Muro bianco, carta di matto (GR 149)
Napolitano, largo di bocca, stretto di mano (SF Ch. 6: 108)	Napolitano, largo di bocca, stretto di mano (GR 161)
Né amor né signoria vuol compagnia (FF Ch. 19: 33r)	Né amor né signoria vuole compagnia (GR 160)
Né donna né gioia né tela non pigliar mai alla candela (SF Ch. 7: 124) Né femina né tela non piglia a la candela (FF Ch. 19: 32v)	Né donne, gioie o tela non pigliar alla candela (GR 160)
Né guanto né beretta mai fu troppo stretta (SF Ch. 7: 122)	Guanto, figa e beretta non fu mai troppo stretta (GR 108)
Nelle guerre d'amor chi la fugge la vince (SF Ch. 12: 170)	Nelle guerre d'amor chi fugge vince (GR 156)

Nel mezzo consiste la virtù, disse il diavolo trovandosi tra due monache (SF Ch. 4: 48)	Virtù consiste in mezzo (GR 213)
Né occhi in lettera né mani in tasca d'altrui (FF Ch. 19: 33r) Non haver mai né occhio in lettere, né mano in tasca, né orecchie in secreti d'altri (SF Ch. 6: 96)	Né occhi in lettera né man in tasca né orecchie in secreti altrui (GR 163)
Né salata né donna né capone non perse mai stagione (SF Ch. 12: 204)	
Nessuno dà quel che non ha (FF Ch. 19: 33r)	Nessuno dà quello che non ha (GR 160)
Non aspettar, s'esser servito vuoi, servitio altrui se tu servir ti puoi (SF Ch. 6: 102)	Non aspettar, s'esser servito vuoi, servitio altrui se tu servir ti puoi (GR 167)
Non ci è mai fumo senza fuoco (FF Ch. 19: 31r)	Non ci è fumo senza fuoco (GR 161)
Non ci sarà mai grido in quella casa dove che il patrone è orbo et la patrona sorda (FF Ch. 19: 28r)	Non può esser guerra in quella casa dove il marito è cieco e la moglie sorda (GR 166)
Non di quelle del dottor Grillo (SF Ch. 4: 60)	Soccorso del dottor Grillo (GR 195)
Non dir mai né donde vieni né dove vai (SF Ch. 6: 98)	
Non dovresti mangiar altro che heleboro (SF Ch. 8: 135)	Haver bisogno di heleboro (GR 112)

Index of Paremias

Non è al mondo né mai fu né sia cuor che da donna alfin vinto non sia (SF Ch. 12: 182)	Non è al mondo né mai fu né fia cuor che d'amor legato al fin non sia (GR 166)
Non è virtù che povertà non guasti (FF Ch. 19: 32r)	Non è virtù che povertà non guasti (GR 160)
Non far ad altri quello che non vuoi per te (SF Ch. 6: 102)	
Non fu mai sì bella scarpa che non diventasse una ciavatta, né si vaga rosa che non diventasse un grattaculo (SF Ch. 6: 104)	Non fu mai sì bella scarpa che non divenisse ciavatta (GR 156) Non fu mai sì vaga rosa che non diventasse grattaculo (GR 156)
Non gittar mai tanto con le mani che tu sii costretto andarlo cercando poi co' piedi (SF Ch. 6: 102)	Non gittar del tuo tanto con le mani che tu lo vadi poi cercando co' piedi (GR 166)
Non hai più ingegno ch'il Savoiano che disfece la sua casa per poter vender il calcinaccio, o Gian de la Vigna che vendette una bella vigna per comprar una cantina (SF Ch. 8: 130)	Romper la casa per vender il calcinaccio (GR 187)
Non mostra mai né il fondo della tua borsa né quello del tuo animo (SF Ch. 6: 100)	
Non scoprir l'ammalato quando suda (SF Ch. 4: 52)	Non discoprir il malato quando suda (GR 156)

Index of Paremias

Non ti disperare per fortuna avversa ché la sua ruota sempre in giro versa (SF Ch. 6: 102) Né disperarsi per fortuna aversa ché la sua rota sempre in giro versa (FF Ch. 19: 30v)	Non ti disperare per fortuna avversa ché la sua ruota sempre in giro versa (GR 166)
Non ti fidar d'amici finti (SF Ch. 6: 100)	
Non ti fidar di donna alcuna ché lei si volta come fa la luna (SF Ch. 3: 28)	Non ti fidar di donna alcuna ché lei si muta come fa la luna (GR 166)
Non ti fidar di nissuno se prima non mangi seco un moggio di sale (SF Ch. 6: 100)	
Non ti metter a giuocare se non vuoi periclitare (SF Ch. 6: 100)	
Non ti motteggiar del vero (SF Ch. 6: 104)	Non ti motteggiar del vero (GR 161; 163)
Non trescar mai con nissuno che doglia (SF Ch. 6: 104)	Non trescar che doglia (GR 163)
Non vogliate mai dar fede a' faremo di Roma, agli adesso adesso d'Italia, a' magnana di Spagna, a' by and by d'Inghilterra, a' warant you di Scotia, a' tantost di Francia, perché tutte sono ciancie (SF Ch. 6: 94)	
Non voler esser troppo pertinace, perché al più potente cede il più prudente (SF Ch. 6: 102)	Al più potente ceda il più prudente (GR 13)

Non voler mai metter liquor pretioso in nuovo ma, inanzi che ci metti vino, guarda se tiene acqua (SF Ch. 6: 98)	
Noze e magistrato sono del ciel destinato (FF Ch. 19: 33r)	Nozze e magistrato dal cielo destinato (GR 160)
Nul bene senza pene (FF Ch. 19: 33r)	Nessun bene senza pene (GR 160)
Occhio bello, animo bello (SF Ch. 12: 196)	
O che tu mi cacci pur le grosse carotte? (SF Ch. 8: 128)	
Odio fra gli amici è soccorso de gli stranieri (FF Ch. 19: 33r)	Odio fra gl'amici è soccorso a' nemici (GR 171)
Odi, vedi et taci se vuoi viver in pace (SF Ch. 6: 100) Odi, vedi e taci se tu vuoi vivere in pace (FF Ch. 19: 31r)	Odi, vedi e taci se vuoi viver in pace (GR 171)
Oglio, ferro e sale, mercantia regale (FF Ch. 19: 33r)	Oglio, ferro e sale, mercantia reale (GR 171)
Ogni carne fa buon bruodo, purché s'habbia fame (SF Ch. 8: 130)	Carne vecchia fa buon brodo (GR 21)
Ogni dieci anni l'uno ha bisogno de l'altro (FF Ch. 19: 33r)	Ogni dieci anni l'uno ha bisogno dell'altro (GR 171)

Ogni dì viene la sera (FF Ch. 19: 33r)	Non vien dì che non venghi sera (GR 160) Ogni bello e gran giorno ha sera (GR 169)
Ogni estremità è vitio (FF Ch. 19: 32v)	Ogni estremo è vitio (GR 171)
Ogni parola non vuol risposta (FF Ch. 19: 32v)	Ogni parola non vuol risposta (GR 171)
Ogni scuffia ti serve di notte (SF Ch. 8: 130)	Ogni lorda scuffia serve di notte (GR 169)
Ogni timidità è vitio (FF Ch. 19: 32v)	Ogni timidità è vitio (GR 171)
Ogni tristo cane mena la coda (FF Ch. 19: 33r)	Ogni tristo cane mena la coda (GR 170)
Ogni ucello non conosce il bon grano (FF Ch. 19: 33r)	Ogni uccello non conosce il buon grano (GR 170)
Ogniuno con arte et con inganno vive mezzo l'anno e con inganno et con arte vive l'altra parte (SF Ch. 6: 104) Con arte e con inganno si vive mezo l'anno, con inganno e con arte si vive l'altra parte (FF Ch. 19: [28]r)	Con arte e con inganno si vive mezzo l'anno (GR 27) Con inganno e con arte si vive l'altra parte (GR 27)
Ogni uno per sé et il diavolo per tutti (FF Ch. 19: 33r)	Ogni un per sé e Dio per tutti (GR 170)

Ogniuno tira l'aqua al suo molino (FF Ch. 14: 14r) Tutti tirano l'aqua al suo molino (FF Ch. 19: 33v)	Ogni uno tira l'acqua al suo molino (GR 168)
O huomo insano e pieno di sciochezza che pensa in donna di trovar fermezza (SF Ch. 12: 182)	O huomo insano e pieno di sciocchezza che pensa in donna di trovar fermezza (GR 173)
O maledetto sesso, abietto et immondo, nato solo per purgar l'huomo al mondo (SF Ch. 12: 172)	
O servi come servo o fuggi come cervo (SF Ch. 6: 104)	O servi come servo o fugge come cervo (GR 171)
O torto o ragione non andar in prigione (SF Ch. 9: 140)	O ragione o non ragione non andar in prigione (GR 168)
Pan padovano, vin vicentino, carne furlana, formaggio piacentino, trippe trevigiane e donne venetiane (SF Ch. 6: 106)	
Parente con parente, guai a chi non ha niente (FF Ch. 19: 32v)	Parente con parente, guai a chi non ha niente (GR 174)
Pari con pari bene sta et dura (FF Ch. 19: 32v)	Pari con pari bene sta e dura (GR 174)
Parole di zuccaro per addolcir gli suoi, se non veneni, almeno purgationi (SF Ch. 12: 196)	

Parole, parole senza sugo, l'amor ci dà la vita et in vita et in morte il tutto amor governa (SF Ch. 12: 176)	
Patisco il male sperando il bene (FF Ch. 19: 33r)	Soffri il male et aspetta il bene (GR 191)
Peccato celato è mezo perdonato (FF Ch. 19: 32v)	Peccato celato è mezzo perdonato (GR 174)
Peccato vechio, penitenza nuova (FF Ch. 19: 32v)	Peccato vecchio, penitentia nuova (GR 174)
Per far una cacciata tale potrebbono esser finte (SF Ch. 9: 138)	
Per ogni verità che ti esce di bocca ti salta fuori una lepre del culo (SF Ch. 8: 132)	
Per tutto c'è da fare, diceva colui che ferrava le oche (SF Ch. 6: 84)	Per tutto c'è da far, diceva colui che ferrava l'oche (GR 175)
Per una o due donne che si trovin ree, che cento buone sian creder si dee (SF Ch. 12: 178)	
Per un piacer mille dolori si truova haver chi segue amore (SF Ch. 12: 176)	
Per un ponto Martin perse la cappa (SF Ch. 5: 68)	Per un ponto Martin perse la cappa (GR 179)
Pesa giusto e vendi caro (FF Ch. 19: 33r)	Pesa giusto e vendi caro (GR 174)

Petto d'alabastro, se lo miri è bellissimo, se lo tocchi è durissimo (SF Ch. 12: 196)	
Piacer preso in fretta riesce in disdetta (SF Ch. 12: 164)	Chi fa in fretta ha disdetta (GR 26)
Piglia il bene quando puoi (SF Ch. 6: 100)	Piglia il bene quando viene (GR 177)
Più ch'il peccato, se la vedeste per fuggirla saltereste in qualche calcinaccio (SF Ch. 9: 144)	
Più morde la penna di un letterato che non fa il dente di alcun serpente (SF Ch. 6: 96)	
Più ne hai manco noia (SF Ch. 5: 66)	
Più per dolcezza che per forza (FF Ch. 19: 33r)	
Più presso la chiesa, più lontano da Dio (FF Ch. 19: 31r)	Più presso alla chiesa, più lontan da Dio (GR 174)
Più tira un sol pelo d'una bella donna che non fanno cento paia di buoi (SF Ch. 12: 182)	Più tira un pel di donna che cento paia di buoi (GR 175)
Più valente che la spada (SF Ch. 7: 116)	
Poche parole bastano fra gli homini savi (FF Ch. 19: 31r)	Poche parole fra gl'huomini savi (GR 174)
Poco fa chi a se non giova (FF Ch. 19: 31r)	Poco fa chi a se non giova (GR 174)

Index of Paremias

Poco senno basta a chi fortuna sona (FF Ch. 19: 33r)	Pocco senno basta a chi fortuna aplaude (GR 174)
Poi c'ha gustato, corre amante con l'amata sua donna a far la tresca (SF Ch. 12: 168)	
Potendo andar per terra, non andar mai per acqua (SF Ch. 2: 16)	
Presto maturo, presto marzo (FF Ch. 19: 34v)	
Punge la bella donna ad una volta occhi più che mille lancie e tanti stocchi (SF Ch. 12: 182)	
Putti e matti indovinano (FF Ch. 19: 33r)	Putti o matti indovinano (GR 174)
Qual è l'arbore, tale è il frutto (SF Ch. 12: 178) Tal è l'arbore, tal è il frutto (FF Ch. 19: 34v)	Qual è l'arbore, tal è il frutto (GR 185)
Qual vita, tal fine (FF Ch. 19: 33r)	Qual vita, tal fine (GR 185)
Quand'il marito fa terra, la moglie fa carne (SF Ch. 12: 192)	
Quando che il cavallo è rubbato, serra la porta de la stalla (FF Ch. 19: 31r)	Quand'il cavallo è rubbato, non val serrar la stalla (GR 185)
Quando il cieco guida il cieco, amenduo si truovan nella fossa (SF Ch. 12: 168)	
Quando la gatta non è in casa, i sorzi b[a]llano (FF Ch. 19: 33r)	Quando la gatta non c'è, i sorgi trescano (GR 185)

Quando l'ha ben tonato, è forza che piovi (FF Ch. 19: 33r)	Quando ha ben tuonato, è forza che piovi (GR 185)
Quando sei incudine ubidisci al martello, ma quando martello attendi a martellare (SF Ch. 6: 100)	Quando s'è incudine, convien soffrire (GR 185) Quando s'è martello, convien percuotere (GR 186)
Quanto in più gioventute et in più bellezza, tanto par che l'honestà sua laude accresca (SF Ch. 12: 194)	
Quanto più si ha, tanto più si desidera (FF Ch. 19: 32r)	
Quantunque la lingua non habbia osso, la fa spesso romper il dosso (SF Ch. 6: 96)	La lingua non ha osso e pur fa romper ossi (GR 137)
Quantunque un gallo basti a dieci galline, dieci huomini non bastano ad una donna (SF Ch. 12: 184)	Un gallo basta a dieci galline, ma non dieci huomini ad una donna (GR 216)
Quel che tu stesso puoi e dire e fare, che altri il faccia mai non aspettare (SF Ch. 6: 102)	Quello che tu stesso puoi e dir e fare, ch'altri il faccia mai non aspettare (GR 187)
Quelli che hanno ducati, signori sono chiamati (SF Ch. 6: 92)	Coloro c'hanno ducati, signori son chiamati (GR 27)
Quello che meno pesa et più vale (SF Ch. 5: [64])	
Questa legna è verde, bruscia e non fa fiamma (SF Ch. 11: 156)	

Questi nostri vini sono buoni Christiani, perché sono ben battezzati (SF Ch. 4: 62)	
Questo vostro servitore è di levante (SF Ch. 4: 56)	
Radigo non fa pagamento (FF Ch. 19: 33r) Radigo non è pagamento (SF Ch. 7: 122)	Radigo non è pagamento (GR 187)
Ragione deve esser in conseglio (FF Ch. 19: 33r)	Ragion deve esser in consiglio (GR 187)
Razza di susagna, chi perde il suo amore assai guadagna (SF Ch. 12: 180)	Gente di susagna, chi perde il suo amore assai guadagna (GR 110)
Recipe delle pillole di gallina, elettuario di cucina, siloppo di cantina, con buona pasta di farina (SF Ch. 4: 60)	
Rendergli pan per focaccia (SF Ch. 2: 18) Mi vorreste render pane per focaccia (SF Ch. 10: 152)	Rendere pane per focaccia (GR 187)
Rendono più frutto donne, asini e noci a chi ver loro ha più le mani atroci (SF Ch. 12: 174)	Rendono più frutto donne, asini e noci a chi ver loro ha più le man atroci (GR 189)
Riescono amici da stranuti, il più che ne hai e un Dio ti aiuti (SF Ch. 6: 100)	Amico da stranuti, il più che n'hai e un Dio t'aiuti (GR 2)

Sangue d'huomo non rompe già diamanti, ma sangue di becco sì (SF Ch. 9: 142)	
Sapientia di pover'huomo e forza di facchino e bellezza di puttana non vaglion un quattrino (SF Ch. 12: [190])	Sapientia di pover huomo, forza di facchino e belezza di puttana non vaglion un quattrino (GR 199)
Scientia non è peso (FF Ch. 19: 34v)	Scientia non è peso (GR 191)
Sciocco è colui che pensa contro amore, o santo o cattivo o sia pien di valore (SF Ch. 12: 182)	Sciocco è colui che pensa contro amore, o santo o cattivo o sia pien di valore (GR 200)
Se brutta ella è un sfinamento e se bella un tormento (SF Ch. 12: [190]) Se brutta non è sfinimento, se bella non è un tormento, se ricca può mantenermi, se povera può piacermi, se vergine è pieghevole, se vedova è esperimentata, se giovane è piacevole, se vecchia è profittevole (SF Ch. 12: [190])	
Secondo il tempo fate et secondo il tempo navigate (SF Ch. 6: 96)	
Se è grande è otiosa, se è picciola è ritrosa. Se è bella, è neghittosa, se è brutta è fastidiosa. Se è vergine è inesperta, se vedova è ostinata, se giovane è lasciva, se vecchia è spiacevole, se grassa è pastosa, se magra è carogna (SF Ch. 12: 188)	

Se hai il lupo per compagno, porta il cane sotto il mantello (SF Ch. 6: 96)	Chi ha il lupo per compagno porti il can sott'il mantello (GR 30)
Sei d'una natura tanto perversa e scialacquata che faresti uscir del seminato un santo (SF Ch. 8: 135) Sete fuori del seminato (SF Ch. 12: 166)	Tu esci del seminato (GR 206)
Sei hore dorme lo studiante, sette il viandante, otto il lavorante et nove ogni furfante (SF Ch. 11: 162)	Cinque hore dorme il viandante, sette il studiante, otto il mercatante et undeci ogni furfante (GR 43)
Se il letto è picciolo mettiti in mezzo (SF Ch. 6: 94)	In letto stretto mettiti in mezzo (GR 123)
Sei più smemorato che l'oblio (SF Ch. 8: 135)	
Se la donna ama lo fa per novità, cioè una volta in sette anni (SF Ch. 12: 174)	
Se la donna fosse così picciola come è buona, il minimo bacello le farebbe una veste et una corona (SF Ch. 12: 174)	Se la donna fosse piccola come è buona, la minima foglia le farebbe una veste et una corona (GR 200)
Se 'l cielo casca, haveremo quaglie (FF Ch. 19: 31r)	Se il ciel casca, haveremo quaglie (GR 191)

Index of Paremias

Se le donne fossero d'argento o d'oro, non varrebbero un quattrino perché non starebbono mai né a tocco né a martello (SF Ch. 12: 180)	Se le donne fossero d'argento, non varrebbon un quattrino perché non starebbon al martello (GR 198)
Se lui mi batte con la spada, io lo batterò con il fodro (SF Ch. 2: 18)	Chi percuote con la spada, sarà percosso col fodro (GR 38)
Se mi bravate con la loica, io vi colpirò con la gramatica (SF Ch. 12: 176)	
Se mortal velo il mio veder appanna, che colpa è delle stelle o delle cose belle? (SF Ch. 12: 194)	Che colpa n'han le stelle e le cose belle? (GR 37)
Sempre a beltà fu leggiezza amica, della beltà compagna è la fierezza (SF Ch. 12: 196)	Sempre a beltà fu leggierezza amica (GR 193) De la beltà compagna è la fierezza (GR 47)
Se non ci fosse vento o femina nata, né in mar né in terra si sentirebbe mai mala giornata (SF Ch. 12: 182)	Se non ci fosse vento o femina nata, non ci saria mai né tempesta né mala giornata (GR 198)
Senza denari non canta Marcantonio (SF Ch. 3: 38)	Senza denari Georgio non canta (GR 190) Haver l'humor di Marcantonio (GR 111)
Senza virtù è viso bello, bella testa non ha cervello (SF Ch. 12: [190])	

Se per sorte se ne truova una che ami, si può dir essere miracolo, e miracoli non duran che nuove giorni (SF Ch. 12: 174)	
Se più che crini havesse occhi il marito, non potria far che non fosse tradito (SF Ch. 12: 192)	Se più che crini havesse occhi il marito, non potria far che non fosse tradito (GR 198)
Sete fuori del seminato (SF Ch. 12: 166) Sei d'una natura tanto perversa e scialacquata, che faresti uscir del seminato un santo (SF Ch. 8: 135)	Tu esci del seminato (GR 206)
Sete nuovo in un mantello vecchio (SF Ch. 12: 168)	
Se vuoi del tuo mestier cavar guadagno, d'un tuo maggiore non ti far compagno (SF Ch. 6: 102)	Se vuoi del tuo mestier cavar guadagno, d'un tuo maggiore non ti far compagno (GR 198)
Se vuoi esser viandante et andare salvo per il mondo, habbi sempre et in ogni luoco: occhio di falcone, per veder lontano; orecchie d'asino per udir bene; viso di cimia per esser pronto al riso; bocca di porcello per mangiar del tutto; spalle di camelo per portar ogni cosa con patientia; e gambe di cervo per poter fuggire i pericoli (SF Ch. 6: 92)	

Se vuoi venir meco, porta teco (FF Ch. 19: 33v)	Chi vuol venir meco porti seco (GR 23)
Siamo al cospetto delle donne, come neve al sole, cera al fuoco o la farfalla alla candela (SF Ch. 12: 170)	
Si danno bene gli offici ma non si dà discretione (FF Ch. 19: 3v)	Si dan gl'offici ma non la discrettione (GR 191)
Siedi e gambetta ché vedrai tua vendetta (SF Ch. 6: 100)	Siedi e gambetta, vedrai tua vendetta (GR 193)
Sienna di sei cose piena, cioè di torri e di campane, di scolari, di puttane, di becchi e di ruffiani (SF Ch. 6: 108)	Siena di sei cose piena, di torri e di campane, di scolari e di puttane, di becchi et di ruffiani (GR 198)
S'io ti comando qualche servigio, tu mi fai fare come il Podestà di Sinigaglia che comanda e bisogna che faccia da se stesso (SF Ch. 8: 135)	Il podestà di Sinigaglia, comanda e poi fa (GR 122)
S'io ti faccio carezze, tu mi mantelizzi (SF Ch. 8: 135)	
S'io ti mando in qualche negotio, tu ritorni col coro (SF Ch. 8: 135)	
Si puol cacciar chiodo con chiodo (FF Ch. 19: 34r)	Si suol cacciar chiodo con chiodo (GR 191)
Sofri il male e aspetta il bene (FF Ch. 19: 33v)	Soffri il male et aspetta il bene (GR 191)

Index of Paremias

Solo bella tella fece, ciò che di giorno fé, la notte poi disfece (SF Ch. 12: 194)	
Solo perché casta visse, Penelope non fu minor d'Ulisse (SF Ch. 12: 194)	Sol perché casta visse, Penelope non fu minor d'Ulisse (GR 195)
Son contento d'haver imparato a mie spese (SF Ch. 8: 132)	Imparare a sue spese (GR 119)
Sono come il sacco d'un mugnaio (SF Ch. 1: 12)	
Sopra Dio non è Signore, sopra negro non è colore, sopra sal non è sapore (FF Ch. 19: 33v; SF Ch. 4: 52)	Sopra Dio non è signore (GR 191) Sopra negro non è colore (GR 191) Sopra sale non è sapore (GR 191)
Speranza conforta l'huomo (FF Ch. 19: 33v)	
Spesso sotto habito vile s'asconde thesor gentile (SF Ch. 6: 98)	
Stolto chi lor dà fede prima che provarle (SF Ch. 12: 178)	
Succia amor la borsa, succia amor il cuore, pazzo è chi compra con duo sangui amore (SF Ch. 12: 176)	Succia amor la borsa e succia il core, pazzo è chi compra con duo sangui amore (GR 198)
Taci caval di cardinale ch'io non ti crederei se tu fossi il credo (SF Ch. 8: 132)	

Taglia la coda al cane e sempre resta cane (FF Ch. 19: 33v)	Taglia la coda al cane e sempre resta cane (GR 202)
Tal biasma altrui che se stesso condanna (FF Ch. 19: 33v)	Tal biasma altrui che se stesso condanna (GR 201)
Tal è l'arbore, tal è il frutto (FF Ch. 19: 34v) Qual è l'arbore, tale è il frutto (SF Ch. 12: 178)	Qual è l'arbore, tal è il frutto (GR 185)
Tal patrone, tal servitore (FF Ch. 19: 34v)	
Tanto è il mal che non mi noce, quanto è il ben che non mi giova (FF Ch. 19: 32r)	Tanto è il male che non mi nuoce, quanto è il bene che non mi giova (GR 208)
Tanto è mio quanto io godo e do per Dio (FF Ch. 19: 32r)	Tanto è mio quanto io godo e do per Dio (GR 202) Quello che io ho, già fu d'altrui, ancor sarà non so di cui, hor'altro haver non mi trovo io che quel ch'io godo e do per Dio (GR 186)
Tardi s'avvede il ratto quando si truova in bocca del gatto (SF Ch. 12: 164)	
Ti dirò bene dove ti tocca il gricciolo se non vedi di emendarti, poltrone in radice, in tronco, in rami, in foglie, in fiori e in frutti che tu sei (SF Ch. 8: 135)	
Tra quali sempre bisogna lasciar del pelo (SF Ch. 5: 66)	

Tra sepolto tesoro et occulta sapientia non si conosce alcuna differentia (SF Ch. 6: 82)	Tra sepolto tesoro et occulta sapientia non si conosce alcuna differentia (GR 208)
Trista quella musa che non [s]a trovar scusa (FF Ch. 19: 33v) Trista quella musa che non ha qualche scusa (SF Ch. 7: 122)	Trista quella musa che non sa trovar sua scusa (GR 201)
Triste quelle case ove le galline cantano et il gallo tace (FF Ch. 19: 33v)	Trista quella casa dove la gallina canta et il gallo tace (GR 201)
Tristo colui che dà esempio altrui (FF Ch. 19: 33v)	Tristo colui che dà essempio altrui (GR 202)
Troppo di una cosa non val niente (FF Ch. 19: 34r)	Troppo non vale nulla (GR 202)
Troppo sperar inganna (FF Ch. 19: 33v)	Troppo sperar inganna (GR 202)
Trotto d'asino, foco di paglia et amor di donna poco durano (FF Ch. 19: 33v)	Trotto di asino, amor di donne, favor di signore, suon di campana, fuoco di paglia, vino di fiasco e vento di dietro poco durano (GR 210)
Tu hai dato il cervello a ripedulare né sai cosa che stia bene (SF Ch. 8: 132)	
Tu hai le mani lunghe e le meni [sic] basse (SF Ch. 8: 135)	
Tu hai tutti i sette peccati in te (SF Ch. 8: 135)	

Tu hai un cervello heteroclito e sregolato (SF Ch. 8: 135)	
Tu la poi slongare ma non scampare (FF Ch. 19: 33*v*)	L'huomo la può slongare ma non fuggire (GR 138)
Tu l'hai sempre in bocca come la canzon dell'uccellaccio (SF Ch. 3: 38)	
Tu mi fai pagar ogni cosa un occhio (SF Ch. 7: 124)	
Tu mi infinocchi (SF Ch. 8: 135)	Lui sa bene infinocchiare (GR 133)
Tu mi ongi i stivalli (SF Ch. 8: 135)	
Tu mi vendi acqua di finocchio (SF Ch. 8: 135)	
Tu non farai mai statuti né casa da tre solari (SF Ch. 1: 6)	
Tu non sei buono né crudo né cotto, né vivo né morto, e sempre sei ubriaco come una suppa (SF Ch. 8: 135)	
Tu sei come l'ancora, la quale sta sempre nell'acqua e mai non impara a nuotare, o come una rapa, che più che sta sotto terra diventa più grossa (SF Ch. 8: 135)	
Tu sei più appricioso che la mula del Papa (SF Ch. 8: 135)	

Index of Paremias

Tu sei più doppio ch'una cipolla (SF Ch. 8: 135)	Lui è più doppio ch'una cipolla (GR 134)
Tu sei più fantastico che tre dadi (SF Ch. 8: 135)	
Tu sei più pigro ch'il sonno o che Lippotopo (SF Ch. 8: 135)	
Tu sei più scaltrito ch'il ladro che rubbò la peste a San Rocco (SF Ch. 8: 135)	Lui torrebbe la peste a San Rocco (GR 137)
Tu sei più sporco ch'un guattaro d'Hongheria (SF Ch. 8: 135)	
Tu sei tanto da poco che moriresti in un forno di pane (SF Ch. 8: 135)	Lui morirebbe di fame in un forno di pane (GR 138)
Tu stai tutto il giorno con le mani a cintola (SF Ch. 8: 135)	
Tutte le arme di Brescia non armeriano la paura (SF Ch. 6: 106) Tutte le arme di Londra non armerion la paura (FF Ch. 19: 32r)	Tutte le arme di Brescia non armerian la paura (GR 202)
Tutti sete macchiati d'una pece (SF Ch. 7: 120)	Tutti siam macchiati d'una pece (GR 203)
Tutti tirano l'aqua al suo molino (FF Ch. 19: 33v) Ogniuno tira l'aqua al suo molino (FF Ch. 14: 14r)	Ogni uno tira l'acqua al suo molino (GR 168)

Tutto è pesce che vi vien alla rete (SF Ch. 7: 120)	
Tutto l'acciaio che hai adosso no[n] farebbe un ago (SF Ch. 8: 135)	Tutto l'acciaio c'hai adosso non farebbe un ago (GR 205)
Tutto quel che luce non è oro (FF Ch. 19: 32r)	Tutto quel che luce non è oro (GR 202)
Una donna m'ha fatto ed una donna m'ha disfatto (SF Ch. 12: 172)	
Una man lava l'altra et tutte due lavano il viso (FF Ch. 19: 34r)	Una man lava l'altra e tutte due il viso (GR 212)
Una pecora rognosa guasta tutto un gregge (FF Ch. 19: 31r)	Una pecora rognosa infetta tutt'un gregge (GR 213)
Una pillola formentina, la giornata d'una gallina, con qualche dramma di sermentina, era una buona medicina (SF Ch. 4: 60)	Una pillola formentina, una dramma sermentina et la giornata d'una gallina fan una buona medicina (GR 217)
Una sola donna si truova netta e pura di tante che ne ha fatte la natura (SF Ch. 12: 182)	
Un avoltor non sarà mai bon sparaviere (FF Ch. 19: 30v)	
Un bel morire tutta una vita honora (FF Ch. 19: 34r)	Un bel morir tutta la vita honora (GR 212)
Un cappello et una borsa più o meno l'anno costano poco et molti amici fanno (SF Ch. 6: 92)	

Un demente non fa inferno (SF Ch. 7: 118)	
Un fiore non fa primavera (SF Ch. 7: 118)	
Un homo val cento e cento non vagliano uno (FF Ch. 19: 32v)	Un huomo ne val cento e cento non ne vagliono uno (GR 213)
Un non ardito cuore di rado gode il suo amore (SF Ch. 12: 164)	
Un signor ch'il tuo ti toglie, il francioso con le doglie, assassin che ti dispoglie è men male che l'haver moglie (SF Ch. 12: 188)	Un signor ch'il tuo ti toglie, il francioso con le doglie, assassin che ti dispoglie è men mal che l'haver moglie (GR 216)
Un ucello in gabbia ne val due del bosco, et pure si è meglio esser ucello di campagna che ucello di gabbia (FF Ch. 19: 34r)	È meglio esser uccello di campagna che di gabbia (GR 97)
Uovo d'un hora, pane d'un dì, capretto a un mese, vino di sei, carne d'un anno, pesce di dieci, donna di quindici et amico di cento bisogna havere chi vuol ben godere (SF Ch. 4: 58)	Pan di un dì, uovo d'un hora, vin d'un anno, pesce di dieci, donna di quindeci, amico di cento (GR 182)
Valente come il poeta da Modona che seminava le fave a cavallo (SF Ch. 7: 112)	Saresti mai il Potta da Modona, che seminava i piselli a cavallo? (GR 193) O che Potta da Modona (GR 169)

Val meglio un huomo di paglia che una donna d'oro (SF Ch. 12: 172)	Un huomo di paglia vale una donna d'oro (GR 216) Huomo di paglia vale una donna d'oro (GR 113)
Val più l'iniquità dell'huomo che la bontà della donna (SF Ch. 12: 172)	
Vanno messeri e tornano seri (SF Ch. 6: 90)	Di questi che vanno messeri e tornano seri (GR 86)
Vegliar a la luna e dormir al sole non fa né profitto né honore (FF Ch. 19: 33v)	Vegliar alla luna e dormire al sole non è né profitto né honore (GR 216)
Venetia, chi non ti vede non ti pretia, ma chi ti vede ben gli costa (FF Ch. 19: 34r; SF Ch. 6: 106)	Venetia chi non ti vede non ti pretia, ma chi ti vede ben gli costa (GR 216)
Vesti caldo, mangia poco, bevi assai che viverai (FF Ch. 19: 34r; SF Ch. 1: 10)	Mangia poco, vesti caldo, bevi assai che viverai (GR 152)
Vesti un zoccarello, e' pare un forfantello (SF Ch. 7: 114)	Chi veste un zoccarello pare un forfantello (GR 34)
Vino adacquato non vale un fiato (SF Ch. 4: 50)	
Viso di calamita per tirar i cuori di ferro come navi a naufragio (SF Ch. 12: 196)	

Vi tirerete la rovina addosso (SF Ch. 12: 172)	
Vive chi vince (FF Ch. 19: 33v)	Vive chi vince (GR 213) Rida chi vince (GR 189)
Vivi con vivi e morti con morti (FF Ch. 19: 34r)	Vivi co' vivi e morti co' morti (GR 212)
Vivono alcuni d'amore come le aloette di porri (SF Ch. 12: 166)	
Voi meritate il paradiso nonché il calendario (SF Ch. 9: 142)	
Voi mi date duro osso da rosegar (SF Ch. 5: 70)	
Voi mi fate lambicar il cervello a sodisfarvi (SF Ch. 8: 132)	
Voi non andate dunque vestito a figura (SF Ch. 1: 8)	
Voi non credete al santo se non fa miracoli et fate come Papa Leone, che donava tutto ciò ch'egli non poteva vendere od havere (SF Ch. 5: 70)	Non credon al santo se non fa miracoli (GR 161) Volentier dona ciò che non puoi vendere (GR 212)
Voi non credete ch'io sia calvo se non mi vedete il cervello (SF Ch. 7: 124)	Non credi che sia calvo se non vedi il cervello? (GR 163)
Voi non havete perso che due poste (SF Ch. 5: 70)	

Voi sete un tristo uccello ad imbrattar il vostro nido (SF Ch. 12: 178)	Tristo quell'uccello che sporca il suo nido (GR 203)
Voi uscite de' gangheri (SF Ch. 12: 166)	Voi uscite sempre de' gangheri (GR 213)
Volontà fa mercato et denari pagano (FF Ch. 19: 34*r*)	Volontà fa mercato e denari pagano (GR 212)
Volto di miele, cuore di fiele (SF Ch. 12: 196)	

Index of Paremias

Numerical Paremias

Aspettar e non venire. Star in letto e non dormire. Ben servir e non gradire. Haver cavallo e non vuol ire; e servitor che non vuol ubidire. Esser in prigione e non poter fuggire; et ammalato e non poter guarire. Smarrir la strada quand'un vuol gire. Star alla porta quand'un non vuol aprire; et haver un amico che ti vuol tradire: son dieci doglie da morire. (SF Ch. 1: 12)

A tre cose non manca mai commedatione, cioè a bon vino quando vien bevuto, una bona sentenza quando vien detta et un bon homo in adversità. (FF Ch. 18: 23*r*)

Cinque cose che non sono necessarie in una republica, un falso giudice in concistorio, un mercante ingannatore nel mercato, un prete avaro in una chiesa, una bella donna in bordello et adulatori ne le corte de' prencepi. (FF Ch. 18: 25*v*)

Cinque sorte di persone dicono la verità spesse volte, un infante, un ebrio, un pazo, un scandalizatore et colui che dorme. (FF Ch. 18: 24*v*)

Ci sono tre cose che mai sono satisfatte et la quarta non dice mai satis, una donna che non è temperata, la terra non è mai sciutta, inferno non è mai satisfatto et il fuoco non ha mai legna assai. (FF Ch. 18: 22*v*)

Ci sono tre cose che non si possono sapere et la quarta nessuno può intendere, i passi de una aquila volante nel aire, la via de un serpente passando una rocca, la via d'una nave sopra il mare e la vita de un giovine passata ne la sua gioventù. (FF Ch. 18: 22*v*)

Colui che cerca di trovar queste cose perde il suo tempo, un porco grasso fra giudei, verità in ipocriti, fede in un adulatore, sobrietà in un ebriaco, danari con un prodigo, sapientia con un matto, richeze in un maestro di scuola, silentio in una donna, virtù in una compagnia cattiva. (FF Ch. 18: 24*v*)

Da tre cose guardate, cioè da un sicophante, da un adulatore, da un presuntuoso. (FF Ch. 33: 74*v*)

Index of Paremias

Da tre cose signor liberaci, da una borsa voda, da un cativo vicino e da una cativa donna. (FF Ch. 19: 30r)

Dio guardi me da cinque F, cioè femine, fuoco, fame, frati et fiume. (SF Ch. 12: 180)

Di tre cose il diavolo si fa insalata, di lingue di avvocati, di dita di notari, la terza è riserbata. (SF Ch. 12: 178)

Due cose, dice Sirach, mi scorrucciano et la terza mi dispiace, quando che homini savii sono disprezati, quando che esperti soldati sono in povertà, quando che un homo declina da la virtù al vitio. (FF Ch. 18: 23r)

Due cose non possono patir equalità, ciò è amor et principalità. (FF Ch. 18: 23v)

I quatro elementi, aqua, foco, aire et terra. (FF Ch. 33: 75r)

I tre corsi dell'huomo, pueritia, gioventù et vechieza. (FF Ch. 33: 75r)

La donna che vuol esser detta bella sopra tutte le bellissime convien haver trenta cose per le quali vien celebrata Helena. Cioè tre bianche, tre negre, tre rosse, tre corte, tre longhe, tre grosse, tre sottili, tre strette, tre larghe e tre picciole. Le bianche sono i denti, le mani et la gola. Le negre sono gli occhi, le ciglia et i peletti c'ascondono diletto. Le rosse sono le labbra, le guancie et i capitelli delle mammelle. Le longhe sono le gambe, le dita et i capelli. Le corte sono i piedi, le orecchie et i denti, ma con misura. Le larghe sono la fronte, il petto et i fianchi. Le strette sono nelle coscie, nel naso et nel luogo di piacere. Le grosse o piene sono le coscie, le groppe et il ventre. Le sottili sono le labbra, le ciglia et i capelli. Le picciole sono la bocca, nel traverso o le pupille de gl'occhi. Et chi manca alcuna di queste parti non può vantarsi d'esser bella, ma chi tutte le possiede si può dir bella in ogni perfettione. (SF Ch. 8: 130)

Non cercar a mover queste quatro cose, un homicido, un homo a chi piace cicalare, una comune cortesana et un cavallo che corre volontariamente in un luogo pericoloso. (FF Ch. 18: 23v)

Non è mai bono per uno a far fretta a quatro luoghi, a una zuffa, a una compagnia de ebriachi o a una festa et non esser invitato et a parlar con un matto. (FF Ch. 18: 23*v*)

Non ti fidar troppo di quatro cose, cioè di un can forastiero, un caval sconosciuto, una donna parlatrice et nel più profondo luogho di una rivera. (FF Ch. 18: 23*v*)

Non ti scorucciar con tre cose, con la verità, con bon conseglio et con il gallo che canta la mattina. (FF Ch. 18: 23*v*)

Per tre cose la terra spesse volte è flagellata, et la quarta è intolerabile, quando che un servitore è fatto signore sopra i beni del suo signore, un pazo cibato con delicateze, un giovine dato a la concupiscentia et una servente fatta herede de la sua signora. (FF Ch. 18: 22*v*)

Quatro cose amazano un huomo inanzi il suo tempo, una bella donna, una casa che non è quiete, mangiar et bever smisuratamente et un aire corotto. (FF Ch. 18: 25*v*)

Quatro cose corompono tutte le sentenze, doni grassi, odio, favore et paura. (FF Ch. 18: 25*v*)

Quatro cose doveriano sempre esser in casa, il polaio, la gatta, il camino et la bona moglie. (FF Ch. 18: 25*v*)

Quatro cose necessarie in una casa, un camino, un gatto, una gallina et una bona donna. (FF Ch. 18: 24*v*)

Quatro fatti che tiranni usano, distruggere li boni, odiare li poveri, inalzar li maligni, annullare virtù. (FF Ch. 19: 28*r*)

Quatro humori regnano nell'huomo secondo i quatro elementi, cioè una complessione è sanguigna, l'altra cholericha, l'altra flemmaticha, l'ultima malinchonicha. (FF Ch. 33: 74*v*)

Quatro sorte de huomini trovano amici, il liberale, il gentile, il potente over richo et color a chi legiermente si può parlare. (FF Ch. 18: 25*v*)

Quatro sorte di tentatione, concupiscentia, ambitione, hipocrisia et vana speranza. (FF Ch. 33: 74*v*)

Quatro vie ci sono che nessuno può star fermo sopra, sopra luoghi bagnati, sopra il giaccio, sopra gloria et ambitione, sopra la beltà di una donna. (FF Ch. 18: 24*r*)

Quattro cose danno noia a la vista di tutti gli huomini, cioè lacrime, fumo, vento et la peggior de tutte è a veder i suoi amici sventurati et i suoi inimici felici. (FF Ch. 18: 23*v*)

Queste otto cose non si accordano mai, un codardo con la guerra, un piccol cavallo con un homo pesante, un homo che ha sete con un piccol potto, un cacciatore con un can pigro, cani e gatti in cucina, un giardinier con una capra, un gran datio ed un povero mercante, un homo vechio con una donna giovine. (FF Ch. 18: 25*r*)

Queste otto cose se vedeno rare volte, una bella figlia senza inamorato, una gran fiera senza ladri, un usuraio senz[a] denari, un giovine senza alegrezza, un granaio senza sorzi, una testa tegnosa senza pedochi, un becco senza barba, un homo sonnolente adorno di sapientia et dottrina. (FF Ch. 18: 24*v*)

Queste cose si accordano insieme, un taglia borsa con una borsa piena di denari, un corridore con una strada piana, bona compagnia et alegreza, un asino et un molinaio, un hoste et un ghiottone, una bella donna con belle vestimenta, una donna ostinata con un bastone, figlioli disobedienti con una scoriada, un ladro con una forca, un bon scolar con i suoi libri, Quaresima et pescatori. (FF Ch. 18: 25*r*)

Questi sono i cinque sensi di natura, cioè vedere, sentire, toccare, gustare et odorare. (FF Ch. 33: 74*r*)

Questi sono i messi di peccato, sugestione, cogitatione, diletto, banchetto, festino, dissolutione, giuoco et ballo, follia, piacere, prodigalità, inconstantia, inconsideratione et cattiva compagnia. (FF Ch. 33: 74*r*)

Index of Paremias

Sei cose ci sono che Iddio ha in odio et la settima lui ha in abominatione, ciò è: ochi alti, la lingua bugiarda, le mani che spargeno il sangue, i piedi veloci per correre a far male, il cuore che macchina iniquità, il testimonio falso, e colui che mette contentione fra fratelli. (FF Ch. 18: 22*v*)

Sei cose ci sono che non si possono mai ascondere, la rogna in mano, la tosse a un banchetto, una fibia in un sacco, una putana a un balcone, povertà in superbia et alegreza ne la libidine. (FF Ch. 18: 24*r*)

Sei cose sono sempre mutabile, il favor de prencipi, il amor di donna, il corso de' dadi, il far caccia a ucelli, il tempo et la primavera de i fiori. (FF Ch. 18: 24*v*)

Sette cose che non sono profitabile in una cosa, una gallina senza ovi, una troia senza porcellini, una vacca senza latte, una figliola che va intorno la notte, un figliolo giuocatore, una donna che spende privatamente, una massara gravida. (FF Ch. 18: 25*v*)

Si vede de gli huomini che diventano poveri per tre cause: alcuni per esser troppo pietosi, ma de quelli ce n'è pochi; alcuni per esser troppo liberali, de quelli ce n'è manco; alcuni per esser troppo prodighi, ma de quelli ce n'è assai in Londra. (FF Ch. 33: 74*v*)

Tre bone cose: verità, charità e virtù. (FF Ch. 33: 74*v*)

Tre bone regole per ogniuno, reggi il tuo volere, tempera la tua lingua, rafrena il tuo ventre. (FF Ch. 33: 75*r*)

Tre cose a nessuno efetto, a tenir acqua in un tamiso, a correre dietro ucelli ne l'aire, a pianger dietro i morti. (FF Ch. 18: 24*r*)

Tre cose apartengono a un conseliere, scientia, benevolentia et libertà in parlar. (FF Ch. 18: 25*r*)

Tre cose bone in un prencipe, misericordia, eloquenza et dotrina. (FF Ch. 33: 75*r*)

Index of Paremias

Tre cose bone per una donna, le richezze di Giuno, la sapientia di Pallas, la belezza di Cerere. (FF Ch. 33: 75*r*)

Tre cose dispiacciono a Dio et a gli huomini, un homo povero superbo, un homo ricco bugiardo et un homo vechio inamorato. (FF Ch. 18: 23*r*)

Tre cose l'huomo non deve prestare, la sua donna, il suo cavallo, le sue arme. (FF Ch. 18: 25*r*)

Tre cose piacciono a Dio et anche a gli huomini, concordia fra fratelli, amicitia fra vicini, accordo fra il marito et moglie. (FF Ch. 18: 23*r*)

Tre sensi dell'huomo, naturale, vitale, ragionevole. (FF Ch. 33: 75*r*)

Tre sorte de huomini che sono da esser tenuti pazzi, un fedel amante di donne, un misericordioso soldato et un bel giuocatore. (FF Ch. 18: 25*v*)

Tre sorte de huomini non vedono niente, l'orbo senza ochi, un pazo senza discretione et colui che si diletta in piaceri mondani senza paura di morte. (FF Ch. 18: 24*r*)

Tre sorte de huomini possono mentire per auctorità, un medico, un vechio et un che è stato lontano. (FF Ch. 33: 75*r*)

Tre sorte de huomini sempre mancano ingegno, colui che non si fida in bugie, colui che non sa vincer la sua ira e colui che mangia assai et non fa niente. (FF Ch. 18: 23*v*)

Tre sorte di beni possiede l'huomo, cioè i beni di fortuna, i beni del corpo et i beni dell'animo. (FF Ch. 24: 42*r*)[10]

Tre sorte di eloquentia, gramatica, retorica, dialettica. (FF Ch. 33: 75*r*)

Tre sorte di filosofia, naturale, morale, loica. (FF Ch. 33: 75*r*)

Index of Paremias

Tre sorte di flagello, fame, peste et guerra. (FF Ch. 33: 75*r*)

Tre sorte de huomini sono sempre sordi, colui che sempre sente boni detti e non semenda, colui che si diletta di scandalizar ogniuno et colui che desidera di sentir i secreti di tutti gli huomini. (FF Ch. 18: 24*r*)

Una cosa in tre fa l'huomo salvo da ogni male, padre, figliolo et lo spirito santo. (FF Ch. 33: 75*r*)

Un homo non si doveria mai vantar di tre cose, di bon vino, de la beleza de la sua moglie et de le sue richezze. (FF Ch. 18: 24*r*)

Tieni le tu[e] orechie da li secreti de altri huomini, i tuoi ochi da gli altrui scriture, le tue mani da gli altrui borse. (FF Ch. 18: 24*v*)

Index of Paremias

Pompeo Sarnelli: A Selection of *Posilecheata*'s Paremias

A l'abbesuogne se canosceno l'ammice (96.3)
A la prova se canosceno li melluno ed a lo spruoccolo lo presutto (194.51)
A lo tuorno se fanno le stròmmola (154.35)
Annigarse dinto a no becchiero d'acqua (189.36)
Arma toia, maneca toja (100.17)
Avere manco jodizio de la mula de lo mulino (105.30)
Avere manco jodizio de 'no cavallo (152.31)
Cadere lo vruoccolo dinto lo lardo, lo maccarone dinto lo ccaso (70.20)
Carne giovane e pesce viecchio (21.29)
Chiantare ardiche e cogliere vruoccole (35.1)
Chi dorme co' cane non se nn'auza senza pullece (141.1)
Chi fa male, male aspetta (35.1)
Chillo de Masto Grillo (18.21)
Chi meglio nasce meglio procede (141.1)
Cinco lettere (7.14)
Comm'è la chianta è la scianta (181.12)
Comme l'urmo e la vite (86.65)
Crederse de fare da cacciatore ed essere cacciato (124.87)
Da dove viene? Da lo molino! (18.22)
Da le cevettole non nasceno aquele, né da le ciavole palumme (141.1)
Da le spine nasceno le rose (181.12)
Da n'erva fetente nasce lo giglio (181.12)
Darele la quatra (37.7)
È meglio la gallina oje che l'uovo craje (152.31)
Essere mogliera e stare pe' bajassa (159.51)
Essere stoccata catalana (104.28)
Fa bene e scordaténne (35.1)
Facevano lo cunto senza lo tavernaro (98.11)
Fare comme fa lo cane ch'abbaja a la luna (169.81)
Fare fuorfece fuorfece (55.63)
Fare lo becco a l'oca (189.35)
Fare na lavatella de capo senza sapone (5.7)
Fare no viaggio e duje servizie (103.24; 143.5)
Fare toccare la coda co le mmano (6.10)
Fare venire tutte le bodella 'ncanna (165.66)

Index of Paremias

Infilare perne a lo junco (123.83)
Io te so' schiavo ed haìme no caucio (192.44)
Lavare la capo senza sapone (200.57)
Lengua che no' la 'ntienne, e tu la caca (6.11)
Li dolure de li pariente muorte songo comme a le tozzate de gúveto, che doleno assai ma durano poco (69.18)
Lo cavallo c'ha uorgio e paglia soperchia tira cauce (158.48)
Lo cuotto e lo crudo (153.32)
Lo grasso dà subbeto a lo core (158.48)
L'ommo comme nasce accossì pasce (141.1)
L'ommo se lega pe le corna e li vuoje pe le parole (161.56)
Longa se vedde, corta se trovaje (38.8)
Lo piso de la corona fa calare tal'ommore all'uocchie che non vedeno lo deritto (74.32)
Lo sazio non crede lo dejuno (74.32)
Magna friddo e bive caudo (198.56)
Maje crapa rognosa facette agniello co lana jentile (181.13)
Maje mora fegliaje e fice no bello nennillo janco commo a lo latto (181.13)
Male e bene a fine vene (82.54)
Nesciuna opera bona non fu premmiata (54.61)
Non capere dinto de la pelle (192.43)
Non c'è peo de pezzente arresagliuto (158.48)
Non chiove, ca delluvia (23.35)
Non se dice lo mutto se non è miezo o tutto (158.48)
Opera lauda lo masto e non parole (53.59)
Pratteca co chi è meglio de tene e falle le spese (141.1)
Quarche strenga rotta se metta 'n dozzana (3.2)
Quarche travo rutto stride (3.2)
Rendere bene per male (58.71; 137.125)
Scotolare sto sacco e bedere se nc'era porvere o farina (182.15)
Semmenare grano e cogliere ardiche (35.1)
Sempe che so' lupe, malannaggia lo meglio (177.1)
Stipare ssa vocca pe le ffico (156.43)
Venne pe' la farina e ce lassaje lo sacco (129.100)

Paremias at the End of the Five *cunti*

Chi vò male ped aute a sè non jova,
E chi fa bene sempre bene trova (61.79; *cunto* 1)

Chi serve fedele aspetta premmio (93.82; *cunto* 2)

'Ncoppa a lo ingannator cade lo 'nganno,
E se tarda, non manca lo malanno (138.127; *cunto* 3)

Non c'è peo de vellane arresagliute (174.92; *cunto* 4)

Lo vizio dello lupo tanto dura,
Che pilo pò mutare e no' natura (207.79; *cunto* 5)

Tripartite Paremias

A tre cose non se deve credere, all'archemista povero, a lo miedeco malato e al remito grasso (13.10)

Pe le tre cannele che s'allumano quanno se fa no strommiento de notte (14.12)

Per li tre parme de funa che danno vota a lo 'mpiso (14.12)

Tre bote tre unnece cose fanno bella na femmiena: azzoè tre cose longhe e tre corte; tre larghe, tre strette e tre grosse, tre sottile; tre retonne, tre piccole, tre ghianche, tre rosse, tre negre (13.11)

Tre cose abbesognano a lo ruffiano: gran core, assai chiacchiare e poca vregogna (14.12)

Tre cose abbesogna tenere a mente: che ammore non vò bellezza, che appetito non vò sauza e che l'accattare non vò ammecizia. ... chi accatta ha da sapere che se deve accattare l'uoglio de coppa, lo vino de miezo e lo mmèle de funno (13.10–11)

Tre cose arroinano la gioventute: juoco, femmena e taverna (14.12)

Tre cose cacciano l'ommo da la casa: fummo, fieto e femmena marvasa (14.12)

Tre cose non possono stare annascose: le fusa dinto de lo sacco, le femmene 'nchiuse 'n casa e la paglia dintro de le scarpe (13.10)

Tre cose non songo stemmate: forze da vastaso, consiglio de poverommo e bellezza de pottana (13.9)

Tre cose osserva lo miedeco: lo puzo, la faccia e lo cantaro (14.12)

Tre cose songo 'nsoffribele: ricco avaro, povero soperbio e biecchio 'nnammorato (13.9)

Index of Paremias

Tre cose songo utele a lo cortesciano: fegnemiento, fremma e sciorte (14.12)
Tre cose squatrano ogne cosa: nummero, piso e mesura (13.9)
Tre cose stanno male a lo munno: n'auciello 'mmano de no peccerillo, no fiasco 'mmano de no Todisco, na zita giovane 'mmano de no viecchio (13.10)
Tre cose strudeno la casa: zeppole, pane caudo e maccarune (14.12)
Tre fff vole avere lo pesce: fritto, friddo e futo (14.12)
Tre le dute prencepale de l'anema de l'ommo: memmoria, 'ntelletto e bolontà (12–13.9)
Tre mmm songo chelle delle quale ognuno n'ha la parte soja: matto, miedeco e museco (14.12)
Tre parme de funa danno vota a lo 'mpiso (14.12)
Tre sciorte de perzune se tene la bonarrobba: smargiasso, bello, giovane e corrivo (14.12)
Tre sciorte de perzune songo patrune de lo munno: pazze, presentuse e sollicete (13.10)
Tre so' le cannelle che s'allummano quando se fa no stromiento de notte (14.12)
Tre songo le sciorte de l'anemale: vegetativo, sensetivo e 'ntellettivo (12.9)
Tre songo li principie naturale: materia, forma e privazione (12.9)
Tre songo li termene d'ogne ncosa: prencipio, miezo e fine (13.9)
Tre sss besognano a lo 'nnammorato: sulo, solliceto e secreto (14.12)

Paremias in Other Languages

Fare de la trippa corazzone (Hazer de tripas corazón; 45.32)
Prossimo accignendo habeto ped accinto (17.21)
Sobre una cosa redonda no haze buen edificio (16.18)

Notes

Foreword

1. Paremiography concerns writing, researching, and gathering paremias, whereas paremiology covers their historical, morphologic, and semantic study.

Chapter One

1. The label "literature of and with proverbs" comes from Alfonso D'Agostino's chapter "Letteratura di proverbi e letteratura con proverbi nell'Italia medievale," in which he offers an overview of paremias in medieval poetry and prose. He demonstrates how, in many works, when the narrative tension coincides with moralizing tones, authors resort to a sententious style and to using paremias (105).

2. For a thorough overview of paremias throughout the centuries beginning with the Sumerians, see Lapucci (*Dizionario dei proverbi italiani* ix–xxiv).

3. For a comprehensive discussion on paremias in the Greek world, their pedagogical use, and their relation to society, religion, and urban life, see Di Capua (57–69) and Vallini (61–85). About Hesiod's influence, see Malerba and Bonardi (vi–vii). One of the first collections of Greek moral *sententiae* is the Pseudo-Phocylides collection (also known as Ποίημα νουζετιχον), claimed to have been written by Phocylides of Miletus under the Alexandrine inclination to catalogue expressions in literary works (A. Farina). Another collection, entitled Μενάνδρου Γνῶμαι Μονόστιχοι or *Menandri sententiae*, gathers maxims and moral precepts alphabetically, mostly one line in iambic trimeters from Euripides and Menander; the collection was progressively enriched with distiches and tetrastiches from subsequent authors, including Christian writers (Pernigotti). A much later collection is that by Lucius Mestrius Plutarchus (50–post 120 AD), whose *Apothegms* gather witty and pleasant expressions as well as notable *sententiae* by Greek and Roman princes, philosophers, orators, and other personalities in a narrative style. For a list of sixteenth- to nineteenth-century editions of Greek paremias, see Gratet-Duplessis (62–72).

4. Beccaria defines *sententiae* as those maxims that are characterized by expressive conciseness like mottos (*Dizionario di linguistica*, s.v. *sentenza*). In her *Manuale di retorica*, Bice Mortara Garavelli offers the same definition and specifies that *sententiae* include paremias and aphorisms. She maintains that, while both are tropes of thought and refer to moral and cultural elements, paremias show a more popular dimension that sometimes draws from traditional superstitions (247); however, aphorisms frequently relate to a specific discipline or field (248). According to Heinrich Lausberg, *sententia*, along with *gnomai*, are *loci communes* or common beliefs, which represent a recognized norm of life, standard of conduct, or knowledge of the world (219–20: par. 398).

5. For a comprehensive analysis of paremias in Greek and Roman literature, see Lelli, vol. 2 (on Greek paremias) and vol. 3 (on Latin paremias), and Tosi (*Dizionario* ix–xxiv). For paremias in Rome up to Tacitus, see Di Capua (69–128) and for collections of Latin expressions in the early modern period, see Gratet-Duplessis (74–110).

6. Balbo's article is an excellent reference on the topic. For a list of Seneca's paremias, see also Di Capua (108–14) and Pientini.

7. The most important edition of Seneca's proverbs is contained in Erasmus von Rotterdam's *L. Annaei Senecae Opera et ad dicendi facultatem et ad bene vivendum utilissima*, which was published in Basel in 1529.

8. For a critical approach to the similarities between proverbs and paradoxes, see Saulnier's article; here he defines paradoxes as doubling proverbs since they reinvigorate the proverbial wisdom in comic, satiric, and laughable instances.

9. On the influence of *Disticha Catonis* in the Middle Ages, see B. Taylor (25). On the specific topic of pedagogical uses of *Disticha* and other similar collections of moral phrases in the Middle Ages, see Di Capua (148–73).

10. An early modern commentary on classical proverbs is contained in Filippo Beroaldo (senior)'s 1496 *Annotationes centum*, a collection and explanation of more than 100 philological issues. For instance, Beroaldo mentions Gaius Valerius Catullus's already then common epigram to Gaius Julius Caesar and its proverbial line *Albus an ater homo* ("white or black man," meaning that it is not important who a person is; 10*r*), which he describes as an example of Catullus's *mordacitas* ("sarcasm"). He also unravels the origins of Cicero's expression in his *Epistulae ad Atticum*, *Omnes enim Coricei subauscultare videntur quod loquor* ("Indeed, all Corinthians seem to eavesdrop what I say"; X.18.1; 15*r*), which Erasmus reports in his *Adagia* (*Collected Works of Erasmus, Adages*, vol. 31, I.ii.44: 185–87). In addition, Beroaldo comments on Cicero's verse in his *Ad familiares*, *Sero sapiunt Phryges* ("The Phrygians learn wisdom too late"; VII.16.1; 95*v*), which Erasmus again explains in his *Adagia* (vol. 31, I.i.28: 76–77). Similarly, Giovanni Battista Pio, in his 1505 *Annotamenta*, discusses Latin and Greek words as well as *sententiae* from a variety of classical, religious, and humanistic works. Among many others, he dedicates an etymological note to a proverb by Cicero in his *Epistulae ad Atticum*, *Dignitatis ἅλις tamquam δρυός* ("As respectable as an oak"; II.19.1; C*v*). Additionally, he reports the Greek origins of a proverb from Saint Jerome in his *Contra Rufinum*, *Manum peteris et pedem porrigis* ("You are asked the hand and you offer the foot"; *Hiir*).

11. For ease of reference, see Di Capua (114–18). He mentions a proverbial phrase inserted within Tibullus's *Elegiae*, *Ardentem flebitur ante rogum* ("[She] will cry in front of the burning pyre"; II.4.1.46; N*v*).

12. The *Prologue* affirms that paremias will make the wise even wiser and the educated man perspicacious (1.5–6). On Solomon's proverbs, see the publications by Niccacci and O'Dowd.

13. Kealy's book offers historical and contemporaneous bibliographical references on all Sapiential books. On the reason that guaranteed the success

of these biblical books in the proverb tradition, see B. Taylor (24–25). For more information on the Book of Wisdom, see Collins.

14. For a few examples of proverbs from Christ's story and from both the Old and New Testament, see Di Capua (128–33) and Lapucci (*Per modo di dire* 11–12). For *sententiae* and proverbs in literature and monastic practices informed by Christian values, see Di Capua (133–48). In England, a *Liber proverbiorum*, falsely attributed to Bede the Venerable Saint (672/3–735), also drew from both Testaments.

15. Garzo's proverbs can be read entirely in the following works: Appel, Brambilla Ageno ("I «Proverbi» di Ser Garzo"), Contini (vol. 2: 295–313, 876–77), and Novati ("Le serie alfabetiche proverbiali" [1909]). G. Sansone reports only those proverbs, fewer in number, that appear in a specific codex transmitting Garzo's expressions, the Alessiano codex.

16. For an analysis of the work and its text, see Schiaffini's edition of da Certaldo's *Libro di buoni costumi*, which contains a list of all its proverbs (263–70). Related to habits and customs are also the paremias that originated at the "School" of Salerno: lawyers, notaries, priests, doctors, and pedagogues contributed with sayings and proverbial expressions in Latin, then translated in vernacular (Lapucci, *Dizionario* xvi–xvii).

17. For the complete Latin and vernacular text of the *Dialogus*, see Q. Marini. In the seventeenth century, G. C. Croce drew inspiration from this model for his cycle of stories on Bertoldo and Bertoldino, including *Le piacevoli et ridicolose semplicità di Bertoldino* (1608) and *Le sottilissime astuzie di Bertoldo* (1609). Both contain a considerable number of proverbs, some featuring in conversations, some listed, some introducing stories or used as their title, and some others generating novellas or fables. For more information, see Malerba and Bonardi (xi–xii). A considerable number of sayings and proverbs for comic purposes characterizes *Novella di Cacasenno figlio del semplice Bertoldino divisa in discorsi e ragionamenti* (before 1620) written by musician Camillo Scaligeri dalla Fratta (born Tommaso Banchieri and also known as Adriano Banchieri); the story describes Croce's same characters plus Cacasenno, Bertoldo's nephew and Bertoldino's son. These three works by Croce and Scaligeri dalla Fratta were published together in 1620 as *Bertoldo, Bertoldino e Cacasenno*. Scaligeri dalla Fratta is also the author of a 1627 collection of "ragionamenti" ("discussions") entitled *Trastulli della villa distinti in sette giornate*, in which one of the topics of the dialogical conversations among different characters deals with "proverbi significanti" ("meaningful proverbs"; frontispiece).

18. On the tradition of learned vis-à-vis popular proverbial wisdom from the fifteenth to eighteenth century, especially in France, see Zemon.

19. It is worth mentioning that in 1536 Brucioli had already translated and commented *Ecclesiastes*: *L'Ecclesiasto di Salomo, tradotto dalla ebraica verità in lingua toscana et con nuovo commento dichiarato* (Venezia: per Bartholomeo Zanetti).

20. To place Brucioli's work within the context of the vernacular translations of the Bible in the fifteenth and sixteenth centuries, see Fragnito (*La Bibbia al rogo* 23–74).

21. The Italian reads: "luoghi privilegiati e riservati dalla dottrina della *dispositio* alla consumata moralità delle sentenze" (Chiecchi, "Sentenze e proverbi" 145). *Dispositio* concerns the organization of the single parts within a discourse, of content within each part, and of words expressing ideas (Beccaria, *Dizionario di linguistica* 248–49; Garavelli 103–10).

22. Among these collections, the most significant are: Franco Sacchetti's *Trecentonovelle* (fourteenth century; see Brambilla Ageno, "Ispirazione proverbiale del Trecentonovelle"); Ser Giovanni Fiorentino's *Il Pecorone* (1378–85); Giovanni Sercambi's *Novelle* (end of the fourteenth century; see Chiecchi, "Sulle moralità"); Masuccio Salernitano's *Il Novellino* (1476); Sabadino degli Arienti's *Porretane* (1483); Pietro Fortini's *Le giornate delle novelle de' novizi* (1530–40) and *Le piacevoli ed amorose notti de' novizi* (1555–61; see Bruscagli, "La novella e il romanzo" 860–62); Anton Francesco Grazzini's (or else Lasca) *Le cene* (1549; see Bruscagli, "La novella" 854–60); Girolamo Parabosco's *I Diporti* (1551); Gianfrancesco Straparola's *Le piacevoli notti* (1550–53; see Bruscagli, "La novella" 866–70); Matteo Bandello's *Novelle* (1554 and 1573; see Bruscagli, "La novella" 870–76; Palma, "Paremiografia e funzioni"); Giovanni Forteguerri's *Novelle* (1556–61); Giambattista Cinzio Giraldi's *Ecatommiti* (1565); Bargagli's *Dialogo de' giuochi che nelle vegghie sanesi si usano di fare* (1572) and *I trattenimenti* (1587); and Tommaso Costo's *Fuggilozio* (1600; see Bruscagli, "La novella" 885–88; Imparato).

23. Here, a novella is said to generate the paremia *L'è fatto il becco a l'oca* ("The goose beak is made"; II.42–115; Bruscagli, "La novella" 839–40). The novella recounts how Cassandro uses a goose as a Trojan horse to introduce himself inside the garden where Alcenia, the woman he loves, is secluded. In the end, Cassandro manages to free Alcenia and marry her. The last stanza of the canto illustrates how the paremia originated: "Così Alcenia, la quale stette rinchiusa / Tanti anni, ebbe d'amor grazia non poca, / Dove nacque il proverbio che ancora s'usa / Fra noi. E non pur sol quando si gioca, / Ma quando un'opra è del tutto conclusa" ("So, Alcenia, who remained secluded / for many years, received the immense grace of Love, / from which the proverb was born and is still used / among us. And it is not only used when you play, / but when a work is completely finished").

24. In the seventeenth century, mock-heroic poems continue this tradition (Malavasi).

25. In his *Etymologiae*, Isidore of Seville comments on maxims by saying that they are impersonal sayings; when a person is added to a maxim, it becomes a χρεία (*chreia*; "purpose, necessity"; II.XI.1–2). For further references on *chreiai*, see Hock and O'Neil.

26. Tesauro groups apothegms with wits in *Il cannocchiale aristotelico*, specifically in the first chapter *Dell'arguttezza et de' suoi parti* ("On Wit and its Parts," par. *Nome dell'arguttezza*, "The Name of the Wit").

27. Pontano specifically argues that the facetious person can attract and please the audience by employing short stories, hilarious remarks, amusing *sententiae*, and proverbs (VI.1.6).

28. Speroni's *Wit and Wisdom* is a valuable resource for collections of *facetiae* and their witticism. For an extended discussion on all these collections and on their translations in the vernacular, see Cherchi ("Alla ricerca di una apoftemmatica moderna" 31–32). For more on Poliziano's work, see Folena's "Sulla tradizione dei *Detti piacevoli*." Likely published at the beginning of the seventeenth century, *Indovinelli, riboboli, passerotti, e farfalloni ... Con alcune cicalate di donne di sentenzie et proverbi posti nel fine* is a collection of riddles, nursery rhymes, *facetiae*, and proverbs, in which the latter two are linked to pleasant conversations by women. This is, as far as it could be researched, the only reference to a gendered use of proverbs. In 1543, Lando adopts the same tradition of *facetiae* in his *Paradossi*, which collects 30 paradoxes and explains them by combining moral precepts, facetious narrations, and fluent style. Castiglione's *Il libro del cortegiano* also contains a discussion on *facetiae*, along with witty remarks and pranks (Book II, ch. XLIV–XCVII).

29. Another example is Geremia da Montagnone's 1505 *Epytoma Sapientie*, which collects paremias mainly in Latin but also in vernacular. The expressions, organized into four books, are extracted mostly from biblical and classical works. Among its sources are Solomon's *Proverbs*, *Psalms*, *Ecclesiasticus*, *Job*, *Libri Paralipomenon*, *Exodus*, *Leviticus*, *Genesis*, the *Gospel according to Matthew*, and many Greek and Latin authors (Novati, "Le serie alfabetiche proverbiali" [1890] 355–56).

30. The first translation in Italian appeared in 1550 by Gabriel Giolito de' Ferrari in Venice and was titled *Proverbi di Erasmo Roterodamo, tradotti per Lelio Carani*.

31. Some of the most cited Greek and Latin authors were, in alphabetical order: Aristophanes, Aristotle, Catullus, Euripides, Gellius, Homer, Horatius, Pindar, Plautus, Plutarchus, Quintilianus, Sophocles, Terentius, and Tibullus.

32. In his *Etimologia e proverbio*, Pignatti offers a thorough examination of Italian (and Latin) paremiography, as well as collections of Italian paremias in and outside Italy in the sixteenth and seventeenth centuries (253–383). Even though not a collection of paremias, F. Guicciardini's *Ricordi* (1530) heavily refers to Erasmus's collection as a source of maxims and proverbial expressions (Palumbo, "Detti, proverbi e allusion" 65–68).

33. Erasmus's paremias also found a place in the visual arts. In the seventeenth century, many of his adages were represented visually in *florilegia* or illustrated collections (Parlato, "Luoghi comuni in immagine"). One of the most well-preserved artistic representations of Erasmus's paremias is in Palazzo Besta in Teglio, Valtellina. Here, selected proverbs from *Adagia* are associated with a fresco representing scenes from Ariosto's *Orlando furioso;* hence, illustrated proverbs moralize the poem and make it more understandable to the public (Caneparo 93–152). Outside of Italy, the famous painting *Netherlandish Proverbs* (1559) by Dutch painter Pieter Bruegel the

Elder represents a visual illustration of those classical, patristic, and popular proverbs that had also informed Erasmus's *Adagia* (M. Sullivan, "Bruegel's Proverbs").

34. Paolo Manuzio's 1575 Venetian edition of *Adagia* was permitted.

35. The long explanation of the expression *Sileni Alcibiadis* appears in Erasmus's *Adagia* (*Collected Works of Erasmus, Adages*, vol. 34, III.iii.1: 262–82). For a modern commentary on this expression and its specificity within *Adagia*, see Margolin.

36. In a lesson on proverbs at the Accademia della Crusca on November 30, 1813, Fiacchi writes that proverbs—even those that, without conveying metaphorical meanings, are characterized by a rhyme—"recar possono un vantaggio singolarissimo alla buona condotta della vita nel basso popolo, che non può leggere e meditare i solenni Trattati della morale Filosofia" ("can uniquely benefit the people's good behavior in life, since they cannot read or ponder the solemn treatises on moral philosophy"; 12). Even in a 1571 treatise on academies and the value of nobility, *Il liceo* by Taegio, proverbs are mentioned as one of the tools that poets use in order to offer useful and agreeable concepts to their readers. Interestingly, proverbs are associated with austerity—as opposed to piquancy, which is typical of *facetiae*—and with entertainment—which characterizes fables (13).

37. In 1454, Cornazzano wrote *De proverbiorum origine*, which led to several publications of its vernacular translation entitled *Proverbi in facetie* (1518–58). This more recent collection contains 16 witty paremias, explained with pleasant stories. Later examples of collections of comic paremias are: Nicolò Liburnio's *Elegantissime sentenze et aurei detti de' diversi antiqui e savi autori*, later translated in vernacular by Marco Cadamosto (1543); Ludovico Domenichi's *Facetie et motti arguti di alcuni eccellentissimi ingegni et nobilissimi signori* (1548); Doni's *La Zucca* (1551–52 and 1565; see Pignatti, "Pratica e ideologia" 328–33) and Orazio Toscanella's *Motti, facezie, burle et altre piacevolezze* (1561; see Bruscagli, "La novella" 882–85). In this perspective, Aretino's and Doni's entire literary productions also represent invaluable sources of proverbial expressions and sententious formulae. For more information on Aretino, see P. Marini and the list of wellerisms and paremias in Aquilecchia's edition of *Sei giornate* (518–22). For further references to Doni's works and his paremiographic tendencies, see Girotto ("Novelle, facezie, apoftegmi"; "Schede sull'uso dei proverbi"); on the sources for his paremias, see Pignatti ("Pratica e ideologia" 333–45). Other minor collections of paremias and moral *sententiae* were published during the sixteenth century. For instance, *Armonia con soavi accenti del nuovo fior di virtù, raccolta da diversi autori. Nella quale si contiene per ordine d'alfabetto molti proverbi, sentenze, motti, et documenti morali. Aggiuntivi di novo molti ammaestramenti et detti di sapientissimi filosofi* (Venezia: Dalla Fede, 1588), gathers 100 paremias and 30 *terza rima* lines, evidently aimed at disseminating virtuous teachings. The section with sayings from philosophers collects 31 numerical paremias based on structures from two to ten members.

38. Because of its extreme eroticism, almost bordering on pornography, and its condemnation of the Church, the Council of Ten in Venice confiscated the book's copies of Cynthio's *Libro* as early as 1527. The book was listed in the 1549 *Le catalogue des livres censurés par la Faculté de théologie de Paris*, published in Rome by Antonio Blado, and it was included among those authored works in Latin to censure (de Bujanda et al., 249–50, 438; Fragnito, *Church, Censorship and Culture* 195–98). As a result, Cynthio's *Libro* was condemned to almost complete oblivion until the twentieth century. This was the fate of other books at the time, which the Inquisition disapproved of due to their witticism, frequently expressed by means of proverbs and sayings, and their mix of sacred and profane content supposedly leading to heretical and dishonest behaviors (Fragnito, "La censura ecclesiastica in Italia" 45–46).

39. Cynthio is also the author of a satire in *terza rima*, which originates from a proverb and presents the same three *cantiche* organization found in his *Libro*: *Satyra nel proverbio Chi prima va al molino prima macina*. The satire includes an "apologhetto" ("fable") in the first *cantica* and another fable in the second and third *cantiche*, which explain the origin of the expression ("He who goes to the mill first, grinds first").

40. He was also known as Vignali di Bonagiunta and the author of a 1525–26 dialogue entitled *La cazzaria* ("Book of the prick").

41. Within the same genre, a similar work occurs in Spanish by Blasco de Garay, who published *Cartas en refranes* in 1541—a few years earlier than Vignali (see Hernando Cuadrado and Rabaey). In Italian, Andrea Calmo's *Lettere* (1547–56) contain a considerable number of proverbial expressions, even though they are not specifically devoted to paremias (D'Onghia). In a different genre, that of an oration, *Oratio proverbialis* (1499) by Beroaldo (already mentioned for his *Annotationes centum*) is a collection of classical paremias, some authorial, some anonymous, interspersed with comments on the nature of proverbs, as well as their different typologies, origins, and uses. In his *Lexicon Tetraglotton* (1660), Howell introduces the section on "Italian Proverbs" with a letter composed of proverbs coherently organized and directed to a gentleman who is on the verge of leaving to go to Italy (*Lettera composta de proverbi, i quali vanno tutti incatinati a far un sentimento intiero et congruo, mandata a un gentilhuomo ch'era su 'l punto de viaggiare et andarsi a Italia*).

42. Concurrent with collections of paremias in Italian, there also existed works gathering regional proverbial expressions. A small collection of 150 paremias published in 1535 (or perhaps earlier) comes from the area of Venice, *Opera quale contiene le diece tavole de' proverbi*. This work was intended to make some paremias more easily readable if compared to its earlier organization into ten large plaques for each letter of the alphabet, though without clear classification. As it gathered all of the Italian proverbs available in the peninsula (A*iv*), *Le dieci tavole* were addressed to those who wished to practice virtue and enrich their talks, while enjoying learning proverbs (A*iir*).

Cortelazzo, the modern editor of the collection, argues that the list of paremias counters the Tuscan tradition both in language and in content. They are undoubtedly Venetian and present the typical voicing of the intervocalic consonant (*Le dieci tavole* 4). However, a considerable number of paremias refer to a Tuscan tradition, meaning that they are Venetian translations of original Tuscan expressions.

43. For more examples, see Gratet-Duplessis (226–76). On a much smaller scale compared to these paremiographers, G. C. Croce, author of the aforementioned works on Bertoldo and Bertoldino, contributed to the field with his *Selva di esperienza* (*L'Eccellenza e trionfo del porco* 150–97; see Gambari and Guerrini 466: entry 232). It is a repository of 1,020 including proverbs, sayings, maxims, and wellerisms, distributed alphabetically in 19 groups, many of which are present in the collections of Salviati, Pescetti, Monosini, Buoni, Serdonati, and Lena (with ca. 20 expressions in Latin). Croce was also the author of a poem entitled *Il mondo alla roversa* (1605), in which rhymed tercets contain moral wisdom and proverbial expressions that denounce the inappropriateness of an upside-down world.

44. For an examination of the philological and paleographic aspects of the manuscript, see D'Eugenio ("Lionardo Salviati"). Salviati's paremias are also available in the database *Proverbi italiani* realized by the Accademia della Crusca. A manuscript copy of Salviati's collection before 1612, Cl. II 25 (Biblioteca Comunale Ariostea in Ferrara) features part of the original paremias in a list format.

45. Pescetti lists his paremias without arranging them alphabetically: expressions starting with the same verb or the same structure as well as synonymic paremias are juxtaposed, often introduced by "Vale lo stesso [del precedente]" ("It has the same meaning [as the previous one]"). However, in the 1611 edition of the collection, proverbs are organized in sections, including *Città, nazioni, e loro qualità* ("Cities, nations, and their qualities"), *Golosità* ("Gluttony"), *Honor e suo contrario* ("Honor and its contrary"), *Puttana* ("Whore"), and *Usanza* ("Habit").

46. In Spanish, Fernando Arce de Benavente compiled a list of paremias translated from Spanish to Latin. A fable introduced all the paremias to motivate the students, teach them grammar, and foster their knowledge of Latin (Messina Fajardo 29–31). For a discussion on the medieval and Renaissance tradition of bilingual Latin-vernacular proverb collections with pedagogical purposes, especially in the Low Countries, see Geudens and Van Hal.

47. See Pignatti and Crimi (341–43) for an analysis of Pescetti's paremias as pedagogical tools in relation to his oration.

48. The books dedicated to paremias are the following: the third book, which offers a definition and many examples of Italian, Latin, and Greek expressions; the fifth book, with examples of equivalent Etruscan and Latin paremias; the sixth book, which presents Italian paremias explained through the Greek ones; the seventh book, which collects Etruscan paremias explained through the Latin ones; and the eighth book, which gathers many typologies of adages, organized in alphabetical order and translated in Latin. Moreover, the second, fourth, and ninth books list many instances of idiomatic expressions and sayings. Pignatti's *Etimologia e proverbio* is the most comprehensive study on Monosini's *Flos*, on his linguistic positions, and on his relationships with contemporaneous paremiographers and linguists.

49. Stobaeus's reference follows: "Si quis suas opes temere dilapidant, laudibus vehantur, id multis obesse potest. Nam qui suam male gubernat vitam, dic quaeso quomodo servabit is alienam?" ("If those who rashly squander the wealth of their own are praised, this can be harmful to many people. Indeed, he who directs his life badly, please tell me how he will preserve another life?"; 127).

50. The same purpose drives Varchi's *L'Hercolano*, published posthumously in 1570. Although not a collection of paremias but a linguistic treatise on the model of Socratic discussions, Varchi's work gathers a considerable number of proverbial expressions with commentary. He employs them to provide instances of the spoken vernacular, explain grammatical aspects of the Florentine language, and promote its eligibility as the language of the peninsula. Despite this similarity, Varchi was an outspoken adversary of etymological research, while Monosini embraced it enthusiastically in his collection and in his collaboration with the Accademia della Crusca (Pignatti, *Etimologia e proverbio* 83).

51. Buoni defines proverbs as "lumi della favella italiana" ("lights of the Italian language") and "chiare luci che abbellendo illumino la natia nostra lingua" ("bright lights that, while embellishing our native language, enlighten it"; a4r).

52. Buoni's *Lettere argute* follow the same criterion as they combine witty and moral aspects that can be useful to anybody. The adjective "arguto" ("witty") does not mean that these letters raise laughter; rather, as the dedicatory letter to the readers states, the epistles are provided with "sali, proverbii, sentenze morali, et detti traslati, i quali rendono dilettevole l'opera, come potranno leggendo avvertire, et perché in breve havranno il *Novo Thesoro* de gli proverbii italiani con la espositione loro" ("clever remarks, proverbs, moral sententiae, and figurative sayings, which make the work delightful, as they can perceive by reading it, and because in a short time they will have the *Novo Thesoro* of the Italian proverbs with their illustration").

53. A thematic organization characterizes a 1642 collection of proverbs by Varrini, *Scuola del volgo*. Varrini does not distinguish between different typologies of paremias or between paremias featuring animals and paremias that convey life precepts. His 28 chapters relate to aspects of everyday life, human body, language, emotions, virtues and vices, habits, human relationships, etc.

54. For further examples, see Ferrato's publications in Works Consulted. Fiorelli's "La raccolta di proverbi di Francesco Serdonati" also contains detailed insight on Serdonati's paremiac production. The publication of

Serdonati's paremias in the Accademia della Crusca's database *Proverbi italiani* is still in progress and curated by Rondinelli under the supervision of Fiorelli and Biffi. For ease of reference, see Rondinelli, "Per l'edizione elettronica" and "Verso l'edizione a stampa"; for further information on Serdonati's collection and the other collections in the database, see Biffi, "La banca dati."

55. For a critical analysis of the major seventeenth-century monolingual, multilingual, printed, and manuscript collections of paremias, see Pignatti (*Etimologia* 253–316).

56. Before gathering this collection, Lena had compiled a *Saggio di proverbi e detti sententiosi italiani e latini*, which might have been the beginning stage of his massive publication 20 years later.

57. *Modi di dire italiani raccolti e dichiarati dal signore Egidio Menagio, gentilhuomo francese* ("Italian sayings collected and explained by Egidio Menagio, French gentlemen") appears at the end of Ménage's etymological dictionary *Le origini della lingua italiana*. It collects 141 expressions, including wellerisms, with commentary and cross references to the *Psalms*, the Crusca's dictionary, Monosini's collection, and many other literary and paremiographic sources. Ménage was appointed member of the Accademia della Crusca on September 2, 1654.

58. In the dedicatory letter, Puccio Lamoni (anagram of Paolo Minucci) declares that his commentaries will benefit those who are not Tuscans and might not have "vera cognizione del valore e senso" ("correct understanding of the value and meaning") of all the Florentine expressions that Lippi uses in his work.

59. In the third edition of the *Vocabolario* (1691), the indices are separate: one for the Latin locutions, one for the Greek proverbs, and one for the Latin proverbs. All of them mention, as in the first and second editions, Erasmus's *Adagia* and Monosini's *Flos* as sources for the dictionary.

60. The original reads: "E perchè intorno a queste non si poteva sempre far quel discorso, che per pieno intendimento di loro derivazioni o origini, sarebbe stato bisogno, abbiamo citato il *Flos Italicae Linguae Angeli Monosinii*, dove il lettore volendo potrà ricorrere" ("And since we could not include those discourses on their sources or origins that are necessary for their understanding, we mentioned Agnolo Monosini's *Flos Italicae Linguae*, to which the reader could refer, if he or she wishes"; a4v). For a description of the relationship between Monosini and the Accademia della Crusca (specifically, an academician's note asking Monosini to list, when possible, paremias in Latin), see Pignatti (*Etimologia* 43–50); for exchanges between Monosini's *Flos* and the *Vocabolario*, see Pignatti (169–88). Aresti mentions 240 explicit references to Monosini's work in the dictionary (296); conversely, Pignatti argues that the total references are 243, of which 40% are devoted to etymology and 60% to paremias (152). More recently, Biffi demonstrates how *Flos* is mentioned 250 times in 214 entries ("La raccolta di proverbi"). Vitale specifies that Monosini's collection was used in the first three editions of the dictionary but was eventually eliminated from the list of approved writers in its 1729–38 fourth edition. This probably occurred because *Flos*, especially its fourth book, was considered to be too popular a work (*L'oro nella lingua* 310).

61. The original says: "De' proverbi di questa lingua s'è proccurato di raccogliere buona parte, e principalmente i significanti e di qualche grazia, così nelle cose gravi come burlesche. Lo stesso abbiam fatto delle maniere del favellare e detti proverbiali, li quali appo di noi son di molte guise" ("We managed to collect a good part of the proverbs of this language, primarily the most significant and those that show some grace, both in the serious and facetious topics. We did the same with various ways of speaking and proverbial sayings, which take on different forms in our language"; a4*v*; S. Parodi 344).

62. Some collections also aimed to revive the efflorescence of the glorious centuries for proverbs, namely the 1500s and the 1600s. In 1874, Romagnoli published a collection of facetious stories from the fifteenth and sixteenth centuries: *Facezie e motti dei secoli XV e XVI*. Here, proverbs introduce, shape, or conclude stories n. 22, 36, 86, and 238. A decade later, Cian released his *Motti inediti e sconosciuti di Messer Bembo* (Marcozzi). In 1872, Tanini published a collection of proverbs and sayings *La donna secondo il giudizio dei dotti e dei proverbi*, which reached 2,000 expressions in its fourth revised edition in 1886. His paremias are all related to the woman and extracted from biblical, classical, humanistic, and contemporaneous Italian, European, and non-European sources. For a list of publications on paremias in the nineteenth and twentieth centuries, also in dialect, see Bonser and Stephens (252–99). The rediscovery of popular origins occurred abroad, too. For instance, Lardelli, a teacher of Italian in Chur, Switzerland, published *Italienische Phraseologie*, a list of Italian idiomatic phrases and paremias, which he divided into 50 groups (in alphabetical order by the initials of the main word of the expression). He translated them into German for the benefit of his students as well as for private use, and combined them with 50 paragraphs (in Italian and German) to show their use in context. The same bilingual structure, yet with a thematic organization (419 categories) appears in an eighteenth-century publication by Pazzaglia, a teacher of the Italian and Spanish languages, in *Ingresso al viridario proverbiale*. The author's intent was representational and celebratory of the proverbial wealth of the Italian language, as he demonstrates in the dedicatory letter to Franz Ernst Freiherr von Platen, Prime Minister for Ernst August von Hannover.

63. Benucci edited the most recent critical edition of Giusti's paremias (*Proverbi*). Her edition gathers Giusti's original paremias without Gino Capponi's additions and new thematic structure. Her choice of the title *Proverbi* follows Giusti's notes in his documents (11) and rejects the version *Proverbi toscani* used in all previous editions (87–88). For additional information on this edition, see Benucci ("Giuseppe Giusti"). In 2014, Fiorelli published *Voci di lingua parlata*, which contains a lexicographical analysis of selected proverbs, proverbial phrases, and sayings from Giusti's collection (*Voci*).

64. Among the collections of regional paremias and aphorisms, it is worth mentioning Frizzi's 1890 *Dizionario dei frizzetti popolari fiorentini*. Technically, a *frizzo* is a clever remark, usually associated with Florentine or Tuscan people, who are renowned for their sharp witticism. Arranged alphabetically, Frizzi's dictionary collects puns, sayings, and proverbs, and provides them with an explanation, a list of contextual uses, literary references, and synonymic expressions. Additionally, the dictionary's entries include equivalent paremias in other vernaculars or dialects, as well as national languages.

65. For a comprehensive analysis of paremiology, see "Introduzione" in Lapucci (*Dizionario dei proverbi italiani* vii–xlii).

66. For a thorough review of the etymology and meanings of παροιμία, see Lippi (*Liber proverbiorum* 160–68) and Rondinelli ("Il concetto di proverbio"). The word *paremia*, for instance, exists in Spanish; the academic world created it to establish order among all the available terms for proverb, including *proverbio* and *refrán*.

67. Another available etymology, which is attributed to Diogenianus of Heraclea, links παροιμία to ὁμοίως, meaning "the same way" (Romero 219). This explanation emphasizes the allegorical and metaphorical interpretation that is necessary to understand the connection of similarity and recognize the paremia's message fully.

68. The very first one to use παροιμία was Aeschylus in his tragedy *Agamemnon*, though without any critical analysis (Romero 219).

69. In modern definitions, adages are related to the person who pronounces them in a specific circumstance, whereas proverbs are anonymous and have a universal appeal (Cherchi, "Tre note" 42). Proverbs are also different from *gnomai*. Generally, *gnomai* present a literary provenance and result from a long work of refinement and reflection; in contrast, proverbs develop from a spontaneous oral utterance, which repetitive use and general acceptance raise to the level of well-recognized structure (Kelso 412–13).

70. For a detailed analysis of the pedagogical application of *sententiae* in oratorical schools during the Roman Empire, see Di Capua (78–108).

71. Franceschi also uses the word "figura" ("trope") to indicate the message that paremias convey. The "figura paremiaca" ("paremiac trope") is the paremia's initial message. This message might not be transparent or immediately understood but is usually rhetorically shaped so that the receiver is able to connect with it ("In margine alle ricerche dell'API" 133).

72. In Quintilianus's definition, brevity seems to characterize both paremias and metaphors, considering that he defines the metaphor as a "similitudo brevior" ("abbreviated simile"; *Institutio oratoria* VIII.6.4).

73. Quintilianus also discusses *sententiae*, which include *gnomai* and aphorisms (VIII.5). He argues that *sententiae* may resemble proverbial phrases, such as *Princeps, qui vult omnia scire, necesse habet multa ignoscere* ("The prince who would know all, must needs ignore much"; VIII.5.3). They may present a comment, for instance, *Nam in omni certamine, qui opulentior est, etiamsi accipit iniuriam, tamen, quia plus potest, facere videtur* ("For in every struggle, the stronger seems not to suffer wrong, even when this is actually the case, but to inflict it, simply in virtue of his superior power"; VIII.5.4). Some *sententiae* show parallelisms, such as Terentius's *Obsequium amicos, veritas odium parit* from *Andria* 1.1.41 ("Complacence wins us friends, truth enmity"; VIII.5.4). Some others express oppositions, such as *Mors misera non est, aditus ad mortem est miser* ("Death is not wretched, but the approach to death"; VIII.5.5; see Tosi, "Gli «Adagia» di Erasmo" 48–50). *Sententiae* may also be embedded in a direct statement. Examples include: *Tam deest avaro, quod habet, quam quod non habet* ("The miser lacks that which he has no less than what he has not"; VIII.5.6) and *Nihil habet, Caesar, nec fortuna tua maius quam ut possis, nec natura melius quam ut velis servare quam plurimos* ("Caesar, the splendor of your present fortune confers on you nothing greater than the power and nothing better than the will to save as many of your fellow-citizens as possible"; VIII.5.7). Di Capua distinguishes between "sentenza" (or "paremia"), which belongs to a community of people, and "periodo," which mostly aims to persuade or excite an emotion (41–49).

74. Wesseling, "Dutch Proverbs and Ancient Sources" and "Dutch Proverbs and Expressions," along with Miller's article, discuss paremias in other works by Erasmus. On the influence of Erasmus's *Adagia* in Italy, see Bainton, Grendler and Grendler, and Menchi.

75. The 1510 edition published in Urbino includes an index of all the commented adages and of all the mentioned names that are not present in the *princeps* (aiiir–aiv).

76. On the presence of Erasmus's *Adagia* in Monosini's *Flos*, see Pignatti (*Etimologia* 203–6).

77. Alunno provides a similar definition in the eighth book, entitled *Qualità* ("Quality") of his encyclopedia *Della fabbrica del mondo* (1546–48). In this work, proverbs are defined "quasi commune omnium verbum vel quod verbum proverbio ponatur" ("as a common word for everything or because a word is put for the proverb"; section *Comparatione* VIII: 223r).

78. Much like for Erasmus, in Garavelli's opinion paremias are forms of allusion ("un dare a intendere"), or ways to appeal to the listener's culture, knowledge, awareness of the world, and memory of the context (257). It follows that paremias are open to polysemy and different interpretations (257–59). Moreover, given their indeterminacy and their cryptic message, paremias are particularly prone to express satire, irony, and sarcasm. Similarly, Lausberg states that allusions blur historical, mythological, and literary facts, as well as everyday and common elements, so that they trigger either detachment or comedy (225–26: par. 404, 232: par. 419).

79. Grimaldi identifies this process as a passage from the sphere of the *parole*, meaning an individual paremiac utterance, to the sphere of the *langue*, suggesting that this utterance becomes an element of an entire community and beyond ("Atlante Paremiologico Italiano" 32).

80. Arora questions the meaning of the adjective "current." In A. Taylor's definition, the word means "generally accepted," but Arora argues that the real issue concerns the modality that brings proverbs to communal acceptance. This can happen inside a small community or at a transcultural level (6).

81. A. Taylor also refers to the etymology of the Greek word αἶνος, ου, ὁ, which means proverb, fable, or laudatory praise to God (in this last meaning it is used in Matthew 21:16 and Luke 18:43). These three meanings refer to morality and ethics, and the difference in their expressive degree depends on the context in which they appear.

82. In his *Il paraverbo*, Menza argues that proverbs are paraverbs. He defines paraverbs as those words or sequences of words that can create a minimum sentence with no or limited relation to the surrounding elements (29). Paraverbs include interjections, formulas of command, imperatives, and different typologies of phrases, such as disjointed, elliptical, pragmatic, prepositional, conjunctional, and verbal phrases. According to Menza, proverbs belong to this category because they can constitute a concluded sentence without introducing external elements (70–76).

83. Grimaldi's approach finds its most significant application in the structure of the questionnaire for the *Atlante paremiologico italiano* ("Atlante Paremiologico Italiano"; for the dictionary, see Franceschi, *Atlante paremiologico italiano*). A question-answer survey does not allow the resurgence of a paremia that is not a direct translation in dialect of a proposed paremia in Italian (34). Grimaldi explains that the interviewer needs to facilitate a spontaneous recollection of the paremias by means of mental associations. Thus, he/she should stimulate the interviewees' reflection over their use, linguistic features, and extra-linguistic components, without heavily influencing them (37).

84. Bronzini advances a similar idea in his 1999 article "La logica del proverbio." His essay is informed by two methods of inquiry, namely the historical contextualization of paremias and their "geochronoparemiological" analysis, which is a combination of regional, synchronic, and diachronic investigations. According to Bronzini, paremias and sayings, more than any other written or spoken elements of the language, are specific to a cultural and social context. Their differences depend on the repetition and commonality of their themes, as well as the multiplicity of their possible meanings (45).

85. Jacqueline and Bernard Cerquiglini express the same idea when they argue that analyzing paremias in literature causes the reader to reflect on the nature of the literary work in its entirety: "S'interroger sur la définition, sur la nature de l'insertion proverbiale dans son œuvre littéraire conduit, par là même, à une réflexion sur le fonctionnement global de cette œuvre" ("To think about the definition, about the nature of proverbial insertion in its literary work leads, by the same token, to a reflection on the global functioning of this literary work"; 360).

86. Grimaldi also speculates that the contextual analysis of paremias is crucial when a text is ironic ("L'ironia nei detti proverbiali" 535). Since irony is inherently ambiguous (Mizzau), Grimaldi argues that its correct interpretation depends on the context, the relationship between speakers, and paralinguistic elements (522). A *pars destruens*, which leads to the refusal of the literal meaning, is followed by a *pars construens*, which implies the

reconstruction of the appropriate contextual meaning (530). When the contextual meaning of the paremia does not comply with the context itself, irony occurs. In spoken utterances, many possible elements may define an ironic paremia: linguistic aspects, such as a pause, interjections, comments; supra-segmental traits, such as intonation; and non-verbal elements, such as mimicry, postures, and gestures. Conversely, in written accounts that do not present pragmatic aspects, irony is expressed through juxtaposition between different contexts, transformation of paremias, interruption of the narrative with the creation of a new perspective, antiphrasis, and dissatisfied expectations.

87. It is not clear what Kelso intends with "sense," but it might concern the reference to moral elements and the presence of pedagogical objectives.

88. Folena talks about "un massimo di brevità formale e di condensazione del significato, e nel contempo di pregnanza e latitudine semantica" ("a maximum of formal brevity and condensed meaning and, simultaneously, of semantic density and extension"; *Quaderni di retorica e poetica* 6).

89. Among the innumerable articles and volumes that Franceschi wrote and curated, the most utilized in this book are the following: "L'atlante paremiologico italiano e la geoparemiologia," "Il proverbio e l'API," "Il proverbio e la Scuola Geoparemiologica Italiana," and *Ragionamenti intorno al proverbio*.

90. The article was previously published in 1994 in *Paremia* (Franceschi, "Il proverbio e la Scuola Geoparemiologica Italiana"). Nonetheless, the essay, "L'atlante paremiologico italiano," will be the most quoted because of its more sequential structure and the greater number of examples. The 1994 publication will be occasionally mentioned when a different concept appears. See also Franceschi (*Ragionamenti*), as well as Miniati and Bucciarelli.

91. Jolles includes proverbs and sayings within his "simple forms," which also incorporate legends, sagas, myths, riddles, cases, memorable events, fairy tales, and jokes. Indeed, proverbs and sayings are structurally simple, but experience multiple actualizations and recall multiple metaphorical meanings (364–78).

92. In her 2006 article "From Usage to Grammar: The Mind's Response to Repetition," Bybee argues that continuous experience allows the human mind to understand when an expression is conventionalized or not (711; see also Langlotz 175–224). This suggests that the human mind recognizes the chain of words in a paremia and analyzes it "as a unit rather than through its individual parts." The mind immediately relates the paremia to a meaning that was systemized either through repetition and continuous usage or else through written codification (Bybee 720).

93. Qualizza refers to the different meanings of a paremia as "*significato generale*" ("general or conventionalized meaning") and "*significati particolari* che pur nella loro particolarità conservano però *l'essenziale* del significato generale" ("specific or contextual meanings, which, despite their specificity, preserve the essential aspects of the general meaning"; 191). The progressive adaptation of a paremia to more contextual instances is, according to

Qualizza, a sign of its antiquity: the more ancient the paremia, the more evolution it has undergone (180). Kirshenblatt-Gimblett supports the same idea in her article "Toward a Theory of Proverb Meaning." Here, she states that the paremia "expresses relative rather than absolute truths and is therefore responsive to the fact that absolute situations, in turn, can be evaluated in more than one way"; "it is not the meaning of the proverb *per se* that need be our central concern but the meaning of proverb performances" (119).

94. Franceschi also defines the "valore paremiologico" as the "insieme di tutte le possibili significazioni traslate che per intuizione o convenzione l'enunciato può suggerire" ("the set of all the possible metaphorical meanings that the utterance may suggest by intuition or convention"; "In margine" 145).

95. Franceschi asserts that, compared to non-metaphorical expressions, paremias are interpreted "per via assai più analogica (irrazionale o pararazionale) che logica" ("in analogical [rational or similar to rational] ways more than logical"; "In margine" 130). Paremias surpass the rules of logic and employ those of analogy, so that they can be associated with a series of events and situations. This aspect distinguishes paremias from didactic sayings or popular aphorisms, which are related mostly to agricultural practices and atmospheric events ("detti didattici," or "detti didascalici," or "aforismi popolari"; Franceschi, "In margine" 14; Franceschi et al., 370; Guazzotti and Oddera 5). Paremias are polysemic, indirect, implicit, and characterized by many possible interpretations. On the contrary, didactic sayings do not follow the rules of analogic representation since they are monosemic and explicit, their meaning coincides with the succession of terms that constitute them, and their content is purely informative.

96. Proverbial expressions reflect "il momento fantastico, poetico, dell'attività linguistica: quello che parla in modo indiretto—analogico e sintetico—per figure o similitudini" ("the fantastic and poetic moment of linguistic activity: that which speaks in indirect—analogic and synthetic—ways via tropes or similitudes"; Franceschi, "L'atlante paremiologico italiano" 7).

97. In their book *Twisted Wisdom*, Mieder and Tóthné Litovkina study expressions that modify traditional and well-known paremias. They call them "anti-proverbs," which means "innovative alterations of and reactions to traditional proverbs" (3). These expressions replace one or more of the original paremia's constituent terms yet maintain the relationship between its component parts and syntactic organization (1–6). Many of the examples they report illustrate how speakers create and invent anti-proverbs to parody the ambiguous didactic wisdom of traditional paremias. The reference to the original expression is necessary to make the entire "new" message recognizable and effective. An example might be *Birds of a feather flop together*, a parody of the well-known expression, *Birds of a feather flock together*. Safian writes on the same topic in his *The Book of Updated Proverbs*. He proposes a well-fitting example, *Man proposes and the computer disposes* (29), whose reference to the traditional paremia *Man proposes, God disposes* is clear, and whose ironic message is incontrovertible.

98. The study of the geographical variation of paremias, based on geolinguistics (or linguistic geography), attests to their dialect variability and offers a detailed description of the socio-cultural aspects of a community (Franceschi, *Ragionamenti* 35–50). For a list of articles and monographs on regional accounts of paremias, see the valuable resources in articles that Franceschi and the researchers at the "Centro Interuniversitario di Geoparemiologia" in Florence wrote on the geographical variations of paremias and their linguistic and cultural idiosyncrasies. Specifically, see Di Natale, Massobrio, Rubano, Salvadori, Tateo, and Tognali in Franceschi, *Ragionamenti*; the bibliography also mentions other articles on the topic by Franceschi, Grimaldi, Mancini, Melis, Miniati, and Porto (48–50). Moreover, Vallini represents a valuable resource (139–76).

99. According to Bakhtin, paremias are placed at one extreme of a continuum of genres, and multivolume novels appear at the other extreme. As such, paremias can be considered a primary or simple speech genre, meaning that they are synthesized within secondary or complex genres (*Speech Genres* 61–62). Hence, primary genres are modified in accordance with the distinctive elements of the secondary genre(s).

100. In the Greek world, three words described textual metamorphoses: "μεταβιξω" ("to transfer"), "μεταφράξω" ("to translate"), "μεταγράφω" ("to transliterate"). Similarly, in order to indicate adaptations of content to different contexts, Latin employed the verbs "convertere" ("to change"), "vertere" ("to turn"), "translatare" ("to transfer"), "transferre" ("to bring across"), "transvertere" ("to transpose"), and "reddere" ("to reproduce"). Both in Greek and Latin, these terms did not suggest a word-by-word translation but rather a transformation of the text so that its general sense could still be transmitted. In *De oratore*, Cicero uses the nouns "translatio" and "traductio" to classify two rhetorical approaches. In book three, while discussing metaphors as a means to refine the orator's style, he states that "translatio" is a synonym for metaphor. Metaphors express a concept by means of a term that shows an affinity ("similitudo") with the original term, even though it refers to a different conceptual and cognitive area ("in alieno loco"; III.38.156). "Traductio," instead, is a synonym for metonymy since it neither invents new words nor implies a metaphor ("translatum"). It rather substitutes ("commutare") one term with another coming from the same conceptual and cognitive area ("proprio"; III.42.167). Metonymy/traductio requires the simple substitution of a word for aesthetic purposes and does not change the content or the meaning of the expression. Metaphor/translation, instead, substitutes a word with another word expressing a different figurative concept. However, if one considers the etymology of the two words, "traductio" (a transference meaning to conduct or lead across; from "ducere") emphasizes the subjectivity of the translator and originality of the process more than "translatum" ("brought across"; from "ferre") and also refers to a more contextualized translation (Berman; Folena, *Volgarizzare e tradurre* 68). Cicero expresses this same concept in his *Epistola ad Pisones*: "Nec verbo verbum reddere fidus interpres" ("Neither does the faithful interpreter translate word by word").

On translation as a cultural adaptation in early modern Europe, see Burke (*Cultural Translation* 7–38); for a history of translation starting from the third millennium B.C.E., see Nocera (27–56).

101. This book adopts the title "proverbial phrase." Compared to "proverbial expression," which refers to a sequence of words governed by rules of textual organization, "proverbial phrase" encompasses other expressions. Among them are the following: nominal phrases whose primary term is a noun or an adjective; expressions containing a simile; individual entries; or expressions with a verb and various complements (for a detailed analysis of the various components and types or proverbial phrases, see Renzi et al., vol. 1: 37–284). "Proverbial phrase" is preferable to "saying" because it underlines the non-literal or figurative meaning that characterizes the structure of these expressions, indeed similar to proverbs. Moreover, it is more comprehensive than "idiomatic expression," which suggests that an expression is just typical of the language. On sayings, Lucilla Pizzoli's 2019 *Modi di dire* is an interesting resource.

102. Franceschi uses the formula "detto proverbiale" or "detto paremiaco" ("proverbial or paremic saying") and includes these expressions inside the paremiac code, which gathers all paremias with figurative meanings (Franceschi et al., 365).

103. In her 1960 article "Premessa a un repertorio di frasi proverbiali," Brambilla Ageno agrees with A. Taylor that proverbial phrases have neither a defined form nor the autonomy of a sentence, yet always maintain a figurative meaning (244). Accordingly, sequences whose terms are not figurative, such as *Dar la soia* ("To give the soy"), *Dar la quadra* ("To give the square"), or *Dar il mattone* ("To give the brick") meaning to tease or to flatter, are not proverbial phrases. In these expressions, the figurative meaning does not derive from the single terms themselves but emerges from the entire sequence. If the expressions were not considered in their entirety, it would be impossible to capture their non-compositional meaning.

104. Serianni refers to the flexibility of the introductory verb in proverbial phrases like "duttilità contestuale" ("contextual ductility"; 71).

105. Cherdantseva finds the aspect that differentiates all sayings from proverbs in emotionality (which is linked to the degree of a certain quality) as opposed to evaluation. Sayings do not moralize, but just show; they "photograph" a fact "emotionally" without expressing an opinion or assessing reality, as do proverbs (342).

106. According to Langlotz, four aspects seem to characterize idiomatic expressions: institutionalization, which is related to their conventionalized status inside a community of speakers; compositeness, since they are multi-word units; frozenness, due to the restricted variability of their lexical elements; and non-compositionality, because of their figurative meaning (4). Not surprisingly, he mentions three of these aspects (institutionalization, compositeness, and non-compositionality) when providing a definition and a classification of proverbs.

107. Proverbs may also be read literally or interpreted metaphorically. One instance is the aforementioned proverb *Chi va al letto la sera senza cena intorno tutta la notte si dimena* ("Who fasting goes to bed, uneasy lies his head around all night"; CN 145). Monna Isabetta is really shaking her bed because she is engaging in sexual intercourse with a monk. By using the proverb, she alludes to her act, but feigns to refer to her hunger and pretends not to speak figuratively (Chiecchi, "Sentenze" 137). The husband is unaware of what is happening in the next room and reads his wife's paremia literally. Thus, he acknowledges that she has been fasting along with him for a long period, and hence is shaking the bed because she is hungry. The equivalence between the literal and the metaphorical reading of the paremia vis-à-vis the reality of the situation emphasizes the comedy stemming from the context.

108. On the topic, specifically on the lexical and grammatical metaphors in idiomatic expressions, see Pamies.

109. Among Casadei's idiomatic expressions, what she calls formulaic and stereotypical expressions, are not considered in the following chapters. Formulaic expressions are related to a specific pragmatic context and include those expressions that are illocutionary (or aim to draw someone's attention), performative (such as certain legal formulas), recurrent formulas in certain communicative contexts (including introductory and conclusive greetings), or textual and conversational transitions and fillers. Stereotypical expressions are those to which the community of speakers, by continuous repetition, gave a fixed meaning as clichés. Both formulaic and stereotypical expressions differ from paremias because they do not actually require a figurative interpretation. Furthermore, their meaning, if not literal, maintains a stronger bond with the original and concrete situation that created them (*Metafore ed espressioni idiomatiche*; Vietri, *Lessico e sintassi*; Elia et al.). What is included in the following chapters are those expressions whose ties are stronger than those of a free combination of terms and that have developed a conventionalized meaning over time and beyond their individual terms.

110. Lapucci proposes "facezia proverbiale" instead of "wellerismo" (*Come disse...* vii). For a thorough bibliography and analysis on wellerisms in many languages up to 1994, see Mieder and Kingsbury.

111. Brambilla Ageno argues that fables and short stories, as well as proverbs and proverbial phrases, are a source for wellerisms, ("Premessa a un repertorio di frasi proverbiali" 253; see also Aquilecchia; Carnes, *Proverbia in Fabula* 11–12). The connection between fables and wellerisms occurs in three ways: either a statement coming from the fable reaches the status of a paremia; or an expression becomes paremiac while preserving a link to the fable; or a paremia generates a story. For these categories, see Bizzarri ("La potencialidad narrativa del refrán" 24–25), Nikolaeva, and A. Taylor (*The Proverb* 27–32).

112. Franceschi distinguishes wellerisms featuring a proverb, such as *Come disse il tale. Chi tardi arriva male alloggia* ("As that person said. He who comes late lodges ill"), from other wellerisms in which the paremiac section does not contain a proverb. He calls the first typology "welleristic proverbs," which do not present the humorous twist that normally characterizes wellerisms. Moreover, their introductory formula is only a later addition aiming to historicize the original portion of the saying and give it authority (Franceschi et al., 372–73; see also A. Taylor, *The Proverb* 220).

113. For more information on wellerisms, see Brambilla Ageno ("A proposito di wellerismi"), Corso, and A. Taylor ("A Bibliographical Note on Wellerisms"). For a brief explanation of five wellerisms in Italian and in dialect, see Speroni, "Five Italian Wellerisms."

114. Borghini mentions wellerisms in some sparing manuscript notes about proverbs (ca. 1570; Borghini, "I proverbi" 165: footnote 1). He states that these paremias belong to a typology of expressions "che è frequente e molto commoda e piacevole insieme, che e' dice il suo concetto ma con un motto già detto da altri e che per la sua piacevolezza o novità sia ito in proverbio" ("that is frequent as well as together convenient and pleasant; it expresses a concept, yet through a quip already used by others that has become a proverb thanks to its pleasantness or novelty"; 172–73).

115. See also Mieder ("Wellerisms"), Mieder and Dundes (8), and A. Taylor (*The Proverb* 217). Different elements can convey humor: a foolish statement or a banal and facetious reply, an obscene remark, use of dialect, or simultaneous presence of different languages (Speroni, *The Italian Wellerism* 7–8).

116. Bizzarri describes wellerisms as "un pequeño y rápido diálogo sin el contexto narrativo" ("a short and quick dialogue without narrative context"; "La potencialidad narrativa del refrán" 17).

117. Speroni argues that not all wellerisms are comedic. Some of them are incomplete, which does not allow for a full understanding of their meaning; others may have been comical when they were first used, but progressively lost their humorous appeal and significance (*The Italian Wellerism* 7–8).

118. This occurs in Salviati's, Serdonati's, Pescetti's, and Lena's collections. For some of Serdonati's wellerisms, see Ferrato's editions of his paremias in Works Consulted; for a concise historical overview and a list of all wellerisms in Serdonati's collection, see Speroni ("Wellerismi tolti dai proverbi inediti di F. Serdonati").

119. The original reads: "It is difficult to appreciate or even to care for the local, and frequently incongruous and untranslatable, phrases that constitute many wellerisms" (Speroni, *The Italiam Wellerism* 6).

Chapter Two

1. Since Brusantino signed three autographed letters as Vincenzo Brusantino (see Works Consulted for the collocation and content of these letters), this spelling is preferred. The linguistic reason behind the other two alternatives also confirms this choice. On one hand, Brusantini is a genitive patronymic, which usually follows the given name but is not used after "messere" or "messer." Brugiantini, on the other hand, is the Florentine version of Brusantino ("brusare," "to burn", which is the Paduan alternative to "bruciare," becomes "brugiare" in Florentine vernacular). In the three autographed letters, the first name is spelled either Vicenzo or Vicentio.

2. Brusantino's biography was almost completely unknown until Pettinelli researched it. Pettinelli indicated 1556 as his date of death (*Forme e percorsi* 71–72: footnote 17), whereas DBI proposes 1570. The Biblioteca Comunale Ariostea preserves some documents concerning the Brusantino family (Brusantino, *Archivio Famiglia Muzzarelli Brusantini*), among which Vincenzo Brusantino is mentioned in genealogical trees, in trials, and in contracts about changes of ownership (see also Pettinelli, *Forme e percorsi* 71). There is, however, a 1544 autographed letter in the collection "Raccolta Autografica Cittadella" at the Archivio di Stato in Ferrara, sent to the judge of the town, Giovanni Paolo Machiavelli (Brusantino, *Lettera al giudice* 563). The letter concerns a credit that Brusantino has with the town and which he asks the judge to disperse by giving portions to different townspeople, including a priest and an estate manager. The Biblioteca Estense Universitaria in Modena also keeps an undated and unsigned letter to Ercole II d'Este (Brusantino, *Lettera a Ercole II*; see Procaccioli, "Nuova veste"). This document deals with the author's copyright on his *L'Angelica innamorata*, defined as the result of "alcuni romanci" "mess[i] insieme" ("some romances assembled together"). Brusantino asks the Duke for a special privilege to preserve his rights for twelve years, so that no one would be able to print or sell his work without his agreement. He also petitions the Duke to apply a fine of 500 gold scudi for each transgressor. Finally, the Archivio di Stato di Modena preserves an autographed letter dated January 8, 1551, which Brusantino sent to the ducal secretary in Ferrara, Bartolomeo Prosperi, along with one of his books, probably *L'Angelica innamorata* (Brusantino, *Lettera a Bartolomeo Prosperi*).

3. For a detailed analysis of Francesco Marcolini's publications from 1534 to 1559 and his engagement with the Venetian literary community, see: Carapezza, Parlato ("L'editoria veneziana e Marcolini"), Pettinelli (*Forme* 167–74), Quondam ("Nel giardino del Marcolini" 78–86, 113–16), Servolini, and Casali (257–60). Particularly remarkable are two of Marcolini's works: *Le sorti di Francesco Marcolino da Forlì intitolate giardino di pensieri* (1540) and *Le ingegnose sorti composte per Francesco Marcolini da Forlì intitulate giardino di pensieri* (1550). Pettinelli demonstrates that Brusantino's introductory paremias may have an antecedent in the *terzine* of Marcolini's *Sorti* (*Forme* 177–78). For this reason, it may be argued that Marcolini, and not Brusantino, introduced both the allegories and the paremias at the beginning of each canto. Since no evidence emerged to support this perspective, in this book both paratextual elements will be considered as the Ferrarese author's own additions.

4. Brusantino's rhymes are contained in a volume that Girolamo Ruscelli commissioned humanist Bona de Boliris to write: *Il tempio della divina signora donna Giovanna d'Aragona, fabbricato da tutti i più gentili spiriti e in tutte le lingue principali del mondo* (Venezia: per Plinio Pietrasanta, 1554). Some of Brusantino's petrarchist rhymes are published in Baruffaldi and

Lanzoni's work *Rime scelte* (113–16). Brusantino also wrote a few poems and maintained an epistolary exchange with Pietro Aretino. In a letter to him on December 22, 1550, from his property called Brusantina, the Ferrarese author praises their friendship and defines the closeness of their souls as an act of transmigration. He looks forward to going back to Venice where he will enjoy illuminating conversations with his friend (this is the only letter by Brusantino published in Aretino, *Lettere*, t. II, b. II: 338–39, letter n. 360).

5. Marcolini reprinted *L'Angelica innamorata* for the second time in 1553; however, there are no modern editions of the work. Its last edition dates to 1837 by Antonelli's Venetian printing press. The integral text of the poem was included in the third volume (1853) of Zanotto's *Parnaso italiano*. References to *L'Angelica innamorata* are also scant. The work is mentioned only in accounts of chivalric poems after *Orlando furioso* or in anthologies of sixteenth-century continuations of Ariosto's masterpiece. In these instances, the text is frequently accused of being incoherent and stylistically unrefined.

6. In this book, all citations come from a copy preserved at the Boston Public Library (G.16.66). The copy, in quarto, consists of 552 numbered pages, with two blank pages at the beginning and two at the end, and eight non-numbered pages. These final pages contain the "Tavola di tutte le novelle, che nelle dieci Giornate del Decamerone si contengono" ("Table of all the stories that are contained in the ten days of the Decameron"). On the first page, Marcolini's emblem appears with the motto "Veritas filia temporis" ("Truth, the Daughter of Time"), included in the external oval and surrounded by the sentence "La verità figliuola è del gran tempo" ("Truth is the daughter of the great time"; see Saxl). For a description of Marcolini's emblem, see Parlato ("L'editoria veneziana e Marcolini" 76–78), Quondam ("Nel giardino" 107), and Servolini (89–90).

7. Prior to the twentieth century, just a few anthologists briefly refer to Brusantino's *Le cento novelle*. Fontanini does not mention *Le cento novelle*, despite describing modern collections of stories, including some rewritings of Boccaccio's *Decameron*. Haym refers to Brusantino's work (*Notizia de' libri rari*, section *Poemi di vario genere*: 121; *Biblioteca italiana*, s.v. *Vincenzo Brugiantino*: 215), and so do Percel (291) and Crescimbeni (129: n. 99). Quadrio only reports that *Le cento novelle* is rare (352), while three other anthologies briefly refer to the work: Mazzucchelli's *Gli scrittori d'Italia* (vol. 3: 2234–36), Tiraboschi's *Storia della letteratura italiana* (vol. 7: 96), and Ughi's *Dizionario storico degli uomini illustri ferraresi* (99).

8. In 1538, Aretino also published a religious work, *I quattro libri de la humanità di Christo*, which was likely part of Brusantino's library and which Florio certainly used as a source for his *A Worlde of Wordes* (Wyatt, "La biblioteca in volgare di John Florio" 434).

9. In 1536 and 1538, Marcolini had published another moral reinterpretation of a canonical text: Franciscan friar Girolamo Malipiero's *Petrarca spirituale*, which, unlike Brusantino's work, received public acclaim and was constantly reprinted, probably thanks to its sublimation of Petrarca's carnal love into a spiritual and Christian one (Fragnito, *Church, Censorship* *and Culture* 210–11; Quondam, "Riscrittura, citazione e parodia" 203–62). Considering the friendship between Marcolini and Aretino, Quondam proposes that Malipiero's operation is parodic and aims to release a work that, by virtue of its spirituality, mocks the original text as well as the entire Petrarchist ideology. It seems hard to consider Brusantino's work as a parodic rewriting of the *Decameron*, especially because *Le cento novelle*'s transformation of the original text is not as pervasive as Malipiero's.

10. A 1492 edition already uses this title in addition to the original: *Decameron o ver Cento novelle del Boccaccio* (Venezia: De Gregoriis). Another work presents the title with "cento:" Francesco Sansovino's 1563 *Delle cento novelle scelte da' più nobili scrittori della lingua volgare* (Venezia: Rampazetto). The text is related to Boccaccio's work only as far as it presents 100 stories. These are taken from the most notable authors of novellas, including Agnolo Firenzuola, Francesco Maria Molza, Parabosco, Masuccio Salernitano, Ser Giovanni Fiorentino, and Straparola.

11. Despite his intent to make Boccaccio's text more ethical, Brusantino's chosen title, *Le cento novelle*, is less "religious" than the *Decameron*. That is, according to Kirkham, the title *Decameron* clearly refers to a ten-day path from the first story to the last one of the collection (264–65).

12. For an overview on the concept of genre, see Pelosi (31–39). On the concept of hybridization of literary genres, Lewalski's book as well as Destro and Sportelli's edited volume are excellent sources.

13. Brusantino alludes very briefly to Boccaccio's lengthy introduction and does not include the "orrido cominciamento" ("grim beginning") of the plague in Florence, probably because its popular memory was lost at that time (Pettinelli, *Forme* 196). The reference to the plague is also absent in Groto's 1588 revision of the *Decameron*.

14. The introductory images of each day depict scenes of social life related to the *brigata*'s activities. Conversely, the introductory images of the first novella of each day (as well as story I.2) represent a scene or simultaneous scenes, usually the central ones, from the story. Favaro argues that many of the illustrations come from Giolito's edition of the *Decameron* and some from *L'Angelica innamorata* (102: footnotes 1, 2). For a detailed illustration of *Le cento novelle*'s iconographic sources, see Carapezza (59-62), and for a more comprehensive analysis of engravings in the fifteenth- and sixteenth-century editions of the *Decameron*, see Pettinelli (*Forme* 173) and Borroni Salvadori. On the artistic exchanges between Brusantino's *L'Angelica innamorata* and Doni's *I marmi* through Marcolini's mediation in his *Sorti*, Plaisance's article deserves mention. The presence of images in sixteenth-century works derives from a trend that applies to both the *Decameron* and *Orlando furioso*. Many editions of *Orlando furioso* feature engravings at the beginning of each canto: the 1536 edition by Nicolò di Aristotile (nicknamed Zoppino); the 1542 edition by Ludovico Dolce and Gabriel Giolito de' Ferrari; the 1553 edition by Giovanni Andrea Valvassori (also known as Guadagnino); and the 1556 edition by Girolamo Ruscelli and Vincenzo Valgrisi. In the Zoppino and Giolito editions, the image is placed at the beginning of the cantos between the title and the allegory; in the Valgrisi edition it extends to the entire page. For images of the different editions, see the website designed by Lina Bolzoni and her group of scholars at the Scuola Normale Superiore di Pisa, entitled *L'Orlando furioso e la sua traduzione in immagini*.

15. The changes from Boccaccio's captions are minimal. At times, Brusantino alters the tense (from past indicative to present indicative) or the mode of verbs (from past participle to gerund; from indicative to subjunctive), their valence, or their pronominal aspect. Sometimes, he adds an adjective (in I.2 the addition of the adjective "molti," "many," before "chierici," "clerics," emphasizes the corruption of the religious members), changes the position of certain clusters, and substitutes or deletes some of them (in IV.2 Boccaccio's "della casa," "from the house," becomes "da una finestra," "from a window"). Moreover, the author of *Le cento novelle* may modify a singular into a plural or vice versa (such as in VIII.3 where Boccaccio's "a' suoi compagni," "to his friends," becomes "a un suo compagno," "to a friend"). Sporadically, Brusantino substitutes a word with a similar one (in IX.10 "'ncantamento," "spell," is substituted for "incantesmo," bearing the same meaning) or a different one (in IV.8 "allato," "on the side," becomes "addosso," "over"). He makes morphological and phonetic modifications and restores some etymological spellings while at the same time introducing more modern words (in II.4 "corsaro" substitutes "corsale," "corsair," and "Corfù" substitutes "Gurfo," "Corfu"). Sometimes, Brusantino makes mistakes. For instance, in II.2 he spells Rinaldo d'Asti as Rinaldo d'Esti and introduces a *saut du même au même* in III.7 and V.10. Other selected mistakes are: the change of Boccaccio's Beltramo into Guglielmo in III.9; the indirect feminine pronoun transformed into the corresponding masculine in IV.5 and IX.7; and "contadini" ("farmers") becoming "cittadini" ("citizens") in VI.10. In story IV.10, Brusantino opts for a synonym: "adoppiato" becomes "alloppiato," both meaning stun or sleeping because of opium. Finally, he introduces Florentine elements, such as "iscampa" ("he escapes") in II.4.

16. Tartaro lists the following stories: I.1.3–6; I.2.3; I.3.4–5; II.7.7; II.9.3; II.10.4; III.1.2–5; III.2.3; III.3.3–4; IV.3.4–7; IV.4.3; IV.7.4–5; IV.8.3–4; V.1.2; V.6.3; VII.5.3–6; VIII.2.3–4; VIII.4.3; VIII.8.3; IX.9.7–9 (663–64). On the incipit of the novellas in general, see Forni.

17. Many of the epithets are feminine plural adjectives, but there are also adverbial clusters. Attributed to the female readers of Brusantino's stories, they commend the praiseworthy qualities of women. Their number varies according to the day, but they do not exceed thirteen and except for a few repetitions, they differ from one day to another. This seems to recall the list of epithets for male characters that Brusantino uses in *L'Angelica innamorata*. On the origins of similar lists, see Perocco ("La moralità rimata" [1987] 297–98).

18. *Le cento novelle*'s layout is similar to that of *L'Angelica innamorata*. Each canto of *L'Angelica innamorata* features a caption in octave ("ottava d'argumento," "octave with the explanation of the topic"), which succinctly describes its topic (a feature that distinguishes it from Cieco's *Mambriano*).

Despite presenting no allegories and paremias, the first octaves of all cantos in *L'Angelica innamorata* contain moral references to various topics (including love, fortune, human cleverness, virtue, glory, honor, and death). In Marcolini's second edition of *L'Angelica innamorata* in 1553, introductory allegories accompany the cantos; it is arguable that Marcolini's paratextual element was transposed into *Le cento novelle* the year after.

19. For a comprehensive discussion of the many European literary filiations from all of Boccaccio's works, see Boitani (99–116) and Mazzoni.

20. Latin translations of Boccaccio's stories were also common, both in prose and in poetry. Some examples are Leonardo Bruni's 1437 translation of Tancredi and Ghismonda's novella (Dec. IV.1), Enea Silvio Piccolomini's, (who became Pope Pius II) 1444 *Historia de duobus amantibus* for the same story VI.1. Another subsequent example is Morata's protestant-driven translation of the collection's first two novellas contained in her posthumous *Latina et graeca quae haberi potuerunt monumenta*.

21. For an overview of novellas reduced in verse, see Beer. Editions in prose of single novellas from the *Decameron* are known as *novelle spicciolate*. One of them is Antonio Manetti's *Il grasso legnaiuolo* (1550s), whose main character draws inspiration from Boccaccio's Calandrino. In the second half of the fifteenth century, Bernardo Giambullari and Bartolomeo Davanzati rendered this same novella in verse (Ascoli). For *novelle spicciolate* in the fifteenth and sixteenth centuries, see the following: Bragantini (*Il riso sotto il velame*), Malato (*La novella italiana* 431–82), and Parma's articles ("Fortuna spicciolata del *Decameron*" [2003]; "Fortuna spicciolata del *Decameron*" ([2005]).

22. Relying on the troubadour tradition of chansons performed in public, *cantari* were mainly recited in squares or church porches and in front of a public who lacked a refined literary knowledge (Favaro 100–1). Parma calls *cantari novellistici* "riscritture–riassunti" ("rewritings–summaries"; "Fortuna spicciolata del *Decameron* [2003] 213), whereas De Robertis refers to them as a "riappropriazione" ("reappropriation") of the original text, which, according to Benucci et al., generates as many different texts as there are different performances in public (xiii).

23. *Cantari novellistici* reproduced Boccaccio's *Decameron* very faithfully but not *verbatim*. They freely elaborated upon the original stories and emphasized certain aspects of the narration, especially salacious and stereotypical ones. Additionally, they abbreviated the references to other events or the psychological description of characters, particularly those belonging to lower societal strata. Specific emphasis was given to dialogues, which allowed for more vivacity and, at the same time, offered space for personal innovations. Theatrical elements were widely present to imitate the spoken language and to reproduce the *Decameron*'s expressionism (Parma, "Una riduzione in ottava rima" 203–5).

24. The most famous *cantari* are renderings of *Decameron*'s novellas I.4, II.9, II.10 (two versions), III.1, III.7, III.10, IV.1 (five versions), IV.4, V.4, V.8, VII.4, VII.7, and X.10 (Rada, *Cantari tratti dal «Decameron»* 17–23;

the article offers detailed analyses and the critical editions of the two *cantari* for stories I.4 and II.10). See also Parma, "Una riduzione in ottava rima" (322–64) for a list of the available *cantari novellistici* and their manuscript or printed tradition (Benucci et al. offers a critical edition of these texts) and Malato (*La novella italiana* 407–30) for their structure and derivation from the *Decameron*.

25. Idiomatic expressions, repetitions of formulas, and paremias testified to the relationship that the performer of *cantari* established with his public on a popular level. For more information, see Matarrese (*Parole e forme* 40) and Villoresi (38–39).

26. In this *cantare*, the husband names "indovinello" ("riddle") what Boccaccio's Rustico calls "diavolo" ("devil").

27. The proverbial phrase opens and concludes the *cantare* as a sort of circular structure. At the beginning, it introduces the topic, whereas in the end, it functions as a concluding device and as a memento of the paremia's message. The expression is also present in Cynthio's *Libro* (308–19).

28. In his collection of Tuscan proverbs, Serdonati explains the expression's origins differently. He begins with an account of a witch from Ravenna named Maria, who was kidnapped by the devil and never found again. The 1691 edition of the Voc. Cr. (s.v. *cercare*) mentions the same proverbial phrase, although it interprets Maria as the Latin word "maria," the plural of "sea." The meaning, therefore, would be to look for the sea in Ravenna, a city that does not connect at all to the Adriatic Sea. In both instances, metaphorically the proverbial phrase suggests that something is particularly difficult to find or is sought in vain.

29. This edition intends to provide a more correct and coherent text than Brucioli's 1538 publication. As Navò declares in his paragraph to "gli osservatori della vera volgar lingua" ("the observers of the true vernacular language"; in Boccaccio, *Il Decamerone* [1541]), Dolce's text is free of all those mistakes that tradition created, especially because "le istesse sentenze in altra guisa formate lo rendevano manchevole della sua propria e natìa chiarezza" ("the same sententious expressions in other forms deprived the text of its own and native clarity"). The list of difficult passages as well as of proverbs and sayings appears at the end of the text, yet their explanation is interspersed within the narrative in a separate paragraph that breaks the continuity of the text. For more information, see P. Trovato (209–40).

30. Brucioli's edition of the *Decameron* (Boccaccio, *Il Decamerone* [1542]) offers a list of annotations, almost at the end of each novella, on single words, clusters of words, idiomatic expressions, sayings, and paremias in order to make Boccaccio's stories more understandable. Specifically, the notes aim to provide explanations of those Florentine words and expressions that might not be intelligible to non-Tuscan speakers and to show the rhetorical strength of Boccaccio's language (Bragantini, *Il riso sotto il velame* 34–36; Pettinelli, *Forme* 167; Richardson, *Print Culture* 99; Rondinelli, "«Ho udito dire mille volte …»" 312: footnote 99). Among the explained proverbs are *Tal asino*

dà in parete, tal riceve ("As the ass gives in the wall, so he may receive"; Dec. II.9.6) and *Fare del pruno un malarancio* ("To make a blackthorn out of a sweet orange tree"; Dec. IV.8.7). Brucioli's glosses are similar to those with which he provides his translation of Solomon's proverbs in *Annotationi sopra i proverbii di Salomo*. For a discussion on the influence of Boccaccio's vernacular on Brucioli's literary activity, see Pierno.

31. This work reproduces the same format of Brucioli's 1538 edition of the *Decameron*. Here, however, Brucioli adds to the end of each novella explanations of the grammatical rules of the Tuscan language in order to make the text, along with its proverbs, words, tropes, and sayings, more intelligible throughout all of Italy. He includes the fourteenth-century words used by Boccaccio, aiming to correct possible mistakes in speaking and writing (dedicatory letter to Maddalena de' Bonaiuti).

32. Just as with previous works, this edition seeks to facilitate a deeper understanding of the *Decameron*, a text that Sansovino knew well since he had written *Le lettere sopra le diece giornate del Decamerone* in 1543. Explanatory elements include: Boccaccio's *Vita*, introductory allegories, a "Dichiarazione di tutti i vocaboli, detti, proverbii e luoghi difficili che sono sparsi nel presente volume per ordine d'alphabetto" ("Explanation of all the words, sayings, proverbs, and difficult places, which are scattered in this volume, listed in alphabetical order"), "I luoghi e gli auttori quali il Boccaccio ha tolto i nomi che sono sparsi in questo volume, così de gli huomini come delle donne" ("The places and the authors from which Boccaccio borrowed the names that are scattered in this volume, for men as well as for women"), and "Epitheti usati da M. Giovanni Boccaccio posti per ordine di alphabeto" ("Epithets used by Sir Giovanni Boccaccio listed in alphabetical order"). Sansovino annotates the text with marginal notes (signaled by an asterisk) that illustrate the differences between his version and previous editions. In 1546, Giolito asks Sansovino to edit the *Decameron* on the basis of the ancient exemplars to obtain a high-quality text. In order to make the edition useful to learners of the vulgar language, Sansovino adds other explanations of words, idioms, and paremias, a note on proper names, and a list of epithets (Richardson, *Print Culture* 111; P. Trovato 220). He gathers information from contemporary dictionaries and encyclopedias, which were still in the process of being printed, including Alberto Acarisio's *Vocabolario, grammatica et orthographia de la lingua volgare* (1543) and Alunno's *Della fabbrica del mondo* (1546–48). Like Brucioli, he introduces some Northern equivalents for Tuscan terms.

33. This text contains textual, moral, and etymological explanations of Boccaccio's work. It features a brief moral statement for each story, which probably comes from the allegories that Dolce introduces in his 1535 edition of *Orlando furioso*.

34. Ruscelli and Valgrisi's edition offers a philologically accurate text, especially in orthography and punctuation, with extensive marginalia on grammatical and textual issues, differences with the precedent tradition, and comparisons with the language of Petrarca. This edition also presents a life of Boccaccio by Sansovino and a "vocabolario generale di tutte le voci usate dal Boccaccio, bisognose di dichiaratione, d'avertimento, o di regole" ("a general dictionary of all the terms used by Boccaccio needing clarifications, explanations, or rules").

35. This edition is based on Sansovino's 1546 text, to which Dolce adds a letter to the readers. Dolce's annotations are in the marginal spaces, signaled by an asterisk as in Sansovino's publication. Many of these notes are shared, but for others Dolce reestablishes the text of previous editions to Sansovino's. For more information, see Pettinelli (*Forme* 171–74).

36. The Bindoni and Pasini 1535 edition of Ariosto's poem (later reprinted in 1540) features a "Dechiarazione di alcuni vocaboli e luoghi difficili dell'opera" ("Explanation of some difficult words and places"), compiled by Dolce. This aspect made this edition easier to use and to disseminate even among non-experts. The 1542 and 1543 editions by Dolce and Giolito feature extensive allegories at the beginning of each canto. In Giolito's 1544 version, Dolce adds extra-textual elements meant to explain *Orlando furioso* in the best way possible. Specifically, he introduces a list of paremias and observations that could help the reader (Richardson, *Print Culture* 98). A similar exposition of Ariosto's text and of its morality through allegories and paratextual elements occurs in the 1553 and 1554 Venetian editions by Valvassori (Javitch 36–39; Richardson, *Print Culture* 118). The later Valgrisi 1556 edition of *Orlando furioso* curated by Ruscelli shares many elements with Giolito's 1552 edition of the *Decameron*, including an introductory "argomento" ("topic") in verse, a summary of the canto, allusions to classical myths, allegories, and a final glossary ("Annotationi") of terms difficult to understand (Javitch 39–41). This also occurs in the 1567 edition of the chivalric poem, which features introductory allegories, final annotations, a list of texts imitating Ariosto's work, historical facts, and fables used by Ariosto.

37. At the end of the poem, Dolce lists all of the challenging words and passages in the book along with some comparisons between Ariosto and other authors that imitate *Orlando furioso*. This edition was frequently reprinted over a twenty-year span (Javitch 31–36; Richardson, *Print Culture* 97).

38. Javitch comments upon the episode of Ricciardetto's transvestism and seduction of Fiordispina in canto XXV. He notes that Dolce leaves out many of Ariosto's sympathetic comments toward the characters and the events and argues that he focuses only on those aspects of the canto that he could moralize and emphasize in the allegories (33).

39. Some examples include: Luigi Alemanni's *Avarchide* (composed in 1548 and published posthumously in 1570); Francesco Bolognetti's *Il Costante* (ca. 1547–48); and Gian Giorgio Trissino's *Italia liberata dai Goti* (started in 1527 but published in 1547–48). All of these texts aimed to substitute Ariosto's contemporary romance with the heroic atmosphere of Homer's and Vergilius's epics (Favaro 100).

40. The adjective "mezzana" comes from Boccaccio's *Filocolo*: "A te bisogna di volare abasso, però che la bassezza t'è mezzana via," meaning that it is not appropriate to seek out higher places ("It is for you to fly low since humbleness is your proper way"; V.97.7).

41. Chiecchi argues that the remarkable presence of paremias in the *Decameron* derives precisely from the collection's appeal to the new pragmatic and practical social class of merchants ("Sentenze" 138). This aspect is evidenced in the great number of copies made after Boccaccio's death for non-aristocratic readers, mostly merchants (Richardson, "The textual history" 43).

42. Perocco emphasizes that the absence of the *Decameron*'s frame makes *Le cento novelle* more appropriate for a median public ("La moralità rimata" [1987] 296).

43. On the chivalric tradition in Ferrara, see Pettinelli (*L'immaginario cavalleresco*). Bruscagli's article "Stagioni della civiltà estense" offers an exhaustive overview of the cultural, literary, and artistic vibrancy in Ferrara and on its distinctive chivalric publications.

44. This aspect derives from the tradition of *cantari*, whose octaves and cantos are concluded in themselves and do not present fluid passages from one stanza to the next (De Robertis 16). Ariosto distinguishes his *Orlando furioso* partially from this tradition. Since he consistently respects the relationship between rhythm and syntax, his text guarantees continuity between the development of events and the meter. However, the author resorts to open octaves when the content requires it, especially in the argumentative and narrative moments (Praloran 21, 191–98, 206–7). Even when he does not use open octaves, he may expand the narration by creating a narrative, lexical, and rhetorical continuum among subsequent stanzas through repeated words or enjambments (Cabani, "Le riprese interstrofiche" and *Costanti ariostesche* 9–259; Roggia 43). In these instances, the clash between the semantic continuity and the metrical discontinuity determines a climax in the narration (Praloran 199–253; Roggia 25–46).

45. For a more detailed discussion on rewritings that moralize *Decameron*, see Torre. Expressing ethical evaluations over a given text is something with which Brusantino had already experimented when writing his *L'Angelica innamorata*. Here, a strong "giudizio morale" ("moral judgement") inspires the events and the characters' behavior (Leo 10). Ruggiero dies violently, poisoned and then killed by Gano, because of his alleged fault of marrying a princess as a foot soldier. Angelica deserves to be punished for her transgressions so that she can purify her mind from the immoral events of her life as narrated in the poems of Boiardo and Ariosto. Under Alcina's spell, she falls in love with any knight but, as in a sort of Dantesque "contrappasso," all of them abandon Angelica before she can satisfy her sexual desires. Finally, she chooses Sacripante as her partner. The need for regularity in religious practices may explain the pervasive presence of marriage in *L'Angelica innamorata*. Ariosto applies this practice to only two couples due to unavoidable narrative and dynastic reasons. Conversely, Brusantino restores marriage as a way to regulate the life of wandering knights and provide a wise and focused conclusion to the vicissitudes of love experienced by the various couples. When marriage does not happen, as in the case of a character called l'Infante, then a spiritual transformation occurs and entails forgoing possessions and privileging religious faith over romantic love.

46. For an analysis of parodic and ironic uses of paremias in chivalric poems, see Matarrese (*Parole e forme* 176–82). Delcorno offers a thorough presentation of irony in the *Decameron*.

47. The link between allegory and paremia is not only in content and ethical attitude, but also in vocabulary (Pettinelli, *Forme* 175).

48. Tartaro discusses the value of the *exemplum* as a timeless life lesson with intellectual, as well as moral and practical purposes. According to him, the *exemplum* transforms past memorable sayings and behaviors into univocal truths in the contemporaneous socio-political contexts (623–33).

49. This is true in the *Decameron*, in which Boccaccio places many paremias at the beginning of his novellas. The stories then develop, confirm, or disapprove of these paremias (for instance, I.10, II.1, II.9, IV.2, VIII.7, VIII.8, and IX.9).

50. For ease of reference, *Le cento novelle*'s captions for the analyzed stories are included after the introductory allegory and paremia.

51. It is worth noting that at the onset of the nineteenth century during the Carnival festivities, a farse in music was represented at the Venetian Teatro San Moisè, based on Giuseppe Foppa's 1801 libretto entitled *Sopra l'ingannator cade l'inganno, over I due granatieri, farsa giocosa per musica*.

52. Pettinelli calls the introductory paremias a "catalogo di virtù e vizi" ("catalogue of virtues and vices"; *Forme* 175–76). This title classifies paremias according to moral schemes and not in accordance with an ethical interpretation of the text.

53. For instance, Brusantino keeps the quarrelling scene between Tindaro and Licisca opening the sixth day (Dec. VI.Intr.4–16; CN 297–98). Although preserving the gist of the event, the author increases the length given to different sections of the two servants' discussion. This is evident both in the description of Licisca's fury and invective against Tindaro and in her point about women who are supposedly virgins on their first night of marriage, but in fact are not.

54. In his article, Bartoli reviews all of the possible interpretations of the paremia. He provides a convincing demonstration of the incongruence of a Pisan obscene and expressive form in "furo."

55. "Loro" for "foro" is probably a typographical error.

56. Boccaccio uses the adverb "sconciamente" in novellas I.1.14, VII.9.54, and IX.8.1.

57. Matarrese demonstrates that the paremia has popular origins. The rhyme in the final distich of the octave is only apparently imperfect because the popular pronunciation of "rana" ("frog") in the Romagna area would have been "rena" in the sixteenth century (*Parole e forme* 85).

58. "Calda" ("hot") refers to a mechanical operation which heats metallic objects in order to shape them into different manufacturing.

59. In the *Decameron*, Friar Alberto goes in front of the crowd dressed up as a "homo salvaticus" ("a feral man"). In *Le cento novelle* he is disguised as a bear. Nevertheless, just a few lines below, Brusantino contradicts himself, since he puts in Friar Alberto's hands a large stick, typical of savage men (CN 204).

60. Boccaccio never uses the word "ingiuria" ("offense") to indicate Monna Ghita's behavior, but rather emphasizes that the only master of her decisions is love: "La donna, alla quale Amore aveva già aguzzato co' suoi consigli lo 'ngegno" ("The lady had all her wits about her, for Love was her counsellor"; Dec. VII.4.16).

61. The *Deputati* edition is the only one, among the various reinterpretations of the *Decameron*, that eliminates this novella entirely (Chiecchi and Troisio 42–44).

62. Brusantino does not eliminate the scene in which the two brothers are surprised before Ciappelletto's confession to the priest. The presence of this part is justified in the *Decameron* because Ciappelletto does not share with the two brothers his intent to confess (Dec. I.1.78–79). However, in *Le cento novelle* Ciappelletto actually warns the brothers about what he is going to say to the priest (CN 19). According to Perocco, this is an instance of how Brusantino's story lacks coherence and generates contradictions ("La moralità rimata" [1987] 300–1), whereas according to Favaro, it is consistent with how the story emphasizes Ciappelletto's hypocrisy (104).

63. Perocco offers a comprehensive analysis of the differences between Boccaccio's novella and Brusantino's canto, as well as of the aspects originating from the Counter-Reformation ideology ("La moralità rimata" [1987] 298–303).

64. Perocco asserts that the octave exhorts the reader to repent all sins for salvation ("La moralità rimata" [1987] 301). However, Brusantino emphasizes the concept of divine justice only for those who engage in a constant relationship with God. He invites them to behave accordingly, otherwise divine grace will not be granted.

65. The second part of the title comes from Praloran's argument that Boiardo and Ariosto "adattano la loro lingua alla forma d'ottava" ("adapt their language to the form of the octave"; 11).

66. On the origins of Boccaccio's paremias and their presence in lexicographic works, see Rondinelli ("«Ho udito dire mille volte …»"). Analysis of *sententiae* is excluded in this discussion; for more on this topic, see Chiecchi ("Sentenze" 124–26).

67. On the paremia's rhythm, see Del Popolo's article, in which the author discusses how, by removing the introductory expression, Brusantino also disregards the elegant *incipit* informed by the *cursus planus* ("slow rhythm") of the *Decameron* (37).

68. The proverbial phrase is extracted from Helen's words to Paris after her abduction: "Si quid ergo mihi captive et aliis captivis mecum boni conferetur a quoquam, sperare poterit talia conferens a diis gratiam, cum *afflictis compati humanitas suggerat* et diis placeant pietates humanae" ("Accordingly, if no one offers anything good to me as a captive and to the other captives with me, he who offers such things can hope for reward from the gods, since human nature prompts one to sympathize with the afflicted, and the compassion of human beings pleases the gods"; delle Colonne, ch. VII: 75–76). For further references on the proverbial phrase, see Hans ("Solamen miseris socios habuisse malorum," entry 43, b. V: 57); for more sources on the expression as it appears in Boccaccio's text, see Fiorilla (129) and Rondinelli ("«Ho udito dire mille volte ...»" 303–4).

69. For a quotation of the proverb, see Merbury (*Proverbi Vulgari* 108). About the presence of the expression in Florio (*Giardino di ricreatione* 94) and Torriano (*Piazza universale* 213), see Merbury (*Proverbi Vulgari* 144).

70. His style drew inspiration from classical figures, including Saint Augustine, Saint Bernardus, and Saint Isidore of Seville, as well as from more contemporaneous rhetoricians, including Giovanni di Garlandia. The works of Paulus Diaconus and Guittone d'Arezzo, as well as Dante's *Vita Nuova* present the same stylistic structure (Branca, *Boccaccio medievale* 60–61).

71. On *cursus* and its influence in medieval times, especially Dante, see Beccaria, *Dizionario di linguistica*, s.v. *cursus*, and also Marigo.

72. In the *Decameron*, Boccaccio uses *cursus*, particularly in the *Introduzione* and in those novellas that he considers to be elevated due to style, setting, and content. Chiecchi's "Sentenze" (132–34) is a good source for accurate examples.

73. For further discussions on the topic, see Beccaria (*Dizionario di linguistica*, s.v. *prosa ritmica*), Branca (*Boccaccio medievale* 45–85), Bruni (*Boccaccio* 380–81), Del Popolo (38–42), and Manni (309).

74. The definition derives from Flamini, who entitled one of his chapters in *Il cinquecento*, "La poesia narrativa," and from Carlo Enrico Roggia's article "Poesia narrativa."

75. In the Greek world, a meter was mostly used for popular poetry and was filled with paremias, hence the title "paremiac meter." It was composed of three ascendant feet (two short and one long) with a final catalepsy. Corazzini offers detailed references on the variety of meters associated with proverbs.

76. For further discussion on the novella and the paremia, see Baratto (94–101), Chiecchi ("Sentenze" 139), and Bragantini ("La spola del racconto" 290–92) who argues for a sarcastic reference to Juvenalis's tenth satire.

77. Goidànich offers a comprehensive discussion on diphthongization in romance languages and, specifically, on the diphthongized results of the Latin vowel ŏ (18–65). On Tuscan diphthongization and its correlation with metaphony, see Maiden's article, which presents "rinnuova" as the less common form vis-à-vis the established form "rinnovare" without the diphthong (218–20).

78. In *Le cento novelle*, the word "fortuna" ("luck") appears in the introductory paremias for novellas II.3, II.4, II.6, V.6, and in rhyme in X.1 (Pettinelli, *Forme* 176). Three out of the five paremias that feature the word introduce stories about the second day, which is devoted to misadventures that suddenly end happily. Additionally, the word "sorte" ("fate") appears in the introductory paremias of novellas II.2, IV.1, IV.7, and X.2.

79. It is interesting to find an element of the Ferrarese *koinè* in the paremia: the article "el" ("the"). Even the word "scioglia" could be influenced by the local dialect: it could be derived from "schiocla," which Nannini attests to in his dictionary and defines as lump, bump, or something swollen (s.v. *schiocla*). The cluster of letters "chi" would have been pronounced with the palatal sound, hence Brusantino's spelling "sci"; the cluster "gli" could be a reproduction of the Tuscan palatal sound (Matarrese, "Saggio di *koinè* cancelleresca" 247–48). This demonstrates how, in some instances, Brusantino resorts to his own vernacular while writing *Le cento novelle*. In the introductory paremias, some examples of dialectal elements of Ferrara include the sonorization in "segondo" ("according to"; II.7), "se deve" instead of "si deve" ("one should"; V.7), and "solazzo" spelled "solaccio" ("mirth"; VIII.5). These linguistic types are frequent in Cieco's *Mambriano* and Boiardo's *Orlando innamorato* (Matarrese, *Parole e forme* 63–82).

80. In all major collections of paremias, this proverb appears with the verb "dare" ("to give"), so it is difficult to find a probable reason for Brusantino's introduction of "urtare" ("to hit"). It might be a way to give the proverb a more formal and elevated appearance.

81. Pettinelli points out that Brusantino, as a special devotee of Venice and its pervasive freedom of thought, softens the harsh tones that Boccaccio uses to illustrate the immoral aspects of the city (*Forme* 189). The Ferrarese author describes Venice as a place of virtue, freedom, and truth in canto XXXII of his *L'Angelica innamorata* (*Forme* 95–112).

82. The story proves the contrary: in fact, as shown before, Friar Alberto's evilness is eventually discovered and punished. The moral is that one should recognize when someone is acting badly, regardless of the general opinion about him (Bragantini, "La spola del racconto" 290).

83. Introductory formulas reveal the author's conscious exhibit of the paremia and his acknowledgment of its metaphorical interpretation (Malavasi 398). In addition, they may emphasize the paremia's dissemination and knowledge among people or delimit the beginning and end of the paremia itself, especially if it features in the final distich of an octave (Chiecchi, "Sentenze" 135).

84. The paremia freely interprets one of Solomon's proverbs: *La sferza al cavallo, la cavezza a l'asino, et il bastone a la schiena de matti* ("The whip with the horse, the halter with the donkey, and the stick in the back of the foolish"; ch. XXVI: v. 3 from Brucioli's *Annotationi*).

85. Boccaccio pays considerable attention to conclusive thoughts expressed through paremias. In these places, according to the art of *dispositio*, paremias could attract the public's attention and allow the exploration of meaningful concepts (Chiecchi, "Sentenze" 142–46). Paremias conclude octaves in *cantari*, as well as *Orlando innamorato* and *Orlando furioso*. The ends of octaves in *Orlando innamorato* consist of popular and proverbial segments that perfectly fit in the metrical system (Pettinelli, *L'immaginario cavalleresco* 101–2). Similarly, Ariosto places paremias in strategic moments of the narration, including the final couplet of the octaves. There, the paremia acts as a brief, detached, and straightforward statement after a long and explanatory thesis (Bigi 171–72; Soletti, "«Come raccende il gusto il mutar esca»" 142). For the structure 6+2 in Ariosto's octaves (as opposed to Boiardo's most common structure 2+2+4), see Praloran (239–44) and Blasucci.

86. The word "gatto" ("a male cat") is an interesting choice by Brusantino. Boccaccio uses the feminine "gatta" in six instances (V.10.20, VII.5.59, VII.9.34, VIII.9.40, IX.6.14, and IX.6.16), but never the masculine "gatto." In the 1612 Voc. Cr., only "gatta" is an entry, whereas "gatto" appears in the dictionary's explanation for "gatta."

87. Boccaccio employs "cauto" ("cautious") in a few instances (I.3.3, II.5.3, III.3.7, IV.3.26, and VII.5.42), as well as "barbiere/a" ("barber"; VIII.10.8 and VIII.10.10), but never combining "cauto barbiere" ("cautious barber") as Brusantino does.

88. For a list of words and clusters of words that Boccaccio inserts in his paremias for the first time, see Rondinelli ("«Ho udito dire mille volte …»" 311–12: footnote 94).

89. The Index of Paremias at the end of the book includes a list of all the introductory proverbs vis-à-vis the final ones.

Chapter Three

1. Florio uses his Italian name, Giovanni Florio, in *Giardino di ricreatione* and in *Firste Fruites*, specifically in the dedicatory letter to Robert Dudley and at the end of its grammatical section. Haller comments on his epithet "John Florio the Resolute" in Florio (*A Worlde of Wordes* [2013] xi).

2. Florio's ambidexterity is mentioned in the "Epistle Dedicatorie" to his *A Worlde of Wordes* ([2013] 3).

3. The OED defines *go-between* as "a person who conveys messages, negotiating terms, etc., between two or more other parties, frequently as a substitute for direct communication when this is difficult or undesirable; an intermediary" (s.v. *go-between*) and simpler as "anything occupying an intermediate position" (s.v. *between*).

4. For an overview of Florio's life, see the following works: Florio (*Giardino di ricreatione* [1993] 11–31), Praz ("Giovanni Florio"), Wyatt (*The Italian Encounter* 1–3), and Yates ("Italian Teachers in Elizabethan England"; *John Florio* 19–26). For a complete overview of studies and monographs on Florio and his works, *Florio's First Fruites* (lv–lxiii) and the extensive bibliography in Wyatt (*The Italian Encounter* 341–65) are good references.

5. Yates (*John Florio* 1–26) and Vischer comment on Michelangelo Florio's life and contemporaneous theological debates.

6. After Henry VIII's separation from the Papal authority and his promotion of the English Reformation (1509–47), the Italian language became inextricably connected to Protestantism during the reign of Edward VI (1547–53) (Simonini, *Italian Scholarship* 24; Rossi, *Ricerche* 62). Many refugees, Michelangelo Florio included, landed in England, encouraged

by Archbishop Thomas Cranmer and Secretary of State Sir William Cecil. Cunningham (137–89) comments on religious refugees in England during the Reformation, while Rossi (*Ricerche* 97–99), along with Yates ("Italian Teachers in Elizabethan England") and Wyatt (*The Italian Encounter* 15–19, 138), discussed the extent of exchanges between Italian and English cultures on a variety of topics and many aspects of intellectual life. For more on the topic, see Einstein's publication.

7. In his grammar book, Michelangelo devotes space to the pronunciation of the Tuscan language, thus establishing his distance from Bembo's literary model (Maraschio, "L'italiano parlato" 57–61; Pellegrini, "Michelangelo Florio" 105–8). Attention to the correct way to pronounce words is likewise privileged in other foreign grammar books of the Italian language, including Thomas's 1550 *Principal rules of Italian grammer*, Grantham's 1575 *An Italian grammer*, and Holyband's 1581 *The Italian Schoole-maister*. Pronunciation also has a strong presence in two works from Torriano, *New and easie directions* (1639) and *The Italian tutor* (1640).

8. Evidently, Florio shares an interest in paremiography with his father, as well. In the preface to his *Regole*, Michelangelo uses a few paremias: *Tre cose governano il tutto, cioè numero, peso et misura*, coming from Alunno's *Della fabbrica del mondo* ("Three things govern the world, which is number, weight, and measure"; see example 7a in Chapter 4 for a reference to the same expression); *Saltar di palo in frasca* ("To jump from one subject to another"); and *Uscir fuori del seminato* ("To wander off the point").

9. Oxford and London were crucial centers for the diffusion of the Italian language, as well as the most vital and vibrant points of intersection among different languages and cultural trends. In London, almost all of the schools in which modern languages were taught alongside Latin opened in the neighborhood of St. Paul's Churchyard (Sumillera, "Language Manuals" 68–69).

10. Giordano Bruno includes Florio in his 1584 *De la causa, principio et uno* (see Franzero 77–81; Spampanato; and Yates, *John Florio* 87–123). In relation to Florio's network, Vedovelli writes that he is a member of "un paradigma di artigianato culturale di alto profilo" ("a paradigm of high-profile cultural craftmanship"; 66).

11. The bibliography abounds with discussions on the exchange between Shakespeare and Florio, including speculations on Florio's identity as Shakespeare (Ashley 49; Franzero 123–27, 177–95; Lawrence 118–36; Orgel; Orsi; and Perini 167–82; Simonini, *Italian Scholarship* 81–109; Yates, *John Florio* 334–36). In *Love's Labour Lost*, Shakespeare employs a paremia that he could read in *Firste Fruites* and *Second Frutes*: *Venetia, chi non ti vede non t'apprezza, ma chi ti vede ben gli costa* ("Venice, who seeth thee not praiseth thee not, but who seeth thee it costeth hym wel"; FF 34r; SF 106; see also Nobili, "Michelangelo Florio"). For more information on Shakespeare's comedy, see Yates (*A Study of Love's Labour's Lost*) and Simonini ("Language Lesson Dialogue" 327–28), which contain a general discussion of Shakespeare's use of proverbs in his works, probably influenced by Florio's *Fruits*.

12. Florio does not translate directly from Cartier's accounts in the eastern coasts of Northern America, originally published in 1545 and entitled *Brief récit de la navigation: Faicte es ysles de Canada*. He bases his English translation on Giovan Battista Ramusio's Italian rendering, inserted in the third volume of his *Terzo volume delle navigationi et viaggi* (369v–85r). Florio opens the dedicatory letter of his *A shorte and briefe narration*, "To the right worshipful Edmond Bray Esquire, High sherife within hir Maiesties Countie of Oxenford," with a proverb: "*None so bolde as blynd Bayard*, nor anye so readye to undertake as the leaste able to performe" (Aii*r*). At the end of each of Cartier's two reports on Northern America contained in *A shorte and briefe narration*, Florio inserts two proverbs, which were absent in Ramusio's translation: *Assai ben balla a chi fortuna suona* ("He dances very well to whom fortune is companion"; Fii*r*) and *Patisco il male sperando il bene* ("I suffer evil hoping for good"; Mii*v*). On the influence that English geographer Richard Hakluyt had on Florio's translation of Cartier's explorations, see Yarrington et al. (27–47).

13. For this translation, Florio refers to Salviati's *rassettatura* (see Boccaccio, *Decameron* [1582]), reproducing it almost faithfully. As a general trend, Salviati chooses settings that are far from the center of Christianity, so that events and characters in Boccaccio's stories are not in contact with those places in which the Christian religion operates. According to Wright, Florio's captions and morals at the beginning of each story come from Antoine Le Maçon's French translation of Boccaccio's collection, *Décaméron, ou cent Nouvelles*, which was published in 1569.

14. The book includes selections from Boccalini's two works, *Ragguagli di Parnaso* and *Pietra del paragone politico*. Florio translated the first part of the texts included in this publication, Thomas Scott translated the second, and William Vaughan translated the third.

15. In the dedicatory letter of the English edition of Epictetus's *Enchiridion*, publisher Thomas Thorpe addresses Florio as a "true favorer of forward spirits" and the most knowledgeable and commendable representative of translations: "For the translation and translator, to whome better recourse, then one so travail'd in translation; both patterne and patron of translators. Artificers' best iudge of arts." Not surprisingly, the work "filles thy head with lessons, nor would bee held in hand, but had by hart to boote" (Healey A4*r–v*). For more information on the relationship between Thorpe and Florio and their connection in the publication of Shakespeare's sonnets, see Rostenberg.

16. In the two editions of the dictionary, Florio seeks Italian regional idioms and words to reevaluate the cultural variety of the peninsula among the Italian community in London (*A Worlde of Wordes* [2013] 5). Accordingly, he includes paremias, mostly proverbial phrases, in the entries and uses them as pedagogical tools. He even employs two paremias in the introductory letter to both editions: *A suo danno* ("To his detriment") and *[A] torto si lamenta del mare chi due volte ci vuol tornare* ("Wrongly complains about the sea he

who wants to go back there twice"; *A Worlde of Wordes* [2013] 9). Another paremia features in the dedicatory epistle of *A Worlde of Wordes*: *Le parole sono femine e i fatti sono maschi* ("Words are feminine and deeds are masculine"; 6). For further information on this paremia, see Frantz ("Negotiating" 8-9), Rondinelli and Vinciguerra. For an analysis of the expression in both *A Worlde of Wordes* and *Second Frutes*, see Florio (*A Worlde of Wordes* [2013] xix–xxxiii) and Wyatt (*The Italian Encounter* 245–46).

17. The collection gathers paremias all written in Italian. However, under letter A, the English translation appears beside an Italian expression: *Affibbia quella, Crack me that nut* ("*Knack me that nut*, much good doyt you all this band"; GR [11]; also in Heywood, *A dialogue* Pt. II, ch. VII). Both the Italian and the English versions metaphorically express the act of fornicating, with the "nut" representing the feminine genitals (Williams, s.v. *nut*: 965–66).

18. The collection is an unsystematic list of around 650 paremias. The expressions are divided into two groups: a list of adages and a list of proverbial phrases titled "Motti brevi ch'hanno del proverbio" ("Brief sayings that are like proverbs"). Sparingly, Merbury adds a commentary on the expression's meaning, typically introducing it with "volevo dire" or "ciò è" ("meaning"). More often, he glosses these paremias with an indication of their regional origins or textual sources; alternatively, he translates a difficult word or the entire expression in English, always satisfying cultural and pedagogical objectives (*Proverbi Vulgari* 63–80; see also Pignatti, *Etimologia* 353–56). Merbury's collection aims to offer members of high society and courts a means to embellish serious as well as familiar conversations, learn useful life precepts, and gain a better knowledge of Italian habits and traditions (*Proverbi Vulgari* 84).

19. For a comparison between Merbury's collection and Florio's paremias in *Firste Fruites* and *Giardino di ricreatione*, see Merbury (*Proverbi Vulgari* 115–49) and Speroni ("Merbury's *Proverbi Vvlgari*" 161–62). In *Second Frutes*, 65 paremias appear to show a resemblance with Merbury's paremias: 32 are identical, whereas 33 are slightly different. The main difference concerns the presence of an introductory formula in Merbury's paremias. At times, two paremias might differ in their vocabulary: one example is *Chi non s'arrischia non guadagna* ("He who does not dare, does not earn"; *Proverbi Vulgari* 89); another is *Chi non s'arischia non s'arichisce* ("His gaines will be but small, who ventures not at all"; SF 70). If Merbury's paremias are associated with a specific person or object, those in *Second Frutes* are not, and hence resemble proverbial phrases more: examples include *Le puttane sono come il carbone che ò coce ò tinge* ("Whores are like charcoal that either burns or dyes"; *Proverbi Vulgari* 104) and *Come il carbone, il quale o tinge o bruscia* ("Like to a coale, which either burneth or besmeareth"; SF 174). Alternatively, the topic of the paremias in the two works may differ: *L'amore infanga il giovane et il vecchio annega* ("Love sullies the young and makes the old drown"; *Proverbi Vulgari* 100) and *Egli è un vero diavolo incarnato che* *infanga i giovani et annega i vecchi* ("He is a devil incarnate who sullies the young and makes the old drown"; SF 166). The structure of Merbury's and Florio's paremias may be the same but vary only in some specific terms, as is the case of *Cinqu'hore dorme il viandante, sette il studiante et undeci ogni forfante* ("The wanderer sleeps five hours, the student sleeps seven, and every rascal sleeps eleven"; *Proverbi Vulgari* 92) and *Sei hore dorme lo studiante, sette il viandante, otto il lavorante et nove ogni furfante* ("The student sleeps six hours, the wanderer seven, the worker eight, and every rascal nine"; SF 162).

20. Florio's most important successor is Torriano. He draws content for his *The Italian reviv'd* (1673) from Florio's dialogues which he adapts to a different time and public. Florio's dictionary also offers materials for Torriano's 1659 *Vocabolario Italiano et Inglese*, which is an expansion of Florio's manuscript notes for the third edition of *A Worlde of Wordes* (Yates, *John Florio* 322–33). Finally, Torriano's works on paremias expand Florio's *Giardino di ricreatione*: *Select Italian proverbs* (with 650 Italian paremias translated into English; see Speroni, "Giovanni Torriano's *Select Italian Proverbs*"); *The second alphabet consisting of proverbial phrases* (a dictionary of Italian proverbial expressions listed by the phrase's primary term, translated into English, and explained in both languages); and *Piazza universale di proverbi italiani* (with 10,000 translated paremias in alphabetical order and for the first time divided between proverbs and proverbial phrases; see Gamberini, *Lo studio dell'italiano* 151–54; Rossi, *Ricerche* 139–42). Speroni argues that Torriano's *Piazza* contains proverbs selected from Merbury's collection that were meant for the English merchants and bourgeoisie in need of the Italian language for business purposes (Merbury, *Proverbi Vulgari* 76–79).

21. For a critical evaluation of English literature in the sixteenth and seventeenth centuries during the Elizabethan period, see Greenblatt, *Representing the English Renaissance*.

22. During the reign of Elizabeth I, the number of religious refugees coming from central and southern Europe corresponded to one-twentieth of the entire population in London (Simonini, *Italian Scholarship* 7).

23. For a discussion of the relationships between Italy and Europe in the Renaissance from a linguistic perspective, see Tavoni. For a testimony of the study of the Italian language during Elizabeth's reign, Petrina's article is a valuable resource; relatedly, Raimondi offers a study of Queen Elizabeth as a polyglot. Finally, for a specific perspective on the role that Italy and the Italian language held in the English court, see Praz ("Fortuna della lingua"), Parks ("The Genesis of Tudor Interest"; "The Decline and Fall"), and Viglione.

24. Italy features in Thomas Nashe's 1594 picaresque novel *The Unfortunate Traveller*, in which the country is associated with evil and violence, such as rape.

25. The proverb, though in a quatrain of verses, also appears in *An italians dead bodie*, edited by Theophilus Field to commemorate Horatio Pallavicino's death in 1600. The quatrain states: "An Englishe man Italianate / becomes a devill incarnate / but an Italian Anglyfide / becomes a Saint Angelifide."

26. For a thorough analysis of Ascham's perspectives on Italy, see De Seta (287–95), Parks ("The First Italianate Englishmen"), Pirillo, and Stammerjohann ("L'immagine della lingua italiana" 15). In *The Italian Encounter*, Wyatt comments on the paradox between Ascham's condemnation of the Italian language and his use of the paremia *Englese italianato è un diabolo incarnato* (162). See Lawrence for a discussion of Ascham's perspective and his relationship to the English context of the sixteenth and seventeenth centuries, particularly in regard to teaching Italian language, translating Italian books into English, and travelling to Italy (1–18). For a history of English anti-Italian statements and a link between travels to Italy and translations of Italian Renaissance literature, see Bartlett; on the opposite perspective about England and English people by Italians, see De Cossart (*This little world*; *This sceptred isle*).

27. In the dedicatory letter *A tutti i gentilhuomini inglesi che si dilettanto de la lingua italiana* in *Firste Fruites*, Florio confirms that proverbs and proverbial phrases enable dedicated students to learn Italian effectively, appropriately, and soon (FF xxir; see also Bocchi 68). During a dialogue from chapter 27 in *Firste Fruites*, an Italian speaker admits that it is possible to become conversant in Italian in three months (FF 51v) and that the best way to learn it is by reading texts, which in turn refines one's oral abilities (FF 50r).

28. Italian refugees were well-known for their translations of masterpieces from the Italian Renaissance. These translations promoted and enriched the relationships between Italy and England and influenced the development of English literature, as well as the country's ideological climate in the second half of the sixteenth century (Rossi, *Ricerche* 69–94). Starting in 1548, refugees began to release translations of anti-Papal and anti-Roman works (mostly by Bernardino Ochino, Francesco Negri da Bassano, and Pietro Martire Vermigli). For a description of the various typologies of Renaissance translators, see Burke ("The Renaissance Translator as Go-Between") and Nocera. In *The Italian Encounter*, Wyatt also discusses Italian humanists and artists in England (28–53), whereas Tedeschi and Biondi explore the role of Italian Protestant emigrants in the diffusion of Italian literature abroad. For a broader contextualization of the Anglo-Italian conversation in Elizabethan England and of the reciprocal relationships between England and Italy, see Elam and Cioni (13–30), as well as Yarrington et al. Lytton Sells's book refers to Englishmen travelling and residing in Italy (92–109).

29. This is the only work that Ascham praises in his *The Scholemaster*, in which he does not even spare Petrarca, Boccaccio, and Machiavelli. According to him, solely Castiglione's translated book, if read appropriately, could implement good manners in the English society (see Yarrington et al., 251–75; Wyatt, *The Italian Encounter* 159–63).

30. Important references on the English translations of Italian courtesy books include: Bartlett (497–506 for Barker's and Hoby's translations), Marrapodi (*Intertestualità shakespeariane* 47–62 for Hoby's and Pettie's works), and Wyatt (*The Italian Encounter* 180–83). Despite not being a courtesy book, Barker's translation of Giovanni Battista Gelli's 1549 *Capricci del Bottaio* contributed to the English experience of Italy and Italian culture.

31. For a detailed analysis of sixteenth-century grammar books including Thomas, Rhys, Grantham, Holyband, and Florio, see Mormile and Matteucci (13–34); for seventeenth-century grammar books including John Sanford, Benvenuto Italiano, and Torriano, see Mormile and Matteucci (37–62). Pizzoli offers a descriptive overview of the same grammar books, along with an investigation of their linguistic choices. For further references, see Bonomi and Castegnaro, Fornara, Paccagnella ("La terminologia"), and Poggi Salani.

32. O'Connor offers a list of bilingual dictionaries (*A History* 173–82). An antecedent for these dictionaries was Ambrogio da Calepio's 1502 successful Latin-Greek dictionary *Calepino*, published in Reggio Emilia by Dionigio Bertocchi.

33. Thomas's grammar also contains the first example of a bilingual dictionary with a list of words in Italian and English to help students better understand Dante, Petrarca, and Boccaccio.

34. Ascham's work is considered to be the first substantial contribution to the field of teaching foreign languages. It became a model for subsequent grammar books aiming to educate the intellectual elite (Mormile and Matteucci 23).

35. Grantham's work is a translation of Scipione Lentulo's 1567 grammar book of the Italian language, *Italice grammatices praecepta et ratio*.

36. By the end of the sixteenth century and the beginning of the next century, the English language started to gain more power in all sectors of life and politics at the expense of other languages (Wyatt, *The Italian Encounter* 158). After the marriage of Charles I and Henrietta Maria of France (1625), which opened up a renewed period of fertile exchange with France, the Italian language lost ground and simply became the representative of a classical world to be appreciated but far from the European political scene (Gamberini, *Lo studio* 11–43). Rome was considered an enemy to the English Puritan orientation and a place of corrupted politics and inadequate poetry (Iamartino 31; Pizzoli 13–22, 26–41).

37. In *The Italian Schoole-maister*, Holyband includes appealing dialogues that could attract prospective learners, mostly merchants and professionals who were about to engage in economic and business enterprises with Italy (Pizzoli 66–67; Rossi, *Ricerche* 109–18). Holyband aims to expose students to the practical use of the language more than its subtleties. Florio's purpose is similar, as he wishes to strengthen the students' language learning process and expose them to actual uses of the target culture (Gamberini, *Lo studio* 69; Wyatt, *The Italian Encounter* 168). Following Holyband's examples, Florio establishes a much higher linguistic level for his students. They are not beginners and should already know the basics of the language in order to grasp the content and profundity of the dialogues, or otherwise learn the content by memory before understanding the lexical components and grammatical

Notes to Page 129

aspects of the language. For this reason, language manuals such as Florio's are frequently compared to contemporaneous books of common prayers. In them, the acquaintance with phraseology came before understanding its meaning, yet maintaining a strong connection with needs that could be both spiritual and related to daily moral conduct. For more information on prayer books, see the publications by Booty and Daniel.

38. On Holyband's innovative method of teaching, which inspires Florio, see Simonini ("The Italian Pedagogy of Claudius Hollyband"). Holyband's and Florio's manuals share a list of decontextualized paremias and a considerable number of numerical paremias. On similarities and differences between the two authors' approaches to language education, see Haller ("John Florio e Claudius Holyband").

39. In his preface to *Choice Proverbs*, Paravicino defines his book as profitable for those who want to learn first Italian proverbs and sayings, and then the Italian language. He offers a list of Italian paremias translated into English (1–41), meaningful dialogues embedded with proverbs useful for wayfarers (49–62), and sayings extracted from Solomon's proverbs and other Sapiential books (285–301). Not dissimilarly from Florio, Paravicino publishes a dictionary of the Italian language in 1660, *A short Italian dictionary*.

40. As Black demonstrates, thirteenth-century elementary education is still founded upon reading Latin texts, including *Disticha Catonis*. However, already in the fourteenth century, vernacular is introduced. While schools outside of Florence rely heavily on grammar instruction, Florentine schools are more oriented toward commercial education in vernacular (abacus schools) and thus are more sensitive to the requests of a society founded on mercantile transactions (43–172).

41. For a general introduction to the "questione della lingua," or controversy on the nature of the Italian language in the first half of the sixteenth century, see Migliorini (*Storia della lingua italiana*); on the English contributions to the Italian "questione della lingua," see Gamberini (*Lo studio* 11–43).

42. In addition to Giovanni Francesco Fortunio's and Bembo's publications, many Italian grammar books displayed a strong linkage between language and literature. Among them are Alberto Acarisio's *Vocabolario, grammatica et orthographia de la lingua volgare, con ispositioni di molti luoghi di Dante, del Petrarca et del Boccaccio* (1543), Giacomo Gabriele's *Regole grammaticali* (1545), Rinaldo Corso's *Fondamenti del parlar thoscano* (1549, which presents a more pedagogical structure that facilitates its consultation), and Lodovico Dolce's *Osservationi nella volgar lingua* (1550). Other grammar books proposed an Italian or national perspective, *in primis* Gian Giorgio Trissino's *Dubbi grammaticali* and *Grammatichetta* (1529). Still others promoted the use of the sixteenth-century spoken Florentine; one example is Pierfrancesco Giambullari's *Regole della lingua Fiorentina* (1552), which intended to teach the non-Florentine speakers of the Italian peninsula how to speak and write appropriately. Along the same lines, Varchi's *L'Hercolano* (1570) offered a comparison between the Florentine vernacular and the classical languages to demonstrate the superiority and appropriateness of the language of Florence spoken at the time (Faithfull).

43. This is also reflected in the language used in foreign grammar books of the Italian language, specifically a "lingua commune" ("common language") which could be understood all over Italy. Grammarians outside Italy opted for more modern choices in diacritical signs and punctuation than their colleagues in Italy or the *Vocabolario degli Accademici della Crusca* (Florio, *A Worlde of Wordes* [2013] xxi). According to Raimondi, this language emerged in Queen Elizabeth I's epistolary correspondence: "a contemporary Italian model of 'moderate' character"; "a norm which is not strictly *bembiana*, but rather open to the innovations produced in the Florentine urban language between the fifteenth and sixteenth centuries" (154).

44. For instance, phonetics was consistently absent in grammar books released in Italy; conversely, in Florio's *Fruits* and in the language manuals preceding them, the proper way to pronounce phonemes was a crucial component of the language learning process. Just a few years before the publication of *Firste Fruites*, Rhys published a language manual of Italian in Latin devoted to foreigners willing to study Italian through the correct pronunciation of the language: *De Italica Pronunciatione* (see Maraschio, *Trattati di fonetica* 91–264). Despite choosing the Tuscan model, Rhys opts for an eclectic approach to pronunciation, emphasizing the practical aspects of speaking languages. He always presents one paragraph on pronunciation and one on orthography and applies a comparative approach to English, French, Polish, Gaelic, Portuguese, Spanish, and German. In spite of the two authors' consonance in foreign language teaching, Florio does not seem to know Rhys's work.

45. That Florio emphasizes the importance of the "true" Italian language portrayed in his two manuals is evident from the grammatical section at the end of *Firste Fruites*: *Necessarie Rules for Englishmen to learne to reade, speake, and write true Italian* (FF 106r–159v; see Gamberini, *Lo studio* 86–89). In this grammar, Florio follows what Bembo prescribes in his *Prose* for the "primatives" ("egli" and the other third person singular and plural subject pronouns), yet declares that "lui" and the other object pronouns are used in all instances: "*Egli, eglino, ella, elleno, e,* and *ei,* are of the first case, but *lui, lei, loro,* are of the obliques, and yet they are otherwise used of the common sort" (FF 128r; original italics). He adopts "lui" and "loro" in all the conjugations of verbs in the grammatical section at the end of *Queen Anna's New World of Wordes*, entitled *Necessarie Rules and Short Observations for The True Pronouncing and Speedy Learning of the Italian Tongue*. Two examples of "lui" as subject pronoun are in chapter 6 of the first manual, specifically in the introductory formula to a paremia: "Come dice lui, vi prego? Lui dice che *è sempre bono per uno haver due corde per il suo archo*, acciò che se una si rompe, lui ne habbia un'altra presta" ("How saith he, I pray you? He saith, it is always good for one to have two stringes to his bowe, to the ende, that if one breake he may have another ready"; FF 6v). In the body of *Firste Fruites*,

Florio never uses "egli" for the third person singular pronoun, except in a few interjections. In the more Tuscanized *Second Frutes*, instead, he resorts to the subject pronoun "egli" and all other third person singular and plural subject pronouns more often. Given the Petrarchan emphasis of the second manual, the language adopted appears free from regionalisms or, at least, generally Tuscan. Another anti-Bembo choice is Florio's use of the future tense. Bembo recommends the suffix "-erò" for the first person singular of verbs from the first conjugation. Conversely, Florio opts for the suffix "-arò," for instance in "A chi domandarò" ("To whom shal I aske?"; FF 6r).

46. Since the Middle Ages, lists of Latin and English paremias, frequently metrical, were common. Their primary intent was pedagogical and included teaching Latin, refining rhetoric, and inculcating common sense. The publications by Whiting and Pantin analyze two such examples from the early eleventh century (in Anglo-Saxon) and the mid-fifteenth century.

47. At the end of *Firste Fruites*, the students could refer to the conclusive grammatical section. The grammatical clarifications occupy a small portion compared to the rest of the book and function as an appendix to the dialogues. As such, they could appropriately answer to the tastes of those Englishmen travelling to Italy and needing an easy, direct, and accessible grammar to learn the language in the fastest way possible (Pizzoli 94). Given the communicative approach that Florio adopts, the explanations occur in the form of a dialogue—which recalls Bembo's *Prose*—between the author and an English speaker who asks him to explain the principles of the Italian language. Practical examples aim to provide the learners with clear-cut rules on how to pronounce words and then, on how to write them correctly. Florio regularly refers to Citolini's *Grammatica de la lingua italiana* (c. 1573–74), which he values for its linguistic originality and distinction from Bembo's ideas (see Antonini; Bellorini, "La *Grammatica de la lingua italiana*"; Cali; Di Felice 93–381). Florio appreciates Citolini's empirical and descriptive aspiration to transmit comprehensible and practical content drawn from different domains. The work also interests him because it does not distinguish between poetry and prose, written and oral language, literary and colloquial registers, or Tuscan and regional vernaculars. Florio adapts Citolini's text for his own students by simplifying the orthographic rules and adding comparative examples with English. In order to satisfy the requests of the Italian people in London, Florio also introduces a grammar section of the English language in his first manual: *Regole necessarie per indurre gl'italiani a proferir la lingua inglese* (FF 160r–63r). In a much more concise way than the grammatical section on the Italian language, Florio attempts to explain the pronunciation of letters in English by providing many examples and practical descriptions of the position of the tongue and lips (Orsini; Wyatt, *The Italian Encounter* 217). For instances of grammatical sections in sixteenth-century grammar books meant to teach the English language to Italophones, see Pizzoli (126: footnote 4); for an overview of the structure of Italian books for foreigners, specifically devoted to the presence of grammatical parts, see Vedovelli (85–106).

48. In *Firste Fruites*, a speaker comments on English society's lack of proper education in foreign languages: he considers his interlocutor an idiot since he speaks only English (FF 20*v*). Chapter 27 contains a dense conversation between an Englishman and an Italian, who expresses his thoughts on England and the English language. English is said to be a disorganized language, made of elements from many different languages and spoken in a limited area. Consequently, merchants are unable to communicate with foreigners in English. The Italian speaker also faults the lack of interest in foreign languages and suggests that parents should make their children learn languages other than English (FF 50*r*–50*v*). In *Second Frutes*, Florio exalts the Italian language at the expense of English (Pizzoli 34). In chapter 2, he states that the comedies and tragedies in England are not true genres because they are rather historical representations without any form of decorum (SF 22).

49. Mormile and Matteucci point out that the presence of more than two speakers in the dialogues was not common before Florio. They consider it a demonstration of Florio's pedagogical orientation exceeding that of his predecessors (30).

50. The topics are listed in the *Tavola de tutti gli capitoli che in questa opera si contengono* ("Table of all the chapters that in this worke are contayned"; FF ***iiv–***iiiir). Chidgey's PhD dissertation presents a classification of these themes in accordance with their reference to "parlar" ("talk/speech"), "discorsi" ("discourses"), and "ragionamenti" ("reasonings"). The titles of the chapters in *Firste Fruites*, along with those from *Second Frutes*, can be read in the Index of Paremias.

51. The classification is not always respected. For instance, a *sententia* in chapter 22 is called "proverbio:" "E anche [è] verificato il proverbio di quel nostro philosopho che dice che *di pace vien prosperità, prosperità porta abondantia, abondantia porta ricchezze, et le ricchezze concupiscentia, concupiscentia porta sdegno, sdegno guerra, guerra povertà, povertà humiltà, humiltà pace, pace prosperità*, et così il mondo va intorno" ("Also [hath] verified the proverbe of that our philosopher that saith that of peace cometh prosperitie, prosperitie bringeth plentie, plentie bringeth riches, riches lust, lust contempt, contempt breedeth warre, of warre cometh povertie, of povertie humilitie, of humilitie peace, of peace prosperity, and so the world goes about"; FF 39*v*).

52. Close to the end of the first manual, in chapter 43, Florio inserts a glossary of 394 Italian words or phrases with corresponding English translation on different aspects of human life (FF 100*r*–03*r*). This can be considered Florio's first lexicographical work preceding his *A Worlde of Wordes*. Many morphological aspects from Northern Italy characterize the list in *Firste Fruites*, which is evidenced by the terms "le ungie" ("the nayles"; FF 100*v*), "una brancada" ("a handfull"; FF 100*v*), and "barba" ("unkle"; FF 101*r*). Among the listed words there are also two Anglicisms that are not recorded in *A Worlde of Wordes*: "pacuzo" for "a warehouse" (FF 102*v*) and "tubbaro" for "a cooper" (from "tub"; FF 103*r*; see O'Connor, *A History* 20–21). The main difference between this lexicographical list in *Firste Fruites* and *A Worlde of Wordes* is the length of each entry's explanation. For instance, in the list from the first manual Florio translates "le chiappe" as "the buttockes" (FF 100*v*), whereas in the dictionary the word's description is more elaborate: "The buttocks or hips. Also splints or rugged stones divided by nature, clifts, crags. Also a kinde of tyle. Also the part of a knife that goes into the handle. Also the breech of a cannon or musket." Another interesting example is "bon mercato." In the lexicographical list, Florio translates it as "good cheape" (FF 102*v*), but in the dictionary he presents it under the entry "mercato" (and not on its own as in the list): "Also cheape, as *Buon mercato*, good cheape." A few entries, though, coincide within the two works; one instance is "barbiere" (FF 103*r*), which Florio translates as "a barber" in both.

53. The introductory caption describing the content of *Novellino* states: "Questo libro tratta d'alquanti fiori di parlare, di belle cortesie e di be' risposi e di belle valentie e doni, secondo che, per lo tempo passato, hanno fatto molti valenti uomini" ("This book is concerned with certain flowers of speech, lovely courtesies and responses, and lovely aptitudes and gifts, as they were set forth by many worthy men in times past").

54. A similar reference is mentioned again in *Firste Fruites*. In chapter 18, one of the speakers proposes to "recitar qualche belle sentenze, qualche belli proverbii, e gentili motti, fatti da qualche gentil poeta e che comunemente si usano ne la lingua italiana" as a way to pass the time before lunch ("rehearse some fine sentences, fine proverbes, and gentle sayeinges, made by some gentle poete, and that commonly are used in the Italian language"; FF 22*r*).

55. Style and language help to create the Stilnovistic ambience of this chapter. For example, there is an abundance of diphthongs typical of the Tuscan tradition ("pruova," "proof") and words common in love poetry ("strali," "darts"). In another instance, specifically chapter 2, a refined tone defines the conversation between a woman and a man, who represents the Stilnovistic humble servant. Sentence balance contributes to the general tone, such as "Io vi ho amato, vi amo, vi amerò" ("I have loved you, I love you, and wil love you"; FF 1*v*) or "Io vi ho odiato, vi odio, vi odierò" ("I have hated you, I hate you, and wyl hate you"; FF 1*v*).

56. Rossi identifies intersections between Florio's dialogues and the Italian theatrical works of the time: *lazzi*, names of characters, comic perspectives in talking about women, betrayed husbands, and unfaithful lovers ("Note sugli italiani" 84). On theater and games in *Second Frutes*, see Arcangeli.

57. Florio is aware of the modern concept of acquisitional sequences and scaffolding. In *Firste Fruites*, he mostly offers accounts of short sentences and lists of names and adjectives. In contrast, the dialogues in *Second Frutes* become more difficult as they deal with more complex topics and show a higher level of formality. However, sometimes the acquisitional process does not appear to be sequential within the same book. For instance, chapter 16 in *Firste Fruites* is evidently characterized by simple sentences and basic grammar, much easier to understand and grasp than the first chapters of the book. In addition, the first manual is culturally more difficult than the second. Since it refers to specific aspects of everyday life in the target society, culture is much more present. In contrast, *Second Frutes* refers to concepts that are almost universally known or experienced. These almost contradictory aspects, according to Simonini, make Florio's *Fruits* "the most interesting of the Elizabethan language lesson manuals" (*Italian Scholarship* 59).

58. Hunter demonstrates that ways to highlight *sententiae* in a text were frequent between 1500 and 1660. Montini argues that the asterisk is "a mark denoting an oral difference, such as a changing intonation when a proverb is quoted in an oral discourse" ("Proverbs in John Florio's *Fruits*" 259; see also Di Martino, "Politeness strategies" 242).

59. According to Florio, learning should be privileged over comprehension; hence, the memorization of formulas useful to enrich everyday speech and embellish courtly conversations is more important than understanding grammatical structures and normative rules. This also illustrates how Florio considers paremias and dialogues primarily as forms of social diversion and cultural wisdom. Only secondarily, he sees them as grammar tools. Such perspective finds substance in what Signor G. ("Mr. G.") states just before chapter 19 in *Firste Fruites* as an introduction to its list of paremias. He admits that their conversation would now feature "certi proverbi che comunemente si usano tanto in Italia, come in Inghilterra … così passeremo via il tempo" ("certaine proverbes that commonly are used as wel in Italie as in Englande … so we wil passe away the time"; FF [26]*v*); indeed, these paremias cannot "se non dare uno certo diletto al ascoltatore" ("but yeelde a certaine delight unto the hearer"; FF 27*r*).

60. If Florio highlights the constant relationship between the two languages of his works (Palermo and Poggiogalli 10), he also determines a clear distinction between them. Italian is the refined language of culture and literature and English is considered to be more practical and less literary. Consequently, as the introductory letters in *Firste Fruites* specify, English is appropriate for gentlemen and merchants alike ("A tutti i gentilhuomini e mercanti italiani che si dilettanto de la lingua inglese," "To all the Italian gentlemen and merchants who delight in the English language"; FF xxii*v*). The Italian language, instead, is addressed to gentlemen only ("A tutti i gentilhuomini inglesi che si dilettano de la lingua italiana," "To all the English gentlemen who delight in the Italian language"; FF xxxiii*r*).

61. In the dedicatory letter to Sir Robert Dudley ("Sr. Roberto Dudleo") in *Firste Fruites*, Florio refers to the benefit that paremias have on both English and Italian language learners: "[N]on ho voluto mancare con il mio debil ingegno di compiacer a certi gentil huomini miei amici ch'ogni giorno mi stimulavano di darli in luce alcuni motti, o vogliam dire proverbii con certo parlar familiare a modo di dialogo, da poter imparare tanto la lingua italiana quanto la inglese, e che tutte dua le nazione potessero alquanto prevalersene" ("I did not want to lack with my feeble talent to please some gentlemen, my friends, who every day used to encourage me to publish some mottoes, or I could say proverbs, within a certain familiar speaking in the form of a dialogue, so to enable people to learn so much the Italian language as much as English, and that both nations could somewhat gain advantage out of it"; FF *ii*v*).

62. Florio is an enthusiast of the language as well as an excellent collator of words, idiomatic expressions, and paremias, according to the Renaissance concept of *copia verborum* (*A Worlde of Wordes* [2013] xxix). He could use these expressions in different works as he was probably structuring his two language manuals, his dictionary, and his *Giardino di ricreatione* simultaneously.

63. For an overview of the sixteenth-century importance in determining future didactic methodologies for language instruction, see Simonini ("The Genesis of Modern Foreign Language Teaching"). The direct method differed greatly from the grammatical approach used to teach Latin in grammar schools (Charlton 89–130). The latter emphasized grammar as the first step in language acquisition before practical application of the language. One of the most frequently used standard Latin school textbooks of the time was William Lily and John Colet's *A shorte introduction of grammar generally to be used, compiled and set forth for the bringing up of all those that intende to attaine the knowledge of the Latine tongue* (Lawrence 22).

64. Florio read Orazio Toscanella's translation of Vives's *Exercitatio*, which might have inspired the titles of his two manuals. Toscanella's rendering was published in 1568 by Vincenzo Valgrisi and titled *Flores Italici ac Latini sermonis; ex hortis exercitationis Joannis Ludovici Vivis excerpti* (Gamberini, "I primi strumenti" 461). For more information, see D'Eugenio ("I «frutti» di Orazio Toscanella, Claudius Holyband e John Florio").

65. The topics discussed in the chapter include: getting up in the morning, greeting, taking kids to school, school subjects, school lunch, returning home, games and their rules, writing, charlatans, alcohol poisoning, walking in the morning, the house, the bedroom, the kitchen, the dining room, the banquet, the royal palace, the prince, the human body, education and its precepts, and the city of Valencia.

66. The numbers refer to the stories in Anne-Marie Van Passen's critical edition of Guicciardini's *L'ore*. Many of Guicciardini's paremias also appear in Florio's *Giardino di ricreatione*; only eleven of Guicciardini's expressions do not feature in Florio's works.

67. For the English translation of these Italian paremias, Florio draws consistently from James Sanford's 1573 edition of L. Guicciardini's *L'ore*. Sanford, who originally titles his translation *The Garden of Pleasure*, reprints it in 1576 as *Houres of recreation*. Florio does not reproduce Sanford's translation literally. Since his pedagogical intent is to provide a meaningful context for the paremias, he changes the original text slightly to fit the paremias in his conversations and also, to avoid being accused of plagiarism (Yates, *John Florio* 37). The following two examples of Florio's adjustments are taken from *Firste Fruites*: *To tary for a thing that cometh not, to lye a bed, and sleepe not, to serve wel and not be accepted, be three things to dy* (FF 27r; *Aspettar e non venire, star nel letto e non dormire, servire e non gradire son tre cose da* *morire*) and *To look for and not to come; to be in bed and not to sleepe; to serve and not to be accepted, are three deadly things* (J. Sanford, *The Garden of Pleasure* 103); *Old sinne and new penance* (FF 32v; *Peccato vechio, penitenza nuova*) and *Olde sinne, new repentaunce* (J. Sanford 98). Other two paremias from chapter 19 demonstrate how Florio may have consulted Sanford's translation but ultimately provides his own translation: *With art and with deceit, halfe the yeere we live; with deceit and with art, we live the other part* (FF [28]r; *Con arte e con inganno si vive mezo l'anno, con inganno e con arte si vive l'altra parte*) and *With art and with deceipte, men live halfe the yeare. With deceite and with arte, men live the other parte* (J. Sanford 101); *Neither a woman nor lynnen chuse thou by a candle* (FF 32v; *Né femina né tela non piglia a la candela*) and *Choose not a woman nor linnen clothe by the candle* (J. Sanford 101).

68. In his *Proverbi Vulgari*, Merbury writes: "Voi sapete, ch'in ogni lingua non c'è più bella gratia, che l'usar, et nel parlar, et nel scrivere, di bei e spessi proverbi: I quali … par che portino seco (non so come) una certa authorità, dignità et maestà a quel che si scrive et si dice" ("You know that in every language there is no more beautiful grace than using beautiful and frequent proverbs, both in speaking and writing. Proverbs seem to bring with them (I do not know how) a certain authoritativeness, dignity, and majesty to what one writes and says"; 84).

69. Many of these paremias are mentioned in chapter 25 in *Firste Fruites*: "Di ira, con certi belli detti di Ariosto e di altri poeti, e che cosa è patientia et adulatione" ("Of wrath, with certaine fyne sayings of Ariosto, and other poets, and what pacience and flattery is"; FF 42v–45v).

70. Florio satirizes the Englishmen who think they are able to speak Italian just by learning phrases from Castiglione's *Il libro del cortegiano* and Guazzo's *La civil conversatione*: "… who think they hath learnt a little Italiano out of Castilions courtier, or Guazzo his dialogues" (SF, dedicatory letter to Saunders A3v). On Florio's borrowings from Guazzo's work in both *Fruits*, see Lievsay ("Florio and His Proverbs").

71. Among those paremias shared by Vignali's letter and *Firste Fruites* are: *Chi ben siede mal pensa* ("Who sitteth wel, thinketh yl"; FF [28]r; Vignali, *Lettera* 33); *Chi ha tempo non aspetti tempo* ("Who hath tyme, let not him tary for tyme"; FF [28]v; Vignali, *Lettera* 6); *È bella cosa pigliar due colombi con una fava* ("It is a prety thing to catch two doves with one beane"; FF 29v; Vignali, *Lettera* 1–2); *L'alegreze di questo mondo duran poco* ("The ioyes of this worlde dure but litle"; FF 32r; Vignali, *Lettera* 5); *L'huomo propone e Dio dispone* ("Man dooth purpose and God dooth dispose"; FF 32v; Vignali, *Lettera* 2); *Ogniuno tira l'aqua al suo molino* ("Every man draweth water to hymselfe"; FF 14r; Vignali, *Lettera* 17); *Peccato vechio, penitenza nuova* ("Old sinne and new penance"; FF 32v; Vignali, *Lettera* 13); *Poco senno basta …* ("Litle wyt serveth"; FF 33r; Vignali, *Lettera* 10).

72. The shared expression is: *Chi lascia la via vechia per la nuova* ("Who leaveth an olde way for a new"; FF 28r; SF 102; Vignali, *Lettera* 17).

73. A selection of the paremias that Vignali and *Giardino di ricreatione* share are: *A buona derrata pensavi su* ("Consider well good things"; GR 2; Vignali, *Lettera* 35); *Far come i pifari da Luca che andaron a sonare e furono sonati* ("To be like the bagpipes of Lucca, which went to play and were played upon"; GR 106; Vignali, *Lettera* 32); *La comodità fa l'huomo ladro* ("Opportunity makes a man committ larceny"; GR 130; Vignali, *Lettera* 16); *Piscia chiaro e fa le fiche al medico* ("Piss clear and bid a fig for the physician," meaning that he who commits a misdeed does not fear any punishment; GR 175; Vignali, *Lettera* 28); *Quando s'è incudine, convien soffrire* and *Quando s'è martello, convien percuotere* ("When you are anvil, you must suffer" and "When you are hammer, you must strike"; GR 185–86; Vignali, *Lettera* 13); *Se vuoi sia secreto non lo dire* ("If you want it to be secret, don't say it"; GR 193; Vignali, *Lettera* 37); *Tutti non son huomini che pisciano al muro* ("Not all those who piss against a wall are men," meaning that it is better not to trust everyone because you may be deceived"; GR 201; Vignali, *Lettera* 35).

74. Some shared paremias between Vignali and *Second Frutes* are: *Ad arca aperta il giusto pecca* ("Open chests do cause to sin the holliest man that looketh in"; SF 168; Vignali, *Lettera* 16); *A' porci cadon le miglior pere in bocca* ("The ripest peares falle to swine," meaning that often good things happen to the unworthy ones; SF 120; Vignali, *Lettera* 10); *Chi fa più carezze che non suole ...* ("Who greets thee with unwonted curtesie ..."; SF 100; Vignali, *Lettera* 25); *Chi non s'arischia non s'arichisce* ("His gaines will be but small, who ventures not at all"; SF 70; Vignali, *Lettera* 9); *Chi pecora si fa il lupo la mangia* ("In his guts the wolfe will creepe that of himselfe doth make a sheepe"; SF 94; Vignali, *Lettera* 11); *Chi si contenta gode* ("Who lives content, hath all the world at will"; SF 10 and 28; Vignali, *Lettera* 4 and 35); *Chi vive a speranza ...* ("He who dooth live in hope"; SF 148; Vignali, *Lettera* 3); *Essendo a tavola, se c'è poco pane tienlo in mano* ("Sitting at board, if there be but little bread, hold it fast in your hand"; SF 94; Vignali, *Lettera* 1); *[N]on ragionar mai de' morti a tavola* ("Never speake of dead men at the board"; SF 94; Vignali, *Lettera* 35); *... pisciar chiaro per poter far le fiche al medico* ("...pisse cleare, that so a man may bid a figg for the phisition"; SF 60; Vignali, *Lettera* 28); *Quantunque la lingua non habbia osso, la fa spesso romper il dosso* ("How be it the tongue be without bone, yet it breaketh manie a one"; SF 96; Vignali, *Lettera* 4 and 35); *Siedi e gambetta ché vedrai tua vendetta* ("Staie at home, sit still and sing, and that is it revenge will bring"; SF 100; Vignali, *Lettera* 24).

75. Another mention of the work appears in Wolfe's 1584 edition of Aretino's *Ragionamenti*. Wolfe promises his readers to publish many works, among which he mentions "il commune de l'Arsitio" ("Arsiccio's well-known work"), which is an evident reference to Vignali's *La cazzaria*.

76. Some of the paremias in the two *Fruits* that derive from Doni's *Zucca* are: *Chi di gallina nasce convien che razzoli* ("What is hatcht by a hen will scrape like a hen"; SF 178); *Chi fa i fatti suoi non s'imbratta le mani* ("He that for himself doth toyle, his hands doth never gather soyle"; SF 10); *Chi ha fiele in bocca non può sputar miele* ("In his mouth who holdeth gall can spit no honie forth at al"; SF 170); *Chi lascia la via vechia per la nuova spesse volte inganato si ritrova* ("Who leaveth an olde way for a new, oftentymes doth finde hymselfe deceyved"; FF 28*r* and SF 102); *Chi non può batter il cavallo batta la sella* ("Who can not beat the horse, let him beat the saddle"; FF 29*r*); *Chi non robba non fa robba* ("Who steals not, makes no robe"; FF 29*r*); *Chi pecora si fa il lupo la mangia* ("In his guts the wolfe will creep that of himselfe doth make a sheep"; SF 94); *Chi tosto dà due volte dà* ("Twice he giveth that soone doth give"; SF 104); *Come la castagna che di fuori è bella e dentro ha la magagna* ("Like chest nutts bin, fayre without and foule within"; SF 184); *È egli de' soldati del Tinca* ("Is your man one of Tinca his souldiers?"; SF 112); *Io non vorrei esser solo in paradiso* ("I would be loth to be alone in Paradise"; SF 14); *I panni rifanno le stanghe* ("Manners makes, yet apparell shapes"; SF 114); *Le parole sono femine et i fatti sono maschi* ("Words are feminine and deedes are masculine"; SF 176); *Tutto quel che luce non è oro* ("Al that glistreth is not gold"; FF 32*r*); *Un bel morire tutta una vita honora* ("A gallant death doth honour a whole life"; FF 34*r*); *Un fiore non fa primavera* ("One swallowe brings not sommer"; SF 118); *Un homo val cento e cento non vagliano uno* ("One man is woorth a hundred and a hundred is not worth one"; FF 32*v*); *Voi non credete al santo se non fa miracoli* ("You beleeve not the Saint unles he work myracles"; SF 70). Florio probably uses Doni's expression *Chi non sa fare i fatti suoi peggio fa quel d'altrui* ("In his owne matter who is negligent, in another man's will never be diligent") for his paremias in *Second Frutes* (*Chi non sa far i fatti suoi peggio farà quegli d'altrui*; SF 104) and *Giardino di ricreatione* (*Chi non sa fare i fatti suoi peggio farà quelli d'altrui*; GR 29).

77. Examples of paremias selected from *L'ore* and listed in *Giardino di ricreatione* are: *Chi cerca truova* ("Who seeketh, fyndeth"; GR 20); *Dal detto al fatto vi è un gran tratto* ("From the said unto the deed there is a gret throw"; GR 47); *Rendere pane per focaccia* ("To give one bread for cake"; GR 187); and *Tal carne, tal cortello* ("To such flesh, such a knife"; GR 202). In one example, *Second Frutes* contains the same expression as in Doni's text, *Ama e sarai amato* ("To love agree, thou lov'd shalt be"; SF 170), whereas *Giardino* lists the expression with a subordinate sentence, *Ama che sarai amato* ("To love agree, so that you'll be loved"; GR 1).

78. For more information on de Guevara, see Grendler (300–4). De Guevara was also the author of a collection of 112 letters, entitled *Epístolas familiares* (1539 and 1542). Within this collection, the epistles of Emperor Caesar Nerva Trajan constitute a block of sequential documents that might have inspired Florio's chapter 37 in *Firste Fruites*: "Parole da Plutarco, scritte da lui a Traiano imperatore, con diversi altri detti di Antonio Guevara" ("Words written by Plutarchus to the Emperor Traianus, with divers sayeinges of Antonio Guevara"; see Cherchi, "Funzione del paratesto" 44–45).

79. A similar expression is also found in Alunno's *Della fabbrica del mondo*: *Tre cose sommamente dispiacciono a Dio, ricco avaro, povero superbo et vecchio lussurioso* ("Three things supremely displease God, a rich avaricious person, a poor proud being, and a lustful old man"; ix: 232*v*).

80. Both the analyzed expressions also feature in Holyband's *The French Littelton*, under the caption *Three things be faire before God and men / Trois choses sont belles devant Dieu et les homes* (*Agreement among brethren, love betwene neighbours, the man and his wife keping faith and lealtie together*; 88) and under the caption *Three things odious and tedious / Trois choses odieuses et fascheuses* (*A begger proude, a rich man a lier, an old man lecherous*; 88).

81. Leopardi's quotation is taken from "Come vada scritta la storia" (*Tutte le opere*, vol. 1: 455, footnote 601).

82. Lepschy comments that an unclear translated expression would stimulate the reader to guess its meaning more than to understand it (*Tradurre e traducibilità* 17–20). For instance, Canepa, when translating Basile's paremias in her edition of *Lo cunto de li cunti* (Basile, *The Tale of Tales*), decided to reproduce the Italian almost literally, although she was aware that her translation would have puzzled the Anglophone readers. Albanese comments that Canepa's English paremias are far from common language and do not coincide with paremiac expressions used in everyday conversations. Hence, they require explicative notes in order to be fully comprehended ("I centomila miliardi di proverbi" and *Metamorfosi del Cunto di Basile* 80–90). According to Albanese, Canepa favors the text over its fluid reading and immediate understanding. She gives more importance to the "restituzione, in forma prosastica, quasi di ogni singola parola" ("a prosaic restitution of almost every single word"), despite losing rhythmic elements, syntactic relationships, and frequently content at large (*Metamorfosi* 83).

83. It is indeed true that Florio first selects the Italian paremias and then translates them into English. However, in two paremias, the Italian words "dangerosa" and "infamosa" are evidently calques from the English terms "dangerous" and "infamous" (FF 66r). As such, these two instances diminish the absolute certainty of how Florio translated his proverbs. For a comprehensive analysis of interference, contact, and shifts between languages, see Weinrich.

84. In Florio's *Fruits*, rendering paremias in another language follows the rules of a "cultural politics of translation." This suggests that paremias become the representative elements of the translation program that informs Florio's profession and career (Wyatt, *The Italian Encounter* 175).

85. Torriano probably refers to Florio's expression when he lists the expression, *Who imbraceth all, nothing grasps*, in the *Appendix of some few choice Italian Proverbs with the English to them* to the 1786 edition of his *Vocabolario Italiano et Inglese* (32).

86. Generally, Florio translates Boccaccio's paremias faithfully. A few examples are: *Umana cosa è aver compassione degli afflitti* ("To take pity on people in distress is a human quality"; Dec. Proemio.2) and *It is a matter of humanity to take compassion on the afflicted* (*The Decameron, The Author's Prologue, to the Lords, Ladies, and Gentlewomen*); *Peccato celato è mezzo perdonato* ("Sin that is hidden is half forgiven"; Dec. I.4.16) and *Sinne so concealed* *is half pardoned* (*The Decameron* 18r); "Acciò che per voi non si possa quello proverbio intendere che comunemente si dice per tutto, cioè che *le femine in ogni cosa sempre pigliano il peggio*" ("In order that people should not associate you with the proverb commonly heard on everyone's lips, namely that women are always worsted in any argument"; Dec. I.10.8) and "To prevent the common proverbe, *That women (in all things) make choyse of the woorst*" (*The Decameron* 26r); *Bocca basciata non perde ventura, anzi rinnuova come fa la luna* ("A kissed mouth doesn't lose its freshness: like the moon it turns up new again"; Dec. II.7.122) and *The mouth wel kist comes not short of good fortune, but is still renewed like the moone* (*The Decameron* 60v); "Suolsi tra' volgari spesse volte dire un cotal proverbio: che *lo 'ngannatore rimane a piè dello 'ngannato*" ("There is a certain proverb, frequently to be heard on the lips of the people, to the effect that a dupe will outwit his deceiver"; Dec. II.9.3) and "It hath passed as a common proverbe: That *the deceiver is often trampled on by such as he hath deceived*" (*The Decameron* 68r); "Come che gli uomini un cotal proverbio usino: *Buon cavallo e mal cavallo vuole sprone e buona femina e mala femina vuol bastone*" ("Although men have a proverb which says: 'For a good horse and a bad, spurs are required; for a good woman and a bad, the rod is required'"; Dec. IX.9.7) and "Albeit men have a common proverb to wit: *As the good horse and bad horse doe both need the spurre, so a good wife and bad wife a wand will make stirre*" (*The Decameron* 131r). Sometimes, Florio adds terms that are not present in the original: "Usano i volgari un così fatto proverbio: *Chi è reo e buono è tenuto, può fare il male e non è creduto*" ("There is a popular proverb which runs as follows: 'He who is wicked and held to be good, can cheat because no one imagines he would'"; Dec. IV.2.5) and "It hath been continually used as a common proverb that *a bad man taken and reputed to be honest and good, may commit evils, yet neither credited or suspected*" (*The Decameron* 148r). In a few instances, he provides a summary of the paremia's content or part of it, thus eliminating the proverb or decreasing its effectiveness: *Quale asino dà in parete tal riceve* ("As the ass gives in the wall, so he may receive"; Dec. II.9.6) and *Offences unknowne are sildome or never called in question* (*The Decameron* 68v); *Chi ha a far con tosco non vuole esser losco* ("Honesty's the better line, when dealing with a Florentine"; Dec. VIII.10.67) and *Whosoever dealt with a Tuscane had neede to have sound sight and judgement* (*The Decameron* 104r). Alternatively, Florio omits the original proverbs: "A chiunque il salutava o d'alcuna cosa il domandava, niuna altra cosa rispondeva, se non: *Il mal furo non vuol festa*" ("Whenever people met him in the street and put any question to him, the only answer they got was: 'There's never any rest for the bar'"; Dec. II.10.42) and "People began to scorne him, demanding dayly of him, what was become of his gallant young wife, making hornes, with ridiculous poitings at him; whereby his sences became distracted" (*The Decameron* 76v); "Per che così vi vo' dire, donne mie care, che *chi te la fa, fagliele*; e se tu non puoi, tienloti a mente fin ché tu possa, acciò che *quale asino dà in parete tal riceva*" ("So my advice to you, dear ladies, is this, that you should always give back as much as you receive; and if you can't do it at once, bear it in mind till you can, so that what you lose on the swings, you gain on the roundabouts"; Dec. V.10.64) and "No complaint passed on either side, but mutuall joy and household contentment, such as ought to be between man and wife" (*The Decameron* 210r). Montini's article "John Florio and the *Decameron*" (99–100) comments on Florio's translation and insertion of proverbs in Boccaccio's work.

87. In his *Three Hundred Epigrammes upon Three Hundred Proverbes* (first appeared in 1552), Heywood writes: "*Soft fire maketh sweet malt*: as malt-makers tell. Then, to make sweet malt fire is too rash in hell; Whereby, since in hell no good ale is to sell, Dry drunken souls cannot like in hell to dwell" (*Proverbs, epigrams, and miscellanies* n. 16). Arthaber also lists related paremias: *Who goes slowly, goes far*; *He that goes softly, goes safely*; *Fair and softly goes far in a way* (1079).

88. Angiolieri's sonnet 87 reads as follows: "Tre cose solamente mi so 'n grado, / le quali posso non ben men fornire: / ciò è la donna, la taverna e 'l dado; / queste mi fanno 'l cuor lieto sentire" ("There are three things that give me great delight, / and none of them come at a handy price: / woman, the tavern and a game of dice; / and these alone can make my heart feel light"; *Rime* 1–4).

89. Montini comments that, more than translating from one language to the other, Florio by virtue of his plurilinguistic abilities "emett[e] simultaneamente un messaggio uguale e diverso" ("emits a message that is simultaneously the same and different"; "John/Giovanni" 53).

90. This expression is modeled on the French "bonne chère," which met-onymically means to eat well with joyful company (TLF, vol. 5 [1977], s.v. *chère*: par. B, 2).

91. In modern times, Lapucci lists the paremia with the verb "propone" ("to propose"; *Dizionario dei proverbi italiani* s.l. U: n. 169–70). He states that the paremia in Latin usually concludes with "nec est in homine via eius" ("and there is no way of their own for men").

92. In *Morgante*, the text reads as follows: "Ma mio costume all'oste è dar le frutte / Sempre al partir, quando il conto facciamo" ("But to innkeep-ers, when they bring the check, / I'm wont to give my money as I leave"; I.18.145.5–6).

93. Engel comments that the paremia contains an allusion to a Memory Palace (512).

94. Salviati and Varchi cite the expression as it appears in Florio's work: *Far come quei da Prato* ("To do as they do at Prato"; Salviati) and *Come quei da Prato quando piove* ("As those by Prato when it rains"; *L'Hercolano* 135). Serdonati, instead, lists the paremia twice, each time with a different initial: *Far come quei da Prato: lasciano piovere quando piove e si stanno in casa* ("To do as they do at Prato: they let it rain when it rains and they stay at home") and *Se piove, facciam come quei da Prato. Lasciam piovere* ("If it rains, let's do it as they do at Prato. Let it rain").

95. Wellerisms in *Giardino di ricreatione* are likewise rare and scattered throughout the collection. Its letter "C" does not have a special section dedicated to them, as happens in other works with paremias. In his *The Italian Wellerism*, Speroni considers some expressions in *Giardino* to be wellerisms when they are in fact proverbial phrases (specifically, the expressions indicated by the numbers 42, 50, 74, 114, 253, 299); indeed, they show neither the formula "come disse" nor the indication of the person or animal that pronounces the expressions. The wellerism *Come disse il Calavrese: Havesti paura?* ("As the Calabrese said: were you afraid?"; Speroni, *The Italian Wellerism* n. 42) is mentioned three times, first as a proverb and the others as a proverbial phrase: *A chi tocca tocca, se nò, havesti paura?* ("Who's next, he is; if not, were you afraid?"; GR [10]); *Havesti paura?* ("Were you afraid?"; GR 113); *Se coglie coglia, se no, havesti paura?* ("If it catches, let it catch; if not, were you afraid?"; GR 197). Furthermore, Speroni includes among wellerisms the phrase, *La padella dice al paiuolo, sta in là, che tu mi tingi* ("The pan says to the pot, stay there that you stain me"; GR 143), but not the similar *La padella dice al manico, tu sei negro* ("The pan says to the handle, you are black"; GR 144), even though both belong to one of four categories of false wellerisms (*The Italian Wellerism* 5). Based on these considerations, the wellerisms in Florio's *Giardino* appear to total twenty-two.

96. This was not the norm at the time considering that, some years later, Torriano translates the Italian paremias in English in his *Piazza universale* (1666).

97. Examples are: *Chi nuoce altrui nuoce se stesso* ("Who hurteth others, hurteth hym selfe"; FF 29r) and *Chi conosce se stesso altrui non nuoce* ("Who knows himself, does not hurt others"; GR 22); *La speranza è l'ultima cosa de l'huomo* ("Hope is the last thynge of a man"; FF 31v) and *L'ultimo riffugio è la speranza o la morte* ("The last refuge is hope or death"; GR 139).

98. Within *Giardino di ricreatione*, Florio collects different formulations of the same paremia, which demonstrates his desire to gather the greatest number of expressions for a future lexicographic intent. The lexical variation, even within the first letter of the alphabet, is well represented. Particularly, one instance is the paremia *A gatto che lecca cenere, non fidar farina* ("To a cat licking ash, do not trust flour"; GR 1) and its alternative *A gatto che lecca il spiede non fidar l'arosto* ("To a cat licking the spit, do not trust the roast"; GR 12). In his collection, Serdonati registers the first expression as an alternative to a more common form featuring "cane" ("dog"): "*A can che lecca cenere non gli fidar farina. Perché, come disse l'Arsiccio, il ciò fare è come porre il lupo per pecoraio, e andare alla gatta pel lardo. Altri dicono A gatto che lecca cenere* ecc.: chi ne fa una piccola ne farà una grande" ("To a dog licking ash, do not trust flour. Because, as Arsiccio said, doing this is like putting the wolf as a shepherd and going to the cat for lard. Others say, To a cat licking ash etc.: whoever makes a small one, will make a big one"). Since neither Buoni nor Pescetti report this variant and Salviati's version is the same as Serdonati's, it is possible that Serdonati read this paremia in Florio's collection. This speculation comes from Speroni's argument that Serdonati explicitly mentions Florio on a few occasions ("Giovanni Torriano's *Select Italian Proverbs*" 156: footnote 18).

99. These words align with the motto and the intent of the Accademia della Crusca to satisfy the ideal of "Il più bel fior ne coglie" ("It picks the most beautiful flower").
100. Hazlitt reports a rhyme created out of the paremia: "He is a fool and ever shall that writes his name upon a wall" (43).

Chapter Four

1. For more on Sarnelli's biography, Malato's introduction to Sarnelli's *Posilecheata* ([1986] xxv–xxix) contains a list of all sources mentioning the author's life. See also Canepa ("Sarnelli, Pompeo") and Iurilli ("I proverbi e le favole"; "Paremìa e favola").
2. Malato reports the date 1692 (Sarnelli, *Posilecheata* [1986] xxvi), whereas Gimma declares that it is instead 1691 (295).
3. Among Sarnelli's erudite works, the most important are: a work on the Greek alphabet *L'alfabeto greco* (1675); translations of Giovanni Battista Della Porta's works including *Della chirofisonomia* and *Della magia naturale* (1677); a Latin grammar book *L'ordinario grammaticale* (1677); *Specchio del clero secolare* (1678–79); *Cronologia de' vescovi ed arcivescovi sipontini* (1680); *Bestiarum Schola* (1680); *Antica basilicografia* (1686); *Lettere ecclesiastiche* (1686–1716); and *Memorie dei vescovi di Bisceglie* (1693). Among his works are also two city guides: *Guida de' forestieri curiosi di vedere ed intendere le cose più notabili della real città di Napoli e del suo amenissimo distretto* (1685; reprinted by Bulifon in 1697) and *Guida de' forestieri curiosi di vedere e considerare le cose notabili di Pozzuolo, Baja, Miseno, Cuma, Gaeta ed altri luoghi circonvicini* (1685; translated into French by Bulifon in 1700). In the introduction to his *Degli avvenimenti di Fortunato*, Sarnelli mentions another work, *Metamorfosi del bue humano, poema*, but its whereabouts are still unknown. For all of Sarnelli's works, see the list of printed books contained in *Istoria delle perrucche* (Bovicelli); see also Gimma (285–301 for an annotated description, 301–3 for a list). Additionally, in the *Catalogo de' libri composti e dati alle stampe dall'illustrissimo e reverendissimo signor Pompeo Sarnelli vescovo di Bisceglia* in the 1685 edition of Sarnelli's *Guida de' forestieri curiosi di vedere ed intendere le cose più notabili della real città di Napoli* (a4r–a5r), Bulifon lists some of Sarnelli's works and refers to the catalogue, *Biblioteca Napoletana*, that biographer Nicolò Toppi produced in 1678.
4. The original text comes from an anonymous story called *Fortunatus* (c. 1509), probably based on one of the tales collected in *Gesta Romanorum* and later translated into Spanish. In 1615, Vion d'Alibray rendered the text in French with the title *Histoire comique, ou Les aventures de Fortunatus*. Sarnelli's translation into Italian is mentioned in Bovicelli's *Istoria delle perrucche*, specifically in its *Catalogo de' libri impressi di Monsignor Sarnelli vescovo di Bisceglia*. Here the title incorrectly appears as *Avvertimenti di Fortunato* (584).

5. Probably founded at the end of the sixteenth century or the beginning of the seventeenth century in Correggio, the Accademia degli Scioperati replaced the Accademia dei Trasformati (Maylender, vol. 5: 132–33).

6. The identity of the author of *Posilecheata* has been the subject of different interpretations throughout the centuries. In the first edition of the collection, Bulifon promotes the idea that Masillo Reppone is not the same person as Sarnelli. Probably, the 1676 edition of *Degli avvenimenti di Fortunato* generated this idea because its colophon reports that Reppone is the editor of both its translation and illustrations. The prefatory letter to this work, which is dedicated to Sarnelli, plays with the two identities: "Ho pensato dedicarlo a me stesso, cioè a te, che, come mio fratello, sei un'altro me" ("I thought to dedicate it to myself, which means to you, who, as a brother of mine, are another me"; †3r). In his 1779 treatise on the Neapolitan dialect *Del dialetto napoletano*, Abbot Ferdinando Galiani names Tommaso Perrone as *Posilecheata*'s author. In *Lo vernacchio*, Serio points out Galiani's mistake and attributes the collection to Sarnelli, while harshly criticizing *Del dialetto napoletano*. If in 1844 Rubini follows Galiani's path in his "Il dialetto napolitano" (374), two years later Raffaele demonstrates Sarnelli's authorship of *Posilecheata* (35). Nonetheless, in 1867 and later in 1874, Martorana contradicts himself in his *Notizie biografiche e bibliografiche*. In Basile's entry, he writes that the 1674 edition of his *Cunto* is by Perrone (23), yet, in Sarnelli's entry, he considers Sarnelli the author of both *Lo cunto de li cunti*'s 1674 edition and *Posilecheata* (371).

7. The 1684 edition of *Posilecheata* contains the following: editor Bulifon's device for the years 1685–97, which is a crowned siren that holds its two tails in its hands; Mount Vesuvio, a rising sun, and ships in the background (see Polito); the initials AB with two crosses on top; and the motto "Sempre non nuoce" ("Not always it harms") surrounded by a vegetal cornice. All of the editions of Sarnelli's work include Bulifon's letter dedicated to Ignazio de Vives; Claudio Ciclirani's dedicatory sonnet to Sarnelli; the letter to the virtuous readers; a celebratory letter by Accademico Sgargiato [E]ugenio Desviati (most certainly a nickname); the book's imprimatur; the licence to print the book granted on August 13, 1684 by Cesare Natale; the introduction; the five fables; the conclusion; and a final section, which contains the index of the various parts of the book followed by "Innece de le ccose notabele" ("Index of the noteworthy aspects of the work"). In the 1885 edition of *Posilecheata*, one of Vittorio Imbriani's illustrations reproduces a long section of the third *cantica* (second proverb) of Cynthio's *Libro della origine delli volgari proverbi*: *Ogni scusa è buona pur che la vaglia* ("Every excuse is good as far as it's worth it"; Sarnelli, *Posilecheata di Pompeo Sarnelli* 155–61). The initial pages of this same edition include an accurate list of all of the copies of Sarnelli's *Posilecheata* until 1885 (v–ix).

8. In 1674, Sarnelli published an edition of Basile's collection with the alternative title *Il Pentamerone*, clearly referring to Boccaccio's *Decameron*. He dedicated it to Pietro Emilio Guaschi, a judge and "eletto del popolo," namely a representative of the Neapolitan citizens.

9. Among the others are Basile Bonsante (actually a concise study on Sarnelli as a moralist); Fulco (863–64), Malato ("La letteratura dialettale campana" 264), Nigro ("*Lo cunto de li cunti*"), Picone and Messerli, and Porcelli ("Alle prese con la lingua").

10. This is similar to what Speroni had done just a decade before with Basile's paremias (Speroni, *Proverbs and Proverbial Phrases*).

11. Used by B. Croce, "dialettalità riflessa" indicates the deliberate use of a dialect when a language standardized by literature is available for use. The complete definition can be found in Croce ("La letteratura dialettale riflessa") and later in *Uomini e cose* (vol. 1: 222–34). For examples of literary works in Neapolitan dialect, see De Blasi and Fanciullo (650–60); for a more general overview of the Neapolitan history and literary enterprises in the fifteenth and sixteenth centuries, including references to the other parts of the reign, see De Blasi and Varvaro.

12. De Rosa's *Ricordi* refers heavily to oral tradition. Many are the examples of discordance between De Rosa's description of an event and its historical and military accounts. This confirms how De Rosa's sources included personal experiences, as well as stories recounted orally and not codified in a written form (Bianchi et al., 72; De Rosa 44–46). *Ricordi* also contains etiologic descriptions of the city of Naples and surrounding areas, reports of supernatural events, and praises of women. The third text of the collection includes an exaltation of the city of Naples, which is defined as the best province in the world and in Italy (653–63: 58*r*–61*v*). On De Rosa's *Ricordi*, see also Ghirelli (535–36).

13. In his book *Spagnolo e spagnoli*, Beccaria offers a comprehensive overview of the contacts between Italian and Spanish in the fifteenth and sixteenth centuries, with many examples concerning the Neapolitan dialect. On Naples and its dialect during the period of the Spanish viceroys, De Blasi's *Storia linguistica* (65–88) is a valuable reference; for a diastratic analysis of the languages spoken in the Neapolitan area in the 1500s, De Blasi ("Notizie") and Radtke ("La questione della lingua") are excellent sources. Ghirelli offers an exploration of the Neapolitan culture and language from the thirteenth century to 1648; within his *Storia di Napoli*, Rak's essay on the popular and dialect tradition from the Spanish conquest in 1503 to 1648 deserves mention (573–747).

14. There were accounts of bureaucratic documents written in Neapolitan, which is evidence of a progressive expansion of the dialect in legal areas. This Neapolitan was highly influenced by Latin, which was the official language of bureaucracy, and thus lacked the most typical aspects of the local dialect (De Blasi, *Storia linguistica* 53).

15. Galiani attacks both Cortese and Basile for their barbarous orthography, which makes their works unintelligible not only to foreigners but also to Neapolitan people. He also blames them because they distort Tuscan words in order to make them more Neapolitan (*Del dialetto napoletano* 30, 121–36). The only merit he recognizes in Basile's text is his extensive use of paremias and idiomatic expressions (123). In *Lo vernacchio*, Serio declares that Basile is

a master of the Neapolitan dialect (31) and could not have written a different collection to express the common people's language. Simultaneously, Serio derides Tuscan speakers and Giovan Battista Marino's followers (38).

16. Despite cataloguing *Posilecheata* as an imitation of Basile's *Lo cunto de li cunti* (*Del dialetto napoletano* 138), Galiani praises the work for preserving the civil memory of Naples and the value of its dialect: "In esse cercò l'autore di conservare la memoria d'alcuni antichi monumenti della nostra città divenuti quasi sacri per noi ... Per l'eleganza del dialetto è da annoverarsi tra' migliori nostri scrittori" ("In them [the five stories] the author tried to preserve the memory of some old monuments of our city, which have almost become sacred ... For the elegance of the dialect, he is to be included among our best writers"; 165–66).

17. Sarnelli's linguistic background included multiple languages. He was undoubtedly exposed to the local dialect spoken in Polignano, although he never manifested it in his works. This dialect was influenced by the Aragonese dynasty in Naples in the second half of the fifteenth century and showed limited influence from the substratum of the Oscan language and from the Greek spoken in the area of Magna Graecia. Other than his "maternal" language, Sarnelli was perfectly fluent in Latin, Greek, and Italian. In Naples, he learned the local dialect used in the streets, as well as literary Neapolitan (Malato, "La letteratura dialettale campana"). For an historical overview of dialects in Apulia and external linguistic influences, see Cortelazzo et al. (*I dialetti italiani* 679–756); Rohlfs (*Studi e ricerche* 231–45), and Valente (*Puglia*).

18. Sarnelli was apparently interested in stories and fables that could convey a moral message through comical topics. An example is *Degli avvenimenti di Fortunato*, the prefatory letter of which combines erudition, witticism, and a strong sense of morality. Another illustration is *Bestiarum Schola*, in which Sarnelli gathers 99 fables in order to castigate the immoral behaviors of the time (Iurilli, "I proverbi e le favole"; "Paremìa e favola").

19. In order to demonstrate his full allegiance to Naples and its language, Sarnelli frequently defends (probably as a literary *topos*) his acquired knowledge and expertise in the Neapolitan dialect. An example of this defense comes from the letter "Al curioso lettore" ("To the curious readers") introducing the *Guida de' forestieri curiosi di vedere ed intendere le cose più notabili della real città di Napoli* (for an excerpt of the letters, see Picone and Messerli 311: footnote 10, and Sarnelli, *Posilecheata* [1986] xii; for its English translation, see Bottigheimer 74). Bulifon reports that Sarnelli protects himself from the accusations of an alleged scarce knowledge of the Neapolitan dialect by declaring a strong linguistic identity. In the prefatory letter *A li vertoluse leieture Napolitane* ("To the virtuous Neapolitan readers") to the 1674 edition of Basile's *Lo cunto de li cunti*, Sarnelli employs paremias to demonstrate that he is a competent writer in Neapolitan. Consequently, he proves to be the best candidate to reproduce Basile's language in its most faithful and philologically-accurate form.

20. In his *L'Eccellenza della lingua napoletana*, Tosco considers the frequency of paremias (as well as tropes) one of the features that makes the Neapolitan dialect superior to all the others (116).

21. For an analysis of some of the paremias, including tripartite ones, that will be mentioned in the following pages, Imbriani's "illustrazioni" ("explanations") are a good source of historical and cultural details (P 105–246). Sarnelli's desire to compile a collection of "Frasi di lingua napoletana" ("Phrases in the Neapolitan language") testifies to his fascination with paremias. As he admits in the preface to his 1674 edition of Basile's *Lo cunto de li cunti* (Bottigheimer 74), he had planned to write a manual on Neapolitan orthography (Valente, "La lingua napoletana") and had been expanding a list of Neapolitan idioms and synonyms over time. Unfortunately, there is no reference to where this work might be preserved. It is arguable that Sarnelli was gathering *sententiae* (and probably paremias) to create a manual to which he could refer when in need of expressing a concept in the most diverse literary occasions.

22. In his research on theoretical approaches to comedy, Ferroni argues that in comedic events, including literary ones, a subject triggers comedy (the actor or the author), a subject laughs (the audience), and a subject or object represents the victim of the comedic act (14).

23. At that time, the academicians were working on the third edition of the *Vocabolario degli Accademici della Crusca* to be eventually published in 1691. Despite the purist ideal that the Crusca followed, its dictionary was more open to regional terms and expressions than what appeared visible in its entries. Cortelazzo demonstrates the presence of regionalisms already in the 1612 edition of the dictionary ("Regionalismi").

24. Caniato explains that at the time, a cognitive process associated dialects with buffoonery and with an exclusively comic representation of life, especially when compared to the presumably dignified literature in Italian. The Neapolitan dialect immediately corresponded to comic and hilarious language, used to entertain and likely to appear in works that were quintessentially connected to a popular sphere. However, Haller argues that there was a considerable tradition of serious texts in prose, poetry, and theatre written in the Neapolitan dialect (*The Other Italy* 243–78).

25. The *Dizionario etimologico italiano* lists the form "strenga" ("shoelace") as a Northern-dialect term in the fourteenth century (s.v. *strenga*).

26. The expression *Nos quoque poma natamus* became common in the Middle Ages through the Latin translation of Aesop's fables by Gaius Julius Phaedrus. Phaedrus entitled this story *Sterquilinum et poma* ("Dung and fruits") and translated it as follows: "Forte sublatum cum pomis sterquilinium subita aquarum eluvione fluitabat in eo loco ubi dudum iacuerat. Tum se illud et in aquis vehi et ferri cum pomis praeclarum existimans, «Quam scite nos,» inquit, «poma natamus.» Sed paulo post, umiditate dissolutum, in aquis evanuit" ("Some dung, which happened to be carried up along with some apples in a sudden runoff of water, was floating in that place where till recently it had been lying. Believing itself so excellent then, in riding on the water and being ferried in the company of apples, it said: 'How skillfully we apples swim!' But a little later, dissolved by the humidity, it vanished in the water"). The fable remained well-known up to the time of Martin Luther, who referred to it in his exposition of Psalm 45: *Enarratio Psalmi XLV ex praelectionibus D.M.L. ab eius auditoribus anno XXXII collecta, edita vero anno MDXXXIIII*. A reference to a pearl found in a dunghill is also in another fable by Aesop, which corresponds to Phaedrus's fable 12 in Book 3, *Pullus ad margaritam* ("The Young Cock to the Pearl"). For the English tradition of the saying, see A. Taylor (*The Proverb* 209).

27. Sarnelli probably refers to chapter 48 of Miguel de Cervantes's *El ingenioso hidalgo*, in which a priest says: "No es posible que esté continuo el arco armado, ni la condición y flaqueza humana se pueda sustentar sin alguna licita recreación" ("It is not possible that the armed bow is continuous, nor the condition and human weakness can be sustained without some legitimate recreation"). In Cervantes's discussion, well-written and well-organized comedies represent precious example of eloquence for intelligent people. Similarly, *Posilecheata* is an appropriate means to take a break from virtuous enterprises in search of the pleasure that *eutrapelia* guarantees (P 4.4). For further elaboration on Cervantes's concept of recreation and usefulness of novellas in relation to his *Novelas ejemplares*, see Zanin. In *Nichomachean Ethics*, Aristotle comments on *eutrapelia* stating that one of its forms consists of distraction accompanied by entertainment (*Opere* IV.1128a–b). However, moderation should inform any behavior because an excess of playfulness transforms the person into a buffoon. Thomas Aquinas, in *Summa Theologica* or *Summa Theologiae*, describes how playfulness can be the subject of virtue (Book 2, part 2, question 168, article 2).

28. This seems to confirm Radtke's idea that "la scelta del dialetto … s'intende come un divertimento intellettuale, come un pretesto, ma non come necessità letteraria" ("choosing dialect … is interpreted as an intellectual *divertissement*, as a pretext, and not as a literary necessity"; "La questione della lingua" 81). Rak comments that the presence of the Tuscan vernacular in the Neapolitan tradition is always comic and parodic (*Napoli gentile* 23); on the topic, see also Brevini (lxxvi–lxxxii).

29. Malato states that Sarnelli takes this anecdote from Book 1, ch. 6, of Summonte's 1601–02 *Historia della città e regno di Napoli* (Sarnelli, *Posilecheata* [1986] 5: footnote 5). In turn, Summonte states that it comes from Book 7 of Cicero's letters *Ad Atticum*; here the only possible reference to Summonte's quotation might be from the second letter (the topic is completely different): "Quo modo expectabam epistulam quam Philoxeno dedisses! Scripseras enim in ea esse de sermone Pompei Neapolitano" ("Impatiently indeed did I await the letter you said you had given to Philoxenus! For you wrote that it contained an account of your conversation with Pompey at Naples").

30. The concept of sweetness comes from Dante's *De Vulgari Eloquentia* and his goal to find the best vernacular in the Italian peninsula. When Dante needs to choose the most suitable words for his works, the only options left are terms that are combed, decorative, glossy, and as sweet as hydromel (II.VII). In his linguistic analysis of the dialects of the peninsula, the poet does not analyze Neapolitan thoroughly. He briefly mentions this dialect when he states that Naples and Gaeta belong to the same tribe (I.IX.4) and places it within the bigger area of Apulia. According to him, the inhabitants of this region use many gross barbarisms, such as "Bolzera che chiangesse lo quatraro" ("I would like the boy to cry"; I.XII.7–8). Galiani quotes Dante's example, saying that "volzera" ("I would like") does not exist in the Neapolitan dialect and must be a copyist mistake (*Del dialetto napoletano* 48).

31. The proverbial phrase also appears in Basile's *Lo cunto de li cunti*, I.1.5, IV.10.29, and V.2.25. Varchi asserts that the expression *Lavargli il capo da' barbieri col ranno caldo* ("To wash someone his/her head with hot ashes and water at the barber's") or *Lavargli il capo col ranno freddo* ("To wash someone his/her head with cold ashes and water") is used to talk ill of someone who is not present (3.55). Similarly, the proverb *Chi lava il capo all'asino perde il ranno e il sapone* ("Who washes the ass his head loses ashes and soap") expresses the waste of time in doing something useless and without profit (Vassano 152–54). In his *Adagia*, Erasmus lists the expression *Asini caput ne laves nitro* ("Do not wash a donkey's head with soap"), metaphorically suggesting that anything similar to this activity is a mean and worthless task (*Collected Works of Erasmus, Adages*, vol. 34, III.iii.39: 295).

32. The derivative process, typical to southern Italy, makes the entire expression more Neapolitan and distinguishes it from the Italian equivalent (Serianni and Castelvecchi 653). For more information, see Renzi et al., vol. 3: 507–09).

33. The opposition between dead and alive languages, which is derived from Tolomei's 1555 *Il Cesano de la lingua toscana* (43), characterizes Citolini's 1540 *Lettera in difesa de la lingua volgare*. Citolini contrasts the rich and dynamic Tuscan vernacular, which thrives and continuously renews itself by drawing from any idiomatic domain, and the bookish Latin, which does not reproduce reality any longer. Much like Sarnelli's creative and fruit-bearing Neapolitan, Citolini's vernacular language "è viva e, come viva, cresce, genera, crea, produce, partorisce, e sempre si fa più ricca e più abondante" ("it is alive and, as such, grows, generates, creates, produces, begets, and always becomes richer and more abundant"; 6v). Citolini innovatively phrases the superiority of the Italian language thanks to its adaptability and its wealth of writers, texts, genres, subjects, registers, and lexicon (see Antonini).

34. In his dictionary, Rocco (s.v. *cinque*) lists an example by Michele Zezza's *Artaserse*, in which *cinco lettere* means "forca" ("death"): "Aggia lo reo la vita o *cinco lettere*" ("May the guilty person have life or five letters"; 2.11). In his *Dizionario dei frizzetti popolari fiorentini*, Frizzi relates the word "cinque" to the vulgar term for the male genital organ "cazzo" ("cock").

35. In his dictionary, D'Ambra (s.v. *chiantuto*) describes "chiantuto" as robust, vigorous, rooted, and well-planted. Rocco (s.v. *chiantuto*) also defines "chiantuto" as big, well-planted, robust, and solid; he reports an example in Niccolò Amenta's comedy *La Fante* (1701): "No lo siente lo parlà chiantuto e aggrazejato?" ("Does he not perceive the robust and graceful way of speaking?"; Act 3, scene 9; see De Blasi, "Notizie" 95-99). In his *Viaggio di Parnaso*, Cortese also uses "chiantuto" to define rumors in Naples: "Vuce chiantute de la maglia vecchia, ch'anno gran forza, ed énchieno l'aurecchia" ("Robust voices of the old intricacy, which have great strength, and fill up the ears"; see Cortese and Sgruttendio de Scafato I.24). Another instance of use is Basile's *Lo cunto de li cunti*, specifically in fable I.1, in which "chiantuto" is associated with Antuono and his gaining weight out of the ogre's plush meals. Similarly, in fable I.2, Basile uses the adjective to describe the beauty of a young woman. Sarnelli refers to the adjective "chiantuto" in *cunto* 4 to present Belluccia's gravestone, on which the proverbial phrase *Non c'è peo de vellane arresagliute* ("There is nothing worse than a wealthy villain") is carved "a lettere chiantute" ("in big letters"; P 174.92). For "majateco," D'Ambra explains that the term carries many meanings, including something fresh, rounded, doughy, juicy, and with nice colors. In his *Nuovo vocabolario*, D'Ascoli proposes that the meaning of "majateco" is robust; the adjective's reference to a flourishing robustness supposedly comes from the cherries in May, which are particularly big and pulpy ("majateco" derives from the Latin *maiaticus* "relative to May" from *maius* "May"). "Maiateco" is used in Sgruttendio de Scafato's *Tiorba a taccone* in the aforementioned sonnet 5 of the first corda (see Cortese and Sgruttendio de Scafato), as well as in two of Capasso's sonnets. The first instance describes the succulent roasted testicles of a ram, in which the adjectives "majateco" and "chiantuto" are ironic references to Petrarchist poets (174). The other instance refers to Petrarchan poetry, which is said to be worthy of cleaning Capasso's posterior (192). Additionally, Galiani links "chiantuto" and "majateco" to those plants or pulpy fruits that please the palate (*Del dialetto napoletano* 11), whereas Serio asserts that the two words come from healthy broccoli with a strong stalk and a thriving top (17).

36. Another reference to Sarnelli's exaltation of the Neapolitan language because of its own substance follows: "E po' co sta lengua Toscana avite frusciato lo tafanario a miezo munno! Vale cchiù na parola Napoletana chiantuta che tutte li vocabole de la Crusca" ("And furthermore, you're breaking the ass of half the world with this Tuscan language! One vigorous Neapolitan word is worth all the vocabulary contained in the Crusca dictionary"; P 5.6; Bottigheimer 76). A similar concept occurs in the prologue to Fiorillo's *L'Amor giusto* (1604): "[V]ale cchiù na scarpa cacata de no napoletano (con leverentia delle faccie vostre) che quanta Toscanicchie se trovano pe lo munno" ("A shit-covered shoe of a Neapolitan is worth more than all the little Tuscans that one can find in the world, with reverence for your faces"; 17). A few years later, G. Fasano expresses an equal contrast between the Crusca in Florence and the richness of the Neapolitan language in his mock epic *Lo Tasso napoletano* (1689): "Tennimoce lo nnuosto, e stia 'n Toscana la Crusca … sta lengua nosta è llengua de tresoro e fuorze ha ccose che no' ll'hanno loro" ("Let's keep what is ours, and let the Crusca stay in Tuscany ... this language of ours is a treasure language and, probably, has things that they don't have"; I.4). On the dichotomy between literature in dialect and Tuscan tradition, see Cortelazzo et al., *I dialetti italiani* 996–1028; on the defense of the Neapolitan dialect and its dignity against the Tuscan vernacular, see Basile, *Lo cunto de li cunti* [2013] xvi–xix.

37. In the *Atlante Linguistico Italiano*, the contemporary extended Lombard area (Brescia, Milan, Bergamo, Como, Trento) is identified by the form "ko" for "capo" ("head"). The pronunciation of "casa" as "ka" ("house") starts in Forlì and includes a large area in Northern Italy, corresponding today to the following areas: Emilia Romagna; Lombardy minus Brescia; Liguria, except a few areas around Genova and Savona; and the Piedmont region, excluding the areas along the border (i.e., Asti and Vercelli).

38. Rocco (s.v. *cacare*) mentions the paremia, which is said to appear both in Sgruttendio de Scafato and in Sarnelli. In Sgruttendio de Scafato's *Tiorba a taccone* the paremia features in a completely different context. Fear in front of the loved one intervenes, ultimately leading to loss of language; thus, the following advice is given: "Parla chiaro, tu saie comm'è lo mutto: *Lengua, che no' la 'ntienne, e tu la caca*" ("Speak clearly, you know how the expression is: 'If you don't understand a language, you shit it right out'"; Cortese and Sgruttendio de Scafato 1.12).

39. Another comic example further explains Sarnelli's attitude since it demonstrates how the further north one goes, the fewer words one uses. The author demonstrates that the Neapolitan word "pane" ("bread") becomes "pan" in an area which can be identified with central Italy and then "pa" in the northern regions of Lombardy. For the traveler, it is better to return home instead of continuing his journey. If he advances any farther, he will find no more bread and will die of hunger (P 7.13). In other words, as one goes further north, one finds less food, hence less linguistic sustenance. As Rak argues, food and hunger become a metaphor for linguistic criticism and language policy (*Logica della fiaba* 257).

40. Eco writes that "il comico pare popolare, liberatorio, eversivo perché dà licenza di violare la regola" ("comedy seems popular, liberating, subversive, because it permits breaking of the rule"; 257).

41. It is interesting to read what Galiani writes about the expressiveness of Neapolitan people: "Ma il Napoletano, l'ente della natura, che forse ha i nervi più delicati e la più pronta irritabilità nelle fibre, se non è tocco da sensazioni, tace; se lo è, e sian queste o di sdegno, o di tenerezza, o di giubilo, o di mestizia, o di gusto, o di rammarico (che ciò non fa gran differenza), subito s'infiamma, si commuove e quasi si convelle. Allora entra in subitaneo desio di manifestar le sue idee. Le parole se gli affollano e fanno groppo sulla lingua. S'aiuta co' gesti, co' cenni, co' moti. Ogni membro, ogni parte è in commozione, e vorrebbe esprimere. Così senza esser facondo è eloquentissimo. Senza ben esprimersi si fa comprender appieno e sovente intenerisce, compunge, persuade" ("But the Neapolitan person, the entity of nature that perhaps has the most delicate nerves and the most prompt irritability in its fibers, if he is not touched by sensations, is silent: if he is, and these may be either outrage, or tenderness, or jubilation, or sadness, or enjoyment, or regret [which does not make much difference], he immediately becomes inflamed, is moved, and almost writhes. Hence, he comes into a sudden desire to manifest his ideas. Words flock to his mouth, and they lump on his tongue. He helps himself with gestures, signals, and motions. Every member, every part is in emotion, and would like to express. So, without being profoundly talkative, he is very eloquent. Without properly expressing himself, he is fully understood, and often softens, empathizes, persuades"; *Del dialetto napoletano* 23).

42. On the *Decameron*'s frame, see Branca (*Boccaccio medievale* 31–44) and on its imitation in Basile's *Lo cunto de li cunti*, see Picone ("La cornice novellistica"). Allasia's article offers a discussion on the connections between Sarnelli's *Posilecheata* and Basile's *Cunto*.

43. Capozzoli lists this sentence in his *Grammatica* when talking about some consonantal substitutions. He refers to the spelling of the word "luongo" ("long") in Sarnelli's introduction to prescribe that *g* should not replace *c*. In Sarnelli's time, the common pronunciation required the velar consonant *g* instead of the palatal one *c*, contrary to the phonetic tendencies common in Capozzoli's time (9–10: footnote 8).

44. This mention appears in Capaccio, *La vera antichità di Pozzuolo*: "... Posilipo, il quale meritamente con questo nome si honora dal toglier la maninconia e la mestitia" ("Posillipo, which deservedly by this name is honored because of its removing melancholy and sadness"; 2). The same Capaccio in his 1634 *Il forastiero* (day X: 100–2) and Celano in his 1692 *Notizie del bello* (day IX: 77–78) describe Posillipo in similarly encomiastic tones. In Imbriani's edition of *Posilecheata*, Desviati's (academician Sgargiato) letter to Reppone refers to Posilleco as a "luoco assaje deliziuso, ca fa sano ogne malato" ("A truly enjoyable place that heals every sick person"; Sarnelli, *Posilecheata di Pompeo Sarnelli* xxiii). Del Tufo celebrates Posillipo as "gran spasso d'un cor ferito e lasso" ("a great amusement for a hurt and tired heart"; 82). In *cunto* 3 of *Posilecheata*, an etiologic explanation on Naples and its gulf includes Posilleco too, which is said to be always green and merry, as well as characterized by entertainment and happiness (P 108.40–41). In the same fable, Posilleco acquires a mythological dimension when the place is said to be a young man transformed into a mountain because of love sickness (P 108.42).

45. In Sarnelli's *Guida de' forestieri curiosi di vedere ed intendere le cose più notabili della real città di Napoli*, editor Bulifon describes *Posilecheata* as follows: "Posilicheata di Masillo Reppone, cioè trattenimento, ed honesta ricreazione in Pausilipo, scritto in lingua Napoletana" ("Masillo Reppone's *Posilecheata*, i.e., entertainment and honest recreation in Posillipo, written in the Neapolitan language"; third page of the *Catalogo de' libri composti, e dati alle stampe dall'illustrissimo et reverendissimo signor Pompeo Sarnelli vescovo di*

Bisceglia). In the third book of the same *Guida*, the first chapter is dedicated to Posillipo (327–31).

46. D'Ambra (s.v. *posellechesco*) comments that "posellechesco" ("at the style of Posillipo") corresponds to pastoral and bucolic or relates to fishing. He mentions that Cortese defined his comedy *La rosa*, "posellechesca," because it was an imitation of Tasso's and Guarino Guarini's dramatic idylls.

47. The description of Marchionno's hunger and eating (P 14.13) resembles that of Cola Iacovo's relative in Basile's *cunto* 2 (CC II.10.7–9).

48. B. Croce describes this typology of paremias as follows: "Sono curiosi per più rispetti e, fra l'altro, perché hanno il carattere comune di contenere non già ciascun proverbio un'idea, ma ciascuno tre idee che vanno a braccetto e s'incontrano poi in una sola" ("They are curious structures for many reasons and, among the others, because they share the notion that each proverb contains not only an idea but three of them, which go arm in arm and eventually meet in one unique idea"; "Proverbi trimembri napoletani" 66). In his edition of Rinaldi's *Dottrina delle virtù e fuga dei vizi* (1585)—a collection of paremias based on the number four—Malato considers these expressions to be products of literary elaborations more than spontaneous formations, hence with limited oral tradition (15–16). Cherchi is engaging in a philological study of Rinaldi's sources, soon to be released.

49. Morel-Fatio offers a thorough overview of collections based on a tripartite structure ("three things are" or "three things do") in the French, Italian, and Catalan traditions. For examples of tripartite paremias in other languages, see A. Taylor (*The Proverb* 159–64).

50. The list of proverbs also features in G. C. Croce's *L'Eccellenza e trionfo del porco* (140–49). Similar paremias were published in the journal *Lo nuovo diavolo zuoppo e Polecenella* (I.6.1866) and in different numbers of the journal *Lo spassatiempo. Vierze e prose nove e Becchie de Luigi Chiurazzi ed autre* (published from 1875–77). They also appeared in n. 146 of the journal *Muode de dire de lo popolo napolitano* (1880). Even modern collections of Neapolitan paremias include expressions with a tripartite structure. Pitrè's *Curiosità popolari tradizionali* contains a considerable number of such expressions; some of them are mentioned in the chapters concerning traditions and practices in the Sorrento peninsula and some others are gathered in a list in chapter 8 (101–30). The more recent Gleijeses's *I proverbi di Napoli* collects many tripartite paremias under the letter T (397–402).

51. The first three proverbs of *Il tre* derives from Alunno's *Della fabbrica del mondo*: a) *Tre sono le parti del mondo, cioè l'Asia, l'Africa, e l'Europa* ("Three are the parts of the world, Asia, Africa, and Europe"; G. C. Croce, *Il Tre* [1960] n. 1) and "Se vogliam parlare del sito nostro trovaremo *Tre essere le parti principali, cioè Asia, Africa, e Europa* ("If we want to talk about our place, we'll find that three are the main parts, that is Asia, Africa, and Europe"; Alunno ix: 232*v*); b) *Tre parti ha l'anima, cioè vegetativa, sensitiva, e rationale* ("Three parts has the soul, that is vegetative, sensitive, and rational");

G. C. Croce, *Il Tre* [1960] n. 2) and "*Tre sono le sorti de gli animali, cioè vegetativo, sensitivo, e intellettivo*, come le piante, animali brutti, et persone rationali" ("Three are the typologies of animals, that is vegetative, sensitive, and intellective, such as the plants, the ugly animals, and the rational people"; Alunno ix: 232*v*); c) *Tre sono le sue potenze, cioè intelletto, memoria e volontà* ("Three are its powers, which are intellect, memory, and will"; G. C. Croce, *Il Tre* [1960] n. 3) and "*Tre ancora sono le doti principali dell'anima, cioè intelletto, memoria e volontà*, mediante le quali tutte le nostre operationi si reggono, et governano" ("Three are the primary gifts of the human soul: memory, intellect, and will, through which all of our actions can be held and controlled"; Alunno ix: 232*v*).

52. As an example, consider numbers 16 and 17 from B. Croce's edition: *Chi ama la maretata, la vita soia la tene prestata; chi ama la donzella, la vita soia la mena in pena; chi ama la vedova, la vita la tene sicura* ("He who loves the married woman, keeps his life as a loan; he who loves the young woman, conducts his life in pain; he who loves the widow, keeps his life safe") and *De la gallina è meglio la nera, de la papara la pardiglia, de la femmena la piccola* ("Among the hens the black one is better, among the ducks the dark gray, among the women the small"; "Proverbi trimembri napoletani" 66).

53. Rinaldi (s.v. *città*) proposes a quadrimember version: *Quattro cose caccian l'uomo di casa. Il troppo fumo, la pioggia che vi entra, la molta puzza e le contese donnesche* ("Four things drive the man out of his house: excessive smoke, rain that soaks, extreme bad smell, and feminine disputes").

54. For a detailed description of the linguistic characteristics of the Neapolitan dialect (spelling, vocalism, consonantism, and other grammatical aspects), Vittorio Formentin's commentary in De Rosa's *Ricordi* and Ledgeway's grammar are fundamental references.

55. The proverb features in Salviati's collection (*Di tre cose non ti fidare, di medico malato, d'alchimista stracciato e romito grasso*, "You should not trust in three things, the sick doctor, the poor alchemist, and the fat hermit") and in Serdonati's *Raccolta* (*Di tre cose non ti fidare, di medico malato, d'alchimista stracciato e di romito grasso*, "You should not trust in three things, the sick doctor, the poor alchemist, and the fat hermit," and *Dio mi guardi da alchimista povero, da romito grasso e da medico infermo*, "May God preserve me from the poor alchemist, the fat hermit, and the sick doctor"). Rocco (s.v. *archemista*) also mentions this paremia.

56. Examples include temporal words (*triennis*, "three years," and *trinoctium*, "three continuous nights"); anatomical words (*trifaux, -cis*, "with three throats or mouths"), and words describing things or facts (*triga*, "a cart with three horses," and *trigamus*, "with three wives").

57. Sarnelli does not list those religious or spiritual paremias that Alunno introduces as "ternari spirituali" ("spiritual ternary expressions"; Alunno, *Della fabbrica* ix: 232*r*). This category includes paremias concerning God and the afterlife, sins and virtues, and a few expressions drawn from Dante.

Additionally, Sarnelli does not consider a paremia on the bell ringing thrice a day for the hymns to the Virgin Mary or Angelus Domini, two paremias regarding the enemies of the soul and the dangers of the world, and one paremia on Christ's disciples. On different topics, he omits geographical paremias along with expressions mentioning the lives of men, astrological matters, and mythological figures (the Moirai, the infernal furies, the gorgons, and the graces). It seems that there is no logical explanation for these choices, except that Sarnelli does not wish to refer to a religious or supernatural subtext among his tripartite paremias.

58. B. Croce writes that, in Imbriani's edition of Sarnelli's *Posilecheata*, there should be a note by the editor on the topic (P 116). However, no reference to the paremia can be found in the entire section dedicated to the virtues of the number three (*Le virtù del tre* P 112–17).

59. The paremia also features in Buoni's *Nuovo thesoro*, yet in a four-member structure: *Quattro cose vuol haver il pesce, fresco, fritto, fermo et freddo* ("Four things the fish wants to have, fresh, fried, still, and cold"). For the word "futo" ("fresh") and paremias containing it, see Malato (*Vocabolarietto napoletano* 139–40).

60. From a linguistic perspective, once the paremia is part of Marchionno's verbal utterance, its Spanish is rendered Neapolitan. For instance, the verb "hacer," which is conjugated in the impersonal way, faces the typical Neapolitan substitution of the unvoiced dental fricative consonant θ with the alveolar fricative consonant z (Ledgeway 99–100). In the introduction, another paremia appears in a phonetic rendering of an untraceable Latin paremia: "E non sapite ca *prossimo accignendo habeto ped accinto?*" ("And don't you know that what is happening soon has already happened?"; P 17.21). The expression anticipates a situation that will soon happen, namely that Marchionno will receive a lot of wine. Marchionno explains that wine is necessary to counteract the dryness of fish, which can disturb the throat. Masillo chides Marchionno saying that he is getting ahead of himself because he has not yet started to eat fish and already fears a dry mouth. Hence, Marchionno uses the paremia to request more wine.

61. In the sonnet that introduces Sarnelli's 1674 edition of *Lo cunto de li cunti*, Basile's collection is said to be able to make its readers laugh and cure them better than mastro Grillo's methods (v. 8). Basile refers to Grillo in the introductory *cunto* of his collection (CC I.2.3, I.4.5).

62. This story is part of a longer poem in 147 rhymed octaves recounting five different episodes (Ulrich): healing the King's daughter (vv. 1–600), healing sick people at the hospital (vv. 601–720), discovering thieves (vv. 721–880), guessing a riddle (vv. 881–928), and helping a farmer to find his donkey (vv. 929–1176).

63. Rocco (s.v. *gatto*) reports a synonymic expression, *A gatto viecchio sorece tenneriello*, used to excuse an old man married or in love with a young girl. In *Posilecheata*, a reference to the two opposing terms, "meat" and "fish," also appears at the beginning of Marchionno's tirade: "Non sapite vuje ca è chiù goliuso lo pesce che la carne? Pe' la quale cosa, li Rommane de la maglia antica chiammavano l'uommene dellecate Ichthiophagi, cioè magna-pisce" ("Don't you know that fish is more gluttonous than meat? For this reason, the Roman people of the past used to call the delicate men Ichthyophagy, which means fish eaters"; P 15.15: footnote 9). One of Erasmus's *Colloquia*—the longest of all probably written around 1526—is entitled with the same word that Sarnelli uses, Ἰκθυοφαγία or "Fish diet," and contains a discussion between a fishmonger and a butcher on some fundamental religious questions (*Collected Works of Erasmus, Colloquies*, vol. 39: 675–762).

64. Rocco (s.v. *delluvio*) lists a similar expression in Serio's *Lo vernacchio*: *Non è chiovere, è delluvio* ("It's not rain, it's a downpour"; IV.29–44). More common is the proverbial phrase *Credere che dovesse piovere, ma non diluviare* ("To believe that it should rain, but not pour down"), which features, for instance, in Vignali's letter: "Credetti bene che piovesse, ma che non diluviasse" ("I thought well that it would rain, but not pour down").

65. A similar accumulation informs Basile's *cunto* IV.2 (*Li dui fratielle*), in which a dying father transmits wisdom to his young children through proverbial expressions.

66. In *Posilecheata*, the proper names of the five storytellers do not carry the same level of comedy as those in Basile's *Cunto*. Picone's article "La cornice novellistica" offers more information on the meaning of Basile's ten women's names.

67. Sarnelli provides a schematic summary and a list of themes for all the five fables in *Posilecheata* ([1986] 227–29).

68. D'Ambra (s.v. *foretana*) explains it as "contadinescamente" ("in the peasant's style").

69. Ghirelli defines final paremias as clever compendiums and perfect equivalents of the narrated fable. They are concluded narrative units, yet capable of originating an infinite number of similar fables, given their applicability to a variety of contexts (675). It is worth noting that final recapitulatory paremias were common in genres typically associated not only with an oral performance or delivery, but also with formal and political discourses, such as the conclusion in Carafa's *Memoriali* (387–408, especially 404–8; see also Montuori 159–62). Zumthor comments that the paremias at the beginning and at the end of a text both achieve a "globalisation thématique" ("thematic globalization"); what changes is their perspective. On one hand, introductory paremias are "annonce prémonitoire" ("premonitory indications") and, hence, they disclose and anticipate the topic. On the other, concluding paremias are "conclusion récapitulative" ("summarizing conclusions") since they summarize the text's topic or a specific line of interpretation (323).

70. Allasia rather argues that the stories are woven so that they can function as comments on their final paremias (258).

71. The etiologic descriptions are Sarnelli's original introduction to *Posilecheata* (they are, for instance, absent in Basile's collection): Neptune's statue outside the castle (*cunto* 1); a bust called the "head of Naples" around the market (*cunto* 2); the river and the gulf of Naples (*cunto* 3); the bronze horse in the surroundings of the Foro Nostriano (*cunto* 4); and the statue of Jupiter, known as the statue of the giant, outside the regal palace (*cunto* 5). Sarnelli must have gathered information on Naples and the surrounding areas when writing his two guides; in fact, *Guida de' forestieri curiosi di vedere ed intendere le cose più notabili della real città di Napoli* is devoted to descriptions of notable places in Naples, such as castles, churches, buildings, and libraries, with a particular attention to artistic aspects and topographic information to foreigners. Before publishing the two guides, Sarnelli had already described, in the pages of his *Degli avvenimenti di Fortunato,* the history of Naples and surrounding towns, including Posillipo, Pozzuoli, Cuma, Baia, and Miseno (181–216). For a more extensive discussion about these topics, see Franzese (115–18) and Giglio.

72. In another article, Albanese defines paremias as "dispositivi di memoria, vere formule mnemoniche" ("devices of remembrance, true mnemonic formulae"; "I centomila miliardi" 4).

73. Lapucci lists a longer paremia, although clarifying that usually only the first part is used: *Fai del bene e scordatelo, fai del male e pensaci* ("Do good and forget about it, do bad and think about it"; *Dizionario dei proverbi italiani*, s.l. B: footnote 335). The antecedent of this proverb can be found in Solomon's *Proverbs*: "L'huomo perverso di cuore non troverà il bene e l'huomo stravolto nel suo parlare caderà nel male" ("The man wicked in his heart will not find good and the man twisted in his speech will fall into evil"; ch. XVII: v. 20 from Brucioli's *Annotationi*).

74. Basile's and Sarnelli's paremias combine two proverbs present in the Florentine vernacular. Lena lists them in his collection: *Chi fa bene ha bene* ("He who does good has good") and *Chi fa male male aspetti* ("He who does bad may he expect bad") or *Chi fa male aspettine altro tale* ("He who does bad may he wait for other similar"; 91).

75. In his fifth book, Monosini lists *Chi dorme coi cani si leva con le pulci, Cum pulicibus surgit, cum canibus dormiens* ("He who sleeps with dogs wakes up with fleas; One wakes with fleas, when sleeping with dogs"; Pignatti, *Etimologia* 241: footnote 18). He also provides a synonymic expression within the same entry: *Cum claudo versans, claudicare discit* ("By living with a cripple, one learns to limp").

76. The word "quatra" indicates a unit used to measure wheat, which corresponds to the fourth part of a bushel.

77. In this meaning, it appears in the fifth fable of the first day: "Conzidera mo chi è Cristiano lo tremmoliccio, lo sorreiemiento, l'assottigliamento de core, lo filatorio, lo spaviento, la quatra de vierme e la cacavessa c'appe la povera figliola: fa' cunto ca no le restaie sango adduosso" ("Anyone who's a Christian can imagine the tremors, the horror, the tightening of the heart, the ruins, the fright, the worms, and the diarrhea that the poor girl experienced: let's just say that there wasn't a drop of blood left in her veins"; CC I.5.23; Basile, *The Tale of Tales* 53).

78. The paremia also features in other Neapolitan works: Basile's *Muse napolitane* 9.75; Cortese's *Vaiasseide* III.26.8; Cortese's Book 4 of his *Li travagliuse ammure de Ciullo e Perna*; Cortese's *Micco Passaro innamorato* VI.17.1; and Andrea Perrucci's *L'agnano zeffonato* I.27.

79. In the word "corazzone" ("heart"), the voiceless alveolar affricate "tts" substitutes the unvoiced dental fricative θ (Ledgeway 99–100) and the word is given the final weakened sound ə (Ledgeway 77–78).

80. Literary works experimenting with combinations of Spanish and Neapolitan languages were common at the time. In 1651, Tauro published *L'Ingelosite speranze*, the Italian and Neapolitan translation of Lope de Vega's comedy *Lo cierto por lo dudoso* (1625), presenting many linguistic hybrid forms between the two languages (Bianconi et al., 34–39; see also the publications by Basalisco and Martinelli).

81. During the Spanish Golden Age, paremias became a constituent part of literary works, and collections and dictionaries of paremias were constantly published. The most extensive collection was Gonzalo Correas's *Vocabulario de refranes i frases proverbiales i otras formulas komunes de la lengua castellana*. It contained more than 25,000 paremias, compiled between 1625 and 1627, but published only in the second decade of the twentieth century. For collections of Spanish paremias in Italy, see Beccaria (*Spagnolo e spagnoli* 309: footnote 114).

82. Sannazaro's original lines in *Arcadia* are: "Nell'onde solca e nell'arena semina / E 'l vago vento spera in rete accogliere / Chi sue speranze funda in cor di femina" ("A furrow in the waves, and seed in the desert sands, / And the wandering wind in a net he hopes to gather / Who builds his trust upon the heart of a woman"; eclogue VIII: vv. 10–12). Petrarca's line in *Rerum Vulgarium Fragmenta* is: "Solco onde, e 'n rena fondo, et scrivo in vento" ("I plow waves and build on sand and write in wind"; 212: v. 4).

83. The two proverbial phrases appear in Basile's first tale of *Lo cunto de li cunti*. Antuono takes advantage of a profitable situation, namely an innkeeper and his wife beaten by his magic club, to have them return all the enchanted objects that they stole from him (CC I.1.53). In *Muse napolitane*, Basile mentions both paremias when he refers to the perfect opportunity that occurred for a recently celebrated marriage: *L'è caduto Lo vroccolo a lo lardo, / Lo maccarone dinto de lo caso* ("Broccoli went with lard, / macaroni with cheese"; 5.152–54). In Cortese's *La rosa*, the paremia is twisted so that it is cheese that falls on top of pasta: *T'è caduto lo ccaso / Ncoppa li maccarune* ("Cheese fell / over macaroni"; Act 1, sc. 1). Finally, in G. Fasano's *Lo Tasso napoletano* the expression has the same structure as Sarnelli's: "*Dinto a lo ccaso a te lo maccarone*, respose, *t'è caduto*" ("She [Sophronia] answered, macaroni went with cheese for you"), which interprets Tasso's original verse in *Gerusalemme liberata*, "Il reo si trova al tuo cospetto" ("The culprit stands before your eyes"; II.21.5–6).

84. Sarnelli plays with culinary metaphors in a variety of ways. In the introductory letter, his book is said to substitute for a meal because it is useful to different typologies of readers (P 8.17). Reppone, who finally accepts his friend's invitation to Posillipo, arrives at Petruccio's house at exactly the right time to eat (P 11.4): his stomach is empty and ready to receive nutrients, i.e., fables. In addition to descriptions of food in the five fables, in the conclusion Reppone goes back home to Naples exhausted by hunger and satisfies his sudden need with honey (P 214.10). By doing so, he replaces the same sweet and pleasant sensation he received from the stories he had just heard with a culinary product (for further references to the teaspoon full of honey, see Allasia 256–57, footnote 8). Finally, at the end of the book, the index's title maintains this food-related metaphor: "Tavola non da magnare ma de li cunte che se fanno dapò magnare" ("Table not to eat but of the tales that one recounts after eating"; P 215). Comically, Sarnelli shifts the semantic area of the word "tavola" as a table of contents to the same word as a table to eat, thus connecting eating with listening to and reading fables.

85. Basile compares wealth and poverty by mentioning this same proverb in *Muse napolitane* (8.219, not 8.332 as mentioned by Rocco, s.v. *diuno* and *satoro*): *Lo satoro non crede a lo diuno* ("A well-fed person does not believe a starving one"). Both Salviati and Serdonati, along with the 1612 Voc. Cr. (s.v. *digiuno*), list a Tuscan variant of the paremia, *Il pasciuto non crede al digiuno*, bearing the same meaning.

86. In this context, the word "corona" indicates a coin (GDLI, s.v. *corona* [2]).

87. In his *Proverbi italiani e latini*, Lena lists the expression: *Male e bene a fin viene, Casura omnia extant* ("Bad and good come to an end; It is known that everything is destined to end"; 408).

88. The translation of the Latin epigram comes from Alciati, *Index emblematicus* (vol. 1, emblem 160; see also Alciati, *Il libro degli emblemi* 87–89). In a 1551 publication in Lyon, *Diverse imprese accomodate a diverse moralità*, the emblem appears twice in two different contexts (Marquale). In the first, the emblem expresses a message on friendship beginning with the motto "Che la vera amicitia mai non muore" ("That true friendship never dies"; 151). The epigram confirms the relationship between the vine and another plant and offers advice about the appropriate choice of friends whose bond can be everlasting: "La vite, che l'ignudo arido legno / abbraccia e stringe, et hor gli rende il merto / d'esser già stato a lei fido sostegno, / e 'l grato animo suo dimostra aperto / ci ammonisce a cercare amici tali, / che i legami d'amor siano immortali" ("The vine, which embraces and squeezes / the naked arid wood, and now recognizes it the value / of having been its trusted support / and clearly shows its grateful soul, / warns us to look for such friends / with whom the bonds of love are immortal"). In the second occurrence, the emblem's message emphasizes instead the brevity of happiness (as the motto declares "In una breve felicità," "In a brief happiness") and the vacuity of the unsubstantiated pride that a pumpkin feels toward a pine tree (122). The epigram confirms it: "Crebbe la zucca a tanta altezza, ch'ella / un altissimo pin passò la cima; / e mentre abbraccia in questa parte e in quella / i rami suoi superba oltre ogni stima, / il pin sen rise, e a lei così favella: / «Breve è la gloria tua, perché non prima / verrà il verno di nevi e ghiacci cinto, / che sia ogni tuo vigor del tutto estinto»" ("The pumpkin grew to such height that it / surpassed the top of a very high pine; / and while it was extending its branches in this and that direction / in a superb attitude beyond all esteem, / the pine laughed about it, and so the pine spoke to the pumpkin: / 'Short is your glory, because, even before / the winter will come girded of snow and ice, / all your strength will be completely extinct'"). In other languages, the image of the elm and the vine appears in different formats and with different messages. One example is Corrozet's 1543 *Hecatongraphie*, which contains 100 emblems with ornamental borders, an image, a motto, and a four-line rhymed description, accompanied by a rhymed commentary on the opposite page. Two emblems depict a scene with two trees and are paired respectively with the mottos "Ingratitude" ("Ingratitude"; *Biiiiv*) and "Le grand ayant affaire du moindre" ("The big one dealing with the lesser"; *Liv*). In the first emblem, the ivy and a tree represent a feeling of unrecognition: the ivy, which the tree sustained since birth, progressively grows around the tree and damages it to such a point to harm its flowers and fruits. The second emblem, whose moral message concerns the superior and powerful entities relying on the inferior, is represented by a vine that does not disdain the help of a small tree, because this allows it to thrive and generate lots of grapes. In his 1620 *Il principe*, Capaccio offers a political explanation to the emblem "Olmo, e vite" ("Elm, and vine"). In "Avvertimento 151," he introduces the emblem with the caption, "Amicitia che anco dopo la morte dura" ("Friendship that lasts even beyond death"; 323–26). The poem in hendecasyllables describes how a vine covers an old elm with its dense foliage to repay the elm for its sustenance when they were young. The metaphorical meaning, as expressed in the poem's last two lines, is that everyone seeks friends who can nourish immortal true love. The subsequent commentary features two different categories of princes: those who consider it convenient not to have friends and those who, upon not being cautious, choose to have many and are later deceived. Capaccio states that the prince should surround himself with good friends to keep everything under control. For more literary instances of this *topos*, see Alfonsi.

89. In his *Grammatica*, Capozzoli mentions the paremia *A l'abbesuogne se canosceno l'ammice* ("When needed one can really value a friend"), to explain how the masculine plural of certain nouns ends in "-ce" ("ammice," "friends") vis-à-vis the feminine plural in "-ca" (46). GDLI (s.v. *asino*, n. 5) lists a similar expression, *Alla prova si scortica l'asino* ("When tested, one can skin the donkey"), suggesting that one can understand and recognize the value of something or someone only in difficult times.

90. The recounted events find an antecedent in Basile's *cunto* IV.9. There, two young adolescents, Iennariello and Liviella, undergo similar events to Jannuzzo and Ninella. Iennariello helps his brother Milluccio, who is devasted by lovesickness, to overcome deadly melancholy. A dove tells him that, upon disclosure of a spell, he will turn into a statue. Only through the intervention of Liviella's father can Iennariello regain his human life.

91. In his work *La rosa*, Cortese uses the expression to refer to incredible things that happen in love matters. However, he introduces a spit as a substitute for the reed (I.3; see D'Ambra, s.v. *perna*).

92. One of them is a statue by Luigi Impò, which is located in a small square at the end of Via della Sellaria. This statue represents a thief who has been transformed into marble after robbing a poor woman's laundry (P 127.96).

93. The paremia also appears in *cunto* 3 of *Posilecheata*, in which it describes the joy of the miller's wife upon breastfeeding Jannuzzo and Ninella. This way, she can get rid of the excessive milk in her breast and feed them "*facenno no viaggio e duje servizie*" ("taking one journey and performing two services"; P 103.24). In Basile's *cunto* IV, instead, the journey is one but the performed services are three: "… io dapo' *avere fatto no viaggio e tre servizie*" ("… after taking a journey and performing three services"; CC IV.9.70; *The Tale of Tales* 370). In G. Fasano's *Lo Tasso napoletano*, the expression is similar to Sarnelli's, even though there is no coordinating conjunction between the two members: "*E fface duie servizie a no viaggio*" ("He performed two services during one journey"; V.2.7).

94. The same names are in Basile's *cunto* V entitled *Sole, Luna e Talia* ("Sun, Moon, and Talia"; CC V.5; *The Tale of Tales* 413).

95. This technique was not unusual in comic works at the time. For instance, in his *L'ingelosite speranze* (1651), Tauro inverts the members of two proverbs for comic effects: *Tanto va lo mastrillo dinto a lo sórece, pe ffi' che nce resta pe la coda* ("So much goes the trap inside the mouse that, in the end, he remains stuck there by the tail") and *Tanto va la lancella dinto la maneca finché nce lassa lo puzzo* ("So much goes the pitcher inside the handle until it does leave there the well"; see Bianconi et al., 35).

96. A paremia explains why barley is mentioned: *L'orzo non è fatto per gli asini* ("Barley does not suit donkeys"). The expression suggests that gross and ignorant people cannot understand the value of what is beautiful and precious (GDLI, s.v. *asino*, n. 5).

97. Later in the narration, an old lady saves Cecca from dying from these serpents. She turns her upside down so that the reptiles, summoned by the smell of the milk below, can exit her body through her mouth. A paremia is associated with the event: *[L]e fece venire tutte le bodella 'ncanna* ("She made her bowels reach her throat"; P 165.66). The expression suggests that Cecca is evidently hung with her head down so that the bowels can almost reach the place where the throat is (GDLI, s.v. *budello*, n. 2). Sarnelli's story derives from Sacchetti's novella CCXIX in his *Trecentonovelle*. Here, two sisters-in-law, longing for a child who would never come, listen to the words of a Hebrew man. He fools them into thinking that a miraculous beverage would make them pregnant. If the eldest of the two refuses to drink the potion, the other imbibes it only to discover that the beverage in fact contains serpents' eggs. For other variants of the fable, see Sarnelli (*Posilecheata di Pompeo Sarnelli* 208–11).

98. Lapucci reports the paremia in his *Dizionario dei proverbi italiani* (s.l. L: footnote 747). He also lists a variant: *Le funi legano i buoi e le parole gli uomini* ("Ropes tie up oxen and words men"; s.l. P: footnote 558).

99. Salviati and Serdonati list a related expression: *La luna non cura l'abbaiar de' cani* or *La luna non si cura dell'abbaiar de' cani* ("The moon does not care about the barking of dogs"), which suggests that powerful people underestimate the menace of low and weak people. The 1612 Voc. Cr. (s.v. *luna*) explains the expression referring to great and valuable things that do not care for the small and vile.

100. This *cunto* is remarkable for the greatest presence of derogatory remarks that feature as a vivid and strong representation of the creativity and potentialities of the Neapolitan dialect, and of the transposition of the spoken language onto the written page. The accumulation of lexical terms was a distinctive feature of works in dialect in the seventeenth century because it demonstrated its richness vis-à-vis the alleged poverty of the Tuscan language (Cortelazzo, *I dialetti e la dialettologia* 86). Moreover, the tendency to express a variety of feelings and emotions undoubtedly answered to the Baroque appetite for marvel and fascination that was "suitable for the plurilingual early-seventeenth century courts for which it [*Posilecheata*] was intended" (Haller, *The Other Italy* 253). The two sections of *cunto* 5 containing a considerable number of derogatory remarks are characterized by theatrical components, as well as a sense of comedy and satire. The first instance occurs when one of the fairies arrives at Nunziella's palace covered in rags. Nunziella's butlers address the fairy with a long list of derogatory remarks. By doing so, the menservants highlight the disgust they feel towards an old and poor woman who dares approach a rich family's house (P 195–96.53). The second instance immediately follows the first, when Nunziella realizes what has happened and responds to her butlers with a similar list of furious and enraged derogatory remarks (P 196–99.54–56). Sarnelli aims to excite an emotional state both through the characters within the narrative context and in the audience. Simultaneously, he wishes to create a playful context in accordance with popular and Baroque expressiveness. On derogatory remarks in Basile's *Lo cunto de li cunti*, which share many aspects with those of Sarnelli, see Stromboli ("Le ingiurie").

101. Her head is full of bumps, her front is wrinkled, her eyebrows are spare, and her ears are long and transparent. Her eyes are like those of a cat, since they try to scrutinize everyone and they are as open as a split, probably recalling the tightness of a greedy person. Her throat is as that of a magpie because she is unappeasable and constantly greedy, and her neck is that of an ostrich, wrinkled and ugly. Her breath smells like a cemetery and her mouth is corrugated and toothless.

102. The Neapolitan paremia features a rhyme that is not present in its Tuscan version: *Comm'è la chiANTA è la sciANTA* vis-à-vis *Com'è la pianta così è il ramo* ("As the plant is, so is the branch"). Alternatives in standard Italian are also: *Il ramo somiglia al tronco* ("The branch resembles the trunk"; Giusti, *Proverbi*) or *Il ramo è come la pianta* ("The branch is like the trunk"; Lapucci, *Dizionario dei proverbi italiani*, s.l. R: footnote 159).

103. The paremia was so common in the Renaissance that in his chivalric poem *Mambriano* (1509), Cieco dedicates an entire novella to explaining the origin of the proverbial phrase (II.42.117). For other sixteenth-century literary works based on the paremia, see Bini (also mentioned in Angeleri, n. 48, 131); on the musical reuse of Cieco's novella, see Everson. Serdonati provides the following explanation for the phrase, *È fatto il becco all'oca*: "La cosa è finita, e se gli è posta l'ultima mano. Uno scultore prese a fare un ritratto d'una oca, e spesso domandato da gli amici se l'oca era finita, rispondeva che le mancava il becco; e finalmente venne a loro e disse ch'era fatto il becco all'oca, mostrando che l'opera era finita; e 'l motto passò in proverbio" ("The thing is over, and one has given it the last check. A sculptor started to make a portrait of a goose and, often asked by his friends if the goose was finished, he replied that his mouth was missing. Eventually he went to his friends and told them that he had added the beak to the goose, showing that the work was finished. And the saying became a proverb").

Conclusion

1. For this expression, which Sacchetti also uses to conclude his eighteenth novella in *Trecentonovelle*, Monosini refers to the Latin source *Fallentem fallens pro poena laudem meret* ("He who deceives the one deceiving deserves praise instead of punishment"; 359).

2. In his *Flos*, Monosini lists two expressions: *Lo 'nganno torna addosso allo 'ngannatore* ("The deceit falls onto the deceiver") and *Lo 'nganno è tornato addosso allo 'ngannatore* ("The deceit fell onto the deceiver"; 238). He traces the second paremia to Seneca's *Thyestes*: "Saepe in magistrum scelera redierunt sua" ("Crimes often return upon the teacher"; Act II: v. 311).

3. Some of the many paremias shared by Florio and Sarnelli are: a) *El pasciuto non crede al digiuno* ("He that is fed beleeveth not the fasting"; FF 29v) and *Lo sazio non crede lo dejuno* ("A well-fed person does not believe a starving one"; P 74.32); b) *Fanno conto inanzi l'hoste* ("Others make their account before the host"; FF 6v) and *Facevano lo cunto senza lo tavernaro* ("They did their calculations without the host"; P 98.11); c) *Non di quelle del dottor Grillo* ("Not doctor Grillo his phisike"; SF 60) and *Chillo de masto Grillo* ("That from doctor Grillo"; P 18.21).

4. A few examples of other paremias that both Brusantino and Florio share are: a) *Basta un gallo a dieci gran galline, ma dieci homin [non] possono il gran peso di una donna satiar* ("One cock is enough for ten big hens, but ten men cannot satisfy the great weight of a woman"; CN 131) and *Quantunque un gallo basti a dieci galline, dieci huomini non bastano ad una donna* ("Although one cock serve many a hen, one woman asketh many men"; SF 184); b) *Chi è tristo e buono vien tenuto ... pol far male ché non gli è creduto* ("He who is wicked and held to be good ... can cheat because no one imagines he would"; CN 199) and *Chi è reo e non è tenuto può far il mal e non è creduto* ("Who is gylty and is not accounted, may do evil and is not suspected"; FF [28]r); c) *Fallo a chi te le fa et, se non poi, tientelo a mente* ("Always give back as much as you receive and, if you can't, bear it in mind"; CN 293) and *A chi te la fa, fagliela, o tientela a mente* ("If any man wrong thee, wrong him againe, or else be sure to remember it"; SF 18); d) *Mi rendete pan per focaccia* ("You give me bread for cake"; CN 421) and *Volete rendergli pane per focaccia* ("What will you give him bread for cake then"; SF 18); e) *Non deve esser losco chi contrattar ne vuol con huomo tosco* ("He who wants to negotiate with a Tuscan needs to be honest"; CN 442) and *Chi ha a far con tosco non convien esser losco* ("Who with a Tuscane hath to mell, had need to heare and see full well"; SF 108).

Index of Paremias

1. Florio's proverbs are listed alphabetically considering the first letter of each expression as it appears in the dialogues of *Firste Fruites* and *Second Frutes*. In the following lists, all the paremias that Florio marks as proverbs in *Second Frutes* are incorporated; from *Firste Fruites*, only those expressions that are actual paremias (proverbs, proverbial phrases, and maxims) are inserted. As for the table of content ("Tavola de tutti gli capitoli che in questa opera si contengono," "Table of all the chapters that in this work are contayned": ***ii*v*–***ii*ir*), the chapters' topics in *Firste Fruites* include: "Parlar familiare" ("Familiar speeche"; ch. 1); "A parlar con donzella" ("To speake with a damsel"; ch. 2); "Parlar familiare con huomo overo con donna" ("Familiar speeche with man or woman"; ch. 3); "Parlar familiare" ("Familiar speech"; ch. 4); "Altro parlar familiare con huomo o con donna" ("Other familiar speach with man or woman"; ch. 5); "Altro parlar familiare" ("Other familiar talke"; ch. 6); "A parlar con un gentilhuomo" ("To speake with a gentleman"; ch. 7); "A parlar con una gentildonna" ("To speake with a gentlewoman"; Ch 8); "A parlar con mercante" ("To speake with a marchant"; ch. 9); "A parlar con donna" ("To speake with a woman"; ch. 10); "A parlar con servitore" ("To speake to a servant"; ch. 11); "Parlar familiare" ("Familiar speach"; ch. 12); "Parlar familiare" ("Familiar talke"; ch. 13); "Parlar amoroso" ("Amarous [sic] talke"; ch. 14); "A parlar d'Inghilterra" ("To speake of England"; ch. 15); "Parlar familiare" ("Familiar talke"; ch. 16); "A parlar al buio" ("To talke in the darke"; ch. 17); "Diverse sentenze divine et profane" ("Divers sentences divine and profane"; ch. 18); "Tre cento belli proverbii" ("Three hundredth fyne proverbes"; ch. 19); "Belli detti" ("Fine sayings"; ch. 20); "Belle domande" ("Prety demands [sic]"; ch. 21); "Discorsi sopra pace, guerra, invidia, et superbia" ("Discourses upon peace, warre, envy, and pride"; ch. 22); "Li abusi del mondo" ("The abuses of the worlde"; ch. 23); "Discorsi sopra belezza, nobilità, povertà, e preghiera necessaria, quali sono i beni di fortuna" ("Discourses upon beautie, nobilitie, poverty, a necessary prayer, and which be the goods of fortune"; ch. 24); "Di ira, con certi belli detti di Ariosto et di altri poeti, et cosa è patientia, et adulatione" ("Of wrath, with certaine fyne sayings of Ariosto, and other poets, and what pacience and flattery is"; ch. 25); "Ragionamenti sopra fortuna et che cosa sia fortuna" ("Reasonynges uppon fortune and what fortune is"; ch. 26); "Ragionamenti sopra dottrina et filosofia, et che cosa siano scrittori et qual è il profitto di leggere et imparare scientie, con certi discorsi in laude de scrittori et filosofi"

("Resonings upon learning and philosophie, and what writers are, and what the profite of reading and learnyng of science is, with certaine discourses in prayse of writers and philosophers"; ch. 27); "Ragionamenti sopra diligentia, humanità, clementia, temperantia, et sobrietà" ("Reasoninges upon diligence, humanitie, clemencie, temperance, and sobrietie"; ch. 28); "Ragionamenti sopra silentio, et liberalità, et in laude di età" ("Reasonings upon silence and liberalitie, and in prayse of age"; ch. 29); "De li costumi de certe genti" ("Of the maners of certaine nations"; ch. 30); "Discorsi sopra musica et amor" ("Discourses upon musicke and love"; ch. 31); "Discorso sopra libidine et la sua forza" ("A discourses upon lust and the force thereof"; ch. 32); "Ragionamenti sopra virtù con sue figlie, che cosa è il fine di guerra, quale sono bone opere, quatordeci bone regole, con altri diversi discorsi" ("Reasonings upon vertue, with her daughters, what is the end of war, which be good woorkes, fourteene good rules, with divers other discourses"; ch. 33); "L'opinione di Marco Aurelio et Ovidio, sopra amore, et che cosa è" ("The opinion of Marcus Aurelius and Ovid upon love and what it is"; ch. 34); "Diversità de gli huomini" ("The diversities of men"; ch. 35); "Certi belli detti et galanti detti, tolti da Antonio Guevara, scritti da lui sopra diverse occasione" ("Certaine fine, learned, and gallant sayings, taken from Antonio Guevara, written by him upon divers occasions"; ch. 36); "Parole di Plutarco, scritte da lui a Traiano imperatore, con diversi altri detti di Antonio Guevara" ("Words written by Plutarchus to the Emperor Traianus, with divers sayeinges of Antonio Guevara"; ch. 37); "Discorso del detto autore sopra beltà" ("A discourse of the said author upon beautie"; ch. 38); "Certi belli brevi detti et belle sentenze del detto autore, degne da esser notate" ("Certaine fine briefe sayings et fine sayings of the saide authour, woorthy to be noted"; ch. 39); "Breve discorso in laude di Henrico ottavo, re di Inghilterra" ("A briefe discourse in prayse of Henry the eight, king of England"; ch. 40); "Belli discorsi di Antonio Guevara sopra diverse occasione" ("Fine discourses of Antonio Guevara upon divers occasions"; ch. 41); "Discorsi del detto autore circa capitani et soldati del nostro tempo, et mostra come bisognerebbe scegliere i giudici" ("Discourses of the said author concernyng captaines and soldiers of our time, and sheweth how judges should be chosen"; ch. 42); "Nomi di tutti i membri che apertengono all'huomo, de i parenti, i giorni della settimana con le stagioni de l'anno, come si debbe numerare, con un certo breve vocabulario" ("Names of the members aperteinyng to man, of al parents, of the dayes of the weeke, of the seasons of the yeere, howe one shall number, with a certaine briefe vocabularie"; ch. 43); "Certe preghiere, come il Padre nostro et il Credo, con altre, et certe regole inglese" ("Certaine prayers, as the Pater noster and the Crede, with others, and certaine English rules"; ch. 44).

2. The chapters' titles in *Second Frutes*, as per the individual sections, are: "Capitolo primo del levare la mattina, e di ciò che appartiene alla camera et al vestire tra Nolano, Torquato, e Ruspa servitore" ("The first chapter of rising in the morning, and of things belonging to the chamber and to

apparrell betweene Nolano, Torquato, and Ruspa their servant"; ch. 1); "Capitolo secondo di parlar famigliare la mattina per strada tra tre amici, ciò è Thomaso, Giovanni, Henrico, et Piccinino servitore, dove vien descritta una partita alla palla" ("The second chapter for common speach in the morning on the way betweene three friends, Thomas, Iohn, Henry, and Piccinino a servant, wherein is described a sette at tenise"; ch. 2); "Capitolo terzo di parlar famigliare la mattina, dove si tratta di molte cortesie e del modo di salutar et visitar gli ammalati e del cavalcare, con tutto ciò che al cavallo appartiene, tra Aurelio, Pompilio, et Trippa servitore" ("The third chapter of familiar morning communication, wherein many curtesies are handled, and the manner of saluting and visiting the sick and of riding, with all that belongeth to a horse, betweene Aurelio, Pompilio and Trippa the servant"; ch. 3); "Capitolo quarto dove vien descritto un descinare al quale intervengono sei persone, cioè Nundinio, Camillo, Horatio, Melibeo, Tancredi et Andrea come convitati e Simone patron di casa e Roberto suo servitore, fra quali seguono molti piacevoli ragionamenti circa il mangiare et pasteggiare" ("The fourth chapter wherein is set downe a dinner, whereat are met sixe persons, to wit Nundinio, Camillo, Horatio, Melibeo, Tancredi, and Andrew as the ghestes, and Simon as good man of the house, and Robert his man, betweene whome there fall many pleasant discourses, concerning meate and repast"; ch. 4); "Capitolo quinto tra Antonio, Samuele, e Crusca servitore, nel quale si ragiona del giuoco e di molte cose a ciò pertinenti, e si descrive una partita a primera, una al tavogliere et una a scacchi con la natura del giuoco de scacchi" ("The fifth chapter betweene Antonio, Samuel, and Crusca the servant, wherein discourse is held of playe and many things therto appertaining, and a game at primero is set downe, another at tables, and the third at chesse, with the nature of chesse plaie"; ch. 5); "Capitolo sesto di molti complimenti famigliari e cerimoniosi tra sei gentilhuomini, cioè Stefano, Nicolò, Daniele, Guglielmo, Michele, Roberto, Pietro, e Losco servitore, tra quali si ragiona di molte cose piacevoli e massimamente d'alcuni necessarii, utili civili e proverbiali ricordi e precetti per un viandante" ("The sixth chapter concerning many familiar and cerimonius complementes, among sixe gentlemen, to wit Stephan, Nicholas, Daniel, William, Michael, Robert, Peeter, and Losco a servant, who talke of many pleasant matters, but especially of divers necessarie, proffitable, civill, and proverbiall precepts for a travailour"; ch. 6); "Capitolo settimo di trattenimenti civili famigliari e piacevoli tra duo gentilhuomini in camera et alla fenestra, e poi spasseggiando fuora si ragiona delle arme e dell'arte della scrimia e di molte altre cose come del vender e comprare, tra Giordano, Edoardo, Tinca servitore et Ulpiano merzaro" ("The seventh chapter of civill, familiar, and pleasant entertainments betweene two gentlemen in their chamber, and at the window, and then walking abroad they talk of armes and of the arte of fencing, and of many other things, as of buying and selling, betweene Giordano, Edward, Tinca a servant, and Ulpian a haberdasher"; ch. 7); "Capitolo ottavo tra Giacomo e Lippa suo servitore, dove si ragiona di molte facete e piacevoli cose, e vien descritta una cattiva stantia, una brutta vecchia, le bellezze che dee haver una donna per esser bella in perfettione et piacevolmente si descrive un infingardo e da poco servitore" ("The eighth chapter betweene Iames, and Lippa his man, wherein they talke of many pleasant and delightsome iestes, and in it is described an unpleasant lodging, an illfavoured olde woman, also the beautifull partes that a woman ought to have to be accounted faire in all perfection, and pleasantlie is blazoned a counterfaite, lazie, and nought-worth servant"; ch. 8); "Capitolo nono tra Cesare e Tiberio, nel quale facetamente si tratta delle novelle, della corte, de' cortegiani hodierni, e di molte altre piacevoli cose" ("The ninth chapter betweene Caesar and Tiberio, wherein they pleasantlie discourse of newes, of the court, of courtiers of this day, and of many other matters of delight"; ch. 9); "Capitolo decimo tra Cosimo, Benedetto, Agostino, Scarpa e Polenta servitori, dove si ragiona dell'andar a cena e del parlar famigliare la sera al tardi" ("The tenth chapter betweene Cosimo, Benedict, Augustine, Scarpa and Polenta two servants, wherein they talk of going to supper and of familiar speech, late in the evening"; ch. 10); "Capitolo undecimo dove si parla d'andar a letto e di molte cose a ciò pertinenti tra Matteo, Ieronimo, e Limbo servitore" ("The eleventh chapter wherein speach is had of going to bed, and many things thereto belonging, between Mathew, Ierome, and Limbo a servant"; ch. 11); "Capitolo duodecimo il quale con una corte o guardia di notte conchiude questa giornata, dove proverbialmente e facetamente si ragiona d'amore e delle donne, tra Pandolpho, Silvestro, Nicodemo, e Dormiglione" ("The twelfth chapter concluding this dayes work, with a night watch, wherein proverbially and pleasantly discourse is held of love and of women, betweene Pandolpho, Silvestro, Nicodemus, and Dormiglione"; ch. 12).

3. In the original, this is page number 12. From now on, in similar occasions both for *Fruits* and *Giardino di ricreatione* the correct pages will be indicated in between square parentheses.

4. In the original, this is page number 16.

5. In the original, this is page number 26.

6. In the original, this is page number 13.

7. In the original, this is page number 182.

8. In the original, this is page number 56.

9. In the original, this is page number 92.

10. This is the only numerical paremia that is not featured in chapters 18, 19, or 33, but in chapter 24.

Works Consulted

Agostiniani, Luciano. "Semantica e referenza nel proverbio." *Archivio Glottologico Italiano* 63 (1978): 78–109.

Albanese, Angela. "I centomila miliardi di proverbi del *Cunto de li Cunti* nella versione inglese di Nancy Canepa." *Italica* 90 (2013): 1–22.

———. *Metamorfosi del Cunto di Basile: traduzioni, riscritture, adattamenti.* Ravenna: Longo, 2012.

Alciati, Andrea. *Emblemata cum commentariis.* New York: Garland, 1976.

———. *Index emblematicus.* Eds. Peter Daly, et al. Toronto: U of Toronto P, 1985.

———. *Il libro degli emblemi, secondo le edizioni del 1531 e del 1534.* Ed. Mino Gabriele. Milano: Adelphi Edizioni, 2015.

Alfonsi, Luigi. "La vite e l'olmo." *Vigiliae Christianae* 21.2 (1967): 81–86.

Allasia, Clara. "La «Posilecheata», una *still life* fiabesca." *I novellieri italiani e la loro presenza nella cultura europea: rizomi e palinsesti rinascimentali.* Eds. Guillermo Carrascón and Chiara Simbolotti. Torino: Accademia UP, 2015. 255–67.

Altamura, Antonio. *Il dialetto napoletano.* Napoli: Il Fiorentino, 1961.

———. *Dizionario dialettale napoletano.* Napoli: Il Fiorentino, 1968.

Altieri Biagi, Maria Luisa. "Dal comico del «significato» al comico del «significante»." *La lingua in scena.* Bologna: Zanichelli, 1980. 1–57.

Alunno, Francesco. *Della fabbrica del mondo di Messer Francesco Alunno da Ferrara, Libri dieci, ne' quali si contengono le voci di Dante, del Petrarca, del Boccaccio et d'altri buoni autthori, mediante le quali si possono esprimere tutti i concetti dell'huomo di qualunque cosa creata.* Venezia: Giovanni Battista Porta, 1584.

———. *Le ricchezze della lingua volgare.* Venezia: in casa de' figliuoli di Aldo Pio Manuzio, 1543.

Andreoli, Raffaele. *Vocabolario napoletano-italiano.* Torino: Paravia, 1889.

Andrews, Richard. "The Canto as a Unit in Ariosto: *Orlando furioso*, XXIV." *Italianist* 3 (1983): 9–29.

Angeleri, Carlo. *Bibliografia delle stampe popolari a carattere profano dei secoli XVI e XVII conservate nella Biblioteca Nazionale di Firenze.* Firenze: Sansoni, 1953.

Angiolieri, Cecco. *Rime.* Ed. Raffaella Castagnola. Milano: Mursia, 1995.

———. *Sonnets. Cecco Angiolieri.* Trans. C.H. Scott and Anthony Mortimer. Richmond: Oneworld Classics, 2008.

Works Consulted

Ankli, Ruedi. *Morgante iperbolico. L'iperbole nel Morgante del Pulci*. Firenze: Olschki, 1993.

Antonelli Giuseppe. *Indice dei manoscritti della Civica Biblioteca di Ferrara*. Ferrara: Antonio Taddei e Figli, 1884.

Antonini, Anna. "La riflessione linguistica di Alessandro Citolini." *Studi di grammatica italiana* 18 (1999): 260–73.

Appel, Carl. "I proverbi di Gharzo." *Il Propugnatore* 3.1 (1890): 49-74.

Apperson, George Latimer. *English Proverbs and Proverbial Phrases: A Historical Dictionary*. London: J.M. Dent and Sons; New York: E.P. Dutton, 1929.

Appiah, Kwame Anthony. "Thick Translation." *The Translation Studies Reader. Second Edition*. Ed. Lawrence Venuti. London-New York: Routledge, 2004. 389–401.

Aquilecchia, Giovanni. "La proverbializzazione del personaggio narrativo nella letteratura italiana del Cinquecento." *Nuove schede di italianistica*. Roma: Salerno Editrice, 1994. 209–21.

Aquinas, Thomas. *Summa Theologiae. The sacraments*. Ed. David John Bourke. Cambridge-New York: Cambridge UP, 2006.

Arcangeli, Alessandro. "Les *Second Fruits* de John Florio ou la vie comme un jeu." *Actes des congrès de la Société française Shakespeare* 23 (2005): 11–24.

Archivio in rete, blog di studi e di divagazioni; coordinated by Alberto Mario Cirese. www.amcirese.it. Accessed 8 June 2019.

Aresti, Alessandro. "Sul patrimonio paremiologico della prima edizione del *Vocabolario degli Accademici della Crusca* (1612)." Tomasin, 295–306.

Aretino, Pietro. *Lettere scritte a Pietro Aretino*. Ed. Paolo Procaccioli. Roma: Salerno Editrice, 2004.

———. *Opere di Pietro Aretino e di Anton Francesco Doni*. Ed. Carlo Cardié. Milano: Ricciardi, 1976.

———. *I quattro libri de la humanità di Christo*. Venezia: Francesco Marcolini, 1538.

———. *Sei giornate*. Ed. Giovanni Aquilecchia. Roma-Bari: Laterza, 1969.

———. *Sonetti lussuriosi e altre opere*. Ed. Piero Lorenzini, et al. Roma: Savelli, 1980.

Ariosto, Ludovico. *Orlando furioso*. 1532. Ed. Lanfranco Caretti. Torino: Einaudi, 1985.

———. *Orlando furioso di messer Lodovico Ariosto, con cinque nuovi canti del medesimo. Ornato di figure. Con queste aggiuntioni. Vita dell'auttore* scritta per messer Simon Fornari. Allegorie in ciascun canto di messer Clemente Valvassori giureconsulto. Argomenti ad ogni canto di messer Giovanni Mario Verdezotti. Annotationi, imitationi, et avvertimenti sopra i luoghi difficili di messer Lodovico Dolce et d'altri. Pareri in duello d'incerto auttore. Dichiaratione d'historie et di favole di messer Thomaso Porcacchi. Ricolta di tutte le comparationi usate dall'auttore. Vocabolario di parole oscure con l'espositione. Rimario con tutte le cadentie usate dall'Ariosto di messer Gio. Giacomo Paruta. Ed. Ludovico Dolce. Venezia: per Giovanni Andrea Valvassori detto Guadagnino, 1567.

———. *Orlando furioso di messer Lodovico Ariosto, tutto ricorretto et di nuove figure adornato. Al quale di nuovo sono aggiunte le annotationi, gli avvertimenti, et le dichiarationi di Girolamo Ruscelli, la vita dell'autore descritta dal Signor Giovambattista Pigna, gli scontri de' luoghi mutati dall'autore doppo la sua prima impressione, la dichiaratione di tutte le favole, il vocabolario di tutte le parole oscure, et altre cose utili et necessarie.* Ed. Girolamo Ruscelli. Venezia: appresso Vincenzo Valgrisi alla bottega d'Erasmo, 1556.

———. *Orlando furioso di Messer Ludovico Ariosto con la giunta, novissimamente stampato e corretto. Con una apologia di messer Lodovico Dolcio contra ai detrattori dell'autore, et un modo brevissimo di trovar le cose aggiunte; e Tavola di tutto quello ch'è contenuto nel libro. Aggiuntovi una breve espositione dei luoghi difficili.* Ed. Ludovico Dolce. Venezia: appresso di Mapheo Pasini et Francesco di Alessandro Bindoni, 1535 and 1540.

———. *Orlando furioso di messer Ludovico Ariosto nobile ferrarese, di nuovo ristampato et historiato. Con ogni diligenza dal suo originale tolto, con la nuova giunta, et le notationi di tutti gli luoghi, dove per lui è stato tal opra ampliata come nella nova tavola nel fine per ordine vedere si puole.* Venezia: per Nicolò di Aristotile detto Zoppino, 1536.

———. *Orlando furioso di messer Ludovico Ariosto novissimamente alla sua integrità ridotto et ornato di varie figure. Con alcune stanze del Signor Aluigi Gonzaga in lode del medesimo. Aggiuntovi per ciascun canto alcune allegorie et nel fine una breve espositione et tavola di tutto quello che nell'opera si contiene.* Ed. Ludovico Dolce. Venezia: appresso Gabriel Giolito de' Ferrari et fratelli, 1542, 1543, and 1544.

———. *Orlando Furioso di messer Ludovico Ariosto. Ornato di nuove figure et allegorie in ciascun canto. Aggiuntovi nel fine l'espositione de' luoghi difficili et emendato secondo l'originale del proprio authore.* Venezia: per Giovanni Andrea Valvassori detto Guadagnino, 1553 and 1554.

Aristotle. *Opere.* Roma-Bari: Laterza, 1997.

Works Consulted

Aristotle. *Rhetoric.* Ed. C.D.C. Reeve. Indianapolis-Cambridge: Hackett, 2018.

Arora, Shirley. "The Perception of Proverbiality." *Proverbium* 1 (1984): 1–38.

Arthaber, Augusto. *Dizionario comparato di proverbi e modi proverbiali italiani, latini, francesi, spagnoli, tedeschi, inglesi e greci antichi, con relativi indici sistematico-alfabetici. Supplemento ai dizionari delle principali lingue moderne ed antiche.* Milano: Hoepli, 1929.

Ascham, Roger. *The Scholemaster or plaine and perfite way of teaching children to understand, write, and speake the Latin tong, but specially purposed for the private bringing up of youth in ientlemen and noble mens houses, and commodious also for all such as have forgot the Latin tonge.* London: printed by Iohn Daye, 1570.

———. *The scholemaster.* Amsterdam: Theatrum Orbis Terrarum; New York: Da Capo Press, 1968.

Ascoli, Albert Russell. "The History of a Story: Manetti's 'La Novella del Grasso Legnaiuolo.'" *Rituals of Politics and Culture in Early Modern Europe: Essays in Honour of Edward Muir.* Eds. Mark Jurdjevic and Rolf Strøm-Olsen. Toronto: Centre for Reformation and Renaissance Studies, 2016. 211–34.

Ashley, Leonard. "Floreat Florio." *The Shakespeare Newsletter* 30 (1980): 49.

Atlante Linguistico Italiano. Roma: Istituto dell'Atlante Linguistico Italiano, 1995–2008.

Auzza, Ginetta. "Gallomania e anglomania." *Storia della cultura veneta.* Eds. Girolamo Arnaldi and Manlio Pastore Stocchi. Vol. 5.1. Vicenza: Neri Pozza, 1985. 579–606.

Bainton, Roland. "Erasmo e l'Italia." Trans. Daniele Pianciola. *Rivista Storica Italiana* 79 (1967): 944–51.

Bakhtin, Mikhail. *Rabelais and His World.* Trans. Helen Iswolsky. Bloomington: Indiana UP, 1984.

———. *Speech Genres and Other Late Essays.* Trans. Vern McGee. Eds. Caryl Emerson and Michael Holquist. Austin: U of Texas P, 1986.

Balbo, Andrea. "Tra sententia e proverbio. Problemi di paremiografia in Seneca il Vecchio." *Philologia Antiqua* 4 (2011): 11–34.

Banchieri, Adriano. *Novella di Cacasenno figlio del semplice Bertoldino divisa in discorsi e ragionamenti. Opera onesta e di piacevole trattenimento, copiosa di motti, sentenze, proverbi ed argute risposte nuovamente aggiunta al Bertoldo del Croce.* Venezia: Sebastiano Tondelli, 1855.

Baratto, Mario. *Realtà e stile nel Decameron.* Vicenza: Neri Pozza, 1970.

Barbe, Katharina. *Irony in Context.* Amsterdam-Philadelphia: John Benjamins Publisher, 1995.

Bargagli, Girolamo. *Dialogo de' giuochi che nelle vegghie sanesi si usano di fare*. Ed. Patrizia Ermini D'Incalci. Siena: Accademia Senese degli Intronati, 1982.

Baricci, Federico. "Dal *Serventese del dio d'Amore* a Nastagio degli Onesti. La punizione dell'amore negato nel medioevo romanzo." *Boccaccio letterato. Atti del convegno internazionale, Firenze-Certaldo 10–12 ott. 2013*. Eds. Michaelangiola Marchiaro and Stefano Zamponi. Firenze: Accademia della Crusca, 2015. 437–51.

Barker, William. *The fearfull fansies of the Florentine couper*. London: by Henry Bynneman, 1568.

Barley, Nigel. "The proverb and related problems of genre-definition." *Proverbium* 23 (1973): 880–84.

Bartlett, Kenneth. "Travel and Translations: The English and Italy in the Sixteenth Century." *Annali d'italianistica* 14 (1996): 493–506.

Bartoli, Lorenzo. "*Il mal furo non vuol festa*: testo, paratesto ed espressivismo linguistico in *Decameron*, II 10 (e IV 5)." *Studi (e testi) italiani. Semestrale del Dipartimento di Italianistica e Spettacolo* 24.2 (2009): 121–34.

Baruffaldi, Girolamo, and Giuseppe Lanzoni. *Rime scelte de' poeti ferraresi antichi e moderni. Aggiuntevi nel fine alcune brevi notizie istoriche intorno ad essi*. Ferrara: per gli eredi di Bernardino Pomatelli, 1813.

Basalisco, Lucio. "L'*Ingelosite speranze* del Tauro e *Lo cierto por lo dudoso* di Lope de Vega." *Quaderni di lingue e letterature* 12 (1987): 109–16.

Basile, Giambattista. *Lo cunto de li cunti*. Ed. Michele Rak. Milano: Garzanti, 1986.

———. *Lo cunto de li cunti: overo Lo trattenemiento de' peccerille*. Ed. Carolina Stromboli. Roma: Salerno Editrice, 2013.

———. *Lo cunto de li cunti, overo lo trattenemiento de peccerille–Le muse napolitane e le lettere*. Ed. Mario Petrini. Roma-Bari: Laterza, 1976.

———. *Le opere napoletane*. Ed. Olga Silvana Casale. Roma: Benincasa, 1989.

———. *Il Pentamerone del cavalier Giovan Battista Basile, overo Lo cunto de li cunte, trattenemiento de li peccerile, di Gian Alessio Abbattutis nuovamente restampato e co' tutte le zeremonie corrietto*. Ed. Pompeo Sarnelli. Napoli: Antonio Bulifon, 1674.

———. *Il Pentamerone, ossia La fiaba delle fiabe. Tradotta dall'antico dialetto napoletano e corredata di note storiche da Benedetto Croce*. Ed. Benedetto Croce. Roma-Bari: Laterza, 1925.

———. *The Tale of Tales, or Entertainment for Little Ones*. Trans. Nancy Canepa. Detroit: Wayne State UP, 2007.

Works Consulted

Basile Bonsante, Mariella. "Appunti su Pompeo Sarnelli, moralista e scrittore d'arte." *Atti del Congresso Internazionale di studi sull'età del Viceregno*. Eds. Francesco De Robertis and Mauro Spagnoletti. Bari: Grafica Bigiemme, 1977. 242–56.

Bassnett, Susan. "Translating Genre." *Genre Matters: Essays in Theory and Criticism*. Eds. Garin Dowd, et al. Bristol: Intellect Books, 2006.

Beccaria, Gian Luigi. *Dizionario di linguistica*. Torino: Einaudi, 1994.

———. *Letteratura e dialetto*. Bologna: Zanichelli, 1975.

———. *Spagnolo e spagnoli in Italia. Riflessi ispanici sulla lingua italiana del cinque e del seicento*. Torino: Giappichelli, 1985.

Beer, Marina. "Alcune osservazioni su oralità e novella italiana in versi (XIX-XV secolo)." *La novella, la voce, il libro. Dal "cantare" trecentesco alla penna narratrice barocca*. Napoli: Liguori, 1996. 5–35.

Bellorini, Maria Grazia. "La *Grammatica de la lingua italiana* di Alessandro Citolini." *English Miscellany* 16 (1965): 281–96.

———. "Le pubblicazioni italiane dell'editore londinese John Wolfe (1580–1591)." *Miscellanea, pubblicazioni dell'Università di Trieste*. Udine: Arti grafiche friulane, 1971. 17–65.

Bembo, Pietro. *Prose e rime*. Ed. Carlo Dionisotti. Torino: UTET, 1966.

Benjamin, Walter. "The Task of the Translator." 1923. *Illuminations*. Trans. Harry Zohn. Eds. Walter Benjamin and Hannah Arendt. New York: Schocken, 1968. 69–82.

Ben Sira, Yeshua. *The Book of Ben Sira: Text, Concordance and an Analysis of the Vocabulary*. Ed. Ze'ev Ben-Hayyim. Jerusalem: The Academy of the Hebrew Language and the Shrine of the Book, 1973.

Benucci, Elisabetta. "Giuseppe Giusti e la «Raccolta di proverbi toscani». Dal manoscritto alla fortuna editoriale del 'repertorio' Giusti-Capponi." Franceschi, *Ragionamenti*, 219–40.

———. "Proverbi italiani dell'Ottocento." *Fraseologia, paremiologia e lessicografia. III convegno dell'Associazione italiana di fraseologia e paremiologia Phrasis (Accademia della Crusca—Università di Firenze, 19–21 ott. 2016)*. Eds. Elisabetta Benucci, et al. Roma: Aracne, 2018. 99–113.

Benucci, Elisabetta, et al. *Cantari novellistici dal Tre al Cinquecento*. Roma: Salerno Editrice, 2002.

Benvenuto Italiano. *Il Passagiere di Benvenuto Italiano, diviso in due parti, che contenguno sette esquisiti dialoghi, in italiana et tradoti nell'inglese favella. / The Passenger of Benvenuto Italian, divided into two parts, containing seaven exquisite dialogues in Italian and English*. London: Thomas Snodham, 1612.

Berman, Antoine. "De la translation à la traduction." *Etudes sur le texte et ses transfomations* 1 (1988): 23–40.

Beroaldo, Filippo. *Annotationes centum*. Brescia: Bernardinus Misinta, 1496.

———. *Oratio proverbialis*. Bologna: Benedictus Hectoris, 1499.

Berruto, Gaetano. "Significato e struttura del significante in testi paremiografici." *Parole e metodi* 4 (1974): 189–211.

Bertinetto, Pier Marco. "Echi del suono ed echi del senso. Implicazioni semantiche in rima." *Parole e metodi* 3 (1972): 47–57.

———. "Per un'analisi quantitativa di certe proprietà semantiche e foniche nei costituenti rimici." *Parole e metodi* 2 (1971): 191–98.

Bessi, Patrizia. *Le strutture del proverbio monofrastico. Analisi di millecinquecento formule tratte dall'Atlante Paremiologico Italiano*. Alessandria: Edizioni dell'Orso, 2004.

Besso, Marco. *Roma nei proverbi e nei modi di dire*. Roma: Loescher, 1889.

Bevilacqua, Mirko. "Il comico, la poetica e la brigata nella sesta giornata del *Decameron*." *Il comico nella letteratura italiana. Teorie e pratiche*. Ed. Silvana Cirillo. Roma: Donzelli, 2005. 37–42.

Biagi, Guido. "La rassettatura del *Decameron*." *Aneddoti letterari*. Milano: Treves, 1896. 282–326.

Bianchi, Patricia, et al. *Storia della lingua a Napoli e in Campania*. Napoli: Pironti, 1993.

Bianconi, Lorenzo, et al. "Lope de Vega napoletanato: *L'ingelosite speranze* di Raffaele Tauro." *Traduzioni, riscritture, ibridazioni prosa e teatro fra Italia, Spagna e Portogallo*. Eds. Michela Graziani and Salomé Vuelta García. Firenze: Olschki, 2016. 17–39.

The Bible. Authorized King James Version. New Scofield study system with introductions, annotations, and subject chain references. Oxford-New York: Oxford UP, 1998.

Bichelli, Pirro. *Grammatica del dialetto napoletano*. Bari: Pegaso, 1974.

Biffi, Marco. "La banca dati *Proverbi italiani*." *Fraseologia, paremiologia e lessicografia. III convegno dell'Associazione italiana di fraseologia e paremiologia Phrasis (Accademia della Crusca—Università di Firenze, 19–21 ott. 2016)*. Eds. Elisabetta Benucci, et al. Roma: Aracne, 2018. 115–28.

———. "La raccolta di proverbi del *Vocabolario degli Accademici della Crusca*." Tomasin, 307–22.

Bigi, Emilio. "Appunti sulla lingua e sulla metrica del *Furioso*." *La cultura del Poliziano e altri studi umanistici*. Pisa: Nistri-Lischi, 1967. 164–86.

Works Consulted

Bini, Ascanio. *La historia perché si dice gli è fatto il becco all'oca. Opera morale, piacevole, vaga e ridicolosa.* Firenze: alle scale di Badia, 1568.

Bizzarri, Hugo. "La potencialidad narrativa del refrán." *Revista de Poética Medieval* 1 (1997): 9–34.

———. "El refràn en el trànsito del Humanismo al Renacimiento (La invención de la ciencia paremiológica)." *Paremia* 17 (2008): 27–40.

Black, Robert. *Education and society in Florentine Tuscany. Teachers, Pupils and Schools, c. 1200–1500.* Leiden: Brill, 2007.

Blasucci, Luigi. "Osservazioni sulla struttura metrica del *Furioso*." *Studi su Dante e Ariosto*. Milano: Ricciardi, 1969. 73–112.

Boccaccio, Giovanni. *Decameron.* Ed. Vittore Branca. Torino: Einaudi, 1980.

———. *The Decameron.* Ed. George McWilliam. London: Penguin, 2003.

———. *Il Decameron di messer Giovanni Boccacci cittadin fiorentino, di nuovo ristampato e riscontrato in Firenze con testi antichi et alla sua vera lettione ridotto dal cavalier Lionardo Salviati.* Ed. Lionardo Salviati. Firenze: Giunti, 1582.

———. *Il Decameron di messer Giovanni Boccacci cittadino fiorentino. Ricorretto in Roma, et emendato secondo l'ordine del Sacro Concilio di Trento, et riscontrato in Firenze con testi antichi et alla sua vera lezione ridotto da' deputati di loro Altezza Sererenissima.* Ed. Vincenzo Borghini. Firenze: Giunti, 1573.

———. *Il Decamerone con nuove e varie figure nuovamente stampato et ricorretto per Antonio Brucioli con la dichiaratione di tutti i vocaboli, detti, proverbii, figure, et modi di dire incogniti et difficili, che sono in esso libro ampliati in gran numero per il medesimo. Con una nuova dichiaratione di più regole de la lingua toscana necessarie a sapere a chi quella vuol parlar o scrivere.* Ed. Antonio Brucioli. Venezia: appresso Gabriel Giolito de' Ferrari et fratelli, 1542.

———. *Il Decamerone di messer Giovan Boccaccio, nuovamente alla sua intera perfettione, non meno nella scrittura che nelle parole ridotto, per Girolamo Ruscelli. Con le dichiarationi, annotationi, et avvertimenti del medesimo, sopra tutti i luoghi difficili, regole, modi, et ornamenti della lingua volgare, et con figure nuove et bellissime, che interamente dimostrano i luoghi ne' quali si riducevano ogni giornata a novellare. Et con un vocabolario generale nel fine del libro.* Ed. Girolamo Ruscelli. Venezia: appresso Vincenzo Valgrisi alla bottega d'Erasmo, 1552.

———. *Il Decamerone di messer Giovanni Boccaccio di nuovo emendato secondo gli antichi essemplari. Con la diversità di molti testi posta nel margine e nel fine con gli epitheti dell'auttore, con la espositione di tutti i proverbii et luoghi difficili, et con la dichiaratione delle historie delle quali il Boccaccio ha tolto il soggetto di far le novelle, e i nomi così de gli huomini come delle donne che nell'opera presente si contengono, con tavole et altre cose notabili et molto utili alli studiosi della lingua volgare.* Ed. Francesco Sansovino. Venezia: Griffio, 1549.

———. *Il Decamerone di messer Giovanni Boccaccio di nuovo emendato secondo gli antichi essemplari, per giudicio et diligenza di più autori, con la diversità di molti testi posta per ordine in margine, et nel fine con gli epitheti dell'autore, espositione de proverbi et luoghi difficili, che nell'opera si contengono, con tavole et altre cose nobili et molto utili alli studiosi della lingua volgare.* Ed. Francesco Sansovino. Venezia: appresso Gabriel Giolito de' Ferrari et fratelli, 1546.

———. *Il Decamerone di messer Giovanni Boccaccio, di nuovo riformato da messer Luigi Groto, Cieco d'Adria con permissione de' superiori et con le dichiarationi, avertimenti, et un vocabolario fatto da messer Girolamo Ruscelli.* Ed. Luigi Groto. Venezia: appresso Fabio et Agostino Zoppini fratelli et Onofrio Fari compagni, 1588 and 1590.

———. *Il Decamerone di messer Giovanni Boccaccio novamente stampato et ricorretto per messer Lodovico Dolce con la dichiaratione di tutti i vocaboli, detti, proverbii, figure, et modi di dire incogniti et difficili che sono in esso libro.* Ed. Ludovico Dolce. Venezia: ad instantia di Curzio Navò et fratelli al Lione, 1541.

———. *Il Decamerone di messer Giovanni Boccaccio nuovamente alla sua vera lettione ridotto. Con tutte quelle allegorie, annotationi, e tavole che nelle altre nostre impressioni si contengono, e di più ornato di molte figure. Aggiuntovi separatamente un indice copiosissimo de i vocaboli e delle materie composto da messer Lodovico Dolce.* Ed. Ludovico Dolce. Venezia: appresso Gabriel Giolito de' Ferrari et fratelli, 1552.

———. *Il Decamerone di messer Giovanni Boccaccio nuovamente corretto et con diligentia stampato.* Firenze: per li heredi di Philippo di Giunta, 1527.

———. *Il Decamerone di messer Giovanni Boccaccio nuovamente stampato et ricorretto per Antonio Brucioli con la dichiaratione di tutti i vocaboli, detti, proverbii, figure, et modi di dire incogniti et difficili che sono in esso libro.* Ed. Antonio Brucioli. Venezia: ad instantia di Messer Giovanni Giolito da Trino, 1538.

———. *Tutte le opere.* Ed. Vittore Branca. Milano: Mondadori, 1964.

Bocchi, Andrea. "I Florio contro la Crusca." *La nascita del Vocabolario. Convegno di studio per i quattrocento anni del Vocabolario della Crusca, Udine, 12–13 mar. 2013.* Eds. Antonio Dan and Laura Nascimben. Padova: Esedra Editrice, 2014. 51–80.

Works Consulted

Bocci, Laura. "Stefano Guazzo e il rinascimento inglese 1575–1675." *Stefano Guazzo e la civil conversazione*. Ed. Giorgio Patrizi. Roma: Bulzoni, 1990. 163–225.

Boggione, Valter, and Lorenzo Massobrio. *Dizionario dei proverbi. I proverbi italiani organizzati per temi. 30.000 detti raccolti nelle regioni italiane e tramandati dalle fonti letterarie*. Torino: UTET, 2004.

Boiardo, Matteo Maria. *Orlando innamorato*. Ed. Charles Stanley Ross. Berkeley-Los Angeles: U of California P, 1989.

———. *Orlando innamorato*. Ed. Riccardo Bruscagli. Torino: Einaudi, 1995.

Boitani, Pietro. "Percorsi europei del Boccaccio." *Boccaccio e i suoi lettori. Una lunga ricezione. Collana del Dipartimento di Italianistica, Università di Bologna, 26*. Eds. Gian Mario Anselmi, et al. Bologna: Il Mulino, 2013. 99–116.

Bongi, Salvatore. *Annali di Gabriel Giolito de' Ferrari da Trino di Monferrato, stampatore in Venezia*. Roma: Ministero della Pubblica Istruzione, 1890–97.

Bonomi, Ilaria, and Cristina Castegnaro. *La grammaticografia italiana attraverso i secoli*. Milano: CUEM, 1998.

Bonser, Wilfrid, and Thomas Arthur Stephens. *Proverb Literature. A Bibliography of Works Relating to Proverbs*. London: Glaisher, 1930.

The Booke of Meery Riddles, together with proper questions and witty proverbs to make pleasant pastime; no lesse usefull then behoovefull for any young man or child to know if he be quick-witted or no. London: printed for John Stafford and W.G., 1629.

Booty, John. *The Book of Common Prayer, 1559. The Elizabethan Prayer Book*. Charlottesville: U of Virginia P, 2005.

Borello, Enrico. "L'italiano come lingua straniera nel '500: John Florio e la glottodidattica." *Quaderni del dipartimento di linguistica dell'Università di Firenze* 5 (1994): 157–66.

Borghini, Vincenzo. *Annotationi et discorsi sopra alcuni luoghi del Decameron, di messer Giovanni Boccacci. Fatte dalli molto magnifici signori deputati da loro Altezze Serenissime, sopra la correttione di esso Boccaccio, stampato l'anno 1573*. Firenze: Giunti, 1573.

———. "I proverbi." *Scritti inediti o rari sulla lingua*. Ed. John Woodhouse. Bologna: Commissione per i testi di lingua, 1971. 165–76.

Borroni Salvadori, Fabia. "L'incisione al servizio del Boccaccio nei secoli XV e XVI." *Annali della Scuola Normale Superiore di Pisa* 7 (1972): 595–734.

Bottigheimer, Ruth. *Fairy Tales Framed: Early Forewords, Afterwords, and Critical Words*. Albany: SUNY UP, 2012.

Boutcher, Warren. "'A French Dexterity, & an Italian Confidence.' New Documents on John Florio, Learned Strangers and Protestant Humanist. Study of Modern Languages in Renaissance England from c. 1547 to c. 1625." *Reformation* 2.1 (1997): 39–109.

———. "Vernacular Humanism in the Sixteenth Century." *The Cambridge Companion to Renaissance Humanism*. Ed. Jill Kraye. Cambridge-New York: Cambridge UP, 1996. 189–201.

Bovicelli, Giuliano. *Istoria delle perrucche, in cui si fa vedere la loro origine, la usanza, la forma, l'abuso e la irregolarità di quelle degli ecclesiastici. Tradotta dal francese per ordine dell'Eminentissimo Arcivescovo Orsini Vescovo Tusculano da Giuliano Bovicelli, Priore della S. Basilica di S. Bartolomeo, Segretario di S. Eminenza, dedicata all'Illustrissimo e Reverendissimo Signore Monsignor Sarnelli Vescovo di Bisceglia*. Benevento: Stamperia Arcivescovile, 1702.

Bowen, Barbara. "Ciceronian Wit and Renaissance Rhetoric." *Rhetorica: A Journal of the History of Rhetoric* 16.4 (1998): 409–29.

Braden, Gordon, et al. *The Oxford History of Literary Translation in English. Volume 2, 1550–1660*. Oxford-New York: Oxford UP, 2015.

Bragantini, Renzo. *Il riso sotto il velame: la novella cinquecentesca tra l'avventura e la norma*. Firenze: Olschki, 1987.

———. "La spola del racconto: dal proverbio alla novella, e viceversa." Pignatti and Crimi, 283–314.

———. "Su alcune edizioni cinquecentesche del *Decameron*." *I dintorni del testo: approcci alle periferie del libro. Atti del convegno internazionale, Roma, 15–17 nov. 2004 – Bologna, 18–19 nov. 2004*. Eds. Marco Santoro and Maria Gioia Tavoni. Roma: Edizioni dell'Ateneo, 2005. 343–48.

Brambilla Ageno, Franca. "Alcune antiche frasi proverbiali." *Lingua Nostra* 15 (1954): 97–99.

———. "A proposito di wellerismi." *Lingua Nostra* 14 (1953): 118–19.

———. "Le frasi proverbiali di una raccolta manoscritta di Lionardo Salviati." *Studi di filologia italiana* 17 (1959): 239–74.

———. "Ispirazione proverbiale del *Trecentonovelle*." *Lettere italiane* 10.3 (1958): 288–305.

———. "Un personaggio proverbiale: il Carafulla." 1959. *Studi lessicali*. Eds. Paolo Bongrani, et al. Bologna: CLUEB, 2000. 352–57.

———. "Premessa a un repertorio di frasi proverbiali." *Romance Philology* 13 (1960): 242–64.

———. "I «Proverbi» di Ser Garzo." *Studi petrarcheschi* 1 (1984): 1–37.

———. "Tradizione favolistica e novellistica nella fraseologia proverbiale." *Lettere Italiane* 8.4 (1956): 351–84.

Works Consulted

Branca, Vittore. *Boccaccio medievale e nuovi studi sul «Decameron»*. Firenze: Sansoni, 1986.

———. "Contemporaneizzazione narrativa ed espressivismo linguistico nel *Decameron*." *Letterature comparate: problemi e metodi. Studi in onore di Ettore Paratore*. Ed. Marcello Aurigemma. Bologna: Patron, 1981. 1283–1305.

———. *Linee di una storia della critica al «Decameron»: con bibliografia boccaccesca*. Milano-Genova: Società anonima editrice Dante Alighieri, 1939.

———. "Registri narrativi e stilistici nel *Decameron*." *Studi sul Boccaccio* 5 (1968): 29–76.

Brand, Peter. "Ariosto and the Oral Tradition." *Opera & Vivaldi*. Eds. Michael Collins and Elise Kirk. Austin: U of Texas P, 1984. 54–63.

Brevini, Franco. *La poesia in dialetto: storia e testi dalle origini al Novecento*. Milano: Mondadori, 1999.

Bronzini, Giovanni Battista. "La logica del proverbio. Problemi e prospettive di classificazione e analisi." S. Trovato, *Proverbi*, 45–55.

Brown, Peter. "Aims and Methods of the Second «Rassettatura» of the *Decameron*." *Studi secenteschi* 8 (1967): 3–41.

———. "I veri promotori della «rassettatura» del *Decameron* nel 1582." *Giornale Storico della Letteratura Italiana* 134.406 (1957): 314–32.

Brucioli, Antonio. *Annotationi di Antonio Brucioli sopra i proverbii di Salomo, tradotti per esso dalla ebraica verità in lingua Toscana*. Venezia: per Aurelio Pincio, 1533.

———. *Commento in tutti i Sacrosanti libri del vecchio et nuovo Testamento, dalla hebraica verità, et fonte greco per esso tradoti in lingua toscana*. Venezia: Brucioli, 1546.

Bruni, Francesco. *Boccaccio. L'invenzione della letteratura mezzana*. Bologna: Il Mulino, 1990.

———. "Caratterizzazione geolinguistica e caratterizzazione stilistica in alcune novelle del *Decameron*." Malato, *La novella italiana*, 657–73.

Brusantino, Vincenzo. *L'Angelica innamorata*. Venezia: Francesco Marcolini, 1550.

———. *L'Angelica innamorata*. Venezia: Antonelli, 1837.

———. *Archivio Famiglia Muzzarelli Brusantini*. Biblioteca Comunale Ariostea, Ferrara, Archivio Pasi, Busta 5, Fasc. 320; Cl. I 222; Cl. I scat. 22. Manuscript.

———. *Le cento novelle da messer Brugiantino dette in ottava rima. Et tutte hanno la allegoria, con il proverbio a proposito della novella*. Venezia: Francesco Marcolini, 1554.

———. *Lettera a Bartolomeo Prosperi*. 8 January 1551. Archivio di Stato, Modena, Letterati, b. 11. Manuscript.

———. *Lettera a Ercole II d'Este*. c. 1550, Biblioteca Estense Universitaria, Modena, It. 883=alfa G.1.1543. Manuscript.

———. *Lettera al giudice Giovanni Paolo Machiavelli*. 1544. Archivio di Stato, Ferrara, Raccolta Autografica Cittadella 563. Manuscript.

Bruscagli, Riccardo. "La novella e il romanzo." *Storia della letteratura italiana*. Ed. Enrico Malato. Vol. 4. Roma: Salerno Editrice, 1996. 835–907.

———. "Stagioni della civiltà estense." *Belfagor* 35 (1980): 517–31.

———. *Studi cavallereschi*. Firenze: Società editrice fiorentina, 2003.

Buoni, Thomas. *Lettere argute scritte da lui a diversi amici et signori padroni*. Venezia: Guarisco, 1603.

———. *Nuovo thesoro de' proverbii italiani del Signor Tomaso Buoni cittadino lucchese. Ove con brieve espositione si mostra l'origine et l'uso accomodato loro, distinto in sei capi*. Venezia: Giovan Battista Ciotti, 1604.

Burke, Peter. *Cultural Translation in Early Modern Europe*. Cambridge-New York: Cambridge UP, 2007.

———. "The Renaissance Translator as Go-Between." *Renaissance Go-Betweens: Cultural Exchange in Early Modern Europe*. Eds. Andreas Höfele and Werner von Koppenfels. Berlin: De Gruyter, 2005. 17–31.

Butler, Kathleen. "Giacomo Castelvetro, 1546–1616." *Italian Studies* 5.1 (1950): 1–42.

Bybee, Joan. "From Usage to Grammar: The Mind's Response to Repetition." *Language* 82.4 (2006): 711–33.

Cabani, Cristina. *Costanti ariostesche: tecniche di ripresa e memoria interna nell'«Orlando Furioso»*. Pisa: Scuola Normale Superiore, 1990.

———. *Le forme del cantare epico-cavalleresco*. Lucca: Pacini, 1988.

———. "Le riprese interstrofiche nella metrica del *Furioso*." *Annali della Scuola Normale Superiore di Pisa* 11 (1981): 469–521.

Cacciari, Cristina. "La comprensione delle espressioni idiomatiche. Il rapporto tra significato letterale e significato figurato." *Lingua e stile* 16.3 (1989): 413–37.

Cacciari, Cristina, and Sam Glucksberg. "Imagining idiomatic expressions: literal or figurative meanings?" *Idioms: Structural and Psychological Perspectives*. Eds. Martin Everaert, et al. London: Psychology Press, 1995. 43–56.

Caiazza, Ida. "Proverbio e sentenza in Alvise Pasqualigo (e una nuova fonte del *Giardino di ricreatione* di John Florio)." Pignatti and Crimi, 315–39.

Calabrese, Stefano. *Gli arabeschi della fiaba: dal Basile ai romantici*. Pisa: Pacini, 1984.

Cali, Piero. "Per un'edizione della grammatica di Alessandro Citolini." *Repertori di parole e immagini, esperienze cinquecentesche e moderni data bases*. Eds. Paola Barocchi and Lina Bolzoni. Pisa: Scuola Normale Superiore, 1997. 235–51.

Calvino, Italo. "Leggerezza." *Lezioni americane: sei proposte per il prossimo millennio*. Milano: Garzanti, 1988. 5–30.

———. *Sulla fiaba*. Milano: Mondadori, 1996.

Canepa, Nancy. "Basile e il carnevalesco." Picone and Messerli, 41–60.

———. "«Entertainment for Little Ones»? Basile's *Lo Cunto de li Cunti* and the Childhood of the Literary Fairy Tale." *Marvels & Tales: Journal of Fairy Tale Studies* 17.1 (2003): 37–54.

———. *From Court to Forest: Giambattista Basile's «Lo Cunto de li Cunti» and the Birth of the Literary Fairy Tale*. Detroit: Wayne State UP, 1999.

———. "Sarnelli, Pompeo (1649–1724)." *The Greenwood Encyclopedia of Folktales and Fairy Tales*. Ed. Donald Haase. Westport, CT: Greenwood Press, 2008. 832.

Caneparo, Federica. *"Di molte figure adornato": L'Orlando furioso nei cicli pittorici tra Cinque e Seicento*. Milano: Officina libraria, 2015.

Caniato, Manuela. "Lingua e dialetto come espressione dell'altro nella commedia del Cinquecento." *Lingue e letterature in contatto: Atti del XV Congresso dell'AIPI, Brunico, 24–27 ag. 2002*. Eds. Bart Van den Bossche, et al. Firenze: Cesati, 2004. 49–54.

Capaccio, Giulio Cesare. *Il forastiero. Dialogi di Giulio Cesare Capaccio Academico otioso*. Napoli: per Giovanni Domenico Roncagliolo, 1634.

———. *Il principe del signor Giulio Cesare Capaccio, gentil'huomo del Serenissimo Signor Duca d'Urbino. Tratto da gli emblemi dell'Alciato, con ducento e più avvertimenti politici e morali, utilissimi a qualunque signore per l'ottima eruditione di costumi, economia e governo di stati, con due copiose tavole, una de gli emblemi et l'altra delle cose più notabili al serenissimo Federico II di Montefeltro della Rovere, principe d'Urbino*. Venezia: appresso Barezzo Barezzi, 1620.

———. *La vera antichità di Pozzuolo, descritta da Giulio Cesare Capaccio secretario dell'inclita città di Napoli ove con l'istoria di tutte le cose contorno si narrano la bellezza di Posillipo, l'origine della città di*

Pozzuolo, Baia, Miseno, Cuma, Ischia, riti, costumi, magistrati, nobiltà, statue, inscrittioni, fabbriche antiche, successi, guerre, e quanto appartiene alle cose naturali di terme, bagni, e di tutte le miniere. A modo d'itinerario, acciò tutti possano servirsene. Napoli: appresso Giovanni Giacomo Carlino e Costantino Vitale, 1607.

Capasso, Niccolò. *Varie poesie di Niccolò Capasso.* Napoli: Stamperia Simoniana, 1761.

Caponetto, Salvatore. "Renata di Francia e il calvinismo a Ferrara e a Faenza." *La riforma protestante nell'Italia del Cinquecento.* Torino: Claudiana, 1992. 279–300.

Capozzoli, Raffaele. *Grammatica del dialetto napoletano.* Napoli: Chiurazzi, 1889.

Carafa, Diomede. *Memoriali.* Ed. Giuseppe Galasso. Roma: Bonacci, 1988.

Carapezza, Sandra. "Il *Decamerone furioso* di Vincenzo Brugiantino." *D'otto in otto versi: il poema in ottave come ricettore di generi.* Eds. Guglielmo Barucci, et al. Firenze: Cesati, 2019. 55–71.

Cardona, Giorgio Raimondo. "Culture dell'oralità e culture della scrittura." *Letteratura italiana.* Ed. Alberto Asor Rosa. Vol. 2. Torino: Einaudi, 1983. 25–101.

Carnes, Pack. "The Fable and the Proverb: Intertexts and Reception." *Proverbium* 8 (1991): 55–76.

———. *Proverbia in Fabula: Essays on The Relationship of the Proverb and the Fable.* Bern: Peter Lang, 1988.

Carron, Jean-Claude. "Imitation and Intertextuality in the Renaissance." *New Literary History* 19 (1988): 565–79.

Casa del Boccaccio, Ente nazionale Giovanni Boccaccio. www.enteboccaccio.it/s/casa-boccaccio/page/home. Accessed 8 June 2019.

Casadei, Federica. "Alcuni pregi e limiti della teoria cognitivista della metafora." *Lingua e stile* 34.2 (1999): 167–80.

———. *Metafore ed espressioni idiomatiche. Uno studio semantico sull'italiano.* Roma: Bulzoni, 1996.

———. "Per una definizione di «espressione idiomatica» e una tipologia dell'idiomatico in italiano." *Lingua e stile* 30.2 (1995): 335–58.

———. "La semantica nelle espressioni idiomatiche." *Studi italiani di linguistica teorica e applicata* 23.1 (1994): 61–81.

Casali, Scipione. *Annali della tipografia veneziana di Francesco Marcolini da Forlì.* Bologna: Gerace, 1953.

Castellani, Arrigo Ettore. "Antroponimia medievale e storia della lingua italiana." *Saggi di linguistica e filologia italiana e romanza (1946–1976).* Vol. 1. Roma: Salerno Editrice, 1980. 457–64.

Castiglione, Baldassare. *Il libro del cortegiano*. Eds. Amedeo Quondam and Nicola Longo. Milano: Garzanti, 1981.

Catford, John Cunnison. *A Linguistic Theory of Translation. An Essay in Applied Linguistics*. Oxford-New York: Oxford UP, 1965.

Celano, Carlo. *Notizie del bello, dell'antico e del curioso della città di Napoli, per i signori forestieri, divise in dieci giornate*. Napoli: Giacomo Raillard, 1692.

Cerquiglini, Jacqueline, and Bernard Cerquiglini. "L'écriture proverbiale." *Revue des sciences humaines* 41.163 (1976): 359–75.

Cervantes, Miguel de Saavedra. *El ingenioso hidalgo don Quijote de la Mancha*. Eds. Thomas Lathrop and Stephen Hessel. Newark, DE: European Masterpieces, Cervantes & Co., 2018.

Charlton, Kenneth. *Education in Renaissance England*. London-New York: Routledge, 2007.

Cherchi, Paolo. "Alla ricerca di una apoftemmatica moderna (1543–1552)." *Rassegna europea di Letteratura italiana* 11 (1997): 29–52.

———. "Il *Decamerone spirituale* di Francesco Dionigi da Fano." *L'onestade e l'onesto raccontare del «Decameron»*. Fiesole: Cadmo, 2004. 1000–09.

———. "Funzione del paratesto nelle *Epistole* di Guevara e nelle *Novelle* di Bandello." *Paratesto* 1 (2004): 41–54.

———. "Tre note al «De vita solitaria»." *Giornale Storico della Letteratura Italiana* 187.617 (2010): 39–49.

Cherdantseva, Tamara. "Proverbio e modo di dire." *Studi di grammatica italiana* 16 (1996): 339–43.

Chidgey, David. *Giovanni Florio's «Firsts Fruites» (1578): dialogue and cultural exchange in Elizabethan England*. 2013. University of Melbourne, PhD dissertation.

Chiecchi, Giuseppe. *Le annotazioni e i discorsi sul "Decameron" nel 1573 dei deputati fiorentini*. Padova: Editrice Antenore, 2001.

———. "Sentenze e proverbi nel *Decameron*." *Studi sul Boccaccio* 9 (1975–76): 119–68.

———. "Sulle moralità in Giovanni Sercambi novelliere." *Lettere Italiane* 29.2 (1977): 133–47.

Chiecchi, Giuseppe, and Luciano Troisio. *Il Decameron sequestrato: le tre edizioni censurate nel Cinquecento*. Milano: Unicopli, 1984. 27–63.

Chlodowski, Ruffo. "Il mondo della fiaba e il *Pentamerone* di Giambattista Basile. Dai sistemi narrativi del Rinascimento classico al sistema narrativo del barocco nazionale italiano." *Cultura meridionale e letteratura italiana: i modelli narrativi dell'età moderna. Atti dell'XI*

Congresso dell'Associazione internazionale per gli studi di lingua e letteratura italiana. Napoli-Castel dell'Ovo, 14–18 apr. 1982. Ed. Giannantonio Pompeo. Napoli: Loffredo, 1985. 191–252.

Cian, Vittorio. *Motti inediti e sconosciuti di Messer Bembo.* Venezia: Tipografia dell'Ancora, 1888.

Cicero, Marcus Tullius. *Letters to Atticus.* Eds. David Shackleton Bailey. Cambridge, MA: Harvard UP, 1999.

———. *On the Ideal Orator (De oratore).* Trans. James May and Jakob Wisse. Oxford-New York: Oxford UP, 2001.

———. *Opere retoriche.* Eds. Giannicola Barone, et al. Milano: Mondadori, 2007.

Cieco, Francesco da Ferrara. *Libro d'arme e d'amore, nomato Mambriano.* Torino: UTET, 1926.

Cirese, Alberto Mario. *Prime annotazioni per una analisi strutturale dei proverbi: appunti del corso tenuto da Alberto M. Cirese.* Cagliari: Università di Cagliari, 1968.

———. *I proverbi: struttura delle definizioni.* Urbino: Università di Urbino, 1972.

———. "Il wellerismo." *Letteratura e cultura popolare.* Ed. Elide Casali. Bologna: Zanichelli, 1982. 156–62.

Citolini, Alessandro. *Lettera in difesa de la lingua volgare scritta al Magnifico messer Cosimo Pallavicino.* Venezia: Francesco Marcolini, 1540.

Civita, Alfredo. *Teorie del comico.* Milano: Unicopli, 1984.

Clarence, Griffin Child. *John Lyly and Euphuism.* Erlangen: G. Böhme, 1894.

Clarke, Derek, et al. *Short-title catalogue of books printed in Italy and of Italian books printed in other countries from 1465 to 1600, now in the British Museum.* London: British Museum, 1958.

Collins, John Joseph. *Jewish Wisdom in the Hellenistic Age.* Louisville, KY: Westminster John Knox, 1997. 178–221.

Coluccia, Rosario. "Storia dei dialetti nella Romania. Italoromania." *Romanische Sprachgeschichte.* Eds. Gerhard Ernst, et al. Vol. 3. Berlin: De Gruyter, 2009. 2478–99.

Comtesse de Chambrun, and Clara Longworth. *Giovanni Florio: un apôtre de la renaissance en Angleterre à l'époque de Shakespeare.* Paris: Payot, 1921.

The Concise Oxford Dictionary of Linguistics. Ed. Peter Hugoe Matthews. Oxford-New York: Oxford UP, 2007.

Conrieri, Davide. "Introduzione." *Novelle italiane. Il Seicento. Il Settecento.* Milano: Garzanti, 1982. vii–lxii.

Considine, John. "Wisdom-literature in early modern England." *Renaissance Studies* 13.3 (1999): 325–42.

Contini, Gianfranco. *Poeti del Duecento.* Milano: Ricciardi, 1960.

Corazzini, Francesco. "Osservazioni sulla metrica popolare. I. La metrica dei Proverbi." *Propugnatore* 13 (1880): 269–78.

Corley, Jeremy. "An intertextual study of Proverbs and Ben Sira." *Intertextual Studies in Ben Sira and Tobit. Essays in Honor of Alexander A. Di Lella.* Eds. Jeremy Corley and Vincent Skemp. Washington, DC: The Catholic Biblical Association of America, 2005. 155–82.

Corona, Oscar. *Proverbi italiani e inglesi. Equivalenti e sinonimi dei più comuni proverbi come espressi nelle due lingue.* Poggibonsi: Lalli, 1985.

Corrozet, Gilles. *Hecatongraphie. C'est à dire les descriptions de cent figures et hystoires, contenants plusieurs appophthegmes, proverbes, sentences et dictz, tant des anciens que des modernes. Le tout reveu par son autheur.* Paris: chez Denys Ianot Imprimeur et Libraire, 1543.

Corsaro, Antonio. "Lettori e editori di Boccaccio nel Cinquecento." *Boccaccio e i suoi lettori. Una lunga ricezione. Collana del Dipartimento di Italianistica, Università di Bologna, 26.* Eds. Gian Mario Anselmi, et al. Bologna: Il Mulino, 2013. 367–80.

Corso, Raffaele. "Wellerismi italiani." *Folklore* 2.3–4 (1947–48): 3–26.

Cortelazzo, Manlio. *I dialetti e la dialettologia in Italia (fino al 1800).* Tübingen: Narr, 1980.

———. *Le dieci tavole dei proverbi.* Vicenza: Neri Pozza, 1995.

———. "Regionalismi nel *Vocabolario della Crusca*." *L'italiano regionale. Atti del XVIII Congresso internazionale di studi, Padova-Vicenza, 14–16 sett. 1984.* Eds. Michele Cortelazzo and Alberto Mioni. Vol. 25. Roma: Bulzoni, 1990. 355–61.

Cortelazzo, Manlio, et al. *I dialetti italiani: storia, struttura, uso.* Torino: UTET, 2002.

Cortese, Giulio Cesare. *Opere di Giulio Cesare Cortese in lingua napoletana.* Napoli: per Novello de Bonis ad istanza d'Adriano Scultore all'insegna di S. Marco, 1666.

———. *La rosa. Favola.* Ed. Andrea Lazzarini. Lucca: Pacini, 2018.

Cortese, Giulio Cesare, and Felippo Sgruttendio de Scafato. *Opere poetiche.* Ed. Enrico Malato. Roma: Edizioni dell'Ateneo, 1967.

Cortini, Maria Antonietta, and Luisa Mulas. *Selva di vario narrare. Schede per lo studio della narrativa breve nel Seicento*. Roma: Bulzoni, 2000.

Crane, Thomas Frederick. "Some Forgotten Italian Storytellers." *The Academy* 717 (1886): 78–79.

Crescimbeni, Giovanni Maria. "De' rimatori del secolo del 1500, Centuria IV." *Istoria della volgar poesia*. Vol. 5. Venezia: presso Basilio Baseggio, 1730.

Crimi, Giuseppe. "Ispirazione proverbiale, polisemia e lessico criptico nei *Sonetti* del Burchiello." *Studi di italianistica per Maria Teresa Acquaro Graziosi*. Ed. Marta Savini. Roma: Aracne, 2002. 69–93.

Croce, Benedetto. "La letteratura dialettale riflessa, la sua origine nel Seicento e il suo ufficio storico." *La Critica* 24 (1926): 334–43.

———. *Nuovi saggi sulla letteratura italiana del seicento*. Roma-Bari: Laterza, 1949.

———. "Proverbi trimembri napoletani." *Giambattista Basile* 1 (1883): 66–67.

———. *Saggi sulla letteratura italiana del seicento*. Roma-Bari: Laterza, 1948.

———. *Storia dell'età barocca in Italia. Pensiero, Poesia e letteratura, Vita morale*. Roma-Bari: Laterza, 1957.

———. *Uomini e cose della vecchia Italia*. Roma-Bari: Laterza, 1927.

Croce, Giulio Cesare. *L'Eccellenza e trionfo del porco, e altre opere in prosa*. Eds. Monique Rouch and Franco Bacchelli. Bologna: Pendragon, 2006.

———. *Il mondo alla roversa, dove con una minutissima ricercata sopra le attioni humane si viene a dimostrar in che stato hoggi sia ridotta la povera virtù*. Bologna: per gli heredi di Giovanni Rossi, 1605.

———. *Selva di esperienza nella quale si sentono mille e tanti proverbi provati et esperimentati da' nostri antichi. Tirati per via d'alfabeto da Giulio Cesare Croce*. Bologna: per Bartolomeo Cochi al Pozzo rosso, 1618.

———. *Il Tre. Operetta dilettevole di Giulio Cesare Croce*. Ed. Charles Speroni. Firenze: Olschki, 1960.

———. *Il tre. Operetta dilettevole nella quale si mostra quante cose si contengono sotto il numero trinario. Con altre cosette belle e da spasso*. Bologna: Vittorio Benacci, 1614.

Croce, Giulio Cesare, and Camillo Scaligeri dalla Fratta. *Bertoldo, Bertoldino e Cacasenno*. Milano: Mondadori, 2018.

Crystal, David. *Dictionary of linguistics and phonetics*. Malden, MA-Oxford: Blackwell, 2008.

Cunningham, William. *Alien immigrants to England*. London: Swan Sonnenschein & Co. Limd; New York: Macmillan, 1897.

Works Consulted

Cuomo, Luisa. "Sillogizzare motteggiando e motteggiare sillogizzando: dal *Novellino* alla VI giornata del *Decameron*." *Studi sul Boccaccio* 13 (1982): 217–65.

Cynthio, Aloyse de gli Fabritii. *Libro della origine delli volgari proverbi*. Ed. Francesco Sardi Saba. Milano: Spirali, 2007.

———. *Satyra nel proverbio Chi prima va al molino prima macina di Aloise Cynthio de gli Fabritii*. Napoli: Gaetano Amalfi, 1901.

da Certaldo, Paolo di messer Pace. *Libro di buoni costumi*. Ed. Alfredo Schiaffini. Firenze: Le Monnier, 1945.

D'Agostino, Alfonso. *Fiori e vita di filosofi e d'altri savi e d'imperadori*. Firenze: La Nuova Italia, 1979.

———. "Letteratura di proverbi e letteratura con proverbi nell'Italia medievale." *Tradition des proverbes et des «Exempla» dans l'occident médiéval / Die Tradition der Sprichwörter und «exempla» im Mittelalter*. Eds. Hugo Bizzarri and Martin Rohde. Berlin: De Gruyter, 2009. 105–29.

D'Ambra, Raffaele. *Vocabolario napolitano-toscano di arti e mestieri*. Bologna: Forni, 1873.

D'Andrea, Antonio. "Le rubriche del *Decameron*." *Yearbook of Italian Studies* 3.3 (1973): 1000–27.

Daniel, Evan. *The Prayer-Book. Its History, Language, and Contents*. London: Wells Gardner, Darton & Co., 1901.

Dante Alighieri. *De vulgari eloquentia*. Ed. Steven Botterill. Cambridge-New York: Cambridge UP, 1996.

———. *The Divine Comedy of Dante Alighieri, Inferno. A Verse Translation, with an Introduction by Allen Mandelbaum*. Ed. Allen Mandelbaum. New York: Bantam Books, 1980.

Da Pozzo, Giovanni. "Il motto arguto nello sviluppo narrativo. Identità e varietà di forme." *La Rassegna della Letteratura Italiana* 108 (2004): 5–28.

D'Aragona, Tullia. *Il Meschino, altramente detto il Guerrino*. Venezia: Giovanni Battista et Melchiorre Sessa, 1560.

D'Ascoli, Francesco. *Lingua spagnuola e dialetto napoletano*. Napoli: Libreria scientifica editrice, 1972.

———. *Nuovo vocabolario dialettale napoletano*. Napoli: Gallina Editore, 1993.

De Blasi, Nicola. "Campania/Kampanien." Eds. Günter Holtus, et al. Vol. 2.2: 174–89.

———. "Notizie sulla variazione diastratica a Napoli tra il '500 e il 2000." *Bollettino Linguistico Campano* 1 (2002): 89–129.

———. *Storia linguistica di Napoli.* Roma: Carocci, 2012.

De Blasi, Nicola, and Franco Fanciullo. "La Campania." *I dialetti italiani: storia, struttura, uso.* Eds. Manlio Cortelazzo, et al. Torino: UTET, 2002. 628–78.

De Blasi, Nicola, and Alberto Varvaro. "Napoli e l'Italia meridionale." *Letteratura italiana.* Ed. Alberto Asor Rosa. Vol. 7. Torino: Einaudi, 1988. 235–325.

de Bujanda, Jesús Martinez, et al. *Index des livres interdits. Index de l'Université de Paris, 1544, 1545, 1547, 1549, 1551, 1556.* Sherbrooke: Centre d'Études de la Renaissance, 1985.

Decameron Web; Brown University, 1994–; coordinated by Massimo Riva and Michael Papio. www.brown.edu/Departments/Italian_Studies/dweb/. Accessed 8 June 2019.

De Cossart, Michael. *This little world: Renaissance Italians' view of English society.* Liverpool: Janus Press, 1984.

———. *This sceptred isle: Renaissance Italians' view of English institutions.* Liverpool: Janus Press, 1984.

De Donato, Nicola. *L'erudito monsignor Pompeo Sarnelli, fra i più moderni del Seicento (Vescovo di Bisceglie).* Bitonto: Garofalo, 1906.

De Falco, Renato. *Proverbi napoletani, raccolti da Renato de Falco; in appendice indovinelli.* Napoli: Colonnese, 1991.

de Guevara, Antonio. *Aureo libro di Marco Aurelio con l'horologio de principi.* Venezia: appresso Francesco Portonaris da Trino, 1553.

———. *Epístolas familiares del illustre señor do[n] Antonio de Guevara, obispo de Modoñedo. Va todo este epistolario al estylo y roma[n]ce de Marco Aurelio porqu'el autor estodo uno.* Valladolid: Juan de Villaquirán, 1539.

———. *The golden boke of Marcus Aurelius Emperour and eloquent oratour.* Trans. Sir John Bourchier. London: in the late house of Thomas Berthelet, 1536.

———. *Libro aureo de Marco Aurelio, emperador y eloquentissimo orador.* Paris: Galleot de Prado, 1529.

———. *Le traduzioni italiane del «Libro aureo de Marco Aurelio» e del «Relox de Principes» di Antonio de Guevara.* Ed. Livia Brunori. Imola: Galeati, 1979.

———. *Vita di Marco Aurelio imperadore, con le alte et profonde sue sentenze, notabili documenti, ammirabili essempi, et lodevole norma di vivere, tradotta di spagnuolo in ligua toscana per Mambrino Roseo da Fabriano.* Trans. Mambrino Roseo da Fabriano. Roma: per Baldasare de Cartolari perugino, 1542.

Works Consulted

Delcorno, Carlo. "Ironia/parodia." Forni and Bragantini, *Lessico critico decameroniano*, 162–91.

Della Porta, Giovanni Battista. *Della chirofisonomia, overo Di quella parte della humana fisonomia che si appartiene allo mano. Libri due*. Trans. and ed. Pompeo Sarnelli. Napoli: Antonio Bulifon, 1677.

———. *Della magia naturale del Signor Giovanni Battista della Porta napolitano libri XX, tradotti da latino in volgare e dall'istesso autore accresciuti sotto nome di Giovanni de Rosa*. Trans. and ed. Pompeo Sarnelli. Napoli: Antonio Bulifon, 1677.

delle Colonne, Guido. *Historia destructionis Troiae*. Trans. Mary Elizabeth Meek. Bloomington: Indiana UP, 1974.

Del Ninno, Maurizio. "Proverbi." *Enciclopedia Einaudi*. Ed. Ruggiero Romano. Vol. 11. Torino: Einaudi, 1980. 385–400.

Del Popolo, Concetto. "La prima stagione. Dalle origini al Trecento." *L'italiano letterario. Profilo storico*. Eds. Gian Luigi Beccaria, et al. Torino: UTET, 1989. 37–42.

Del Tufo, Gioan Battista. *Ritratto o modello delle grandezze, delizie e maraviglie della nobilissima città di Napoli*. Eds. Olga Silvana Casale and Maria Teresa Colotti. Roma: Salerno Editrice, 2007.

De Ritis, Vincenzio. *Vocabolario napoletano lessicografico e storico*. Napoli: Stamperia reale, 1845.

De Robertis, Domenico. "Nascita, tradizione e venture del cantare in ottava rima." Picone and Bendinelli Predelli, 9–24.

De Rosa, Loise. *Ricordi*. Ed. Vittorio Formentin. Roma: Salerno Editrice, 1998.

de' Rossi, Bastiano. *Diario dell'Inferigno*. 1585–1613, Accademia della Crusca, Firenze, codex 23, now n. 74. Manuscript.

De Seta, Cesare. "Il mito Italia." *Storia della letteratura italiana*. Ed. Enrico Malato. Vol. 12. 261–98.

Destro, Alberto, and Annamaria Sportelli, eds. *Ai confini dei generi: casi di ibridismo letterario*. Bari: Graphis, 1999.

D'Eugenio, Daniela. "Fra Italia e Inghilterra: Considerazioni contestuali e linguistiche su proverbi e locuzioni proverbiali di Lionardo Salviati e John Florio." *«Acciò che 'l nostro dire sia ben chiaro». Scritti per Nicoletta Maraschio*. Eds. Marco Biffi, et al. Firenze: Pubblicazioni dell'Accademia della Crusca, 2018. 383–93.

———. "I «frutti» di Orazio Toscanella, Claudius Holyband e John Florio." *Italia, Italie. Studi in onore di Hermann W. Haller*. Eds. Daniela D'Eugenio, et al. Milano: Mimesis, 2021.

———. "*Lengua che no' la 'ntienne, e tu la caca*. Irony and Hilarity of Neapolitan Paroemias in Pompeo Sarnelli's *Posilecheata* (1684)." *Humour in Italy Through the Ages, Part I of a double special issue. International Studies in Humour* 5.1 (2016): 74–111.

———. "Lionardo Salviati and the collection of *Proverbi toscani*: Philological Issues with Codex Cl. I 394." *Forum Italicum* 48.3 (2014): 495–521.

Di Capua, Francesco. "Sentenze e proverbi nella tecnica oratoria e loro influenza sull'arte del periodare (studi sulla letteratura latina medievale)." *Scritti minori*. Vol. 1. Roma-Parigi: Desclée, 1959. 41–188.

Di Felice, Claudio. *Alessandro Citolini. Scritti linguistici*. Pescara: Libreria dell'Università, 2003.

Di Martino, Gabriella. "Florio's *Firste Fruites*." *Words in action. Diachronic and synchronic approaches to English discourse. Studies in honour of Ermanno Barisone*. Eds. John Douthwaite and Domenico Pezzini. Genova: ECIG, 2008. 75–91.

———. "Politeness strategies in 17th century didactic dialogues." *English Diachronic Pragmatics*. Eds. Gabriella di Martino and Maria Lima. Napoli: CUEN, 2000. 227–46.

Diodati, Giovanni. *La Bibbia, cioè I libri del Vecchio e del Nuovo Testamento*. Geneva: Jean de Tournes, 1607.

Dionigi, Francesco da Fano. *Il Decamerone spirituale, cioè le diece spirituali giornate*. Venezia: apresso gl'Heredi di Giovanni Varisco, 1594.

Dionisotti, Carlo. *Geografia e storia della letteratura italiana*. Torino: Einaudi, 1967.

Dizionario biografico degli italiani (DBI). Roma: Istituto dell'Enciclopedia Italiana, 1960–.

Dizionario dei proverbi italiani e dialettali. Eds. Riccardo Schwamenthal and Michele Straniero. Bologna: BUR, 2013.

Dizionario della lingua italiana. Eds. Niccolò Tommaseo, et al. Torino: UTET, 1861–79.

Dizionario etimologico della lingua italiana (DELI). Eds. Manlio Cortelazzo, et al. Bologna: Zanichelli, 1999.

Dizionario etimologico italiano (DEI). Eds. Carlo Battisti and Giovanni Alessio. Firenze: Barbèra, 1950–57.

Donatus, Aelius. *Excerpta de comoedia (Hoc est: praefationis commento Terentii Donatiano in codicibus praemissae pars posterior)*. Turnhout: Brepols, 2010.

D'Onghia, Luca. "Sull'uso dei proverbi nelle *Lettere* di Andrea Calmo." Pignatti and Crimi, 161–81.

Doni, Anton Francesco. *I marmi*. Bologna: Zanichelli, 2011.

———. *Le novelle*. Ed. Elena Pierazzo. Roma: Salerno Editrice, 2003.

———. *Opere di Pietro Aretino e di Anton Francesco Doni*. Ed. Carlo Cordié. Milano: Ricciardi, 1976.

Doyle, Charles Clay, et al. *The Dictionary of Modern Proverbs*. New Haven: Yale UP, 2012.

Dundes, Alan. "On the Structure of the Proverb." *Proverbium* 25 (1975): 961–73.

Early English Books Online. eebo.chadwyck.com/home. Accessed 8 June 2019.

Eco, Umberto. "Il comico e la regola." *Sette anni di desiderio*. Milano: Bompiani, 1983.

Einstein, Lewis. *The Italian Renaissance in England*. New York: Burt Franklin, 1902.

Elam, Keir, and Fernando Cioni. *Una civile conversazione. Lo scambio letterario e culturale anglo-italiano nel rinascimento. / A civil conversation. Anglo-Italian literary and cultural exchange in the Renaissance*. Bologna: CLUEB, 2003.

Elia, Annibale, et al. "Tre componenti della sintassi italiana: frasi semplici, frasi a verbo supporto e frasi idiomatiche." *Sintassi e morfologia della lingua italiana d'uso. Teorie e applicazioni descrittive*. Eds. Annalisa Franchi De Bellis and Leonardo Maria Savoia. Roma: Bulzoni, 1985. 311–25.

Emblematica ONLINE. emblematica.grainger.illinois.edu/. Accessed 8 June 2019.

Enciclopedia italiana di scienze, lettere ed arti (*Enciclopedia Treccani*). Roma: Istituto dell'Enciclopedia Italiana, 1929–.

Engel, William Edward. "Knowledge That Counted: Italian Phrase-Books and Dictionaries in Elizabethan England." *Annali d'Italianistica* 14 (1996): 507–21.

Erasmus von Rotterdam. *The Adages of Erasmus*. Ed. William Barker. Toronto: U of Toronto P, 2001.

———. *Collected Works of Erasmus*. Toronto: U of Toronto P, 1982–2017.

———. *Desiderii Erasmi Roterodami Opera Omnia emendatiora et auctiora ad optimas editiones praecipue quas ipse Erasmus postremo curavit summa fide exacta, doctorumque virorum notis illustrata*. Ed. Jean Le Clerc. Leiden: Petri Vander Aa, 1703–06.

Essary, Brandon. "Between two sad love songs: the trials and tribulations of marriage in *Decameron* 5." *Annali d'Italianistica* 31 (2013): 258–87.

Everson, Jane. "Fare il becco all'oca: Mozart e il «Mambriano» di Francesco Cieco da Ferrara." *Italianistica* 25.1 (1996): 65–81.

Facchetti, Vittorio. "Il *Pentamerone* del Basile nel contesto storico-culturale." *Cultura meridionale e letteratura italiana: i modelli narrativi dell'età moderna. Atti dell'XI Congresso dell'Associazione internazionale per gli studi di lingua e letteratura italiana. Napoli-Castel dell'Ovo, 14–18 apr. 1982.* Ed. Giannantonio Pompeo. Napoli: Loffredo, 1985. 253–73.

Faithfull, Glynn. "The Concept of 'Living Language' in Cinquecento Vernacular Philology." *The Modern Language Review* 48.3 (1953): 278–92.

Faloppa, Federico. "Modi di dire." *Enciclopedia dell'italiano*. Ed. Raffaele Simone. Roma: Istituto dell'Enciclopedia italiana, 2011. 908–11.

Farina, Antonio. *Silloge Pseudofocilidea*. Napoli: Libreria scientifica editrice, 1962.

Farina, Domenico. *Guida ai detti napoletani*. Milano: Sugar Editore, 1971.

Fasano, Gabriele. *Lo Tasso napoletano, zoè La Gierosalemme libberata de lo sio Torquato Tasso votata a llengua nosta*. Napoli: Stamperia de Iacovo Raillardo, 1689.

Fasano, Pino. "Gli incunaboli della letteratura dialettale napoletana («chelle lettere che fecero cammarata co *La Vaiasseida*»)." *Letteratura e critica. Studi in onore di Natalino Sapegno*. Ed. Walter Bini. Roma: Bulzoni, 1975. 443–88.

Favaro, Maiko. "Il *Decameron* in veste di poema: *Le cento novelle* di Vincenzo Brusantini." *Italianistica* 39.3 (2010): 97–109.

Ferme, Valerio. "Ingegno and Morality in the New Social Order: The Role of the *Beffa* in Boccaccio's *Decameron*." *Romance Language Annual* 4 (1992): 248–53.

Ferrario, Giulio. *Storia ed analisi degli antichi romanzi di cavalleria e dei poemi romanzeschi d'Italia*. Milano: Tipografia dell'autore, 1828–29.

Ferrato, Pietro. *Alcuni proverbi inediti*. Padova: Salmin, 1870.

———. *Novellette tratte dai proverbi inediti di Francesco Serdonati—Per le nozze Pizzati-Brunello*. Padova: Penada, 1873.

———. *Proverbi fiorentini*. Padova: Salmin, 1871.

———. *Proverbi inediti aggiuntivi una supplica dello stesso Consiglio dei CC*. Padova: Penada, 1873.

Ferrato, Pietro. *Saggio di proverbi inediti*. Bologna: Fava e Garfagnani, 1873.

Ferroni, Giulio. *Il comico nelle teorie contemporanee*. Roma: Bulzoni, 1974.

Fiacchi, Luigi, *Dei proverbii toscani, lezione di Luigi Fiacchi detta nell'Accademia della Crusca il dì 30 novembre 1813, con la dichiarazione de' proverbi di Giovanni Maria Cecchi*. Milano: Silvestri 1838.

Field, Theophilus. *An italians dead bodie stucke with English flowers, On the death of Sir Horatio Pallavicino*. London: Printe[d] by Thomas Creede for Andrew Wise, 1600.

Fierro, Aurelio. *Grammatica della lingua napoletana*. Milano: Rusconi, 1989.

Fiorelli, Piero. "La raccolta di proverbi di Francesco Serdonati." S. Trovato, *Proverbi*, 219–30.

———. "Tra il proverbio e la regola di diritto." *Scritti in memoria di Dino Pieraccioni*. Eds. Michele Bandini and Federico Pericoli. Firenze: Istituto Papirologico Girolamo Vitelli, 1993. 189–212.

Fiorilla, Maurizio. "Decameron." *Boccaccio autore e copista*. Eds. Teresa De Robertis, et al. Firenze: Mandragora, 2013. 129–36.

Fiorillo, Silvio. *L'Amor giusto, egloga pastorale in napolitana e toscana lingua*. Milano: per Pandolfo Malatesta, 1605.

Fiume, Emanuele. "Giovanni Diodati: Il creatore della Bibbia evangelica italiana nel XVII secolo." *Bibelübersetzungen und (Kirchen-) Politik*. Eds. Markus Mülke and Lothar Vogel. Göttingen: V & R Unipress, 2015. 95–104.

———. *Giovanni Diodati: un italiano nella Ginevra della Riforma: traduttore della Bibbia e teologo europeo*. Roma: Società Biblica Britannica & Forestiera, 2007.

Flamini, Francesco. *Il cinquecento*. Milano: Vallardi, 1898–1902.

Flonta, Teodor. *A Dictionary of English and Italian Equivalent Proverbs*. Hobart, Tasmania: DeProverbio.com, 2001.

———. *A Dictionary of English and Romance Languages Equivalent Proverbs*. Hobart, Tasmania: DeProverbio.com, 2001.

Florio, John. *The Decameron, containing an hundred pleasant novels. Wittily discoursed betweene seven honourable ladies and three noble gentlemen*. London: printed by Isaac Iaggard, 1620.

———. *The essayes or morall, politike and millitarie discourses of Lord Michaell de Montaigne, Knight of the noble Order of St. Michaell, and one of the gentlemen in ordinary of the French king, Henry the third his chamber. The first booke. First written by him in French. And now done into English by him that hath inviolably vowed his labors to the aeternitie of their honors, whose names he hath severally inscribed on these his consecrated altares*. London: Edward Blount dwelling in Paules churchyard, 1603.

———. *Firste Fruites*. 1578. Amsterdam-New York: Da Capo Press, 1969.

———. *Florio's First Fruites; facsimile reproduction of the original edition*. Ed. Arudel Del Re. Vol. 3.1 (*Memoirs of the Faculty of Literature and Politics*). Formosa, Japan: Taihoku Imperial University, 1936.

———. *Florio his firste fruites which yeelde familiar speech, merie proverbes, wittie sentences, and golden sayings. Also a perfect induction to the Italian and English tongues, as in the table appareth. The like heretofore never by any man published*. London: Dawson Thomas for Woodcock Thomas, 1578.

———. *Florios Second Frutes, to be gathered of twelve trees, of divers but delightsome tastes to the tongues of Italians and Englishmen. To which is annexed his Gardine of Recreation yeelding six thousand Italian Proverbs*. London: Dawson Thomas for Woodcock Thomas, 1591.

———. *Giardino di ricreatione nel quale crescono fronde, fiori e frutti, vaghe, leggiadri, e soavi, sotto nome di sei mila proverbii e piacevoli riboboli italiani, colti e scelti da Giovanni Florio, non solo utili ma dillettevoli per ogni spirito vago della nobil lingua italiana*. London: Dawson Thomas for Woodcock Thomas, 1591.

———. *Giardino di ricreazione*. Ed. Luca Gallesi. Milano: Greco e Greco, 1993.

———. *A letter lately written from Rome, by an Italian gentleman to a freende of his in Lyons in Fraunce, wherein is declared the state of Rome, the suddaine death and sollemne buriall of Pope Gregory the thirteenth, the election of the newe Pope, and the race of life this newe Pope ranne before hee was advanced. Thereto are adioyned the accidentes that have fallen out, not onely in Rome, but in Naples and other parts of the worlde also*. London: by Iohn Charlewoode dwelling in Barbican, 1585.

———. *The new-found politicke. Disclosing the secret natures and dispositions as well of private persons as of statesmen and courtiers; wherein the governments, greatnesse, and power of the most notable kingdomes and common-wealths of the world are discovered and censured. Together with many excellent caveats and rules fit to be observed by those princes and states of Christendome, both Protestants and papists, which have reason to distrust the designes of the King of Spaine, as by the speech of the Duke of Hernia, uttered in the counsell of Spaine, and hereto annexed, may appeare. Written in Italian by Traiano Boccalini and now translated into English for the benefit of this kingdome*. London: printed at Eliot's Court Press for Francis Williams, 1626.

———. *Perpetuall and natural prognostications of the change of weather. Newly translated out of Italian into English by John Florio*. London: Dawson Thomas for Woodcock Thomas, 1591.

Florio, John. *Second Frutes*. 1591. Amsterdam-New York: Da Capo Press, 1969.

———. *A shorte and briefe narration of the two navigations and discoveries to the Northweast partes called Newe Fraunce. First translated out of French into Italian by that famous learned man Giovanni Baptista Ramutius, and now turned into English by Iohn Florio, worthy the reading of all venturers, travellers, and discoverers*. London: by Henry Bynneman, 1580.

———. *A Worlde of Wordes*. Ed. Hermann W. Haller. Toronto: U of Toronto P, 2013.

———. *A Worlde of Wordes, or most copious and exact Dictionarie in Italian and English*. London: Edward Blount, 1598.

Foffano, Francesco. *Il poema cavalleresco dal XV al XVIII secolo*. Milano: Vallardi, 1904.

Folena, Gianfranco. *Quaderni di retorica e poetica. La lingua scorciata: detto, motto, aforisma*. Vol. 2. Padova: Liviana, 1986.

———. "Sulla tradizione dei *Detti piacevoli* attribuiti al Poliziano." *Studi di filologia italiana* 11 (1953): 431–48.

———. *Volgarizzare e tradurre*. Torino: Einaudi, 1994.

Fontanini, Giusto. *Della eloquenza italiana. Ragionamento steso in una lettera al Marchese Giangiuseppe Orsi, aggiuntovi un catalogo delle opere più eccellenti che intorno alle principali arti e facoltà sono state scritte in lingua italiana*. Roma: per Francesco Gonzaga a S. Marcello al Corso, 1706.

Foppa, Giuseppe. *Sopra l'ingannator cade l'inganno, over I due granatieri, farsa giocosa per musica*. Venezia: per il Casali, 1801.

Fornara, Simone. *Breve storia della grammatica italiana*. Roma: Carocci, 2009.

Forni, Pier Massimo. "Come cominciano le novelle del *Decameron*." Malato, *La novella italiana*, 689–700.

Forni, Pier Massimo, and Renzo Bragantini. *The Decameron: A Critical Lexicon*. Trans. Michael Papio. Ed. Christopher Kleinhenz. Tempe: ACMRS, 2019.

———. *Lessico critico decameroniano*. Torino: Boringhieri, 1995.

Forteguerri, Giovanni. *Novelle e ragguaglio sopra gli avvenimenti di Pistoia*. Eds. Tommaso Braccini and Giampaolo Francesconi. Pistoia: Società pistoiese di storia patria, Fondazione Cassa di risparmio di Pistoia e Pescia, 2011.

Fragnito, Gigliola. *La Bibbia al rogo: la censura ecclesiastica e i volgarizzamenti della Scrittura (1471–1605)*. Bologna: Il Mulino, 2015.

———. "La censura ecclesiastica in Italia: volgarizzamenti biblici e letteratura all'Indice. Bilancio degli studi e prospettive di ricerca." *Reading and Censorship in Early Modern Europe (Barcelona, 11–13 dic. 2007).* Eds. Maria José Vega and Julian Weiss. Bellaterra: Universitat Autònoma de Barcelona, 2010. 39–56.

———. *Church, Censorship and Culture in Early Modern Italy.* Trans. Adrian Belton. Cambridge-New York: Cambridge UP, 2001.

Franceschi, Temistocle. "L'atlante paremiologico italiano e la geoparemiologia." S. Trovato, *Proverbi,* 1–22.

———. *Atlante paremiologico italiano: ventimila detti proverbiali raccolti in ogni regione d'Italia.* Alessandria: Edizioni dell'Orso, 2000.

———. "La formula proverbiale." Boggione and Massobrio, ix–xviii.

———. "In margine alle ricerche dell'API." *Studi linguistici offerti a Gabriella Giacomelli dagli amici e dagli allievi.* Eds. Amalia Catagnoti and Gabriella Giacomelli. Padova: Unipress, 1997. 129–45.

———. "Il proverbio e l'API." *Archivio Glottologico Italiano* 63 (1978): 110–47.

———. "Il proverbio e la Scuola Geoparemiologica Italiana." *Paremia* 3 (1994): 27–36.

———, ed. *Ragionamenti intorno al proverbio. Atti del II Congresso internazionale dell'Atlante paremiologico italiano. Andria, 21–24 apr. 2010.* Alessandria: Edizioni dell'Orso, 2011.

Franceschi, Temistocle, et al., eds. *Pagine sparse.* Alessandria: Edizioni dell'Orso, 2008.

Franciosini, Lorenzo. *Vocabulario italiano e spagnuolo, nel quale con agevolezza si dichiarano e con propietà convertono tutte le voci toscane in castigliano e le castigliane in toscano, con infinite frasi e molti proverbi; s'è aggiunto la grammatica della lingua spagnuola [et] alcuni dialoghi che facilitano sommamente l'apprendere l'uno e l'altro idioma.* Venezia: presso il Barezi, 1645.

Frank, Thomas. "The First Italian Grammars of the English Language." *Historiographia Linguistica* 10 (1983): 25–61.

Frantz, David. "Florio's Use of Contemporary Italian Literature in *A Worlde of Wordes*." *Dictionaries: Journal of the Dictionary Society of America* 1 (1979): 47–56.

———. "Negotiating Florio's *A Worlde of Wordes*." *Dictionaries: Journal of the Dictionary Society of America* 18 (1997): 1–32.

Franzero, Carlo Maria. *John Florio a Londra ai tempi di Shakespeare.* Parma: Guanda, 1969.

Franzese, Rosa. "Luoghi favolosi nella *Posilicheata* di Sarnelli." *Napoli Nobilissima* 23 (1984): 114–23.

Works Consulted

Fries, Udo. "Dialogue in instructional texts." *Historical Pragmatics. Anglistentag (1997 Giessen). Proceedings.* Eds. Raimund Borgmeier, et al. Trier: Wissenschaftlicher Verlag Trier, 1998. 85–96.

Frizzi, Giuseppe. *Dizionario dei frizzetti popolari fiorentini.* Roma: Multigrafica, 1975.

Fulco, Giorgio. "La letteratura dialettale napoletana. Giulio Cesare Cortese e Giovan Battista Basile. Pompeo Sarnelli." *Storia della letteratura italiana.* Ed. Enrico Malato. Vol. 5. Roma: Salerno Editrice, 1997. 813–67.

Fumagalli, Giuseppe. *Chi l'ha detto?: tesoro di citazioni italiane e straniere, di origine letteraria e storica, ordinate e annotate.* Milano: Hoepli, 1989.

Fumagalli, Giuseppina. *La fortuna dell'Orlando furioso in Italia nel secolo XVI.* Ferrara: Zuffi, 1912.

Galiani, Ferdinando. *Del dialetto napoletano. Edizione seconda corretta ed accresciuta.* Napoli: Porcelli, 1779.

———. *Vocabolario delle parole del dialetto napoletano, che più si scostano dal dialetto toscano con alcune ricerche etimologiche sulle medesime degli accademici Filopatridi.* Napoli: Porcelli, 1789.

Gallagher, John. "The Italian London of John North: Cultural Contact and Linguistic Encounter in Early Modern England." *Renaissance Quarterly* 70 (2017): 88–131.

Gambari, Stefano. "La «Selva» di proverbi di Giulio Cesare Croce." *«Strada maestra». Quaderni della Biblioteca comunale «G. C. Croce» di San Giovanni in Persiceto* 36–37 (1994): 85–144.

Gamberini, Spartaco. "I primi strumenti dell'italianistica in Inghilterra." *Belfagor* 24.4 (1969): 446–70.

———. *Lo studio dell'italiano in Inghilterra nel '500 e nel '600.* Messina-Firenze: Casa Editrice G. D'Anna, 1970.

Garavelli, Bice Mortara. *Manuale di retorica.* Firenze: Giunti, 2012.

Garzoni, Tommaso. *La piazza universale di tutte le professioni del mondo.* Ed. Paolo Cherchi. Torino: Einaudi, 1996.

Gehl, Paul. *Humanism for Sale. Making and Marketing Schoolbooks in Italy, 1450–1650.* Chicago: Newberry Library Center for Renaissance Studies, 2008–. www.humanismforsale.org/. Accessed 8 June 2019.

Genette, Gerard, and Marie Maclean. "Introduction to the Paratext." *New Literary History* 2 (1991): 261–79.

Getto, Giovanni. *Il Barocco letterario in Italia. Barocco in prosa e poesia.* Milano: Mondadori, 2000.

Geudens, Christophe, and Toon Van Hal. "The Role of Vernacular Proverbs in Latin Language Acquisition, c. 1200–1600." *Historiographia Linguistica* 44.2 (2017): 278–305.

Ghinassi, Ghino. "Incontri tra toscano e volgari settentrionali in epoca rinascimentale." *Archivio glottologico italiano* 61 (1976): 86–100.

Ghirelli, Antonio. *Storia di Napoli*. Torino: Einaudi, 1973.

Giannetto, Nella. "Madonna Filippa tra 'Casus' e 'Controversia'. Lettura della Novella VI, 7 del *Decameron*." *Studi sul Boccaccio* 32 (2004): 81–100.

Gibellini, Pietro. "Satira e dialetto dalle origini all'età romantica." *Letteratura e dialetti* 3 (2010): 11–26.

Giglio, Raffaele. "Il cunto 'dotto' di Pompeo Sarnelli." *La tradizione del "cunto" da Giovan Battista Basile a Domenico Rea. Giornate di studio, 19 e 20 genn. 2006, Palazzo du Mesnil*. Ed. Caterina De Caprio. Napoli: Edizioni Libreria Dante & Descartes, 2007. 141–56.

Gimma, Giacinto. *Elogi Accademici della società degli spensierati di Rossano*. Napoli: Carlo Troise, 1703.

Giovanardi, Claudio. "Pedante, arcipedante, pedantissimo. Note sulla morfologia derivativa nella commedia del Cinquecento." *Nuovi Annali della Facoltà di Magistero dell'Università di Messina* 7 (1989): 1–22.

Giraldi, Giambattista Cinzio. *Discorsi di messer Giovambattista Giraldi Cinthio nobile ferrarese e segretario dell'illustrissimo et eccellentissimo Duca di Ferrara intorno al comporre de i romanzi, delle comedie, e delle tragedie, e di altre maniere di poesie*. Venezia: appresso Gabriel Giolito de' Ferrari et fratelli, 1554.

Girotto, Carlo Alberto. "Novelle, facezie, apoftegmi: ancora sul tessuto narrativo della «Seconda libraria» di Anton Francesco Doni." *Archivio novellistico italiano* 1 (2016): 68–113.

———. "Schede sull'uso dei proverbi nelle opere di Anton Francesco Doni." Pignatti and Crimi, 113–38.

Giusti, Giuseppe. *Proverbi*. Ed. Elisabetta Benucci. Firenze: Le lettere, 2011.

———. *Voci di lingua parlata*. Ed. Piero Fiorelli. Firenze: Accademia della Crusca, 2014.

Givón, Talmy, and Bertram Malle. *The Evolution of Language out of Pre-Language*. Amsterdam-Philadelphia: John Benjamins Publisher, 2002.

Gleijeses, Vittorio. *I proverbi di Napoli con ventiquattro litografie fuori testo di Gatti e Dura*. Napoli: Società editrice napoletana, 1978.

Gluski, Jerzy. *Proverbs: A Comparative Book of English, French, German, Italian, Spanish, and Russian Proverbs with a Latin Appendix*. Amsterdam-London-New York: Elsevier, 1971.

Works Consulted

Goidànich, Pietro Gabriele. *L'origine e le forme della dittongazione romanza. Le qualità d'accento in sillaba mediana nelle lingue indeuropee.* Halle: Niemeyer, 1907.

Gorni, Guglielmo. "Un'ipotesi sull'origine dell'ottava rima." *Metrica* 1 (1978): 79–94.

Grande dizionario della lingua italiana (GDLI). Eds. Salvatore Battaglia and Giorgio Bàrberi Squarotti. Torino: UTET, 1961–2002.

Grantham, Henry. *An Italian grammer written in Latin by Scipio Lentulo a Neapolitane and turned in English by Henry Grantham.* London: Thomas Vautrollier, 1575.

Gratet-Duplessis, Pierre-Alexandre. *Bibliographie parémiologique. Études bibliographiques et littéraires sur les ouvrages, fragmens d'ouvrages et opuscules spécialement consacrés aux proverbes dans toutes les langues, suives d'un appendice contenant un choix de curiosités parémiographiques.* Paris: Potier, 1847.

Green, Thomas, and William Pepicello. "The Proverb and Riddle as Folk Enthymemes." *Proverbium* 3 (1986): 33–45.

Greenblatt, Stephen, ed. *The Forms of Power and the Power of Forms in the Renaissance.* Norman: University of Oklahoma, 1982.

———, ed. *Representing the English Renaissance.* Berkeley-Los Angeles: U of California P, 1988.

Grendler, Marcella, and Paul Grendler. "The Survival of Erasmus in Italy." *Erasmus in English* 8 (1976): 2–22.

Grendler, Paul. *Schooling in Renaissance Italy. Literacy and Learning, 1300-1600.* Baltimore: Johns Hopkins UP, 1989.

Grimaldi, Mirko. "Atlante Paremiologico Italiano (API), questionario e metodi di ricerca sul campo." S. Trovato, *Proverbi*, 23–43.

———. "L'ironia nei detti proverbiali fra citazione e metafora." *Lares* 62 (1997): 521–43.

Guaragnella, Pasquale. "Motti, sentenze e proverbi in «novella». Su *Lo cunto de li cunti* di Giambattista Basile." *InVerbis* 2 (2011): 123–42.

———. "Rassegna di proverbi e sentenze ne *Lo cunto de li cunti* di Giambattista Basile." Franceschi, *Ragionamenti*, 329–46.

Guazzo, Stefano. *La civil conversatione del signor Stefano Guazzo, gentilhuomo di Casale di Monferrato, divisa in quattro libri.* Venezia: presso Altobello Salicato, 1574.

———. *Dialoghi piacevoli del sig. Stefano Guazzo.* Venezia: Bertano, 1586.

Guazzotti, Paola, and Maria Federica Oddera. *Il grande dizionario dei proverbi italiani.* Bologna: Zanichelli, 2010.

Guerrini, Olindo. *La vita e le opere di Giulio Cesare Croce*. Bologna: Zanichelli, 1879.

Guicciardini, Francesco. *Ricordi*. 1530. Ed. Carlo Varotti. Roma: Carocci, 2013.

Guicciardini, Lodovico. *Detti et fatti piacevoli et gravi di diversi principi, filosofi, et cortigiani raccolti dal Guicciardini et ridotti a moralità*. Ed. Francesco Sansovino. Venezia: appresso Domenico Nicolini, 1565.

———. *L'ore di ricreazione*. 1568. Ed. Anne-Marie Van Passen. Roma: Bulzoni; Leuven: Leuven UP, 1990.

Guidotti, Gloria. "I 'proverbi' e il *Vocabolario degli Accademici della Crusca* del 1612." *Paremia* 6 (1997): 313–16.

Haemerkken (à Kempis), Thomas. *Of the imitation of Christ. Four books*. London: Oxford UP, 1996.

Haller, Hermann W. *La festa delle lingue: la letteratura dialettale in Italia*. Roma: Carocci, 2002.

———. "John Florio e Claudius Holyband. I dialoghi didattici di due maestri nell'Inghilterra rinascimentale." *Maestri di lingue tra metà Cinquecento e metà Seicento. Atti del convegno di studi. Università per Stranieri di Siena, 12–13 apr. 2018*. Eds. Giada Mattarucco and Félix San Vicente. Firenze: Le lettere, 2018. 59–74.

———. "Lingua, società e letteratura dialettale in Italia." *Atti dell'Istituto veneto di scienze, lettere ed arti. Classe di scienze morali, lettere ed arti* 150 (1991–92): 399–410.

———. *The Other Italy: The Literary Canon in Dialect*. Toronto: U of Toronto P, 1999.

Halpert, Herbert. "Folktale and 'Wellerism'—A note." *Southern Folklore Quarterly* 7 (1943): 75–76.

Hans, Walther. *Proverbia sententiaeque Latinitatis Medii Aevi; Lateinische Sprichwörter und Sentenzen des Mittelalters in alphabetischer Anordnung*. Göttingen: Vandenhoeck & Ruprecht, 1963–69.

Hay, Denys. *Polydore Vergil: Renaissance Historian and Man of Letters*. Oxford: Clarendon Press, 1952.

Haym, Nicolas François. *Biblioteca italiana; o sia Notizia de' libri rari italiani divisa in quattro parti, cioè istoria, poesia, prose, arti e scienze. In questa impressione corretta, ampliata e di giudizi intorno alle migliori opere arricchita. Con tavole copiosissime e necessarie*. Milano: appresso Giuseppe Galeazzi, 1771–73.

———. *Notizia de' libri rari nella lingua italiana divisa in quattro parti principali; cioè, istoria, poesia, prose, arti e scienze*. London: Jacob Tonson-Giovanni Watts, 1726.

Works Consulted

Hazlitt, William Carew. *English proverbs and proverbial phrases collected from the most authentic sources alphabetically arranged and annotated with much matter not previously published.* London: J. R. Smith, 1869.

Healey, John. *Epictetus his manuall. And Cebes his table. Out of the Greeke originall.* London: Thomas Thorpe, 1610.

Hermans, Theo. "The Task of the Translator in the European Renaissance." *Translating Literature.* Ed. Susan Bassnett. Cambridge: Brewer, 1997. 14–40.

Hernando Cuadrado, Luis Alberto. "Las *Cartas en refranes* de Blasco de Garay. Aspectos paremiológicos y sintácticos." *Boletín de la Real Academia de Extremadura de las Letras y las Artes* 17 (2009): 181–92.

Heywood, John. *A dialogue conteinyng the nomber in effect of all the prouerbes in the Englishe tongue, compacte in a matter concernyng two maner of mariages, made and set foorth by Iohnn Heywood.* London: imprinted at London in Fletestrete by Thomas Berthelet printer, 1546.

———. *John Heywood's A Dialogue of Proverbs. Edited, with Introduction, Commentary, and Indexes by Rudolph Habenicht.* Berkeley-Los Angeles: U of California P, 1963.

———. *Proverbs, epigrams, and miscellanies, comprising a dialogue of the effectual proverbs in the English tongue concerning marriages; first hundred epigrams; three hundred epigrams on three hundred proverbs; the fifth hundred epigrams; a sixth hundred epigrams; miscellanies; ballads; notebook and word-list.* Ed. John Farmer. London: Early English Drama Society, 1906.

Hock, Ronald, and Edward O'Neil. *The Chreia and Ancient Rhetoric. Classroom Exercises.* Atlanta: Society of Biblical Literature, 2002.

Hockett, Charles Francis. "Idiom Formation." *For Roman Jakobson. Essays on the occasion of his sixtieth birthday, 11 Oct. 1956.* Eds. Morris Halle, et al. The Hague: Monton, 1956. 222–29.

Holtus, Günter, et al., eds. *Lexikon der Romanistischen Linguistik.* Tübingen: Niemeyer, 1988.

Holyband, Claudius. *Campo di fior, or else, The flourie field of foure languages of M. Claudius Desainliens, alias Holyband. For the furtherance of the learners of Latine, French, English, but chieflie of the Italian tongue.* London: Thomas Vautrollier, 1583.

———. *The French Littelton. A most easie, perfect, and absolute way to learne the French tongue.* London: Thomas Vautrollier, 1566.

———. *The French Schoole-master. Wherin is most plainlie shewed the true and perfect way of pronouncinge the Frenche tongue, without any helpe of maister or teacher, set foorthe for the furtherance of all those whiche *doo studie privatly in their owne study or houses, unto the which is annexed a vocabularie for al such woordes as bee used in common talkes*. London: by William How for Abraham Veale, 1573.

———. *The Italian Schoole-maister, contayning rules for the perfect pronouncing of the Italian tongue, with familiar speeches and certaine phrases taken out of the best Italian authors. And a fine Tuscan historie called Arnalt and Lucenda. Set forth by Claudius Holliband Gentlemen of Bourbonnois*. London: by Thomas Purfoot, 1581.

———. *The pretie and wittie historie of Arnalt and Lucenda, with certen rules and dialogues set foorth for the learner of the Italian tong and dedicated unto the worshipfull Sir Hierom Bowes Knight. By Claudius Hollyband scholemaster, teaching in Paules Churcheyarde by the signe of the Lucrece*. London: by Thomas Purfoot, 1575.

Horatius, Quintus Flaccus. *Satires, Epistles and Ars poetica*. Trans. Rushton Fairclough. Cambridge, MA: Harvard UP, 2005.

Howatt, Anthony Philip Reid, and Henry George Widdowson. "«Refugiate in a strange country»: the refugee language teachers in Elizabethan London." *A history of English language teaching*. Oxford-New York: Oxford UP, 2011. 18–36.

Howell, James. *Lexicon Tetraglotton, an English-French-Italian-Spanish dictionary, whereunto is adjoined a large nomenclature of the proper terms (in all the four) belonging to several arts and sciences, to recreations, to professions both liberal and mechanick, and co., divided into fiftie two sections; with another volume of the choicest proverbs in all the said toungs (consisting of divers compleat tomes) and the English translated into the other three to take off the reproach which useth to be cast upon her, that she is but barren in this point and those proverbs she hath are but flat and empty. Moreover, there are sundry familiar letters and verses running all in proverbs with a particular tome of the British or old Cambrian sayed sawes and adages, which the author thought fit to annex hereunto and make intelligible for their great antiquity and weight. Lastly, there are five centuries of new sayings, which, in tract of time, may serve for proverbs to posterity. By the labours and lucubrations of James Howell*. London: printed by John Grismond for Samuel Thomson at the Bishop head in St. Paul's Churchyard, 1660.

Huffman, Clifford Chalbers. *Elizabethan Impressions: John Wolfe and his Press*. New York: AMS Press, 1988.

Hunter, George. "The Marking of Sententiae in Elizabethan Printed Plays, Poems, and Romances." *The Library* 6.3–4 (1951): 171–88.

Hutcheon, Linda. *Irony's Edge: The Theory and Politics of Irony*. London-New York: Routledge, 1995.

Iamartino, Giovanni. *Da Thomas a Baretti: i primi due secoli della lessicografia angloitaliana*. Milano: Pubblicazioni dell'I.S.U. Università Cattolica, 1994.

Imparato, Emilia. *La prima giornata del Fuggilozio*. Napoli: Società editrice napoletana, 1979.

Indovinelli, riboboli, passerotti, e farfalloni. Nuovamente messi insieme e la maggior parte non più stampati, parte in prosa e parte in rima, et hora posti in luce per ordine d'alfabeto. Con alcune cicalate di donne di sentenzie et proverbi posti nel fine. N.p.: n.p., c. 1600.

Isidore of Seville. *Isidore of Seville's Etymologies. The complete English translation of Isidori Hispalensis Episcopi Etymologiarum sive Originum Libri XX*. Trans. Priscilla Throop. Charlotte, VT: MedievalMS, 2005.

Iurilli, Antonio. "Paremìa e favola. La *Bestiarum schola* di Pompeo Sarnelli." Franceschi, *Ragionamenti*, 315–28.

———. "I proverbi e le favole. La *Bestiarum schola* di Pompeo Sarnelli." *Gutta cavat lapidem. Indagini fraseologiche e paremiologiche*. Eds. Elena Dal Maso and Carmen Navarro. Mantova: Universitas studiorum, 2016. 207–22.

Jakobson, Roman. "Results of a joint conference of anthropologists and linguists." *Selected Writings. Volume II, Word and Language*. Berlin: De Gruyter, 1971. 554–67.

Javitch, Daniel. *Proclaiming a Classic: The Canonization of «Orlando Furioso»*. Princeton: Princeton UP, 1991.

Jeffery, Violet May. *John Lyly and the Italian Renaissance*. New York: Russell & Russell, 1969.

Jente, Richard. "El refrán." *Folklore Americas* 7 (1947): 1–11.

Jolles, André. *Simple forms*. Trans. Peter Schwartz. London-New York: Verso, 2017.

Jones, William. "Two Learned Italians in Elizabethan England." *Italica* 32 (1955): 242–47.

Kealy, Sean. *The wisdom books of the Bible—Proverbs, Job, Ecclesiastes, Ben Sira, Wisdom of Solomon. A Survey of the History of their Interpretation*. Lewiston, NY: Edwin Mellen Press, 2012.

Kelso, James. "Proverbs." *Encyclopedia of Religion and Ethics*. Eds. James Hastings, et al. Edinburgh: Clark; New York: Charles Scribner's Sons, 1908–26. 412–15.

Kindstrand, Jan Fredrik. "The Greek Concept of Proverbs." *Eranos. Acta Philologica Suecana Uppsala* 76.2 (1978): 71–85.

Kirkham, Victoria. "Morale." Forni and Bragantini, *Lessico critico decameroniano*, 249–68.

Kirshenblatt-Gimblett, Barbara. "Toward a Theory of Proverb Meaning." *The Wisdom of Many: Essays on the Proverb*. Eds. Wolfgang Mieder and Alan Dundes. New York: Garland, 1981. 111–21.

Knox, Norman. "Irony." *Dictionary of the History of Ideas. Studies of Selected Pivotal Ideas*. Ed. Philip Wiener. Vol. 2. New York: Charles Scribner's Sons, 1973–74. 626–34.

Kristeller, Paul Oskar. *Renaissance Thought and the Arts. Collected Essays*. Princeton: Princeton UP, 1990.

Labov, William. *Sociolinguistic Patterns*. Philadelphia: U of Pennsylvania P, 1972.

La Mantia, Benito, and Gabriella Cucca. *Libri proibiti. Quattro secoli di censura cattolica*. Viterbo: Stampa Alternativa, 2007.

Lando, Ortensio. *Paradossi, cioè sententie fuori del comun parere novellamente venute in luce, opra non men dotta che piacevole et in due parti separata*. Lione: per Gioanni Pullon da Trino, 1543.

Langland, William. *Piers Plowman*. Eds. Talbot Donaldson and George Kane. London: Athlone Press, 1988.

Langlotz, Andreas. *Idiomatic Creativity: A Cognitive-Linguistic Model of Idiom-Representation and Idiom-Variation in English*. Amsterdam-Philadelphia: John Benjamins Publisher, 2006.

Lapucci, Carlo. *Come disse... Dizionario delle facezie proverbiali della lingua italiana*. Firenze: Valmartina, 1978.

———. *Dizionario dei proverbi italiani: con saggio introduttivo sul proverbio e la sua storia*. Firenze: Le Monnier, 2006.

———. *Per modo di dire. Dizionario dei modi di dire della lingua italiana*. Firenze: Valmartina, 1969.

Lardelli, Giovanni. *Italienische Phraseologie. Manualetto degli italicismi, proverbi e modi proverbiali più frequenti con relativi temi italiani e tedeschi ad uso delle scuole e per lo studio privato*. Davos: Hugo Richter Verlagsbuchhandlung, 1885.

Larson, Pär. "Pai Gomez Charinho al di là del bene e del male." *Revista de Literatura Medieval* 28 (2016): 225–34.

Lausberg, Heinrich. *Elementi di retorica*. Bologna: Il Mulino, 1969.

Lavinio, Cristina. *La magia della fiaba: tra oralità e scrittura*. Firenze: La Nuova Italia, 1993.

Lawrence, Jason. *"Who the Devil taught there so much Italian?" Italian Language Learning and Literary Imitation in Early Modern England*. Manchester: Manchester UP, 2005.

Lazar, Kristina. "Stilemi manieristici in un capolavoro trecentesco: il *Decameron* censurato di Luigi Groto (1541–1584)." *Giovanni Boccaccio. Tradizione, interpretazione e fortuna*. Ed. Antonio Ferracin. Udine: Forum, 2014. 393–404.

Lean, Vincent Stuckey. *Lean's collectanea; collections of proverbs (English and foreign), folklore, and superstitions, also compilations towards dictionaries of proverbial phrases and words, old and disused*. Bristol: James William Arrowsmith, 1902–04.

Ledgeway, Adam. *Grammatica diacronica del napoletano*. Tübingen: Niemeyer, 2009.

Lefevere, André. "Translation: Its genealogy in the West." *Translation, history, and culture*. Eds. Susan Bassnett and André Lefevere. London-New York: Pinter Publishers, 1990. 14–28.

Lelli, Emanuele, ed. *Paroimiakòs. Il proverbio in Grecia e a Roma*. Vols. 2–3. Pisa-Roma: Serra, 2010.

Lena, Francesco. *Proverbi italiani e latini raccolti già da Francesco Lena della Congregazione della Madre di Dio*. Bologna: per il Longhi, 1694.

———. *Saggio di proverbi o detti sentenziosi italiani e latini, raccolti da diversi autori per uso della gioventù studiosa*. Lucca: Iacinto Paci, 1674.

Leo, Ulrich. *Angelica ed i "migliori plettri". Appunti allo stile della Controriforma*. Krefeld: Scherpe, 1953.

Leopardi, Giacomo. *Poesie e prose*. Ed. Siro Attilio Nulli. Milano: Hoepli, 1997.

———. *Tutte le opere. Volgarizzamenti in prosa*. Eds. Enrico Ghidetti and Walter Binni. Firenze: Sansoni, 1993.

Lepschy, Giulio. *Tradurre e traducibilità. Quindici seminari sulla traduzione*. Torino: Nino Aragno Editore, 2009.

———. "Traduzione." *Enciclopedia Einaudi*. Ed. Ruggiero Romano. Vol. 14. Torino: Einaudi, 1981. 446–59.

Lessico Etimologico Italiano (LEI). Eds. Max Pfister and Wolfgang Schweickard. Wiesbaden: Reichert, 1979–.

Lessicografia della Crusca in rete, Accademia della Crusca. www.lessicografia.it. Accessed 8 June 2019.

Lévi, Israel. "Sirach, The Wisdom of Jesus the Son of." *The Jewish Encyclopedia* 11 (1905): 388–97.

Lewalski, Barbara Kiefer. *Renaissance Genres: Essays on Theory, History, and Interpretation*. Cambridge, MA: Harvard UP, 1986.

Lievsay, John Leon. *The Elizabethan Image of Italy*. Ithaca: published for the Folger Shakespeare Library by Cornell UP, 1964.

———. *The Englishman's Italian Books, 1550–1700.* Philadelphia: U of Pennsylvania P, 1969.

———. "Florio and His Proverbs." *Stefano Guazzo and the English Renaissance, 1575–1675.* Chapel Hill: U of North Carolina P, 1961. 127–32.

Limentani, Alberto. *Il racconto epico: funzioni della lassa e dell'ottava.* Firenze: Olschki, 1984.

Lippi, Lorenzo. *Liber proverbiorum di Lorenzo Lippi.* Ed. Paolo Rondinelli. Bologna: Bononia UP, 2011.

Lombardi, Nicolò. *La cucceide, o puro la reggia de li ciucce conzarvata, poemma arrojeco di Nicolò Lombardi.* Napoli: Porcelli, 1783.

Lovarini, Emilio. "Per la storia della paremiografia italiana nei secoli XV e XVI." *Il libro e la stampa* 4 (1910): 118–20; 125–42.

Luchi, Marco. *Il patrimonio paremiaco nella "Cena di Trimalchione." Proverbi e modi di dire in funzione della mimesi linguistica in Petronio.* 2015. Università degli Studi di Siena, MA thesis.

Lurati, Ottavio. *Per modo di dire... Storia della lingua e antropologia nelle locuzioni italiane ed europee.* Bologna: CLUEB, 2002.

Luzio, Alessandro. "L'*Orlandino* di Pietro Aretino." *Giornale di filologia romanza* 6 (1880): 68–84.

Lytton Sells, Arthur. *The Paradise of Travellers. The Italian Influence on Englishmen in the Seventeenth Century.* Bloomington: Indiana UP, 1964.

Maffei, Sonia. "«Qua bisogna invenzione non piccola…». Il manoscritto delle *Nuove pitture* del Doni e i suoi percorsi di lettura." *Le nuove pitture del Doni fiorentino. Libro primo consacrato al mirabil signore donno Aloise da Este illustrissimo et reverendissimo.* Eds. Sonia Maffei, et al. Napoli: La stanza delle scritture; Città del Vaticano: Biblioteca apostolica vaticana, 2006. 157–220.

Maiden, Martin. "Italo-Romance Metaphony and the Tuscan Diphthongs." *Transactions of the Philological Society* 114.2 (2016): 198–232.

Maino, Paolo. "Un caso particolare tra i podromi del *Vocabolario della Crusca*: la lingua della censura nella rassettatura del *Decameron* di Salviati." Tomasin, 105–15.

Malato, Enrico. "La letteratura dialettale campana." *Lingua e dialetto nella tradizione letteraria italiana. Atti del Convegno di Salerno, 5–6 novembre 1993.* Roma: Salerno Editrice, 1996. 255–72.

———. *Vocabolarietto napoletano.* Napoli: Edizioni scientifiche italiane, 1965.

Works Consulted

Malato, Enrico, ed. *La novella italiana. Atti del convegno di Caprarola, 19–24 sett. 1988*. Roma: Salerno Editrice, 1989.

Malavasi, Massimiliano. "«Son sentenze i proverbi arciprovate». Il proverbio nel poema eroicomico secentesco." Pignatti and Crimi, 395–427.

Malerba, Luigi, and Giovanna Bonardi. *Proverbi italiani*. Roma: Istituto Poligrafico e Zecca dello Stato, 1999.

Mancini, Anna Maria. "L'Atlante Paremiologico Italiano (API): un'innovazione nello studio del proverbio." *Italienische Studien* 4 (1981): 141–49.

———. "Esperienze di ricerche dialettologiche e paremiologiche." *Quaderni dell'Istituto di Linguistica dell'Università di Urbino* 4 (1986): 369–90.

Mango, Achille. "Wellerismi e farsa cavaiola." *Problemi* 9 (1968): 425–27.

Manley, Lawrence. "Proverbs, Epigrams, and Urbanity in Renaissance London." *English Literary Renaissance* 15.3 (1985): 247–76.

Manni, Paola. *Il Trecento toscano: la lingua di Dante, Petrarca e Boccaccio*. Bologna: Il Mulino, 2003.

Maraschio, Nicoletta. "L'italiano parlato nell'Europa del Cinquecento." *Eteroglossia e plurilinguismo letterario. L'italiano in Europa. Atti del XXI Convegno interuniversitario di Bressanone (2–4 lug. 1993)*. Eds. Furio Brugnolo and Vincenzo Orioles. Vol. 1. Roma: Il Calamo, 2002. 51–69.

———. *Trattati di fonetica del Cinquecento*. Firenze: Accademia della Crusca, 1992.

Maraschio, Nicoletta, and Marco Biffi. *La lingua di Giovanni Boccaccio*. Firenze: Università di Firenze, 2002.

Marazzini, Claudio. "Grammatica e scuola dal XVI al XIX secolo." *Norma e lingua in Italia: alcune riflessioni fra passato e presente*. Milano: Istituto Lombardo di Scienze e Lettere, 1997. 7–27.

———. "The teaching of Italian in 15th and 16th century Europe." *History of the language science. An international handbook on the evolution of the study of language from the beginnings to the present*. Ed. Sylvain Auroux. Vol. 1. Berlin: De Gruyter, 2000. 699–705.

Marchiaro, Michaelangiola, and Stefano Zamponi, eds. *Boccaccio letterato. Atti del convegno internazionale. Firenze-Certaldo, 10–12 ott. 2013*. Firenze: Accademia della Crusca, 2015.

Marcozzi, Luca. "*Minima adnotanda* sui *Motti* di Pietro Bembo." Pignatti and Crimi, 47-65.

Margolin, Jean-Claude. *I Sileni di Alcibiade*. Trans. Stefano Ugo Baldassarri. Napoli: Liguori, 2002.

Marigo, Aristide. *Il "cursus" nella prosa latina dalle origini cristiane ai tempi di Dante*. Padova: Penada, 1932.

Marini, Paolo. "«Più pro fa il pane asciutto in casa sua...» Formule proverbiali e sentenziose in Pietro Aretino." Pignatti and Crimi, 67–111.

Marini, Quinto. *Il Dialogo di Salomone e Marcolfo*. Roma: Salerno Editrice, 1991.

Marquale, Giovanni. *Diverse imprese accomodate a diverse moralità, con versi che i loro significati dichiarano insieme con molte altre nella lingua italiana non più tradotte, tratte da gli Emblemi dell'Alciato*. Lione: Mathias Bonhomme, 1551.

Marrapodi, Pietro, ed. *Intertestualità shakespeariane. Il Cinquecento italiano e il Rinascimento inglese*. Roma: Bulzoni, 2003.

———, ed. *Shakespeare and Intertextuality: The Transition of Cultures Between Italy and England in the Early Modern Period*. Roma: Bulzoni, 2000.

Martinelli, Rita. "Notizie su Raffaele Tauro." *Studi bitontini* 30–31 (1980): 136–41.

Martorana, Pietro. *Notizie biografiche e bibliografiche degli scrittori del dialetto napolitano*. Bologna: Forni, 1874.

Matarrese, Tina. *Parole e forme dei cavalieri boiardeschi: dall'«Inamoramento de Orlando» all'«Orlando innamorato»*. Novara: Interlinea Edizioni, 2004.

———. "Saggio di *koinè* cancelleresca." *Koinè in Italia dalle origini al Cinquecento. Atti del convegno di Milano e Pavia, 25–26 sett. 1987*. Ed. Glauco Sanga. Bergamo: Pierluigi Lubrina, 1991. 241–62.

———. "Il volgare a Ferrara fra corte e cancelleria." *Rivista di Letteratura Italiana* 8 (1990): 515–60.

Matthiessen, Francis Otto. *Translation: An Elizabethan Art*. Cambridge, MA: Harvard UP, 1965.

Maylender, Michele. *Storia delle Accademie d'Italia*. Bologna: Licinio Cappelli Editore, 1926–30.

Mazzoni, Francesco. *Il Boccaccio nelle culture e letterature nazionali*. Firenze: Olschki, 1978.

Mazzotta, Giuseppe. *The World at Play in Boccaccio's «Decameron»*. Princeton: Princeton UP, 2014.

Mazzucchelli, Giammaria. *Gli scrittori d'Italia cioè notizie storiche e critiche intorno alle vite e agli scritti dei letterati italiani del Conte Giammaria Mazzucchelli bresciano*. Brescia: presso Giambactista Bossini, 1753–63.

Melis, Luisa. "Pertinenza della struttura tema/rema nell'analisi della frase proverbiale." *Paremia* 6 (1997): 377–82.

Ménage, Gilles. *Le origini della lingua italiana, compilate dal Signore Egidio Menagio, gentiluomo francese. Colle giunta de' modi di dire italiani, raccolti e dichiarati dal medesimo.* Paris: S. Mabre-Cramoisy, 1669.

Menchi, Silvana Seidel. *Erasmo in Italia, 1520–1580.* Torino: Boringhieri, 1987.

Menichetti, Aldo. *Metrica italiana. Fondamenti metrici, prosodia, rima.* Padova: Editrice Antenore, 1993.

Menza, Salvatore. *Il paraverbo: l'interiezione come sottoclasse del verbo.* Alessandria: Edizioni dell'Orso, 2006.

Merbury, Charles. *A briefe discourse of royall monarchie, as of the best common weale, wherein in the subiect may beholde the sacred maiestie of the princes most royall estate. Written by Charles Merbury Gentlemen in duetifull reverence of her Maiesties most princely Highnesse. Whereunto is added by the same gentlemen a collection of Italian proverbs, in benefite of such as are studious of that language.* London: Thomas Vautrollier, 1581.

———. *Proverbi Vulgari: A i nobili et illustri signori di corte et altri gentil'huomini honorati della lingua italiana intendenti.* Ed. Charles Speroni. Vol. 28.3. Berkeley-Los Angeles: U of California P, 1946. 63–157.

Meschonnic, Henri. "Les proverbes, actes de discours." *Revue des sciences humaines* 163 (1976): 419–30.

Messina Fajardo, Luisa. *Paremiografía, paremiología y literatura.* Roma: Nuova Cultura, 2012.

Meyer, Paul. *La manière de langage qui enseigne à parler et à écrire le français. Modèles de conversations composés en Angleterre à la fin du XIVe siècle et publiés d'après le ms. du musée britannique Harl. 3988.* Paris: Franck, 1873.

Mieder, Wolfgang. *International Bibliography of Paremiography. Collections of Proverbs, Proverbial Expressions and Comparisons, Quotations, Graffiti, Slang, and Wellerisms.* Burlington, VT: University of Vermont, 2011.

———. *Proverbs in Literature: An International Bibliography.* Bern: Peter Lang, 1978.

———. *Selected Writings on Proverbs by Archer Taylor.* Helsinki: Suomalainen Tiedeakatemia, Academia scientiarum fennica, 1975.

———. "Wellerisms." *American Proverbs: A Study of Texts and Contexts.* Bern: Peter Lang, 1989. 223–38.

Mieder, Wolfgang, and Alan Dundes, eds. *The Wisdom of Many: Essays on the Proverb.* New York: Garland, 1981.

Mieder, Wolfgang, and Stewart Kingsbury. *A Dictionary of Wellerisms*. Oxford-New York: Oxford UP, 1994.

Mieder, Wolfgang, and Anna Tóthné Litovkina. *Twisted Wisdom: Modern Anti-Proverbs*. Burlington: University of Vermont, 1999.

Migliorini, Bruno. *The Italian language*. Trans. Griffith Gwynfor. London-Boston: Faber and Faber, 1984.

———. *Storia della lingua italiana*. Firenze: Sansoni, 1961.

Miller, Clarence. "The Logic and Rhetoric of Proverbs in Erasmus's *Praise of Folly*." *Essays on the Works of Erasmus*. Ed. Richard DeMolen. New Haven: Yale UP, 1978. 83–98.

Miniati, Valeria, and Lucrezia Porto Bucciarelli. "Osservazioni su alcune strutture paremiologiche." *Il dialetto dall'oralità alla scrittura. Atti del XIII Convegno per gli studi dialettali italiani (Catania-Nicosia, 28 sett. 1981)*. Pisa: Pacini, 1984. 107–23.

Mizzau, Marina. *L'ironia: la contraddizione consentita*. Milano: Feltrinelli, 1986.

Moll, Otto. *Sprichvörter bibliographie*. Frankfurt am Main: Klostermann, 1958.

Monosini, Agnolo. *Angeli Monosinii Floris Italicae Linguae libri novem, quinq[ue] de congruentia Florentini, sive Etrusci sermonis cum Graeco-Romanoque, ubi praeter dictiones, phraseis, ac syntaxin conferruntur plus mille proverbia et explicantur. in quatuor ultimis enodatae sunt pro uberiori copia ad tres adagiorum chiliades*. Venezia: Guerigli, 1604.

Montanari, Massimo. *Il formaggio con le pere: la storia in un proverbio*. Roma-Bari: Laterza, 2008.

Montini, Donatella. "John Florio and the *Decameron*: Notes on Style and Voice." *Boccaccio and the European Literary Tradition*. Eds. Pietro Boitani and Emilia di Rocco. Roma: Edizioni di storia e letteratura, 2014. 89–104.

———. "John/Giovanni: Florio mezzano e intercessore della lingua italiana." *Memoria di Shakespeare* 6 (2008): 47–59.

———. "Proverbs in John Florio's *Fruits*: Some Pragmatic Aspects." *Historical Perspectives on Forms of English Dialogue*. Eds. Gabriella Mazzon and Luisanna Fodde Melis. Milano: Franco Angeli, 2012. 248–64.

———. "Teaching Italian as a Foreign Language: Notes on Linguistic and Pragmatic Strategies in Florio's *Fruits*." *Textus* 24.3 (2011): 517–36.

Montuori, Francesco. "Sui proverbi della Campania." *La fortuna dei proverbi, identità dei popoli. Marco Besso e la sua collezione*. Ed. Laura Lalli. Roma: Artemide, 2014. 153–63.

Works Consulted

Morata, Olympia Fulvia. *Latina et Graeca quae haberi potuerunt monumenta eaque plane divina cum eruditorum de ipsa iudiciis et laudibus*. Basel: Pietro Perna, 1558.

Mordenti, Raul. "Le due censure: la collazione dei testi del *Decameron* «rassettati» da Vincenzio Borghini e Lionardo Salviati." *Le Pouvoir et la plume: Incitation, contrôle et repression dans l'Italie du XVIe siècle*. Paris: Université de la Sorbonne nouvelle, 1982. 253–73.

Morel-Fatio, Alfred. "Le livre des trois choses." *Romania* 12 (1883): 230–42.

Mormile, Mario, and Riccarda Matteucci. *Le grammatiche italiane in Gran Bretagna. Profilo storico: secoli XVI, XVII, XVIII*. Lecce: Argo, 1997.

Moro, Anna. *Aspects of Old Neapolitan: The Language of Basile's «Lo cunto de li cunti»*. München: Lincom Europa, 2003.

Morri, Antonio. *Vocabolario romagnolo-italiano*. Faenza: dai tipi di Pietro Conti all'Apollo, 1840.

Musarra, Franco. "L'«Orazione in lode della fiorentina lingua e de' fiorentini autori»: un momento cruciale della storia della lingua del Rinascimento." *Il Rinascimento: aspetti e problemi attuali*. Ed. Vittore Branca. Firenze: Olschki, 1982. 553–65.

Muscetta, Carlo. "Introduzione alla Sesta Giornata del *Decameron*." *Ritratti e Letture*. Milano: Marzorati, 1961. 195–211.

Mussafia, Adolfo. *Sopra il «Decameron» di Giovanni Boccacci riscontrato coi migliori testi e postillato da Pietro Fanfani (Firenze, 1857). Osservazioni di Adolfo Mussafia*. Milano: Tipografia di Zaccaria Brasca, 1857.

Nannini, Francesco. *Vocabolario portatile ferrarese-italiano, ossia raccolta di voci ferraresi le più alterate, alle quali si sono contrapposte le corrispondenti voci italiane, dell'abbate Francesco Nannini, operetta utilissima ad ogni classe di persone*. Ferrara: per gli eredi di Giuseppe Rinaldi, 1805.

Nashe, Thomas. *The Unfortunate Traveller, or The life of Jacke Wilton*. London: printed by Thomas Scarlet for Cuthbert Burby, 1594.

Nasi, Franco. "L'onesto narrare, l'onesto tradurre: il *Decameron* in italiano." *Specchi comunicanti: traduzioni, parodie, riscritture*. Eds. Franco Nasi and Stefano Bartezzaghi. Milano: Medusa, 2010. 85–126.

———. *Poetiche in transito: Sisifo e le fatiche del tradurre*. Milano: Medusa, 2004.

Nencioni, Giovanni. *Di scritto e di parlato: discorsi linguistici*. Bologna: Zanichelli, 1983.

Niccacci, Alviero. "Proverbi 1–9. Testo, traduzione, analisi, composizione." *Liber Annuus* 64 (2014): 45–126.

Nigro, Salvatore. "*Lo cunto de li cunti* di Giovan Battista Basile." *Letteratura italiana*. Ed. Alberto Asor Rosa. Vol. 2. Torino: Einaudi, 1993. 867–91.

———. "Il regno di Napoli." *Letteratura italiana. Storia e geografia*. Ed. Alberto Asor Rosa. Vol. 2. Torino: Einaudi, 1988. 1147–92.

Nikolaeva, Giulia. "Genesi del proverbio secondo le fonti paremiologiche italiane del cinquecento." S. Trovato, *Proverbi*, 65–72.

Nobili, Massimo Oro. "A 500 anni dalla nascita di Michelangelo Florio: Aretino, i Florio, *Amleto*." 2018. 1–135. www.shakespeareandflorio.net. Accessed 8 June 2019.

———. "Michelangelo Florio e la celebre frase: «Venezia, chi non ti vede non ti pretia, ma chi ti vede ben gli costa.»" 2017. 1–53. www.shakespeareandflorio.net. Accessed 8 June 2019.

Nocentini, Alberto, and Alessandro Parenti. *L'etimologico: vocabolario della lingua italiana*. Firenze: Le Monnier, 2010.

Nocera, Carmela Avila. *Studi sulla traduzione nell'Inghilterra del Seicento e del Settecento*. Caltanissetta: Sciascia, 1990.

Norrik, Neal. *Proverbial Linguistics: Linguistic Perspectives on Proverbs*. Trier: Linguistic Agency University of Trier, 1981.

Novati, Francesco. "Le serie alfabetiche proverbiali e gli alfabeti disposti nella letteratura italiana dei primi tre secoli." *Giornale Storico della Letteratura Italiana* 15 (1890): 337–401.

———. "Le serie alfabetiche proverbiali e gli alfabeti disposti nella letteratura italiana dei primi tre secoli." *Giornale Storico della Letteratura Italiana* 54 (1909): 36–58.

The Novellino, or One Hundred Ancient Tales. An Edition and Translation based on the 1525 Gualteruzzi editio princeps. Ed. Joseph Consoli. New York: Garland, 1997.

Nuccorini, Stefania. "Phraseology and Lexicography. English and Italian Dictionaries of Collocations: A Comparison." *Gutta cavat lapidem. Indagini fraseologiche e paremiologiche*. Eds. Elena Dal Maso and Carmen Navarro. Mantova: Universitas studiorum, 2016. 325–49.

———. "The translation of English Idiomatic and metaphorical expressions in bilingual (English-Italian and Italian-English) dictionaries." *Metamorfosi. Traduzione / Traduzioni. Atti del IX Congresso dell'Associazione Italiana di Anglistica (Pescara, 25–26 ott. 1986)*. Ed. Elizabeth Grass. Pescara: CLUA, 1988. 215–22.

Obelkevich, James. "Proverbs and Social History." *The Social History of Language*. Eds. Peter Burke and Roy Porter. Cambridge-New York: Cambridge UP, 1987. 43–72.

Works Consulted

O'Connor, Desmond. "Florio, John." *Oxford Dictionary of National Biography.* Eds. Henry Colin Gray Matthew and Brian Harrison. Vol. 20. Oxford-New York: Oxford UP, 2004. 165–68.

———. *A History of Italian and English Bilingual Dictionaries.* Firenze: Olschki, 1990.

———. "John Florio's Contribution to Italian-English Lexicography." *Italica* 41 (1972): 49–67.

O'Dowd, Ryan. *Proverbs.* Grand Rapids: Zondervan, 2017.

Oesterley, William Oscar Emil, ed. *The Wisdom of Ben-Sira (Ecclesiasticus).* London: Society for Promoting Christian Knowledge, 1916.

Opera del vocabolario italiano; Istituto del consiglio nazionale delle ricerche. www.ovi.cnr.it. Accessed 8 June 2019.

Opera quale contiene le diece tavole de' proverbi, sententie, detti et modi di parlare che hoggi dì da tutt'homo nel comun parlare d'Italia si usano. Molto utili e necessarii a tutti quelli gentili spiriti che di copioso et ornatamente ragionare procaciano. Torino: per Martino Cravoto et soi compagni a la instantia de Jacobino Dolce, c. 1535.

Ordine, Nuccio. *Teoria della novella e teoria del riso nel '500. Omaggio a Carlo Muscetta.* Vol. 2. Napoli: Liguori, 1996.

Ordine, Nuccio, and Nicola Merola. *La novella e il comico. Da Boccaccio a Brancati. Omaggio a Carlo Muscetta.* Vol. 1. Napoli: Liguori, 1996.

Orgel, Stephen. *Imagining Shakespeare: A History of Texts and Visions.* New York: Macmillan, 2003.

L'Orlando furioso e la sua traduzione in immagini; coordinated by Lina Bolzoni, Alessandro Benassi, and Serena Pezzini. www.orlandofurioso.org/. Accessed 8 June 2019.

Orsi, Laura. "William Shakespeare e John Florio: una prima analisi comparata linguistico-stilistica." *Atti e Memorie dell'Accademia Galileiana di Scienze, Lettere ed Arti, vol. CXXVIII (2015–2016), Parte III, Memorie della Classe di Scienze Morali, Lettere ed Arti.* Padova: presso la sede dell'Accademia, 2016. 139–280.

Orsini, Giordano. "Un trattatello sconosciuto di Giovanni Florio." *La cultura* 10 (1931): 483–89.

Ovidius, Publius Naso. *Metamorphoses. A New Verse Translation.* Trans. David Raeburn. London: Penguin, 2014.

The Oxford Dictionary of English Proverbs (ODEP). Eds. Frank Percy Wilson and Joanna Wilson. Oxford-New York: Oxford UP, 1995.

The Oxford English Dictionary (OED). Oxford-New York: Oxford UP, 1884–.

Paccagnella, Ivano. *Plurilinguismo letterario: lingue, dialetti, linguaggi.* Torino: Einaudi, 1983.

———. "La terminologia nella trattatistica grammaticale del primo trentennio del Cinquecento." *Tra Rinascimento e strutture attuali: saggi di linguistica italiana. Atti del Primo Convegno della Società Internazionale di Linguistica e Filologia Italiana, Siena, 28–31 mar. 1989.* Ed. Luciana Giannelli. Torino: Rosenberg & Sellier, 1991. 119–30.

———. "Uso letterario dei dialetti." *Storia della lingua italiana.* Eds. Luca Serianni and Pietro Trifone. Vol. 3. Torino: Einaudi, 1994. 495–539.

Palermo, Massimo, and Danilo Poggiogalli. *Grammatiche di italiano per stranieri dal '500 a oggi. Profilo storico e antologia.* Pisa: Pacini, 2010.

Palma, Flavia. "Paremiografia e funzioni del proverbio nelle *Novelle* di Matteo Bandello." *Lettere italiane* 71.2 (2019): 293–315.

Palsgrave, John. *L'esclaircissement de la langue francoyse, compose par maistre Iohan Palsgrave Angloyse natyf de Londres et gradue de Paris.* London: by Richard Pynson, 1530.

Palumbo, Matteo. "Detti, proverbi e allusioni: sul riuso delle fonti nei 'Ricordi' di Francesco Guicciardini." *Tempo e memoria. Studi in ricordo di Giancarlo Mazzacurati.* Eds. Matteo Palumbo and Antonio Saccone. Napoli: Fridericiana Editrice Universitaria, 2000. 47–74.

———. "I motti leggiadri nella sesta giornata del *Decameron.*" *Esperienze letterarie* 33 (2008): 3–23.

Pamies, Antonio. "Metafora grammaticale e metafora lessicale: implicazioni teoriche per la fraseologia." *Gutta cavat lapidem. Indagini fraseologiche e paremiologiche.* Eds. Elena Dal Maso and Carmen Navarro. Mantova: Universitas studiorum, 2016. 87–120.

Pantin, William Abel. "A medieval collection of Latin and English proverbs and riddles from the Rylands Latin MS 394." *Bulletin of the John Rylands Library* 14 (1930): 81–114.

Paravicino, Pietro. *Choice Proverbs and Dialogues in Italian and English. Also, delightfull stories and apophthegms, taken out of famous Guicciardine. Together with the history of the warres of Hannibal against the Romans.* London: printed by E.C. and are to be sold by Robert Horn, 1660.

———. *A short Italian dictionary expounded into English in the which is contained all the words that are used in the Italian tongue ending in the vowel (e).* London: printed for Thomas Clark, 1660.

Parks, George. "The Decline and Fall of the English Admiration of Italy." *Huntington Library Quarterly* 32 (1969): 341–57.

———. "The First Italianate Englishmen." *Studies in the Renaissance* 8 (1961): 197–216.

Works Consulted

Parks, George. "The Genesis of Tudor Interest in Italian." *Publications of Modern Language Association* 77.5 (1962): 529–35.

Parlato, Enrico. "L'editoria veneziana e Marcolini." *Francesco Salviati «spirito veramente pellegrino ed eletto»*. Eds. Antonio Geremicca and Barbara Agosti. Roma: Campisano, 2015. 75–144.

———. "Luoghi comuni in immagine. Da Erasmo ai florilegi secenteschi." Pignatti and Crimi, 449–68.

Parma, Michela. "Fortuna spicciolata del *Decameron* fra Tre e Cinquecento. Per un catalogo delle traduzioni latine e delle scritture italiane volgari." *Studi sul Boccaccio* 31 (2003): 203–70.

———. "Fortuna spicciolata del *Decameron* fra Tre e Cinquecento. II. Tendenze e caratteristiche delle rielaborazioni." *Studi sul Boccaccio* 33 (2005): 299–364.

———. "Una riduzione in ottava rima della novella di Nastagio degli Onesti (Decameron, V, 8) (dal ms Londra, British Library Additional 25487)." *Studi sul Boccaccio* 34 (2006): 199–243.

Parodi, Ernesto Giacomo. "Osservazioni sul «cursus» nelle opere latine e volgari del Boccaccio." *Lingua e letteratura. Studi di teoria linguistica e di storia dell'italiano antico*. Eds. Ernesto Giacomo Parodi and Gianfranco Folena. Venezia: Neri Pozza, 1957. 480–92.

Parodi, Severina. *Gli atti del primo vocabolario*. Firenze: Sansoni, 1974.

Pastorello, Ester. *Bibliografia storico-analitica dell'arte della stampa in Venezia*. Venezia: Reale Deputazione Editrice, 1933.

Pazzaglia, Giovanni Antonio. *Ingresso al viridario proverbiale, aperto a curiosi amatori della vera moralità, insegnata da proverbi antichi e moderni, con la traduzione tedesca et l'indice*. Hannover: Freytag, 1702.

Pellegrini, Giuliano. *John Florio e il Basilicon Doron di James VI: un esempio inedito di versione elisabettiana*. Milano: Feltrinelli, 1961.

———. "Michelangelo Florio e le sue *Regole de la lingua thoscana*." *Studi di filologia italiana* 12 (1954): 72–201.

Pelosi, Pietro. *Teoria dei generi letterari e critica contemporanea*. Napoli: Federico & Ardia, 1992.

Percel, Gordon. *Bibliothèque des romans, avec des remarques critiques sur leur choix et leurs différentes éditions*. Amsterdam: chez la Veuve De Poilras à la Vérité sans fard, 1734.

Perini, Giovanna. "Dialogo didattico e dialogo drammatico: John Florio e William Shakespeare." *Studi Secenteschi* 33 (1992): 167–82.

Pernigotti, Carlo. *Menandri Sententiae*. Firenze: Olschki, 2008.

Perocco, Daria. "La moralità rimata: V. Brusantini riscrittore del *Decameron*." *Viaggiare e raccontare. Narrazione di viaggio ed esperienze di racconto tra Cinque e Seicento*. Alessandria: Edizioni dell'Orso, 1997. 109–18.

―――. "La moralità rimata: Vincenzo Brusantini riscrittore del «Decameron»." *Scritture di scritture. Testi, generi, modelli nel Rinascimento.* Eds. Giancarlo Mazzacurati and Michel Plaisance. Roma: Bulzoni, 1987. 293–305.

Perseus Digital Library. www.perseus.tufts.edu/. Accessed 8 June 2019.

Pescetti, Orlando. *Orazione dietro al modo di istituire la gioventù.* Verona: Girolamo Discepolo, 1592.

―――. *Proverbi italiani e latini per uso de' fanciuli che imparan grammatica.* Verona: nella stamperia di Francesco dalle Donne, 1602.

―――. *Proverbi italiani raccolti per Orlando Pescetti.* Verona: Girolamo Discepolo, 1598.

Petrarca, Francesco. *Canzoniere.* Ed. Marco Santagata. Milano: Mondadori, 1996.

―――. *The Canzoniere, or Rerum Vulgarium Fragmenta.* Trans. Mark Musa. Bloomington: Indiana UP, 1999.

Petrina, Alessandra. "«Perfit readiness»: Elizabeth Learning and Using Italian." *Elizabeth I's Foreign Correspondence. Letters, Rhetoric, and Politics.* Eds. Carlo Bajetta, et al. New York: Macmillan, 2014. 93–113.

Petrini, Mario. *Il gran Basile.* Roma: Bulzoni, 1989.

―――. "La sesta giornata." *Nel giardino di Boccaccio.* Udine: Del Bianco, 1986. 77–90.

Pettinelli, Rosanna. *Forme e percorsi dei romanzi di cavalleria: da Boiardo a Brusantino.* Roma: Bulzoni, 2004.

―――. *L'immaginario cavalleresco nel rinascimento ferrarese.* Roma: Bonacci, 1983.

Pfister, Manfred. "Inglese italianato-Italiano anglizzato." *Renaissance Go-Betweens: Cultural Exchange in Early Modern Europe.* Eds. Andreas Höfele and Werner von Koppenfels. Berlin: De Gruyter, 2005. 32–54.

Phillips, Margaret Mann. *The «Adages» of Erasmus; a study with translations.* Cambridge-New York: Cambridge UP, 1964.

―――. *Erasmus on his times. A shortened version of the «Adages» of Erasmus.* Cambridge-New York: Cambridge UP, 1967.

Picone, Michelangelo. *Boccaccio e la codificazione della novella. Letture del «Decameron».* Eds. Nicole Coderey, et al. Ravenna: Longo, 2008.

―――. "La cornice novellistica dal *Decameron* al *Pentamerone*." *Modern Philology* 101.2 (2003): 297–315.

Picone, Michelangelo, and Maria Bendinelli Predelli, eds. *I cantari: struttura e tradizione. Atti del Convegno Internazionale di Montreal, 19–20 mar. 1981.* Firenze: Olschki, 1984.

Picone, Michelangelo, and Alfred Messerli, eds. *Giovan Battista Basile e l'invenzione della fiaba*. Ravenna: Longo, 2004.

Pientini, Michele, ed. *I proverbi di Seneca: scrittura inedita del buon secolo di nostra lingua estratta da un codice riccardiano*. Firenze: Giuseppe Mariani, 1858.

Pierno, Franco. "Il modello linguistico decameroniano e il suo rapporto con il volgare nel pensiero di Antonio Brucioli." *Cahiers d'études italiennes* 8 (2008): 99–114.

Pignatti, Franco. *Etimologia e proverbio nell'Italia del XVII secolo – Floris Italicae Linguae libri novem. Ristampa anastatica*. Manziana: Vecchiarelli, 2010.

———. "Frottola e proverbio nel XVI secolo. Con qualche notizia sulla perduta raccolta paremiografica di Marcantonio Piccolomini." Pignatti and Crimi, 247–82.

———. "Pratica e ideologia del plagio nelle raccolte facete e apoftegmatiche." *Furto e plagio nella letteratura del Classicismo*. Ed. Roberto Gigliucci. Roma: Bulzoni, 1998. 323–45.

Pignatti, Franco, and Giuseppe Crimi, eds. *Il proverbio nella letteratura italiana dal XV al XVII secolo. Atti delle Giornate di studio, Università degli studi Roma Tre—Fondazione Marco Besso, Roma, 5–6 dic. 2012*. Manziana: Vecchiarelli, 2014.

Pike, Kenneth. *Language in Relation to a Unified Theory of the Structure of Human Behavior*. The Hague: Mouton De Gruyter, 1967.

Pinnavaia, Laura. "Teaching Italian (and English) through proverbs in conversation: a case study of Pietro Paravicino's «Choice Proverbs and Dialogues in Italian and English» (1660)." *Historical Perspectives on Forms of English Dialogue*. Eds. Gabriella Mazzon and Luisanna Fodde Melis. Milano: Franco Angeli, 2012. 265–82.

Pio, Giovanni Battista. *Annotamenta*. Bologna: appresso Giovanni Antonio de' Benedetti, 1505.

Pirillo, Diego. "«Inglese italianato è un diavolo incarnato». In margine ad un recente studio su John Florio e la cultura italiana in Inghilterra." *Rinascimento* 46 (2006): 585–93.

Pitrè, Giuseppe. *Curiosità popolari tradizionali. Tradizioni ed usi nella penisola sorrentina*. Vol. 8. Torino-Palermo: Carlo Clausen, 1890.

Pizzoli, Lucilla. *Le grammatiche di italiano per inglesi, 1550–1776: un'analisi linguistica*. Firenze: Accademia della Crusca, 2004.

Plaisance, Michael. "Il riuso delle immagini ne *I marmi* del Doni." *Percorsi tra parole e immagini, 1400–1600*. Eds. Angela Guidotti and Massimiliano Rossi. Lucca: Pacini, 2000. 9–18.

Poggi Salani, Teresa. "Italienisch: Grammatikographie. Storia delle grammatiche." Eds. Günter Holtus, et al. Vol. 4: 774–86.

Policardi, Silvio. *John Florio e le relazioni culturali anglo-italiane agli albori del XVII secolo*. Venezia: Montuoro, 1947.

Polito, Armando. "Il Vesuvio e la sirena." www.vesuvioweb.com/it/wp-content/uploads/Armando-Polito-Il-Vesuvio-e-la-sirena-vesuvioweb.pdf. Accessed 8 June 2019.

Pollard, Alfred William, et al. *A short-title catalogue of books printed in England, Scotland & Ireland and of English books printed abroad 1475–1640*. London: The Bibliographical Society, 1976–91.

Pontano, Giovanni. *De sermone*. Ed. Alessandra Mantovani. Roma: Carocci, 2002.

Porcelli, Bruno. "Alle prese con la lingua di autori napoletani del Seicento." *Studi e problemi di critica testuale* 15 (1997): 104–43.

———. "Il lessico erotico nelle novelle di Celio Malespini fra *Cent nouvelles nouvelles* e Aretino." *Italianistica* 41.2 (2012): 13–20.

———. "Il senso del molteplice nel *Pentamerone*." *Novellieri italiani. Dal Sacchetti al Basile*. Ravenna: Longo, 1969. 193–236.

Portonaris, Francesco. *Libro di Marco Aurelio con l'horologio de' principi distinto in quatro volumi. Composto per il molto reverendo Signor Don Antonio di Guevara, Vescovo di Mondogneto, predicatore et scrittore delle croniche della Maestà Cesarea di Carlo Quinto. Nel quale sono comprese molte sententie notabili et essempi singolari appertinenti non solamente a i prencipi christiani, ma a tutti color che desiderano di vivere civilmente e da veri et honorati gentil'huomini. Con l'aggiunta del quarto libro novamente tradotto di lingua spagnola in italiano da la copia originale di esso auttore*. Venezia: apresso Francesco Portonaris, 1562.

Pötters, Wilhelm. "«Quale asino dà in parete, tal riceve». Funzione metapoetica di una frase proverbiale del *Decameron*." *La parola del testo* 24.1–2 (2020): 83–98.

Praloran, Marco. *Le lingue del racconto: studi su Boiardo e Ariosto*. Roma: Bulzoni, 2009.

Prandi, Michele. "Dall'analogia all'inferenza: la motivazione delle espressioni idiomatiche." *Quaderni di semantica* 20 (1999): 131–45.

Praz, Mario. "Fortuna della lingua e della cultura italiana in Inghilterra." *Machiavelli in Inghilterra, ed altri saggi*. Roma: Tumminelli, 1942. 269–328.

———. "Giovanni Florio." *Machiavelli in Inghilterra, e altri saggi*. Roma: Tumminelli, 1942. 165–72.

Praz, Mario. "The Italian Element in English." *Ricerche Anglo-Italiane*. Roma: Edizioni di storia e letteratura, 1944. 1–62.

———. "Shakespeare's Italy." 1954. *The Flaming Heart: Essays on Crashaw, Machiavelli, and Other Studies in the Relations between Italian and English Literature from Chaucer to T. S. Eliot*. Gloucester, MA: Peter Smith, 1966. 146–67.

Procaccioli, Paolo. "Dai *Modi* ai *Sonetti lussuriosi*. Il «capriccio» dell'immagine e lo scandalo della parola." *Italianistica* 38.2 (2009): 219–37.

———. "Nuova veste, nuova via o nuova vita? L'illusione di Vincenzo Brusantino riscrittore in ottave del *Decameron*." *Leggere, interpretare, riscrivere. Poeti, filologi, traduttori alla prova del Decameron (1313-2013). Atti del VII Seminario di Letteratura italiana (Helsinki, 29 ott. 2013)*. Ed. Enrico Garavelli. Helsinki: Publications romanes de l'Université de Helsinki, 2014. 49–78.

Procaccioli, Paolo, et al., eds. *Un giardino per le arti. Francesco Marcolino da Forlì, la vita, l'opera, il catalogo. Atti del Convegno internazionale di studi (Forlì, 11–13 ott. 2007)*. Bologna: Editrice Compositori, 2009.

Proverbi italiani; Accademia della Crusca. www.proverbi-italiani.org/index.asp. Accessed 8 June 2019.

Pulci, Luigi. *Morgante*. Trans. Giuliano Dego. Milano: Biblioteca Universale Rizzoli, 2019.

———. *Morgante. The Epic Adventures of Orlando and His Giant Friend Morgante*. Trans. Joseph Tusiani. Ed. Edoardo Lèbano. Bloomington: Indiana UP, 2000.

Puoti, Basilio. *Vocabolario domestico napoletano e toscano*. Napoli: Stamperia Simoniana, 1841.

Quadrio, Francesco Saverio. *Della storia e della ragione d'ogni poesia dell'Abate Francesco Saverio Quadrio dove le cose all'epica appartenenti sono comprese alla Serenissima Altezza di Francesco III Duca di Modana, Reggio, Mirandola etc*. Bologna: per Ferdinando Pisarri all'insegna di S. Antonio, 1739–52.

Quaglio, Antonio Enzo. "Parole del Boccaccio." *Lingua Nostra* 26 (1965): 73–80.

Qualizza, Giorgio. "Per una definizione del proverbio." *Scienze umane* 3 (1980): 175–97.

Quintilianus, Marcus Fabius. *The Institutio Oratoria of Quintilian*. Ed. Harold Edgeworth Butler. Cambridge, MA: Harvard UP, 1920–22.

Quondam, Amedeo. "Nel giardino del Marcolini. Un editore veneziano tra Aretino e Doni." *Giornale Storico della Letteratura Italiana* 157.497 (1980): 75–116.

———. "Riscrittura, citazione e parodia. Il *Petrarca spirituale* di Girolamo Malipiero." *Il naso di Laura. Lingua e poesia lirica nella tradizione del Classicismo*. Modena: Panini, 1991.

Rabaey, Hélène. "El ingenioso inventor Blasco de Garay, autor de las «Cartas en refranes» y traductor de Erasmo." *ehumanista* 31 (2015): 674–702.

Rada, Paola. "Cantari tratti dal *Decameron*: modalità di riscrittura della novella di Paganino e Ricciardo (II.10)." *Il cantare italiano fra folklore e letteratura. Atti del convegno internazionale di Zurigo, Landesmuseum, 23–25 giu. 2005*. Eds. Michelangelo Picone and Luisa Rubini. Firenze: Olschki, 2007. 339–53.

———. *Cantari tratti dal «Decameron». Modalità di riscrittura ed edizione della «Storia di Messer Ricciardo» (II, 10), della «Novella di Paganino» (II, 10) e della «Novella Bellissima d'uno monaco e uno abbate» (I, 4)*. Pisa: Pacini, 2009.

Radtke, Edgar. *I dialetti della Campania*. Roma: Il Calamo, 1997.

———. "Kampanien." Eds. Günter Holtus, et al. Vol. 4: 652–61.

———. "La questione della lingua e la letteratura dialettale a Napoli nel Seicento." *Italica et Romanica. Festschrift für Max Pfister zum 65. Geburtstag. Band. 3, Dialektologie und Soziolinguistik. Onomastik. Literatur- und Kulturgeschichte. Wissenschaftsgeschichte*. Eds. Günter Holtus, et al. Tübingen: Niemeyer, 1997. 75–86.

Raffaele, Liberatore. "Del dialetto napoletano." *Annali civili del Regno delle due Sicilie* 14 (1837): 28–41.

Ragone, Giovanni. "Le maschere dell'interprete barocco. Percorsi della novella secentesca." *La novella, la voce, il libro. Dal 'cantare' trecentesco alla penna narratrice barocca*. Ed. Marina Beer. Napoli: Liguori, 1996. 137–201.

Raimondi, Gianmario. "Elizabeth's Italian: Linguistic Standards and Interlingual Interference." *Elizabeth I's Foreign Correspondence. Letters, Rhetoric, and Politics*. Eds. Carlo Bajetta, et al. New York: Macmillan, 2014. 151–65

Rak, Michele. *Logica della fiaba. Fate, orchi, gioco, corte, fortuna, viaggio, capriccio, metamorfosi, corpo*. Milano: Mondadori, 2005.

———. *Napoli gentile: la letteratura in 'lingua napoletana' nella cultura barocca (1596–1632)*. Bologna: Il Mulino, 1994.

Ramusio, Giovan Battista. *Breve et succinta narratione della navigatione fatta per ordine della Maestà Christianissima all'isole di Canada, Hochelaga, Saguenai, et altre, al presente dette la nuova Francia con particolari costumi et cerimonie de gli habitanti*. Venezia: Giunti, 1565.

Works Consulted

Ramusio, Giovan Battista. *Prima relazione di Iacques Carthier della Terra Nuova detta la nuova Francia trovata nell'anno 1534*. Venezia: Giunti, 1565.

———. *Terzo volume delle navigationi et viaggi*. Venezia: Giunti, 1565.

Ray, John. *A complete collection of English proverbs and also the most celebrated proverbs of the Scotch, Italian, French, Spanish, and other languages. The whole methodically digested and illustrated with annotations and proper explications*. London: Allman, 1818.

Rees, D. G. "John Florio and Anton Francesco Doni." *Comparative Literature* 15.1 (1963): 33–38.

Reif, Arno. "Interpretatio, imitatio, aemulatio." *Studi di Estetica* 7 (1993): 41–54.

Renzi, Lorenzo, et al. *Grande grammatica italiana di consultazione*. Bologna: Il Mulino, 1988–95.

Rhys, Siòn Dafydd. *De Italica Pronunciatione*. Padova: Lorenzo Pasquato ad instantia di Pietro Antonio Alciati, 1569.

Richardson, Brian. "Editing the *Decameron* in the Sixteenth Century." *Italian Studies* 45 (1990): 13–31.

———. *Print Culture in Renaissance Italy: The Editor and The Vernacular Text, 1470–1600*. Cambridge-New York: Cambridge UP, 2003.

———. "The textual history of the *Decameron*." *Boccaccio: A Critical Guide to the Complete Works*. Eds. Victoria Kirkham, et al. Chicago: The U of Chicago P, 2013. 41–49.

Rico, Francisco. *El sueño del humanismo: de Petrarca a Erasmo*. Barcelona: Crítica, 2014.

Rigg, James Macmullen. *The Decameron of Giovanni Boccaccio*. London: Bullen, 1903.

Rinaldi, Orazio. *Dottrina delle virtù e fuga dei vizi*. Ed. Enrico Malato. Roma: Salerno Editrice, 1990.

Rocco, Emmanuele. *Vocabolario del dialetto napolitano. A-FEL*. Napoli: Chiurazzi, 1882–91.

———. *Vocabolario del dialetto napolitano*. Ed. Antonio Vinciguerra. Firenze: Accademia della Crusca, 2018.

Roggia, Carlo Enrico. "Poesia narrativa." *Storia dell'italiano scritto*. Eds. Giuseppe Antonelli, et al. Roma: Carocci, 2014. 85–153.

Rohlfs, Gerhard. *Grammatica storica della lingua italiana e dei suoi dialetti*. Trans. Temistocle Franceschi. Torino: Einaudi, 1970.

———. *Studi e ricerche su lingua e dialetti d'Italia*. Firenze: Sansoni, 1972.

Romagnoli, Gaetano. *Due opuscoli rarissimi del secolo XVI*. Bologna: Romagnoli, 1865.

———. *Facezie e motti dei secoli XV e XVI, codice inedito magliabechiano.* Bologna: Romagnoli, 1874.

———. *La istoria di Maria per Ravenna, scritta nel secolo XV da ignoto autore.* Bologna: Romagnoli, 1864.

Romani, Werther. "La traduzione letteraria nel Cinquecento: note introduttive." *La traduzione. Saggi e studi.* Ed. Bertil Malmberg. Trieste: LINT, 1973. 389–402.

Romero, Fernando García. "Sobre la etimología de «paroimía»." *Paremia* 8 (1999): 219–23.

Rondinelli, Paolo. "Il concetto di proverbio nell'antichità e nel Rinascimento." Franceschi, *Ragionamenti,* 167–78.

———. "«Ho udito dire mille volte...» Presenza dei proverbi nel *Decameron* e loro fortuna in lessicografia." *Boccaccio letterato. Atti del convegno internazionale, Firenze-Certaldo 10–12 ott. 2013.* Eds. Michaelangiola Marchiaro and Stefano Zamponi. Firenze: Accademia della Crusca, 2015. 297–317.

———. "Il *Liber proverbiorum* di Lorenzo Lippi e la paremiografia umanistica." Pignatti and Crimi, 11–34.

———. "Per l'edizione elettronica dei *Proverbi* di Francesco Serdonati." *Fraseologia e paremiologia. Passato, presente e futuro.* Ed. Cosimo De Giovanni. Milano: Franco Angeli, 2017. 185–94.

———. "La presenza della lingua spagnola nell'opera di Francesco Serdonati." *Artifara* 18 (2018): 37–45.

———. "Verso l'edizione a stampa dei *Proverbi* di Francesco Serdonati." *Fraseologia, paremiologia e lessicografia. III convegno dell'Associazione italiana di fraseologia e paremiologia Phrasis (Accademia della Crusca—Università di Firenze, 19–21 ott. 2016).* Eds. Elisabetta Benucci, et al. Roma: Aracne, 2018. 185–202.

Rondinelli, Paolo, and Antonio Vinciguerra. "«Le parole son femmine e i fatti son maschi». Storia e vicissitudini di un proverbio." *Studi di lessicografia italiana* 33 (2016): 21–37.

Rosenberg, Eleanor. "Jacopo Castelvetro; Italian Publisher in Elizabethan London and his Patrons." *Huntington Library Quarterly* 6 (1942–43): 119–48.

Rossi Sergio. "Note sugli italiani in Inghilterra nell'età del Rinascimento." *Saggi sul Rinascimento.* Milano: Unicopli, 1984. 55–115.

———. *Ricerche sull'umanesimo e sul rinascimento in Inghilterra.* Milano: Società editrice Vita e Pensiero, 1969.

Rostenberg, Leona. "Thomas Thorpe, Publisher of 'Shake-Speares Sonnets.'" *The Papers of the Bibliographical Society of America* 54.1 (1960): 16–37.

Works Consulted

Roth, Wolfgang. *Numerical Sayings in the Old Testament. A Form-Critical Study.* Leiden: Brill, 1965.

Roveri, Alessandro. *Renata di Francia.* Torino: Claudiana, 2012.

Rubini, Cesare. "Il dialetto napolitano (osservazioni estetiche)." *Napoli e sue province: album per l'anno 1844.* Napoli: Barel et Bompard, 1844. 197–207.

Sabatini, Francesco. "Prospettive sul parlato nella storia linguistica italiana (con una lettura dell'*Epistola napoletana* del Boccaccio)." *Italia linguistica: idee, storia, strutture.* Ed. Federico Albano Leoni. Bologna: Il Mulino, 1983. 167–201.

Sabbatino, Pasquale. "Lingua letteraria e idioma napoletano nel cinquecento (con un inedito di Velardiniello)." *Lingua e dialetto nella tradizione letteraria italiana. Atti del Convegno di Salerno, 5–6 nov. 1993.* Roma: Salerno Editrice, 1996. 473–524.

Sacchetti, Franco. *Le Trecento Novelle.* Ed. Michelangelo Zaccarello. Firenze: SISMEL, 2014.

Sacchi, Guido. *Fra Ariosto e Tasso: vicende del poema narrativo. Con un'appendice di studi cinque-secenteschi.* Pisa: Edizioni della Normale, 2007.

Safian, Louis. *The Book of Updated Proverbs.* New York: Abelard-Schuman, 1967.

Salviati, Lionardo. *Raccolta di proverbi toscani.* 1588–ante 1612, Biblioteca Comunale Ariostea, Ferrara, Cl. II 25. Manuscript.

———. *Raccolta di proverbi toscani.* 1588–post 1612, Biblioteca Comunale Ariostea, Ferrara, Cl. I 394. Manuscript.

Sammartino, Alberto. "Polemica letteraria antitoscana e produzione dialettale a Napoli nel tardo '600." *Annali della Facoltà di Lettere e Filosofia dell'Università di Napoli* 20 (1977–78): 215–35.

Sanders, Jack. *Ben Sira and Demotic Wisdom.* Chico, CA: Scholars Press, 1983.

Sanford, James. *The Garden of Pleasure, contayninge most pleasante tales, worthy deeds and witty sayings of noble princes learned philosophers, moralized. No less delectable than profitable. [By Lodovico Guicciardini.] Done out of Italian into English by James Sanforde.* London: Bynneman, 1573.

———. *Houres of recreation, or afterdinners, which may aptly be called The garden of pleasure, containing most pleasant tales, worthy deedes, and wittie sayings of noble princes et learned philosophers with their morals. No lesse delectable than profitable. Done firste out of Italian into Englishe by Iames Sandford gentleman and now by him newly perused, corrected, and enlarged. Wherein are also set foorth divers verses and sentences in Italian, with the English to the same for the benefit of students in both toungs.* London: Bynneman, 1576.

Sanford, John. *A grammer or Introduction to the Italian Tongue.* Oxford: printed by Joseph Barnes, sold by Simon Waterson, 1605.

Sanguineti-White, Laura. "Spazio, tempo e personaggi ne «Lo cunto de li cunti»." *Forma e parola. Studi in memoria di Fredi Chiappelli.* Ed. Dennis Dutschke. Roma: Bulzoni, 1992. 467–80.

Sannazaro, Jacopo. *Arcadia and Piscatorial Eclogues.* Trans. Ralph Nash. Detroit: Wayne State UP, 1966.

Sansone, Giuseppe. "Garzo e Guidotto nell'alfabeto paremiografico dell'Alessiano." *Dal Medioevo al Petrarca: Miscellanea di studi in onore di Vittore Branca.* Ed. Armando Balduino. Vol. 1. Firenze: Olschki, 1983. 47–56.

Sansone, Mario. "Cultura napoletana e letteratura nazionale." *Culture regionali e letteratura nazionale. Atti del VII Convegno dell'AISLLI (Bari, 31 mar.–4 apr. 1970).* Bari: Adriatica Editrice, 1973. 81–118.

———. "Relazioni fra la letteratura italiana e le letterature dialettali." *Problemi ed orientamenti critici di lingua e letteratura contemporanea. Letterature comparate.* Ed. Attilio Momigliano. Vol. 4. Milano: Marzorati, 1948.

Sansovino, Francesco. *Le lettere sopra le diece giornate del Decamerone di Messer Giovanni Boccaccio.* Ed. Christina Roaf. Bologna: Commissione per i testi di lingua, 2003.

Santa Cruz de Dueñas, Melchor de, and Francisco Asensio y Mejorado. *Floresta española de apotegmas ó sentencias, sabia y graciosamente dichas de algunos españoles.* Madrid: Joachin Ibarra, 1777.

Sarnelli, Pompeo. *Alfabeto greco con grandissima facilità ordinato da Pompeo Sarnelli e così chiaramente spiegato che potrà ciascuno imparare a leggere la lingua greca.* Roma: per il Mascardi ad istanza di Antonio Bulifon, 1675.

———. *Antica basilicografia di Pompeo Sarnelli dottor della Santa teologia e delle leggi, dedicata all'eminentissimo Vincenzo Maria cardinale Orsini.* Napoli: Giuseppe Roselli, 1686.

———. *Bestiarum schola ad homines erudiendos ab ipsa rerum natura provide instituta.* Cesena: presso Pietro Paolo tipografo episcopale, 1680.

———. *Cronologia de' vescovi et arcivescovi sipontini colle notitie historiche di molte notabili cose ne' loro tempi avvenute tanto nella vecchia e nuova Siponto quanto in altri luoghi della Puglia.* Manfredonia: nella stamperia arcivescovale, 1680.

———. *Degli avvenimenti di Fortunato e de' suoi figli. Historia comica tradotta et illustrata da Masillo Reppone da Gnanopoli. Libri due. Al molto Illustrissimo e Reverendissimo Signore e Padrone Osservandissimo il signor Pompeo Sarnelli Dottor delle Leggi e Protonotario Apostolico.* Napoli: Antonio Bulifon, 1676.

Works Consulted

Sarnelli, Pompeo. *Guida de' forestieri curiosi di vedere e considerare le cose notabili di Pozzuolo, Baja, Miseno, Cuma, Gaeta ed altri luoghi circonvicini.* Napoli: Giuseppe Roselli, 1685.

———. *Guida de' forestieri curiosi di vedere ed intendere le cose più notabili della real città di Napoli e del suo amenissimo distretto, ritrovata colla lettura de' buoni scrittori e colla propria diligenza dall'Abate Pompeo Sarnelli.* Napoli: Giuseppe Roselli, 1685.

———. *La guide des etrangers curieux de voir et de connoitre les choses les plus memorables de Poussol, Bayes, Cumes, Misene et autres lieux des environs. Expliquée a l'aide des bon auteurs et par la propre recherche de l'Abbé Pompee Sarnelli. Traduite en françois par Antoine Bulifon.* Trans. Antonio Bulifon. Napoli: Antonio Bulifon, 1700.

———. *Lettere ecclesiastiche di monsignor Pompeo Sarnelli vescovo di Bisceglia.* Napoli: nella Stamperia di Felice Mosca, 1686–1716.

———. *Memorie de' vescovi di Bisceglia e della stessa città. Ricercate dal vescovo Pompeo Sarnelli.* Napoli: Giuseppe Roselli, 1693.

———. *Ordinario grammaticale utilissimo ad ogni studioso della lingua latina, precise a chi vuole imparare a tradurre.* Napoli: Antonio Bulifon, 1677.

———. *Posilecheata.* Ed. Enrico Malato. Roma: Benincasa, 1986.

———. *Posilecheata de Masillo Reppone de Gnanopoli.* Napoli: Giuseppe Roselli, 1684.

———. *Posilecheata di Pompeo Sarnelli.* Ed. Vittorio Imbriani. Napoli: Domenico Morano, 1885.

———. *Posilecheata. Testo, traduzione, introduzione e note di Enrico Malato.* Ed. Enrico Malato. Firenze: Sansoni, 1963.

———. "Posillecheata de Masillo Reppone de Gnanopole." *Collezione di tutti i poemi in lingua napoletana.* Vol. 22. Napoli: Porcelli, 1788. 135–322.

———. *Specchio del clero secolare, overo Vite de SS. cherici secolari.* Napoli: Antonio Bulifon, 1678–79.

Saulnier, Voir. "Proverbe et paradoxe du XVe au XVIe siècle." *Pensée humaniste et tradition chrétienne aux XVe et XVIe siècles. Essais, notes et documents.* Ed. Henri Bédarida. Paris: Boivin, 1950. 87–104.

Saxl, Fritz. "Veritas filia temporis." *Philosophy and History. Essays presented to Ernst Cassirer.* Eds. Raymond Klibansky and Herbert James Paton. New York-London: Harper & Row, 1963. 197–222.

Scaligeri dalla Fratta, Camillo (aka Adriano Banchieri and Tommaso Banchieri). *Trastulli della villa distinti in sette giornate.* Venezia: appresso Giovanni Antonio Giuliani, 1627.

Schiaffini, Alfredo. *Tradizione e poesia nella prosa d'arte italiana dalla latinità medievale al Boccaccio*. Roma: Edizioni di storia e letteratura, 1969.

Schifanoia. Notizie dell'Istituto di studi rinascimentali di Ferrara. 28/29. Modena: Panini, 2005.

Segre, Cesare. "Comicità strutturale nella novella di Alatiel." *Le strutture e il tempo. Narrazione, poesia, modelli*. Torino: Einaudi, 1974. 145–59.

———. *Lingua, stile e società. Studi sulla storia della prosa italiana*. Milano: Feltrinelli, 1974.

———. *Le strutture e il tempo*. Torino: Einaudi, 1993.

Segre, Cesare, and Mario Marti. "I «Conti morali» di Anonimo senese." *La prosa del Duecento*. Ed. Cesare Segre. Vol. 3. Milano: Ricciardi, 1959. 489–509.

Seneca, Lucius Annaeus. *Ad Lucilium Epistulae Morales with an English Translation*. Trans. Richard Gummere. Cambridge, MA: Harvard UP; London: William Heinemann, 1953.

———. *Tragedies*. Trans. John Fitch. Eds. John Fitch and Jeffrey Henderson. Cambridge, MA: Harvard UP, 2018.

Serdonati, Francesco. *Raccolta di proverbi*. c. 1650–1700, Biblioteca Medicea Laurenziana, Firenze, Mediceo Palatino 62. Manuscript.

———. *Raccolta di proverbi*. 1877. Accademia della Crusca, Firenze, ms. 47. Manuscript.

Serianni, Luca. "Sulla componente idiomatica e proverbiale nell'italiano di oggi." *Lingua, storia, cultura: una lunga fedeltà per Gian Luigi Beccaria. Atti del convegno internazionale di studi di Torino 16–17 ott. 2008*. Eds. Pier Marco Bertinetto, et al. Alessandria: Edizioni dell'Orso, 2010. 69–88.

Serianni, Luca, and Alberto Castelvecchi, eds. *Grammatica italiana: italiano comune e lingua letteraria, suoni, forme, costrutti*. Torino: UTET, 1988.

Serio, Luigi. *Lo vernacchio. Risposta al Dialetto napoletano (dell'abate Galiani)*. N.p.: n.p., 1780.

Servolini, Luigi. "Edizioni di Francesco Marcolini nella biblioteca di Forlì." *Bollettino dell'istituto di patologia del libro* 1.4 (1950): 86–133.

Simonini, Rinaldo Jr. "The Genesis of Modern Foreign Language Teaching." *Modern Language Journal* 35 (1951): 179–86.

———. "Italian-English Language Books of the Renaissance." *Romanic Review* 42 (1951): 241–44.

———. "The Italian Pedagogy of Claudius Hollyband." *Studies in Philology* 49.2 (1952): 144-54.

Works Consulted

Simonini, Rinaldo Jr. *Italian Scholarship in Renaissance England.* Chapel Hill: U of North Carolina P, 1952.

———. "John Florio, Scholar and Humanist." *A Tribute to George Coffin Taylor. Studies and Essays Chiefly Elizabethan by his Students and Friends.* Eds. George Coffin Taylor and Arnold Williams. Chapel Hill: U of North Carolina P, 1952. 67–82.

———. "Language Lesson Dialogue in Shakespeare." *Shakespeare Quarterly* 2.4 (1951): 319–29.

Singer, Samuel, et al. *Thesaurus proverbiorum medii aevii: Lexikon der Sprichwörter des romanisch-germanischen Mittelalters.* Berlin: De Gruyter, 1995–2002.

Skehan, Patrick William, and Alexander Di Lella. *The Wisdom of Ben Sira. A New Translation with Notes.* Vol. 39. New York: Anchor Bible, 1987.

Skuza, Sylwia. "Le tecniche della traduzione. Come, se e quando tradurre i proverbi?" *Fraseologia, paremiologia e lessicografia. III convegno dell'Associazione italiana di fraseologia e paremiologia Phrasis (Accademia della Crusca—Università di Firenze, 19–21 ott. 2016).* Eds. Elisabetta Benucci, et al. Roma: Aracne, 2018. 369–81.

Soletti, Elisabetta. "«Come raccende il gusto il mutar esca». Allusione e parodia nei proverbi del *Furioso*." *Boiardo, Ariosto e i libri di battaglia. Atti del convegno Scandiano-Reggio Emilia 3–6 ott. 2005.* Eds. Andrea Canova and Paola Vecchi Galli. Novara: Interlinea Edizioni, 2007.

———. "Proverbi." *Enciclopedia dell'italiano.* Ed. Raffaele Simone. Roma: Istituto dell'Enciclopedia Italiana, 2011. 1182–85.

Spampanato, Vincenzo. "Giovanni Florio. Un amico del Bruno in Inghilterra." *La Critica* 21 (2008): 113–25.

Spera, Lucinda, ed. *La novella barocca, con un repertorio bibliografico.* Napoli: Liguori, 2001.

Speroni, Charles. "Five Italian Wellerisms." *Western Folklore* 7 (1948): 54–55.

———. "Giovanni Torriano's *Select Italian Proverbs*." *Italica* 34.3 (1957): 146–57.

———. *The Italian Wellerism to the End of the XVII Century.* Berkeley-Los Angeles: U of California P, 1953.

———. "Merbury's *Proverbi Vvlgari*: A Rare 16th Century Collection of Italian Proverbs." *Italica* 20.4 (1943): 157–62.

———. "Proverbi che si trovano nel dizionario del Petrocchi e non nella raccolta del Giusti." *Folklore* 3–4 (1950–51): 13–53.

———. "Proverbi della *Posilecheata*." *Folklore Napoletano* 8 (1953): 3–22.

———. *Proverbs and Proverbial Phrases in Basile's «Pentameron»*. Berkeley-Los Angeles: U of California P, 1941.

———. "Wellerismi tolti dai proverbi inediti di F. Serdonati." *Folklore* 4 (1949): 12–31.

———. *Wit and Wisdom of the Italian Renaissance*. Berkeley-Los Angeles: U of California P, 1964.

Sportelli, Annamaria, ed. *Generi letterari: ibridismo e contaminazione*. Roma-Bari: Laterza, 2001.

Staël, Madame de. "De l'esprit des traductions." *Oeuvres completes de la Madame la Baronne de Staël, Publiées par son fils. Précédées d'une notice sur le caractère et les écrits de Madame de Staël par Madame Necker de Saussure*. Eds. Anne-Louise-Germaine de Staël, et al. Vol. 17. Paris: Treuttel et Würtz, 1821. 387–99.

Stammerjohann, Harro. "L'immagine della lingua italiana in Europa." *Lingua e cultura italiana in Europa. Atti del congresso di Amsterdam (ott. 1988)*. Ed. Vincenzo Lo Cascio. Firenze: Le Monnier, 1990. 11–34.

———. "L'italiano alla corte inglese." *Italiano & Oltre* 8 (1993): 303.

Starnes, DeWitt. "John Florio Reconsidered." *Texas Studies in Literature and Language* 6 (1965): 407–22.

Stefanini, Alberta. "Illustrazioni marcoliniane e testi doniani." *Riscrittura, intertestualità transcodificazione. Atti del Seminario di studi (Pisa, genn.-magg. 1991)*. Eds. Emanuela Scarano and Donatella Diamanti. Pisa: Tipografia editrice pisana, 1992. 145-66.

Stevenson, Burton. *The Home Book of Proverbs, Maxims, and Familiar Phrases*. New York: Macmillan, 1948.

Stobaeus, Joannes. *Keras amalthaias. Ioannou tou Stovaiou eklogai apophthegmaton. Ioannis Stobaei Sententiae ex thesauris Graecorum delectae, quarum autores circiter ducentos et quinquaginta citat, et in sermones sive locos communes digestae*. Zurich: Christoph Froschauer, 1543.

Stocchi, Manlio Pastore. "Appunti su il *Decameron* e la letteratura italiana." *Il Decameron nella letteratura europea. Atti del convegno organizzato dall'Accademia delle Scienze di Torino e dal Dipartimento di Scienze Letterarie e Filologiche dell'Università di Torino. Torino, 17–18 nov. 2005*. Ed. Clara Allasia. Roma: Edizioni di storia e letteratura, 2006. 129–40.

Stoppelli, Pasquale, and Eugenio Picchi. *Letteratura Italiana Zanichelli*. Bologna: Zanichelli, 2001.

Strafforello, Gustavo. *La sapienza del mondo, ovvero Dizionario universale dei proverbi di tutti i popoli, raccolti, tradotti, comparati e commentati da Gustavo Strafforello con l'aggiunta di aneddoti, racconti, fatterelli e di illustrazioni storiche, morali, scientifiche, filologiche, ecc*. Torino: Augusto Federico Negro, 1883.

Stromboli, Carolina. "Le ingiurie." *Le parole del "Cunto." Indagini sul lessico napoletano del Seicento*. Firenze: Cesati, 2017. 103–34.

———. "La lingua de *Lo Cunto de li cunti* di Giambattista Basile." 2005. Università degli Studi di Napoli Federico II, PhD dissertation.

———. "La lingua de *Lo cunto de li cunti* tra fiaba e realtà." *La tradizione del "cunto" da Giovan Battista Basile a Domenico Rea. Giornate di studio 19 e 20 genn. 2006, Palazzo Du Mesnil*. Ed. Caterina De Caprio. Napoli: Edizioni Libreria Dante & Descartes, 2007. 67–91.

Stussi, Alfredo. "Lingua." Forni and Bragantini, *Lessico critico decameroniano*, 192–221.

———. "Scelte linguistiche e connotati regionali nella novella italiana." *Lingua, dialetto e letteratura*. Torino: Einaudi, 1993. 129–53.

Sullivan, Constance. "Gender Markers in Traditional Spanish Proverbs." *Literature among Discourses: The Spanish Golden Age*. Eds. Wlad Godzich and Nicholas Spadaccini. Minneapolis: U of Minnesota P, 1986. 82–102.

Sullivan, Margaret. "Bruegel's Proverbs: Art and Audience in the Northern Renaissance." *The Art Bulletin* 73.3 (1991): 431–66.

Sumillera, Rocío. "Language Manuals and The Book Trade in England." *Translation and the Book Trade in Early Modern England*. Eds. José Maria Pérez-Fernàndez and Edward Wilson-Lee. Cambridge-New York: Cambridge UP, 2014. 61–80.

———. "Sixteenth-Century Italian, French, Spanish and English Language Material. A Bibliographical Study." *Sederi* 23 (2013): 139–58.

Summonte, Giovanni Antonio. *Historia della città e regno di Napoli di Giovanni Antonio Summonte napolitano, ove si trattano le cose più notabili accadute dalla sua edificatione sin a' tempi nostri*. Napoli: appresso Giovanni Iacomo Carlino, 1601–02.

Taegio, Bartolomeo. *Il Liceo di Messer Bartolomeo Taegio, dove si ragiona dell'ordine delle academie et della nobiltà*. Milano: appresso Pietro et Francesco Tini, 1571.

Tanini, Francesco. *La donna secondo il giudizio dei dotti e dei proverbi*. Firenze: presso Felice Paggi, 1872.

Tartaro, Achille. "La prosa narrativa antica." *Letteratura italiana*. Ed. Alberto Asor Rosa. Vol. 3. Torino: Einaudi, 1984. 623–713.

Tarzia, Fabio. "Il *Cunto* di Giovan Battista Basile e l'ideazione di un nuovo genere letterario." *Letteratura italiana e utopia*. Ed. Alberto Asor Rosa. Roma: Editori Riuniti, 1996. 177–200.

Tassinari, Lamberto. *John Florio. The Man Who Was Shakespeare*. Montréal: Giano Books, 2009.

Tasso, Torquato. *Gerusalemme liberata*. Ed. Lanfranco Caretti. Torino: Einaudi, 2007.

———. *Jerusalem Delivered*. Trans. Joseph Tusiani. Rutherford: Fairleigh Dickinson UP, 1970.

Tauro, Raffaele. *L'Ingelosite speranze, comedia del signor Rafaele Tauro*. Napoli: per Ettore Cicconio e di nuovo per Giovanni Francesco Paci ad istanza di Adriano Scultore, 1670.

Tavoni, Mirko, ed. *Italia ed Europa nella linguistica del Rinascimento: confronti e relazioni. Atti del Convegno internazionale, Ferrara, Palazzo Paradiso, 20–24 mar. 1991*. Modena: Panini, 1996.

Taylor, Archer. "A Bibliographical Note on Wellerisms." *The Journal of American Folklore* 65.258 (1952): 420–21.

———. *An Index to «The Proverb»*. Helsinki: Suomalainen Tiedakatemia, Academia scientiarum fennica, 1934.

———. "An Introductory Bibliography for the Study of Proverbs." *Modern Philology* 30.2 (1932): 195–210.

———. "Problems in the Study of Proverbs." *The Journal of American Folklore* 47.183 (1934): 1–21.

———. *The Proverb*. Cambridge, MA: Harvard UP, 1931.

———. "The Wisdom of Many and the Wit of One." *The Wisdom of Many: Essays on the Proverb*. Eds. Wolfgang Mieder and Alan Dundes. New York: Garland, 1981: 3–9.

Taylor, Barry. "Medieval Proverb Collections: The West European Tradition." *Journal of the Warburg and Courtauld Institutes* 55 (1992): 19–35.

Tedeschi, John, and Grazia Biondi. "I contributi culturali dei riformatori protestanti italiani nel tardo Rinascimento." *Italica* 64.1 (1987): 19–61.

Terracini, Benvenuto. *Lingua libera e libertà linguistica*. Torino: Einaudi, 1963.

Tesauro, Emanuele. *Il cannocchiale aristotelico, o sia Idea dell'arguta et ingegniosa elocutione che serve a tutta l'arte oratoria, lapidaria, et simbolica*. Venezia: Valvasense, 1688.

Theocritus. *Idylls. A Verse Translation*. Trans. Barriss Mills. West Lafayette, IN: Purdue University Studies, 1963.

Thomas, William. *Principal rules of Italian grammer, with a dictionarie for the better understanding of Boccacce, Petrarcha, and Dante, gathered into this tongue by William Thomas*. London: Thomas Berthelet, 1550.

Tilley, Morris Palmer. *Elizabethan Proverb Lore in Lyly's "Euphues" and in Pettie's "Petite Pallace" with Parallels from Shakespeare*. New York: Macmillan, 1926.

Works Consulted

Tiraboschi, Girolamo. *Storia della letteratura italiana*. Napoli: a spese di Giovanni Muccis, 1774–81.

Tobler, Adolf. "Proverbia que dicuntur super natura feminarum." *Zeitschrift für romanische Philologie* 9 (1885): 287–331.

Tolomei, Claudio. *Il Cesano de la lingua toscana*. Ed. Ornella Castellani Pollidori. Firenze: Accademia della Crusca, 1996.

———. *Il Cesano, dialogo di Messer Claudio Tolomei, nel quale da più dotti huomini si disputa del nome col quale si dee ragionevolmente chiamare la volgar lingua*. Venezia: appresso Gabriel Giolito de' Ferrari et fratelli, 1555.

Tomasi, Franco. "Osservazioni sul proverbio nella lirica quattro-cinquecentesca." Pignatti and Crimi, 217–46.

Tomasin, Lorenzo, ed. *Il «Vocabolario degli Accademici della Crusca» (1612) e la storia della lessicografia italiana. Atti del X Convegno ASLI, Associazione per la Storia della Lingua Italiana (Padova, 29–30 nov. 2012–Venezia, 1 dic. 2012)*. Firenze: Cesati, 2013.

Tomaszczyk, Jerzy. "On bilingual dictionaries. The case for bilingual dictionaries for foreign language learners." *Lexicography: Principles and Practice*. Ed. Reinhard Hartmann. London: Academic Press, 1983. 41–51.

Toppi, Nicolò. *Biblioteca Napoletana et apparato a gli huomini illustri in lettere di Napoli e del regno delle famiglie, terre, città, e religioni, che sono nello stesso regno, dalle loro origine per tutto l'anno 1678*. Napoli: Antonio Bulifon, 1678.

Torre, Andrea. *Scritture ferite: innesti, doppiaggi e correzioni nella letteratura rinascimentale*. Venezia: Marsilio, 2019.

Torriano, Giovanni. *The Italian reviv'd, or The introduction to the Italian tongue, containing such grounds as are most immediately useful and necessary for the speedy and easie attaining of the same, as also a new store-house of proper and choice dialogues most useful for such as desire the speaking part*. London: printed by Thomas Roycroft for John Martyn, 1673.

———. *The Italian tutor or a new and most compleat Italian grammer. Containing above others a most compendious way to learne the verbs, and the rules of syntax. To which is annexed a display of the monosyllable particles of the language, by way of alphabet, as also certaine dialogues made up of italianismes or neicities of the language, with the English to them. Studied and compiled with much more time and labour, and now published for the speede and ease of such as desire to attaine the perfection of said language; with an alphabet of primitive and original Italian words, underivable from the Latin. By Giovanni Torriano, an Italian and professor of the same within the city of London*. London: Thomas Paine sold by Henry Robinson, 1640.

Works Consulted

———. *New and easie directions for attaining the Thuscan Italian tongue. Comprehended in necessary rules of pronunciation, rules of accenting by way of alphabet. With a nomenclator, or little dictionarie, set forth for the especiall use of such as are desirous to bee proficients in the said language. By Giovanni Torriano, an Italian and professour of the same within the city of London.* London: by Richard Oulton for Ralph Mab, 1639.

———. *Piazza universale di proverbi italiani, or A common place of Italian proverbs and proverbial phrases, digested in alphabetical order by way of dictionary, interpreted, and occasionally illustrated with notes, together with a supplement of Italian dialogues.* London: Francis and Thomas Warren for the author, 1666.

———. *The second alphabet consisting of proverbial phrases interpreted and illustrated where most necessary, with pleasant and usefull annotations, Italian and English.* London: printed by A. Warren for the author, 1662.

———. *Select Italian proverbs, the most significant, very useful for travellers, and such as desire as language; the same newly made to speak English and the most obscurest places with notes illustrated, use full for such as happily aim not at the language, yet would see the genius of the nation.* Cambridge: Roger Daniel, 1642.

———. *Vocabolario Italiano et Inglese, A dictionary Italian and English formerly compiled by John Florio, and since his last edition, Anno 1611, augmented by himselfe in his life time, with many thousand words and Thuscan phrases, now most diligently revised, corrected, and compared with la Crusca and other approved dictionaries extant since his death, and enriched with very considerable additions; whereunto is added a dictionary English and Italian, with several proverbs and instructions for the speedy attaining to the Italian tongue, never before published by Giovanni Torriano.* London: printed by Thomas Warren for John Martin, James Allestry, and Thomas Dicas, 1659.

Toschi, Paolo. *Guida allo studio delle tradizioni popolari.* Torino: Boringhieri, 1962.

Tosco, Partenio. *L'Eccellenza della lingua napoletana con la maggioranza alla toscana.* Napoli: Il Fiorentino, 1662.

Tosi, Renzo. "Gli «Adagia» di Erasmo e la presenza di τόποι classici nella letteratura europea." *Erasmo da Rotterdam e la cultura europea. Atti dell'Incontro di Studi nel V Centenario della Laurea di Erasmo all'Università di Torino (Torino, 8–9 sett. 2006).* Eds. Enrico Pasini and Pietro Rossi. Firenze: SISMEL, Edizioni del Galluzzo, 2008. 43–59.

———. *Dizionario delle sentenze latine e greche: 10.000 citazioni dall'antichità al Rinascimento nell'originale e in traduzione con commento storico, letterario e filologico.* Milano: BUR, 2000.

Works Consulted

Tosi, Renzo. *La donna è mobile e altri studi di intertestualità proverbiale.* Bologna: Pàtron, 2011.

———. "Precedenti classici di proverbi italiani." Franceschi, *Ragionamenti,* 179–94.

Trésor de la langue française. Dictionnaire de la langue du XIXe et du XXe siècle (1789–1960). Paris: Centre de recherche pour un trésor de la langue française; Editions du Centre national de la recherche scientifique, 1971–.

Trovato, Paolo. *Con ogni diligenza corretto: la stampa e le revisioni editoriali dei testi letterari italiani (1470–1570).* Ferrara: UnifePress, 2009.

Trovato, Salvatore. "Il proverbio come oggetto lessicografico (quasi una norma redazionale)." Franceschi, *Ragionamenti,* 83–91.

———, ed. *Proverbi locuzioni modi di dire nel dominio linguistico italiano.* Roma: Il Calamo, 1999.

Tschiesche, Jacqueline. "Il rifacimento del *Decameron* di Luigi Groto." *Luigi Groto e il suo tempo (1541–1585). Atti del convegno di studi (Adria, 27–29 apr. 1984).* Eds. Giorgio Brunello and Antonio Lodo. Rovigo: Minelliana, 1984. 236–69.

Turrini, Giovanna. *Capire l'antifona. Dizionario dei modi di dire con esempi d'autore.* Bologna: Zanichelli, 1995.

Ughi, Luigi. *Dizionario storico degli uomini illustri ferraresi nella pietà, nelle arti e nelle scienze colle loro opere o fatti principali.* Ferrara: per gli eredi di Giuseppe Rinaldi, 1804.

Ulrich, Giacomo. *Opera nuova e da ridere o Grillo medico. Poemetto popolare di autore ignoto.* Livorno: Raffaello Giusti, 1901.

Valente, Vincenzo. "La lingua napoletana di Pompeo Sarnelli." *Archivio storico pugliese* 30 (1977): 255–65.

———. "Per una migliore intelligenza del napoletano di G. Basile." *Lingua Nostra* 40 (1979): 43–49.

———. *Puglia.* Pisa: Pacini, 1975.

Valesio, Paolo. *Strutture dell'allitterazione. Grammatica, retorica e folklore verbale.* Bologna: Zanichelli, 1968.

Vallini, Cristina, ed. *La pratica e la grammatica. Viaggio nella linguistica del proverbio.* Napoli: Istituto Universitario Orientale, 1989.

Vannucci, Atto. *Proverbi latini illustrati.* Milano: Brigola, 1880–83.

Vanossi, Luigi. "Valori iconici della rima nell'*Orlando furioso.*" *Lingua Nostra* 45 (1984): 35–47.

Varchi, Benedetto. *L'Hercolano.* Ed. Antonio Sorella. Pescara: Libreria dell'Università, 1995.

Varrini, Giulio. *Scuola del volgo, cioè scielta de' piu leggiadri e spiritosi detti, aforismi, e proverbi, tolti da varie lingue particolarmente dall'hebrea, araba, chaldea, greca, latina, todesca, francese, spagnuola, fiamenga, inglese e molt'altre, e trasportati nell'italiana, oltre quelli che in questa nati, da questa sono stati colti. Tutti disposti con certo ordine e ridotti a capi, per instruttione dell'huomo e regola delle attioni humane. Opra in cui l'utile contrasta co 'l curioso, l'acuto co 'l facile, et il vago co 'l breve*. Verona: per Francesco Rossi, 1642.

Vassano, Pico Luri di. *Modi di dire proverbiali e motti popolari italiani, spiegati e commentati da Pico Luri di Vassano*. Roma: Tiberina, 1875.

Vecchi, Giuseppe. "Il «proverbio» nella pratica letteraria dei dettatori della scuola di Bologna." *Studi mediolatini e volgari* 2 (1954): 283–302.

Vecchio, Paola. "Storia linguistica e letteratura dialettale riflessa. Il caso dei pronomi personali in napoletano." *Bollettino linguistico campano* 9–10 (2006): 97–142.

Vedovelli, Massimo. *L'italiano degli stranieri: storia, attualità e prospettive*. Roma: Carocci, 2002.

Vergili, Polidoro. *Polydori Vergilii Urbinatis praesbyteri proverbiorum liber, quo paroemiae insigniores omnium fere scriptorum luculentissima enarratione explicantur*. Strasbourg: Matthias Schürerius, 1510.

———. *Proverbiorum libellus*. Venezia: per Cristoforo de' Pensi, 1498.

Vietri, Simonetta. *Lessico e sintassi delle espressioni idiomatiche: una tipologia tassonomica dell'italiano*. Napoli: Liguori, 1985.

———. "La sintassi delle frasi idiomatiche." *Studi italiani di linguistica teorica e applicata* 1 (1990): 133–46.

Viglione, Francesco. *L'Italia nel pensiero degli scrittori inglesi*. Milano: Fratelli Bocca, 1946.

Vignali, Antonio. *La cazzaria*. Ed. Pasquale Stoppelli. Roma: Edizioni dell'elefante, 1984.

———. "Lettera di Antonio Vignali Arsiccio Intronato in proverbii." *Aggiunta di proverbi toscani di Giuseppe Giusti. Compilata per cura di Aurelio Gotti e corredata d'un indice generale de' proverbi contenuti nelle due raccolte*. Ed. Aurelio Gotti. Firenze: Le Monnier, 1855. 11–20.

———. *Lettera in proverbi*. Ed. Giampaolo Pecori. Firenze: Società editrice fiorentina, 2012.

Villoresi, Marco. *La letteratura cavalleresca: dai cicli medievali all'Ariosto*. Roma: Carocci, 2000.

Vinciguerra, Antonio. "Per un'edizione critica della parte inedita (F-Z) del *Vocabolario del dialetto napolitano* (1891) di Emmanuele Rocco." *Actes du XXVIIe Congrès international de linguistique et de philologie romanes (Nancy, 15–20 juil. 2013). Section 5: Lexicologie, phraséologie, lexicographie*. Eds. Rosario Coluccia, et al. Nancy: ATILF, 2016. 547–57.

Works Consulted

Vinciguerra, Antonio. "Spigolature lessicali napoletane dalle «Carte Emmanuele Rocco» dell'Accademia della Crusca." *Studi di lessicografia italiana* 32 (2015): 197–222.

Vischer, Lukas. "Michelangelo Florio tra Italia, Inghilterra e Val Bregaglia." *Il protestantesimo di lingua italiana nella Svizzera. Figure e movimenti tra cinquecento e ottocento.* Eds. Emidio Campi and Giuseppe La Torre. Torino: Claudiana, 2000. 67–76.

Vitale, Maurizio. *Il capolavoro del Boccaccio e due diverse redazioni. I. La riscrittura del «Decameron» e i mutamenti linguistici. II. Variazioni narrative e stilistiche.* Venezia: Istituto Veneto di Scienze, Lettere ed Arti, 2002.

———. "Di alcune rivendicazioni secentesche della «eccellenza» dei dialetti." *La veneranda favella. Studi di storia della lingua italiana.* Napoli: Domenico Morano, 1988. 305–24.

———. *L'oro nella lingua: contributi per una storia del tradizionalismo e del purismo italiano.* Milano: Ricciardi, 1986.

Vives, Juan Luis. *Los diálogos (Linguae latinae exercitatio).* Ed. María del Pilar García Ruiz. Navarra: Eunsa, 2005.

———. *Linguae latinae exercitatio Ioannis Lodovicus Vivis Valentini. Libellus valde doctus et elegans, nuncque primum in lucem editus. Eiusdem In Vergilii Bucolica expositio, potissimum allegorica.* Basel: Oporin, 1538.

Vocabolario degli Accademici della Crusca con tre indici delle voci, locuzioni, e proverbi latini, e greci posti per entro l'opera. Con privilegio del Sommo Pontefice, del Re Cattolico, della Serenissima Repubblica di Venezia e degli altri Principi e Potentati d'Italia e fuori d'Italia, della Maestà Cesarea, del Re Cristianissimo, e del Serenissimo Arciduca Alberto. Venezia: Tipografia Alberti, 1612.

von Hutten, Ulrich. *Trias Romana.* Mainz: Johann Schöffer, 1519.

Weinrich, Uriel. *Languages in contact: Findings and problems.* The Hague-Paris: Mouton, 1968.

Wesseling, Ari. "Dutch Proverbs and Ancient Sources in Erasmus's *Praise of Folly.*" *Renaissance Quarterly* 47.2 (1994): 351–78.

———. "Dutch Proverbs and Expressions in Erasmus' *Adages, Colloquies,* and *Letters.*" *Renaissance Quarterly* 55.1 (2002): 81–147.

Whiting, Jere Bartlett. "A Collection of Proverbs in BM Additional MS. 37075." *Frangiplegius. Medieval and Linguistic Series in Honor of Francis Peabody Magoun Jr.* Eds. Jessy Bessinger and Robert Creed. New York: New York University, 1965. 274–89.

Whiting, Jere Bartlett, and Helen Wescott Whiting. *Proverbs, sentences, and proverbial phrases from English writings mainly before 1500.* Cambridge, MA: Harvard UP, 1968.

Williams, Gordon. *A dictionary of sexual language and imagery in Shakespearean and Stuart literature*. London: Athlone Press, 1994.

Wright, Herbert. *The first English translation of the "Decameron"*. Upsala: Lindequist, 1953.

Wyatt, Michael. "La biblioteca in volgare di John Florio. Una bibliografia annotata." *Bruniana e Campanelliana* 9.2 (2003): 409–34.

———. *The Italian Encounter with Tudor England: A Cultural Politics of Translation*. Cambridge-New York: Cambridge UP, 2005.

Yarrington, Alison, et al., eds. *Travels and Translations. Anglo-Italian Cultural Transactions*. Amsterdam-New York: Rodopi, 2013.

Yates, Frances Amelia. "An Italian in Restoration England." *Journal of the Wartburg and Courtauld Institute* 4 (1943): 216–20.

———. "Italian Teachers in Elizabethan England." *Journal of the Warburg Institute* 1.2 (1937): 103–16.

———. "Italian Teachers in England." 1955. *Renaissance and Reform: The Italian Contribution*. London-New York: Routledge, 1983. 161–64.

———. *John Florio. The Life of an Italian in Shakespeare's England*. Cambridge-New York: Cambridge UP, 1934.

———. *A Study of «Love's Labour's Lost»*. 1936. Cambridge-New York: Cambridge UP, 2013.

Yver, Jacques. *A courtlie controversie of Cupids cautels*. London: imprinted by Francis Coldock and Henry Bynneman, 1578.

Zanin, Enrica. "Cervantes, i novellieri e la finalità delle novelle: dall'utilità all'eutrapelia." *eHumanista/Cervantes* 6 (2017): 183–96.

Zanotto, Francesco. *Parnaso italiano: raccolta delle opere dei poeti italiani dai primi secoli ai tempi moderni*. Venezia: Antonelli, 1832–55.

Zemon, Natalie Davis. "Proverbial wisdom and popular errors." *Society and Culture in Early Modern France*. Stanford: Stanford UP, 1975. 227–67.

Zolkovskij, Alexandr. "At the Intersection of Linguistics, Paremiology and Poetics: on the Literary Structure of Proverbs." *Poetic* 7.3 (1978): 309–32.

Zumthor, Paul. "L'epiphonème proverbial." *Revue des Sciences Humaines* 51.163 (1976): 313–28.

Index of Names

Acarisio, Alberto, 411n32, 425n42
Accademia degli Intronati, *xiii*
Accademia degli Scioperati, 196, 440n5
Accademia dei Trasformati, 440n5
Accademia della Crusca (also "Accademici della Crusca" in text), *xii*, 9, 12–13, 22–23, 124, 199–200, 202, 390n36, 392n44, 393n50, 394n54, 394n57, 394n60, 426n43, 439n99, 443n23, 446–47n36
Acciaioli, Donato, 198
Acciaioli, Jacopo, 198
Aeschylus, 1, 396n68
Aesop, 204, 443–44n26
Agricola, Georgius, 122
Albanese, Angela, 32, 435n82, 453n72
Alciati, Andrea, 143, 239, 455n88
Aldobrandini, Ippolito. *See* Clement VIII
Alemanni, Luigi, 412n39
Alfonso I of Aragon (king), 198
Allasia, Clara, 197, 448n42, 452n70
Alunno, Francesco, 47, 216–21, 264–65, 397n77, 411n32, 419n8, 434n79, 449–50n51, 450n57
Amenta, Niccolò, 446n35
Andreoli, Raffaele, 232, 240
Angeli, Niccolò, 7
Angiolieri, Cecco, *xxii*, 159, 437n88
Anne of Denmark (queen), 123–24
Antonelli, Giuseppe, 406n5
Apuleius, Lucius Madaurensis, 2
Aquinas. *See* Thomas Aquinas, Saint
Arce de Benavente, Fernando, 392n46
Aresti, Alessandro, 14, 394n60
Aretino, Pietro, 41–42, 57, 79, 390n37, 406n4, 406n8, 407n9, 433n75
Ariosto, Ludovico, 6, 41–43, 48, 50–52, 104, 120, 143, 389n33, 406n5, 407n14, 411n33, 412nn36–39, 413nn44–45, 415n65, 417–18n85, 432n69, 460n1
Aristophanes, 1, 389n31
Aristotle, 17–18, 21, 255, 389n31, 444n27
Arora, Shirley, 397n80
Arthaber, Augusto, 154, 157, 437n87
Ascham, Roger, 126, 128, 130, 423n26, 423n29, 424n34
Asensio y Mejorado, Francisco, 224
Augustine of Hippo, Saint, 416n70
Aurelius, Marcus Antoninus, 144–45, 461n1
Auriemma, Luca, 215–16
Awdeley, John, 146

Bailey, David, *xxii*
Bakhtin, Mikhail, 210, 213, 401n99
Banchieri, Adriano/Tommaso. *See* Scaligeri dalla Fratta, Camillo
Bandello, Matteo, 388n22
Baratto, Mario, 100
Bargagli, Girolamo, *xiii–xiv*, 21, 388n22
Barker, William (modern critic), *xxi*
Barker, William, 423–24n30
Bartoli, Lorenzo, 414n54
Basile, Giambattista, *xv–xvi*, *xxi–xxii*, 196–97, 200–03, 209–10, 221–23, 227, 229–32, 237–38, 241–42, 244, 246, 250, 255, 259, 435n82,

535

Basile (*continued*)
440n6, 440–41nn8–10, 441–42nn15–16, 442n19, 443n21, 445n31, 446n35, 448n42, 449n47, 451n61, 452nn65–66, 452n71, 453n74, 453–54nn77–78, 454n83, 455n85, 456n90, 457nn93–94, 458n100
Battaglia, Salvatore, 254
Beccaria, Gian Luigi, 233, 385n4, 441n13
Bede the Venerable, Saint, 387n14
Bembo, Pietro, 48, 122, 129, 199, 395n62, 419n7, 425n42, 426–27n45, 427n47
Benucci, Elisabetta, 395n63, 409n22, 410n24
Benvenuto da Imola, 248–49
Benvenuto Italiano, 129, 424n31
Bernardus, Saint, 416n70
Berni, Francesco, 52
Beroaldo, Filippo, 386n10, 391n41
Bertocchi, Dionigio, 424n32
Biffi, Marco, 394n54
Bindoni, Francesco di Alessandro, 412n36
Bizzarri, Hugo, 404n116
Black, Robert, 425n40
Blado, Antonio, 391n38
Blount, Edward, 127
Boccaccio, Giovanni, *xv–xvi*, *xviii*, *xxi–xxii*, 4–5, 8, 31–32, 41–120, 123, 134, 141, 143, 157, 160, 186, 196, 198, 200, 209–10, 244, 254–57, 260–65, 406nn6–7, 406–07nn09–11, 407nn13–14, 408n15, 409nn19–21, 409–10nn23–24, 410n26, 410–12nn29–34, 412n36, 412–13nn40–41, 413–14nn45–46, 414n49, 414n56, 414–15nn59–63, 415nn66–67, 416n68,
416n72, 417n81, 417n85, 418nn86–88, 420n13, 423n29, 424n33, 435–37n86, 440n8, 448n42
Boccalini, Traiano, 123, 420n14
Boggione, Valter, 254
Boiardo, Matteo Maria, *xxii*, 6, 52, 57, 73–74, 413n45, 415n65, 417n79, 417–18n85
Bolognetti, Francesco, 412n39
Bolzoni, Lina, 408n14
Bonciani, Francesco, 53
Borghini, Francesco, 54–55, 60, 404n114
Botterill, Steven, *xxii*
Bottigheimer, Ruth, *xxi*, 197
Bourchier, John, 145
Bovicelli, Giuliano, 439nn3–4
Bracciolini, Poggio, 6
Brambilla Ageno, Franca, 37, 387n15, 402n103, 403n111
Branca, Vittore, *xxi*, 100, 108
Bronzini, Giovanni Battista, 398n84
Brucioli, Antonio, 4, 50, 57, 105, 147–49, 165, 262, 387n19, 388n20, 410–11nn29–32, 417n84, 453n73
Bruegel, Peter (the Elder), 389n33
Bruni, Francesco, 51
Bruni, Leonardo, 409n20
Bruno, Giordano, 123, 132, 143, 419n10
Brusantino, Vincenzo (aka Vincenzo Brusantini and Vincenzo Brugiantini), *xv–xviii*, *xxi–xxiii*, 6, 31–34, 39, 41–120, 134, 157, 160, 228, 243, 251, 253–67, 404–06nn1–5, 406–07nn7–9, 407n11, 407nn13–14, 408n15, 408–09nn17–18, 413n42, 413n45, 414n50, 414n53, 415n59, 415nn62–64, 415n67, 416n78, 417nn79–81, 418nn86–87, 459n4

Index

Bruscagli, Riccardo, 413n43
Bulifon, Antonio, 195, 439n3, 440nn6–7, 442n19, 448n45
Buoni, Tomaso, 9, 11–12, 392n43, 393nn51–52, 438n98, 451n59
Burchiello (born Domenico di Giovanni), 74
Butler, Harold, *xxi*
Bybee, Joan, 399n92

Cadamosto, Marco, 390n37
Caecus, Appius Crassus Claudius, 1
Caesar, Julius Gaius, 386n10
Calepio, Ambrogio da, 424n32
Calmo, Andrea, 391n41
Calvin, John, 52
Canepa, Nancy, *xxi*, 226, 435n82
Caniato, Manuela, 443n24
Capaccio, Giulio Cesare, 448n44, 456n88
Capasso, Niccolò, 446n35
Capozzoli, Raffaele, 197, 448n43, 456n89
Capponi, Gino, 15, 395n63
Carafa, Diomede, 452n69
Carafa, Gian Pietro. *See* Paul IV
Carapezza, Sandra, 43
Carbone, Ludovico, 6
Cardona, Giorgio Raimondo, 227
Cartier, Jacques, 123, 420n12
Casadei, Federica, 36, 403n109
Cassio da Narni, 6
Castelvetro, Giacomo, 124
Castiglione, Baldassare, 116, 127, 389n28, 423n29, 432n70
Castiglione, Giovanni Battista, 126
Cato, Dionysius, 2, 4, 39, 386n9, 425n40
Catullus, Gaius Valerius, 386n10, 389n31
Cecil, Robert, 123
Cecil, William, 419n6
Celano, Carlo, 448n44
Cerquiglini, Bernard, 398n85
Cerquiglini, Jacqueline, 398n85

Cervantes, Miguel de, 444n27
Charles I (king), 424n36
Charles I of Anjou, 103
Cherdantseva, Tamara, 402n105
Chiecchi, Giuseppe, 5, 413n41
Cian, Vittorio, 395n62
Cicero, Marcus Tullius, *xxii*, 18, 107, 205–06, 210, 386n10, 401n100, 444n29
Ciclirani, Claudio, 440n7
Cieco d'Adria. *See* Groto, Luigi
Cieco da Ferrara, Francesco, 6, 408n18, 417n79, 458–59n103
Cirese, Mario Alberto, 16, 25–26
Citolini, Alessandro, 124, 427n47, 445n33
Claude de Sainliens. *See* Holyband, Claudius
Clement VII (pope; born Giulio de' Medici), 8
Clement VIII (pope; born Ippolito Aldobrandini), 7, 54
Colet, John, 431n63
Consoli, Joseph, *xxii*
Corazzini, Francesco, 416n75
Cornazzano, Antonio, 6, 143, 390n37
Correas, Gonzalo, 454n81
Corrozet, Gilles, 456n88
Corso, Raffaele, 37
Corso, Rinaldo, 425n42
Cortelazzo, Manlio, 199, 392n42, 443n23
Cortese, Giulio Cesare, 200, 233, 441n15, 446n35, 449n46, 454n78, 454n83, 456n91
Costo, Tommaso, 199, 388n22
Crane, Thomas Frederick, 196
Cranmer, Thomas (archbishop), 419n6
Crescimbeni, Giovanni Maria, 406n7
Croce, Benedetto, 196, 215–16, 222, 441n11, 449n48, 450n52, 451n58

Index

Croce, Giulio Cesare, 214–15, 387n17, 392n43, 449–50nn50–51
Cynthio, Aloyse de gli Fabritii, 8, 391nn38–39, 410n27, 440n7

da Barberino, Andrea, 52–53
D'Agostino, Alfonso, 385n1
d'Alibray, Vion, 439n4
D'Ambra, Raffaele, 216, 232, 236, 240, 245, 247, 445–46n35, 449n46, 452n68, 456n91
Dante Alighieri, *xxii*, 78, 101, 143, 200, 248, 413n45, 416nn70–71, 424n33, 425n42, 444–45n30, 450n57
D'Aragona, Tullia, 52–53
d'Arezzo, Guittone, 416n70
D'Ascoli, Francesco, 446n35
da Strada, Zanobi, 198
Davanzati, Bartolomeo, 409n21
Davanzati, Bernardo, 116
de Boliris, Bona, 405n4
de' Bonaiuti, Maddalena, 411n31
De Donato, Nicola, 196
degli Arienti, Sabadino, 388n22
de Guevara, Antonio, 144–46, 434n78, 461n1
della Casa, Giovanni, 127
della Porta, Giovanni Battista, 439n3
delle Colonne, Guido, 101, 416n68
Del Tufo, Gioan Battista, 448n44
de Robertis, Domenico, 409n22
de Rosa, Loise, 198, 441n12, 450n54
de' Rossi, Bastiano, 14
Desviati, Eugenio (aka Sgargiato), 440n7, 448n44
de Vega, Lope, 454n80
de Vives, Ignazio, 440n7
Diaconus, Paulus, 416n70

Di Capua, Francesco, 386nn5–6, 386n9, 386n11, 387n14, 396n70, 397n73
Dickens, Charles, 36
Diodati, Giovanni, 147
Diogenianus of Heraclea, 396n67
Dionigi da Borgo San Sepolcro, 103
Dionigi, Francesco da Fano, 55
Dionisotti, Carlo, 55
Dolce, Ludovico, 50–51, 407n14, 410n29, 411n33, 412nn35–38, 425n42
Domenichi, Ludovico, 390n37
Domenico di Giovanni. *See* Burchiello
Doni, Anton Francesco, 143–44, 246, 390n37, 407n14, 433–34nn76–77
Dudley, Robert, 123–24, 133, 418n1, 430n61
Dyer, Edward, 124

Eco, Umberto, 447n40
Edward VI (king), 418n6
Elizabeth I (queen), 122, 126–27, 422n22, 426n43
Engel, William, 437n93
Ennius, Quintus, 1
Epictetus, 420n15
Epicurus, 101
Erasmus von Rotterdam, *xxi*, 7, 14, 20–22, 34, 140, 158, 178, 250, 253, 264, 386n7, 386n10, 389–90nn32–33, 390n35, 394n59, 397n74, 397n76, 397n78, 445n31, 452n63
Ercole II d'Este (duke), 41, 52, 59, 405n2
Euripides, 1, 385n3, 389n31

Farnese, Ottavio, 42
Fasano, Gabriele, 446n36, 454n83, 457n93

538

Index

Favaro, Maiko, 42, 59–60, 407n14, 415n62
Ferdinand II of Aragon (king) ["Ferdinand the Catholic" in text], 198
Ferroni, Giulio, 443n22
Fiacchi, Luigi, 390n36
Field, Theophilus, 422n25
Fiorelli, Piero, 393–94n54, 395n63
Fiorillo, Silvio, 446n36
Firenzuola, Agnolo, 407n10
Fitch, John, *xxii*
Flamini, Francesco, 416n74
Flonta, Teodor, 1
Florio, John (a.k.a. Giovanni Florio), *xv–xviii, xxi–xxiii*, 11, 23, 29, 31–33, 35, 38–39, 121–93, 220, 228, 240, 251, 253–67, 406n8, 416n69, 418nn1–2, 418nn4–8, 419nn10–11, 420–21nn12–16, 421–22nn19–20, 423n27, 424n31, 424–25nn37–39, 426–27nn43–45, 427n47, 428nn48–49, 428n50, 428–29n52, 429n54, 429–31nn56–62, 431n64, 431–32nn66–67, 432nn69–71, 433n74, 434nn76–78, 435–37nn83–86, 437n89, 437n94, 438n95, 438n98, 459nn3–4, 460–63nn1–2, 463n3
Florio, Michelangelo, 121–22, 418nn5–6, 419nn7–8
Folena, Gianfranco, 32, 399n88
Fontanini, Giusto, 406n7
Foppa, Giuseppe, 414n51
Forteguerri, Giovanni, 388n22
Fortini, Pietro, 388n22
Fortunio, Giovanni Francesco, 129, 425n42
Franceschi, Temistocle, *xiv–xv, xvii*, 17, 26–30, 35, 396n71, 399nn89–90, 400nn94–96, 401n98, 402n102, 403n112
Franzese, Rosa, 196
Frizzi, Giuseppe, 396n64, 445n34
Frontinus, Sextus Julius, 3
Fulco, Giorgio, 197

Gabriele, Giacomo, 425n42
Galiani, Ferdinando, 440n6, 441n15, 442n16, 445n30, 446n35, 447n41
Garavelli, Bice Mortara, 385n4, 397n78
Garay, Blasco de, 391n41
Garzo (aka Garço dottore), 3, 387n15
Garzoni, Tommaso, 124
Gelli, Giovanni Battista, 424n30
Gellius, Aulus, 389n31
Geremia da Montagnone, 389n29
Getto, Giovanni, 201
Gherardo, Paolo, 54
Ghirelli, Antonio, 441n13, 452n69
Giambullari, Bernardo, 409n21
Giambullari, Pierfrancesco, 425n42
Giglio, Raffaele, 197
Giolito, Gabriel de' Ferrari, 50, 389n30, 407n14, 411n32, 412n36
Giolito, Giovanni da Trino, 50
Giovanni di Garlandia, 416n70
Giovanni Fiorentino (ser), 388n22, 407n10
Giraldi, Giambattista Cinzio, 388n22
Giusti, Giuseppe, 15, 34, 38, 41, 395n63, 458n102
Gleijeses, Vittorio, 449n50
Gluski, Jerzy, 154, 156
Goidànich, Pietro Gabriele, 416n77
Grantham, Henry, 128, 419n7, 424n31, 424n35
Grazzini, Anton Francesco (aka Lasca), 388n22

539

Index

Griffio, Giovanni, 50
Grimaldi, Mirko, 24–25, 30, 35, 397n79, 398n83, 398n86
Groto, Luigi (aka Cieco d'Adria), 54–55, 407n13
Guadagnino. *See* Valvassori, Giovanni Andrea
Guarini, Guarino, 449n46
Guaschi, Pietro Emilio, 440n8
Guazzo, Stefano, 127, 143, 432n70
Guicciardini, Francesco, 195, 389n32
Guicciardini, Lodovico, 141–42, 253, 431nn66–67
Gummere, Richard, *xxii*

Hakluyt, Richard, 420n12
Haller, Hermann W., 197, 418n1, 443n24
Haupt, Moritz, 36
Haym, Nicolas François, 406n7
Hazlitt, William Carew, 439n100
Henderson, Jeffrey, *xxii*
Henrietta Maria of France (queen), 424n36
Henry VIII (king), 418n6
Herodotus, 1
Hesiod, 1, 385n3
Heywood, John, 158–59, 167, 421n17, 437n87
Hoby, Thomas, 127, 423n30
Hockett, Charles, 35
Holyband, Claudius (aka Claudius Hollyband, Claudius Holiband, Claudius Holliband; born Claude de Sainliens), 128, 130, 137, 419n7, 424n31, 424n37, 425n38, 435n80
Homer, 389n31, 412n39
Horatius, Publius Cocles, 389n31
Howell, James, 391n41
Hunter, George, 430n58

Imbriani, Vittorio, 215, 440n7, 443n21, 448n44, 451n58

Innocent XII (pope; born Antonio Pignatelli), 195
Isidore of Seville, Saint, 416n70

James I (king), 123
Javitch, Daniel, 60, 412n38
Jerome, Saint, 386n10
Jesus Ben Sira. *See* Yeshua Ben Sira
John the Evangelist, 3
Jolles, André, 399n91
Juvenalis, Junius Decimus, 416n76

Kelso, James, 25, 399n87
Kirshenblatt-Gimblett, Barbara, 400n93

Labov, William, 24–25
Lando, Ortensio, 398n28
Langland, Thomas, 165
Langlotz, Andreas, 35, 402n106
Lapucci, Carlo, 38, 403n110, 437n91, 453n73, 457n98
Lardelli, Giovanni, 395n62
Lasca. *See* Grazzini, Anton Francesco
Lausberg, Heinrich, 385n4, 397n78
Ledgeway, Adam, 197, 216, 450n54, 451n60, 454n79
Le Maçon, Antoine, 420n13
Lena, Francesco, 9, 12–13, 248, 392n43, 394n56, 404n118, 453n74, 455n87
Lentulo, Scipione, 424n35
Leopardi, Giacomo, 121, 151, 435n81
Lepschy, Giulio, 435n82
Liburnio, Nicolò, 390n37
Lily, William, 431n63
Lippi, Lorenzo, 6–7, 13, 19–20, 394n58
Litovkina, Anna Tóthne, 400n97
Loffredo, Ferrante, 195
Lorenzo il Magnifico. *See* Medici, Lorenzo de'
Luke the Evangelist, 3

Index

Luther, Martin, 444n26
Lyly, John, 146

Machiavelli, Giovanni Paolo, 405n2
Machiavelli, Niccolò, 116, 143, 423n29
Maiden, Martin, 416n77
Mainardi, Arlotto, 6
Malato, Enrico, *xxi*, 196, 204, 206, 209, 232–33, 439nn1–2, 444n29, 449n48
Malipiero, Girolamo, 406–07n9
Mandelbaum, Allen, *xxii*
Manetti, Antonio, 409n21
Manners, Roger ["Earl of Rutland" in text], 124
Manni, Paola, 5
Manuzio, Aldo, 7
Manuzio, Paolo, 390n34
Marcolini, Francesco, 41–43, 118, 405n3, 406nn5–6, 406–07n9, 407n14, 409n18
Marino, Giovan Battista, 134, 442n15
Mark the Evangelist, 3
Martorana, Pietro, 440n6
Mary I of Tudor (queen), 122
Masillo Reppone. *See* Sarnelli, Pompeo
Massobrio, Lorenzo, 254
Masuccio Salernitano, 388n22, 407n10
Matarrese, Tina, 414n57, 417n79
Matteucci, Riccarda, 428n49
Matthew the Evangelist, 3
Maximus, Valerius Lucius, 2–3, 107
May, James, *xxii*
Mazzucchelli, Giammaria, 406n7
McWilliam, George, *xxi*
Medici, Cosimo I de', 54
Medici, Francesco I de', 55
Medici, Giovanni Angelo. *See* Pius IV
Medici, Giulio de'. *See* Clement VII
Medici, Leopoldo de', 13
Medici, Lorenzo de' (a.k.a. Lorenzo il Magnifico), 7, 19
Ménage, Gilles, 13, 394n57
Menander, 1, 11, 385n3
Menza, Salvatore, 398n82
Merbury, Charles, 125, 416n69, 421–22nn18–20, 432n68
Mieder, Wolfgang, 400n97
Minucci, Paolo (pseud. Puccio Lamoni), 394n58
Molza, Francesco Maria, 407n10
Monosini, Agnolo (a.k.a. Angelo Monosini), 9, 11, 13–14, 22–23, 263, 392n43, 393n48, 393n50, 394n57, 394nn59–60, 397n76, 453n75, 459nn1–2
Montaigne, Michel Eyquem de, 123
Montini, Donatella, 135, 430n58, 437n86, 437n89
Montuori, Francesco, 197
Morata, Olimpia, 409n20
Morel-Fatio, Alfred, 449n49
Mormile, Mario, 428n49
Mortimer, Anthony, *xxii*
Musa, Mark, *xxii*

Nannini, Francesco, 417n79
Nashe, Thomas, 422n24
Nash, Ralph, *xxii*
Natale, Cesare, 440n7
Navò, Curzio Traiano, 50, 410n29
Negri da Bassano, Francesco, 423n28
Nencioni, Giovanni, 140
Nicolò di Aristotile (pseud. Zoppino), 407n14
North, Thomas, 146

Ochino, Bernardino, 423n28
Orsini, Vincenzo Maria (cardinal), 195
Ovidius, Publius Naso, *xxii*, 238, 461n1

541

Index

Quintilianus, Marcus Fabius, *xxi*, 18–19, 21–22, 389n31, 396–97nn72–73
Quondam, Amedeo, 407n9

Pallavicino, Horatio, 422n25
Palsgrave, John, 165
Paolo da Perugia, 103
Paolo di messer Pace da Certaldo, 3–4
Parabosco, Girolamo, 388n22, 407n10
Paravicino, Pietro, 129, 425n39
Parma, Michela, 409n22, 410n24
Pasini, Mapheo, 412n36
Patecchio da Cremona, Girardo, 4
Paul IV (pope; born Gian Pietro Carafa), 55
Pazzaglia, Giovanni Antonio, 395n62
Percel, Gordon, 406n7
Perocco, Daria, 78, 115, 413n42, 415nn62–64
Perrone, Tommaso. *See* Sarnelli, Pompeo
Perrucci, Andrea, 454n78
Pescetti, Orlando, 9–10, 13, 21, 130, 165, 392n43, 392n45, 392n47, 404n118, 438n98
Peterson, Richard, 127
Petrarca, Francesco, *xiii–xiv, xxii*, 3, 143, 200, 234, 406n9, 412n34, 423n29, 424n33, 425n42, 454n82
Petronius, Gaius Arbiter (a.k.a. Titus Arbiter Petronius), 3
Pettie, George, 127, 423n30
Pettinelli, Rosanna, 42, 50, 58, 118, 259, 405nn2–3, 414n52, 417n81
Phaedrus, Gaius Julius, 443–44n26
Phocylides of Miletus, 385n3
Piccolomini, Enea Silvio. *See* Pius II
Picone, Michelangelo, 452n66

Piergentile, Felice. *See* Sixtus V
Pignatelli, Antonio. *See* Innocent XII
Pike, Kenneth, 24–25
Pincio, Aurelio, 4
Pindar, 389n31
Pio, Giovanni Battista, 386n10
Pitrè, Giuseppe, 449n50
Pius II (pope; born Enea Silvio Piccolomini), 409n20
Pius IV (pope; born Giovanni Angelo Medici), 7, 55
Pizzoli, Lucilla, 402n101, 424n31
Plato, 143, 165
Plautus, Titus Maccius, 1, 389n31
Plutarchus, Lucius Mestrius, 107, 143, 145, 385n3, 389n31, 434n78, 461n1
Poliziano, Angelo, 6–7, 389n28
Pompeius, Gnaeus Magnus, 204–06
Pontano, Giovanni, 6, 389n27
Ponze de Soto, Manuel, 222
Portonaris da Trino, Francesco, 144
Pötters, Wilhelm, 109
Praloran, Marco, 415n65
Procaccioli, Paolo, 43
Prosperi, Bartolomeo, 405n2
Puccio Lamoni. *See* Minucci, Paolo
Pulci, Luigi, *xxii*, 6, 58, 167

Quadrio, Francesco Saverio, 406n7
Qualizza, Giorgio, 26, 30–31, 399–400n93

Rabelais, François, 213
Radtke, Edgar, 444n28
Raeburn, David, *xxii*
Raffaele, Liberatore, 440n6
Raimondi, Gianmario, 422n23, 426n43
Rak, Michele, 202, 208, 441n13, 444n28, 447n38
Raleigh, Walter, 123
Ramusio, Giovan Battista, 420n12

Index

Renée of France, 4, 50, 52
Rhys, Siòn Dafydd, 424n31, 426n44
Rinaldi, Orazio, 449n48, 450n53
Rocco, Emmanuele, *xxi*, 197, 205–06, 208, 233, 236–37, 240, 244–46, 250, 445nn34–35, 447n38, 450n55, 451n63, 452n64, 455n85
Romagnoli, Gaetano, 49, 221, 395n62
Rondinelli, Paolo, 394n54, 396n66, 415n66, 416n68, 418n88
Roseo, Mambrino da Fabriano, 144
Rossi, Sergio, 419n6, 429n56
Rubini, Cesare, 440n6
Ruscelli, Girolamo, 50, 405n4, 407n14, 411n34, 412n36
Russell, Lucy ["Countess of Bedford" in text], 124

Sacchetti, Franco, 58, 388n22, 457n97, 459n1
Safian, Louis, 400n97
Salviati, Lionardo, 9–10, 12, 14, 54–55, 167, 232, 392nn43–44, 404n118, 420n13, 437n94, 438n98, 450n55, 455n85, 457n99
Sanford, James, 125, 137, 154, 431–32n67
Sanford, John, 128, 424n31
Sannazaro, Jacopo, *xxii*, 199, 234–35, 238, 454n82
Sansovino, Francesco, 50, 57, 407n10, 411n32, 411–12nn34–35
Santa Cruz de Dueñas, Melchor de, 224
Sarnelli, Pompeo (pseud. Masillo Reppone and Tommaso Perrone), *xv–xviii, xxi–xxiii*, 13, 31–33, 35, 39, 193, 195–252, 253–67, 439nn1–4, 440–41nn6–9, 442–43nn16–19, 443n21, 444n27, 444n29, 445n33, 446nn35–36, 447nn38–39, 448–49nn42–45, 450–51nn57–58, 451n61, 452n63, 452nn66–67, 452–53n71, 453n74, 454–55nn83–84, 457n93, 457n97, 458n100, 459n3
Saunders, Nicholas, 124, 133
Scaligeri dalla Fratta, Camillo (a.k.a. Adriano Banchieri; born Tommaso Banchieri), 387n17
Scott, C. H., *xxii*
Scott, Thomas, 420n14
Segre, Cesare, 151
Seneca, Licius Annaeus, *xxii*, 2, 18, 386nn6–7, 459n2
Sercambi, Giovanni, 388n22
Serdonati, Francesco, 9, 12, 108, 165, 167, 232, 392n43, 393–94n54, 404n118, 410n28, 437n94, 438n98, 450n55, 455n85, 458n99, 459n103
Serianni, Luca, 402n104
Serio, Luigi, 440n6, 441–42n15, 446n35, 452n64
Sgargiato. *See* Desviati, Eugenio
Sgruttendio de Scafato, Felippo, 200, 233, 446n35, 447n38
Shakespeare, William, 123, 419n11, 420n15
Simonini, Rinaldo Jr., 135, 419n11, 430n57
Sixtus V (pope; born Felice Piergentile), 55
Solomon, 3–4, 55, 58, 105, 113, 143, 146–49, 165, 214, 262, 386n12, 387n19, 398n29, 411n30, 417n84, 425n39, 453n73
Sophocles, 1, 389n31

543

Index

Speroni, Charles, 38–39, 181, 197, 214, 389n28, 404n113, 404nn117–19, 422n20, 438n95, 438n98, 441n10
Stanley, Charles Ross, *xxii*
Stobaeus, Joannes, 11, 393n49
Strafforello, Gustavo, 15, 59
Straparola, Gianfrancesco (a.k.a. Giovanni Francesco Straparola), 388n22, 407n10
Stromboli, Carolina, *xxi*, 197, 458n100
Sullivan, Constance, 254
Summonte, Giovanni Antonio, 195, 444n29

Tacitus, Publius Cornelius (a.k.a. Gaius Cornelius Tacitus), 386n5
Taegio, Bartolomeo, 390n36
Tanini, Francesco, 395n62
Tartaro, Achille, 408n16, 414n48
Tasso, Torquato, 143, 199, 449n46, 454n83
Tauro, Raffaele, 454n80, 457n95
Taylor, Archer, 16, 23–24, 35, 37, 181, 397n80, 398n81, 402n103
Terentius, Publius, 2, 389n31, 397n73
Tesauro, Emanuele, 388n26
Theocritus, 36
Thomas Aquinas, Saint, 444n27
Thomas Haemerkken (a.k.a. Thomas à Kempis), 165
Thomas, William, 128, 419n7, 424n31, 424n33
Thorpe, Thomas, 420n15
Tibullus, Albius, 386n11, 389n31
Tiraboschi, Girolamo, 406n7
Tolomei, Claudio, 445n33
Toppi, Nicolò, 439n3
Torriano, Giovanni, 1, 128–29, 154, 416n69, 419n7, 422n20, 424n31, 435n85, 438n96

Toscanella, Orazio, 390n37, 431n64
Tosco, Partenio, 199, 443n20
Trajanus, Caesar Nerva, 145, 434n78, 461n1
Trissino, Gian Giorgio, 412n39, 425n42
Trovato, Salvatore, 24
Tusiani, Joseph, *xxii*

Ughi, Luigi, 406n7

Valente, Vincenzo, 197
Valgrisi, Vincenzo, 50, 407–08n14, 411n34, 412n36, 431n64
Valvassori, Giovanni Andrea (pseud. Guadagnino), 407n14, 412n36
Van Passen, Anne-Marie, 431n66
Varchi, Benedetto, 393n50, 425n42, 437n94, 445n31
Varisco, Giovanni, 55
Varrini, Giulio, 393n53
Vaughan, William, 420n14
Vedovelli, Massimo, 419n10
Vergili, Polidoro, 7, 21, 23
Vergilius, Publius Maro, 2, 412n39
Vermigli, Pietro Martire, 423n28
Vignali, Antonio Bonagiunti (a.k.a. Antonio di Bonagiunta Vignali and Arsiccio Intronato), 8–9, 143–44, 391nn40–41, 432nn71–72, 433nn73–75, 452n64
Vinciguerra, Antonio, *xxi*
Vitale, Maurizio, 394n60
Vives, Juan Luis, 140–42, 431n64
von Hannover, Ernst August, 395
von Hutten, Ulrich, 214
von Platen, Franz Ernst Freiherr, 395

Weller, Sam, 36
Wisse, Jakob, *xxii*
Wolfe, John, 127, 433n75
Woodcock, Thomas, 127

Wright, Herbert, 420n13
Wriothesley, Henry [also "Earl of Southampton" in text], 123–24
Wyatt, Michael, 133, 160, 175, 423n26, 423nn28–30, 424nn36–37, 435n84

Yeshua Ben Sira (a.k.a. Jesus Ben Sira), 146, 149–51, 264
Young, Bartholomew, 127
Yver, Jacques, 154

Zanotto, Francesco, 406n5
Zezza, Michele, 445n34
Zino, Pier Francesco, 130
Zoppino. *See* Nicolò di Aristotile
Zumthor, Paul, 452n69

About the Book

Paremias (proverbs and proverbial phrases) constitute a rich, underexplored archive of historical, cultural, and linguistic significance. Despite intercultural similarities, they are adapted to and affect specific genres, linguistic codes, and contexts. They circulate through writers, texts, and communities in a process that ultimately results in modifications in their structure and meaning. Vincenzo Brusantino's *Le cento novelle* (1554), John Florio's *Firste Fruites* (1578) and *Second Frutes* (1591), and Pompeo Sarnelli's *Posilecheata* (1684) offer clear representation of how paremias embed the authors' personal interpretations of society, culture, and literature, but also disguise their voice behind communal wisdom and knowledge. The analysis of the three authors' paremias through comparisons with classical and contemporaneous collections of maxims and *sententiae* illustrates how their perspectives inform the content, language, and structure of their works. Brusantino's proverbs introduce ethical interpretations to the 100 novellas of Boccaccio's *Decameron*, which he rewrites in octaves of hendecasyllables. His text appeals to Counter-Reformation society and its demand for a comprehensible and immediately applicable morality. In Florio's two language manuals, proverbs and proverbial phrases fulfill a need for language education in Elizabethan England through authentic and communicative instruction. Florio manipulates the proverbs' vocabulary and syntax to fit the context of his dialogues, best demonstrating the cultural and linguistic value of learning Italian in a foreign country. Sarnelli's expressions illustrate the inherent creative and expressive potentialities of the Neapolitan dialect vis-à-vis languages with a more robust literary tradition. Paremias, interpreted as moral maxims, ironic assessments, or witty insertions, characterize the local Neapolitan context in which the collection's frame and fables take place.

About the Author

Daniela D'Eugenio is Assistant Professor of Italian at the University of Arkansas. She studied at the University of Florence, Italy (Laurea Specialistica in Filologia e Linguistica) and at the University of Padua, Italy (Master in didattica dell'italiano come L2). In 2017, she completed her PhD at the City University of New York (Comparative Literature—Italian Specialization). Her research interests focus primarily on the study of proverbs in the context of Renaissance and Baroque literature, paleography, irony and humor, and pedagogical approaches in the foreign language classroom. Her articles and entries appeared in *Guida alla formazione del docente di lingue all'uso delle TIC—Le lingue straniere e l'italiano L2*, *Italian Language and Culture Conference—Challenges in the 21st Century Italian Classroom*, *Encyclopaedia of the Medieval Chronicle* (*Brill Online Reference Works*), *Forum Italicum*, *International Studies in Humour*, *Italica*, the Newberry Library *Italian Paleography* project, and the Accademia della Crusca *Proverbi italiani* database. Currently, she is examining the intersections and cross-fertilizations between the verbal and the visual for proverbs in calligraphy manuals and emblem books.

Dr. D'Eugenio has authored an exceptional scholarly monograph on Italian proverbial language based on a close analysis of three selected texts from the sixteenth and seventeenth centuries. Her use of interdisciplinary research to illustrate how Italian proverbs function as flexible literary instruments provides new insights into their meaning and function (individual, societal, and cultural perspectives, ethical commentary, regional dialects). Moreover, the author's interpretive and analytical ability enhances our understanding of the malleable nature of this significant literary, linguistic, and cultural form.

—Frank Nuessel, University of Louisville

www.ingramcontent.com/pod-product-compliance
Lightning Source LLC
Chambersburg PA
CBHW071430300426
44114CB00013B/1380